Recent Developments in the Economics of Training
Volume I

The International Library of Critical Writings in Economics

Series Editor: Mark Blaug

Professor Emeritus, University of London, UK
Professor Emeritus, University of Buckingham, UK
Visiting Professor, University of Amsterdam, The Netherlands

This series is an essential reference source for students, researchers and lecturers in economics. It presents by theme a selection of the most important articles across the entire spectrum of economics. Each volume has been prepared by a leading specialist who has written an authoritative introduction to the literature included.

A full list of published and future titles in this series is printed at the end of this volume.

Wherever possible, the articles in these volumes have been reproduced as originally published using facsimile reproduction, inclusive of footnotes and pagination to facilitate ease of reference.

For a list of all Edward Elgar published titles visit our site on the World Wide Web at
www.e-elgar.com

Recent Developments in the Economics of Training Volume I

Recent Developments in the Theory of Training

Edited by

Francis Green

Professor of Economics
University of Kent, UK

THE INTERNATIONAL LIBRARY OF CRITICAL WRITINGS IN ECONOMICS

An Elgar Reference Collection
Cheltenham, UK • Northampton, MA, USA

Published by
Edward Elgar Publishing Limited
Glensanda House
Montpellier Parade
Cheltenham
Glos GL50 1UA
UK

Edward Elgar Publishing, Inc.
William Pratt House
9 Dewey Court
Northampton
Massachusetts 01060
USA

A catalogue record for this book is available from the British Library.

Library of Congress Control Number: 2007925026

ISBN 978 1 84542 546 3 (2 volume set)

Printed and bound in Great Britain by MPG Books Ltd, Bodmin, Cornwall.

Contents

Acknowledgements

The editor and publishers wish to thank the authors and the following publishers who have kindly given permission for the use of copyright material.

Blackwell Publishing Ltd for articles: Francis Green (1993), 'The Determinants of Training of Male and Female Employees in Britain', *Oxford Bulletin of Economics and Statistics*, **55** (1), February, 103–22; Paul Osterman (1995), 'Skill, Training, and Work Organization in American Establishments', *Industrial Relations*, **34** (2), April, 125–46; John Paul MacDuffie and Thomas A. Kochan (1995), 'Do U.S. Firms Invest Less in Human Resources? Training in the World Auto Industry', *Industrial Relations*, **34** (2), April, 147–68; Josef Zweimüller and Rudolf Winter-Ebmer (1996), 'Manpower Training Programmes and Employment Stability', *Economica*, **63** (249), February, 113–30; Alison L. Booth and Monojit Chatterji (1998), 'Unions and Efficient Training', *Economic Journal*, **108** (447), March, 328–43; James J. Heckman and Jeffrey A. Smith (1999), 'The Pre-programme Earnings Dip and the Determinants of Participation in a Social Programme: Implications for Simple Programme Evaluation Strategies', *Economic Journal*, **109** (457), July, 313–48; Margaret Stevens (2001), 'Should Firms be Required to Pay for Vocational Training?', *Economic Journal*, **111** (473), July, 485–505; M.J. Andrews, S. Bradley and D. Stott (2002), 'Matching the Demand for and Supply of Training in the School-to-Work Transition', *Economic Journal*, **112** (478), March, C201–C219; Wiji Arulampalam, Alison L. Booth and Mark L. Bryan (2004), 'Training and the New Minimum Wage', *Economic Journal*, **114** (494), March, C87–C94; René Böheim and Alison L. Booth (2004), 'Trade Union Presence and Employer-Provided Training in Great Britain', *Industrial Relations*, **43** (3), July, 520–45; Filipe Almeida-Santos and Karen A. Mumford (2004), 'Employee Training in Australia: Evidence from AWIRS', *Economic Record*, **80**, Special Issue, September, S53–S64; Edwin Leuven (2005), 'The Economics of Private Sector Training: A Survey of the Literature', *Journal of Economic Surveys*, **19** (1), February, 91–111.

Econometric Society for article: John C. Ham and Robert J. LaLonde (1996), 'The Effect of Sample Selection and Initial Conditions in Duration Models: Evidence from Experimental Data on Training', *Econometrica*, **64** (1), January, 175–205.

Elsevier for articles: Håkan Regnér (2002), 'A Nonexperimental Evaluation of Training Programs for the Unemployed in Sweden', *Labour Economics*, **9** (2), April, 187–206; Anders Holm (2002), 'The Effect of Training on Search Durations: A Random Effects Approach', *Labour Economics*, **9** (3), July, 433–50; James M. Malcomson, James W. Maw and Barry McCormick (2003), 'General Training by Firms, Apprentice Contracts, and Public Policy', *European Economic Review*, **47** (2), April, 197–227.

Industrial and Labor Relations Review for article: Francis Green, Stephen Machin and David Wilkinson (1999), 'Trade Unions and Training Practices in British Workplaces', *Industrial and Labor Relations Review*, **52** (2), January, 179–95.

Lucius and Lucius Verlagsgesellschaft mbH for article: Florian Kraus, Patrick Puhani and Viktor Steiner (1999), 'Employment Effects of Publicly Financed Training Programs – The East German Experience', *Jahrbücher für Nationalökonomie und Statistik*, **219** (1 + 2), July, 216–48.

Oxford University Press for article: Margaret Stevens (1994), 'A Theoretical Model of On-the-Job Training with Imperfect Competition', *Oxford Economic Papers*, **46** (4), October, 537–62.

Review of Economic Studies Ltd for articles: Daron Acemoglu (1997), 'Training and Innovation in an Imperfect Labour Market', *Review of Economic Studies*, **64** (3), July, 445–64; Liliane Bonnal, Denis Fougère and Anne Sérandon (1997), 'Evaluating the Impact of French Employment Policies on Individual Labour Market Histories', *Review of Economic Studies*, **64** (4), October, 683–713.

Southern Economic Association for article: David Fairris and Roberto Pedace (2004), 'The Impact of Minimum Wages on Job Training: An Empirical Exploration with Establishment Data', *Southern Economic Journal*, **70** (3), January, 566–83.

University of Chicago Press for articles: Chun Chang and Yijiang Wang (1996), 'Human Capital Investment under Asymmetric Information: The Pigovian Conjecture Revisited', *Journal of Labor Economics*, **14** (3), July, 505–19; Ann P. Bartel and Nachum Sicherman (1998), 'Technological Change and the Skill Acquisition of Young Workers', *Journal of Labor Economics*, **16** (4), October, 718–55; Daron Acemoglu and Jörn-Steffen Pischke (1999), 'The Structure of Wages and Investment in General Training', *Journal of Political Economy*, **107** (3), June, 539–72; David Neumark and William Wascher (2001), 'Minimum Wages and Training Revisited', *Journal of Labor Economics*, **19** (3), July, 563–95.

Every effort has been made to trace all the copyright holders but if any have been inadvertently overlooked the publishers will be pleased to make the necessary arrangement at the first opportunity.

In addition the publishers wish to thank the Library of Indiana University at Bloomington, USA, for their assistance in obtaining these articles.

Introduction

Francis Green

The training of individuals after they have left school has assumed, in recent years, a huge importance in industrialised economies. First, the acquisition of 'human capital' is seen to be paramount in the 'knowledge economy', wherein human resources, rather than privileged access to materials and equipment, are the main determinants of economic success. Second, given the drive to become more skilled, the importance of post-school learning has increasingly become recognised. The main reason is that many work skills cannot easily be acquired in classrooms – they are learned in the context of work, whether through formal or informal training (Streeck, 1989). In addition, as new skills are demanded and others discarded, no economy can wait until new cohorts emerge from the education system with the requisite skill supplies. The existing workforce has to learn. It is thus not surprising that the training industry now absorbs very considerable resources.

Economics has a substantive role in explaining this phenomenon, in laying bare the theoretical rationales for training, and developing a methodology for evaluating training in both the private and public spheres. Yet economics is not alone in this endeavour among the social sciences. Training is also a concern for industrial relations and human resource management scientists. And, of course, the substance of training – its forms of delivery, curricula and so on – are important areas for development by educationalists. This collection concentrates, however, on the economic aspects of training, while drawing on contributions from the human resource management literatures that have a distinct set of implications for the economics of training.

The economic study of training concerns a number of key questions:

1. Who gets training at work, and how much training do they receive? Economic theory answers this question on the basis of the assumptions that firms and workers are maximising their profits and their wages respectively.
2. What are the effects of training on workers, firms and the economy generally? As often happens this question is more difficult to frame than may at first appear. Analysing the effects means, in principle, specifying a counter-factual – in this case, what would have happened to the workers/firms/economy if the training had not taken place; alternatively, what would have been the impact if more training had taken place than actually did?
3. Are there reasons to think that private individuals will undertake a socially sub-optimal volume of training? If so, is social intervention warranted?
4. Do social interventions into training work in practice? Economists' methods have been applied to public interventions, mainly in respect of the unemployed.

Since the last collection of critical writings on the economics of training (Ashenfelter and Lalonde, 1996), there has been a considerable output of further theoretical and empirical research on these four training issues. The papers selected for reprinting in this volume give a good overall perspective on this burgeoning literature, but they by no means cover everything that has been written on the subject.

The Theory of Training

For most of the two decades following publication of Becker's seminal work on training (Becker, 1964), the core formal theory of training remained unchanged: Becker's model had become the conventional economic wisdom. According to this theory, training could be divided into two types: general and firm-specific. General training produced skills that were as useful in many other firms as they were in the training firm. This definition implied that the worker could in a competitive labour market bid up the wage to its market value (its marginal revenue product). Firms would have no incentive to fund the training since workers received all the benefit. Workers, however, would be willing to pay, either in the form of fees or through foregone wages. They would do so if the benefit exceeded the opportunity cost.

Firm-specific training, by contrast, would need to be funded, at least in part, by firms. This type of training generated skills that were only of use in the firm providing the training. If workers are paid their marginal product in other firms they would receive no benefits from the training, and therefore be prepared to pay no costs. However, to deter quitting, firms will nevertheless offer a somewhat higher wage, and normally share the benefit and costs with workers. But, whatever the share, the investment is socially efficient (Hashimoto, 1982).

In short, whether the training was general or firm-specific there was no case (in the Becker model) for public intervention in the private arrangements for skill acquisition made between employers and employees. The exception was made in the case of training for unemployed workers. These could be legitimated by the credit constraints facing the unemployed, by equity considerations or by macroeconomic concerns for the management of unemployment. For the most part, interventions by governments in private training were seen as politics-led aberrations, leading to distortions of the labour market. Lees and Chiplin (1970), for example, famously castigated the grant-levy system that underpinned industrial training in 1960s Britain, on grounds that it was not economically justified.

Notwithstanding the technical erudition of the existing neoclassical economic theory of training that still predominated in the 1980s, the overall stance was a scientifically uncomfortable one, in at least two respects. First, the proposition that firms normally do not pay for general training did not stand up to serious scrutiny of the facts. While one could always find examples of employees paying all the costs of training, it was clear to most serious observers that employer-sponsoring of general training is widespread, and far from being an exception. One might, for example, refer to the relatively good rates of pay afforded to apprentices. Relatedly, researchers have found that most incidences of reported training tend not to be firm-specific – the paper by Loewenstein and Spletzer (1998; Chapter 7, Volume II) is one example of such a finding. Green, Ashton and Felstead (2001) found, in a similar vein, that training had a substantive impact on skills even when undertaken with a previous employer. Second, social intervention in training – in whatever form, be it government subsidies, levy systems or a regulated tripartite system – was in practice widespread. It seemed to be stretching credulity to imply that all this was necessarily inefficient, on account of a rather abstract neoclassical economic model. What was needed was a more realistic conceptualisation of the labour markets and workplaces in which training took place. Critics of neoclassical economics could point to the unduly individualistic perspective, which did not take account of the way that institutions shape both the incentives and the preferences and attitudes of trainees and trainers. While maintaining its individualistic approach, economics nevertheless responded with a recasting of the theory of training, in the light of new theories of imperfect competition. In some of these new approaches, explicit attention is paid to the consequences of there being incomplete, usually asymmetric, information about training's effects or about something that is complementary to them.

An early hint of how incomplete information could foil the generality of training was the analysis by Katz and Ziderman (1990), which focused on the consequences if employers could not assess the quality of training received in other firms. But it was Margaret Stevens, two of whose papers appear in Part I of Volume I, who first showed that a not-unrealistic relaxation in the assumptions of perfect competition implied that Becker's dichotomy of general and firm-specific training was inadequate. Becker had argued that all forms of training could be categorised as some combination of the two types he had defined – general and firm-specific. Stevens, however, showed that this was wrong. She introduced a further category of 'transferable' training, where skills acquired were productive in at least one outside firm. Transferable training could also be general training, but her focus was on training that was transferable but not general. Workers receiving transferable-but-not-general training could not raise their pay up to the level of their new marginal revenue product, so they would invest less in skill acquisition than if they could receive the full benefits. Training firms would gain some benefit from workers who do not quit. So, as long as at least some workers remained with the training firm, employers would be prepared to contribute towards the cost of training. In other words, the costs would be shared. However, as long as some workers did indeed quit (for exogenous reasons) other firms who take on the skilled workers would get to hire below marginal revenue product without bearing any of the training cost – a free-riding bonus. This externality implied that training investment would be below the socially efficient level, even if there were no liquidity constraints facing workers or firms.

In Stevens' model (1994; Chapter 1, Volume I) the key feature is the gap that emerges between the marginal revenue product and the wage, as a result of the training. This feature, referred to as 'wage compression' (Acemoglu and Pischke, 1999; Chapter 2, Volume I), is common to other recent models of firm-sponsored training. Wage compression can result from a number of labour market imperfections. In Acemoglu's 1997 paper (Chapter 3, Volume I), search frictions are the source. Other models focus on asymmetric information, either with regard to training quality (such as the 1996 paper by Chang and Wang (Chapter 5, Volume I) which builds on Katz and Ziderman, 1990), or with regard to work effort (as with the 1999 paper by Acemoglu and Pischke) or with regard to ability when it is complementary with the effectiveness of training (see Acemoglu and Pischke, 1999). The 2005 paper by Leuven (Chapter 4, Volume I) provides a good overview of these different, but related, reasons for wage compression.

Also common to these models is the finding that, in the presence of market imperfections, various forms of social intervention may act to shift the amount of training towards the social optimum. The 2003 paper by Malcomson, Maw and McCormick (Chapter 7, Volume I) gives an economic rationale for regulation of the length of apprenticeships in an efficiency wage model. Stevens' 2001 paper (Chapter 6, Volume I) considers the case for government subsidies of vocational training.

Evidence

A potential weakness of all these economic models of training lies in the simplification they make in considering the firm's training decision in isolation, rather than as part of a set of human resource practices. The economists' approach contrasts with that of human resource management (HRM) theorists who see training as potentially integrated with a human resource strategy that affects, not just skills, but also the organisational commitment of employees. One consequence may be that effects attributed in empirical research to training are more appropriately associated with a broader set of HR practices, including appraisal and other consultation mechanisms, and with various correlated forms of work organisation such as team working. The omission of these other factors could bias estimates of the impact of training if considered in isolation.

Empirical research on training has, nevertheless, blossomed in the last decade, and this collection includes several important selections from this recent literature. One aim of these studies has been to provide evidence for the theoretical models being developed, but a prime objective has been to build up a body of knowledge on the key empirical questions, which could then be used to support training policies.

Studies of the determinants of training typically construct a reduced form model that combines both supply-side and demand-side effects in a single equation for estimating participation, intensity or duration. One issue is whether the assumed exogenous determinants affect training as predicted by the human capital model. For example, it is widely found that training participation declines with age. This is hardly a surprising finding, but it is at least consistent with seeing training as future-oriented, as all theories maintain. Another issue is whether training is, as hypothesised, 'bundled' with other HR policies. The study by MacDuffie and Kochan (1995; Chapter 9, Volume I) is an example of research that broadly supports this idea. Also on the demand side, there is evidence in favour of the view that technological change requires more skills, as is shown by the link between technological change and training (Bartel and Sicherman (1998; Chapter 10, Volume I).

Many studies focus on particular determinants of training. For example, there is evidence of a changing degree of discrimination in access to training, as is shown in the 1993 paper by Green (Chapter 17, Volume I). However, as it happens training participation in Britain was equalised between the sexes during the 1990s (Green and Zanchi, 1997). The catch-up of women in training, from an earlier position in which men had greater access, is associated with the growing participation of women in the labour market, including the changing composition of occupations. Gender differences in training need to be analysed separately in each country, as they will depend on institutional differences in the labour markets. Women are found to receive more training than men in the United States (Simpson and Stroh, 2002), but less in Sweden (Evertsson, 2004).

Another set of studies included in Part II of Volume I examines whether unions affect training, and if so how. A simple human capital model predicts a negative effect, while either the 'voice' model of unionism, or the non-competitive theories of training can imply a positive impact. The papers by Green, Machin and Wilkinson (1999; Chapter 12, Volume I) and by Böheim and Booth (2004; Chapter 13, Volume I) are examples that demonstrate a robust positive impact of unions on training in Britain, and the same is true for Osterman's paper (1995; Chapter 11, Volume I) on the United States. But Almeida-Santos and Mumford (2004; Chapter 18, Volume I) come to a different conclusion for Australia, finding little link between training and unionism. These differences again point to the need for studies in a range of countries, where national-specific institutions like unions are concerned.

A third issue, with important policy implications, is whether minimum wages encourage or discourage training. The verdict in the United States is mixed, as shown in the two studies reproduced here (Fairris and Pedace (2004; Chapter 14, Volume I), and Neumark and Wascher (2001; Chapter 15, Volume I)). In Britain, the introduction of the minimum wage was found not to decrease training and possibly to increase it (paper by Arulampalam, Booth and Bryan (2004; Chapter 16, Volume I)), again consistent with non-competitive models of training.

Recent studies have also made some progress in understanding the relationship between training and economic performance. A number of studies have found a positive link between training and wages or wage growth. Illustrations in this collection are the studies by Parent (1999; Chapter 3, Volume II), by Booth and Bryan (2005; Chapter 8, Volume II), and by Loewenstein and Spletzer. Training appears to raise wages even when it was sponsored by a previous employer, providing support for the non-competitive models of training. Nevertheless, assessments of the causal impact of training need to address the econometric problems that arise because the training decision is an inherent part of a firm's strategy. Because training participation and training intensity are thus endogenous, typical regression parameter estimates are better interpreted as a conditional association of training with wages, rather than as unbiased estimates of the treatment effect of training. Researchers' strategies have been to instrument training wherever possible, given the data available, or to run separate selection equations and allow for covariance between error terms in the selection equation and the wage equation. In the papers by Vignoles, Galindo-Rueda and Feinstein (2004; Chapter 6, Volume II), and by Goux and Maurin (2000; Chapter 5, Volume II), both of which account for selection into training, the wage effects of private training on the non-trained are much less than the effect on those workers who are trained.

Researchers have also looked at the effect of training on productivity and, while the same issue of selectivity bias applies, these studies often find larger effects of training on productivity than on wages – again vindicating non-competitive theories that attribute net gains to firms in providing general training. For example, the paper by Conti (2005; Chapter 18, Volume II) in this collection found that training in Italian industries had a substantial impact on productivity, while the impact on wages was smaller and statistically insignificant. The evidence from France and Sweden also suggests that training has a large impact on productivity (Ballot, Fakhfakh and Taymaz, 2001). Yet training's effect could be over-estimated in such studies, if training is part of a bundle of human resource practices which together yield higher economic performance. Zwick's paper (2005; Chapter 17, Volume II) using German data is an example of one where estimates of the productive impact of training are obtained, yet found to be reduced once certain human resource practices are controlled for. Moreover, some studies fail to detect a major influence of training on productivity (for example, the much-cited 1996 study by Black and Lynch (1996; Chapter 16, Volume II)). There is no consensus, as yet, as to how bundles of the human resource practices are constructed, or on how they are to be measured, or on which interactions are most salient. This collection includes some widely cited studies in this mould, those by Huselid (1995; Chapter 10, Volume II), by MacDuffie (1995; Chapter 14, Volume II), by Huselid and Becker (1996; Chapter 11, Volume II), by Ichniowski, Shaw and Prennushi (1997; Chapter 12, Volume II), and by Ichniowski and Shaw (1999; Chapter 13, Volume II). A critique of this high-performance paradigm is provided by Godard (2004).

The issue about which least is known by training researchers is the economic returns to training for profit-maximising employers. A general presumption of economic theory is that in a competitive market investments would receive a normal risk-adjusted return on capital. Investments in human capital, however, are subject to great uncertainty, so the returns can deviate from a normal rate without there being a market-equilibriating reaction. The effect is that the amount of training can be influenced by the 'culture' of a firm, and more particularly by the beliefs of managers about training's effectiveness. Moreover, shifts in those beliefs which resulted in more or less training could then be reflected in market returns that deviate from the normal return: 'too little' training would have a high return, while 'too much' training would yield a return lower than normal. In practice, little is known about the returns to training achieved by private companies, in part because adequate data has usually not been available. Some companies do their own private evaluations of their training, in terms of their internal objectives. The paper by Bartel (2000; Chapter 19, Volume II) overviews some attempts to measure a rate of return to training, using a within-firm econometric approach. An alternative approach is to examine how far training is associated with the long-term commercial survival of firms: this approach is taken in the 2005 paper by Collier, Green and Peirson (2005; Chapter 20, Volume II). They find that training of white-collar workers is indeed associated with subsequent commercial survival. However, the impact varies somewhat according to which group is trained, and the size of establishment; moreover, this study was unable to secure an adequate instrument to take account of possible endogeneity biases in training.

With respect to the effects of training and other human resource practices in private organisations the findings of economists' research are likely to have only indirect implications for public policy. Interventions by governments depend in part upon whether training access is restricted by market failures, and on whether training is found to generate private benefits (and if so for whom and how much). In contrast, the effects of public-funded training programmes are of major importance for policymakers concerned to know what works and where to allocate the public purse. There are all too many cases of government training interventions that have 'failed' just as much as the market to deliver what is needed. Methodologies for evaluating public training programmes (and other 'active labour market' policies) were already well developed by the start of the 1990s. They are broadly divided into those using experimental data, derived from random assignment of participants to programmes, and those relying on non-experimental data using econometric methods to attempt to allow for the endogeneity of training. Experimental studies largely drew on US programmes, since random assignment was considerably rarer elsewhere. Overall assessments of the microeconomic impact of public training programmes have not generally been favourable, though there are exceptions (LaLonde, 1995, gives an overview). Nevertheless, the econometric problems of generating unbiased estimates of the treatment effect of directing unemployed persons to a public training programme remain formidable (Dolton, 2004).

Recent developments have seen a diffusion of attempts to evaluate training programmes in several countries with contrasting institutional frameworks. Differences between countries' training programmes as well as in the labour market environment mean that valid generalisations about the effectiveness of recent programmes are difficult to arrive at. Nevertheless, progress towards making policy development more soundly evidence-based is being made in various ways. Experimental data are being combined with econometric methods to generate improved estimates, as in Ham and LaLonde's paper (1996; Chapter 24, Volume I). Progress is also facilitated by the collection of richer data sets that combine employer and matched employee variables, and in some countries by harnessing and combining administrative data sets, thereby avoiding the usual problems of surveys and delivering very large numbers of cases. Computation constraints that might earlier have limited the exploitation of these new methods and data sets are being relegated to the past by the increasing speed of processors and low cost of computer memory space. Illustrations of these recent developments are provided in the selected contributions in Part III of Volume I, which in addition to US studies includes analyses of public training programmes in Sweden, Austria, France and, as an example of a transition economy, East Germany.

References

Acemoglu, D. and J.S. Pischke (1999), 'Beyond Becker: Training in imperfect labour markets', *Economic Journal*, **109** (453), F112–F142.

Ashenfelter, O.C. and R.J. LaLonde (eds) (1996), *The Economics of Training*, Cheltenham, UK: Edward Elgar.

Ballot, G., F. Fakhfakh and E. Taymaz (2001), 'Firm's human capital, R&D and performance: A study on French and Swedish firms', *Labour Economics*, **8** (4), 443–62.

Becker, G.S. (1964), *Human Capital*, New York: National Bureau of Economic Research.

Dolton, P. (2004), 'The economic assessment of training schemes', *International Handbook on the Economics of Education*, edited by G. Johnes and J. Johnes, Cheltenham: Edward Elgar, 101–63.

Evertsson, M. (2004), 'Formal on-the-job training: A gender-typed experience and wage-related advantage?', *European Sociological Review*, **20** (1), 79–94.

Godard, J. (2004), 'A critical assessment of the high-performance paradigm', *British Journal of Industrial Relations*, **42** (2), 349–78.

Green, F., D. Ashton and A. Felstead (2001), 'Estimating the determinants of supply of computing, problem-solving, communication, social and teamworking skills', *Oxford Economic Papers*, **53** (3), 406–33.

Green, F. and L. Zanchi (1997), 'Trends in the training of male and female workers in the United Kingdom', *British Journal of Industrial Relations*, **35** (4).

Hashimoto, M. (1982), 'Firm-specific human-capital as a shared investment', *American Economic Review*, **71** (3), 475–82.

Katz, E. and A. Ziderman (1990), 'Investment in general training: the role of information and labour mobility', *The Economic Journal*, **100**, (September), 1147–58.

LaLonde, R.J. (1995), 'The promise of public sector-sponsored training-programs', *Journal of Economic Perspectives*, **9** (2), 149–68.

Lees, D. and B. Chiplin (1970), 'The economics of industrial training', *Lloyds Bank Review*, **96**, 29–41.

Simpson, P.A. and L.K. Stroh (2002), 'Revisiting gender variation in training', *Feminist Economics*, **8** (3), 21–53.

Streeck, W. (1989), 'Skills and the limits of neoliberalism: The enterprise of the future as a place of learning', *Work, Employment and Society*, **3** (1), 89–104.

Part I
Recent Developments in the Theory of Training

[1]

Oxford Economic Papers 46 (1994), 537–562

A THEORETICAL MODEL OF ON-THE-JOB TRAINING WITH IMPERFECT COMPETITION

By MARGARET STEVENS

Trinity College, Oxford OX1 3BH
and
Institute of Economics and Statistics, St Cross Building, Oxford OX1 3UL

1. Introduction

IN HIS book *Human Capital*, Gary Becker (1964, 1975) classified on-the-job training as 'general' if it raises the worker's productivity equally in many firms, and 'specific' if it is of value only in the training firm. Becker suggested that most training was some combination of the two types. His most important conclusion was that workers, and not firms, receive the whole of the return to general training, and will therefore bear the costs. Moreover, since firms do not, and need not, invest in general training (although they may supply it) there is no problem of under-investment due to poaching of trained workers by other firms.

Becker's argument was convincing and has been influential not only in the economics literature—in which almost any discussion of training uses the general/specific classification as a starting point—but also on training policy. For example, it was used by Lees and Chiplin (1970) to support their claim that the grant-levy system of the 1964 Industrial Training Act had 'no basis in economic logic'.

Yet some unresolved puzzles remain. Much effort has been expended in trying to explain the empirical finding that firms do, apparently, invest in general training.[1] Furthermore, it is widely believed that there is under-investment in training, and in spite of the theoretical argument, many authors seem reluctant to abandon the notion that this is in part due to a poaching externality (for example, Finegold and Soskice, 1988).

The contention of this paper is that there is a simple and plausible theoretical explanation for these problems. The general/specific classification does not encompass all types of training—in particular that which takes place in the context of imperfect competition between firms in the labour market. When firms have labour market power, a firm may obtain some return to an investment in training, in spite of the fact that the skills are transferable to some other firms; in addition, since those other firms can also benefit from the investment there is an externality which may lead to under-investment.

The paper is organised as follows. In Sections 2 and 3 the classical theory of training is discussed, and extended to allow for imperfect competition. The conditions under which an externality exists are identified. In the remainder

---

[1] See, for example, the collection of papers edited by Stern and Ritzen (1991).

of the paper a formal model is developed, to demonstrate some of the implications for training decisions by workers and firms.

2. General, specific and transferable training

Although the terms 'general' and 'specific' are widely used in discussion of training, there are some surprising differences in interpretation by different authors. But Becker is unambiguous about the meaning of 'perfectly general' and 'completely specific' training:[2]

Definition G. A training programme is 'perfectly general' if it increases the worker's marginal product by exactly the same amount in many firms (p. 20). Examples: clerical training; brick-laying.

Definition S. A training programme is 'completely specific' if it increases the worker's productivity in the firm providing the training, but has no effect on his productivity in any other firm (p. 26). Example: familiarisation programme for new employees.

However, it is when training is neither perfectly general nor completely specific that ambiguities arise. For example, Becker asserts at one point that training which raises productivity more at the firm providing it falls within the definition of specific training (p. 26). Others have tended to expand the definition of general training: Jones (1988), Ritzen (1991), and Hyman (1992) (and many others) define it as of use to some other firms, and Shackleton (1992) says that it is training of use to at least one other firm. Such definitions may be reasonable, and suggest that these authors believe that, in practice, some types of training are of use to small numbers of firms. But the inconsistencies become important if results obtained under one definition are assumed to apply when a different definition is used.

Becker's famous and influential result for general training can be summarised as:

Becker's Result for General Training. If a training programme is perfectly general, and if the labour market for trained workers is perfectly competitive, then the worker's post-training wage is equal to his marginal product, so the whole of the return to the investment in the training programme accrues to the worker.

The implication of this result (p. 25) is that there is no positive externality between firms which would lead to under-investment in general training. Neither the training firm nor any other firm obtains any part of the return to the training investment. The training firm will not, therefore, be prepared to incur training costs, but the investment can be financed by the worker since he captures the full return, and hence an optimal level of investment will occur.

---

[2] In what follows, page numbers refer to the 2nd (1975) edition of *Human Capital*.

The result is often quoted more briefly as 'the return to general training accrues to the worker'—on the assumption, perhaps, that if the training is equally useful to many firms the labour market must be competitive. But the definitional inconsistencies noted above have lead to misuse of this result: those authors who define general training as of use to some other firms frequently make the implicit assumption that Becker's result extends to such training. Yet to do so without considering the characteristics of the corresponding labour market is highly questionable. Becker does not make this claim: indeed, he states that the effect on training when firms possess monopsony power (but are not pure monopsonists) is 'difficult to assess' (p. 36).

Discussing completely specific training, Becker used an informal argument to hypothesise that the wage of a specifically trained worker would lie somewhere between his marginal product and the market wage available to him elsewhere. Thus, the return to an investment in specific training would be shared between worker and firm, and the costs of that investment would also be shared. Also (p. 30) since such training is of no value to other firms, there is no associated externality which could lead to sub-optimal investment.

The final step in Becker's analysis is the recognition that in practice, training is often neither perfectly general, nor completely specific, raising the worker's productivity in other firms but by less than in the training firm. He claims (p. 30) that such training can be regarded as 'the sum of two components, one completely general, the other completely specific'. This claim is important, because it gives the impression that, having understood the economic characteristics of these two polar cases, we can, almost trivially, derive results for any other type of training. So, for example, we know that there is no positive externality between firms associated with either general or specific training. If we believe that all types of training are a 'sum' of general and specific components, we may conclude that the much-discussed 'poaching externality' does not exist—for any type of training.[3] However, it is argued below that both this belief and this conclusion would be false.

As a first step, we will formalise the analysis as follows. Suppose that there are many firms in the economy, and consider a single worker who undertakes a training programme in firm 0. Assume, for simplicity, that before undertaking training, the worker's productivity is zero in every firm. Let v_i be the productivity of the worker after training if he works in firm i. Then the value of the training programme can be described by the vector

$$v = (v_0, v_1, v_2, \ldots, v_n, \ldots)$$

where the length of the vector is large, and corresponds to the total number of firms in the economy. So, using Becker's definitions, a perfectly general training programme can be described by

$$v_g = (g, g, g, \ldots, g, \ldots) \quad \text{for some } g > 0$$

---

[3] Becker did not make this assertion.

and completely specific training by

$$v_s = (s, 0, 0, \dots, 0, \dots) \quad \text{for some } s > 0$$

A sum of general and specific training would have a vector of the form

$$v_{s,g} = (s + g, g, g, \dots, g, \dots)$$

This formulation immediately indicates that there are many other possibilities which cannot be regarded as the sum of a general and a specific component. For example

$$v_{t1} = (t, t, t, 0, 0, \dots, 0, \dots) \qquad \text{where } t > 0,$$

or

$$v_{t2} = (v_0, \lambda v_0, \lambda^2 v_0, \dots, \lambda^n v_0, \dots) \quad \text{where } v_0 > 0 \quad \text{and} \quad 0 < \lambda < 1$$

According to the alternative definition discussed above, v_{t1} would correspond to general training. But we will continue to use Becker's definition, reserving the term general for vectors of the form v_g above, and use the term transferable (often used interchangeably with general) for training corresponding to vectors such as v_{t1} and v_{t2}.

Definition T. A training programme is transferable if it is of some value to at least one firm in addition to the training firm.

Having recognised that not all transferable training can be regarded strictly as a sum of general and specific components, we should ask whether this matters. If, in fact, transferable training programmes such as v_{t1} above have economic properties which are 'intermediate' between the general and specific polar cases, then the distinction would not be of much value. But, as will be shown, in one important respect this is not the case.

In order to analyse the return to any training programme, we require to know not only its value v, but also how the wage of a trained worker will be determined—that is, we need to know how the labour market for this type of worker operates. If training is general, it is usual to suppose that the labour market is perfectly competitive. Specific training, on the other hand, corresponds to a situation of pure monopsony: specific skills are those for which there is no competition between firms in the labour market. But for training programmes such as v_{t1} and v_{t2} which are transferable but not general, we should consider the possibility that the labour market is imperfectly competitive: v_{t1} corresponds to oligopsony; v_{t2} models a situation in which firms have differentiated skill requirements.

It is natural to consider imperfect competition in the context of training, since the acquisition of specialised skills by workers, and the requirement for particular skills by firms, can be regarded as reducing competition in the labour market. In the classical perfectly competitive labour market there are many identical workers and many identical firms, but as workers acquire different bundles of skills, they differentiate themselves from each other. Similarly, firms who use different combinations of specialised technology, or different patterns of work organisation, require workers with particular sets of skills and job experience. Specific skills represent the extreme example of the association between training and imperfect competition, although as pointed out by Chapman (1991) it is difficult to think of many examples of purely specific skills. That some skills are required by small numbers of employers is a rather more plausible hypothesis. Furthermore, as in the product market, if firms can gain labour market power by differentiating themselves from others, they may choose to do so.

The inherent competition-reducing effects of training may be further compounded by lack of worker mobility. If workers face high moving-costs to other areas, or are prevented from moving by family commitments, their set of potential employers may be further reduced. Even if skills are very general, lack of mobility may mean that their value is effectively represented by a vector such as v_{t1}, rather than v_g. The importance of mobility in the analysis of training was emphasized by Oatey (1970). We could incorporate this concept formally by defining the value vector as representing the total value of the training to firms and worker, inclusive of all switching costs. When defined in this way, purely specific human capital may become relatively more important: it can include (as Becker pointed out) recruitment costs, and the costs to a firm of discovering the ability and potential of new employees.

3. The implications of imperfect competition for training

It has been argued firstly that the analysis of the returns to training depends on labour market conditions, and secondly that there is a natural link between training and an imperfectly competitive labour market. When we consider the effects of imperfect competition an important result emerges immediately:

3.1. *Basic Result for Transferable Training*

If, when an investment in transferable skills is made, the training firm and worker are uncertain about whether the worker will remain with the firm after training or move to an alternative firm which values the skills, and if the labour market is such that alternative firms are able to pay a wage less than marginal product, then part of the total expected return to the investment is captured by alternative firms.

That is, the total private return (the joint return to the worker and training firm) is smaller than the social return which includes that obtained by alternative firms: there is an externality associated with transferable training, which may lead to underinvestment.

This result will be demonstrated in this paper using a particular model, but it is a very general one: any source of imperfect competition leading to wages below marginal product, combined with any source of uncertainty about labour turnover, gives rise to this externality. Becker (p. 29) discusses the importance of labour turnover, arguing that although it can be ignored in traditional competitive analysis, it is an essential element of the analysis of specific training. Here, we simply extend this argument: labour turnover has important implications whenever the labour market is less than perfectly competitive.

In the special cases in which training is perfectly general or perfectly specific the externality disappears: for general training this is because we then assume a perfectly competitive labour market, and for specific training because there is no possibility that the worker can move to an alternative firm which values these skills. Nor will the externality exist for training which is strictly a sum of general and specific components, represented by the vector $v_{g,s}$ above. With many external firms for which the worker has identical value, $\mathbf{g}$, the external wage will be equal to $\mathbf{g}$ so these firms cannot obtain any part of the return. It is when training is transferable but not simply a combination of general and specific that the externality problem can arise.

4. A Model of Training with Imperfect Competition Between Firms

We will now develop a model which allows investigation of how the returns to a transferable training programme are shared, and demonstrates the existence and implications of the externality identified above. Two features are therefore required: some form of uncertainty generating labour turnover, and imperfect competition between firms in the labour market. In the following model these features are generated by supposing that there are a small number of firms, which are subject to independent productivity or demand shocks, leading to short-run heterogeneity of firms and hence imperfect labour market competition. In other respects the labour market in this model is competitive: firms set wages in a 'Bertrand' manner, and workers are perfectly sensitive to any difference in wages.[4]

We will consider an economy in which there may be many workers and firms, but make a simplifying assumption of constant returns to labour which allows us to focus on the training taking place at a single firm, firm 0. That is, the productivity of any worker in any firm is unaffected by the number of other workers employed in that firm. Since workers do not then compete for jobs, the training decisions made at an individual firm can be made independently of those at other firms.

4.1. *The Workers*

Suppose that, initially, all workers are untrained and a random group of workers is attached to firm 0. Untrained workers have constant productivity, initialised to zero, in all firms. Workers differ from each other only in their

---

[4] Stevens (1994) demonstrates how similar results can be obtained when it is the propensity of workers to change jobs which is uncertain, and their lack of perfect sensitivity to wage differences which gives market power to the firms.

'trainability', which affects the cost of training them, and is represented by a continuously distributed parameter α.

4.2. *Timing*

There are two periods: a training period and a work period. At the start of the first period each worker and firm 0 make a joint decision on whether the worker should be trained, and if so, choose the amount of training and decide how to share the costs. At the start of the second period the worker enters the labour market; he then works either in the training firm, or for some other firm.

4.3. *Training programmes*

Firm 0 offers a type of training which is of potential positive value in **n** other firms in the economy; in all other firms its value is identically zero. So the post-training productivity of a worker is described by the vector

$$v = (v_0, v_1, v_2, \ldots, v_n, 0, 0, \ldots)$$

During training the values v_i are uncertain, since the firms are subject to random independent and identically distributed productivity or demand shocks. So v is a random vector, whose actual value is realised at the start of the second period.[5]

Suppose that the expected value of the training is equal in all external firms, but may be higher in the training firm

$$E(v) = (m + a, m, m, m, \ldots, m, 0, 0, \ldots) \quad \text{for some } m \geqslant 0, a \geqslant 0$$

Let the independent and identically distributed shocks be represented by random variables ε_i, for $i = 0, \ldots, n$, with mean zero, support $[-1, 1]$ and continuous distribution and density functions $F(.)$ and $f(.)$. Then:

$$v = (m + a + \varepsilon_0, m + \varepsilon_1, m + \varepsilon_2, \ldots, m + \varepsilon_n, 0, \ldots)$$

So, for a given distribution F, the training programme is represented by a set of parameters, $\{m, a, n\}$. Looking at the expected value vector, it would be natural to describe **m** as the level of a transferable element, **a** as the level of a specific element, and **n** as a parameter of transferability—the higher it is, the more transferable is the training in the sense that there is a larger external market for the resultant skills. When $n = 0$ the programme is purely specific; when **n** is very large the transferable element becomes general, and only then might the programme be regarded as a combination of general and specific elements.

In this analysis, it will be assumed that the size of the external market, **n**, is

[5] The independence assumption is made for convenience; it is only necessary that the v_i's are not perfectly correlated. In interpreting the variation between firms as arising from demand or productivity shocks, it can be noted that these firms are not necessarily operating in the same product market. For example, consider a training programme for the use of a particular computer package which is used by a variety of firms in one locality.

544   A THEORETICAL MODEL OF ON-THE-JOB TRAINING

exogenous, given the type of training,[6] but that the levels of training, **m** and **a**, are chosen optimally when training decisions are made. The cost of the training programme depends on the levels chosen, and the worker's trainability, and is represented by a function $C(m, a; \alpha)$, which is assumed to be increasing and convex in **m** and **a**, and to decrease with α.

The specific element, **a**, may include, in addition to specific skills, switching costs for both the worker and the firms. Some such costs may not be under the control of the agents, in which case they can be regarded as exogenous when the programme is chosen, but it is possible that the worker and firm will choose to increase **a** through some means not classified as training. For example, the firm might encourage the worker to take out a mortgage on favourable terms, thus increasing his future moving costs.

4.4. *The labour market*

At the start of the second period the worker enters the labour market, then works for one of the $n + 1$ firms. Although the external firms have identical distributions of value for the worker, the actual values v_i will be different when labour market competition takes place, and this short-run heterogeneity gives the firms some market power. We will assume that the labour market operates as follows. The firms observe the worker's actual value, v. There are no information asymmetries—firm i observes not only the value, v_i, of the worker to itself, but also his value to its competitors. Then each of the $n + 1$ firms simultaneously makes a wage offer, $w_i (i = 0, \ldots, n)$, and the worker chooses to work for the one offering the highest wage.

4.5. *The training decision*

Consider the decisions made in respect of a worker of type α. Figure 1 summarises the timing of events. Both worker and firm are assumed to be risk-neutral, and to make training desisions to optimise their joint net return. It they decide to undertake a training programme, they will bargain as to how the costs should be shared, and this will depend on their individual returns, but the training outcome will not be affected by the sharing of costs provided that neither party is credit-constrained. In the present paper, we will assume perfect capital markets (although the model could easily be adapted to allow for credit constraints) and so will not analyse the cost bargaining stage.

Clearly untrained workers work at a zero wage in both periods. If training occurs, the levels **m** and **a** will be chosen to maximise the joint net return on the investment

$$\max_{\mathbf{m, a}} R_p(\mathbf{m, a, n}) - C(\mathbf{m, a}; \alpha)$$

---

[6] It may in practice be possible to vary transferability: for example, inclusion in the training of tests leading to some form of certification could be a way of increasing n.

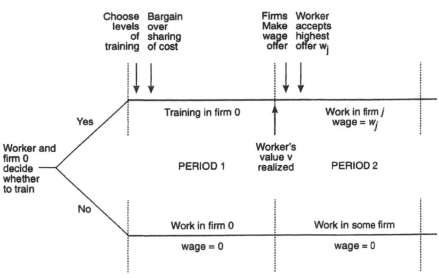

Fɪɢ. 1. Decisions and timing

where R_p is the joint expected return in the second period and there is no discounting between periods. So training will be undertaken if and only if the optimal net return is positive. Note that when the training externality exists the private return R_p will differ from the social return, so private training decisions will not be socially optimal.

The analysis proceeds as follows: in Section 5 we evaluate the outcome of the labour market stage, given a particular realisation of v, and use this to calculate the expected returns to all parties for a training programme of given parameters. Then in Section 6 we examine how these returns vary with the parameters. Finally, in Section 7 we analyse the maximisation problem above, to evaluate the training investment decisions and the consequences of the training externality.

5. Calculation of expected returns

At the labour market stage, the $n + 1$ firms observe the realised value vector v of the worker and make simultaneous wage offers. Let v^1 and v^2 be the order statistics representing the highest and second highest of the values v_i. Since the firms know all the v_i's before making their wage offers, this is a standard full information price game. The following two propositions hold for any continuously distributed random vector v—they do not require the particular parameterisation chosen in the previous section.

Proposition 1. The outcome of the second-period labour market competition is that the worker works for the firm for which he has highest value, v^1, at a wage equal to the second highest value v^2.

Proof. The following strategy for firm $i(i = 0, \ldots, n)$ constitutes a Nash equilibrium of this game, and leads to an outcome with the above properties:

> If v_i is the highest value $(v_i = v^1)$ offer $w_i = v^2 + \varepsilon$ (ε small and positive); otherwise $w_i = v_i$.

This is not the only equilibrium strategy, since when v_i is less than the second highest value firm i can offer any $w_i \leqslant v_i$ without affecting the outcome. But it can be shown, following the usual argument for asymmetric Bertrand competition and abstracting from some technical problems (see, for example, Tirole, 1989) that the equilibrium outcome is unique.   □

So, *ex-post*, the total value of the training programme is v^1, which is shared between the worker, who receives v^2, and the firm that has the highest value, which receives $v^1 - v^2$. Taking expectations we have:

Proposition 2. Any firm which has positive probability of having the highest value for the worker receives a positive share of the expected return to the training programme. The expected returns to each party are given by:

Total expected return: $R = E[v^1]$

Return to worker: $R_w = E[v^2]$

Return to firm i: $R_i = E[v^1 - v^2 | v_i = v^1] Pr[v_i = v^1]$

Proposition 2 demonstrates the condition for the existence of a training externality in this model. If there is any probability that the training firm will lose the worker to one of its competitors in the labour market, part of the expected return to training accrues to alternative firms: the externality exists. If, on the other hand, the training firm will have the highest value with probability 1 (perhaps due to a large element of specificity) then it is known with certainty when the investment is undertaken that the worker will not leave, and there is no externality.[7]

To calculate expected returns for the programme with parameters {**m, a, n**}, let $F_n(y) = F(y)^n$. This function is the distribution function of $y = \max\{\varepsilon_1, \varepsilon_2, \ldots, \varepsilon_n\}$. The corresponding density is $f_n(y) = nf(y)F(y)^{n-1}$. Then, using the algebraic manipulation given in the appendix, the expected returns can be shown to be (for $n \geqslant 1$)

Total Expected Return: $$R = m + 1 + a - \int_{a-1}^{1+a} F_n(y)F(y-a)\,\mathrm{d}y$$

Return to Training Firm: $$R_0 = \int_{-1}^{1+a} F_n(y)(1 - F(y-a))\,\mathrm{d}y$$

---

[7] This is an example of the association between externalities and uncertainty identified by Rasmusen (1989) in a variety of other contexts. The common feature is that in the absence of uncertainty there is a critical investment level at which private incentives are aligned with social incentives, which is smoothed away if uncertainty is introduced.

Sum of Returns to External Firms: $X = \displaystyle\int_{a-1}^{1} nF_{n-1}(y)(1 - F(y))F(y - a)\,dy$

Return to worker: $R_w = m + \displaystyle\int_{-1}^{1} yf_n(y)\,dy - X$

The probability that the worker moves to another firm in the second period is given by:

$$P = \int_{a-1}^{1} f_n(y)F(y - a)\,dy$$

and the joint private return to the worker and training firm is:

$$R_p \equiv R_0 + R_w \equiv R - X$$

6. Dependence of the returns on the parameters of the training programme

6.1. *The level of transferable training,* **m**

The parameter **m** represents the expected value of the transferable part of the training. In this model it simply shifts the distributions of value v_i upwards in all $(n + 1)$ firms, and the following result holds:

Proposition 3. The marginal benefit of the transferable element of training is equal to one, accrues to the worker only (provided $n \geqslant 1$) and has no effect on the returns to any of the firms

$$\frac{\partial R}{\partial m} = \frac{\partial R_w}{\partial m} = 1 \qquad \frac{\partial R_0}{\partial m} = \frac{\partial X}{\partial m} = 0$$

Hence the existence of the externality, represented by the term X, will not affect the choice of the level of **m**. To some extent, this result it an artefact of the model, since with many training programmes it may not be possible to vary **m** without affecting other characteristics of the training. For example, higher levels of transferable training may be associated with greater uncertainty, or with either a larger or smaller external market, both of which would affect the return to external firms. However, within the limitations of this model, it is clear that the level of **m** has no effect on the degree of competition between firms, and is not, therefore, related to the externality problem.

6.2. *The specific element of training,* **a**

An additional unit of specific training raises the value of the worker by one unit, if he remains in the training firm; otherwise its value is lost. This is the direct effect of specific training. But it also has an indirect effect, since the higher is the parameter **a**, the higher is the chance that, *ex-post*, the worker will have highest value in the training firm. Thus, the specific element also affects the probability of movement. The following proposition summarises the impact of specific training on the social return, R.

Proposition 4. (i) The marginal benefit of specific training is equal to the probability that the worker remains in the training firm. (ii) The probability of the worker leaving decreases with the level of specific training. (iii) There are increasing returns to specific training.

Proof. (i) Differentiating the total return, R, with respect to **a** gives

$$\frac{\partial R}{\partial a} = \int_{a-1}^{1+a} F_n(y) f(y - a) \, dy$$

$$= 1 - \int_{a-1}^{1} f_n(y) F(y - a) \, dy \quad \text{(integrating by parts)}$$

$$= 1 - P \text{ (where } P \text{ is the probability of movement, defined above)}$$

$$= \text{the probability of remaining in the training firm}$$

(ii) $\dfrac{\partial P}{\partial a} = -\displaystyle\int_{a-1}^{1} f_n(y) f(y - a) \, dy \leqslant 0$

(iii) Follows immediately since $\dfrac{\partial^2 R}{\partial a^2} = -\dfrac{\partial P}{\partial a} \geqslant 0$ □

The first part of this proposition formalises the statement by Becker (p. 32) that there are external diseconomies associated with specific training—part of its potential value may be lost due to turnover. The 'increasing returns' effect happens because an additional unit of specific training not only increases the direct value of the worker, but also increases the return to earlier units, because there is a lower probability that their value will be lost through turnover.

The results of Proposition 4 do not depend on the existence of an externality: it will be shown below that they hold even in the limiting case as **n** approaches infinity. But the specific element is also important in relation to the externality problem:

Proposition 5. (i) The total return to external firms, X, falls with the level of specific training. Hence the marginal private benefit of specific training is greater than the marginal social benefit. (ii) There are increasing private returns to specific training.

Proof. (i) Differentiating the expression for X gives

$$\frac{\partial X}{\partial a} = -\int_{a-1}^{1} n(F(y))^{n-1}(1 - F(y)) f(y - a) \, dy \leqslant 0$$

and since $R_p = R - X$ we have

$$\frac{\partial R_p}{\partial a} = \frac{\partial R}{\partial a} - \frac{\partial X}{\partial a} \geqslant \frac{\partial R}{\partial a}$$

that is, the marginal private benefit is greater than the marginal social benefit.

(ii) It is proved in the appendix that $\partial^2 R_p / \partial a^2 \geqslant 0$.   □

Next, we can ask how the private return to specific training is shared between the firm and the worker. Since they optimise their joint net return when choosing a training programme, this division does not affect the investment decision in the present model, but it is interesting to ask whether Becker's sharing hypothesis holds here.

Consider what happens if the worker has higher value in the training firm than elsewhere—which is more likely if there is a large element of specific training. Then the training firm pays a wage equal to the best available elsewhere, and so does not appear to share any of the return to the specific part of the training with the worker. This is consistent with later work on the sharing hypothesis by Hashimoto (1981), who showed that further assumptions about asymmetry of information and transaction costs are required to justify the use of a long-term contract which results in sharing. Here, with the assumption of symmetric information, there are no inefficiencies requiring a long-term contract. The firm makes a single take-it-or-leave-it offer so is effectively assumed to possess all the bargaining power, and need not share the worker's specific value with him.

The following proposition follows immediately from differentiation of the expressions for the returns.

Proposition 6. The direct marginal benefit of specific training accrues to the firm: $\partial R_0 / \partial a = \partial R / da$. The worker benefits indirectly, from the reduction in return to external firms:

$$\partial R_w / \partial a = -\partial X / \partial a \geqslant 0.$$

Thus, although in one sense the assumption that the firm sets the wage does result in non-sharing, the worker is not indifferent to the level of specific training when an externality exists.

Finally, consider the case when **a** is so large that the range of the distribution of value in the training firm does not overlap with the distribution in other firms: that is, $a \geqslant 2$. Then, the probability of a move to another firm is zero and the marginal benefit of specific training is equal to one. Both the externality and the increasing returns effect disappear. In this case, the benefit of specific training accrues entirely to the training firm.

6.3. *The size of the external market,* **n**

The parameter **n** represents the transferability of the training—the higher it is, the more potential employers there are who value the training. It might also be regarded as an index of competition, since as **n** increases, we would expect the difference between wage and marginal product—the margin between v_1 and v^2—to fall. In fact, this does not necessarily happen, but it is true for many well-behaved distributions.[8] In what follows, **n** is initially treated as a continuous parameter, to obtain some comparative statics results.

Proposition 7. As the transferability, n, of the training increases:
  (i) the total return to the training programme increases: $\partial R/\partial n \geqslant 0$;
  (ii) the return to any individual firm falls: $\partial R_0/\partial n \leqslant 0$ and $\partial(X/n)/\partial n \leqslant 0$;
  (iii) the probability of the worker moving to another firm increases: $\partial P/\partial n \geqslant 0$;
  (iv) the return to the worker increases ($\partial R_w/\partial n \geqslant 0$) if the distribution F is log-concave;
  (v) the marginal benefit of specific training falls: $\partial^2 R/\partial a \partial n \leqslant 0$.

Proof.

  (i) $\dfrac{\partial R}{\partial n} = -\displaystyle\int_{a-1}^{1+a} \log(F(y))F_n(y)F(y-a)\,\mathrm{d}y \geqslant 0$

  (ii) $\dfrac{\partial R_0}{\partial n} = \displaystyle\int_{-1}^{1+a} \log(F(y))F_n(y)(1 - F(y-a))\,\mathrm{d}y \leqslant 0$

  Firm $i(i = 1, \ldots n)$ obtains expected return X/n and

  $$\frac{\partial(X/n)}{\partial n} = \int_{a-1}^{1} \log(F(y))(F(y))^{n-1}(1 - F(y))F(y-a)\,\mathrm{d}y \leqslant 0$$

  (iii) Integrating by parts, the moving probability, P, can be written

  $$P = F(1 - a) - \int_{a-1}^{1} F_n(y)f(y-a)\,\mathrm{d}y$$

  and hence

  $$\frac{\partial P}{\partial n} = -\int_{a-1}^{1} \log(F(y))F_n(y)f(y-a)\,\mathrm{d}y \geqslant 0$$

  (iv) Proved in appendix.

  (v) $\dfrac{\partial^2 R}{\partial a\,\partial n} = \displaystyle\int_{a-1}^{1+a} \log(F(y))F_n(y)f(y-a)\,\mathrm{d}y \leqslant 0$ □

These results are intuitive: the greater the number of firms for which the training has value, the more socially valuable it is, and the more likely it is that some firm other than the training firm has highest value for the worker. Since the worker is more likely to leave, specific training is less

---

[8] It can be shown that, for a set of n i.i.d. random variables, a sufficient condition for the expectation of the difference between the first two order statistics to decrease with n is that the distribution be log-concave. This is a wide class which includes the normal, truncated normal, and uniform distributions. See Caplin and Nalebuff (1991) and Stevens (1993).

valuable. The return to any individual firm falls because of increased competition, and this does not require any condition on the distribution because even if the margin between wage and marginal product increases, the probability of that firm obtaining the worker falls, and the latter effect always dominates. The worker does not necessarily benefit from increased competition, but if the distribution is such that the difference between the wage and marginal product falls he will certainly do so.

Note that there is a divergence here (which does not occur with respect to the levels **m** and **a**) between the interests of the worker and training firm: the worker prefers training with a large external market, while the firm prefers less transferable training. This divergence does not matter when training is chosen to optimise the joint return and capital markets are perfect, but would affect the training chosen if, for example, there were asymmetries of information between the investing parties.

Although the return to individual firms falls with increasing transferability, it does not follow that the externality problem, represented by the total return to external firms, X, is necessarily alleviated, since there are a larger number of firms obtaining a share of the expected return. The following proposition shows that increasing competition can worsen the problem.

Proposition 8. The total return to external firms, X, achieves a maximum value for some number of firms $N \in [1, \infty)$. There is no upper bound on N: that is, for any $N_0 \in [1, \infty)$ there exists some **a** such that the maximum of X occurs at $N > N_0$.

Proof. Consider X as a function of n and a

$$X = \int_{a-1}^{1} n(F(y))^{n-1}(1 - F(y))F(y - a)\,dy$$

X is a continuous function of n on $[0, \infty)$, zero at $n = 0$ and approaching zero as n tends to infinity. For all intermediate values of n, X is positive. Hence the maximum occurs at some finite positive N, which depends on the parameter a (and the shape of the distribution F).

$$\frac{\partial X}{\partial n} = \int_{a-1}^{1} (1 + n \log F(y))F(y)^{n-1}(1 - F(y))F(y - a)\,dy$$

Consider a particular N_0. The term $(1 + N_0 \log F(y))$ is monotonically increasing on $(-1, 1]$, positive when y is close to 1, and negative at low y. So, there exists $z \in (-1, 1)$ such that $1 + N_0 \log F(y) > 0$ *iff* $y > z$. Let $a - 1 = z$. Then the integrand is positive throughout the range, so $\partial X/\partial n > 0$ at N_0, and furthermore, $\partial X/\partial n > 0$ for all $n < N_0$. Hence the maximum of X occurs at $N > N_0$. Since this is true for any finite N_0, there is no upper bound on the maximand N ☐

Figure 2 shows the function X for the uniform distribution. The return to

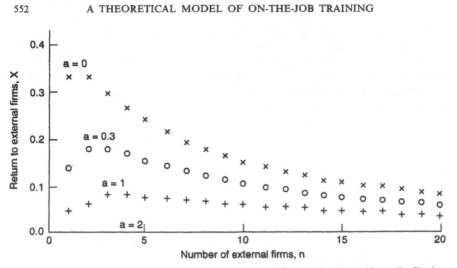

FIG. 2. Total return to external firms, X, as a function of firms, n, for the uniform distribution

external firms is highest when there is no specific element in the training, and the number of competing firms is 1 or 2. When the specific element, a, is positive, increasing competition initially increases X: for example, when $a = 1$, the maximum occurs when $n = 4$. But (as we know from proposition 5(i)) for given $\mathbf{n}$, X is smaller at higher values of $\mathbf{a}$ and reduces to zero at $a = 2$.

6.4. *Two special cases*

6.4.1. *Fully transferable training,* $\boldsymbol{a} = 0$. If the training contains no specific element, it might be described as 'fully transferable', in the sense that its value has identical distribution in the training firm and the n external firms. The terminology causes some problems here—it may not be 'highly transferable', and certainly not general, if n is small.

The point to be emphasised is that the training firm still obtains a positive expected return—the incentive for a firm to invest in training does not depend on there being some purely specific element.

6.4.2. *The limiting case,* $\boldsymbol{n} \to \infty$. The case of a large number of firms might be thought of as approximating a competitive labour market. This is only an approximation: what happens in the limit is that the highest external wage offer will be (with certainty) at the upper limit of the range of values, and equal to the marginal product, $m + 1$. However, the heterogeneity of firms does not disappear in the limit, so this is not really a classical labour market.

When $\mathbf{n}$ is large, any uncertainty about the external labour market disappears: the worker will definitely leave if the wage is less than $m + 1$, and stay otherwise.

Proposition 9. In the limit, as $\mathbf{n}$ approaches infinity, the total return to external firms tends to zero. The return to the training programme is the sum of a general component (the competitive wage) which accrues to the worker, and a specific component which accrues to the firm.

Proof.

$$X = \int_{a-1}^{1} n(F(y))^{n-1}(1 - F(y))F(y - a)\,\mathrm{d}y$$

As $n \to \infty$, $nF(y)^n \to 0\ \forall\ y < 1$; hence $X \to 0$.
Integrating the expression for the worker's return by parts gives

$$R_w = m + 1 - \int_{-1}^{1} F_n(y)\,\mathrm{d}y - X$$

So $\lim_{n \to \infty} R_w = m + 1 \equiv w$

That is, the worker's return is exactly equal to the external wage and is unaffected by the specific element. He receives the same wage whether he stays in the training firm or not. The training firm's return is

$$R_0 = \int_{-1}^{1+a} F_n(y)(1 - F(y - a))\,\mathrm{d}y$$

$$\lim_{n \to \infty} R_0 = \int_{1}^{1+a} (1 - F(y - a))\,\mathrm{d}y$$

$$= \int_{1}^{1+a} (y - 1)f(y - a)\,\mathrm{d}y$$

$$= E[v_0 - w|v_0 > w]\,Pr[v_0 > w]$$

So, the return to the training firm is the expectation of the worker's additional value in the training firm, given that this is positive so that he will stay, multiplied by the probability that he will stay. The firm's return arises only from the specific element of the training; in particular, if $a = 0$, $R_w = 0$. □

This result is not very surprising: the parameterisation of the model was chosen so that the expected value would have the form $v_{s,g}$ in the limit, so could then be regarded as the sum of two components. But it is important to stress that it is only in the limiting case that the returns can be decomposed in this way: otherwise, part of the return accrues to other firms, the training firm obtains some return even if there is no specific element, and the worker's return is affected by the specific element.

Finally, note that Proposition 4 still holds in the limit as **n** tends to infinity since the marginal benefit of specific training is then

$$\frac{\partial R}{\partial a} = 1 - F(1 - a) = Pr[v_0 > w] = \text{Probability that the worker stays}$$

and this increases with **a**, as for finite **n**. This means that, in the limit, the marginal benefit of specific training is zero at $a = 0$. The implications of this result will be discussed below.

7. The choice of a training programme

Now consider the choice of training programme for a worker of trainability α. Suppose that, given the type of training programme, the transferability **n** is fixed, and there is some minimum level of specific human capital a_0, perhaps due to unavoidable switching costs. The training firm and worker are able to choose the levels of transferable training **m** and additional specific human capital **a**. The first step in the decision is to find the optimal levels of training for this worker; then they can decide whether it is worthwhile to undertake such a programme.

7.1. *Choice of training levels*

The optimisation problem is

$$\max_{m,\,a} R_p(m, a + a_0, n) - C(m, a, n; \alpha) \text{ subject to } a \geqslant 0$$

Since $R_p = R - X$ the first order conditions for an interior private optimum are

$$1 = \frac{\partial R}{\partial m} = \frac{\partial C}{\partial m}$$

$$\frac{\partial R}{\partial a} - \frac{\partial X}{\partial a} = \frac{\partial C}{\partial a}$$

The social optimum satisfies the same conditions but without the term $\partial X / \partial a$. Recall from Proposition 5 that there are increasing private and social returns to specific training ($\partial^2 R_p / \partial a^2 \geqslant 0$ and $\partial^2 R / \partial a^2 \geqslant 0$) so that a unique solution is not guaranteed. An optimum will exist, since if $a \geqslant 2$ (in which case there is no probability of the worker leaving) the increasing returns effect disappears: $\partial R / \partial a = \partial R_p / \partial a = 1$ if $a \geqslant 2$. But it may either occur at $a = 0$, or have the property that **a** is so large as to prevent any labour turnover.

First consider the socially optimal levels (m^*, a^*). The following result is proved in the appendix but follows directly from the earlier comparative statics results.

Proposition 10. The socially optimal amount of specific training, a^*, increases with exogenous switching costs, a_0, and decreases with the size of the external market, n.

This proposition tells us, in particular, that when the conditions for a highly competitive labour market prevail—many firms and low exogenous switching costs—there should be little investment in specific human capital. And in such conditions the social optimum will be achieved since the externality disappears.

In fact, it is likely that the optimum level of specific investment will then be zero; as shown in Section 6.4 the marginal benefit of specific training is zero at $a = 0$. It is only when the external labour market is less competitive, so turnover is low, or when there is a need to reduce turnover because of switching costs, that investment in specific human capital becomes worthwhile.

Now consider how the existence of the externality affects the choice of a and m.

Proposition 11. If there is a unique solution to the first order conditions for the socially optimal (m^*, a^*), then (for finite n) the private choice (m_p, a_p) will be such that $a_p > a^*$. Thus, there will be over-investment in specific training. m_p may be greater or less than m^*.

Proof. If the solution for a^* is unique, then

$$\forall\ (a, m) \text{ such that } a < a^* \text{ and } \partial C/\partial m = 1 \text{ we must have } \frac{\partial R}{\partial a} - \frac{\partial C}{\partial a} > 0$$

$$\text{But } (m_p, a_p) \text{ satisfies } \partial C/\partial m = 1 \text{ and } \frac{\partial R}{\partial a} - \frac{\partial C}{\partial a} = \frac{\partial X}{\partial a} \leqslant 0$$

Hence $a_p \geqslant a^*$. From the condition $\partial C/\partial m = 1$ it is clear that m_p is either greater than or less than m^* according to the sign of $\partial^2 C/\partial a\ \partial m$. $\square$

It was shown (Proposition 8) that the total return to external firms is greatest for some intermediate value of **n**. Following an identical argument it can be shown that magnitude of the distortionary term $\partial X/\partial a$ is also greatest for intermediate **n**, so that it is possible for increasing competition to worsen the over-investment in specific training, although it disappears as **n** becomes very large.

Combining the results of Propositions 10 and 11 suggests that privately-chosen training programmes will tend to fall into one of two categories. If the exogenous conditions favour a highly competitive labour market, the training programme will be chosen optimally and will include little or no specific training. Thus, a training programme with a substantial perfectly general component will include little specific training. But in the presence of non-competitive influences, such as switching costs or training of a specialised type, the training programme will also include substantial amounts of specific human capital leading to a further reduction in turnover and competition in the labour market. In particular, when the training is of a type which is of use to a small number of employers, it will be accompanied by specific human capital (which may or may not be training) in order to reduce turnover and protect the investment in transferable training. In such a case the parties to the training investment could be said to be erecting socially costly mobility barriers.

7.2. *Decision whether to train*

For a worker of type α, training will be undertaken if, at the levels of training which are privately optimal for this worker, the net private return is positive.

556   A THEORETICAL MODEL OF ON-THE-JOB TRAINING

This decision will not be socially optimal, and it is intuitively obvious that the following proposition holds.

Proposition 12. If the training programme is transferable, but not a combination of general and specific (that is, if n is finite), too few workers will be trained.

Proof. Consider the net social return to training, as a function of trainability α

$$T(\alpha, n) = R(m^*, a^*, n) - C(m^*, a^*; \alpha)$$

Since m^* and a^* are chosen optimally for a worker of type α, and since $\partial C/\partial \alpha < 0$, the envelope theorem implies that T is a strictly increasing function of α. Hence, training will be socially optimal for any worker with $\alpha \geqslant \alpha^*$, where $T(\alpha^*, n) = 0$. Similarly the net private return $T_p(\alpha, n)$ is strictly increasing in α, and training will be privately optimal if $\alpha \geqslant \alpha_p$ where $T(\alpha_p, n) = 0$.

But $T_p(\alpha, n) = R(m_p, a_p, n) - C(m_p, a_p; \alpha) - X(a_p, n) \leqslant T(\alpha, n)$
$$- X(a_p, n) < T(\alpha, n)$$

Since both functions are continuous, this proves that $\alpha_p > \alpha^*$, and hence that the number of workers trained will be too low.   □

Note that, since X may initially increase with **n**, the problem of too few workers trained may (like the problem of over-investment in specific training) be most serious for intermediate values of transferability, **n**.

To summarise the results of Section 7, it has been shown that, when training is transferable, but is not a combination of general and specific, the number of workers trained will be too small, and that those who are trained will receive training which has too great a specific element, resulting in a skilled labour market characterised by low turnover. On the other hand, if the transferable element of training is truly general, socially optimal training decisions will be made, training programmes will not include much specific training (unless it happens that exogenous switching costs are also high) and the corresponding labour market will be characterised by high turnover. Since the distortions are most severe for training programmes of intermediate transferability, we would expect in practice to observe training programmes of either low transferability, with a substantial specific component, or very general programmes with little specific training.

There is an interesting link between these ideas and the theory of internal labour markets (ILMs) (Doeringer and Piore, 1971) which relies upon the assumption of a high degree of specificity in training. An ILM is one in which firms recruit and train unskilled workers, higher level jobs are filled by internal promotion, and mobility of workers above entry level is low. The present analysis suggests that the endogenous choices of workers and firms may lead to the development of labour markets characterised by low transferability of training, mobility barriers and low turnover. According to Marsden and Ryan (1990) occupational labour markets (OLMs), characterised by general training and high mobility, 'are unstable, and tend to degenerate into internal markets'.

Some support is offered here for that view, in the sense that the requirements for an OLM are stringent (perfectly general training, financed by the worker, and low switching costs) and unless all these are fulfilled, private choices will lead to the development of ILMs.

8. Conclusions

The most important result of this paper is the simplest: that not all transferable skills are general, and for some types of on-the-job training for transferable skills, firms—both the training firm and external firms—can obtain a positive share of the return to the training investment. This may explain why firms have been found to invest in transferable training. It also means that there is an externality—of the type sometimes referred to as a poaching externality—associated with some types of on-the-job training programmes, which may lead to under-investment in training.

It has been shown that the classical analysis using a combination of general and specific cannot describe all types of training—for example, training for skills which are of value to a small number of firms. The term transferable has been used to designate training which is of some use to at least one firm in addition to the training firm. Skills for which there is a larger external market can then be described as 'more transferable' than those which are valued by only two or three employers. Specific skills are those for which there is no external market, and general skills correspond to the other limiting case in which the external market is very large.

The size of the external market is important insofar as it affects the degree of competition between employers. It is imperfect competition between employers in the labour market on which the existence of an externality depends: if there is a possibility that the worker will move after training to a a firm which can pay him less than his marginal product, that firm obtains a positive share of the expected return to training. Furthermore, it was argued in Section 2 that this is not merely a theoretical curiousity. Rather, there is a natural link between training and imperfect competition, in that the acquisition of skills, and skill requirements, differentiate workers and firms: training can be a competition-reducing process.

The relationship of the externality problem to transferability is illustrated by Figure 2, in which the horizontal axis represents the number of firms in the external market for some type of training. This can be regarded as an index of transferability, or of the degree of competition. When this index is zero, the training is purely specific, and there is no externality. As the index increases, the externality problem, represented by the total return to external firms, initially increases, reaching a maximum at some intermediate level of competition, then falling towards zero again as the labour market approaches the limiting case of perfect competition, in which case the training is either perfectly general, or a combination of general and specific.

The arguments presented in this paper do not conflict strongly with those made by Becker, except to the extent that he implied that all types of training were covered by his analysis in terms of general and specific. Becker did not show, or claim (although it is frequently asserted that he did) that a poaching externality did not exist. In fact, he stated clearly that his conclusions with respect to the non-existence of a poaching externality applied to a competitive labour market. Nor did he deny the possibility that some training would take place in the presence of imperfect competition between firms—he conjectured that such training would be more like specific, less like general training. In this paper, his analysis has been extended by focusing directly on imperfect competition, and, in one sense his conjecture has been shown to be correct. For if we consider training which is transferable to a small number of other firms and has no specific element, the training firm is able to capture more of the return than it would if the training were completely general, and less than it would if the training were completely specific. But it has been shown that in another sense the conjecture was misleading: training in the presence of imperfect competition differs from both the limiting cases of monopsony and perfect competition, in that part of the return accrues to alternative firms.

In the second part of this paper a model has been developed in order to explore the properties of transferable training, and the consequences of the externality in particular. Analysis of imperfect competition between firms, which has been more common in the industrial economics literature than in labour economics, frequently requires some apparently drastic simplifying assumptions, and this model is no exception. Despite these, the predictions of the model accord well with intuition. It demonstrates how, as the size of the external market for some type of training increases, firms (individually) capture less of the return to training and the worker captures more. It illustrates the relationship between labour turnover, the level of purely specific training, and the size of the external market, and shows how this relationship may distort private training choices. Other authors have hypothesised that there is an incentive to over-invest in specific training (for example, Hyman, 1992): this model demonstrates it explicitly. Furthermore, it shows that the training firm benefits, at the expense of the worker, from reducing the transferability of training; this result could be used to explore the idea that firms may choose to differentiate their skill requirements in order to obtain market power in the labour market.

The effect of the externality is that too few workers receive training which is valued by small numbers of employers. One important prediction is that it is not necessarily the case that increasing competition reduces distortions. It can happen that the increased probability of turnover dominates the reduction in market power and worsens the problem.

If firms and workers are unable to undertake the socially optimal training programme because of the externality, they may choose instead either training which is completely general (or at least highly transferable) or training of low transferability. If training of low transferability is chosen it may not be completely specific, but if not, there is an incentive to include a high specific element, or some other kind of mobility barrier, in order to protect the investment from appropriation by rival employers.

ACKNOWLEDGEMENTS

An earlier version of this paper was presented at the Oxford Economic Papers Conference on Vocational Training, and at the Labour Market Imperfections Group seminar at Birkbeck College. The paper has benefited greatly from the comments of the participants, and from those of two anonymous referees. Thanks are also due to my supervisor, Meg Meyer, for her help and advice.

REFERENCES

BECKER, G. (1964, 1975). *Human Capital*, Columbia University Press, New York.
CAPLIN, A. and NALEBUFF, B. (1991). 'Aggregation and Social Choice: A Mean Voter Theorem', *Econometrica*, **59**, 1–23.
CHAPMAN, P. G. (1991). 'Institutional Aspects of Youth Employment and Training Policy in Britain: A Comment', *British Journal of Industrial Relations*, **29**, 491–5.
DOERINGER, P. and PIORE, M. (1971). *Internal Labour Markets and Manpower Analysis*, Lexington.
FINEGOLD, D. and SOSKICE, D. (1988). 'The Failure of Training in Britain: Analysis and Prescription', *Oxford Review of Economic Policy*, **4**, 21–53.
HASHIMOTO, M. (1981). 'Firm Specific Human Capital as a Shared Investment', *American Economic Review*, **71**, 475–82.
HYMAN, J. (1992). *Training at Work*, Routledge, London and New York.
JONES, I. (1988). 'An Evaluation of YTS', *Oxford Review of Economic Policy*, **4**, 54–71.
LEES, D. and CHIPLIN, B. (1970). 'The Economics of Industrial Training', *Lloyds Bank Review*, **96**, 29–41.
MARSDEN, D. and RYAN, P. (1990). 'Institutional Aspects of Youth Employment and Training Policy in Britain', *British Journal of Industrial Relations*, **28**, 351–69.
OATEY, M. (1970). 'The Economics of Training with the Firm', *British Journal of Industrial Relations*, **8**, 1–21.
RASMUSEN, E. (1989). *Games and Information*, Blackwell, Oxford, 172–3.
RITZEN, J. (1991). 'Market Failure for General Training, and Remedies', in D. Stern and J. Ritzen (eds), *Market Failure in Training*, Springer-Verlag, Berlin Heidelberg.
SHACKLETON, J. R. (1992). 'Training Too Much? A Sceptical Look at the Economics of Skill Provision in the UK', Hobart Paper 118, Institute of Economic Affairs, London.
STERN, D. and RITZEN, J. (1991). *Market Failure in Training*, Springer-Verlag, Berlin Heidelberg.
STEVENS, M. (1993). 'Some Issues in the Economics of Training', University of Oxford D. Phil thesis.
STEVENS, M. (1994). 'Transferable Training and Poaching Externalities', in A. Booth and D. Snower (eds). *Acquiring Skills: Market Failures, their Symptoms, and Policy Responses*, Cambridge University Press.
TIROLE, J. (1989). *The Theory of Industrial Organization*, The MIT Press, Cambridge, MA, 211.

APPENDIX

An outline of proofs is provided here. Further details of the algebraic manipulation can be found in Stevens (1993).

1. Derivation of expressions for returns to training in Section 5

Let u^1 and u^2 be the first two order statistics for the values in the external firms only $(v_1, \ldots, v_n)$. Then the expressions for the returns obtained in Proposition 2 can be written:

Total return, $R = E[\max(v_0, u^1)]$
Return to worker, $R_w = R_{0w} + R_{1w}$, the sum of the returns received in the training firm and

560   A THEORETICAL MODEL OF ON-THE-JOB TRAINING

elsewhere, where:

$R_{0w} = E[u^1|v_0 > u^1]Pr[v_0 > u^1]$

Return to training firm, $R_0 = E[v_0|v_0 > u^1]Pr[v_0 > u^1] - R_{0w}$

$R_{1w} = E[u^2|u^2 > v_0]Pr[u^2 > v_0] + E[v_0|u^1 > v_0 > u^2]Pr[u^1 > v_0 > u^2]$

Sum of returns to external firms, $X = E[u^1|u^1 > v_0]Pr[u^1 > v_0] - R_{1w}$

The density functions for $(v_0\text{-}m\text{-}a)$, $(u^1\text{-}m)$ and $(u^2\text{-}m)$ are $f(.)$, $f_n(.) = nf(.)F(.)^{n-1}$ and $f_n^2(.) = n(n-1)F(.)^{n-2}f(.)(1 - F(.))$ respectively. Hence, evaluating these expressions

$$R_{0w} = \iint_{a+x>y} (m + y)f_n(y)f(x) = \int_{-1}^{1} (m + y)f_n(y)(1 - F(y - a))\,dy$$

$$R_0 + R_{0w} = \iint_{a+x>y} (m + a + x)f_n(y)f(x)\,dx\,dy = \int_{a-1}^{1+a} (m + y)F_n(y)f(y - a)\,dy$$

$$\mathbf{R_0} = (R_0 + R_{0w}) - R_{0w}$$

$$= \int_{-1}^{1+a} (m + y)\frac{d}{dy}\{-F_n(y)(1 - F(y - a))\}\,dy = \int_{-1}^{1+a} F_n(y)(1 - F(y - a))\,dy$$

$$R_{1w} = \iint_{a+x<y} (m + y)f_n^2(y)f(x)\,dx\,dy + \iiint_{y<a+x<z} (m + a + x)f(x)f_{n-1}(y)nf(z)\,dx\,dy\,dz$$

$$= \int_{-1}^{1} (m + y)f_n(y)F(y - a)\,dy - \int_{-1}^{1} n(1 - F(y))F(y - a)F(y)^{n-1}\,dy$$

$$X + R_{1w} = \iint_{a+x<y} (m + y)f_n(y)f(x)\,dx\,dy = \int_{a-1}^{1} (m + y)f_n(y)F(y - a)\,dy$$

$$\mathbf{X} = (X + R_{1w}) - R_{1w} = \int_{a-1}^{1} n(1 - F(y))F(y - a)F(y)^{n-1}\,dy$$

$$\mathbf{R_w} = R_{0w} + (X + R_{1w}) - X = m + \int_{-1}^{1} y f_n(y)\,dy - X$$

$$\mathbf{R} = (R_0 + R_{0w}) + (X + R_{0w})$$

$$= \int_{a-1}^{1+a} (m + y)\frac{d}{dy}\{F_n(y)F(y - a)\}\,dy = m + 1 + a - \int_{a-1}^{1+a} F_n(y)F(y - a)\,dy$$

Finally, the probability that the worker moves is

$$P = Pr[u^1 > v_0] = \iint_{a+x<y} f_n(y)f(x)\,dx\,dy = \int_{a-1}^{1} f_n(y)F(y - a)\,dy$$

M. STEVENS   561

2. Proof of Proposition 5(ii) $\dfrac{\partial^2 R_p}{\partial a^2} \geqslant 0$

$$\frac{\partial X}{\partial a} = -\int_{a-1}^{1} n(1 - F(y))f(y-a)F(y)^{n-1}\,\mathrm{d}y$$

Integrating by parts gives

$$\frac{\partial X}{\partial a} = \int_{a-1}^{1} F(y-a)\{f_n^2(y) - f_n(y)\}\,\mathrm{d}y$$

$$\frac{\partial^2 X}{\partial a^2} = \int_{a-1}^{1} f(y-a)\{f_n(y) - f_n^2(y)\}\,\mathrm{d}y$$

We know from proposition 4(i) that $\dfrac{\partial^2 R}{\partial a^2} = \displaystyle\int_{a-1}^{1} f(y-a)f_n(y)\,\mathrm{d}y$

Hence, $\dfrac{\partial^2 R_p}{\partial a^2} = \dfrac{\partial^2 R}{\partial a^2} - \dfrac{\partial^2 X}{\partial a^2} = \displaystyle\int_{a-1}^{1} f(y-a)f_n^2(y)\,\mathrm{d}y \geqslant 0$

3. Proof of Proposition 7(iv) $\dfrac{\partial R_w}{\partial n} \geqslant 0$ if F is log-concave

From the expression for R_w, integrating by parts gives

$$R_w = m + 1 - \int_{-1}^{1} F_n(y)\left(1 - \frac{\partial}{\partial y}\left[\frac{(1 - F(y))F(y-a)}{f(y)}\right]\right)\mathrm{d}y$$

$$\frac{\partial R_w}{\partial n} = -\int_{-1}^{1} \log(F(y))F_n(y)\left(1 - \frac{\partial}{\partial y}\left[\frac{(1 - F(y))F(y-a)}{f(y)}\right]\right)\mathrm{d}y$$

It can be shown (Stevens, 1993) that for log-concave distributions

$\dfrac{\partial}{\partial y}\left[\dfrac{(1 - F(y))F(y-a)}{f(y)}\right] \leqslant 1$ $\forall y$, from which the result follows immediately.

4. Proof of Proposition 10 $\dfrac{\mathrm{d}a^*}{\mathrm{d}a_0} \geqslant 0, \dfrac{\mathrm{d}a^*}{\mathrm{d}n} \leqslant 0$

Suppressing the other arguments we can write the first order condition for a^*

$$\frac{\partial R}{\partial a}(a_0 + a^*) = \frac{\partial C}{\partial a}(a^*)$$

562   A THEORETICAL MODEL OF ON-THE-JOB TRAINING

Differentiating with respect to a_0 gives:

$$\left[1 + \frac{\mathrm{d}a^*}{\mathrm{d}a_0}\right]\frac{\partial^2 R}{\partial a^2} = \frac{\mathrm{d}a^*}{\mathrm{d}a_0}\frac{\partial^2 C}{\partial a^2}$$

$$\frac{\mathrm{d}a^*}{\mathrm{d}a_0}\left[\frac{\partial^2 C}{\partial a^2} - \frac{\partial^2 R}{\partial a^2}\right] = \frac{\partial^2 R}{\partial a^2}$$

Since the term in square brackets must be positive at a^*, and $\partial^2 R/\partial a^2 \geqslant 0$, $\mathrm{d}a^*/\mathrm{d}a_0 \geqslant 0$. Differentiating the first order condition with respect to n

$$\frac{\partial^2 R}{\partial n\,\partial a} + \frac{\mathrm{d}a^*}{\mathrm{d}n}\frac{\partial^2 R}{\partial a^2} = \frac{\mathrm{d}a^*}{\mathrm{d}n}\frac{\partial^2 C}{\partial a^2}$$

and since $\partial^2 R/\partial n\partial a \leqslant 0$ (Proposition 7), $\mathrm{d}a^*/\mathrm{d}n \leqslant 0$

[2]

The Structure of Wages and Investment in General Training

Daron Acemoglu and Jörn-Steffen Pischke

Massachusetts Institute of Technology

In the human capital model with perfect labor markets, firms never invest in general skills and all costs of general training are borne by workers. When labor market frictions compress the structure of wages, firms may pay for these investments. The distortion in the wage structure turns "technologically" general skills into de facto "specific" skills. Credit market imperfections are neither necessary nor sufficient for firm-sponsored training. Since labor market frictions and institutions shape the wage structure, they may have an important impact on the financing and amount of human capital investments and account for some international differences in training practices.

I. Introduction

The distinction between general and specific skills is the cornerstone of the standard theory of human capital as developed by Becker (1964). Specific skills are useful only with the current employer, whereas general skills are as useful with other employers. In competitive labor markets, workers capture all the returns to their general human capital, and employers have no incentive to pay for investments in these skills. In this paper, we show that if labor market frictions reduce the wages of skilled workers relative to wages of un-

We thank an anonymous referee, Joshua Angrist, Alan Krueger, Kevin Lang, Andrew Oswald, Sherwin Rosen, Eric Smith, Robert Topel, Michael Waldman, and various seminar participants for helpful comments. Financial support from the German Federal Ministry for Research and Technology and National Science Foundation grant SBR-9602116 (Acemoglu) is gratefully acknowledged.

[*Journal of Political Economy*, 1999, vol. 107, no. 3]

skilled workers (i.e., compress the structure of wages), firms may provide and pay for general training. Credit market problems and the presence of a long-term attachment between the worker and the firm are neither necessary nor sufficient to generate firm-sponsored training. The key is labor market imperfections, which imply that trained workers do not get paid their full marginal product when they change jobs, making *technologically general* skills de facto *specific.*[1]

There is a variety of evidence that suggests that, in line with our approach, firms provide and pay for general training. For example, in Germany, firms voluntarily offer apprenticeships to young workers, and general skills are an important component of these programs as evidenced by the fact that apprentices are given exams by outside boards at the end of their programs. The mere fact that firms provide general training does not establish that they pay the costs since workers may be taking a correspondingly lower wage relative to their marginal product. Nevertheless, most calculations suggest that employers pay for at least part of the costs. For example, the data reported in von Bardeleben, Beicht, and Fehér (1995) show that, even under conservative estimates, the *net* cost of an apprentice to a large German firm is over DM 7,500 a year (see also Harhoff and Kane 1997; Acemoglu and Pischke 1998*b*). Similarly, Ryan (1980) reports sizable net costs of apprenticeship training in a U.S. shipyard. An interesting example of firm-sponsored training is the case of temporary help agencies in the United States, which provide general training to new employees, such as computer and typing skills, and bear the full monetary costs (Krueger 1993; Autor 1998).

The main idea of our paper can be explained using figure 1, which draws the (marginal) product of a worker, $f(\tau)$, as a function of his or her skills, τ. Suppose that workers can quit and work for another firm and, in the process, incur a cost $\Delta \geq 0$. Under the assumption that workers will receive their full product on quitting, their outside option is $v(\tau) = f(\tau) - \Delta$. Suppose that the current employer can keep them by paying this outside option, so their wage is $w(\tau) = f(\tau) - \Delta$. The employer has no incentive to invest in the workers' skills because its profits are $f(\tau) - w(\tau) = \Delta$ irrespective of the value of τ. This is true despite the fact that when $\Delta > 0$, there are mobility

---

[1] In the standard theory, firms pay for skills that are specific, and which skills are specific is determined by technology. In contrast, we focus on skills that are technologically general in the sense that, without frictions, they will be as useful with other employers. Market structure and institutions determine, in equilibrium, which skills are turned into effectively "specific" skills. Becker realized that this may happen when he wrote that "in extreme types of monopsony . . . job alternatives for trained and untrained workers are nil, and all training, no matter what its nature, would be specific to the firm" ([1964] 1993, p. 50), but he did not pursue this further.

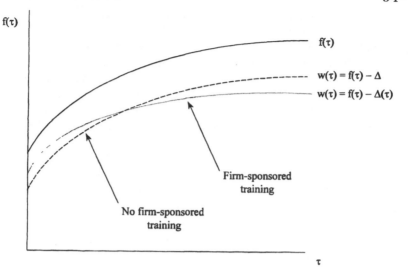

FIG. 1.—Wage structure and training

costs creating an attachment between workers and the firm. Also, notice that a perfectly competitive labor market corresponds to the case with $\Delta = 0$, and employers once again do not invest in general skills. Next, consider the main focus of our analysis, a labor market with a compressed wage structure.[2] Specifically, let the mobility cost be $\Delta(\tau)$, with $\Delta'(\tau) > 0$ as shown with the dotted curve in the figure. Since firms pay workers their outside options, profits are $f(\tau) - w(\tau) = \Delta(\tau)$. Because skilled workers face relatively worse outside opportunities, the equilibrium wage structure is compressed relative to productivity differentials, that is, $w'(\tau) < f'(\tau)$, and the firm makes greater profits from more skilled workers. Therefore, as long as training costs are not too large, the firm will find it profitable to invest in τ. This is the basic story of our paper, which is analyzed in more detail in Section II. In that section, we shall also establish a key comparative static result: even when workers are not credit constrained, as the wage structure becomes more compressed, firms pay for a larger fraction of the costs of general training, and when the structure of wages is sufficiently distorted, they may pay for all the costs.

Our partial equilibrium analysis in Section II assumes that, as in figure 1, the *external wage structure*, $v(\tau)$, is distorted, inducing em-

[2] The evidence in Bishop (1987) and Barron, Berger, and Black (1997) shows that wages across workers doing the same job in the same firm differ much less than their productivities, suggesting that the structure of wages in practice is compressed.

ployers to compress the internal wage structure, and shows how this wage compression leads to firm-sponsored training. In Section III, we investigate why a distorted external wage structure may emerge. We show that a range of plausible frictions, such as search, informational asymmetries, and efficiency wages, lead to this type of distortion. Furthermore, even when the labor market is frictionless, complementarities between technologically general and specific skills may induce firms to invest in the general skills of their workers. Finally, we also show that labor market institutions such as union wage setting and minimum wages, which also compress the structure of wages, may encourage firms to invest in the general skills of their employees. Therefore, our model predicts that in a variety of circumstances, we should observe firm-sponsored investments in general training.

The link we draw between labor market institutions and human capital accumulation may be useful in evaluating international patterns in training provision. There are important differences between labor market institutions of Anglo-Saxon economies, continental Europe, and Japan. For example, in contrast to the United States and the United Kingdom, in Germany and Sweden, unions play an important role in wage determination, and there are relatively high wage floors set by minimum wages and unemployment benefits (e.g., OECD 1994). Many economists believe that these institutions compress returns to skills (e.g., Blau and Kahn 1996; Edin and Topel 1997). Comparisons of wage dispersion and returns to education support this view. For example, in the mid-1980s, the log difference of ninetieth and tenth percentile wages was 1.73 in the United States and 1.11 in the United Kingdom as opposed to 0.83 in Germany, 0.67 in Sweden, 1.22 in France, and 1.01 in Japan (OECD 1993). It has also been argued that wage compression reduces not only employment but also investments in human capital (e.g., Lindbeck et al. 1993). In contrast, in our theory a compressed wage structure may induce firms to provide and pay for general training. Therefore, we expect that European and Japanese labor market institutions may increase one of the components of investment in human capital, firm-sponsored general training, and possibly even contribute to total human capital accumulation.[3]

---

[3] The incidence of company-provided *formal* training appears to be higher in Europe and Japan than in the United States: OECD (1994, table 4.7) reports that 23.6 percent of young workers in France, 71.5 percent of those in Germany, and 67.1 percent of new hires in Japan receive formal training. By way of comparison, only 10.2 percent of U.S. workers receive any formal training during their first 7 years of labor market experience. These data are collected using different methods, however, and are not easily comparable. Using the U.S. National Longitudinal Survey of Youth (NLSY), e.g., Loewenstein and Spletzer (1999) report the incidence of

STRUCTURE OF WAGES   543

Since labor market distortions make general skills firm-specific, our model is consistent with a variety of evidence traditionally used to support the presence of firm-specific human capital. But it suggests that many of these apparently specific skills may be more general, which is in line with the fact that in surveys workers claim that most of the training they receive provides skills useful with other employers. For example, Barron, Berger, and Black (1997) find that employers claim that training is valuable with other firms, but productivity growth associated with training exceeds wage growth by a factor of 10. Also, in our economy, as in models of specific training, employers recoup the costs of general training later during the tenure of the workers, which is consistent with Loewenstein and Spletzer's (1998b) finding that wage returns to general and specific training provided by the current employer are quite similar. Finally, since training is general, our model predicts an experience premium: wages are higher during the later career of workers because of the investments during the early years. Furthermore, because market frictions make these skills partly specific, there is also a tenure premium (see Altonji and Shakotko 1987; Topel 1991; Altonji and Williams 1997). We discuss other empirical predictions of our analysis and the relevant evidence in Section III.

II. Partial Equilibrium

A. The Environment

We work with the following two-period model throughout this section. In period 1, which we view as the early career of the worker, the employer or the worker or both choose how much to invest in the worker's general human capital, denoted by $\tau \in R_+$. We normalize production during this period to zero and denote the worker's first-period wage by W. In period 2, the worker either stays with the firm at a wage $w(\tau)$ or decides to quit and obtains an outside wage, $v(\tau)$. We also assume that with probability q, the firm and the worker receive an adverse shock, cease to be productive together, and separate. With probability $1 - q$, they can continue their productive relation. Therefore, q is a measure of (expected) turnover in our model. We ignore discounting and assume that all agents are risk-neutral and have preferences defined over the single good of this economy.

Each worker produces output $f(\tau)$ independent of the number

---

formal training as 17 percent. There are also important differences between numbers for formal and informal training. Loewenstein and Spletzer discuss various data sources on informal training for the United States. They find the incidence of informal training to be between 28 percent and 38 percent in the NLSY.

and human capital of other workers.[4] The function $f(\cdot)$ is increasing, differentiable, and concave. If he receives no training, the worker is as productive as during his early career, $f(0) = 0$. The cost of acquiring τ units of skill is $c(\tau)$ in terms of the final good and is incurred by the firm (although the worker can pay for it by having $W < 0$). We assume that $c(\tau)$ is everywhere strictly increasing, differentiable, and convex, with $c'(0) = c(0) = 0$ and $\lim_{\tau \to \infty} c'(\tau) = \infty$. These conditions ensure that the first-best training level, τ^*, is given by $c'(\tau^*) = f'(\tau^*)$, and from the assumptions on the cost of training, $\tau^* > 0$.

The productivity of the worker is the same in all firms since τ is general human capital. The assumption that there are no (technologically) firm-specific skills is extreme but serves to highlight our focus: the presence of frictions may transform technologically general capital into firm-specific human capital. We discuss how technologically specific and general skills interact in Section III C.

We distinguish three cases below. In the first, which we call the *constrained regime,* a worker cannot take a wage cut during the first period in order to compensate the firm for the expenses of training, so only the firm makes training investments. The most satisfactory justification for this is contractual problems between the firm and the worker; for example, the employer may not be able to commit to providing training after the worker makes a wage concession. A more common explanation in the literature for why workers do not make contributions to training investments has been the idea that young workers may be credit constrained (see, e.g., Ritzen and Stern 1991). However, since zero output in the first period is only a normalization, it is possible that the worker produces some amount $y_1 > 0$ in the first period and can contribute to training expenses by taking a wage lower than y_1. Nevertheless, such a wage concession would still be costly in the absence of perfect capital markets because it would lead to a nonsmooth consumption profile. Therefore, credit constraints also provide a justification for the constrained regime.

Despite these possible justifications, it should be clear that the constrained regime is an extreme case, and we consider it only to focus on our main innovation—firms' incentives to invest in general training—and to highlight the contrast between perfect and imperfect labor markets. In the second case we consider, the *noncooperative*

---

[4] This assumption is not as restrictive as it appears. For example, if total output is a function of human capital H and physical capital K, $F(H, K)$ exhibits constant returns to scale, and K can be adjusted freely, then the marginal contribution of a worker with human capital τ, $y = f(\tau)$, will be independent of the level of H. The reason is that an optimizing firm will keep the ratio of physical to human capital, K/H, constant.

regime, firms can credibly commit to a level of training, and workers are not credit constrained. However, firms and workers make decisions about training unilaterally, and we allow firms to make positive profits. In particular, we start with a first-period wage $W = 0$, but the worker chooses how much to contribute to training by taking a wage cut. So the level of training is $\tau = c^{-1}(\gamma_f + \gamma_w)$, where c^{-1} is the inverse function of the cost of training, $c(\tau)$; γ_f is the firm's contribution to training costs; and γ_w is the contribution of the worker, so his first-period wage is $W = -\gamma_w$. Our analysis of the noncooperative regime will show that the main results of the constrained regime carry over to this case, demonstrating that contractual problems or credit constraints are not essential for our results.

The third case is the *full-competition regime*, where firms compete in the first period by offering training-wage combinations $\{W, \tau\}$ to workers, and in equilibrium they make zero profits. Contractual problems and credit constraints are once again absent, so $W < 0$ is allowed. This case leads to a number of different results, but our main conclusions that firms may pay for general training and that the extent of their payments depends on the degree of wage compression continue to apply. The assumption that contractual problems are absent in the noncooperative and the full-competition regimes is reasonable when firms have long-term reputations but might be harder to justify in other circumstances, for example when firms are small or face a high probability of failure. We therefore believe that different regimes may be more reasonable descriptions for particular labor markets or episodes.

B. Training in a Perfectly Competitive Labor Market

If a worker quits after the first period, she receives a wage of $v(\tau)$ in the outside labor market. Before discussing labor market frictions, we set the stage by reviewing the case of a competitive labor market. Since all skills are general and the worker can quit at no cost, we have $v(\tau) = f(\tau)$. This implies that workers have to be paid their full marginal product,[5] that is, $w(\tau) = v(\tau) = f(\tau)$. The following result is immediate.

PROPOSITION 1. Suppose that we are in the constrained regime and labor markets are competitive. Then the equilibrium training level is $\hat{\tau} = 0$ (and $W = 0$).

In this case, the worker cannot contribute to training costs, so the firm chooses the level of training unilaterally. Since $w(\tau) = f(\tau)$, the firm cannot recoup the costs of training during the later career of

---

[5] Recall that the marginal product of the worker is equal to $f(\tau)$, not $f'(\tau)$.

the worker, so no investment takes place, even though the optimal amount of training, τ^*, is strictly positive. It is sometimes asserted that credit constraints faced by workers may induce firms to invest in general training. Proposition 1 shows that such constraints are not sufficient for firm-sponsored training.

We next analyze the noncooperative and full-competition regimes.

PROPOSITION 2. In both the noncooperative and the full-competition regimes, when labor markets are competitive, the equilibrium level of training is $\hat{\tau} = \tau^*$ and $W = -c(\tau^*)$.

Consider first the noncooperative regime. Here the worker realizes that the firm will not contribute to training, so $\gamma_f = 0$ and $\tau = c^{-1}(-W)$. Hence, the worker chooses $W = -c(\tau^*)$, which induces training τ^*, and achieves the highest lifetime payoff. Intuitively, since the worker is the full residual claimant of returns from training, he has the right incentives to invest.

In the full-competition regime, firms compete to attract workers in the first period and are forced to offer the highest lifetime utility, which in this case is $f(\tau^*) - c(\tau^*)$. So firms provide training τ^* and ensure that the worker pays for the cost by offering $\{W, \tau\} = \{-c(\tau^*), \tau^*\}$. Workers, who are paying the costs of general training, again have the right incentives to invest, and the first-best level of training is achieved.

Therefore, when labor markets are competitive and workers are allowed to contribute to training, the equilibrium achieves first-best training and the worker bears the full costs, as emphasized in Becker's (1964) seminal analysis. Note that the presence of separations with probability q is of no consequence because the worker gets exactly the same returns for his general human capital in the outside market.

C. Frictional Labor Markets in the Constrained Regime

We now model frictional labor markets by assuming that $v(\tau) < f(\tau)$. Despite the fact that τ is general human capital, when the worker separates from his employer, he receives a wage lower than his marginal product. In the next section, we discuss in detail how different types of frictions and institutions determine $v(\tau)$ and its relation to $f(\tau)$. For now, we take $v(\tau)$ as given and assume that $v''(\tau) \geq f''(\tau)$, which is a sufficient (but not necessary) restriction for the second-order conditions to hold. In the specific examples in Section III, this restriction will hold. Since $v(\tau) < f(\tau)$, there is a surplus that the firm and the worker can share when they are together. For the exposition in this section, we adopt the Nash bargaining approach. We also start with the constrained regime and return to the other cases below.

Asymmetric Nash bargaining and risk neutrality imply that $w(\tau)$, the second-period wage at the current firm, is

$$w(\tau) = v(\tau) + \beta[f(\tau) - v(\tau) - \pi_0], \qquad (1)$$

where $\beta \in [0, 1]$ is the bargaining power of the worker, and π_0 is the outside option of the firm, which we normalize to zero. The equilibrium wage rate $w(\tau)$ is independent of the cost of training, $c(\tau)$. This is a feature of the temporal structure of our economy. The level of training is chosen by the firm, and then the worker and the firm bargain over the wage rate. At this point, training costs are already sunk.

Profits of the firm are

$$\pi(\tau) = (1 - q)[f(\tau) - w(\tau)] - c(\tau)$$
$$= (1 - \beta)(1 - q)[f(\tau) - v(\tau)] - c(\tau),$$

where we have incorporated the fact that, with probability q, there will be an involuntary separation. In this regime the firm decides the level of training and bears all the costs, so it chooses τ to maximize $\pi(\tau)$, which gives the first-order condition

$$(1 - \beta)(1 - q)[f'(\hat{\tau}) - v'(\hat{\tau})] - c'(\hat{\tau}) = 0. \qquad (2)$$

The necessary condition for the firm to invest in the general human capital of the worker, that is, for $\hat{\tau} > 0$, is $\pi'(0) > 0$. Since $c'(0) = 0$, firms will invest in training if and only if $f'(0) > v'(0)$ and $(1 - \beta)(1 - q) > 0$.

PROPOSITION 3. Suppose that we are in the constrained regime, labor markets are frictional, $\beta < 1$, and $q < 1$. Then as long as $f'(0) > v'(0)$, the firm invests a positive amount in general skills, that is, $\hat{\tau} > 0$.

In contrast to the case of competitive labor markets, the firm may now have an incentive to invest in the general skills of its workers. The condition $f'(0) > v'(0)$ implies that the wage structure is compressed (at the point of $\tau = 0$), so an increase in the worker's productivity increases profits, encouraging the firm to invest in training.[6] What is relevant to the firm is the wage it pays, $w(\tau)$, that is, the internal wage structure. However, the internal wage structure is endogenous and is linked to the external wage structure, $v(\tau)$. In particular, the wage rule (1) implies $w'(\tau) = \beta f'(\tau) + (1 - \beta)v'(\tau)$.

---

[6] The additional requirements that $\beta < 1$ and $q < 1$ ensure that the firm gets some rents from the relation and that the employment relationship does not end with probability one.

Therefore, $f'(\tau) > v'(\tau)$ is equivalent to $f'(\tau) > w'(\tau)$, so that wages increase less with skills than productivity does, and the firm makes higher profits from trained workers. In other words, the internal wage structure is distorted only when the external wage structure is.[7] Note, however, that $v'(\tau) < f'(\tau)$ does *not* imply that training is less productive with other firms: since τ is general skills, the worker produces $f(\tau)$ with outside firms; but moving to a new firm is costly, and more so for more skilled workers. More explicit microfoundations for these costs will be given in the next section.

Although a distorted wage structure encourages firms to pay for training, equilibrium training, $\hat{\tau}$, is generally less than the first-best, τ^*. In particular, as long as $\beta > 0$ and $v'(\tau^*) > 0$, or if $q > 0$, equation (2) implies that $\hat{\tau} < \tau^*$.

A key comparative static result is immediate from our analysis so far. Let $v(\tau) = a\bar{v}(\tau)$. Then everything else being equal, a reduction in a increases firms' investments in training, $\hat{\tau}$ (see eq. [2]). A decrease in a reduces the outside option of skilled workers relative to the outside opportunities of the unskilled, compressing the wage structure. This implies that the firm can capture additional rents from the skilled, so it invests more in its employees' skills. Therefore, contrary to conventional wisdom, a more compressed wage structure may improve human capital investments.

This result implies that the distortion of the wage structure may actually improve welfare. This is the well-known theory of the second-best at work. Since in the constrained regime training outcomes are inefficient, another distortion, in this case in the labor market, may induce firms to undertake some of these investments and improve output and welfare. For example, a move from $v(\tau) = f(\tau)$ to $v(\tau) = af(\tau) + b$ with $a < 1$ increases human capital investments and does not affect other margins, so it increases net output (since $\hat{\tau} = 0 < \tau^*$). Naturally, in practice, increased frictions will have a number of allocative costs, such as lower employment. These costs need to be compared to the benefits in terms of better training incentives. Also our simple example in which workers cannot take wage cuts to bear the costs of training exaggerates the potential benefits from a distortion in the wage structure (see the next two subsections). In any case, the implications of labor market frictions on

[7] This is a feature of Nash bargaining. Other bargaining solutions give similar results but make the dependence of the internal on the external wage structure less transparent. Notice also that $v(\tau)$ and $w(\tau)$ are the wage structures "off the equilibrium path" because all workers and firms are homogeneous. So they invest the same amount, and in equilibrium we observe only $v(\hat{\tau})$ and $w(\hat{\tau})$. It is straightforward, but not very instructive, to introduce worker or firm heterogeneity so that in equilibrium we observe different workers paid different wages.

training are worth bearing in mind when suggesting labor market reforms. For example, proposals for reducing union power and removing other regulations in the German labor market, which are on the current political agenda, could have unforeseen consequences regarding the German apprenticeship system, where employers pay for the general training of their workers.

Another useful comparative static result pertains to turnover, q. Equation (2) immediately implies that $d\hat{\tau}/dq < 0$, so turnover reduces training. The reason is that the firm benefits from training only when the worker does not change jobs, and higher turnover makes this less likely. Since the equilibrium level of training, $\hat{\tau}$, is already less than the first-best τ^*, an increase in q makes training suboptimally low. It is often argued that high-turnover economies such as the United States do not generate sufficient investments in worker skills and that this represents an important market failure (e.g., Blinder and Krueger 1996). Indeed, cross-sectional comparisons reveal that high-turnover countries or industries have lower training. For example, Topel and Ward (1992) find that the median number of jobs held by a male worker with 10 years of experience is six in the U.S. labor market, whereas it is one (Acemoglu and Pischke 1998*b*) or two (Dustmann and Meghir 1997) in Germany, where young workers are much more likely to receive formal training (see also OECD 1994). Our model explains these correlations and suggests why high turnover causes less training in general skills, and why this may represent a market failure. Standard theory predicts a negative correlation between specific skills and turnover but suggests that such a negative correlation is optimal.

While we find a link between general training and turnover, it should be stressed that it is not the attachment between firms and workers that leads to firm-sponsored training. To see this, suppose that $q = 0$ and outside employers offer wages equal to $f(\tau)$, but there is a cost of moving to a new employer, Δ, so that the worker receives $v(\tau) = f(\tau) - \Delta$. In this case, $w(\tau) = f(\tau) - (1 - \beta)\Delta$, and all workers stay with their initial firms. Although workers never leave their employer, there is no firm-sponsored investment in training because there is no distortion in the wage structure, that is, $v'(\tau) = w'(\tau) = f'(\tau)$.

It is also worth noting that when $v'(0) < f'(0)$ so that firms invest in training, there is both an experience premium and a tenure premium. The experience premium, conditional on tenure, is given by the change in wages for a worker who switches employers, that is, $EP = v(\hat{\tau}) - W$. Since $W = 0$, $EP > 0$ except in the extreme case in which the outside wage structure does not reflect any of the general skills. The tenure premium, on the other hand, is the additional wage increase that workers staying with their initial employers receive compared to switchers, which in this case is equal to $w(\hat{\tau}) - v(\hat{\tau}) = \beta[f(\hat{\tau}) - v(\hat{\tau})]$. Estimates in the literature suggest that an increase in profit per worker increases wages, and the coefficient, which corresponds to β, varies between 0.003 and 0.3 (see Abowd and Lemieux 1993; Blanchflower, Oswald, and Sanfey 1996). This suggests possible tenure effects ranging from quite small to sizable, consistent with empirical evidence that finds different tenure effects depending on specification and sample (e.g., Altonji and Shakotko 1987; Topel 1991; Altonji and Williams 1997).

Proposition 3 shows that firms prefer to pay for the training rather than employ an unskilled work force when wage differentials are compressed. However, there might be another, more profitable, strategy, which is to hire (poach) trained workers in the second period. In order to understand this poaching problem, notice that workers have no incentive to quit in equilibrium since $w(\tau) > v(\tau)$, but firms would like to hire trained workers because $w(\tau) < f(\tau)$. Whether poaching trained workers from other firms is profitable or not depends on the source of the distortion causing $v(\tau) < f(\tau)$. Since we take the external wage structure as given, we delay a more detailed discussion of this possibility until we analyze more specific mechanisms in the next section.

D. *Firm-Sponsored Training in the Noncooperative Regime*

We now discuss the impact of labor market frictions on training when both firms and workers can contribute to training investments. We find that, contrary to common beliefs, credit market problems are *not* necessary for firms to bear the cost of general training. Whether they do or not is once again determined by the structure of wages.

Recall that in this regime, training investments by firms and workers are chosen *noncooperatively*. In particular, we start with a first-period wage $W = 0$, and the worker and the firm simultaneously choose the amount of money they wish to spend on training, γ_w and γ_f. The amount of training is τ_{nc} such that $c(\tau_{nc}) = \gamma_w + \gamma_f$ or $\tau_{nc} = c^{-1}(\gamma_w + \gamma_f)$, and the worker's first-period wage is $W = -\gamma_w$. Therefore, the worker maximizes $v(\tau_{nc}) + (1 - q)\beta[f(\tau_{nc}) - v(\tau_{nc})] - \gamma_w$ by choosing $\gamma_w \geq 0$ and takes γ_f as given. Intuitively, with probability $1 - q$, the worker stays with the firm at the wage $w(\tau) = \beta f(\tau) + (1 - \beta)v(\tau)$. With probability q, he is forced to quit and receives $v(\tau)$. The first-order condition for the worker's contribution is

STRUCTURE OF WAGES   551

$$v'(\tau_{nc}) + (1 - q)\beta[f'(\tau_{nc}) - v'(\tau_{nc})] - c'(\tau_{nc}) = 0 \quad \text{if } \gamma_w > 0$$
$$\leq 0 \quad \text{if } \gamma_w = 0. \tag{3}$$

Similarly, the firm maximizes $(1 - q)(1 - \beta)[f(\tau_{nc}) - v(\tau_{nc})] - \gamma_f$ by choosing $\gamma_f \geq 0$ and taking γ_w as given. The first-order condition for the firm is

$$(1 - q)(1 - \beta)[f'(\tau_{nc}) - v'(\tau_{nc})] - c'(\tau_{nc}) = 0 \quad \text{if } \gamma_f > 0$$
$$\leq 0 \quad \text{if } \gamma_f = 0, \tag{4}$$

which is essentially the same as (2). Inspection of equations (3) and (4) implies that, generically, only one of them holds as an equality, so one of the parties bears the full cost of training. The reason is that the contributions of the worker and the firm are perfect substitutes. More precisely, let τ_w be the level of training that satisfies (3) as an equality and τ_f be the solution to (4) as an equality. Then we get the following proposition.

PROPOSITION 4. Suppose that we are in the noncooperative regime. If $\tau_f > \tau_w$, then the firm bears all the cost of training, $W = \gamma_w = 0$, and $\tau_{nc} = \tau_f$. In contrast, if $\tau_w > \tau_f$, then $\gamma_f = 0$, the worker bears all the cost of training, $W = \gamma_w = -c(\tau_{nc})$, and $\tau_{nc} = \tau_w$.

Despite the fact that training is general and the worker is *not* credit constrained, the firm may bear all the costs of training. When $\tau_f > \tau_w$, the results in Section IIC continue to hold. Therefore, for our results that firms pay for general training to be true, we do not need the assumption that workers cannot contribute to the costs of training: as long as the structure of wages is sufficiently distorted, firms will be more willing to invest in training than workers, and they will bear all the costs.

An important result of this analysis is that the more distorted the wage structure is (i.e., the lower v' is relative to f'), the more likely the firm, rather than the worker, is to pay for training. Therefore, our model predicts that in economies with compressed wage structures such as Germany and Sweden, employers should pay for general training, whereas in the United States it may be the workers who bear the cost of a range of training investments (such as vocational courses). Also, when the firm is paying for training, a further distortion in the wage structure increases training, whereas when workers are bearing the costs, a distortion in the structure of wages reduces training. Finally, inspection of (3) and (4) shows that a larger bargaining power for the firm, that is, a lower value of β, makes it more likely that the firm will finance the costs of training. The reason is that for a given $v(\tau)$, a decline in β makes the *internal wage structure* more compressed, encouraging the firm to make a larger contribution to training.

Hashimoto (1979, 1981) and Hashimoto and Yu (1980) have previously analyzed how costs of investments in specific training are shared between the firm and the worker. Since labor market imperfections turn τ into de facto specific skills, our analysis is related to this work. Hashimoto's work assumes that there are transaction costs, causing inefficient separations later in the career of workers. In particular, workers and firms receive idiosyncratic taste and productivity shocks and can unilaterally decide to end the relation. The firm-worker pair therefore shares productivity gains to minimize inefficient separations, and this sharing rule for returns from training dictates how the costs of investments should be shared. Our analysis differs in that there are no transaction costs after investment and, thus, no inefficient separations in the second period. However, one might view our model as including "transaction costs" at the point of training, which force workers and firms to make their contributions to training investments *noncooperatively* (in the next subsection, we remove these transaction costs). This feature implies that the expectation of future returns, partially shaped by outside wages, determines the willingness of the parties to invest. When the external wage structure is highly distorted, the resulting internal wage structure does not reward the worker for his skills, so the firm has to pay all the cost. In this setup, either the firm or the worker pays for all the costs because investments by the two parties are perfect substitutes. With a modified setup in which $\tau = h(\gamma_w, \gamma_f)$ and the cross-partial derivative of h is nonzero, both the firm and the worker contribute to training as in Hashimoto's papers.

E. Training Investments in the Full-Competition Regime

Now workers can contribute to training costs and firms can commit to providing training, but in contrast to the noncooperative regime, firms compete for workers by offering wage-training packages, $\{W, \tau\}$, taking workers' valuation of the training into account. Firms maximize profits, which are (by substitution for the wage rule [1])

$$\pi(\tau, W) = (1 - q)(1 - \beta)[f(\tau) - v(\tau)] - c(\tau) - W, \quad (5)$$

by choosing W and τ, subject to the constraint that workers receive as much utility as that offered by other firms, U, which is

$$v(\tau) + (1 - q)\beta[f(\tau) - v(\tau)] + W \geq U. \quad (6)$$

Competition ensures that U is high enough so that $\pi = 0$.[8] This implies the following proposition.

PROPOSITION 5. In the full-competition regime, all firms offer first-period wage-training combination $\{W_{fc}, \tau_{fc}\}$ such that $c'(\tau_{fc}) = (1 - q)f'(\tau_{fc}) + qv'(\tau_{fc})$ and $W_{fc} = (1 - q)(1 - \beta)[f(\tau_{fc}) - v(\tau_{fc})] - c(\tau_{fc})$.

To understand the level of training in this case, note that full competition induces a "cooperative" choice of training.[9] In particular, in the noncooperative regime, the firm considered only its own profits when choosing its contribution to training. However now, via the participation constraint of the worker, (6), the firm takes into account how much the utility of the worker increases as a result of a marginal increase in training. This turns the problem into one of maximizing joint surplus, $(1 - q)f(\tau) + qv(\tau)$ (i.e., with probability $1 - q$, the pair remains together and the joint return is $f(\tau)$; and with probability q, there is a separation, and the firm receives no return from training whereas the worker receives $v(\tau)$).

Notice that as long as $q > 0$, the external wage structure continues to matter for training. However, a more distorted external wage structure now reduces training. Also when $q > 0$ and $f'(\tau) > v'(\tau)$, the level of training investment is generally less than the first-best amount, because with probability q the worker is employed by another firm. So ex ante investments create positive externalities on his potential future employers (this is not the case when $f'(\tau) > v'(\tau)$ is caused by complementarities between general and specific skills as in Sec. IIIC but is true in the other cases discussed in the next section). In particular, if $v(\tau)$ is the wage that future employers pay the worker, then their profit is equal to $f(\tau) - v(\tau)$, and a higher level of τ increases future employers' profitability. The worker and the firm do not take this into account in their training decisions, making training suboptimally low (see Acemoglu [1997] for further details).

More important, notice that as long as β is sufficiently less than one, we have $W > 0$. Therefore, the worker receives a positive salary, despite the fact that he is not credit constrained and his net output is $-c(\tau_{fc})$. In particular, the larger the gap between marginal product and the outside wage at the level of equilibrium training, $f(\tau_{fc}) - v(\tau_{fc})$, the greater the first-period wage. The gap $f(\tau_{fc}) - v(\tau_{fc})$ tends

---

[8] Otherwise, another firm would offer $U + \epsilon$, for ϵ sufficiently small and positive, attract all the workers, and make positive profits.

[9] We obtain very similar results when W and τ are determined by Nash bargaining in the first period. In particular, the presence of the first-period wage W makes utility fully transferable, so the choice of training would be "cooperative," i.e., maximize joint surplus.

to be larger when the external wage structure is more distorted (especially if we start with $f(0) = v(0)$). Therefore, our analysis with full competition also suggests that when the wage structure is more distorted, firms pay for a larger fraction of training costs. Intuitively, with imperfect labor markets, the worker has an attachment to his employer, enabling the firm to make positive profits in the second period. Competition then forces the firm to pay these profits in the first period. The firm's monopsony power in the second period originates from the gap between $f(\tau_{fc})$ and $v(\tau_{fc})$. So the more distorted $v(\tau)$ is (or the lower $v(\tau_{fc})$ is), the greater the rent the firm expects, and competition forces it to pay a larger fraction of the costs of training. In fact, if $f(\tau_{fc}) = v(\tau_{fc})$ as in competitive markets, the firm earns no rents in the second period, so $W = -c(\tau_{fc})$; that is, the firm pays nothing toward general training. Therefore, the important conclusion overall is that although the assumption of full competition modifies our analysis, as long as the labor market is imperfect, firms continue to contribute to the cost of general training, and their contribution tends to be larger when the (external) wage structure is more compressed. Hence, except for the impact of wage compression on the total amount of training, our qualitative results from the constrained regime continue to hold.[10]

Our analysis of full competition is closer in spirit to Hashimoto's work. In particular, now there are no transaction costs in the first period, and so the level of training is chosen "cooperatively." While there are no inefficient separations, the firm cannot choose and commit to future wages, so returns from training are shared by Nash bargaining in the second period. Given this sharing rule, training costs are shared in the first period so as to ensure zero profits for the firm.

III. Specific Mechanisms and the Role of Institutions

The previous section described our simple theory of firm-sponsored investment in general training. The key ingredient was a compressed wage structure such that $f'(\tau) > w'(\tau)$. We found that the crucial condition to ensure this is $f'(\tau) > v'(\tau)$; that is, outside opportunities for the worker should improve less than his productivity as he acquires more skills. Although the structure of wages is taken as given by the firm and the worker, it is an equilibrium object. In this

---

[10] Also notice that the tenure premium, $\beta[f(\tau_{fc}) - v(\tau_{fc})]$, is again positive. The experience premium, $v(\tau_{fc}) - W_{fc}$, on the other hand, may be negative, but if β is sufficiently high, it will be positive.

section we discuss how a range of plausible labor market frictions lead to a distortion in the external wage structure, $v(\tau)$, inducing firm-sponsored training. Throughout this section, we simplify our discussion by focusing on the constrained regime, so we study only firms' incentives to invest in skills. Our analysis in Sections II*D* and II*E* shows that firms continue to pay for general training in the noncooperative and full-competition regimes. But in the full-competition regime a distortion in the external wage structure reduces training, whereas in the noncooperative regime it may reduce or increase investments. This has to be borne in mind when one interprets our results in this section. Our aim here is to bring out the major ideas rather than analyze each model fully. For this reason we keep the exposition as simple as possible.

A. Search and Monopsony

Consider the same setup as in Section II, but in the second period the worker has to find a new firm if he quits. With probability p_w, the worker is successful and finds a new employer; with probability $1 - p_w$, he is unemployed and receives unemployment benefit $b(\tau)$. If he finds an employer, he has to bargain with this firm to determine wages. The worker's outside option in this second and final bargain is zero. With the same bargaining power, β, for the worker as above, he will get a wage $w_2(\tau) = \beta f(\tau)$, and his new employer will capture a proportion $1 - \beta$ of the output. The fact that there is no further period is a special, but nonessential, feature. In the Appendix we analyze the infinite-horizon case and establish the same results.

The outside option of the worker in the bargain of the first period is therefore $v(\tau) = p_w \beta f(\tau) + (1 - p_w) b(\tau)$. The first-order condition for the firm's investment in training is therefore $(1 - \beta)[(1 - p_w\beta)f'(\tau) - (1 - p_w)b'(\tau)] = c'(\tau)$. As in Section II, firms invest in general training if the external wage structure is distorted against skilled workers (i.e., $f'(0) > v'(0)$). In this model, this is equivalent to $p_w\beta f'(0) + (1 - p_w)b'(0) < f'(0)$, which will be satisfied if $b'(0) < f'(0)$ and $p_w < 1$, or $\beta < 1$. Most unemployment insurance systems are progressive, so $b'(0) < f'(0)$ is a weak requirement, and $p_w < 1$ and $\beta < 1$ are almost always true in models with frictions. Therefore, under fairly weak conditions, this model predicts firm-sponsored investments in general training.

We refer to this situation as search-induced monopsony: because it is costly for the worker to change employers, the firm has some monopsony power and captures part of the higher output due to the worker's higher productivity. There are two costs of leaving the current employer that underlie the monopsony power of the firm.

First, the worker anticipates that his future employers will capture a certain fraction of his productivity, so the monopsony power of potential future employers contributes to the monopsony power of the current employer. Second, a worker who quits can suffer unemployment, which reduces the return to quitting. Both costs increase with skills, which compresses the equilibrium wage structure and induces firm-sponsored training (see the Appendix and also Acemoglu [1997] for further details).

This model predicts that when the labor market is more "frictional" in the sense that p_w, the exit rate from unemployment, is lower and unemployment higher, we should observe more firm-sponsored training. The reason is that a lower exit rate from unemployment, p_w, makes the wage structure more distorted since $b'(\tau) < f'(\tau)$. According to OECD (1993), monthly exit rates from unemployment are 48.2 percent in the United States, 22 percent in Japan, 7.6 percent in Germany, and 6.7 percent in France. Therefore, in line with our theory, the numbers reported in note 3 suggest that economies with more frictional markets may have more firm-sponsored formal training programs.

It is also instructive to contemplate whether poaching of trained workers may change the implications of this specific mechanism. The answer depends on the exact specification of the poaching process. A reasonable first pass is to consider a situation in which a new firm contacts and makes a poaching offer to an already-employed trained worker. This will create Bertrand competition between the two firms for this particular worker, increasing the worker's wage to his marginal product. Recall that in this model there are search frictions, so it is plausible that it would be costly for firms to find trained workers to make poaching offers to. Hence, anticipating that after a poaching offer there are no profit opportunities, firms would not make such offers. Therefore, introducing the possibility of poaching in the simplest way does not affect our main results.

B. Asymmetric Information

Skills may be technically general, but outside employers may be unable to ascertain whether a worker actually possesses these skills, or in what amount or quality. If this is the case, the outside wage will not reflect these uncredentialed skills, or not reflect them fully so that $f'(\tau) > v'(\tau)$. This has been suggested by Katz and Ziderman (1990) and analyzed by Chang and Wang (1996). Bishop (1994) finds empirical support for this notion using data from the National Federation of Independent Business Survey.

Information advantages of the incumbent employers may lead to firm-sponsored training even if the skills are observable. For example, the content of German apprenticeship programs is well known; thus τ is observed by outside firms, but the initial employer still has superior information regarding the ability of its workers. We have analyzed this case in Acemoglu and Pischke (1998*b*). The following adverse selection model is based on our previous work.

Workers have two different abilities denoted by η. A proportion p have low ability normalized to $\eta = 0$. The remaining proportion $1 - p$ have high ability with $\eta = 1$. The production function is $f(\tau, \eta) = \tau\eta$. The incumbent firm does not know the ability of a particular worker at the beginning of period 1 when it must decide about training. At the end of period 1, it learns the worker's type and offers a wage that can be contingent on ability, $w(\tau, \eta)$. Outside firms do not know worker ability but observe the level of training the worker has received. They offer a wage, $v(\tau)$, conditional on training. Workers quit their original employer whenever the outside wage is higher, that is, when $v(\tau) > w(\tau, \eta)$. We also assume that there are other (exogenous) reasons for quits, so that even when $w(\tau, \eta) \geq v(\tau)$, workers separate with probability λ.

To avoid issues of bargaining with asymmetric information, we give all the bargaining power to the incumbent firm by setting $\beta = 0$. Therefore, the firm will offer a wage $w(\tau, \eta = 0) = 0$ to low-ability workers and the lowest possible wage to high-ability workers that will prevent them from leaving, that is, $w(\tau, \eta = 1) = v(\tau)$. At this wage, only the fraction λ of the high-ability workers who are unhappy in this firm would quit. The outside market is competitive but, as noted above, cannot distinguish high-ability workers, so the outside wage is equal to the expected productivity of workers who separate. Since some high-ability workers quit (i.e., $\lambda > 0$), we have $v(\tau) > 0$. This implies that all low-ability workers will also quit to take advantage of the higher outside wage. In equilibrium, expected productivity and the wage in the outside market are

$$v(\tau) = \frac{\lambda(1 - p)\tau}{p + \lambda(1 - p)}.$$

The incumbent employer keeps a fraction $(1 - \lambda)(1 - p)$ of workers, all of whom are high-ability. Therefore, profits are given by

$$\pi(\tau) = (1 - \lambda)(1 - p)[\tau - w(\tau, 1)] - c(\tau)$$
$$= (1 - \lambda)(1 - p)[\tau - v(\tau)] - c(\tau).$$

In words, the firm pays the cost of training for all workers because worker ability is not observed before training. After training, all low-ability and a proportion λ of high-ability workers leave and the firm pays $v(\tau)$ to the remaining workers and makes profits equal to $\tau - v(\tau)$ per retained worker. Therefore, the first-order condition for training is

$$\pi'(\tau) = (1 - \lambda)(1 - p)[1 - v'(\tau)] - c'(\tau) = 0. \qquad (7)$$

The firm retains only highly skilled workers, so $f'(\tau) = 1$. Since we also have $c'(0) = 0$, the necessary and sufficient condition for firm-sponsored training is $v'(0) < 1$, our familiar condition that the wage structure should be compressed. It is immediate to see that this condition is always satisfied because $v'(\tau) = \lambda(1 - p)/[p + \lambda(1 - p)] < 1$. Intuitively, the presence of low-ability workers in the second-hand labor market implies that firms view workers in this market as "lemons." They are therefore unwilling to increase their wage offers by much for workers with higher τ because training is not useful to low-ability workers, who are the majority of those in the secondhand market.

Many of the assumptions in this example are inessential and were made only to simplify the exposition. The crucial ingredient is that training and ability are complements, as captured by the multiplicative production function $f(\tau, \eta) = \tau\eta$. To see the importance of complementarity between unobserved ability and training, consider instead $f(\tau, \eta) = \tau + \eta$. The outside wage in this case is

$$v(\tau) = \frac{p\tau + \lambda(1 - p)(1 + \tau)}{p + \lambda(1 - p)} = \tau + \frac{\lambda(1 - p)}{p + \lambda(1 - p)}.$$

The outside wage now increases one for one with τ, that is, $v'(\tau) = 1$. Therefore, (7) is satisfied at $\tau = 0$, and the firm does not invest in the training of its workers. The reason is that training raises the productivity of the more and less able workers by an equal amount. Asymmetric information still leads to rents for the incumbent firm, but it does *not* lead to a distortion of the wage structure.

In Acemoglu and Pischke (1998*b*), we discuss the case in which outside firms can make poaching offers, and we show that the results discussed here are robust to this extension. The intuition is that the superior information of the incumbent firm creates a "winner's curse": the incumbent would stop competing against the raiding firm only when the raider's offer exceeds the worker's productivity. As a result, the raider will attract the worker only when his productivity falls short of his wage. Also in that paper we present empirical evidence for adverse selection among German apprentices. We show that apprentices who leave their training firm because of the military draft (an exogenous separation) earn more than those who stay at the apprenticeship firm and other quitters. Unlike other quitters *and* stayers, military quitters are freed from the adverse selection problem because the reason for their separation is observed by the outside market.

C. Firm-Specific Human Capital

Our analysis has so far concentrated on general human capital for clarity. However, it is undoubtedly true that there exist skills that are more useful in the current firm than in outside firms. Becker's (1964) classic analysis discussed investment in such skills and concluded that the firm should pay for at least part of the costs, and Hashimoto (1979, 1981) showed how the costs of these investments are shared. In the presence of purely specific skills, markets are not competitive in the most usual sense; if a worker has some skills that can be used in only one firm, then for one of the commodities there is only one buyer and one seller, so price-taking behavior does not apply. In this subsection we show that this deviation from pure competition also leads to firm-sponsored investments in general training.

Assume that output in the second period is now given by $y = f(\tau, s)$, where s is firm-specific human capital. Once again, in the first period the firm chooses τ at cost $c(\tau)$, and there is an exogenous probability q that the pair will separate in the second period. The source of the firm-specific skill, s, is inessential: it could be acquired during the first period that the worker spends with the firm (e.g., via a learning mechanism as in Jovanovic [1979]), so $s > 0$. Alternatively, the firm may choose how much to invest in these skills with some cost function $\phi(s)$ such that $(1 - q)\partial f(\tau, 0)/\partial s > \phi'(0)$, which ensures that the firm would always like to invest a positive amount in firm-specific skills. Both scenarios are equivalent for the purposes of this section.

Since there is competition among outside firms, we have $v(\tau) = f(\tau, 0)$. Generally, $v(\tau)$ is independent of s because s is useful only in the current firm. This is the crucial ingredient creating a distortion in the internal wage structure. Assuming Nash bargaining once more, we have $w(\tau, s) = \beta f(\tau, s) + (1 - \beta)f(\tau, 0)$. The firm will solve

$$\max_{\tau} \pi(\tau, s) = (1 - q)[f(\tau, s) - w(\tau, s)] - c(\tau)$$
$$= (1 - q)(1 - \beta)[f(\tau, s) - f(\tau, 0)] - c(\tau).$$

As before, this implies that the firm invests $\hat{\tau} > 0$ only if $\beta < 1$, $q < 1$, and $\partial f(0, s)/\partial \tau > v'(0)$ or if $\partial f(0, s)/\partial \tau > \partial f(0, 0)/\partial \tau$. Therefore, for firm-sponsored investment in general training, we need

$\partial^2 f(\tau, s)/\partial\tau\partial s > 0$, that is, a *complementarity between firm-specific and general skills*. In fact, since $c'(0) = 0$, it is necessary and sufficient for firm-sponsored investments in general training that $\partial^2 f(\hat{\tau}, s)/\partial\tau\partial s > 0$, $q < 1$, and $\beta < 1$.

To summarize, if firm-specific skills and general skills are complements in the production function, increasing general skills raises productivity more than outside wages, encouraging the firm to invest in these general skills.[11] If specific and general skills do not interact, the outside wage function has the same slope in τ as the production function. In this case, specific skills generate rents from the current employment relationship, but these rents are the same at all levels of skill. The firm therefore has no incentive to invest in general skills.

Notice also that standard theory suggests that there should be less investment in firm-specific skills when turnover is higher. Our model points out that there should be more firm-sponsored investments in general skills when there are more firm-specific skills. Therefore, our analysis in this subsection suggests another reason to expect more general training in economies with low turnover.

The formulation above is also useful in contexts other than merely specific training. For example, s above could be physical capital of the firm. If firms have different levels of physical capital and physical and general human capital are complements, then firms with more physical capital would like to employ workers with more human capital. Suppose that there is one firm that has a higher stock of physical capital than other firms. It would be profitable for this firm to invest in the workers' human capital if physical capital is not perfectly mobile. This conclusion again crucially depends on the existence of some frictions, in this case in the credit market. With perfect markets, a new employer could buy additional physical capital (from the previous employer or another source) and pay the worker his full marginal product, which would prevent the initial employer from recouping training costs. At first sight, this example seems to contradict our general premise that *labor market imperfections* are needed for firm-sponsored investments in general human capital. However, if capital is immobile, then the employer with a larger stock of physi-

---

[11] Related ideas have been discussed in other papers. Stevens (1994) considers skills that are neither completely general nor completely specific and notes that this will mean that workers are unlikely to face a perfect outside labor market for these skills. However, she does not consider the interaction between specific and general skills as a source for firms' investments in general training. Franz and Soskice (1995) discuss the case in which general training is a by-product of specific training; i.e., the complementarity is on the cost side rather than on the output side as in our analysis above. Bishop (1997) points out that individual skills may be general, but the particular mix of these general skills used by any single employer could be firm-specific.

STRUCTURE OF WAGES   561

cal capital has monopsony power over the human capital of the worker, which is the source of the distortion in the wage structure. In other words, the imperfection in the capital market spills over into the labor market.

Finally, note that poaching is not a problem here. Because of firm-specific skills, outside firms could not offer higher wages to trained workers and make positive profits.

D. Efficiency Wages

Our analysis in subsection B considered asymmetric information between the current employer of the worker and other firms. Another important asymmetry of information exists between the worker and the firm. Principal-agent, efficiency wage, and personnel economics literatures analyze how the structure of wages can be designed to avoid adverse selection and encourage effort (see, e.g., Weiss 1990; Lazear 1995). Incentive compatibility constraints in these models often distort the structure of wages, which we illustrate here with a simple example.

Suppose that the firm invests in general training in the first period. In the second period, it chooses what wage to offer to the worker, but there is a moral hazard problem that requires the firm to pay an efficiency wage. Either the worker can exert effort at cost e and produce $f(\tau)$, where, as before, τ is general human capital, or he exerts no effort and produces nothing. If e or a variable highly correlated with e were contractible, there would be no moral hazard.[12] Instead, a worker who exerts no effort has a probability p of getting caught. We assume that both the firm and the worker are risk-neutral, and there is a limited liability constraint, so that the worker cannot be paid a negative wage. Finally, to simplify the analysis, we assume that the firm has all the bargaining power and that there are no other reasons for a separation (i.e., $q = 0$).

Since a worker caught shirking will receive zero, when he shirks he saves the effort cost, e, but risks losing his wage with probability p. The incentive compatibility condition to exert effort is therefore $w - e \geq (1 - p)w$. The firm, trying to minimize costs, would choose $w = e/p$ if it can. Notice that the incentive compatibility constraint is independent of skill, which creates the necessary distortion in the

---

[12] It is natural that the effort level of the worker is not always observed. Also, in most firms, rather than the output of an individual worker, only the output of a whole division is observed, and this is not easy to use to provide incentives to individual workers.

wage structure.[13] There is also a participation constraint for the worker to be satisfied. We assume that the worker can obtain his net marginal product $f(\tau) - e$ by quitting but would incur some cost $\Delta > 0$, independent of skills, in the process. Therefore, the participation constraint takes the form $w \geq f(\tau) - \Delta$. The important point to notice is that without moral hazard considerations, the presence of Δ does not induce the firm to invest in general skills (i.e., $\hat{\tau} = 0$).

It is clear that the optimal wage structure, which satisfies the incentive and participation constraints above, is

$$w(\tau) = \max\left\{\frac{e}{p}, f(\tau) - \Delta\right\}. \tag{8}$$

The firm then chooses τ to maximize profits $f(\tau) - w(\tau) - c(\tau)$. It should be clear that this distortion will encourage the firm to invest in general training (as long as e/p is not so high as to shut down production). So in general $\hat{\tau}$ will be positive.[14]

Notice at this point a feature that distinguishes this mechanism (and the minimum-wage and union examples that follow) from the others we have discussed. There is no distortion in the external wage structure $(v'(\tau) = f'(\tau))$, but efficiency wages (or minimum wages or unions) distort the internal wage structure. In contrast, in the other examples, labor market frictions distort the external wage structure and, via this channel, compress the internal wage structure. Nevertheless, in the efficiency wage example, when there are moral hazard problems in other firms as well, the external wage structure will also be distorted, but this does not affect our results. In fact, more generally, (8) will take the form $w(\tau) = \max\{e/p, v(\tau)\}$, which continues to be compressed at low wages irrespective of the form of $v(\tau)$. For example, when all other firms in the economy have exactly the same moral hazard problem, we have $v(\tau) = p_w w(\tau) - \Delta$, where p_w is the probability of employment, which may be less than one as a result of unemployment caused by efficiency wages. It is straightfor-

---

[13] The assumption that the incentive compatibility constraint is independent of future job opportunities, and thus of skills, is not crucial. The result holds as long as the constraint induces a relation between wages and skills less steeply sloped than $f(\tau)$. The model by Loewenstein and Spletzer (1998a) has a similar flavor. In their model, firms can commit ex ante to pay a certain wage in the second period in order to reduce turnover. Whenever this constraint is binding for the firm, it has an incentive to invest in the worker's general skills.

[14] The exact level of training depends on the relative positions of the kink in the wage function (8) and τ^*. In particular, let $\bar{\tau}$ be such that $f(\bar{\tau}) - \Delta = e/p$. Then if $\bar{\tau} \leq \tau^*$ and $c(\bar{\tau}) \leq \Delta$, the firm will operate and choose $\hat{\tau} = \bar{\tau}$. If $\bar{\tau} > \tau^*$ and $f(\tau^*) \geq c(\tau^*) + (e/p)$, then the firm will operate and choose $\hat{\tau} = \tau^*$. Finally, if $\bar{\tau} > \tau^*$ and $f(\tau^*) < c(\tau^*) + (e/p)$ or if $\bar{\tau} \leq \tau^*$ and $c(\bar{\tau}) > \Delta$, then the firm will choose not to operate.

STRUCTURE OF WAGES   563

ward to see that firms continue to invest in general training, so whether the rest of the economy is subject to moral hazard is not crucial. Also in this case, the compressed external wage structure induces the internal wage structure to be compressed further and increases firms' incentives to sponsor training.

Finally, there will be no poaching in this case either because Δ is a mobility cost or a premium to specific skills, and the worker loses this amount when he changes jobs. Therefore, an outside firm would need to pay a wage that is at least higher than the current wage by Δ, so poaching is not profitable.

E.   Minimum Wages and Other Wage Floors

The next two mechanisms we discuss are labor market institutions that create wage distortions. Perhaps the most common intervention in the labor market is the imposition of wage floors, due to minimum wages and high reservation wages caused by unemployment benefits. Minimum wages are relatively low in the United States and the United Kingdom as compared to the higher levels in many continental European economies.

It is well known that the imposition of a minimum wage can never lead to more training when labor markets are competitive (Rosen 1972). Because workers pay for training through lower wages, a minimum wage may prevent the firm from reducing wages enough during the training period. This is the rationale behind the introduction of "training subminima" in many recent U.S. minimum-wage laws.

Now consider a labor market with frictions, where $v(\tau) = f(\tau) - \Delta$, due to a mobility cost unrelated to skill. It is once again important to emphasize that this distortion does not by itself lead to firm-sponsored training because $v(\tau)$ is not distorted. Also suppose that the firm has all the bargaining power ($\beta = 0$) so that $w(\tau) = v(\tau)$.

Next consider a wage floor w_M due to either minimum wages or unemployment benefits. The structure of wages now becomes

$$w(\tau) = \max\{w_M, f(\tau) - \Delta\}, \tag{9}$$

which is kinked at w_M and thus distorted at low levels of τ. The firm then chooses τ to maximize $f(\tau) - w(\tau) - c(\tau)$. Observe that this wage function is identical to (8) in the case of efficiency wages, with w_M replacing e/p. The condition for a positive training level, a distortion in the structure of wages, is satisfied, so equilibrium training is $\hat{\tau} > 0$ as long as the firm chooses to operate.[15] Note that as in the

[15] The exact conditions for training are very similar to those given in n. 14. In particular, w_M replaces e/p, and the no-shutdown conditions become $w_M + c(\bar{\tau}) \leq \Delta$ when $\bar{\tau} < \tau^*$ and $2w_M + c(\tau^*) \leq f(\tau^*)$ when $\tau^* \leq \bar{\tau}$, because the firm has to pay the minimum wage w_M in both periods.

case of efficiency wages, if Δ is interpreted as a mobility cost for the worker, there are no poaching opportunities.

Notice the stark contrast of the predictions in this case to those of the standard human capital model. With competitive markets, a minimum wage just below $f(0)$ is detrimental to the accumulation of general human capital because it prevents the worker from taking a wage cut in the first period to compensate the firm for the costs of training. With frictions, in contrast, such a minimum wage could imply $f'(0) > w'(0) = 0$ and induce the firm to invest in general training.[16]

Given the contrast between our results and those based on Becker's theory of general training in which workers bear the costs, it is instructive to look at the empirical evidence regarding the impact of minimum wages on training. The micro evidence is mixed. Leighton and Mincer (1981) and Neumark and Wascher (1998) find negative effects of minimum wages on training, whereas Grossberg and Sicilian (1999) and Acemoglu and Pischke (1998a) find no effects of minimum wages. Only our own study uses within-state variation in the minimum wage from one year to the next, which seems the most convincing way of getting at the effect of the minimum wage. This absence of negative effects of minimum wages on training suggests that as well as preventing some workers from financing their own training, minimum wages may also be inducing firm-sponsored training as implied by our theory.

F. Unions

Another important institutional difference across economies is the role played by unions. In Germany and Scandinavian countries, unions are heavily involved in wage determination, whereas in the United States they have traditionally been less prominent, and their importance has been declining. Since unions tend to compress the wage structure among covered workers (Freeman and Medoff 1984), they are relevant for our theory.

---

[16] There are additional results when we consider the case in which workers can also contribute to training (see Acemoglu and Pischke [1998a] for details). For example, if there was no minimum wage previously and workers were able to pay for their own training, then the introduction of a minimum wage leads to firm financing of the training. But the training level never goes up and may go down. On the other hand, an increase in a previously binding minimum wage may lead to more investment. In this case, worker financing through lower wages was already impossible, so that the firm paid for training before the minimum-wage increase. Because a higher minimum wage moves the kink in the wage function (9) to the right, the firm will now choose more training unless it was already providing the first-best amount.

STRUCTURE OF WAGES   565

We therefore consider union wage setting as an alternative to individual Nash bargains discussed above. A union with N members can set the entire wage structure $w(\tau)$ at the beginning of the period, and then the firm chooses training. Hence, this model is an analogue to the standard monopoly union (right-to-manage) model, except that because of constant returns, all N union members are employed, but the firm's labor demand decision is replaced with the training decision. The firm maximizes profit per worker $\pi(\tau) = f(\tau) - w(\tau) - c(\tau)$ and chooses to shut down if maximum profits are negative.

We start with the simple case in which the union can choose only one wage for all training levels, $w(\tau) = w$. We shall see that the union cannot improve over this situation. Also suppose that the rest of the economy is not unionized and has a wage structure $v(\tau) < f(\tau)$. The union anticipates the behavior of the firm, which can be summarized by the first-order condition $f'(\tau) - w'(\tau) = c'(\tau)$. Since the wage does not vary with skill (i.e., $w(\tau) = w$), the firm will choose first-best training, τ^*.

The union simply maximizes the wage income of workers and has to make sure to obey $\pi(\tau^*) \geq 0$ so that the firm does not shut down. This implies that the union will set w so as to extract all the rents and force the firm down to zero profits. Therefore, the optimal wage is $w^* = f(\tau^*) - c(\tau^*)$.[17]

The reason for first-best training is that the union is choosing the wage structure before the training decisions. The firm invests τ^* because $f'(\tau) > w'(\tau) = 0$; in other words, workers get a fixed payment and the firm is the full residual claimant. This immediately implies that the union cannot do better by choosing a wage schedule that is different from $w(\tau) = w^*$. It is also important to note that if the firm had the option to set the wage structure itself and *commit* to this ex ante, we would not obtain the same results because the union is not only committing to a wage structure but also choosing one that forces the firm to pay less skilled workers more than their marginal product. The firm would never find this profitable without the union.

Next consider the case in which the rest of the economy is unionized, with other unions choosing the same wage policy. Therefore, a worker who quits the firm will either be unemployed (probability $1 - p_w$) or find a job paying w^* (probability p_w). Therefore, $v(\tau) = p_w w^*$. It is clear that for all values of p_w, this does not change the optimal wage policy of the union, which is again to set w^* and ensure first-best training.

---

[17] As long as $w^* \geq v(\tau^*)$, which we assume to be the case.

This analysis also suggests a new reason why unions may like to compress the wage structure. Such behavior is usually explained with reference to unions' political preferences (e.g., the median union member chooses the wage structure, and the distribution of marginal products may be skewed to the left) or ideological reasons (see, e.g., Freeman and Medoff 1984). Our analysis points out that when unions take into account the impact of the wage structure on the training decisions of firms, there is another reason for choosing a compressed wage structure. It is also interesting to note that in this case there may be room for poaching since $w^* < f(\tau^*)$. So if the firm anticipates that trained workers will be poached by other firms, it would choose not to invest and shut down. Thus unions might have an additional role in preventing mobility of trained workers, which is sometimes suggested as a role of German works councils.

Notice finally that if there were ex ante heterogeneity among covered workers, the union would no longer choose a single wage. However, it can be shown in this case that the union would still choose to compress the wage structure and induce training.

The predictions of our model once again are different from those of the standard theory, where wage compression would reduce workers' investments in general training. In contrast, we predict that by compressing the wage structure, unions may encourage firms to sponsor training programs. The micro evidence is once again mixed. Studies by Duncan and Stafford (1980) and Mincer (1983) based on the Panel Study on Income Dynamics, Lillard and Tan (1992) based on the Current Population Survey, and Barron, Fuess, and Loewenstein (1987) based on the Employment Opportunity Pilot Project (EOPP) find negative effects of union status on training. Barron, Berger, and Black (1997), on the other hand, report insignificant union effects using the EOPP data and find positive effects for formal training in the Small Business Administration survey. Lynch (1992) also finds positive effects for formal training in the NLSY. For the United Kingdom, Booth (1991) reports more training for union workers, and Green (1993) finds more training for unionized workers in small establishments but not in large establishments.

IV. Conclusion

When the wage structure is distorted away from the competitive benchmark and in favor of less skilled workers, firms may want to invest in the general skills of their employees. For this result to hold, workers do not need to be credit constrained. What matters is the form of labor market frictions and institutions. These results contrast with the standard theory based on Becker's seminal work in which firms would never invest in general skills. We also found that more frictional and regulated labor markets may encourage more firm-sponsored training.

We view the presence of many firm-sponsored general training programs, such as the German apprenticeship system, and the fact that U.S. employers send their workers to vocational and technical training facilities without reducing their wages as evidence that the forces we emphasize are present. Also, the fact that firms appear to contribute more toward general skills training in Europe and Japan, which have more regulated and frictional markets and more distorted wage structures, is in line with our approach. Future empirical work should test the more micro-level implications that follow from our analysis and contrast them with those of the standard theory.

This paper also has implications for the interpretation of empirical results on the returns to training (e.g., Lynch 1992). Wage returns to training reflect the total increase in productivity only if labor markets are competitive. Our work predicts that, whenever employers pay for training, true returns will exceed wage returns, which are often estimated to be quite large already.

We have discussed a number of reasons why wages may be compressed, but our list is by no means exhaustive. Lazear (1989) argues that pay compression may arise so as to encourage workers to cooperate, or at least to discourage sabotaging their coworkers. Optimal pay compression may also arise when workers can direct their effort between different tasks; the output of only some tasks is easily measured whereas others have an effect on firm profits that is harder to detect. In this case, it may be optimal not to reward observed performance differences, which again compresses the structure of wages (e.g., Holmstrom and Milgrom 1991; Baker 1992). Any of these and other reasons for wage compression may also encourage firms to invest in training. In future work, the link between these stories and training can be more carefully derived, yielding empirical predictions to determine which sources of wage compression, if any, are important in encouraging firm-sponsored training.

Finally, an important development in the theory of contracts in recent years has been the literature on incomplete contracts and property rights (e.g., Grossman and Hart 1986; Hart and Moore 1990). As in the earlier papers by Hashimoto (1979, 1981), Hashimoto and Yu (1980), and Grout (1984), this literature focuses on relationship- or asset-specific investments and analyzes how property rights and other features of organizations can be designed to maximize efficiency. By its nature, this literature has been partial equilibrium. Our analysis was a first attempt at investigating how market structure can turn general skills into effectively relationship-specific skills, but we have ignored how organizational forms or property rights *within firms* matter for these investments. Combining these two types of analyses may yield new insights into thinking about organizations and markets. For example, how do organizational choices vary with the extent of market frictions? Is it beneficial to make skills more specific? Do different forms of organizations lead to different paths of training, productivity, and wage growth?

Appendix

Dynamic Version of the Search Model

Consider a continuous-time infinite horizon version of the model of Section IIIA. Namely, each worker is matched with a firm, and the firm decides whether and how much to invest in the general skills of the worker. The worker has no funds and cannot commit to a lower wage in the future in return for training now. The productivity of a worker who receives training τ is $f(\tau)$ in every period. For simplicity, training is possible only in period $t = 0$. Both firms and workers are risk-neutral and discount the future at the rate r. All worker-firm matches come to an end at the exogenous rate q. Also a worker, once unemployed, finds a new firm at the rate p_w, which is independent of his training level, and a firm after losing its worker finds a new worker at the rate p_f. We set the unemployment benefit to $b = 0$ to simplify the expressions. The worker that the firm finds will be a random draw from the pool of unemployed workers, irrespective of the value of training. So workers with different levels of training have the same probability of getting a job.

Suppose that all workers have training $\bar{\tau}$, and consider a worker with training τ. Then the value of being employed for this worker as a function of his training level τ, $J^E(\tau)$, is

$$rJ^E(\tau) = w(\tau) + q[J^U(\tau) - J^E(\tau)],$$

where $J^U(\tau)$ is the present discounted value of being unemployed for a worker of training τ. This equation is a standard dynamic programming equation (see, e.g., Pissarides 1990). The worker gets $w(\tau)$ every instant he is with the firm and loses his job at the flow probability q, in which case he gets J^U and loses J^E. In turn we have

$$rJ^U(\tau) = p_w[J^E(\tau) - J^U(\tau)].$$

And for the firm, the value of employing a worker with training τ is

$$rJ^F(\tau) = f(\tau) - w(\tau) + q[J^V - J^F(\tau)],$$

and the value of having an unfilled vacancy is

$$rJ^V = p_f[J^F(\bar{\tau}) - J^V].$$

Nash bargaining in this context implies that the present discounted values should be shared. Therefore, $w(\tau)$ will be chosen so as to maximize

STRUCTURE OF WAGES   569

$$[J^E(\tau) - J^U(\tau)]^\beta [J^F(\tau) - J^V]^{1-\beta}.$$

This gives a standard wage rule:

$$w(\tau) = \beta f(\tau) + (1 - \beta) r J^U(\tau) - \beta r J^V$$

or, with substitution for $rJ^U(\tau)$,

$$w(\tau) = \frac{(p_w + r + q)\,[\beta f(\tau) - \beta r J^V]}{r + q + \beta p_w}.$$

Now in period $t = 0$, since the worker is credit constrained and cannot invest in training, the firm will maximize

$$J^F(\tau) - c(\tau) \qquad\qquad\qquad (A1)$$

by choosing training τ and taking the training level of all other workers, $\bar\tau$, as given. The term $\bar\tau$ influences only J^V, which is in turn independent of the value of τ. So the level of $\bar\tau$ does not influence the choice of τ. For this reason, the first-order condition of (A1) takes the simple form

$$(1 - \beta) f'(\hat\tau) = (r + q + \beta p_w) c'(\hat\tau).$$

Since $c'(0) = 0$, for all $\beta < 1$ and $r + q + \beta p_w < \infty$, the firm will choose $\hat\tau > 0$. Since all other firms are solving a similar problem, we also have $\bar\tau = \hat\tau$ and a unique symmetric equilibrium.

The reason why $\beta < 1$ is necessary for firm-sponsored training is familiar from the text. However, the second condition is interesting. First, it requires that $r < \infty$; thus the future needs to feature in the calculations. A value of $q < \infty$ is also required, which means that the worker should not be leaving the firm for sure. Finally, $p_w < \infty$ is necessary. In fact, $p_w \to \infty$ is the case of perfectly competitive labor markets: the worker finds an employer immediately. Therefore, this last requirement reiterates that labor market imperfections are necessary for firms to invest in the general skills of their workers. Moreover, it is clear that as p_w increases, there is less investment in training. Since steady-state unemployment in this economy is equal to $u = q/(q + p_w)$, this implies that higher unemployment is associated with more investment in training. The reason is that a higher rate of unemployment leads to a more distorted wage structure by reducing the outside option of more skilled workers.

References

Abowd, John, and Lemieux, Thomas. "The Effects of Product Market Competition on Collective Bargaining Agreements: The Case of Foreign Competition in Canada." *Q.J.E.* 108 (November 1993): 983–1014.

Acemoglu, Daron. "Training and Innovation in an Imperfect Labour Market." *Rev. Econ. Studies* 64 (July 1997): 445–64.

Acemoglu, Daron, and Pischke, Jörn-Steffen. "Minimum Wages and On-the-Job Training." Manuscript. Cambridge: Massachusetts Inst. Tech., Dept. Econ., 1998. (*a*)

———. "Why Do Firms Train? Theory and Evidence." *Q.J.E.* 113 (February 1998): 79–119. (*b*)

Altonji, Joseph G., and Shakotko, Robert A. "Do Wages Rise with Job Seniority?" *Rev. Econ. Studies* 54 (July 1987): 437–59.

Altonji, Joseph G., and Williams, Nicolas. "Do Wages Rise with Job Seniority? A Reassessment." Working Paper no. 6010. Cambridge, Mass.: NBER, April 1997.

Autor, David. "Why Do Temporary Help Firms Provide Free General Skills Training?" Manuscript. Cambridge, Mass.: Harvard Univ., Kennedy School Government, October 1998.

Baker, George P. "Incentive Contracts and Performance Measurement." *J.P.E.* 100 (June 1992): 598–614.

Barron, John M.; Berger, Mark C.; and Black, Dan A. *On-the-Job Training.* Kalamazoo, Mich.: Upjohn Inst. Employment Res., 1997.

Barron, John M.; Fuess, Scott M., Jr.; and Loewenstein, Mark A. "Further Analysis of the Effect of Unions on Training." *J.P.E.* 95 (June 1987): 632–40.

Becker, Gary S. *Human Capital: A Theoretical and Empirical Analysis, with Special Reference to Education.* New York: Columbia Univ. Press (for NBER), 1964; 3d ed. Chicago: Univ. Chicago Press (for NBER), 1993.

Bishop, John H. "The Recognition and Reward of Employee Performance." *J. Labor Econ.* 5, no. 4, pt. 2 (October 1987): S36–S56.

———. "The Impact of Previous Training on Productivity and Wages." In *Training and the Private Sector: International Comparisons,* edited by Lisa M. Lynch. Series in Comparative Labor Markets. Chicago: Univ. Chicago Press (for NBER), 1994.

———. "What We Know about Employer-Provided Training: A Review of the Literature." In *Research in Labor Economics,* vol. 16, edited by Solomon W. Polachek. Greenwich, Conn.: JAI, 1997.

Blanchflower, David G.; Oswald, Andrew J.; and Sanfey, Peter. "Wages, Profits, and Rent-Sharing." *Q.J.E.* 111 (February 1996): 227–51.

Blau, Francine D., and Kahn, Lawrence M. "International Differences in Male Wage Inequality: Institutions versus Market Forces." *J.P.E.* 104 (August 1996): 791–837.

Blinder, Alan S., and Krueger, Alan B. "Labor Turnover in the USA and Japan: A Tale of Two Countries." *Pacific Econ. Rev.* 1 (June 1996): 27–57.

Booth, Alison L. "Job-Related Formal Training: Who Receives It and What Is It Worth?" *Oxford Bull. Econ. and Statis.* 53 (August 1991): 281–94.

Chang, Chun, and Wang, Yijiang. "Human Capital Investment under Asymmetric Information: The Pigovian Conjecture Revisited." *J. Labor Econ.* 14 (July 1996): 505–19.

Duncan, Greg J., and Stafford, Frank P. "Do Union Members Receive Compensating Wage Differentials?" *A.E.R.* 70 (June 1980): 355–71.

Dustmann, Christian, and Meghir, Costas. "Wages, Experience and Seniority." Manuscript. London: Univ. Coll. London, Dept. Econ., 1997.

Edin, Per-Anders, and Topel, Robert H. "Wage Policy and Restructuring: The Swedish Labor Market since 1960." In *The Welfare State in Transition: Reforming the Swedish Model,* edited by Richard B. Freeman, Robert H. Topel, and Birgitta Swedenborg. Chicago: Univ. Chicago Press (for NBER), 1997.

Franz, Wolfgang, and Soskice, David. "The German Apprenticeship System." In *Institutional Frameworks and Labor Market Performance: Comparative Views on the U.S. and German Economies,* edited by Friedrich Buttler et al. London: Routledge, 1995.

Freeman, Richard B., and Medoff, James L. *What Do Unions Do?* New York: Basic Books, 1984.

Green, Francis. "The Impact of Trade Union Membership on Training in Britain." *Appl. Econ.* 25 (August 1993): 1033–43.

Grossberg, Adam J., and Sicilian, Paul. "Minimum Wages, On-the-Job Training, and Wage Growth." *Southern Econ. J.* 65 (January 1999).

Grossman, Sanford J., and Hart, Oliver D. "The Costs and Benefits of Ownership: A Theory of Vertical and Lateral Integration." *J.P.E.* 94 (August 1986): 691–719.

Grout, Paul A. "Investment and Wages in the Absence of Binding Contracts: A Nash Bargaining Approach." *Econometrica* 52 (March 1984): 449–60.

Harhoff, Dietmar, and Kane, Thomas J. "Is the German Apprenticeship System a Panacea for the U.S. Labor Market?" *J. Population Econ.* 10 (May 1997): 171–96.

Hart, Oliver D., and Moore, John. "Property Rights and the Nature of the Firm." *J.P.E.* 98 (December 1990): 1119–58.

Hashimoto, Masanori. "Bonus Payments, On-the-Job Training, and Lifetime Employment in Japan." *J.P.E.* 87, no. 5, pt. 1 (October 1979): 1086–1104.

———. "Firm-Specific Human Capital as a Shared Investment." *A.E.R.* 71 (June 1981): 475–82.

Hashimoto, Masanori, and Yu, Ben T. "Specific Capital, Employment Contracts, and Wage Rigidity." *Bell J. Econ.* 11 (Autumn 1980): 536–49.

Holmstrom, Bengt, and Milgrom, Paul. "Multitask Principal-Agent Analyses: Incentive Contracts, Asset Ownership, and Job Design." *J. Law, Econ., and Organization* 7 (special issue, 1991): 24–52.

Jovanovic, Boyan. "Job Matching and the Theory of Turnover." *J.P.E.* 87, no. 5, pt. 1 (October 1979): 972–90.

Katz, Eliakim, and Ziderman, Adrian. "Investment in General Training: The Role of Information and Labour Mobility." *Econ. J.* 100 (December 1990): 1147–58.

Krueger, Alan B. "How Computers Have Changed the Wage Structure: Evidence from Microdata, 1984–1989." *Q.J.E.* 108 (February 1993): 33–60.

Lazear, Edward P. "Pay Equality and Industrial Politics." *J.P.E.* 97 (June 1989): 561–80.

———. *Personnel Economics.* Cambridge, Mass.: MIT Press, 1995.

Leighton, Linda, and Mincer, Jacob. "The Effects of Minimum Wages on Human Capital Formation." In *The Economics of Legal Minimum Wages*, edited by Simon Rottenberg. Washington: American Enterprise Inst. Public Policy Res., 1981.

Lillard, Lee A., and Tan, Hong W. "Private Sector Training: Who Gets It and What Are Its Effects?" In *Research in Labor Economics*, vol. 13, edited by Ronald G. Ehrenberg. Greenwich, Conn.: JAI, 1992.

Lindbeck, Assar, et al. "Options for Economic and Political Reform in Sweden." *Econ. Policy* 18 (October 1993): 219–46.

Loewenstein, Mark A., and Spletzer, James R. "Dividing the Costs and Returns to General Training." *J. Labor Econ.* 16 (January 1998): 142–71. (*a*)

———. "General and Specific Training: Evidence from the NLSY." Manuscript. Washington: Bur. Labor Statis., 1998. (*b*)

———. "Formal and Informal Training: Evidence from the NLSY." In *Research in Labor Economics*, vol. 18, edited by Solomon W. Polachek. Greenwich, Conn.: JAI, 1999, in press.

Lynch, Lisa M. "Private-Sector Training and the Earnings of Young Workers." *A.E.R.* 82 (March 1992): 299–312.

Mincer, Jacob. "Union Effects: Wages, Turnover, and Job Training." In *New Approaches to Labor Unions,* edited by Joseph D. Reid, Jr. Research in Labor Economics, suppl. 2. Greenwich, Conn.: JAI, 1983.

Neumark, David, and Wascher, William. "Minimum Wages and Training Revisited." Working Paper no. 6651. Cambridge, Mass.: NBER, July 1998.

OECD. *Employment Outlook.* Paris: OECD, 1993, 1994.

Pissarides, Christopher A. *Equilibrium Unemployment Theory.* Cambridge: Blackwell, 1990.

Ritzen, Jozef M. M., and Stern, David. "Introduction and Overview." In *Market Failure in Training? New Economic Analysis and Evidence on Training of Adult Employees,* edited by David Stern and Jozef M. M. Ritzen. Berlin: Springer Verlag, 1991.

Rosen, Sherwin. "Learning and Experience in the Labor Market." *J. Human Resources* 7 (Summer 1972): 326–42.

Ryan, Paul. "The Costs of Job Training for a Transferable Skill." *British J. Indus. Relations* 18 (November 1980): 334–52.

Stevens, Margaret. "A Theoretical Model of On-the-Job Training with Imperfect Competition." *Oxford Econ. Papers* 46 (October 1994): 537–62.

Topel, Robert H. "Specific Capital, Mobility, and Wages: Wages Rise with Job Seniority." *J.P.E.* 99 (February 1991): 145–76.

Topel, Robert H., and Ward, Michael P. "Job Mobility and the Careers of Young Men." *Q.J.E.* 107 (May 1992): 439–79.

von Bardeleben, Richard; Beicht, Ursula, and Fehér, Kálmán. *Betriebliche Kosten und Nutzen der Ausbildung: Repräsentative Ergebnisse aus Industrie, Handel und Handwerk.* Berichte zur beruflichen Bildung Heft 187. Bielefeld: Bertelsmann, 1995.

Weiss, Andrew. *Efficiency Wages: Models of Unemployment, Layoffs, and Wage Dispersion.* Princeton, N.J.: Princeton Univ. Press, 1990.

Review of Economic Studies (1997) **64**, 445–464
© 1997 The Review of Economic Studies Limited

0034-6527/97/00220445$02.00

Training and Innovation in an Imperfect Labour Market

DARON ACEMOGLU
Massachusetts Institute of Technology

First version received June 1995; final version accepted January 1997 (Eds.)

This paper shows that in a frictional labour market part of the productivity gains from general training will be captured by future employers. As a result, investments in general skills will be suboptimally low, and contrary to the standard theory, part of the costs may be borne by the employers. The paper also demonstrates that the interaction between innovation and training leads to an amplification of this inefficiency and to a multiplicity of equilibria. Workers are more willing to invest in their skills by accepting lower wages today if they expect more firms to innovate and pay them higher wages in the future. Similarly, firms are more willing to innovate when they expect the quality of the future workforce to be higher, thus when workers invest more in their skills.

1. INTRODUCTION

In modern economies, a large portion of human capital investments takes place within firms in the form of training. Most economic analyses of training are based on the paradigm introduced by Becker (1964) which suggests that a worker should pay for any general training which allows him/her to use the new skills when employed by other firms. Inefficiency occurs mainly because workers may be unable to pay for their training, and also unable to commit to not quitting their firm after employer sponsored training. Yet this source of inefficiency does not seem particularly relevant for many instances of training in the real world. For example, in Germany which has the most developed system of privately funded training, firms bear a large part of the cost of training while apprentices are often paid attractive wages (see for instance Harhoff and Kane (1994)) and also in the U.S. firms often pay for the vocational training courses of their employees (see Bishop (1991) or Acemoglu and Pischke (1996) for some numbers).

This paper argues that the focus on credit market imperfections ignores an important source of market failure in training. Although workers may be willing to pay the present-discounted value of their increased future earnings to a firm which offers training,[1] this present discounted value is only equal to the social value of training in a frictionless labour market. As soon as the hypothetical world of the Walrasian auctioneer is abandoned and labour markets characterized by costly mobility and search are considered, workers will not receive their full marginal product in future jobs. Because employer rents do not feature in workers' calculations, underinvestment in training will result. In other words, in an imperfect labour market future employers of a worker will also benefit from his skills. This is an externality that the decentralized market will not be able to internalize. It is important to contrast this mechanism to the one emphasized by the previous literature.

---

1. Throughout the paper, I will be talking of a firm "offering" training with the understanding that this is mostly on-the-job training, thus a worker cannot buy the same training in a school. Since the model has perfectly transferable utility, the addition of such an option would not change the results.

In this paper the externality is between the worker and his *future* employer whereas previous literature has concentrated on the inefficiencies in investment, due to incomplete contracts and credit market imperfections, between the worker and his current employer (see Becker (1964), pp. 93–95, Grout (1984)). These inefficiencies often have simple solutions as soon as the extreme incompleteness of contracts is relaxed (for instance in the form of exit penalties for workers who quit their firms). In contrast, contractual arrangements to deal with the externality proposed here are not easy to develop; the worker cannot contract with his future employer because at the investment stage it is unknown who this future employer will be. This is not only a more appealing source of inefficiency than the one emphasized by the previous literature, but also I will argue that it offers possible explanations to a number of otherwise puzzling observations, such as the willingness of employers to bear part of the costs of general training, and the absence of significant wage increases after such training is completed.

Training is most essential when new technologies are adopted, or in the process of a radical change of environment, for example, the shift from low- to high-skill jobs taking place in most OECD countries today. In support of this view, survey evidence suggests that the availability of appropriate skills is a key determinant of innovation and technology adoption decisions (e.g. see Northcott and Walling (1988), Northcott and Vickrey (1993)), and the efficient adoption of new technologies by Japanese firms is often attributed to their effective training strategies (e.g. Hashimoto (1991)). My analysis will establish not only that innovation decisions will be distorted due to labour market imperfections, but also that the interaction of innovation and training decisions leads to an amplification of inefficiencies and to a multiplicity of equilibria. Intuitively, skills are more valuable to a firm which has the new technology, thus the expected future wages of a worker depend on how many of his potential future employers have adopted the innovation. Similarly, expected profits depend on how skilled the future workforce is. As a result, when a greater number of firms adopt the innovation, workers expect higher wages from training and invest more in skills, and the profits from the new technology are higher. Therefore, the profitability of innovation and of training will increase with the *thickness* of the market for trained labour. An often-made claim is that capital investments in less developed economies are limited because the workforce is not sufficiently skilled (for instance this is suggested in Rosenstein–Rodan's famous 1943 article pp. 204–205). My analysis formalizes this claim and shows that the workforce may be unskilled because of lack of capital investments. Moreover, I also demonstrate that this result crucially relies on labour market frictions.

This paper is related to a number of contributions in the literature. First, a number of recent papers have analysed the physical capital investments and schooling decisions in labour markets characterized by search, e.g. Acemoglu (1996a), Burdett and Smith (1996), Laing, Palivos and Wang (1995), Robinson (1995) and Saint-Paul (1996). For instance, Acemoglu (1996a) shows how the return to a worker can be increasing in the skill level of competing workers. Laing, Palivos and Wang (1995) demonstrate how education choices interact with wage determination and affect the growth rate in a search economy. In their paper, a more efficient matching technology encourages workers to invest more in education, and increases the growth rate. However, these papers neither deal with training choices nor identify the externality proposed in this paper. It is therefore not possible to understand why firms pay for training and whether training decisions will be efficient. Also, the interactions between adoption of new technologies and skills of workers, which appear to be important in practice, are not treated in the previous literature. Acemoglu and Pischke (1996) develop a model where workers do not pay for their general training, but the key ingredient is the superior information that the initial employer has over future employers regarding the ability of their employees.

Another closely related literature concerns multiple equilibria in macroeconomics. This literature has identified two channels for agglomeration of activity and multiplicity of equilibria; the first is technological externalities, as in Durlauf (1993), and the second is aggregate demand externalities as in Kiyotaki (1988) or Murphy, Shleifer and Vishny (1989). This paper proposes a new source of multiplicity in macro-models arising from labour market imperfections. In my model there are neither technological externalities nor aggregate demand spillovers, but multiplicity of equilibria is likely to exist because skills are more valuable to workers when a greater number of potential employers with the new technology are hiring. Diamond's famous (1982) contribution on search is also motivated by a labour market analogy, but the source of multiplicity is increasing return (externalities) in the matching technology. There are other examples of multiplicity in frictional labour markets but the mechanisms are rather different. In Laing, Palivos and Wang (1995) and Robinson (1995) more schooling leads to higher firm profits; this induces further entry by firms, increasing the likelihood of employment and the incentives to invest in skills for workers. In contrast, the source of multiplicity in this paper is the fact that skills are more valuable to firms with the new technologies combined with the externality identified between the worker and his *future* employers.

The plan of the paper is as follows. Section 2 presents the environment, derives the efficient allocation and characterizes the Walrasian equilibrium. Section 3 contains the main results of this paper. First, I abstract from innovation decisions and show how underinvestment in training occurs, then I illustrate how multiple equilibria can emerge from the interaction of training and innovation. Section 4 includes some extensions. The appendix contains a more detailed analysis of the equilibrium of the economy in the absence of labour market frictions.

2. THE MODEL AND COMPETITIVE EQUILIBRIUM

2.1. *Description of the environment*

Consider an economy consisting of a continuum of risk-neutral workers and risk-neutral firms. Each group has mass 1. All agents have discount rate equal to r and enjoy the consumption of the only good of this economy. The economy lasts for T periods. I will start with the case of $T=2$ and will later consider $T=\infty$ to give an idea of the possible magnitude of the effects discussed here and also to illustrate the possibility of delay. Each firm has access to a Leontieff production function which requires one worker and produces per period output equal to y. A worker or firm on its own produces nothing.

Output of a pair can be increased by investment. There are two types of investments which can only be undertaken in period 1 and affect productivity in periods $t \geq 2$. The first is an investment in new technology (or innovation). At cost δ the firm can acquire a new machine. The important assumption here is that it is necessary for the property rights over the machine to be vested in the firm. If the employment relation between the firm and the worker ends, the machine will stay with the firm. The second type of investment is in the *general* human capital of the worker. The worker can acquire τ units of general human capital, but this reduces the output of the firm in the first period by $c(\tau)$. Whether the firm or the worker incurs this cost is immaterial since throughout the paper I assume that there are no credit constraints or equivalently that utility is transferable. Human capital is general in the sense that the worker can use his skills with any firm. Also

Assumption 1. $c(\cdot)$ is differentiable, strictly increasing and convex and $c(0)=0$,

$$\text{and } \exists \bar{\tau} \quad \text{s.t. } \lim_{\tau \to \bar{\tau}} c(\tau) = \infty.$$

Therefore, the level of training is chosen from a set $[0, \bar{\tau}]$ and the cost function is strictly convex. Let $\gamma_j = 0$ denote that firm j does not have the new technology and $\gamma_j = 1$ that it has the new technology, and τ_i is the training level of worker i. The productivity of worker i and firm j in all periods $t \geq 2$ is assumed to be equal to $y + \alpha(\gamma_j, \tau_i)$.

Assumption 2. $\alpha(0, \tau) = \alpha_0 \tau$ and $\alpha(1, \tau) = \alpha_1 \tau$, $\forall \tau$, and $\alpha_0 \leq \alpha_1$.

This assumption implies that training and investment in new technology are complements. This is important for the multiplicity result, but also very plausible. A sizeable empirical literature starting with Grilliches (1969) establishes the complementarities between physical and human capital, and Bartel and Lichtenberg (1989) show that firms which adopt new technologies are more likely to train their workers.

There is a final feature of the technology which needs to be specified. At the end of every period that worker i and firm j are together, there is a probability $s \in (0,1)$, that the pair receives an adverse match-specific shock which reduces their output to 0 in all future periods. After such a shock, both parties can try to find new partners for production.

It is important to reiterate that since the output of a pair does not depend on the decisions of other agents in this economy, there are no technological externalities. Further, since utility is perfectly *transferable* across all agents, there are no credit market constraints nor aggregate demand externalities.

2.2. *The Pareto optimal allocation*

Since there are no social costs of allocating workers to different firms in the second period (i.e. s does not matter), the efficient allocation can be determined by maximizing the joint surplus of the partnership with respect to γ and τ, which is

$$\max_{\gamma, \tau} \alpha(\gamma, \tau) - (1+r)(c(\tau) - \gamma \delta). \tag{1}$$

This problem will have a solution with either $\gamma = 0$ or 1. It is clear that if $\gamma = 0$, the optimal level of training is given by τ^l such that

$$\alpha_0 = (1+r)c'(\tau^l).$$

In contrast, when $\gamma = 1$, the efficient level of training is τ^h such that

$$\alpha_1 = (1+r)c'(\tau^h).$$

Given the strict convexity of $c(\cdot)$, both τ^l and τ^h are uniquely defined.

Assumption 3.

(i) $\alpha_1 \tau^h - (1+r)(c(\tau^h) + \delta) > \alpha_0 \tau^l - (1+r)c(\tau^l)$.
(ii) $\alpha_1 \tau^l - (1+r)(c(\tau^l) + \delta) < \alpha_0 \tau^l - (1+r)c(\tau^l)$.

Part (i) of the assumption ensures that (1) has a unique solution where $\gamma = 1$ and $\tau = \tau^h$, thus investment in the new technology and training are socially efficient. If Assumption

3 did not hold, then $\gamma = 0$ and $\tau = \tau'$ would give the Pareto optimal allocation. The second part of the assumption restricts attention to the area of the parameter space where the effects emphasized in this paper can be seen most clearly: it ensures that when all workers choose τ', investment in the new technology is no longer desirable.

2.3. *Equilibrium without frictions*

I now characterize the equilibrium of this economy in the absence of labour market frictions. In this subsection, I will only state the existence of a unique and Pareto optimal Walrasian allocation, which is not surprising in view of the second welfare theorem. The Walrasian allocation is not the only possible benchmark equilibrium in the frictionless case, and it is in fact quite a stringent equilibrium concept as it requires all trades to take place at time $t = 1$. An alternative is to characterize the subgame perfect equilibria of the game in which firms and workers trade in each period and there are no frictions nor costs of changing partners. This different approach is taken in the Appendix and will yield the same result.

To define the equilibrium concept more formally, let $w(\tau)$ be the price at which the labour services of a worker with training τ is traded at time $t = 2$, and $v(\tau)$ be the price at which a firm can hire the labour services of a worker at time $t = 1$ if it promises to provide an amount of training τ to this worker (note that there is no enforceability problem related to this promise). Also denote the excess demand for the services of workers with training τ at time $t = 2$ by $e_2(\tau)$, and the excess demand from firms offering training τ at time $t = 1$ by $e_1(\tau)$. A Walrasian equilibrium is a set of wage functions $w(\tau)$ and $v(\tau)$ such that $w: [0, \bar{\tau}] \to \mathbb{R}^+$ and $v: [0, \bar{\tau}] \to \mathbb{R}$ (thus v can take negative values—the worker paying to receive the training), such that $\forall t, \tau, e_t(\tau) \leqq 0$, and if $w(\tau) > 0$, then $e_2(\tau) = 0$ and if $v(t) > 0$, then $e_1(\tau) = 0$.

Proposition 1. *There exists a unique Walrasian equilibrium allocation in which all firms adopt the new technology and all workers choose $\tau = \tau^h$.*

The proof follows immediately from the discussion in the Appendix. This proposition states that the unique Walrasian equilibrium is Pareto optimal. Therefore, in the rest of the paper, I will take the Pareto efficient allocation as the unique benchmark equilibrium in the absence of labour market frictions. It is also straightforward to see that in this unique equilibrium, the worker is bearing the full cost of training, in the sense that $v(\tau) = v(0) - c(\tau)$. In other words, in the first period, the worker takes a wage cut equal to the cost of training he is receiving. This is an important, and well known (see Becker (1964)), feature of the frictionless economy.

3. EQUILIBRIUM IN AN IMPERFECT LABOUR MARKET

3.1. *Description*

All the technological features are the same as above but the market mechanism is different. In particular, there is no spot labour market with an auctioneer calling out wage functions to regulate trade. Instead, in each period, workers and firms looking for a new partner have to engage in costly search as in the models of Diamond and Maskin (1979), Diamond (1982), Mortensen (1982) and Pissarides (1990). In particular, agents will be matched one to another randomly, and all parties will have a partner, thus there will be no unemployment. The assumption that every agent finds a partner is in order to demonstrate that the difference between the competitive and non-competitive economies is not due to the presence of unemployment (see Section 4.3 for unemployment). There is however no guarantee that the firm with the investment in the new technology will be matched with the worker who has more training: thus the matching technology is random (as is the norm in this type of models, see for instance, Sattinger (1995), Burdett and Coles (1995), or Acemoglu (1996*b*)). This is an important difference between the competitive and frictional environments since in the absence of frictions, the high-training workers will always produce with the firms which possess the new technology (see Lemma 1 in the Appendix for more details). This aspect of the technology will be discussed in more detail later. Finally, to simplify the analysis I assume that after the initial random match between a firm and a worker, breaking the match and looking for a new partner within the same period is excessively costly, thus workers and firms who are matched together will find it profitable to reach agreement.[2]

How are wages determined? Since there is no spot labour market, wages cannot be equal to the opportunity cost (outside option) of both sides. This implies that there will be some *rent-sharing*. The most common way of dealing with this is bargaining, and any bargaining rule will yield the same results. Here I adopt the bargaining solution suggested by Shaked and Sutton (1984) [see Acemoglu (1996*a*) Appendix A for details and a game-theoretic derivation in the context of search models, see also Binmore, Rubinstein and Wolinsky (1985)]. According to this bargaining rule, as long as both parties are getting more than their outside options, the gross surplus of the partnership is shared. In the current context this simply implies that the worker will get a proportion β of the total surplus and the firm obtains the remaining $1 - \beta$ proportion. Also, in order to emphasize the novel source of inefficiency in this paper, rather than simply force the firm and the worker to bargain over current output, I assume that a firm and a worker who are together can write a *completely enforceable and binding long-term contract* to determine the future divisions of surplus. More explicitly, worker i and firm j, if together at time $t = 1$, can write a contract that specifies future contingent transfers between themselves and therefore will share the present discounted value of the total surplus of the partnership.

3.2. *Underinvestment in training*

This subsection will demonstrate inefficiency in training investments due to labour market imperfections. We will also find that firms could now be willing to bear part of the costs of general skills as we observe in practice. To focus on the main point, I assume that $\alpha_0 = \alpha_1$, and $\delta = 0$, thus the decision to invest in the new technology is irrelevant. In this case the Pareto optimal (and Walrasian equilibrium) amount of training is given by $\tau^h = \tau^l$ (since $\alpha_1 = \alpha_0$).

---

2. Formally, a firm and a worker incur a cost ζ when they break a match within a period and find a new partner (for instance, the value of foregone production in the process of search). The limit point with $\zeta = 0$ is the competitive equilibria analysed in the Appendix. Here, I am assuming that ζ is large enough that no break-up ever occurs. This assumption is of no major importance. Appendix A of Acemoglu (1996*a*) proves, in a similar setting, that even for very small costs of breaking-up, the same equilibrium will be obtained. The same proof can be applied in this setting quite easily, but since it is of tangential interest for this paper, I will only give the intuition. All the equilibria of interest will be symmetric in the sense that all workers will have the same level of training and all firms will have the same technology. Thus, by breaking up, the firm will find itself in exactly the same bargaining situation with another worker, and in the subgame perfect equilibrium, it will get the same share of the surplus (see Shaked and Sutton (1984)). This reasoning also applies to workers. Therefore, for all positive values of ζ, the conclusions of the analysis of large ζ will apply. Only at the limit point of no frictions, $\zeta = 0$, the results of the previous section and the Appendix will be valid.

To characterize the equilibrium, start with the problem of worker i and firm j' who meet in period $t = 2$ after being separated from their respective partners. Given the assumptions, they will simply split the overall surplus which is equal to $y + a_0 \tau_i$, thus the worker gets a wage $\hat{w}_i = \beta(y + a_0 \tau_i)$. I can now analyse the problem of worker i and firm j at $t = 1$. Recall that this pair can write a long-term contract which specifies; (i) a first-period wage; (ii) training level; (iii) a second-period wage if the firm and the worker are together in the second period; (iv) when to terminate the relation; (v) a transfer from one party to the other if there is a termination.

If the adverse shock causes the productivity of the pair to diminish to zero, it is mutually beneficial to terminate the relation (by terminating both parties will get a positive return whereas without termination, they will both get zero), and the worker pays the firm the agreed transfer f. If there is no adverse shock, worker i and firm j produce together in the second period and the firm pays the worker the contractually determined wage w. Let us denote the training level by τ, the first period wage by v, and the distribution function for training among workers by $q(\tilde{\tau})$. Since the firm and the worker can write a long-term contract and utility is perfectly transferable, τ, v, w and f will simply be chosen to maximize the total surplus of the relationship. This total surplus is given as

$$TS = \frac{(1-s)[y + a_0 \tau] + s[\beta(y + a_0 \tau) + (1-\beta)(y + a_0 \int \tilde{\tau} dq(\tilde{\tau}))]}{1 + r} - c(\tau). \qquad (2)$$

Let us now carefully review the terms that make up (2). The last term is the cost of training that the relationship incurs immediately. All benefits accrue in the second period, hence the discounting. With probability $(1 - s)$, there is no adverse shock and the relationship continues. In this case, irrespective of the value of the second period wage w, the total surplus is $y + a_0 \tau$, thus w only determines the distribution of the surplus. The more involved case occurs with probability s, when there is a separation. In this case the worker pays f to the firm. Nevertheless, f does not feature in expression (2) since it is a pure transfer.[3] This is similarly the reason why w and v are not in (2); they do not influence the marginal incentive to invest in training. After the separation, the firm and the worker find new partners and bargain. The worker obtains a proportion β of the surplus with his new firm which gives $\hat{w} = \beta(y + a_0 \tau)$ as his second-period wage. Similarly, the firm obtains a proportion $1 - \beta$ of the output that the new worker produces, thus its return is $(1 - \beta)(y + a_0 \tau)$. (2) is obtained by taking expectations over $\tilde{\tau}$ and noting that the subsample of workers who are looking for a match in the second period is randomly drawn from the population of workers since all pairs face the same probability of separation. The following proposition is immediate[4]:

Proposition 2.   *There is a unique equilibrium in which all pairs choose a level of training $\hat{\tau}$ in the first period such that $a_0[(1 - s) + s\beta] = (1 + r)c'(\hat{\tau})$ and thus $\hat{\tau} < \tau^h = \tau^l$. In this unique equilibrium, $(1 + r)v + (1 - s)w - sf = \beta[(1 + r)y + y + a_0 \hat{\tau}]$.*

3. The reason I have included f in the discussion so far is that the presence of such an exit fee would prevent most of the inefficiencies in training in models with competitive labour markets and credit constraints, thus the presence of this variable emphasizes that this type of incompleteness of contracts is not related to the mechanism proposed here.

4. Note that the separation decision is assumed to be specified and committed to. In the absence of this assumption none of the results would change but w and f need to be restricted to $w = \beta(y + a_0 \hat{\tau}) - f$ because with a lower second period wage, the worker would prefer to leave the firm and find a new employer, and similarly for a higher wage, knowing that all other workers also have training $\hat{\tau}$, the firm would prefer to separate.

Proof. Differentiating (2) with respect to τ gives a unique solution $\tau = \hat{\tau}$, thus all workers choose this level of training. Comparison with the F.O.C. of the planner's problem immediately implies that $\hat{\tau} < \tau' = \tau^h$. Finally, given $\hat{\tau}$, the total surplus to be divided is $y + (y + \alpha_0 \hat{\tau}/1 + t)$ and the worker gets a share β of this which can be made up of different linear combinations of v, w and f. ∥

There is a unique equilibrium with underinvestment in training. The reason is intuitive. In the competitive equilibrium, in the second period the worker obtained 100% of the increase in productivity due to training, and was therefore willing to pay the cost. In contrast, here with probability s an *unknown third-party*, the future employer, is getting a proportion $(1 - \beta)$ of the benefit. Underinvestment in training results because the rents accruing to this third party do not feature in the calculations of the worker and his current employer.

Although the firm and the worker can write complicated and binding contracts, the externality is not internalized. The positive externality is onto the future employer, therefore the crucial variable that the firm and the worker would like to contract upon is $\hat{w}$, the wage in the second period *after* the worker separates from the current firm and finds a new employer. However, at the time of training it is not known who this future employer will be, thus contracting with this firm is not possible. This incompleteness of contracts between the worker and his future employers is therefore crucial for the underinvestment result.

This discussion also implies that there are two types of contracts, not allowed in the analysis, which would help with the inefficiency. The first, *contract* 1, would involve the firm and the worker writing in their contract that if in the second period the worker has a new employer, this new employer has to pay a certain amount, $P(\tau)$, to the initial firm, otherwise the worker is not allowed to work. The second, *contract* 2, works similarly, but requires the new employer of the worker to pay a certain wage to the worker. For instance, conditional on a separation in the second period, if $\hat{w} < x$, then $\hat{f} = F$ and if $\hat{w} \geq x$, then $\hat{f} = 0$ where $\hat{f}$ is the punishment imposed on the worker for breaking the terms of the contract (say as a payment to his initial employer). It is straightforward to obtain the following corollary to Proposition 2.

Corollary 1. *If contract* 1 *can be written and enforced, then* $P(\tau) = \alpha_0 \tau$ *would implement the efficient training* τ^h. *If contract* 2 *can be written and enforced, then the efficient level of training,* τ^h, *can be implemented with* $x = \alpha_0 \tau$, *and F large enough.*

The proof of this corollary is immediate from the discussion and is thus omitted. Both contracts work in the same way: they impose an obligation on the future employer by forcing it to make a higher payment. This is of course intuitive since as noted above, training creates a positive externality on the future employer, and these contracts ensure that this firm contributes to the costs of training. In the first case, the payment imposed on the future employer is a transfer fee to the initial employer, and in the second it is a sufficiently high wage payment to the worker. Since complete contracts between the worker and his initial employer are possible, whether the initial firm or the worker gets the future payments is of no consequence, hence both contracts essentially achieve the same goal.

However, both types of contracts are very difficult to implement precisely because they impose obligations on a party who is not part of the contract, and are thus not legally enforceable. In fact, contracts which enable a worker to unilaterally determine his future wages (by committing not to work for less) would certainly distort a number of important

ACEMOGLU   TRAINING AND INNOVATION   453

economic decisions (e.g. firm entry and investments), and would be very hard to enforce. Also in a more general model, contracts of this type will often hurt the worker by reducing his future employment opportunities. There will also be some more specific problems with these contracts, for instance, with *contract* 2 if the worker and the new firm can distort the observation of $\hat{w}$, the bargaining between them will lead to a wage less than x, but they will report the wage to be x. When this possibility is present, anticipating that the equilibrium wage $\hat{w}$ will be less than x, training investments in the first period will still be suboptimal.

It is also interesting to note that an example of *contract* 1 was actually used in the market for European football players. This contract which required a new team to pay a transfer fee to the player's previous club has been recently challenged and declared unlawful in European courts precisely on such grounds (the Bosman Case, September, 1995). Overall, it is safe to presume that such contracts are not possible and that there will therefore be underinvestment in training. Nonetheless, despite the implementation difficulties, the fact that such contracts were tried suggests that the externality this paper emphasizes is important. Interestingly, if the market failure emphasized by the previous literature (i.e. externalities between the worker and his initial employer) was substantial, we would expect the transfer fee to be from the player to his previous club. Although star soccer players are far from being liquidity constrained, such contracts are not observed.

The emphasis on the inability to contract with future employers does not however imply that the results are driven by incomplete contracts rather than frictional labour markets. Both the need to write such a contract and the inability to do so are intimately related to the frictions in the labour market: in the perfectly competitive economy of Section 2.5, because all workers are always paid their marginal product, there was no need to write a contract with the future employers. Also, it is precisely the decentralized nature of the labour market which makes it impossible for the worker to sign a contract at $t = 1$ with all possible future employers (i.e. a grand contract between all workers and all firms). Therefore, the key results of this paper are driven by labour market frictions, but they also rely on the impossibility to write contracts with future employers.

Another important implication of this approach is that v, w and f are not individually determined; the only equilibrium requirement is that the overall share of the worker be equal to a proportion β of the total surplus. Therefore, it is not possible to infer the productivity of training from the wage-profile of the worker. This observation explains a number of otherwise puzzling findings. For instance, Pischke (1996) looks at the further training offered by German firms. Because this is a voluntary activity on both sides, both the worker and the firm must benefit. Yet, although workers report that the skills they acquire are general, there is no increase in the wage after training. My model suggests that this puzzling observation may be due to the fact that the worker is paid for his future productivity increase during training (i.e. high v and low w), and more importantly, in contrast to the economy with perfectly competitive labour markets, he cannot costlessly change employer and obtain his full marginal product after training; in other words, the firm is able to capture some of the increase in productivity due to the additional skills. Therefore, in contrast to the competitive benchmark as analysed by Becker (1964), the firm will often have an incentive to bear part of the training costs, because due to hold-up by future employers, the worker will only have limited mobility. Therefore, the model offered in this paper is capable of explaining the prevalence of firm sponsored general training (see Harhoff and Kane (1994) for German, Jones (1986) for British, and Bishop (1991) for U.S. evidence on this).

Finally, the model also predicts an inverse relation between s (turnover) and train-
In particular, when $s = 0$, there are no external effects on future employers, and the

equilibrium is efficient. The greater is s, the larger is the likelihood that the skills of the worker will be used by some future employer, and the more serious is the inefficiency. This negative correlation between training and turnover is often found in the data (see for instance OECD (1994)) and is argued to be related to market failure in training in Anglo-Saxon economies (e.g. Blinder and Krueger (1991)). Although the standard Becker-ian model of training would predict an inverse relation between turnover and *firm-specific* human capital, a large portion of the investments that take place in German and Japanese firms appears to be general (see for instance Tan (1990), Harhoff and Kane (1994), Acemoglu and Pischke (1996)). Moreover, it is socially optimal to have an inverse relation between firm-specific training and turnover. Therefore, existing models neither explain the high levels of general training in low turnover markets nor substantiate the claim that low training induced by high turnover is a market failure. My model accounts for the negative correlation and suggests why this may be indicative of inefficiencies in the amount of general training.

3.3. *New technologies and multiple equilibria*

In this subsection I reintroduce the technology choice as in Section 2 and demonstrate that the interaction between innovation and training can lead to the existence of multiple equilibria. The presence of multiple equilibria can be interpreted to imply that similar economies may have very different outcomes due to small differences in environments; or that the inefficiency introduced in the last subsection is much amplified as a result of the new interactions; and/or that some less developed economies do not generate investments in new technologies and have highly unskilled labour forces as a result of a coordination failure.

The same ingredients as before lead us to write a programme similar to (2) to be maximized with respect to γ and τ (again w, v and f are just transfers)

$$\max_{\gamma, \tau} TS = \frac{(1-s)(y + \alpha_0 \tau + \gamma(\alpha_1 - \alpha_0)\tau)}{1+r}$$

$$+ \frac{s(\beta[y + (1-\phi)\alpha_0\tau + \phi\alpha_1\tau] + (1-\beta)[y + ((1-\gamma)\alpha_0 + \gamma\alpha_1) \int \tilde{\tau} dq(\tilde{\tau})])}{1+r}$$

$$- [c(\tau) + \gamma\delta], \tag{3}$$

where ϕ is the proportion of firms with the new technology, and since s hits pairs irrespec-tive of their characteristics, ϕ is also the proportion of firms with the new technology in the subsample of firms looking for a new worker in period $t = 2$. The rest of the expression (3) has exactly the same intuition as (2), the only new feature being that when $\gamma = 1$, there is an increase in productivity equal to $(\alpha_1 - \alpha_0)\tilde{\tau}$ for a firm employing a worker with training $\tilde{\tau}$. Note that if the adverse productivity shock does not hit a pair, they are assumed not to separate (see next section).

The next result characterizes the equilibrium of this economy. First I introduce two conditions which will be useful in the statement of this proportion.

Condition 1.

$$\alpha_1 \hat{\tau}^h - (1+r)(\delta + c(\hat{\tau}^h)) > (1-s)\alpha_0\bar{\tau}^l + s\beta\alpha_1\bar{\tau}^l + s(1-\beta)\alpha_0\hat{\tau}^h - (1+r)c(\bar{\tau}^l).$$

Condition 2.

$$a_0 \hat{t}^l - (1+r)c(\hat{t}^l) > (1-s)a_1 \bar{\tau}^h + s\beta a_0 \bar{\tau}^h + s(1-\beta)a_1 \hat{t}^l - (1+r)(\delta + c(\bar{\tau}^h));$$

where $\hat{t}^h$, $\bar{\tau}^h$, $\hat{t}^l$ and $\bar{\tau}^l$ are defined as: $(1-s)a_1 + s\beta a_1 = (1+r)c'(\hat{t}^h)$, $(1-s)a_0 + s\beta a_0 = (1+r)c'(\hat{t}^l)$, $(1-s)a_0 + s\beta a_1 = (1+r)c'(\bar{\tau}^l)$ and $(1-s)a_1 + s\beta a_0 = (1+r)c'(\bar{\tau}^h)$.

In words, $\hat{t}^h$ is the level of training a pair would choose when they decide to adopt the new technology and when they anticipate $\phi = 1$ (i.e. all other firms are also adopting the new technology). The only difference between $\hat{t}^h$ and the efficient amount τ^h arises because of the underinvestment effect identified in the previous subsection; the firm and the worker recognize that with probability s, the worker will have a new employer who will capture a proportion $1 - \beta$ of his additional productivity. In contrast, $\bar{\tau}^h$ is the level of training when they decide to adopt the new technology but anticipate $\phi = 0$. Similarly $\hat{t}^l$ is the level of training when the pair decides not to adopt the new technology and anticipates $\phi = 0$. And $\bar{\tau}^l$ is the level of training if the innovation is not adopted but $\phi = 1$. It is straightforward to see that $\tau^h > \hat{t}^h > \bar{\tau}^h$ and $\tau^l > \hat{t}^l$ and $\bar{\tau}^l > \hat{t}^l$. Therefore, Condition 1 is more restrictive than Assumption 3(i), and although Assumption 3 still holds, Condition 1 may not be satisfied. Also Conditions 1 and 2 can hold together, but not that given Assumption 3, it is not possible that both conditions be violated at the same time. Then, we have:

Proposition 3.   *There can be two types of pure strategy symmetric equilibria*:

A: *All pairs innovate* ($\phi = 1$) *and all workers choose* $\tau = \hat{t}^h$.
B: *No pair innovates* ($\phi = 0$) *and all workers choose* $\tau = \hat{t}^l$.

  (i) *If Conditions 1 and 2 hold, then both* A *and* B *are equilibria and* A *Pareto dominates* B.[5]
 (ii) *If Condition 1 holds and 2 does not, then* A *is the unique equilibrium*,
(iii) *If Condition 2 holds and 1 does not, then* B *is the unique equilibrium*.

Proof. Suppose $\phi = 1$ and worker i and firm j decide to adopt the technology. Then the F.O.C. of (3) with respect to τ gives $\hat{t}^h$. When all other pairs expect $\phi = 1$ and innovate they will also choose $\hat{t}^h$, thus $q(\tau)$ has all its mass at $\hat{t}^h$, therefore the return from adopting the innovation is given by the LHS of Condition 1. Now suppose that worker i and firm j deviate and do not innovate. Since $\phi = 1$, the F.O.C. will give $(1-s)a_0 + \beta s a_1 = c'(\tau)$ which is $\bar{\tau}^l$. Because all other workers have training level $\hat{t}^h$, in case of separation the firm expects an additional $(1-\beta)a_0 \hat{t}^h$, thus the profit to deviating is given by the RHS of Condition 1. If Condition 1 holds, then deviating is not profitable and there exists an equilibrium with $\phi = 1$ and $\tau = \hat{t}^h$. Similarly, if $\phi = 0$, a pair not innovating would choose $\hat{t}^l$ and anticipating that $\tau_i = \hat{t}^l$ for all workers, the expected surplus will be given by the LHS of Condition 2. If a pair deviates and decides to innovate, then they will choose a level of training $\bar{\tau}^h$, and the total surplus is the RHS of Condition 2. Thus when this condition holds, there is an equilibrium with $\phi = 0$ and $\tau = \hat{t}^l$. If both conditions hold, both allocations are equilibria. Since Assumption 3(i) holds, high training is preferred and thus at $\hat{t}^l$ and $\gamma = 1$, all agents are better off compared to an allocation with $\hat{t}^l$ and no innovation. ∥

5. In this case, there also exists a mixed strategy equilibrium where firms are indifferent between $\gamma = 1$ and $\gamma = 0$ and all workers choose $\tau^m \in (\hat{t}^l, \hat{t}^h)$.

For the set of parameter values at which there is a unique Pareto optimal competitive equilibrium, the economy with costly search can have multiple Pareto ranked equilibria or can have a unique equilibrium with no innovation and low training. The failure to capture all the rents created by training which led to underinvestment in the previous subsection is still present, thus training and innovation are less profitable than in the competitive equilibrium. Moreover, the private benefits from training depend on the expected wage of the worker in the case of separation. From expression (3), this expected wage is $\beta[y + (1 - \phi)a_0\tau + \phi a_1\tau]$ and is increasing in ϕ. If a greater number of firms possess the new technology, it is more likely that the marginal product of the worker will be $a_1\tau$ rather than $a_0\tau$. Hence the larger is ϕ, the higher is the desired level of training. Now let us look at the problem facing the firm. The profitability of innovation will depend on expected profits in case of separation which is $(1 - \beta)[y + ((1 - \gamma)a_0 + \gamma a_1) \int \bar{\tau} dq(\bar{\tau})]$. Therefore, expected profits after a separation are increasing faster in γ when the expected skill level of the *future* workforce, $\int \bar{\tau} dq(\bar{\tau})$, is higher. Thus, firms are more willing to invest in new technologies when they expect future employees to be skilled. Further, when other firms are adopting the innovation, a pair that adopts the technology will choose a higher level of training, ϕ will be larger, average training will be higher, and innovation will be more profitable hence the *multiplicity of equilibria*. Therefore, in the range of parameter values where it is socially beneficial to innovate, there can now be two equilibria: in one all firms innovate and workers have a relatively high level of skill, $\hat{\tau}^h$. In the other, there is a coordination failure, firms do not innovate expecting their future recruits to only have a low level of skill, $\hat{\tau}^l$, and workers expecting the firms not to innovate choose $\hat{\tau}^l$. Note again that as s tends to zero, the inefficiencies disappear, and Conditions 1 and 2 become identical. Thus, without separations, there are no inefficiencies nor multiple equilibria because there are no interactions with future employers, and so the externality identified in this paper disappears.

An interesting question is whether the random matching assumption, that a high-training worker has exactly the same probability of matching with a firm with the new technology as a low-skill worker, is important for our results. It is first easy to see that the results of subsection 3.2 on inefficient training investments are not affected: these results were derived with all firms having the same technology, and were driven only by the impossibility to write contracts with future employers. In this subsection, in contrast, random matching plays an important role since there is potential heterogeneity on both sides. In particular, the intuition for the multiplicity of equilibria is that the *thickness* of the market for skilled labour, ϕ, matters: when only a few firms have the new technology, it is not worthwhile to acquire additional skills. This intuition does not hold with competitive markets because as Lemma 1 in the Appendix proves, irrespective of the value of ϕ, the same wage rule applies. However, the extreme random matching assumption is of no major consequence. This is because both Conditions 1 and 2 are for the cases in which all firms make the same decision. Therefore, irrespective of the matching technology (as long as we are not in a fully Walrasian market), these conditions will be valid.[6] Thus even when the assumption of random matching is relaxed (e.g. high skill workers having a higher probability of matching with high technology firms, see Acemoglu (1997)), the results of this paper would not be affected at all. This again reiterates the main conclusion of the previous subsection that some degree of labour market frictions and the inability

6. Although Conditions 1 and 2 would not change, equation (3) would change, in particular, the term $\int \bar{\tau} dq(\bar{\tau})$ would be replaced with one which takes the differential matching probabilities into consideration.

to write contracts with future employers are the crucial ingredients for the results of this paper.

3.4. *A simple example and some numbers*

To obtain the intuition more clearly, and to help us assess the possible magnitude of the mechanism proposed here, consider the following simple example where τ takes the values 0 and 1 with $c(0) = 0$ and $c(1) = c$. Thus if there is training and innovation, productivity goes up by α_1 and because skills and technology are strongly complementary, without either training or innovation there is no change in productivity. It is immediate to see that Assumption 3(i) now takes the form of $\alpha_1 > (1 + r)(\delta + c)$. Let us write the expected increase in surplus due to innovation. This will be equal to $(1 - s)\alpha_1 + s\beta\phi\alpha_1 + s(1 - \beta)\alpha_1 \int \tilde{\tau} dq(\tilde{\tau}) - (1 + r)(\delta + c)$. Since in this case a pair would only invest in training when they adopt the new technology, we have $\int \tilde{\tau} dq(\tilde{\tau}) = \phi$, and thus innovation and training are profitable if $[(1 - s) + s\phi]\alpha_1 > (1 + r)(\delta + c)$. By substituting $\phi = 1$, we can see that Condition 1 is exactly the same as Assumption 3(i). Therefore, an equilibrium with high training and innovation always exists. Similarly, Condition 2 becomes $(1 - s)\alpha_1 < (1 + r)(\delta + c)$. In this case Conditions 1 and 2 are satisfied for $(1 - s)\alpha_1 < (1 + r)(\delta + c) < \alpha_1$, which is a non-empty set of parameter values. The under-training result of the previous subsection does not arise here and Assumption 3(i) and Condition 1 coincide because training decisions are binary, and as a result the loss of surplus to the future employer does not influence the marginal training decision.

In this simple example it is easier to see the exact reason for the multiplicity of equilibria. In the Walrasian economy a trained worker will always find a firm with the new technology which can make use of his skills, thus the marginal return to more training is always α_1 irrespective of the value of ϕ (see Lemma 1 in the Appendix). In contrast, in the economy with frictional labour markets, the likelihood of finding a firm with the new technology is ϕ, and the likelihood of finding the right worker for the firm is ϕ. Therefore, the *thickness* of the market for trained workers (and for firms with the new technology) plays a crucial role in the absence of the Walrasian auctioneer. This reasoning also establishes that for the claim that less developed economies may have limited investment because of a low-skill workforce to be true, labour market imperfections are necessary; this claim is not true in a competitive labour market.

How important is this interaction? Take $T = \infty$, and consider the example with only $\tau = 0$ and $\tau = 1$ discussed above. When all other firms adopt the innovation, the profit is equal to $\alpha_1/r - c - \delta$. Whereas when no other firm adopts the innovation, the return is equal to $(1 - s)\alpha_1/(r + s) - c - \delta$. Thus, the expected return from innovation and training will be higher by a factor of $s(1 + r)/(r + s)$ when all other firms invest compared to when they do not. Studies such as Leonard (1987) and Blanchard and Diamond (1990) find monthly separation rates as high as 4·5%. A recent study by Andersen and Meyer (1994) calculates a total quarterly separation rate of 23%. For my calculation it is more appropriate to concentrate on the permanent part of this rate which is 17%. Also in line with other evidence, Andersen and Meyer find that the likelihood of permanent separations fall with tenure. To arrive at a conservative estimate I use the lowest hazard rate that Andersen and Meyer calculate for workers who have been with their firm for more than 16 quarters. This gives a quarterly value of 5·7% for s. I take the quarterly real interest rate to be 1%. These numbers imply that the return from new technology will be higher by roughly 86% when all other firms adopt the new technology and train their workers compared to the case in which no other firm invests. This suggests that the mechanism proposed in this paper can be a very important determinant of innovation and training decisions.

4. EXTENSIONS

4.1. *Delay and inefficiencies*

The assumption so far has been that all investments have to be made during period $t = 1$. If a firm does not adopt the innovation at this date, it can never adopt it in the future. This is a strong assumption since most new technologies can be adopted any time after they become available. To show how the results change, I use the simple example introduced at the end of Section 3 where $\tau = 0$ or $\tau = 1$ and take the horizon to be infinite, i.e. $T = \infty$. I also assume that the firm and the worker can decide to adopt the new technology and invest in training at any point. If training and innovation are adopted at time t^*, productivity is equal to $y + \alpha_1$ in all periods $t > t^*$. Without either training or innovation, output is equal to y.

Let us suppose that all other pairs adopt the new technology at date $t = 1$, thus the proportion of firms with the new technology and the proportion of workers with high training are both equal to $\phi_t = 1$ for all $t > 1$. Now consider worker i and firm j. First look at the strategy of never adopting the innovation and never training. The return from this strategy is $TS_0 = (1 + r)y/r$. If the firm adopts the innovation and trains the worker immediately, the return is $TS_1 = (1 + r)y + \alpha_1/r - c - \delta$. If only these two options were being compared, the condition for investment and training to be an equilibrium would be (conditional on coordinating on the better equilibrium): $\alpha_1/r > \delta + c$, the only difference from Section 3.4 being that revenues from innovation and training are accruing for all $t > 1$ here, thus α_1/r rather than $\alpha_1/(1 + r)$. I assume in the rest of this section that this inequality holds so that $TS_1 > TS_0$, and I will then show that this is not sufficient to ensure the adoption of the new technology when delay is possible.

When the firm has an option to delay, it can follow the strategy of adopting the new technology whenever it receives a worker who is already trained. The firm will produce y until the worker leaves and a new worker arrives, and this happens with probability s. Since $\phi_t = 1$ for all t, the new worker will be trained, thus only the adoption cost has to be incurred.[7] Therefore, the surplus from that point onwards is $TS_f = (1 + r)y + \alpha_1/r - \delta$. The firm will get a proportion $(1 - \beta)$ of this amount. Turning to the worker, as soon as he is separated from his initial firm, he will meet a firm with the new technology and the total surplus to be shared at this point between this worker and his new firm is $TS_w = (1 + r)y + \alpha_1/r - c$; because the firm already has the innovation, the partnership only needs to pay the cost of training. The worker will receive a proportion β of TS_w. Then, the total surplus of worker i and firm j who choose to delay at time $t = 1$ is given as TS_d where

$$TS_d = y + \frac{1}{1+r} [(1 - s)TS_d + s(\beta TS_w + (1 - \beta)TS_f)]. \qquad (4)$$

In words, in every period there is a probability s that the worker and the firm will separate. If separation, occurs, the firm will get $(1 - \beta)TS_f$ and the worker will get βTS_w.

---

7. As it is already assumed that $TS_1 > TS_0$, it is immediate that TS_f is positive, thus the innovation will be adopted. Similarly, TS_w is positive and an untrained worker will be trained immediately by a firm which possesses the new technology.

Substituting for TS_w and TS_f gives

$$TS_d = \frac{(1+r)y}{r} + \frac{s}{r+s}\left(\frac{\alpha_1}{r} - \beta c - (1-\beta)\delta\right). \tag{5}$$

For the innovation to be adopted immediately, it is also necessary that $TS_1 \geq TS_d$. Given $TS_1 > TS_0$, it is immediate that $TS_d > TS_0$. Therefore, the condition for all firms to adopt the new technology and train their workers has become tighter. More specifically, when firms can delay innovation and training decisions, an equilibrium in which all firms invest at $t=1$ requires $\alpha_1 > r(\delta + c) + s(1 - \beta)c + s\beta\delta$ which is considerably more restrictive than the condition for innovation and training to be an equilibrium in the absence of the option to delay which was $\alpha_1 > (\delta + c)$.

Intuitively, the skill level of the future workforce of this economy is a *public good* from which all firms benefit (and similarly, the innovation level of firms is a public good from which all workers benefit). When the investment opportunities can be delayed, agents can *free-ride* and reduce their contribution to these public goods by delaying their adoptions and this increases the extent of the inefficiency.[8]

4.2. *Opportunistic separations*

The analysis in Section 3 assumed that worker i and firm j only separate if they receive the adverse productivity shock. This can be formalized by assuming that both sides incur a cost equal to B when they end their current relation and look for a new partner. If B is sufficiently large, they will not want to separate in the absence of an adverse shock, but when such a shock arrives, they are foced to end the relation. If B is not too large, then the possibility of voluntary separations may affect innovation decisions. In particular, suppose that worker i and firm j who have not invested in the innovation, and all other pairs have. In this case, after a separation worker i will get a firm with the new technology, and firm j will get a more trained worker. Therefore, the incentives not to invest in the first period and separate opportunistically at $t=2$ will be stronger. The previous version of the paper established that with this modification, Proposition 3 still applies as before, but a more stringent condition replaces Condition 1. Condition 2 will remain unchanged since a firm and a worker choosing innovation and high training while others do not will never want to separate voluntarily. Because the new condition is more stringent, it is possible that the multiplicity of equilibria is replaced by a unique equilibrium with low training and no innovation. In any case, inefficiencies are now more serious.[9]

4.3. *Unemployment*

The analysis so far has not allowed for unemployment. The main reason was to clarify the crucial differences between a competitive economy and one characterized by frictional labour markets. The presence of unemployment does not change any of the key results, but yields some additional insights. To illustrate the effects in the simplest possible way, consider the case in which workers anticipate that if they separate they face a probability

---

8. Gale (1995) contains a more general analysis of the efficiency consequences of delay in a model with pay-off externalities. Chamley and Gale (1995) illustrate the consequences of delay in a model with informational externalities. Shleifer (1986) shows the possibility of delay in the context of a model with aggregate demand externalities.

9. Details are available from the author upon request.

460   REVIEW OF ECONOMIC STUDIES

of unemployment, $p_u > 0$, and that training is useless to an unemployed worker (and also unrealistically that training does not change the probability of unemployment). This formulation immediately implies that a higher probability of unemployment, p_u, which is naturally associated with a higher unemployment rate, reduces the incentives to invest in training, and therefore, the incentives to invest in new technologies.[10]

This insight also sheds light on a famous debate started by Habakkuk (1962). Habakkuk claimed that the reason technological progress was faster in the U.S. than in the U.K. during the nineteenth century was the shortage of labour in the U.S. which forced firms to innovate. However, this thesis is not consistent with the fact that most new technologies during this period were not labour saving (see MacLeod (1988)). The model of this paper implies that high unemployment discourages innovation despite the fact that new technologies and labour are complementary, and it offers an explanation for why the lack of labour shortage in nineteenth century Britain may have slowed down labour augmenting technological change.

5. CONCLUSION

This paper analysed innovation and training decisions in a frictional labour market and offered two key results. First, workers do not have the right incentives to invest in general training because they anticipate that part of the productivity gains created by training will be captured by their future employers. This inefficiency in training, in contrast to others proposed in the literature, does not depend on an extreme form of incompleteness of contracts between a worker and his employer, nor does it require credit market imperfections. Also with competitive markets, workers bear the full costs of general training, whereas with labour market frictions, firms may be willing to pay part of the costs of training. Second, if there are also investment decisions in new technology complementary to the skills of the workers, then the inefficiency in training is increased and a multiplicity of equilibria emerges. If a large number of firms are expected to adopt the new technology, workers expect their future productivity to be higher and are more willing to pay for general training. In contrast, there can also be a coordination failure equilibrium where firms do not adopt the innovation and workers choose a low level of skills. The multiplicity of equilibria does not rely on technological spillovers or aggregate demand externalities, it is instead driven by labour market frictions.

APPENDIX: NON-WALRASIAN EQUILIBRIA WITHOUT FRICTIONS

The analysis in subsection 2.3 treated a frictionless labour market as a market coordinated by a Walrasian auctioneer. This is not the only possible interpretation. The crucial imperfection in the economy of Section 3 is that workers and firms cannot costlessly change partners (within a period). Thus a natural benchmark is the limit point where there are no costs of changing partners. However, this is not necessarily the same as a Walrasian equilibrium. Instead it is the (subgame perfect) equilibrium of a game in which firms compete *a la* Bertrand in each period for all the workers. Let me refer to this equilibrium as a *weak competitive equilibrium*[11] and characterize these equilibria in this Appendix.

10. Also this channel can lead to a further multiplicity of equilibria. In one equilibrium, unemployment is high, therefore workers do not want to invest in skills, this reduces profitability of firms, and as a result, few firms enter, supporting an equilibrium with high unemployment. Details, which were included in previous versions, are available upon request.

11. This is an equilibrium concept first proposed by Hart (1979) and Makowski (1980) in the context of monopolistic competition, and referred to by Allen and Gale (1988) as *conjectural equilibrium*. I use the term *weak competitive equilibrium* to emphasize the fact that this concept is used implicitly as the competitive equilibrium concept but it is weaker than the *Walrasian equilibrium*.

ACEMOGLU   TRAINING AND INNOVATION   461

The game underlying the *weak competitive equilibrium* is as follows: at all times $t \geq 2$, firms hire labour with training τ at the wage $w_t(\tau): [0, \bar{\tau}] \to \mathbb{R}^+$. Then all agents take the sequence of future equilibrium wage functions $\{w_t(\tau)\}$ as given, and workers are hired at time $t = 1$ at wage $v(\tau): [0, \bar{\tau}] \to \mathbb{R}$ where τ is the amount of training that the employer will provide during this period. An equilibrium is a sequence of functions $\{w_t(\tau)\}_{t=2}^{T}$ and $v(\tau)$ such that all agents' demands are satisfied at the time t spot labour market for all t.[12] Note the difference between this equilibrium concept and the Walrasian one: here the market for worker with training τ only needs to clear if there are workers of training level τ. In contrast, with the Walrasian equilibrium, even if there are no workers with training level τ, we still have to find a price $w(\tau)$ such that at this price, no firm wants to hire workers with training level τ and no worker wants to obtain training τ rather than some other level. Thus, it must be clear that a *Walrasian equilibrium* is a *weak competitive equilibrium* but not vice versa.

Let me start with the last period of this economy, $t = T = 2$, and denote the proportion of firms with $\gamma = 1$ (i.e. the firms with the new technology) by ϕ. There will be some pairs of workers and firms who cannot work together [that is, if worker i and firm j were together in period $t = 1$ and received the adverse shock], but this will not create any problem unless $\phi = 0$ or $\phi = 1$ because there will be a continuum of firms that can employ each worker. Before the next result, I also define, as in the text, $q(\bar{\tau})$ as the distribution function of workers with training $\bar{\tau}$ in period $t = 2$.

Lemma 1. *Suppose $0 < \phi < 1$, then in all $t = 2$ weak competitive equilibria, workers with $r \geq \tau^*$ work with firms that have $\gamma = 1$ and workers with $\tau < \tau^*$ work with firms that have $\gamma = 0$ where τ^* is such that $q(\tau^*) = 1 - \phi$. For any training level τ at which there exist a positive measure of workers, wages are given by*

$$w(\tau) = y + a_1\tau - a \qquad \text{if } \tau \geq \tau^*$$
$$w(\tau) = y + a_0\tau - b \qquad \text{if } \tau < \tau^*, \tag{6}$$

where $a - (a_1 - a_0)\tau^* = b$.

Proof. The proof is by contradiction. I first prove that no other allocation rule can be equilibrium, then given the allocation rule, I show that only the wage function in (6) is equilibrium.

Suppose that a worker with $\tau' > \tau^*$ is employed by a firm without the innovation, j'. Let the profit of this firm be $\pi(j')$, then $\pi(j') = y + a_0\tau' - w(\tau')$. Let the profit of this firm from hiring worker τ^* be $\pi^*(j')$, then $\pi^*(j') = y + a_0\tau^* - w(\tau^*)$. For equilibrium, it is necessary that $\pi(j') = y + a_0\tau' - w(\tau') \geq \pi^*(j') = y + a_0\tau^* - w(\tau^*)$ which implies that $w(\tau') - w(\tau^*) \leq a_0(\tau' - \tau^*)$. Suppose this last inequality is true. Then because a firm with the innovation must be indifferent between hiring τ^* and τ', $w(\tau') - w(\tau^*) \geq a_1(\tau' - \tau^*)$ which, since $a_1 > a_0$, gives a contradiction. This implies that all workers with $\tau \geq \tau^*$ are hired by firms that have $\gamma = 1$, and therefore, all workers with $\tau < \tau^*$ must be hired by firms with $\gamma = 0$.

Now take this allocation rule as given. Take two training levels $\tau'' > \tau' \geq \tau^*$. Then firms with the innovation must be indifferent between hiring any of these two workers, thus $w(\tau'') - w(\tau') = a_1(\tau'' - \tau')$ which gives the first part of (6). Next consider two workers with $\tau' < \tau'' < \tau^*$. The same reasoning implies $w(\tau'') - w(\tau') = a_0(\tau'' - \tau')$. Thus the second part of (6) is obtained. Now consider $\tau'' \geq \tau^* > \tau'$. Since a firm with $\gamma = 1$ is hiring τ'', we require $\pi_1(\tau'') \geq \pi_1(\tau')$ where $\pi_1(\tau)$ denotes the profit that a firm with the new technology makes from a worker with training equal to τ. Thus, it is necessary that $w(\tau'') - w(\tau') \leq a_1(\tau'' - \tau')$. This implies that $b \leq a - (a_1 - a_0)\tau'$. Since this has to be true for all $\tau' \leq \tau^*$, then we also have $b \leq a - (a_1 - a_0)\tau^*$. Next a firm without the technology can always hire τ^*, and obtain profits equal to $\pi_0(\tau^*) = a_0\tau^* - w(\tau^*) = a - (a_1 - a_0)\tau^*$. This firm is currently making profits equal to $\pi_0(\tau') = b$, therefore, $\pi_0(\tau') \geq \pi_0(\tau^*)$, hence $b \geq a - (a_1 - a_0)\tau^*$. Combining this with the previous inequality, we get $b = a - (a_1 - a_0)\tau^*$, which completes the proof. ‖

An important result contained in this lemma is that the allocation of workers to firms will be optimal; high-training workers will be employed by firms that have the new technology. Moreover, irrespective of the skill distribution of workers, firms with the new technology will pay the marginal product of a worker, thus they will be indifferent to the exact training of the worker they hire in equilibrium. Also note the statement in the lemma which requires some positive measure of workers to have training τ for the above wage rules to apply. This requirement is not necessary when we are considering a Walrasian equilibrium. But as noted above, with the weaker definition, only commodities which are actively traded can be priced.

12. Since firms are competing *a la* Bertrand, the requirement that markets clear, and the offers are best-response to each other are equivalent.

462   REVIEW OF ECONOMIC STUDIES

Also, the above lemma is for $0 < \phi < 1$. If instead $\phi = 0$, there is no demand from firms that have the new technology, thus wages are simply given as

$$w(\tau) = y + a_0 \tau - \tilde{a},$$

and similarly when $\phi = 1$, $w(\tau) = y + a_1 \tau - \hat{a}$, for $\tilde{a}$ and $\hat{a}$ non-negative.

Proposition 4. *Assume that Assumption 3 holds, then there exist exactly two weak competitive equilibrium allocations.*

(i) $\phi = 1$, *and all workers choose* τ^h.
(ii) $\phi = 0$, *and all workers choose* τ^l.

Proof. Part A shows that (i) above is an equilibrium. *Part B* shows that (ii) is an equilibrium and *Part C* shows that there are no others.

Part A: Suppose all firms choose to invest in the new technology so that $\phi = 1$. Then $w(\tau) = y + a_1 \tau - a$, and each worker knowing that his wages will be higher by $a_1 \tau$ is willing to pay up to the point where $a_1 = (1 + r)c'(\tau)$ which gives the training level equal to τ^h (and workers pay $c(\tau^h)$ in the first period to the firm to compensate it for the cost of training). Since all workers have training τ^h, the profit levels to the alternative strategies of a firm are given as $\pi_1 = a - (1 + r)\delta$ and $\pi_0 = a - (a_1 - a_0)\tau^h$. Assumption 3(i) implies that $a_1 \tau^h - a_0 \tau^l > (1 + r)[c(\tau^h) - c(\tau^l) + \delta]$. Given the strict convexity of $c(\cdot)$, it is also the case that $(1 + r)[c(\tau^h) - c(\tau^l)] > a_0(\tau^h - \tau^l)$, thus $a_1(\tau^h - \tau^l) > (1 + r)\delta$. Hence (i) above is an equilibrium.
Part B: Now suppose all firms choose $\gamma = 0$, then second period wages are $w(\tau) = y + a_0 \tau - \tilde{a}$ because there is no firm with the advanced technology that may get additional marginal product a_1 from training. Anticipating this wage function, workers choose τ^l. With a similar argument to *Part A* above, it follows from Assumption 3(ii) that firms are happy to choose $\gamma = 0$.
Part C: Next suppose that there is an equilibrium with $\phi \in (0, 1)$. Then the wage function in Lemma 1 applies. Therefore, $\pi_1 = a$ and $\pi_0 = b$. If $a - b < (1 + r)\delta$, then the firms that choose $\gamma = 1$ can increase their profits by not investing. If $a - b > (1 + r)\delta$, then firms with $\gamma = 0$ can increase their profits by investing. Finally $a - b = (1 + r)\delta$ can only be an equilibrium if a proportion $(1 - \phi)$ of the workers choose τ^l. In this equilibrium, $w(\tau^h) - w(\tau^l) = a_1(\tau^h - \tau^l) - (1 + r)\delta$, thus the net return to choosing τ^h rather than τ^l is $a_1(\tau^h - \tau^l) - (1 + r)\delta - (1 + r)[c(\tau^h) - c(\tau^l)]$, which by Assumption 3(i) is positive, thus no worker chooses τ^l, hence there are no equilibria with $\phi \in (0, 1)$. ‖

This proposition establishes that as well as the Pareto optimal equilibrium there is a coordination-failure equilibrium. In this second equilibrium, (ii), investment in the new technology is not undertaken and a lower than socially optimal level of training is chosen. The existence of this "coordination-failure" equilibrium is due to the fact that the right markets are not open at time $t = 2$. In particular, when all workers choose τ^l, there is no one hiring or supplying labour in the market for workers with training τ^h, thus this market is closed and the appropriate price signals are not being transmitted. In contrast, suppose the wage determination rule in the lemma applies to τ^h even when there are no workers with training τ^h, then it is clear that workers would prefer to obtain training τ^h rather than τ^l. In other words, in a Walrasian equilibrium, if the market for workers with training τ^h is closed, then their price (wage) must be zero and there must be excess supply at this price. Yet at zero price, firms will naturally want to hire workers with training level τ^h at $t = 2$ [see also the discussion in Allen and Gale (1988)]. Therefore, if labour with training τ^h were priced (even when there are no workers at this training level), the allocation with τ^l and $\phi = 0$ would not be an equilibrium. This reasoning immediately establishes Proposition 1 in the text: there is a unique Pareto optimal Walrasian equilibrium.
Nevertheless, the concept of *weak competitive equilibrium* may appear more relevant than the abstract notion of *Walrasian equilibrium* which seems to demand even more than usual from the auctioneer (i.e. to price commodities not traded along the "equilibrium path"). In fact, in many economic applications, the concept of weak competitive equilibrium is used implicitly rather than the Walrasian equilibrium. However, the allocation with $\gamma = 0$ and $\tau = \tau^l$ is not even a robust weak competitive equilibrium. In a game-theoretic sense it is "unstable" because it does not survive arbitrarily small perturbations.
To demonstrate this in the simplest way, consider an economy E_ε which is the same as the economy above except that firms make a mistake/tremble with probability ε and choose the opposite of the investment choice they intended (e.g. they invest if they intended not to invest). Then:

Definition 1. Let A be an equilibrium allocation and $\tau_A : [0, 1] \to \mathbb{R}$ be a mapping that allocates a training level to each worker in this equilibrium. A satisfies *stability iff* $\forall \nu > 0$, $\exists \bar{\varepsilon} > 0$ such that $\forall \varepsilon < \bar{\varepsilon}$, A_ν is an equilibrium of E_ε where in A_ν training levels are given by τ_ν such that $\|\tau_\nu - \tau_A\| < \nu$.

In words, an equilibrium satisfies stability if a small change in the behaviour of the firms leads to a small change in the behaviour of the workers.[13]

Proposition 5. *Suppose Assumption 3 holds, then the allocation $\phi = 1$ and $\tau = \tau^h$ is the unique weak competitive equilibrium which satisfies stability.*

Proof. It is necessary to establish that for all $v > 0$, there exists τ_v that is best response to $\phi = 1 - \varepsilon$ for all $\varepsilon < \bar{\varepsilon}$ such that $\|\tau^h - \tau_v\| \le v$. Let $w(\tau^h) = y + a_1\tau^h - a$ as in Lemma 1. A worker who deviates and chooses $\tau < \tau^h$ will have the lowest training level and thus by Lemma 1 will be matched with the firms that have $\gamma = 0$. He will therefore have a wage rate $w(\tau) = y + a_1\tau - b$ for all $\tau < \tau^h$. Since the marginal return to τ is still a_1, $\tau = \tau^h$ is the best-response, thus $\tau_v = \tau^h$. Therefore, the requirement is satisfied for all $v > 0$, and the equilibrium allocation with $\phi = 1$ and $\tau = \tau^h$ satisfies stability.

Next consider the equilibrium allocation with $\phi = 0$ and $\tau = \tau^l$. From Lemma 1, $\forall \phi = \varepsilon > 0$, by the same argument as in *Part C* of Proposition 4, $\tau = \tau^h$ is best-response, thus $\tau_v = \tau^h$. So let $v < \tau^h - \tau^l$, then $\|\tau^l - \tau_v\| > v$ and this allocation does not satisfy stability. ‖

The intuition of this result is quite simple. The coordination failure equilibrium was pathological as it relied on one of the markets not transmitting price signals. As soon as there is some activity in all markets such that even commodities not traded along the equilibrium path have the right prices, this equilibrium disappears.

Therefore, the analysis of this Appendix confirms the conclusion reached in subsection 2.3 that in the absence of labour market frictions, there is a unique efficient equilibrium.

It is also straightforward to see that the "coordination failure' equilibrium of Section 3 when labour markets are imperfect satisfies the notion of stability introduced in this Appendix. A small fraction of firms investing in the new technology would only have a minimal impact on the expected return to training, and thus workers will only respond by a very small amount to such changes.

Acknowledgements. I am grateful to Charlie Bean, Peter Diamond, Oliver Hart, Steve Pischke, Kevin Roberts, Jim Robinson, Andrew Scott and three anonymous referees. I also thank seminar participants at Boston College, Chicago, LSE, Northwestern, MIT, Princeton, UCL and Yale.

REFERENCES

ACEMOGLU, D. (1996a), "A Microfoundation For Increasing Returns in Human Capital Accumulation", *Quarterly Journal of Economics*, **111**, 779–804.
ACEMOGLU, D. (1996b), "Changes in Unemployment and Wage Inequality: An Alternative Theory and Some Evidence" (CEPR Discussion Paper, No. 1459).
ACEMOGLU, D. (1997), "Matching, Heterogeneity and the Evolution of Income Distribution", *Journal of Economic Growth*, **1**, 40–65.
ACEMOGLU, D. and PISCHKE, S. (1996), "Why Do Firms Train? Theory and Evidence" (National Bureau of Economic Research, Working Paper No. 5605).
ALLEN, F. and GALE, D. (1988), "Optimal Security Design", *Review of Financial Studies*, **1**, 229–263.
ANDERSEN, P. M. and MEYER, B. D. (1994), "The Extent and Consequences of Job Turnover", *Brookings Papers on Economic Activity, Microeconomics*, 177–248.
BARTEL, A. and LICHTENBERG, F. (1987), "The Comparative Advantage of Educated Workers in Implementing New Technologies", *Review of Economics and Statistics*, **69**, 1–11.
BECKER, G. (1964) *Human Capital* (Chicago: University of Chicago Press).
BINMORE, K., RUBINSTEIN, A. and WOLINSKY, A. (1986), "The Nash Bargaining Solution in Economic Modelling", *Rand Journal of Economics*, **17**, 176–188.
BISHOP, J. (1991), "On-the-Job Training of New Hires", in Stern, D. and Ritzen, J. M. (eds.), *Market Failure in Training*? (Berlin: Springer-Verlag).
BLANCHARD, O. and DIAMOND, P. (1990), "The Cyclical Behavior of the Gross Flows of U.S. Workers", *Brookings Papers On Economic Activity*, **2**, 85–155.

13. An alternative definition of stability can be given in terms of the slopes of best-response functions, see for instance Fudenberg and Tirole (1991) pp. 23–28). The notion of stability used here is related to refinements such as Trembling Hand Perfection and is therefore weaker than the definition of asymptotic stability given there, and thus, the result that the coordination failure equilibrium is not stable derived here is a stronger result. In particular, it is straightforward to see that the best-response functions of workers in this case are discontinuous: when no firm adopts the innovation, they all want to receive training equal to τ^l but as soon as there is even a very small proportion of firms adopting the innovation, all workers would like to obtain τ^h. Thus, as soon as there is a very small number of firms who demand the new technology, the best-response of the workers jumps from τ^l to τ^h.

BLINDER, A. S. and KRUEGER, A. B. (1991), "International Differences in Turnover: A Comparative Study with Emphasis on the U.S. and Japan" (mimeo, Princeton University).

BURDETT, K. and COLES, M. (1995), "Marriage and Class" (mimeo, University of Essex).

BURDETT, K. and SMITH, E. (1996), "Education and Matching Externalities", in Booth, A. and Snower, D. (eds.), *Skills Gap and Economic Activity* (Cambridge: Cambridge University Press).

CHAMLEY, C. and GALE, D. (1994), "Information Revelation and Strategic Delay in a Model of Investment", *Econometrica*, **62**, 1065–1085.

COOPER, R. and JOHN, A. (1988), "Coordinating Coordination Failures in Keynesian Models", *Quarterly Journal of Economics*, **103**, 441–465.

DIAMOND, P. (1982), "Aggregate Demand Management in a Search Equilibrium", *Journal of Political Economy*, **90**, 881–894.

DIAMOND, P. and MASKIN, E. (1979), "An Equilibrium Analysis of Search and Breach of Contract, I: Steady States", *Bell Journal of Economics*, **10**, 282–316.

DURLAUF, S. (1993), "Non-ergodic Growth", *Review of Economic Studies*, **60**, 349–366.

FUDENBERG, D. and TIROLE, J. (1991) *Game Theory* (Cambridge: MIT Press).

GALE, D. (1995), "Dynamic Coordination Games", *Economic Theory*, **5**, 1–18.

GRILLICHES, Z. (1969), "Capital and Skill Complementarity", *Review of Economics and Statistics*, **51**, 465–468.

GROUT, P. (1984), "Investment and Wages in the Absence of Binding Contracts: A Nash Bargaining Approach", *Econometrica*, **52**, 449–460.

HABAKKUK, H. J. (1962) *American and British Technology in the Nineteenth Century (Cambridge: Cambridge University Press)*.

HARHOFF, D. and KANE, T. J. (1994), "Financing Apprenticeship Training: Evidence from Germany" (NBER Working Paper No. 4557).

HART, O. D. (1979), "Monopolistic Competition in a Large Economy With Differentiated Commodities", *Review of Economic Studies*, **46**, 1–30.

HASHIMOTO, M. (1991), "Training and Employment Relations in Japanese Firms", in Stern, D. and Ritzen, J. M. (eds.), *Market Failure in Training?* (Berlin: Springer-Verlag).

JONES, I. (1985), "Apprentice Training Costs in British Manufacturing Establishments: Some New Evidence", *British Journal of Industrial Relations*, **24**, 333–362.

KIYOTAKI, N. (1988), "Multiple Expectational Equilibria under Monopolistic Competition", *Quarterly Journal of Economics*, **103**, 695–713.

LAING, D., PALIVOS, T. and WANG, P. (1995), "Learning, Matching and Growth", *Review of Economic Studies*, **62**, 115–131.

LEONARD, J. S. (1987), "In the Wrong Place at the Wrong Time: The Extent of Frictional and Structural Unemployment", in Lang, K. and Leonard, J. S. (eds.), *Unemployment and the Structure of the Labor Markets* (Oxford: Basil Blackwell).

MacLEOD, C. (1988) *Inventing the Industrial Revolution* (Cambridge: Cambridge University Press).

MAKOWSKI, L. (1980), "Perfect Competition, the Profit Criterion and the Organization of Economic Activity", *Journal of Economic Activity*, **22**, 222–242.

MORTENSEN, D. (1982), "Property Rights and Efficiency in Mating, Racing and Related Games", *American Economic Review*, **72**, 968–979.

MURPHY, K., SHLEIFER, A. and VISHNY, R. (1989), "Industrialization and the Big Push", *Journal of Political Economy*, **97**, 1003–1026.

NORTHCOTT, J. and WALLING, A. (1988), "The Impact of Microelectronics; Diffusion Benefits and Problems in British Industry (Policy Studies Institute, London).

NORTHCOTT, J. and VICKREY, G. (1993), "Surveys of the Diffusion of Microelectronics and Advanced Manufacturing Technology" (Paper presented at MIT/NSF/OECD Workshop on "The Productivity Impact of Information Technology Investments").

OECD (1994) *Employment Outlook*.

PISCHKE, S. (1996), "Continuous Training in Germany" (NBER Working Paper No. 8529).

PISSARIDES, C. (1990) *Equilibrium Unemployment Theory* (Oxford: Basil Blackwell).

ROBINSON, J. A. (1995), "Unemployment and Human Capital Accumulation" (mimeo, USC).

ROSENSTEIN-RODAN, P. (1943), "Problems of Industrialization of Eastern and Southern-Eastern Europe", *Economic Journal*, **53**, 202–211.

SAINT-PAUL, G. (1996), "Unemployment, Wage Rigidity and the Returns to Education", *Journal of Public Economics* (forthcoming).

SHAKED, A. and SUTTON, J. (1984), "Involuntary Unemployment as a Perfect Equilibrium in a Bargaining Model", *Econometrica*, **52**, 1341–1364.

SHLEIFER, A. (1986), "Implementation Cycles", *Journal of Political Economy*, **94**, 1163–1190.

TAN, H. W. (1991), "Technical Change and Human Capital Acquisition in the U.S. and Japanese Labor Markets", in Hulten, C. R. (ed.), *Productivity Growth in Japan and the United States* (Chicago: University of Chicago Press).

[4]

THE ECONOMICS OF PRIVATE SECTOR TRAINING: A SURVEY OF THE LITERATURE

Edwin Leuven

Universiteit van Amsterdam

Abstract. This survey organizes and summarizes existing theoretical work on private sector training. The theoretical models focus on investment efficiency, finance and turnover. Recent developments in the on-the-job training literature are characterized by strategic interaction between employers and employees and emphasize market imperfections.

Keywords. Human capital; Investment; Training

1. Introduction

This paper provides a survey of the economic literature on private sector training. It therefore considers on-the-job training and does not discuss formal education or training of the unemployed or any learning activities that workers undertake independently from their employer. This of course does not imply that insights from the on-the-job training literature are not relevant for other types of training and education.

Human capital theory as formalized by Becker (1962) is the dominant perspective on on-the-job training. This theory views training as an investment; it raises expected future productivity but at a cost. The key distinguishing feature of a human capital investment as opposed to an investment in capital concerns property rights. A machine can be sold, but in modern society, men cannot. As individuals have the discretion over the deployment of their own human capital, workers and firms will need to agree on an exchange in the labour market. This implies that how the costs and returns to training are shared between workers and firms is a central concern in the on-the-job training literature.

Human capital theory has been further developed in the 1970s to explain the life-cycle pattern of earnings. This literature analyses the human capital investment decision of individuals in a competitive environment. One may argue that, in this model, the distinction between education and training is an artificial one. Workers choose the investment as a function of prices (and ability). Through

0950-0804/05/01 0091–21   JOURNAL OF ECONOMIC SURVEYS Vol. 19, No. 1

these prices, the demand side enters. There is no strategic interaction between workers and firms. Weiss (1986) surveys this literature.

In the beginning of the 1990s, the new field of economics of information resulted in applications to on-the-job training. We will see that these recent developments in the training literature focus on the strategic interaction between employers and employees, and as such stands apart from life-cycle theories of earnings. The focus is on market imperfections and information asymmetries. This review restricts itself to the core of private sector training theory. The reason for this focus is the scattered nature of this literature. The studies in this field differ in many modelling assumptions that complicate comparison. Yet, some common themes can be distinguished. The main concerns of the theoretical economic literature on training are the following:

- Investment efficiency,
- Separation efficiency,
- Division of costs and returns.

The review will therefore present the results in these terms and highlight additional insights where necessary.

The outline of this paper is as follows. The next section presents an overview of models of training. Section 3 presents the standard model of general training. After which specific training will be discussed in section 4. Section 5 considers the impact of contract (re)negotiations on investment incentives and hold-up, after which section 6 discusses market imperfections and specific sources thereof in more depth. Section 7 offers a brief summary of the main insights and discusses implications for policy and further research.

2. Models of Training

Becker (1962) is the first reference for anyone interested in the economics of training.[1] In this seminal paper, a simple two-period model is presented. Becker assumes that labour and product markets are perfectly competitive and distinguishes two types of training: general training and specific training (definitions are given in the next section). The analysis of Becker has subsequently been extended and refined by other authors to take imperfect competition and the role of information asymmetries into account. In many respects, these models still resemble Becker's analysis. The distinction of general and specific is still important, and most models in this literature are two-period models.

Figure 1 gives a description of the timing of events in the prototypical model of on-the-job training. There is a training period and a production period, and each of them can be preceded by contract negotiations (wages are set and training can be contractible). Most models are of a non-cooperative nature, and other modelling assumptions vary more widely. Some models assume free entry at the first stage, thereby imposing a zero profit condition on the firm and creating a cooperative outcome. Models also vary in the extent to which they allow ex-ante uncertainty, thereby justifying the renegotiation of the initial contract

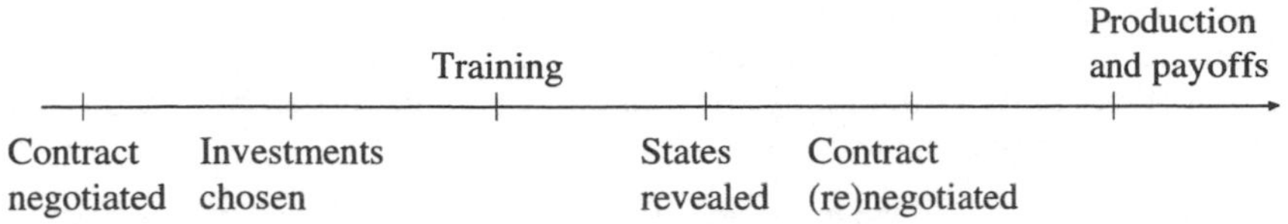

PRIVATE SECTOR TRAINING 93

Figure 1. Timing of Events in Prototypical Models of Training.

after the arrival of new information. Finally, the different analyses vary in the assumptions they make about the observability of training and/or ability, and who has this information and when.

Contract negotiations typically take the form in which the firm proposes an initial contract (possibly in the presence of competition or strategic bidding of outside firms). The worker may then accept the contract or take-up his market alternative. On accepting, the worker is automatically trained if the contract specifies a training level, otherwise the firm or the worker may decide to invest. After training, ex-ante uncertain information may become known to one or more parties. Examples of sources of uncertainty are the worker's ability, an outside option or the value of the match. Then, before entering second period employment, there may be, again, a contracting phase in which the second period wage is (re)negotiated and the worker may separate from the training firm. After this, production takes place and the parties retire.

It will be convenient to introduce some notation at this point. Throughout the paper we will use s to denote training. Training s can be continuous or dichotomous depending on the specific model under consideration. Cost of training is $c(s)$. Output in period t in the training firm given training s is denoted by $y_t(s)$ and similarly market productivity in period t equals $\bar{y}_t(s)$. Finally, period t wages are written as $w_t(s)$ and market wages are $\bar{w}_t(s)$. Table 1 provides an overview of the notation.

The following assumptions are made:

Assumption 1.1. Firms maximize expected profits and workers maximize expected lifetime earnings.

Insurance motives are typically ignored:

Table 1. Overview of Notation.

Quantity	Description
s	Amount of training (time),
$y_t(s)$	Period productivity in training firm, $(t=1,2)$
$\bar{y}_t(s)$	Period productivity in alternative employment, $(t=1,2)$
$w_t(s)$	Period wage in training firm, $(t=1,2)$
$\bar{w}_t(s)$	Period wage in alternative employment, $(t=1,2)$
$c(s)$	Training cost

Assumption 1.2. Firms and workers are risk neutral.

There is no discounting. In addition, to avoid corner solutions, the following (standard) regularity assumptions are made to ensure the existence of a positive training level in equilibrium:

Assumption 1.3. $c(s)$ is increasing and strictly convex in s. In addition, $c(0) = 0$, $\lim_{s\to 0} c'(s) = 0$ and $\lim_{s\to\infty} c'(s) = \infty$
and

Assumption 1.4. $y_2(s)$, $\bar{y}_2(s)$ are non-decreasing and concave in s.

It is also assumed that training (as compared with no training) is socially optimal.

These are the most important assumptions. They will be augmented with other assumptions where necessary. The next section starts with the standard model of training where it is assumed that markets are perfectly competitive.

3. Perfect Competition

The standard model of training is a model of full competition where training is general. Becker (1962) defined general training as training that it is equally useful in many firms:

Definition 1. *Training is general if $\bar{y}_2(s) = y_2(s)$.*

Becker argued that if training is general and labour (and product) markets are perfectly competitive, then firms will not be prepared to finance this training. Workers will reap all the returns and will therefore bear all the training costs. The basic argument runs as follows. With competitive labour markets, workers can receive a market wage that is equal to the value of their marginal product in the market. As training is general, the value of their marginal productivity is the same in the training firm and the market, the training firm will be obliged to pay workers their full marginal productivity. Because the firm does not reap any of the benefits, it will not be prepared to finance general training. If it would, the worker could leave after training and capture the full returns without reimbursing the cost of training to the firm (in the absence of a contract specifying a breach remedy). Becker showed that workers may pay for the general training they receive through lower wages during the training period.

The structure of Becker's model is shown in Figure 2. A firm offers training amount s and starting wage w_1. The worker accepts (A) or rejects ($\sim A$). If the worker rejects, he enters the market and receives the wage of an unskilled worker. If the worker accepts, he is trained. After training, the firm offers a second-period wage. The worker quits (Q) if the firm's wage offer is less than what the worker can earn in the market and stays ($\sim Q$) otherwise. In the second period, production takes place after which the parties receive their payoffs and retire.

In addition to definition 1, it is also assumed that there is perfect competition in the labour market. This can be modelled by assuming that there is free entry. As a result, Bertrand competition at the start of the second period will drive the market wage $\bar{w}_2$ to the value of worker productivity $\bar{y}_2$.[2] The training firm is

PRIVATE SECTOR TRAINING   95

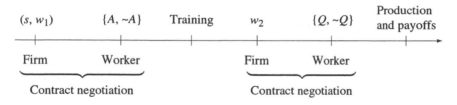

Figure 2. Timing in the Standard Competitive Model of General Training.

therefore obliged to offer at least the market wage $\bar{w}_2$ because the worker will quit otherwise. However, as training is general, it follows that the training firm will offer exactly $w_2 = \bar{w}_2 = y_2$; the worker is paid his marginal product. Similarly, free entry in the first stage, where firms will compete to attract workers, results in zero profits and will drive down the first-period wage to $w_1 = y_1 - c$; workers pay for training through lower starting wages.

Finally, note that investment is also efficient. As the worker receives $w_1 + w_2 = y_1 - c(s) + w_2(s)$, he is prepared to pay for investment up to the level s that solves the first-order condition $w'_2(s) = c'(s)$. As the labour market is competitive ($w_2 = y_2$), this is identical to $y'_2(s^*) = c'(s^*)$, the first order condition for socially efficient investment s^*.

The firm will offer exactly s^* of training. Offering more will result in a lower profit, and the firm will be driven out of the market by new entrants. If the firm offers less, other firms have an incentive to offer slightly more training. This will drive the equilibrium investment level to s^*. This proves the following proposition:

Proposition 1. *If training is general and labour markets are perfectly competitive then*

(i)   The worker will be the full residual claimant and receive all the returns and will also pay the full costs through lower wages.

(ii) Investment is efficient.

Proof. See text above or Becker (1962, 1993).

Moreover, in equilibrium, all workers are trained and all firms train.[3]

Pigou (1912) argued that under-investment in general training would occur, as firms in competitive labour markets have no incentive to provide training. This is the famous poaching externality: outside firms hire the trained workers away, thereby inflicting a capital loss on the training firms who, anticipating this, will not train their workers. Proposition 1 shows that although firms do not have an incentive to pay for general training, workers do. Moreover, workers can finance this training by taking a wage cut. As a consequence, the poaching externality disappears and there is no under-investment. The under-investment problem re-surfaces, however, if the worker is liquidity constrained. Minimum wages may also give rise to under-investment, as these may prevent wages to fall to levels necessary to pay for training.[4]

4. Imperfect Competition

Not all training will be equally productive in all firms as is the case with general training. Clearly, training exists which will increase productivity by a different amount in the firm where training takes place compared with other firms. An example is the extreme case in which training is specific to the firm where training takes place.

Although not clear in his definition of general training, Becker (1962) recognized that, if training is technologically general, the degree of competition in the labour market determines whether it is general in an economic sense:

> In extreme types of monopsony [...] all training, no matter what its nature, would be specific. [...] The effect on training of less extreme monopsony positions is more difficult to assess. [...] But monopsony power as a whole, including the more extreme manifestations, would appear to increase the importance of specific training and the incentive for firms to invest in human capital (Becker, 1962, pp. 50–51).

Becker's (1962) analysis of general training rests on the assumption that labour markets are competitive. Yet, there are many reasons why labour markets are not competitive, examples are asymmetric information, institutions and search frictions. To illustrate how imperfect competition changes investment incentives, it is useful to start with the extreme case in which there is only one buyer for a particular type of skill: specific training.

Timing is again as in Figure 2, but now training is specific. Specific training can be defined as training that is only useful in the training firm and has no effect on the worker's productivity in other firms:

Definition 2. *Training is specific if* $\bar{y}_2 (s) = y_2(0)$.

When training is specific, workers will not pay for this training (either through accepting lower wages or directly) but firms will. To see this, consider what happens if the firm refuses to pay the worker the value of his marginal product $y_2(s)$. In the case of general training, we saw above that the worker could just leave and receive his marginal product in the market $\bar{w}_2 = y_2(s)$, but this is no longer possible when training is specific. As labour markets are competitive, the outside wage that the worker can receive equals the value of his marginal productivity in the market $\bar{w}_2 = \bar{y}_2 = y_2(0)$. Assume that the firm makes a take-it-or-leave-it wage offer (the firm sets wages). There is no reason for the incumbent firm to offer more than the market wage and the worker will accept this wage.[5] The worker does not receive part of the returns on specific training and is therefore not prepared to finance (part of) this training. The firm on the other hand captures the full return to specific training, and as it also pays the full cost, investment is efficient. This gives us the following result.

Proposition 2. *If training is specific and the firm sets wages then*

(i) *The firm will be the residual claimant and receive all the returns. It will also pay the costs.*

(ii) *Investment is efficient.*

At this point, Becker introduced turnover in his argument. If the worker and the firm separate after training, the (specific) investment is effectively lost, as it is only of value within the match. Becker conjectured that the firm and the worker will share the return. By paying the worker a higher wage, the firm reduces (costly) turnover. Because there will now be an excess supply of trainees, workers will need to share part of the costs in order to re-establish equilibrium. This sharing argument is not made in a formal manner. Regarding the exact size of the share, Becker remarks that 'the shares of each depend on the relation between quit rates and wages, layoff rates and profits, and on other factors not discussed here, such as the cost of funds, attitudes toward risk, and desires for liquidity'. (p. 44)[6]

Hashimoto (1981) formalized Becker's conjecture in a model with transaction costs. The timing in this model is shown in Figure 3. At the start of period 1, the worker and the firm write a long-term contract specifying the investment level and wages in period 1 and 2. The worker and the firm are ex-ante uncertain about the outside opportunities $\overline{w}_2$ and the period 2 productivity of the worker y_2. At the start of the second period, the worker learns the value of his market alternative $\overline{w}_2$, the firm does not. The firm, however, learns the value of the worker's product y_2; yet, the worker does not.[7] The firm will now lay off the worker if $w_2 < y_2$, whereas the worker on his side will quit if $w_2 < \overline{w}_2$.[8] Note that the worker may quit inefficiently ($\overline{w}_2 > w_2$ but $y_2 > \overline{w}_2$) and the firm may lay off (L) inefficiently ($y_2 < w_2$ but $\overline{w}_2 < y_2$). In fact, as renegotiation is not possible, separation will typically be inefficient.

To solve the model, Hashimoto assumes that the worker and firm maximize joint surplus and w_2 is therefore set in such a way as to minimize the ex-ante expected (social) cost of this inefficient turnover by balancing the cost of inefficient quits vs. the cost of inefficient layoffs. Free entry at the start of period 1 makes that w_1 is set such as to drive expected profits to zero.

It is important to note that as, by definition, the investment has no externalities, investment is efficient, even if there is ex-post inefficient turnover. In general,

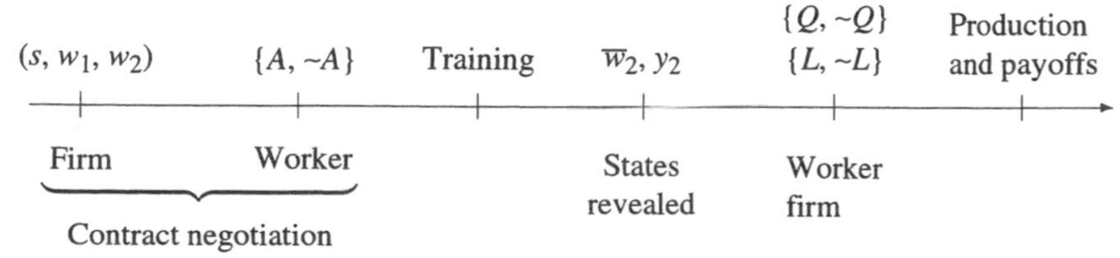

Figure 3. Timing of Events in Transaction Cost Model of Specific Training.

as the investment is specific, increasing the level of s will reduce the probability of a separation. Investment and turnover are therefore not independent. Solving the model gives the following result:

Proposition 3. *If training is specific, long-term contracting is possible (no renegotiation) and there are costs of evaluating and agreeing on the worker's productivities in the firm and elsewhere,*

  (i)   *The returns will be shared between the worker and the firm and so will the costs.*

  (ii) *Investment is efficient.*

Proof. See Hashimoto (1981).

One might wonder whether the sharing results hold for other wage setting schemes. Leuven and Oosterbeek (2001) presented comparative statics results in the Hashimoto model both under the predetermined wage and the firm-sets-wage contract (see below). They also showed that the sharing argument is still valid under the latter contract.

Hashimoto's model has been influential, and subsequent research has extended it in various ways.[9] Carmicheal (1983), for example, showed that, if one allows that a worker is promoted with probability p during period 2 (based on a seniority rule where the number of senior jobs are fixed), wages can be set in such a way as to induce efficient turnover. To see this, suppose that the wage in the entry job is w_2 and in the senior job $w_2 + B$. At the start of the second period, the firm will now fire the worker if $y_2 < w_2$ and the employee will quit if $\bar{w}_2 > w_2 + p \cdot B$. Because the number of senior jobs is fixed, another employee will get promoted if the employee under consideration is not. This means that the firm only saves w_2 with a lay-off and not $w_2 + B$. With this extra degree of freedom, w_2 will be set such as to induce ex-ante efficient lay-offs and B such as to induce ex-ante efficient quits (note that ex-post there are still inefficient separations in the absence of renegotiation).

Hall and Lazear (1984) investigated how other contracts than the long-term (predetermined) wage contract analysed above perform in terms of separation efficiency. In particular, they analyse unilateral wage setting contracts which they call firm-sets-wages and worker-sets-wage contracts. In the firm-sets-wages contract, the incumbent firm observes the worker's productivity y_2 and makes a wage offer w_2 which the worker can accept or reject. In the worker-sets-wage contract, the worker observes his market alternative and posts a wage demand w_2 at which the firm can hire the worker or not. Hall and Lazear (1984) showed that the firm always proposes a wage which is less than the worker's marginal product and, similarly, the worker always sets a wage above the value of his market alternative, even though this sometimes will result in an inefficient separation. This reflects that, in these unilateral wage-setting schemes, the wage-setting party acts as a monopolist. Which of the three contracts perform best in term of separation efficiency depends on the joint distribution of y_2 and $\bar{w}_2$. Full separation efficiency is, however, never obtained. This is implied by the analysis of Myerson and

Satterthwaite (1983) who have shown that, in the presence of two-sided asymmetric information, there does not exist an efficient trading mechanism. Hall and Lazear (1984) do not discuss investment efficiency.[10]

Hashimoto precluded renegotiation of the second-period wage because of excessive transaction costs. Malcomson (1997) argued that the firm-sets-wage contract is in fact a good description of the 'employment at will' practice in American labour markets and as such the above model can be a good approximation of real-world situations. However, one can imagine many relevant situations in which renegotiation will occur. The next sections consider the consequences of such renegotiation for training investment.

5. Hold-Up

Little attention has been paid so far to the effect of contract (re)negotiations on investments. There are, of course, many situations in which contracts are renegotiated after specific investments have been made. Renegotiation occurs because a contingent contract can not be written and because without renegotiation the parties will separate inefficiently.[11] In the renegotiation process, the non-investing party will often be able to capture part of the returns. As the investor no longer receives the full marginal return on his investment, he will under-invest. Williamson (1985) has coined this phenomenon 'hold-up' (Grout, 1984). Renegotiation therefore typically has adverse effects on investment incentives.

Renegotiation involves bargaining. In a bargaining situation, it is important to distinguish between the payoffs the parties get during bargaining and the payoffs they receive when bargaining breaks down and the parties take up other opportunities. The former type of payoffs arc called default payoffs or threat points, and the latter type are called outside options. Bargaining can be explicitly modelled as an alternating offers game (Rubinstein, 1982). It has been shown that, when bargaining becomes frictionless, the equilibrium outcome in this game is equivalent to the Nash Bargaining Solution which tells us that bargaining will split the surplus (gains of trade relative to default payoffs) according to the parties' bargaining power, except if the outside options are binding (e.g. Binmore *et al.*, 1986). Denote the worker's bargaining power by α, $\alpha \in [0,1]$. If $\alpha = 0$ then the firm has all bargaining power. This is equivalent to the firm-sets-wage contract in the previous section. If $\alpha = 1$, the worker has all bargaining power and this is equivalent to the worker-sets-wage contract.

To show that renegotiation typically has adverse effects on investment incentives suppose that, in the notation of this paper, an enforceable contract specifying a specific investment s cannot be written. Moreover, assume that it is the worker who invests and that the worker and the firm have the possibility to renegotiate the second-period wage. Efficient investment s^* equates marginal cost to marginal return: $c'(s^*) = y_2'(s^*)$.

If the default payoffs for both parties during bargaining are normalized to zero and outside options are not binding, then the worker's (renegotiated) second-period wage in the training firm will be equal to a share α of the surplus y_2:

$$w_2 = \alpha y_2$$

As $w_2 > \overline{w}_2$, the worker will not quit. To see what happens to the worker's investment, incentives in the case of renegotiation write down the worker's (indirect) utility function:

$$U = w_2 - c(s)$$
$$= \alpha y_2(s) - c(s)$$

Inspection of the first-order condition, $c'(s^{**}) = \alpha y_2'(s^{**})$, shows that, if the worker does not have all bargaining power ($\alpha < 1$), the investment level in the presence of hold-up s^{**} is less than the efficient level s^*.

In this example, we assumed that outside options were not binding. When the firm's outside option ($\overline{\pi}$) is binding, we get a strikingly different result (still assuming that it is efficient for the parties to trade). The firm's outside option is binding if $\pi = y_2 - w_2 = (1 - \alpha)y_2 < \overline{\pi}$. From bargaining theory, we know that the wage will be renegotiated down to: $w_2 = y_2 - \overline{\pi}$ and now the worker chooses s to maximize:

$$U = w_2 - c(s)$$
$$= y_2(s) - \overline{\pi} - c(s)$$

The first order condition is $c'(s) = y_2'(s)$, which shows that the worker will invest efficiently.[12]

We have seen that when contracts can be renegotiated workers may have insufficient incentives to collect firm-specific skills. If firms get a reputation for rewarding skill collection, the hold-up problem might be less severe or even non-existent (given that their discount rate is low enough). There is of course no guarantee that this is the case.[13] In a related paper, Leuven *et al.* (2004) showed that worker reciprocity can play a similar role as firm reputation in improving investment incentives for the other (investing) party.

5.1 *Contractual Solutions to Hold-Up*

Absence of reputation does not imply that workers and firms have no means to circumvent the hold-up problem. Sometimes it is possible to find a (contractual) solution for hold-up by employing compensation schemes for workers that are designed to induce them to collect non-verifiable firm-specific human capital. One example is the well-known up-or-out practice (Kahn and Huberman, 1988), and another example is a credible up-or-stay promotion rule (Prendergast, 1993). Both schemes depend on the assumption that, although firms cannot attach wages to skills, they can attach wages to tasks.[14]

First consider up-or-stay. There are two tasks, an easy (E) and a difficult (D) one. Instead of offering a uniform second-period wage w_2, the firm can now offer the worker a contract which specifies the wage for each task $\{w_E, w_D\}$. Assume for ease of exposition that training is indivisible $s \in \{0,1\}$. If the worker accepts the contract, he can either invest at cost c or not. Output in job D is denoted by $y_D(s)$ and $y_E(s)$ in job E. The production technology is such that within a job a trained worker is more productive than an untrained worker. A trained worker is also assumed to be more productive in the difficult job, while an untrained worker is more productive in the easy job:

$$y_D(1) > y_E(1) > y_E(0) > y_D(0) \tag{1}$$

As usual, it is also assumed that training is efficient:

$$y_D(1) - y_E(0) > c \tag{2}$$

A worker will invest (i) if the wage increase on promotion is greater than the cost of investment:

$$w_D - w_E > c$$

and (ii) if the firm will promote him after training. The firm has an incentive to promote a trained worker if:

$$y_D(1) - y_E(1) > w_D - w_E$$

A contract that satisfies these two conditions solves the hold-up problem: the firm has an incentive to promote the worker, who then has an incentive to invest. The feasibility of the up-or-stay promotion rule depends on (i) whether firms can assign wages to tasks and (ii) whether the production technology allows credible assignment of workers to tasks. Note that the latter is not necessarily true, even if investment is efficient, as this requires that $y_D(1) - y_E(1) > c$ which is not implied by the efficiency condition (2).

If wages cannot (credibly) be assigned to different jobs which satisfy (1), the up-or-stay rule cannot be implemented. This will happen if the two jobs are just job titles with the same production technology or if they are quite similar. In this situation, the hold-up problem might be solved through an up-or-out rule (Kahn and Huberman, 1988). The idea here is that, after a fixed period of time, the firm either pays the worker a high wage w^* or fires him. For this to happen, w^* must satisfy the following condition $y_D(1) > w^* > y_E(0)$. The first inequality requires the worker to be productive enough in the difficult task, whereas the second inequality implies that an untrained worker is not productive enough in the easy task. The worker on his part will train if $> w^*; > c$. If investment is efficient, such a wage can always be found. As a consequence, all workers train and all workers are promoted.

If workers are heterogeneous, then the up-or-out rule performs not always that well. The reason for this is that if a worker can choose various levels of investment (training is no longer indivisible), some of the workers who invested, but not enough, will be fired and specific investments are lost. Moreover, if uncertainty is introduced, for example if training is not necessarily successful, then the investment efficiency of up-or-out typically comes at the cost of separation inefficiency.

6. Sources of Imperfect Competition

The previous sections reviewed human capital investment when there is only one buyer. This section shows that it is the degree of market competition for a particular skill that determines whether training is, *de facto*, either general, specific, or somewhere in between.

Consider the case where there is more than 1 buyer, but competition is less than perfect. Training is assumed to be technologically general but, to illustrate the mechanism, assume that frictions (for the moment, of an undefined nature) lead to a market wage lower than the worker's productivity: $\overline{w}_2(s) < y_2(s)$. Moreover, suppose that the worker separates with exogenous probability q from the training firm, and that the firm invests in training. Assuming that the firm has all bargaining power, it will pay the worker his market alternative $w_2 = \overline{w}_2(s)$ and choose s such as to maximize its profits:

$$\pi = (1 - q)(y_2(s) - \overline{w}_2(s)) - c(s)$$

The first-order condition is $(1 - q)(y_2'(s) - \overline{w}_2(s)) = c'(s)$. For the firm to invest in training, the left-hand side of the first-order condition must be strictly greater than 0. This implies the following:

Proposition 4. *The firm invests in technologically general training if,*

(i)   *There is a positive probability that the worker stays with the training firm:* $q < 1$.
(ii) *The marginal increase in a worker's productivity is not fully reflected in his best opportunity in the market:* $y_2'(s) > \overline{w}_2(s)$.
(iii) *The firm makes a positive profit if it trains and employs the worker:* $y_2(s) - \overline{w}_2(s) - c(s) > 0$.[15]

Proof. See text or Acemoglu and Pischke (1999b).

Hence, if skill markets are non-competitive, firms may pay for technologically general training. This is a strikingly different result compared to the competitive model analysed above. The non-competitive model differs also in a second respect, highlighted by the following proposition.

Proposition 5. *Under imperfect competition, training investment is inefficient because of the poaching externality when*

(i) *The worker has a positive probability of leaving the training firm:* $q > 0$.
(ii) *It is profitable for the poaching firm to employ the trained worker:* $\overline{y}_2(s) - \overline{w}_2(s) > 0$.

Proof. See Stevens (1994b).

This is an important point. Becker argued that all training can be regarded as a sum of a general and a specific component. As a consequence, there is no positive externality and under-investment does not arise. The analysis of Stevens (1994b) shows that this is potentially misleading and that imperfect competition may cause training to have a transferable character, meaning that it is neither perfectly general nor perfectly specific, nor a convex combination of the two. If the market for skills is such that firms pay wages below marginal productivity and if there is uncertainty about labour turnover then outside firms earn a positive expected profit on training. But these are externalities that are not internalized by the worker and the training firm when they decide on training, as they maximize their own joint surplus and not social surplus. Investment will therefore be inefficient, and the poaching externality reappears. Stevens does not discuss any specific market frictions, she notes that 'any source of imperfect competition leading to wages below marginal product, combined with any source of uncertainty about labour turnover, gives rise to this externality' (p. 541).

We have seen how imperfect competition generates different results compared to the competitive model without being explicit about the specific market frictions involved. The next subsections review, more in depth, specific sources of market imperfection.[16]

6.1 *Asymmetric Information*

Information asymmetries between the training firm and the market are such a mechanism. Two main cases can be distinguished. Firstly, the case where the training firm is better informed about the training of its employees than the market. Secondly, the case in which the training firm is better informed about the abilities of its workers giving rise to adverse selection.

6.1.1 *Training Not Observable by Outside Employers*

Katz and Ziderman (1990) forwarded the argument that, if incumbent firms have superior information about the training of their workers, then it might not be possible for those workers to capture the full return to technologically general training in the market. Potential recruiters, so they argued, are unlikely to know very much about the extent and type of training workers received with their current/previous employer(s). The result of this will be that a recruiting firm will place a lower (expected) value on a recruited worker with general training than the firm that trained him. The information asymmetry between the training firm and outside employers renders general training thus effectively specific.

Katz and Ziderman discussed the implications of this information asymmetry regarding liquidity constraints and certification. In the standard model of general training, if workers are liquidity constrained (either directly or indirectly when training can not be financed through wage cuts because of a binding minimum wage), they will not invest in general training. In the model of Katz and Ziderman, this under-investment problem is actually less severe, as employers will be prepared to participate in the cost of training.

Finally, certification may overcome the information asymmetry and thereby reduce firms' incentives to pay for general training. As a consequence, the under-investment problem will be aggravated by certification if workers are liquidity constrained.

Chang and Wang (1996) presented a formal model that borrows from Katz and Ziderman.[17] The timing of the model is shown in Figure 4. The first thing to note is that the first period wage w_1 is not made contingent on s. Chang and Wang

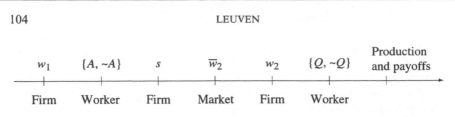

Figure 4. Timing of Events When Training Is Not Observed by Outside Employers.

(1996) made two other important assumptions: (i) they assume that $y_2 = s + \varepsilon$ and $\bar{y}_2 = \delta s + \eta$, which implies that in addition to a general investment δs there is a complementary specific investment $(1 - \delta)s$, and (ii) $w_2 = \bar{w}_2 + \alpha(y_2 - \bar{w}_2)$, the worker and firm share the surplus through Nash bargaining. Both ε and η are random job-match components.

Because outside firms do not observe the amount of training a worker received, they cannot base their wage offer $\bar{w}_2$ on s but only on the expected training level $E[s]$ (which equals the actual training level in equilibrium). As a consequence, the market wage is independent of the investment level that the firm chooses, and the firm has an incentive to pay (part) of the general component of training as long as there is a positive probability that the worker stays. The rational expectations equilibrium in the market is defined by

$$\bar{w}_2 = \delta E[s]$$

and $E[s] = s^*$, where s^* is the firms' optimal investment level. Note that the marginal increase of the worker's productivity is not fully reflected in his best market opportunity $\bar{w}'_2(s) = 0 < 1 = y'_2(s)$ as in condition (*ii*) of proposition 4.

The worker and the firm will separate if $y_2 < \bar{w}_2$; hence, the probability of separation is $q = \Pr(y_2 < \bar{w}_2)$. The firm's (second period) profit therefore becomes[18]

$$\pi = -w_1 + E[y_2 - w_2 | 1 - q] \cdot (1 - q) - c(s)$$

and, the firm maximizes profit subject to the worker's participation constraint,

$$w_1 + E[w_2 | 1 - q](1 - q) + \bar{w}_2 q \geq U$$

which is binding in the optimum. Substituting the binding participation constraint in the profit function it can be show that the first-order condition becomes

$$(1 - \alpha)(1 - q) = c'(s) \tag{3}$$

the optimal s^* solves (3). Like in Katz and Ziderman (1990) and as shown above, the most important result is that there is positive investment $s^* > 0$ if there is a positive probability that the worker stays with the firm and does not have all bargaining power q, $\alpha < 1$, which implies that the firm invests in general training. A number of additional results follow. First, note that the socially efficient level of investment s^e maximizes $\pi + (1 - q)w_2 + qE[\bar{y}_2]$ and therefore solves $1 - (1 - \delta)q = c'(s)$. Comparing this with (3) shows that there are two sources of under-investment. Firstly, the firm under-invests because of hold-up if $\alpha > 0$. Secondly, the firm under-invests because of externalities. This is illustrated by the fact that the severity of the under-investment increases with the degree of generality of the human capital δ. To see this, suppose that the worker has no bargaining power ($\alpha = 0$) and under-investment because of hold-up is thus ruled out. The first-order condition under asymmetric information (3) then becomes $1 - q = c'(s)$. If training is completely specific ($\delta = 0$), then the firm's investment will be socially efficient. If training is general ($\delta = 1$), then the firm will under-invest. The intuition lies in the fact that the investment has positive externalities (if $\delta > 0$) that increase with δ. The training firm does not internalize these extern-alities and under-invests. This mechanism is identical to the one in Stevens (1994b).

6.1.2 *Ability Not Observable by Outside Employers*

Another information asymmetry that may lead to firm-sponsored general training investment occurs if current employers are better informed about the abilities of their workers than potential future employers. Adverse selection then dampens the response of market wages to human capital investments. This idea can be traced back to Greenwald (1986), who applied the adverse selection problem described in Akerlof (1970) to labour markets. He noted that employers may find it beneficial to finance general human capital accumulation of their workers as, 'adverse selection with its entry-level bonuses and tendency to tie workers to firms would rule out [these] possible job-changes and rationalize such investments by firms'.

Chang and Wang (1995) were the first to present a formal model with adverse selection and training. The adverse selection model that follows can be found in Acemoglu and Pischke (1999b). Figure 5 shows the order of events. Workers are heterogeneous in ability η, with probability p a worker is of low ability ($\eta = 0$) and with probability $1 - p$ the worker is of high ability ($\eta = 1$). Productivity of a worker after training equals $y_2 = \eta s$, and training and ability are therefore complements in production. Ability is not observed by the firm or the worker at the moment of hiring. The firm offers a first-period wage that the worker can accept or reject. Because ability is unknown at this point, the firm either offers training to all its workers or does not train at all. After the training ends, the firm observes the worker's ability and makes a second-period wage offer contingent on ability and training. The firm offers low-ability workers a second-period wage that equals their productivity ($w_2 = 0$) and high-ability workers the market wage ($w_2 = \overline{w}_2$, assuming that the firm has all the bargaining power).

Outside firms observe only the worker's training level s and not his ability. Their wage offer therefore depends only on s. The worker chooses to work for the party that offers him the highest wage. There is also exogenous turnover, with probability q (independent of ability), a worker quits the training firm and enters the market. As a result, there are at least some high-ability workers in the market.

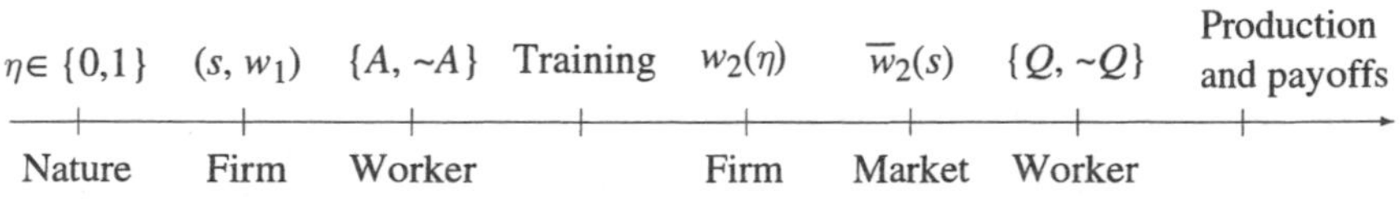

$\eta \in \{0,1\}$	(s, w_1)	$\{A, \sim A\}$	Training	$w_2(\eta)$	$\overline{w}_2(s)$	$\{Q, \sim Q\}$	Production and payoffs
Nature	Firm	Worker		Firm	Market	Worker	

Figure 5. Timing of Events When Ability Is Not Observed by Outside Employers.

The expected productivity of a worker in the market is therefore strictly greater than the productivity of a low-ability worker. As a consequence, all low-ability workers will leave the training firm.

Assuming that workers get trained, then a fraction p of these workers is of low ability and profits for them equal $0 - \overline{w}_2$. These workers always separate because the market wage is higher than the wage offer from the incumbent firm. A fraction $1 - p$ consists of high-ability workers and profits for them equal $s - \overline{w}_2$. These workers separate for exogenous reasons with probability q. This gives the expected profit for an outside employer:

$$\overline{\pi} = p \cdot (0 - \overline{w}_2) + (1 - p) \cdot q \cdot (s - \overline{w}_2) \qquad (4)$$

It is assumed that competition in the second period drives expected profits in the market to zero. This determines the equilibrium wage in the market for skills. Equating (4) to zero and solving for $\overline{w}_2$ gives the equilibrium market wage

$$\overline{w}_2 = \frac{(1-p)qs}{(1-p)q+p}$$

The training firm's profit function now becomes

$$\pi = (1 - q)(1 - p)(y_2 - \overline{w}_2) - c(s)$$
$$= (1 - q)(1 - p)\frac{p}{(1-p)q+p}s - c(s)$$

The optimal investment level s^* is again strictly positive. The firm invests in technologically general training because it is able to earn a positive marginal return on this investment because the worker does not receive his full marginal product in the market.

A number of papers explore this information asymmetry and its consequences for human capital investment. Acemoglu and Pischke (1998) and Chang and Wang (1995) both presented models where adverse selection creates firm-sponsored human capital investment; in Acemoglu and Pischke (1998), training is contractable, whereas in Chang and Wang (1995), this is not the case. Acemoglu and Pischke (2000) presented a model in which workers have to exert effort for training to be successful. This creates a hold-up opportunity for the firm. The workers anticipating this will put forward suboptimal effort. Certification may be necessary to encourage workers to exert effort. Firms may then be willing to finance training. Schlicht (1996) and Su (1996) investigated what happens if the firm is subject to a moral hazard problem in training provision. Finally, Autor (2001) presented an asymmetric information model where credit-constrained workers can signal their ability through training choices; training therefore acts as a screening device and explains firms' (temporary help supply establishments in Autor's paper) investment in apparently general human capital.

6.2 *Other Sources of Market Imperfection*[19]

If it is costly for an employee to change jobs, the firm has some monopsony power and is able to capture part of the returns to training. If a worker quits, he has to find a new match. Suppose that as a result of search frictions the worker succeeds but not always; he finds a new firm with probability $\lambda < 1$. If he finds a new job, he bargains over his wage with the new firm and $w_2 = \alpha y_2(s)$ (assuming Nash bargaining and bargaining power α). If the worker does not find a new job, he is unemployed and receives unemployment benefits $b(s)$. As a consequence, his expected market wage in the second period equals

$$\overline{w}_2 = \lambda \alpha y_2(s) + (1 - \lambda) b(s)$$

This serves as the worker's outside option when he bargains over his wage: $w_2 = \overline{w}_2 + \alpha(y_2 - \overline{w}_2)$. The firms profit function therefore becomes $\pi = (1 - \alpha)(y_2(s) - \overline{w}_2) - c(s)$. The first-order condition is

$$(1 - \alpha)((1 - \lambda \alpha) y'_2(s) - (1 - \lambda) b'(s)) = c'(s)$$

The marginal return to training for the firm is positive if $b'(s) < y'_2(s)$, which implies that the worker does not receive the full marginal return on his productivity in the unemployment benefits. This would imply full insurance which seems to be a weak condition, as most insurance systems are regressive.[20]

If general training is complementary to specific capital, the firm also has an incentive to invest in technologically general human capital. The complementarity makes that the productivity of the worker increases more in the incumbent firm than in the market. Note that the specific capital does not need to be specific human capital. If the general skills of the worker are complementary with specific physical capital, then the only requirement is that a new firm cannot buy additional physical capital and pay the worker his full marginal product. This again requires frictions of some sort, in particular credit constraints on the part of the new firm. The capital market imperfection therefore has spill-overs on the labour market.

As mentioned in section 3, if labour markets are competitive, then minimum wages lower general human capital investment because it may prevent workers from taking a wage cut to pay for this training. Now suppose that there are some frictions that in itself do not affect investment incentives: $\overline{w}_2 = y_2(s) - \Delta$, where Δ denotes, for example, fixed turnover cost. In this case, the worker still gets the full marginal product in the market. But now there is a minimum wage w_m. The second-period wage that the training firm pays is

$$w_2 = \max\{w_m, \overline{w}_2\}$$

If $\overline{w}_2 < w_m$ and $y_2 > w_m$, then the firm employs the worker at a wage $w_2 = w_m$ and therefore has an incentive to invest in general training, because the minimum wage is independent of the workers productivity. Market imperfections may therefore reverse the effect of minimum wages on general training investment.

A final example concerns unions. The basic idea is that, as unions compress wages among covered workers, this implies that the firm does not pay the most productive worker his full marginal product. The simplest case is the one in which all covered workers receive a uniform wage $w_2 = w$. The firm will then invest the efficient level, as $\pi = y_2(s) - w - c(s)$, and the first-order condition is

$y'_2(s) = c'(s)$. Note that if the workers are the investing party then union wage compression reduces their incentives to invest.[21]

7. Summary and Conclusion

This paper has presented a review of the economics of training. Standard competitive theory, as in Becker (1962), distinguishes between general training and specific training. General training is of equal value in many firms, whereas specific training is only useful in one firm. In this competitive world, workers reap all the returns to general training and consequentially finance it, either directly or through lower wages. Under-investment in general training occurs therefore only if workers are liquidity constrained. As firms will not finance general training, the negative poaching externality in which firms under-invest in general training because of the poaching of trained workers by other firms disappears. Finally, firms finance specific on-the-job training but might let workers share in the returns to reduce inefficient turnover.

The recent literature demonstrates how market imperfections may render training that is technologically general *de facto* specific because wages will be below marginal product. This restores investment incentives for technologically general training for the employer and may alleviate under-investment in such training. The poaching externality, however, reappears, as any source of imperfect competition leading to wages below marginal product, combined with any source of uncertainty about labour turnover, makes that the worker and the firm do not internalize positive externalities and under-invest.

It is difficult to arrive at unambiguous policy recommendations from the literature reviewed above. First of all, theory alone does not tell us whether and where there is (sufficient) under-investment to intervene. Under-investment crucially depends on the extent to which credit constraints and labour market imperfections impede investment, the practical significance of which, as Stevens (2001) points out, is difficult to assess.

A second complication in devising policy is that, depending on the particular market failure at work, solutions will differ. To illustrate this, take the example of training certification. The analysis of Katz and Ziderman (1990) showed that increased certification may lead to less investment in training by firms because training then becomes more visible to other employers. Acemoglu and Pischke (2000) on the other hand argue that certification may in fact be necessary to encourage firm-sponsored training if the success of training depends on the effort of workers. To arrive at a well-argued policy recommendation (certification or not), one would need to know which mechanism is more important in practice.

It is an empirical issue how the mechanisms reviewed above net out in practice. It is also an empirical question in which imperfections are important, where under-investment arises and where specifics will likely vary between markets. A challenging avenue for future research would be the unravelling of these issues empirically. This would further our understanding of training markets, close the

PRIVATE SECTOR TRAINING 109

gap between theory and empirics and finally allow policy makers to effectively address real problems.

Acknowledgements

I gratefully acknowledge valuable comments from Hessel Oosterbeek, Steve Pischke and Randolph Sloof.

Notes

1. Many of the ideas found in Becker are also present in Oi (1962).
2. From a modelling point of view, it will suffice to assume that there is one alternative employer.
3. One might wonder why firms provide general training to their workers and why there is no separate training market. Becker explained this by complementarities between learning and working (Becker, 1993, footnote 3, p. 34).
4. Acemoglu and Pischke (1999a) note that, if loan markets are not perfect and individuals smooth consumption, then wage cuts are costly and investment will not be efficient.
5. Here, it is assumed, without loss of generality, that in case of a tie the worker joins the training firm.
6. This sharing argument is also present in Oi (1962). See Parsons (1972) for an early formal discussion of the sharing hypothesis.
7. The firm and the worker could bargain over the surplus. Hashimoto, however, assumes that transaction costs are prohibitively high. Renegotiation could result in separation efficiency at the cost of investment inefficiency and transaction costs. Which of these two options is more expensive is an open question.
8. In the formulation of Carmichael (1983), quits are the result of low job satisfaction. The exposition here follows Becker *et al.* (1977) who argued that 'a quit could be said to result from an improvement in opportunities elsewhere and a layoff from a (usually unexpected) worsening in opportunities in this job...'. Unlike Becker *et al.* (1977), the model here allows inefficient separations.
9. Not discussed here are Hashimoto and Yu (1980) on wage indexing and MacLaughlin (1991) on the distinction between layoffs and quits.
10. Stevens (1994a), in a related model, considers jointly separation and investment efficiency. Instead of an exogenous stochastic market alternative for the worker, Stevens (1994a) models the labour market as a first-price sealed bid auction. As a consequence, the worker is no longer perfectly informed about his alternative value, and the outside firms behave strategically ($\overline{w}_2$ is no longer independent of w_2).
11. It may be impossible to write a contingent contract because investments may be too complicated or multidimensional.
12. See MacLeod and Malcomson (1993a), MacLeod and Malcomson (1993b) and Malcomson (1997) for models featuring hold-up in this vein.
13. Note that reputation does not play a role in the two-period models discussed here.
14. This resembles the analysis of Carmichael (1983) discussed above, although in his analysis wages could be attached to job titles, whereas it is crucial here that wages are attached to tasks.
15. With Inada conditions, $y_2(0) - \overline{w}_2(0) > 0$ is sufficient.
16. See also Acemoglu and Pischke (1999a) for a review of this literature.

110   LEUVEN

17. Chang and Wang (1995) is a related model where future employers are also uninformed about workers' abilities.
18. To simplify notation, we also use q to refer to the event of a separation.
19. Acemoglu and Pischke (1999b) give many examples of market frictions leading to firm-sponsored general training, this section discusses some of them.
20. See the appendix of Acemoglu and Pischke (1999b) and Acemoglu (1997) for more details.
21. Booth and Chatterji (1998) present an alternative model where the presence of a union solves hold-up of the workers by the firm.

References

Acemoglu, D. (1997). Training and innovation in an imperfect labour market. *Review of Economic Studies* 64: 445–464.

Acemoglu, D. and Pischke, J.-S. (1998). Why do firms train? Theory and evidence. *Quarterly Journal of Economics* 113(1): 79–119.

Acemoglu, D. and Pischke, J.-S. (1999a). Beyond Becker: Training in imperfect labor markets. *Economic Journal* 109: F112–F142.

Acemoglu, D. and Pischke, J.-S. (1999b). The structure of wages and investment in general training. *Journal of Political Economy* 107(3): 539–572.

Acemoglu, D. and Pischke, J.-S. (2000). Certification of training and training outcomes. *European Economic Review* 44(4–6): 917–927.

Akerlof, G. (1970). The market for 'lemons': Quality uncertainty and the market mechanism. *Quarterly Journal of Economics* 84(3): 488–500.

Autor, D. (2001). Why do temporary help firms provide free general skills training? *Quarterly Journal of Economics* 116(4): 1409–1448.

Becker, G. S. (1962). Investment in human capital: A theoretical analysis. *Journal of Political Economy* 70: 9–49.

Becker, G. (1993). *Human Captial: A Theoretical and Empirical Analysis with Special Reference to Education*, 3rd edn. Chicago: The University of Chicago Press.

Becker, G., Landes, E. and Michael, R. (1977). An economic analysis of marital instability. *Journal of Political Economy* 85(6): 1141–1188.

Binmore, K., Rubinstein, A. and Wolinksy, A. (1986). The Nash bargaining solution in economic modelling. *RAND Journal of Economics* 17: 176–188.

Booth, A. and Chatterji, M. (1998). Unions and efficient training. *Economic Journal* 108: 1–16.

Carmichael, H. L. (1983). Firm specific capital and promotion ladders. *Bell Journal of Economics* 14: 251–258.

Chang, C. and Wang, Y. (1995). A framework for understanding differences in labor turnover and human capital investment. *Journal of Economic Behavior and Organization* 28: 91–105.

Chang, C. and Wang, Y. (1996). Human capital investment under asymmetric information: The Pigovian conjecture revisited. *Journal of Labor Economics* 14: 505–519.

Greenwald, B. (1986). Adverse selection in the labour market. *Review of Economic Studies* 53(3): 325–347.

Grout, P. (1984). Investment and wages in the absence of binding contracts. *Econometrica* 52(2): 449–460.

Hall, R. E. and Lazear, E. P. (1984). The excess sensitivity of layoffs and quits to demand. *Journal of Labor Economics* 2(2): 233–257.

Hashimoto, M. and Yu, B. T. (1980). Specific capital, employment contracts, and wage rigidity. *Bell Journal of Economics* 2: 536–549.

Hashimoto, M. (1981). Firm-specific human capital as a shared investment. *American Economic Review* 71(3): 475–482.

Kahn, C. and Huberman, G. (1988). Two-sided uncertainty and Up-or-Out contracts. *Journal of Labor Economics* 6(4): 423–444.

Katz, E. and Ziderman, A. (1990). Investment in general training: The role of information and labour mobility. *Economic Journal* 100: 1147–1158.

Leuven, E. and Oosterbeek, H. (2001). Firm-specific human capital as a shared investment: Comment. *American Economic Review* 91(1): 342–347.

Leuven, E., Oosterbeek, H., Sloof, R. and van Klaveren, C. (2004). Worker reciprocity and employer investment in training. *Economica* (forthcoming).

MacLaughlin, K. (1991). A theory of quits and layoffs with efficient turnover. *Journal of Political Economy* 99(1): 1–29.

MacLeod, W. and Malcomson, J. (1993a). Specific investment and wage profiles in labour markets. *European Economic Review* 37: 343–354.

MacLeod, W. B. and Malcomson, J. M. (1993b). Investment, holdup, and the form of market contracts. *American Economic Review* 83(4): 811–837.

Malcomson, J. M. (1997). Contracts, hold-up, and labor markets. *Journal of Economic Literature* XXXV: 1916–1957.

Myerson, R. and Satterthwaite, M. (1983). Efficient mechanisms for bilateral trading. *Journal of Economic Theory* 29(2): 265–281.

Oi, W. (1962). Labor as a quasi-fixed factor. *Journal of Political Economy* 70(6): 538–555.

Parsons, D. (1972). Specific human capital: An application to quit rates and layoff rates. *Journal of Political Economy* 80(6): 1120–1143.

Pigou, A. (1912). *Wealth and Welfare*. London: Macmillan.

Prendergast, C. (1993). The role of promotion in inducing specific human acquisition. *Quarterly Journal of Economics* 108: 522–534.

Rubinstein, A. (1982). Perfect equilibrium in a bargaining model. *Econometrica* 50: 97–110.

Schlicht, E. (1996). Endogenous on-the-job training with moral hazard. *Labour Economics* 3: 81–92.

Stevens, M. (1994a). Labour contracts and efficiency in on-the-job training. *Economic Journal* 104: 408–419.

Stevens, M. (1994b). A theoretical model of on-the-job training with imperfect competition. *Oxford Economic Papers* 46: 537–562.

Stevens, M. (2001). Should firms be required to pay for vocational training? *Economic Journal* 111: 485–505.

Su, T. L.-J. (1996). *On-the-Job Training in a Labor Market with Adverse Selection*. Manuscript: UCLA.

Weiss, Y. (1986). The Determination of Life Cycle Earnings: A Survey. In O. Ashenfelter and R. Layard (eds), *Handbook of Labor Economics*, pp. 603–640. Amsterdam: North-Holland.

Williamson, O. (1985). *The Economic Institutions of Capitalism: Firms, Markets, Relational Contracting*. New York: Free Press.

[5]

Human Capital Investment under Asymmetric Information: The Pigovian Conjecture Revisited

Chun Chang, *University of Minnesota*

Yijiang Wang, *University of Minnesota*

This article investigates how human capital investment, labor turnover, and wages are jointly determined when the current employer knows more about a worker's productivity than potential employers. Results derived are quite different from, or unexplored by, the standard human capital theory. We show that the information asymmetry can cause *an externality distortion in human capital investment because higher* productivity due to the investment may not be recognized by the market. The investment level increases in the degree of firm specificity of human capital. The underinvestment problem is more severe when human capital is general than when it is firm-specific.

In a book on welfare economics published in 1912, Pigou conjectured that the training provided by employers to workers is likely to fall considerably short of the social optimal level. His reasoning is as follows: "Since workpeople are liable to change employers, and so to deprive . . . [employers] of their investment, the private net product is apt to fall considerably short of the social net product. Hence, socially profitable expenditure by employers in the training of their workpeople . . . does not carry a corresponding private profit" (Pigou 1912; p. 153). Half a century later,

An earlier version of this paper was presented at the Federal Reserve Bank of Minneapolis and a workshop at the Industrial Relations Center, the University of Minnesota. We thank John Budd, Ed Green, John Kareken, John Krainer, Brian McCall, Ed Prescott, Michael Waldman, and Neil Wallace for comments.

[*Journal of Labor Economics*, 1996, vol. 14, no. 3]

the works of Becker (1962), Oi (1962), Parsons (1972), and the literature that followed have demonstrated the importance of human capital investment to workers' productivity, labor turnover, wage determination, and other labor market phenomena. The human capital theory has since become a cornerstone of the modern labor economics. An important result of the theory is that, since training can increase a worker's future wage, competition among untrained workers for jobs with more training will lower the starting wage. Consequently, it is the worker who pays the cost of training, and the externality problem conjectured by Pigou cannot exist.

In the past 2 decades, economists have become increasingly aware of the significance of various asymmetric information problems in the labor market. One such problem arises when a worker's current employer has better information about the worker's productivity than other potential employers. Models exploring the implications of this informational problem have deepened our understanding of labor turnover patterns (Greenwald 1986; Lazear 1986), job assignments (Waldman 1984), job discrimination (Milgrom and Oster 1987), wage changes following layoffs (Gibbons and Katz 1991), labor contracts (Kahn and Huberman 1988; Waldman 1990), and other important labor market phenomena. However, the effects of information asymmetry on human capital investment and the relationships among human capital investment, wages, and labor turnover in the presence of asymmetric information have not been adequately explored.

In this paper, we study the private incentives to make human capital investment when a worker's current employer knows more about the amount of human capital that the worker possesses than other potential employers. We show that, compared to the socially optimal (first-best) outcome under the assumption of symmetric information, the asymmetric information problem distorts the incentives for human capital investment in two ways. First, when the market wage for a job-changing worker is based on the conjectured rather than the actual amount of human capital that the worker possesses, the marginal social benefit of an additional investment is not recognized, and therefore not compensated for, by the market. Thus the asymmetric information problem can cause the externality distortion suggested by Pigou. Second, when information is asymmetric, a wage contract contingent on a worker's actual productivity is not enforceable. Even if a worker does not change jobs, the employer and the worker will share the rent created by the investment in future wage bargaining. The sharing prospect dampens investment incentives and gives rise to the sharing distortion.[1]

---

[1] Such a distortion is the focus of Williamson (1985), Grossman and Hart (1986), and Hart and Moore (1990). They study the role of ownership structure in reducing this distortion.

Our approach yields several important findings that are quite different from the standard human capital theory. Under the assumption of frictionless economy, the standard theory shows that investment decisions and turnover decisions can be separately analyzed. This separation result no longer holds under information asymmetry. When potential employers cannot observe the actual investment, the investing party, a firm or a worker, cannot reap the marginal benefit of an investment if the worker leaves the firm. Thus, the marginal benefit of human capital investment depends only on the retention rate (one minus the turnover rate). In this sense, one can say that a higher turnover rate leads to less human capital investment.[2]

Since, as we will show, the negative relationship between human capital investment and turnover can hold regardless of the degree of (exogenous) firm specificity of human capital, it can hold even when human capital is completely general. We thus establish a negative relationship between *general* human capital and labor turnover, while the standard theory implies that turnover is independent of general human capital investment.

Although government-sponsored job training programs receive much attention in policy debates, little is known about the kinds of training the private sector has the least incentives to provide. We show that, under asymmetric information, the investment level is increasing in the firm specificity of human capital. The underinvestment problem is less severe when human capital is more firm-specific. This is so because firm-specific human capital provides little benefit to other firms, and consequently the externality distortion is small. In contrast, if information is symmetric, the investment level is higher when human capital is general than when it is firm-specific because the former has a greater market value.

Scoones and Bernhardt (1995) investigate workers' incentive to make human capital investment under asymmetric information. There are two main differences between their model and ours. First, while we assume that firms are asymmetrically informed about the amount of human capital a worker has acquired, they assume that firms are asymmetrically informed about workers' innate ability.[3] Second, we identify the incentive to underinvest given the degree of firm specificity of human capital, whereas they focus on the choice between general investment and firm-specific investment given the quantity of investment. As a result, our results are complimentary to, but different from, theirs.

---

[2] Blinder and Krueger (1992) raised the question of whether it is the human capital investment that determines turnover or the other way around. They suspect that the latter is true, while traditional human capital theory tends to support the former.

[3] Chang and Wang (1995) develop a model in which both types of asymmetric information are present. In that setting, Pareto-rankable multiple equilibria can exist. The model can be used to explain the international differences in human capital investment and labor turnover levels.

This article proceeds as follows. The model and assumptions are laid out in the next section. Section II characterizes the equilibrium. Section III studies the effects of asymmetric information and the degree of firm specificity on human capital investment. It also examines the relationship between labor turnover and human capital investment. Section IV concludes the article.

I. The Model

A. Technology, Preferences, and Information

In the economy there are many similar firms and workers. A worker's productivity depends on the level of human capital investment and the quality of a random job match. Initially, we assume that the employer makes the human capital investment. In Section IV below, we show that, when the worker rather than the firm makes the investment, the results are essentially unchanged. For simplicity, we refer to the firm's human capital investment as "training."

There are three dates, dates 0, 1, and 2, and two periods given by these three dates, that is, period 1 between dates 0 and 1 and period 2 between dates 1 and 2. The timing of events is as follows. At date 0, the firm offers a first-period wage. The worker can either accept or reject the offer. If the offer is accepted, the first-period employment relation begins. In this period, the worker's productivity equals the quality of the job match with the firm. Also in this period, the firm provides training to the worker. At date 1, the market (other potential employers) can bid the worker away at a market wage. The worker's productivity in the second period will depend on whether he moves to another firm or not. His second-period wage may be either a wage negotiated with the current employer or the market wage offered by a new employer. The worker retires from the labor market at date 2.

Training at a level h increases the worker's second-period productivity by h. It costs the firm $c(h)$, where the function $c(h)$ has the standard properties that $c'(h) > 0$ and $c''(h) > 0$ for $h > 0$. To avoid corner solutions, we also assume that $c'(0) = 0$.

Formally, if a worker stays with the same employer in both periods 1 and 2, his productivity is given by

$$x_1 = m + \xi, \quad \text{and} \quad x_2 = h + m + \xi,$$

where ξ is a zero-mean random variable representing the job match (or other firm-specific productivity) quality and m is the mean productivity of an untrained worker.[4] Without loss of generality, we assume that $m = 0$.

The random variable, ξ, has a continuously differentiable cumulative distribution function $F(\xi)$ defined on the real line. The realization of this random variable is assumed to be the same in both periods if the worker does not change jobs.

If the worker changes jobs, the productivity with the new employer will be

$$y = \delta h + \eta,$$

where η is a zero-mean random variable that measures the quality of the job match with the new employer and δ, a fixed number in $[0, 1]$, measures the degree of firm specificity of training. The degree of firm specificity of training δ is exogenous to our model. The random variables η and ξ are independent.

For simplicity, the worker is assumed to be risk-neutral and to maximize a utility function of the form $w_1 + w_2$, where w_t is the worker's wage in period $t = 1, 2$. We assume that a new worker will accept a firm's offer for employment if $E[w_1 + w_2]$ is no less than the reservation utility level u. Demand for and supply of new workers determine u, which we take as exogenous to the model.

Firms are assumed to maximize expected profit, which is the sum of a worker's two-period productivities net of the wage payments and the training cost.

In the spirit of the asymmetric information models mentioned in the introduction, we assume that the worker's current employer has an information advantage over other potential employers about the worker's human capital investment and productivity. In particular, we assume that the training level h and the realization of the job match quality ξ become known to the worker and his current employer but are too costly for outsiders to evaluate.[5]

B. Wages, Profit, and Participation Constraint

Because the realized match quality and the training level h cannot be observed by outsiders, enforceable contracts cannot be made contingent on them. This means that the first-period wage has to be a constant.

---

[4] This technology is similar to the one used by Jovanovic (1979, p. 1250) to study the relationships among worker's job search, firm-specific human capital investment, wage, and turnover under symmetric information.

[5] To be sure, job-changing workers can be screened at a cost. One might also argue that the screening cost is increasing in the specificity of training so that the degree of information asymmetry may increase with specificity. These issues can affect some of our results. The basic point that information asymmetry introduces externality is unaffected, however.

However, since the firm and the worker both know the worker's second-period productivity if the worker stays with the firm as well as the wage offer the worker can obtain from the market, the second-period wage can be negotiated through bargaining. We assume that the outcome is determined by the Nash bargaining solution (Nash 1950).[6]

Suppose that the market wage for a job-changing worker is w (w will be specified shortly). That is, if a worker and his current employer cannot agree on a wage level after the first period and the worker leaves, the worker will receive w from a new employer. The firm's expected net profit in the second period will be zero if the worker leaves. Thus, the disagreement point for the bargaining problem between the worker and his current employer is $(w, 0)$. The Nash solution implies that the worker's second period wage is

$$w_2 = \begin{cases} w + [x_2 - w]/2 & \text{if } x_2 \geq w, \\ w & \text{if } x_2 < w, \end{cases} \tag{1}$$

where $x_2 = \xi + h$ is known to the worker and his current employer at the time of bargaining.[7]

Equation (1) states that, when the worker's second-period productivity is lower than the market wage, he will leave and receive wage w from the market. Otherwise, he will receive w plus half of the rent of staying with the firm.

The firm's second-period profit p_2 is the difference between x_2 and w_2 when the worker stays and is zero otherwise:

$$p_2 = \begin{cases} [x_2 + w]/2 - w & \text{if } x_2 \geq w, \\ 0 & \text{if } x_2 < w. \end{cases} \tag{2}$$

Since the firm's choice of h is not observable by outsiders, the labor market will use its conjecture about h to determine w. Let h^c be the market's conjecture about the worker's training level. The conjectured productivity of a job-changing worker at a new firm is δh^c. Assume that the market for

---

[6] Allowing for other bargaining solutions or sequential bargaining (Rubinstein 1982) only changes the weights in which the rent is divided.

[7] The sharing rule here is not the same as that in Hashimoto (1981). There the problem is how to share the cost of a human capital investment when the worker and the employer have different evaluations of the employment relationship and make quit or layoff decisions unilaterally. Our model does not distinguish between quits and layoffs. Separation follows the principle of "joint wealth maximization" as in Mortensen (1978) and is socially optimal.

experienced workers is competitive. The job-changing worker's wage will be equal to his conjectured productivity in a new firm:[8]

$$w = \delta h^c. \tag{3}$$

Note that, since there is no bargaining cost, separation occurs when the worker's conjectured productivity is higher outside ($x_2 < \delta h^c$). As in many models based on asymmetric information, there is no distinction between a layoff and quitting in our model.

We can now write a new worker's voluntary participation constraint. The worker will receive w_1 in the first period. His second-period wage is determined by (1) (the condition $x_2 \geq w$ is equivalent to $\xi \geq \delta h^c - h$). Note that, instead of using the firm's actual choice h, the worker uses the market expectation h^c in deciding whether to participate. This is because, at the time a new worker decides to join the firm, h has not been chosen yet. The new worker's participation constraint is

$$w_1 + \int_{\delta h^c - h^c}^{\infty} \{w + [(1 - \delta)h^c + \xi]/2\}dF(\xi) + F(\delta h^c - h^c)w \geq u. \tag{4}$$

II. Training Levels under Symmetric and Asymmetric Information

We first derive the socially optimal (first-best) training level. The expected second-period social return from training is the weighted average of the returns when a worker separates, $F(\delta h - h)\delta h$, and when he does not separate, $E[h + \xi | \xi \geq \delta h - h]\mathrm{pr}(\xi \geq \delta h - h)$. We have assumed that separation occurs efficiently, that is, it occurs when $x_2 = h + \xi$ is lower than δh. The social cost of training is $c(h)$. The socially optimal (first-best) training level is the one that provides

$$\max_h \int_{\delta h - h}^{\infty} (h + \xi)dF(\xi) + F(\delta h - h)\delta h - c(h) - u. \tag{5}$$

Let h^* denote the training level that is socially optimal. The first-order condition that gives h^* is

---

[8] If the number of experienced workers and the number of positions for them are about the same, the gain δh^c can be divided between the worker and his new employer. That case is considered in an earlier version of this article. In that case, a firm that loses a worker will get a worker from another firm. The same results are obtained.

$$1 - (1 - \delta)F(\delta h^* - h^*) - c'(h^*) = 0. \qquad (6)$$

Since the lost value of training due to a job change is $1 - \delta$, the marginal social benefit of training is $[1 - (1 - \delta)F(\delta h^* - h^*)]$, while marginal social cost is $c'(h^*)$.

Under asymmetric information about h, the situation is more complex. An equilibrium consists of the firm's choice of training level h^e, its choice of first period wage w_1, and the market's expectation h^c such that (*a*) given h^c, w_1, and h^c maximize the firm's expected profit subject to the worker's participation constraint (4); and (*b*) the market's expectation is correct: $h^c = h^e$.

Using (2), the firm's profit maximization problem can be written as

$$\max_{w_1, h} - w_1 - c(h) + \int_{\delta h^c - h}^{\infty} [(\delta h^c + h + \xi)/2 - w]dF(\xi)$$
$$+ F(\delta h^c - h)[\delta h^c - w]. \qquad (7)$$

subject to equation (4).

It is easy to see that the participation constraint (4) is binding in equilibrium. Otherwise, w_1 can always be reduced to increase the firm's profit. The constraint (4) is thus replaced with

$$w_1 = u - \int_{\delta h^c - h^c}^{\infty} \{w + [(1 - \delta)h^c + \xi]/2\}dF(\xi) - F(\delta h^c - h^c)w. \qquad (8)$$

Note that the firm's equilibrium level of training h^e is not affected by (8), for (8) involves only h^c, the conjectured level of h. By differentiating the objective function in (7) with respect to h, we obtain the first-order condition for the equilibrium h under asymmetric information,

$$[1 - F(\delta h^c - h)]/2 - c'(h) = 0, \qquad (9)$$

in which $[1 - F(\delta h^c - h)]/2$ is the marginal benefit of training to the firm, and $c'(h)$ the marginal cost. In the term that stands for marginal benefit, a factor $1/2$ is present because any gain in second-period productivity is divided equally between the firm and the worker through Nash bargaining. A closer look at condition (9) reveals the many factors that determine the firm's training level are subsumed in the turnover rate. The firm only needs to see the turnover rate to determine the equilibrium training level. This is important later when we study the relationship between investment and turnover.

An equilibrium now becomes a solution of w_1, h^e, and h^c to the three equations, (8), (9), and $h^c = h^e$. Note that the wage for job-changing workers w is given by (3) once h^c is determined.

By substituting $h^c = h^e$ into (9), we obtain the equilibrium condition

$$[1 - F(\delta h^e - h^e)]/2 - c'(h^e) = 0. \tag{10}$$

Proposition 1 below gives the condition under which the equilibrium level of training is unique. The condition is the second-order sufficient condition for the optimization problems (5) and (7). That is, $f(\xi) - c''(h) < 0$ for all ξ and h.[9] As an example, the second-order condition holds if $f(\xi)$ is bounded above by M and $c''(h)$ is bounded below by M. When the second-order condition holds, both (6) and (10) have a unique solution.

PROPOSITION 1.   Suppose that the second-order condition holds. Then both the socially optimal training level h^* and the equilibrium training level h^e exist, and both are unique.

The proof of proposition 1 and those of all other propositions are in the appendix. For the remainder of this article, we assume that the second-order condition is satisfied.

III. Asymmetric Information, Specificity of Training, and Turnover

A. The Effects of Information Asymmetry on Training

When information is symmetric, many arrangements can be used to achieve the socially optimal training level h^*. For example, one arrangement is as follows: the firm pays a new worker $u/2$ in the first period; in the second period the firm pays the worker $w_2 = u/2$ if there is no separation, or $[(u/2) - w]$ if there is separation (w being the worker's market wage). Under this arrangement, if the training level is at h^*, the market wage will be δh^* under symmetric information. Since the worker's second period wage is $u/2$ whether he leaves or not, the firm will let him leave whenever $x_2 - u/2 < 0 - [u/2 - w]$ or $h^* + \xi < \delta h^*$. That is, the separation decision is socially optimal. Moreover, since the worker's total compensation is always u, the firm will receive all the benefit of choosing h^*. Thus, it will do so, and the first-best is achieved under symmetric information.

When the worker's potential employers cannot observe h, the first-best training level h^* can no longer be achieved. We can compare (6) and (10) to see the effects of asymmetric information on training. Two differences are found from the comparison. First, (10) derived under asymmetric information does not have a factor $1 - \delta$ before $F(\ )$, that is, it lacks a term

---

[9] The second-order conditions needed for (6) and (7) are in fact weaker. They are, respectively, $(1 - \delta)f(\xi) - c''(h)$ and $f(\xi)/2 - c''(h) < 0$ for all ξ, δ, and h.

like $\delta F(\quad)$ as found in (6). This term represents the marginal benefit of the investment to other employers when the worker changes job. When information is symmetric, the firm receives the social benefit of a marginal increase in training because the resulting higher w received by the job-changing worker allows the firm to reduce the first-period wage w_1. Under asymmetric information, w cannot depend on the actual investment level. Consequently, the firm will ignore the marginal social benefit of investment, leading to an *externality distortion.*

Second, the first term in (10), which represents the marginal benefit of investment, is divided by two. This is so because no contract contingent on realized productivity can be signed, and the part of the benefit of investment that exceeds the outside alternative has to be shared with the worker. This creates a *sharing distortion* in the firm's investment incentives.

Both the externality distortion and the sharing distortion reduce the firm's incentive to provide training to the worker. We have our second result.

PROPOSITION 2. Under symmetric information, the firm's training level equals the socially optimal level h^*. Under asymmetric information, the equilibrium level of training h^e is lower than h^*.

B. The Effects of Firm Specificity of Human Capital on Training

Proposition 2 tells us that, with a given degree of firm specificity of training measured by δ (a larger δ means that human capital is more general), asymmetric information leads to an equilibrium training level lower than what is socially optimal. The effect of a change in δ on the level of training also depends on whether information is symmetric or asymmetric, as shown in proposition 3.

PROPOSITION 3.   Under symmetric information, the training level is higher when human capital is completely general than when it is completely firm-specific; that is, $h^*(1) > h^*(0)$. Under asymmetric information, the equilibrium training level decreases in δ, that is, $h^{e\prime}(\delta) < 0$.

Proposition 3 implies that $[h^*(1) - h^e(1)] > [h^*(0) - h^e(0)]$. We thus know that the underinvestment problem under asymmetric information is more severe when human capital is completely general than when it is completely firm-specific.

The intuition for the second part of proposition 3 is fairly straightforward. An inspection of equation (10) reveals that a change in δ affects the externality distortion caused by the informational asymmetry. A larger δ means that the market wage for a job-changing worker is higher. Job change is thus more likely and the expected return to the training firm becomes lower. This means that the externality distortion is more severe, leading to a lower equilibrium training level. A smaller δ has exactly the opposite effect.

The intuition for the first part of proposition 3 is as follows. When information is symmetric, there is no externality distortion. However, some value of training is lost in labor turnover due to the specificity of training. Besides $c'(h)$, the marginal cost of training under symmetric information is the expected marginal loss of value due to training specificity, that is, the product of the probability of turnover, $F(\delta h - h)$, and the marginal loss, $l - \delta$ (the second term in the square brackets in equation (6)). In the extreme when $\delta = 0$, training is worth nothing to another employer, whereas when $\delta = 1$ there is no loss of training investment. When the training is completely general ($\delta = 1$), this expected marginal loss is zero. When it is completely specific ($\delta = 0$), the expected loss is $F(-h) > 0$. Thus, the firm has a stronger incentive to invest in human capital when $\delta = 1$ than when $\delta = 0$.[10]

C. The Relationship between Training and Turnover

In the standard human capital theory derived under symmetric information, investment decisions and turnover decisions can be separated. Consequently, the existing literature has studied the relationship between human capital investment and labor turnover by taking the amount of human capital as given. The standard theory implies that the labor turnover rate is unrelated to the training level if training is not firm-specific and is negatively related to the training level otherwise. We now reexamine this relationship under asymmetric information. Since the investment level and the turnover rate are determined simultaneously, we need to look at their relationship as the model's exogenous variables (such as δ, the distribution function of the job match quality, the reservation utility level u, or the training cost function) change.

Since the turnover rate in our model is $F(\delta h - h)$, (10) can be rewritten as

$$c'(h^e) = [1 - \text{Labor Turnover Rate}]/2. \qquad (11)$$

Equation (11) is a direct consequence of the externality effect due to asymmetric information. At the margin the firm can obtain the benefit of its investment, regardless of the degree of specificity, only when the worker stays with the firm. Since exogenous variables (except the cost function $c(h)$) of the model influence the training level through the turnover rate, in one sense one can say that the training level is determined by the labor turnover rate.

---

[10] Although we can show that the first-best training level h^* is higher when δ is near one than when δ is near zero, we cannot in general reach the conclusion that the relationship between the first-best h^* and δ is monotone without further restrictions on the distribution function $F(\xi)$.

One interesting aspect of equation (11) is that, except for the cost function $c(h)$, none of the model's other exogenous variables directly appears in (11). Since $c''(h) > 0$, the relationship between h^e and the turnover rate is negative when a change in any of the model's exogenous variables, except the cost function, leads to changes in h^e and the turnover rate. When the cost function $c(h)$ changes, it has a direct influence on the relationship (11) between training and turnover. An increase in the marginal cost $c'(h)$ (for all h) will directly reduce the turnover rate. At the same time, an increase in $c'(h)$ will also reduce h^e, which indirectly increases the turnover rate through (11). We can prove, however, that the direct effect is larger than the indirect effect. We thus have proposition 4.

PROPOSITION 4.   For a given cost function, if a change in the model's exogenous variables leads to a higher (lower) turnover, it also leads to a lower (higher) equilibrium level of training. A higher (lower) marginal training cost $c'(h)$ leads to a lower (higher) level of training and a higher (lower) rate of turnover.

Since the result of proposition 4 holds regardless of the specificity of human capital, it has an implication that is different from the standard human capital theory that turnover is independent of general human capital investment.

COROLLARY.   Even when the firm's training is completely general ($\delta = 1$), there can be a negative relationship between the turnover rate and the training level.

IV. Concluding Remarks

Unlike the standard human capital theory, we have shown that the incentives to make human capital investment can be distorted by an externality. The cause of the externality, however, is not exactly the one suggested by Pigou (1912); that is, the employer will lose its investment in a worker when the worker leaves. More precisely, the externality is due to potential employers' inability to compensate fully for the investment in the presence of asymmetric information. This logic suggests that who makes the investment is not crucial to the existence of the externality.

In fact, we can show that our results are not affected if the cost of human capital investment is directly borne by the worker. The reason is that, under asymmetric information, the worker, like the firm, cannot expect the market to fully recognize the value of, and thus to reward, the investment. To see this more clearly, let the worker choose h and the firm choose w_1 to meet the worker's ex ante participation constraint. In this case, once h is invested, the second-period bargaining problem is exactly the same as before so that the sharing rules are given again by (1) and (2). In addition, equation (3) that determines the market wage is unchanged. The worker's choice problem is

$$\max_{h} w_1 + \int_{\delta h^c - h}^{\infty} [w + (h - \delta h^c + \xi)/2] dF(\xi) + F(\delta h^c - h)w - c(h). \quad (12)$$

Note that the difference between the worker's expected payoff in (12) and in (4) is that, while the worker still takes the market conjectured gain from turnover δh^c as given, he does not take as given the effect of an increase in h on his second-period wage within the firm. This is because the choice of h is his. Thus, there are several places where h^c is replaced with h. The first-order condition for (12) is exactly the same as equation (9) because, as before, the worker has to share the benefit whenever his second-period productivity is above his market value. Since the first-order condition is the same and w_1 is still determined by the constraint (4), the analysis is exactly the same as before.

Of course, that the analysis is quantitatively the same is due to the fact that the worker and the firm have equal bargaining power. Otherwise, the sharing distortion would depend on who makes the investment. The results would be the same qualitatively, but not quantitatively.

The result linking training to the degree of firm specificity of human capital has implications for policies regarding government-sponsored training programs. The model has shown that under asymmetric information private incentive for human capital investment is weaker when human capital is more general than when it is more firm-specific. Thus, if the government is to intervene, our model suggests that training programs that provide more general skills are likely to yield greater social gains, other things being equal.[11]

Appendix

Proofs

Proof of Proposition 1. Since conjectured training level is involved in defining an equilibrium, the existence and uniqueness of an equilibrium are not so trivial. An equilibrium exists if equation (10) has a solution. Let us denote the left-hand side of (10) by $S(h^e)$. It is positive when $h^e = 0$ because $c'(0) = 0$. Since $c''(h) > 0$, $c'(h)$ approaches infinity as h increases. The first term in (10) is bounded by $1/2$. Thus, $S(h^e)$ is negative for h sufficiently large. Consequently, there exists an $h^e > 0$ that satisfies $S(h^e) = 0$. When the second-order condition is met, $S(h^e)$ is decreasing. Thus, the equilibrium is unique. When we replace equation (10) with

[11] We do not address why the government should intervene in the first place. Nor do we address the potential bureaucratic inefficiency that is associated with many government-run programs.

equation (6), we obtain the proof for the existence and uniqueness of the first-best outcome. Q.E.D.

Proof of Proposition 2. The left-hand side of (10), $[1 - F(\delta h - h)]/2 - c'(h)$, is less than that of (6), $1 - (1 - \delta)F(\delta h - h) - c'(h)$, for all δ and h. Thus, by the second-order condition, $h^* > h^e$. Q.E.D.

Proof of Proposition 3. When $\delta = 1$, the first term in (6) becomes one, which is greater than $1 - F(-h)$, the value of the first term when $\delta = 0$. Thus, $h^*(1) > h^*(0)$.

An increase in δ in (10) will reduce the left-hand side of (10). Since the second-order condition holds, the equilibrium h^e will be reduced. Q.E.D.

Proof of Proposition 4. Note that except for the cost function $c(h)$, none of the model's other exogenous variables directly appears in (11). Since $c''(h) > 0$, the relationship between h^e and the turnover rate is negative when any of the model's exogenous variables, except the cost function, changes.

We now prove that when $c(h)$ changes, the same negative relationship holds. Since $c''(h) > 0$, the derivative of the turnover rate with respect to h in (11) is $-c''(h^e) < 0$. Thus the relationship between the training level and the turnover rate is negative when the cost function does not change.

Let the cost function be indexed by I, namely, cost $= c(h, I)$. Assume that an increase in I increases the marginal cost. That is, $c_{hI}(h, I) > 0$ for all h and I. By differentiating (10) with respect to I (we will drop the superscript e on h for simplicity), we have

$$f(\delta h - h)(1 - \delta)h_I/2 - c_{hh}h_I - c_{hI} = 0. \tag{A1}$$

The second-order condition and $c_{hI} > 0$ imply that $h_I < 0$.

Let T denote the turnover rate. By differentiating (11) with respect to I, we have

$$T_I = -2[c_{hI} + c_{hh}h_I]. \tag{A2}$$

Substituting in (A1), we have $T_I = -f(\delta h - h)(1 - \delta)h_I > 0$. Thus, as I increases, h decreases, and the turnover rate increases. Q.E.D.

Proof of Corollary. Since the proof of proposition 4 is valid for any value of δ, it is true when $\delta = 1$. Q.E.D.

References

Becker, Gary. "Investment in Human Capital: A Theoretical Analysis." *Journal of Political Economy* 70, Suppl. (1962): 9–49.

Blinder, Alan, and Krueger, Alan. "International Differences in Labor Turnover: A Comparative Study with Emphasis on the U.S. and Japan." Paper for Harvard University Research Conference," The Labor Market in International Perspective." Cambridge, Mass.: Harvard University, 1992.

Chang, Chun, and Wang, Yijiang. "A Framework for Understanding Differences in Labor Turnover and Human Capital Investment." *Journal of Economic Behavior and Organization* 28 (1995): 91–105.

Gibbons, Robert, and Katz, Lawrence. "Layoffs and Lemons." *Journal of Labor Economics* 9, no. 4 (1991): 351–80.

Greenwald, Bruce. "Adverse Selection in the Labor Market." *Review of Economics Studies* 53 (1986): 325–47.

Grossman, Sanford, and Hart, Oliver. "The Costs and Benefits of Ownership: A Theory of Vertical and Lateral Integration." *Journal of Political Economy* 94, no. 4 (1986): 691–719.

Hart, Oliver, and Moore, John. "Property Rights and the Nature of the Firm." *Journal of Political Economy* 98 (1990): 1119–58.

Hashimoto, Masanori. "Firm-Specific Human Capital as a Shared Investment." *American Economic Review* 71, no. 3 (1981): 475–81.

Jovanovic, Boyan. "Firm-Specific Capital and Turnover." *Journal of Political Economy* 87 (1979): 1246–60.

Kahn, Charles, and Huberman, Gur. "Two-Sided Uncertainty and 'Up-or-Out' Contracts." *Journal of Labor Economics* 6, no. 4 (1988): 423–43.

Lazear, Edward. "Raids and Offer Matching." *Research in Labor Economics* Vol. 8, pt. A, ed. Ronald G. Ehrenberg, pp. 141–65. Greenwich, CT: JAI Press, 1986.

Milgrom, Paul, and Oster, Sharon. "Job Discrimination, Market Forces, and the Invisibility Hypothesis." *Quarterly Journal of Economics* 102, no. 3 (1987): 453–76.

Mortensen, Dale. "Specific Capital and Labor Turnover." *Bell Journal of Economics* 9 (1978): 572–86.

Nash, John. "The Bargaining Problem." *Econometrica* 18 (1950): 155–62.

Oi, Walter. "Labor as a Quasi-Fixed Factor." *Journal of Political Economy* 70 (1962): 538–55.

Parsons, Donald. "Specific Human Capital: An Application to Quit Rates and Layoff Rates." *Journal of Political Economy* 80 (1972): 1120–43.

Pigou, A. *Wealth and Welfare.* London: Macmillan, 1912.

Rubinstein, Ariel. "Perfect Equilibrium in a Bargaining Model." *Econometrica* 50, no. 1 (1982): 97–109.

Scoones, David, and Bernhardt, Dan. "Promotion, Turnover and Human Capital Acquisition." Kingston, Ontario: Queen's University, 1995.

Waldman, Michael. "Job Assignments, Signalling, and Efficiency." *Rand Journal of Economics* 15, no. 2 (1984): 255–67.

Waldman, Michael. "Up-or-Out Contracts: A Signaling Perspective." *Journal of Labor Economics* 8 (1990): 230–50.

Williamson, Oliver. *The Economic Institutions of Capitalism.* New York and London: Free Press, 1985.

[6]

The Economic Journal, 111 (*July*), 485–505. © Royal Economic Society 2001. Published by Blackwell Publishers, 108 Cowley Road, Oxford OX4 1JF, UK and 350 Main Street, Malden, MA 02148, USA.

SHOULD FIRMS BE REQUIRED TO PAY FOR VOCATIONAL TRAINING?*

Margaret Stevens

Failure in the training market may result from credit constraints and other capital market imperfections, deterring potential trainees, or labour market imperfections creating external benefits for firms. This paper presents a model of a training market affected by both problems, and examines their impact, and the impact of various policy measures, on the welfare of workers and firms. It is shown that there is a rationale for imposing training costs on firms, irrespective of the cause of under-investment. However, training levy schemes in which the levy depends upon the wage bill are shown to address capital market imperfections only.

Policy-makers in several countries have attempted to increase investment in vocational training by imposing a training levy on firms. In the United Kingdom a policy of this type operated between 1964 and 1982. For each of 28 industries, an Industrial Training Board was given statutory powers to raise a levy from the firms within the industry, and redistribute it in the form of grants to those firms deemed to train their employees to an appropriate level. In 1971 France instituted a similar policy requiring employers to spend a certain percentage of payroll costs on training. The required percentage has gradually been raised, standing now at $1\frac{1}{2}\%$, and the system continues to operate with little political controversy. In contrast, the very similar Australian Training Guarantee Scheme faced strong opposition from employers' organisations and was suspended in 1994, after only four years.[1]

The supposed economic rationale for such intervention is that training creates external benefits for other firms. A firm will be deterred from investing sufficiently in training because trained workers might leave, and the firm would then be unable to capture the benefits. A mechanism is needed to ensure that firms cannot free-ride by 'poaching' skilled labour from other firms. But this argument has found little favour with economists in recent years, and few have defended the use of levy schemes.

Perfectly competitive markets ensure optimal investment in training as follows. Provided that the skills are 'general'[2] (Becker, 1962) they can be traded in a competitive labour market: a generally-trained worker is paid his marginal product, and thus receives the full return from the training investment. Moreover, he is fully informed about the expected return, and can borrow at a competitive interest rate in order to finance the investment. The

* I would like to thank participants in seminars at the Universities of Oxford and Stirling for useful comments on an earlier version of this paper, and two anonymous referees for extensive and helpful suggestions.

[1] See Finegold and Crouch (1994) for discussion of levy schemes in these and other countries. Greenhalgh (1999) describes the current French system in detail. Green *et al.* (1999) discuss the use of training levies and workplace regulation in Korea, Singapore, and Taiwan.

[2] Specific skills will not be considered in this paper; although investment in specific training may be sub-optimal (due to a hold-up problem, for example) there are fewer compelling arguments for public intervention.

486   THE ECONOMIC JOURNAL   [JULY

decision as to whether to undertake training is his alone; even if training takes place 'on-the-job' the firm is involved only passively, as the supplier of the training which the worker demands, and the worker pays by accepting lower wages during the training period. The firm will not invest in training, since it cannot obtain a return. But optimal investment follows from the decisions of rational workers.

There are two principal theoretical explanations for failure in the market for vocational training. One is that potential trainees do not invest in training because of capital market problems: they cannot borrow against human capital, or insure against associated risks. The second is that the skilled labour market is not perfectly competitive, so that the wage is not equal to the marginal product of the worker. Then, both the worker and the firm where he trains may obtain part of the expected return to a training investment, so they will share the costs. However, if it is possible that the worker will move to an alternative firm that will pay him a wage below marginal product, this constitutes an external benefit which will lead to under-investment.

These market failure arguments seem to suggest that a training levy can be justified if the cause of under-investment is an imperfectly competitive labour market, but is inappropriate if the problem originates in the capital market. In this paper I investigate this proposition, and explore the impact of different types of training policy.

I construct a model of the market for vocational training allowing for both labour and capital market imperfections. A policy of requiring firms to increase training expenditure beyond their private choice is a first-best response to under-investment caused by labour market imperfections, and can also be a second-best response to problems originating in the capital market. While this provides a rationale for imposing training costs on firms, a levy scheme does not necessarily have that effect; if the firm's liability to train is assessed as a proportion of wages, the scheme acts instead like a training subsidy financed by a tax on wages. I show that such a policy addresses capital market problems only.

1. Explanations for Training Market Failure[3]

Having demonstrated the absence of external benefits to general training, Becker (1962) concluded that under-investment in general skills must be due to the credit constraints facing trainees. Human capital cannot normally be used as security for a loan. The source of the problem is the asymmetries of information and associated moral hazard that make it infeasible to write complete loan contracts. A related problem (Layard *et al.*, 1995; Hamilton, 1987) is the uncertainty in the return to a training investment (due, for example, to shocks to the demand for particular skills), and the lack of insurance against such risks.

Becker's analysis presumes that the labour market for generally skilled

[3] See Booth and Snower (1996), Bishop (1997) and Stevens (1999) for more extensive discussion.

workers is perfectly competitive. Stevens (1994; 1996) and Acemoglu (1997) both show that an imperfectly competitive labour market may cause under-investment in training. In Stevens' models the market for skilled workers is oligopsonistic – due to mobility costs and the nature of the skills, skilled workers have a limited number of potential employers. Acemoglu's model has many employers but search frictions in the skilled labour market. In both models the effect of imperfect competition is that a worker may move after training to an employer who can pay him a wage lower than productivity, although his skills are useful in all firms – training has external benefits for these firms, so the incentive to invest in training is too low. This has been described (Booth and Snower, 1996; Stevens, 1996; Booth and Zoega, 1999) as a 'poaching externality' (although the term can be misleading, as discussed below).

More precisely, the externality arises when training increases the actual or potential monopsony rents of future employers. Stevens (1996) argues that training has this effect because firms are differentiated in their skill require-ments and so skilled workers have a reduced set of potential employers. Similarly, in a search market, it may take longer to find an appropriate skilled job than an unskilled one – this is the assumption adopted in the model developed in Section 2 below. In the frictional labour market in Acemoglu's (1997) model, the wage is assumed to be an exogenous fraction of the worker's output, so all firms obtain higher rents from trained workers.

Acemoglu and Pischke (1999 *a*, *b*) argue that imperfect competition in the labour market is a necessary condition for firms to invest in 'technologically general' training; with a perfectly competitive labour market, firms will not invest even if trainees are severely credit-constrained (see also Stevens, 1996). Firms have an incentive to invest whenever training 'compresses the wage structure' – that is, raises productivity more than the market wage. They suggest several types of labour market distortion with this feature; in most but not all of these, training compresses the external wage structure as well as the wage structure in the training firm, and hence has potential benefits for external firms.[4]

One example of wage compression (Chang and Wang, 1996; Acemoglu and Pischke, 1998) occurs as a result of an information asymmetry, when outside firms cannot observe workers' skills or ability. The wage is reduced by adverse selection. Firms obtain no external benefits in equilibrium: in this respect these models differ from the oligopsony and search models. Nevertheless, the level of training is too low. At the equilibrium, the worker and firm will not

---

[4] As noted above, this is sometimes described as a poaching externality, yet for some of their examples, Acemoglu and Pischke suggest that poaching is not a problem, even when the external wage structure is compressed. They are using the term 'poaching' in a stronger sense, to mean the adoption by firms of a strategy of poaching skilled workers instead of training. In Stevens (1994), Chang and Wang (1996) and Acemoglu (1997) there is a poaching externality in the weaker sense that investment in training is too low because workers may (whether or not they do so in equilibrium) move to other firms who will benefit from the training, and who might therefore be seen as 'poachers'. In equilibrium it can happen (as in Acemoglu, 1997) that all firms both invest in training and employ workers trained in other firms.

increase their investment because if they did so, external firms would benefit. Acemoglu and Pischke demonstrate that this information asymmetry can be beneficial when no training would otherwise occur because trainees are severely credit-constrained. By diverting part of the return from worker to firm, it gives firms an incentive to invest. Other types of labour market imperfection can be expected to act similarly.

It is difficult to assess the practical significance of the externality problem. There are plausible arguments that training reduces labour market competition, but we have no direct evidence to support them (although the finding that firms *do* pay for general training (Acemoglu and Pischke, 1998) constitutes indirect evidence). Surveys of employers' attitudes to training and poaching are hard to interpret. A finding that employers are deterred from providing training because they may lose workers to other firms is consistent with a competitive labour market – it does not necessarily constitute evidence of an externality. On the other hand a survey by the Confederation of British Industry (1997) found that employers believe themselves to provide training which is highly transferable, but nevertheless increases the likelihood of retaining employees by instilling 'greater organisational commitment'. The CBI interpreted this as evidence against a poaching problem, but it does suggest that training increases the labour market power of employers, in which case there may be under-investment due to an externality.

Bishop (1997) discusses other explanations for training market failure: information problems, distortions arising from the tax system, and network externalities. However, it is under-investment arising from capital market imperfections and/or externalities between firms that has been the basis of calls for large-scale public intervention in the training market (for example, Chapman, 1993; Layard *et al.*, 1995), and which is therefore the focus of this paper.

The objective is to construct a simple and tractable 'supply and demand' model of a training market affected by both types of problem. This can be used to clarify the differing impact of capital and labour market imperfections on training, to examine the interaction between them, and to explore the impact of policy. In particular, the model allows us to analyse the effects of policies on the welfare of workers and firms separately, which (as explained in the next section) is not possible in most existing models of training, but is important for the political implications of training policy.

2. The Model

Consider a particular skill, which is of potential value to many firms. There is a continuum of workers, initially unskilled and not attached to firms, with productivity normalised to zero, who have identical productive characteristics but may differ in their disutility of training. The disutility of the jth worker is $D(j)$ where $D'(j) \geqslant 0$.

Suppose that workers possessing this skill are one of many possible inputs to production. There is a continuum of firms, differing in technology and the choice of other inputs. If firm i wishes to use this particular skill, it must incur an investment cost $E(i)$, where $E'(i) \geqslant 0$. Thus $E(i)$ is an entry cost to the skilled labour market (although it may be negative, representing a benefit of entry). Having incurred this cost, all firms have identical production functions $f(N_i)$ where N_i is the mass of skilled workers employed, and $f' > 0$, $f'' \leqslant 0$, with constant labour demand elasticity

$$|\varepsilon| \equiv \frac{-f'(N_i)}{N_i f''(N_i)} \geqslant 1.$$

The specification of the technology is unusual, so deserves some comment. The aim is to capture in a simple way[5] two possible features of the skilled labour market which are not present in most training models. First, the demand for skilled labour may be downward-sloping, so that when skilled workers are scarce the wage will be higher. Second, heterogeneity in entry costs allows for infra-marginal firms to earn rents from training and employing skilled workers. This makes it possible to consider the 'welfare' of firms, without arbitrarily fixing the number of firms – otherwise, with homogeneity and entry, all firms make zero profits in equilibrium, and are indifferent to policy decisions.

In general, the welfare of firms and workers must depend on the elasticity of the entry of each group to the market. Existing models of training assume either that the populations of firms and workers are fixed (inelastic), or free (perfectly elastic) entry by one group only, so that the other group necessarily obtains all the rents. The specification here, with E' and $D' \geqslant 0$, is more general and includes free-entry of either group as a special case, although we require either $E' > 0$ or $D' > 0$ to close the model.

There are two periods, a training period and an employment period. In the first period firm i chooses whether to enter, and if so, how many workers to train. If it trains T_i workers the cost of training is $C(T_i)$: $C' > 0$, $C'' \geqslant 0$.

Unskilled workers are perfectly mobile between firms, and will wish to train in the firm where the expected utility of training is highest (provided that net utility is positive after allowing for the disutility of training). This means that the training market is effectively competitive. In the second period firms compete for the services of the skilled workers. The skilled labour market is imperfectly competitive: skilled workers care about the non-wage characteristics of jobs, and take time to find a preferred job, and this gives firms some wage-setting power. Thus the model has the characteristic of wage-compression (Acemoglu and Pischke (1999a) discussed above): the effect of training is to raise productivity more than the wage.

Workers' decisions are affected by capital market imperfections, which are modelled very simply, as follows. All agents are risk-neutral, and there is no discounting between periods. Firms maximise the sum of expected profits over the two periods, and can borrow and save at a zero interest rate. Workers

---

[5] The alternative would be a more complete general equilibrium model, with capital and skilled and unskilled labour in the production function, together with heterogeneity of the production function itself.

maximise the sum of utility, but have no initial resources so must borrow to finance training, and face an interest rate $r \geqslant 0$ on loans. It is possible to extend the model to allow for the effect of uncertainty on risk-averse workers (Stevens, 1999); the effects of increasing uncertainty on training decisions are similar to the effects of increasing r. Here, for simplicity, we represent the degree of capital market imperfection by the single parameter r.

We will look for a symmetric equilibrium in which every firm that enters trains the same number, T, of workers. The first step is to analyse the skilled labour market assuming that a mass m of firms has entered the market, that firm k has trained T_k workers, and that all other firms have trained T workers.

2.1. *The Skilled Labour Market*

The labour market is subject to frictions, which give firms some market power. At the start of period two firm i sets wage W_i. Frictions arise because skilled jobs differ in non-wage characteristics, and each worker must search for a job that suits him.

We will suppose that the worker knows the wage and non-wage character-istics in the firm where he trained, but inspecting an alternative firm takes time $\eta \leqslant 1$, and all search must take place within a time interval of unit length at the start of the second period. So the worker takes a random sample of $n \equiv 1/\eta$ alternative firms,[6] then chooses the best of the $n + 1$ firms available to him. Thus η represents the degree of labour market friction. As η approaches zero the worker samples all firms.

The non-wage characteristics of firm i are represented by a random variable $y_i \sim U[0, h]$, independent across firms, and the worker's utility from a job in firm i is:

$$U(W_i, y_i) \equiv W_i y_i.$$

His realisation of y_i is independent of the realisation for any other worker. We choose $h = (n+2)/(n+1)$ to normalise the expected maximum value of y_i in the sample to be one. This means that y_i captures the worker's assessment of the non-wage utility in firm i relative to the pleasantest job he can expect to find by sampling $n + 1$ firms.

Suppose that firm k has trained T_k workers and sets a wage W_k, and that all the other firms (except possibly for a set of firms of mass zero) have each trained T workers and set a wage W. To find the equilibrium wage-setting strategies we first determine the supply of labour to firm k.

Consider a worker who samples firm k, and n other firms. He prefers firm k if $W_k y_k > W y_i$ for all the other firms, i, in his sample. So the probability, P, that he prefers firm k depends on the relative wage $w_k \equiv W_k/W$, and is given by:

$$P(w_k) = \frac{1}{h} \int_0^h F^n(w_k y_k) \, dy_k$$

---

[6] More precisely $n \equiv \text{int}(1/\eta)$, but for the derivation of the labour market equilibrium we will simply assume that $1/\eta$ is an integer.

where F is the uniform distribution function. Evaluating this:

$$P(w) \equiv \begin{cases} \dfrac{\eta}{1+\eta}\, w^{1/\eta} & \text{if } w \leqslant 1, \\[3mm] \dfrac{\eta}{1+\eta}\left[1 + \dfrac{1}{\eta}\left(1 - \dfrac{1}{w}\right)\right] & \text{if } w > 1. \end{cases} \tag{1}$$

Firm k is sampled by all the workers that it trained, together with a mass nT of those trained in other firms – that is by $T_k + T/\eta$ workers. Hence the supply of labour to firm k is:

$$N_k = P(w_k)\left(\frac{\eta T_k + T}{\eta}\right). \tag{2}$$

The market is monopsonistically competitive: each firm faces an upward-sloping labour supply function but its choice of wage does not affect any other firm. As the search friction η approaches zero, it can be verified from (1) and (2) that the firm's labour supply becomes perfectly elastic at the market wage W. If the firm trains the same number of workers as all other firms, T, and sets the market wage, it can expect to recruit T skilled workers. However, training gives workers a degree of attachment to the training firm because they know the job characteristics there, but have to search for alternatives. Hence, when η is high, workers trained by firm k have a significant effect on its own supply of skilled labour, but when the labour market becomes more competitive the firm's hold over its own workers diminishes – in the limit, all firms compete on equal terms for all workers.

It helps to simplify the analysis if we linearise the labour supply function around the market wage. The function $P(w)$ given by (1) is continuous, with continuous first derivative, so we avoid having to treat the two segments of the function separately by using an approximation valid for w close to 1 (that is, in the neighbourhood of the symmetric equilibrium):

$$P(w) \approx \frac{\eta}{1+\eta}\left[1 + \frac{1}{\eta}(w-1)\right]$$

and hence replacing (2) by the labour supply function:[7]

$$N_k = \left[1 + \frac{1}{\eta}(w_k - 1)\right]\left(\frac{\eta T_k + T}{\eta + 1}\right). \tag{3}$$

Now consider the firm k's choice of wages. It chooses W_k to maximise profits in the skilled labour market, Ψ_k:

$$\Psi_k \equiv f(N_k) - W_k N_k$$

taking the market wage W as given. The first order condition is:

$$f'(N_k) = (1+\eta) W_k \tag{4}$$

[7] This step is convenient because it avoids some additional analysis needed to allow for the discontinuity in the second derivative of P, but it is not essential for evaluating the equilibrium: without it, we obtain the same qualitative results.

where N_k is given by (3). Putting $T_k = T$ and $W_k = W$ in (4) gives the corresponding condition for firms that have trained T workers and set a wage W:

$$f'(T) = (1 + \eta) W. \tag{5}$$

So, in a symmetric equilibrium in which almost all firms have trained T workers, the market wage W is determined by (5). If firm k has trained a different number of workers T_k, it sets a different wage W_k determined by (4). Clearly, all firms set a wage below marginal product when the search friction η is positive.

2.1.1. The firm's private benefit from training

Consider the effect of the firm's own training, T_k, on its second-period profit when wages are optimally chosen, $\Psi_k^*(T_k)$. By the envelope theorem the effect acting through wages disappears, so:

$$\frac{d\Psi_k^*}{dT_k} = [f'(N_k) - W_k] \frac{\partial N_k}{\partial T_k}. \tag{6}$$

The benefit from training an additional worker is the difference between the wage and the marginal product, multiplied by the probability of keeping the worker after training. At the symmetric equilibrium when all firms have trained T workers:

$$\frac{d\Psi_k^*}{dT_k} = \left(\frac{\eta}{1 + \eta} \right)^2 f'(T). \tag{7}$$

Clearly the marginal benefit of training depends on the existence of frictions, and disappears as $\eta \to 0$.

2.1.2. The worker's expected utility in the skilled labour market

A worker who has trained in firm k samples n other firms and works in the one that gives him highest utility. Let U_k^e be his expected utility in the skilled labour market. At the equilibrium described by (4) and (5):

$$U_k^e = \iint \max(W_k y_k, \ Wy) \, g_n(y) \, g_1(y_k) \, dy \, dy_k \tag{8}$$

where $g_n(y) = ny^{n-1}/h^n$ is the density function of the maximum of the non-wage characteristics variable in a sample of n firms. Evaluating the integral (see Appendix):

$$U_k^e = \begin{cases} \dfrac{W}{(\eta + 1)^2} \left[1 + 2\eta + \eta^2 w_k^{1+(1/\eta)} \right] & \text{if } w_k \leqslant 1, \\[2ex] \dfrac{W}{2(\eta + 1)} \left[(1 + 2\eta) w_k + \dfrac{1}{w_k} \right] & \text{if } w_k \geqslant 1. \end{cases} \tag{9}$$

At the symmetric equilibrium when all firms have trained T workers:

$$U^e_k = W = \frac{f'(T)}{1+\eta}. \tag{10}$$

But if firm k trains a different number of workers, this affects the wage there, and hence the worker's utility. Differentiating (9) with respect to W_k, and (4) with respect to T_k, we obtain the overall effect of the firm's training on the worker's utility. Evaluated at the symmetric equilibrium, this is:

$$\frac{\partial U^e_k}{\partial T_k} = \frac{\partial U^e_k}{\partial W_k}\frac{dW_k}{dT_k} = -\left(\frac{\eta}{1+\eta}\right)^3\frac{f'(T)}{(1+\eta|\varepsilon|)\,T}. \tag{11}$$

So from (10), the worker's expected utility is equal to the equilibrium wage, which approaches the competitive wage as $\eta \to 0$. From (11), when $\eta > 0$, the worker would benefit if the firm reduced the number of other trainees, since this would raise the skilled wage in that firm, and hence his expected utility.

Note that the result that expected utility equals expected wage arises because the worker's utility is dependent on the non-wage characteristics of firms *relative* to what he can expect given his sample size, so expected non-wage utility does not increase as the sample size increases. Hence frictions do not cause allocative inefficiency in the labour market. This allows us to focus on the effects of labour market frictions on training decisions only, and to clarify the extent to which training policy can improve the outcome *given the existence of frictions* – clearly training policy cannot help to allocate the worker to his best job if the worker is unable to inspect all the possible jobs. The alternative specification, in which the absolute level of non-wage characteristics determines utility, is algebraically more complex but gives the same qualitative results.

2.2. *The Training Market*

In the first period each firm that has entered chooses its training programme, then trainees evaluate the training offered by firms and decide whether to train, and if so, where. Specifically, firm k chooses the number of trainees T_k, and the price of training P_k. Since the productivity of unskilled workers and trainees is normalised to zero, this is equivalent to setting a trainee wage of $(-P_k)$.[8]

When the number of trainees in each firm has been decided, trainees can form an expectation U^e_k of their utility in the skilled labour market if they train in firm k. This depends on the wages that they expect each firm to set, which in turn depends on the number of trainees in each firm. Workers must borrow to finance training, and repay the loan in the second period at interest rate r.

---

[8] Note that we are ruling out training contracts in which the firm sets a fee to be paid by the worker if he leaves after training. Such contracts are not normally legally enforceable, although the British government did consider changing the law (Employment Department *et al*, 1992). They can be expected to reduce the externality problem, but would not, in the present model, eliminate it. In the second period, firms would make different offers to workers trained inside and outside the firm, but the search friction would still give firms some labour market power over workers trained elsewhere.

Hence the net second-period expected utility for any worker choosing to train in firm k is:

$$u_k \equiv U_k^e - (1 + r) P_k \tag{12}$$

(provided that $P_k \geqslant 0$).[9] Since there are many firms and workers, and all workers who choose to train will wish to do so at the firm offering the training package with the highest level of second-period utility, the training market is effectively competitive. However the firms are not price-takers; rather, they must offer the market level of expected future utility, $u_k = \bar{u}$.

Hence firm k chooses T_k and P_k to maximise its two-period profit, subject to the constraint that the combined effect of these decisions is to provide utility $\bar{u}$. To find the symmetric equilibrium, assume that all other firms choose the same price, P, and quantity, T, giving utility $\bar{u}$. Then the problem for firm k is:

$$\max_{P_k, T_k} \Psi^*(T_k) + P_k T_k - C(T_k) \text{ subject to } U_k^e - (1 + r) P_k = \bar{u}. \tag{13}$$

The first-order condition is:

$$\frac{d\Psi^*}{dT_k} + P_k - C'(T_k) + \frac{T_k}{1 + r} \frac{\partial U_k^e}{\partial T_k} = 0 \tag{14}$$

where $d\Psi^*/dT_k$ and $\partial U_k^e/\partial T_k$ are given by (7) and (11). In equilibrium $T_k = T$ and $P_k = P$ so the firm's optimal choice satisfies:

$$P - C'(T) + \left(\frac{\eta}{1 + \eta}\right)^2 f'(T) - \frac{\eta^3}{(1 + r)(1 + \eta)^3 (1 + \eta|\varepsilon|)} f'(T) = 0. \tag{15}$$

On the demand-side, the expected future utility for trainees is:

$$\bar{u} = \frac{f'(T)}{1 + \eta} - (1 + r) P$$

($P \geqslant 0$) and workers will wish to train if their individual disutility of training is less than $\bar{u}$. In equilibrium, when m firms each train T workers, the disutility of the marginal worker equals $\bar{u}$:

$$\frac{f'(T)}{1 + \eta} - (1 + r) P = D(mT). \tag{16}$$

Finally, firms enter the market until the two-period profit is zero for the marginal firm:

$$f(T) - \frac{f'(T)}{1 + \eta} T + PT - C(T) = E(m). \tag{17}$$

Equations (15) and (16) can be regarded as the firm's supply function and the market demand function for training, although some care is required in this

---

[9] In the following analysis we ignore the case in which the equilibrium price set by firms is strictly negative. This is straightforward to analyse, but occurs only if both labour and capital market imperfections are very high.

interpretation since it is utility, not price, that is taken as given by firms. The number of firms, and hence market supply, is determined by (17).

Consider now the effects of capital and labour market frictions on the supply and demand for training. Looking first at the supply function (15), note that when $\eta = 0$ the firm supplies training at marginal cost. As in Stevens (1996) and Acemoglu and Pischke (1999a), when the labour market is competitive firms will not invest in training even if workers are credit-constrained $(r > 0)$. The third term in (15) represents an increase in training supply due to labour market frictions $(\eta > 0)$. The firm will finance part of the cost of training because it has a positive probability of keeping the worker at a wage below marginal product.

There is a secondary, negative, effect of η on training supply, represented by the fourth term in (15). In the presence of frictions, a firm that reduces the quantity of training below that of its competitors raises the expected wage of its workers and hence the price that trainees will pay. Thus labour market frictions give firms some derived power in the training market, tending to reduce training supply. This effect is most severe when there is a perfect capital market (so that trainees are able to pay more), but is always outweighed by the primary effect – that is, the sum of the third and fourth terms in (15) is positive. But it means that in the presence of labour market frictions, credit constraints do tend to increase the supply of training.

The effects of capital and labour market imperfections on the demand for training (16) are more straightforward. Credit constraints reduce demand because they raise the effective price. Labour market frictions reduce the expected benefit for trainees, and hence demand.

In summary, imperfections in capital and labour markets increase the firm's supply of training and reduce market demand. In the next section we examine the overall effect on equilibrium training and welfare, allowing also for the entry decisions of firms.

2.3. *Welfare and Comparative Statics*

The demand function (16) and supply functions (15) and (17), together determine the equilibrium number of trainees per firm, $T^*(r, \eta)$, the number of firms $m^*(r, \eta)$, and the price of training.

The welfare of firms and workers at the market equilibrium is represented by producer surplus and 'worker surplus' respectively:

$$\Omega_f(m^*) \equiv \int_0^{m^*} [E(m^*) - E(i)]\, di, \tag{18}$$

$$\Omega_w(m^* T^*) \equiv \int_0^{m^* T^*} [D(m^* T^*) - D(j)]\, dj. \tag{19}$$

Ω_f and Ω_w are increasing functions of m^* and $m^* T^*$ respectively.

2.3.1. *First-best outcome*

If there is perfect competition in the labour and capital markets, $(r = \eta = 0)$, we have the first-best training outcome:

$$f'(T_f) - C'(T_f) = D(m_f T_f),$$
$$f(T_f) - C(T_f) = TD(m_f T_f) + E(m_f), \qquad (20)$$
$$P = C'(T_f); \; W = f'(T_f).$$

Workers pay the full marginal cost of training, and reap the full return in the form of enhanced wages.

2.3.2. *Comparative statics: labour market imperfections*

Differentiating (15) to (17) with respect to η (see appendix A.2.) gives:

$$\text{If } r = 0, \; \frac{\partial(m^* T^*)}{\partial \eta} < 0; \frac{\partial m^*}{\partial \eta} \text{ is ambiguous.} \qquad (21)$$

$$\text{For } r \text{ sufficiently high, } \frac{\partial(m^* T^*)}{\partial \eta} > 0 \text{ and } \frac{\partial m^*}{\partial \eta} > 0. \qquad (22)$$

With a perfect capital market (or for small r, by continuity), labour market frictions decrease the quantity of training. They decrease demand and increase supply, but the decrease in demand always dominates the increase in supply. The intuition is simple: frictions reduce the wage, raising the return to training for firms and lowering it for workers. But a worker loses whether or not he changes firm after training, whereas his training firm gains only if the worker stays, which he does with probability less than one. In other words, there is an external benefit to outside firms. The overall effect on firm welfare is ambiguous: they lose from the decline in the supply of skilled workers, but gain directly from the lower wage.

However, (22) shows that labour market imperfections can benefit both workers and firms, by mitigating the effects of capital market problems. When demand for training is already low because of credit constraints, an increase in friction and consequent reduction in the wage has little effect on demand. Then the increase in supply outweighs the fall in demand, and the overall effect on training is positive.

These results illustrate the discussion of employers' attitudes in Section 1 above. It is when labour market frictions are high that employers are not deterred from paying for training by the fear of losing the trained workers. The employer does not perceive training as a problem (although correspondingly he may perceive a difficulty of recruiting skilled workers). So frictions increase supply. But, if there are no credit constraints, the increase in supply is always outweighed by a fall in demand, so the overall effect of frictions is to reduce equilibrium training. The joint return to training for the firm and the trainee falls, because some of the benefit accrues to external firms. On the other hand, when demand is already low due to capital market imperfections, the net effect of labour market frictions can be positive. There is still an externality – investment in training is lower than it would be if the benefits to other firms were taken into account – but there is more training than would occur without frictions.

2.3.3. *Comparative statics: capital market imperfections*

Similarly, differentiating (15) to (17) with respect to r gives (see appendix A.3.):

$$\frac{\partial(T^* m^*)}{\partial r} < 0 \text{ and } \frac{\partial m^*}{\partial r} < 0 \text{ provided that } C'(T^*) > \left(\frac{\eta}{1+\eta}\right)^2 f'(T^*). \quad (23)$$

When there are no labour market frictions, credit constraints decrease training in the obvious way: they reduce demand and have no effect on supply. In the presence of frictions credit constraints also increase supply (by limiting the firm's incentive to exploit the worker's future attachment and push up the price); however (23) tells us that the decrease in demand normally dominates, reducing training. Specifically, it states that credit constraints cannot increase the welfare of firms or workers unless labour market frictions are so high, and the equilibrium quantity of training per firm is so low, that the second-period marginal private benefit *to the firm* of training a worker is greater than the marginal cost of training.

2.3.4. *Summary of the effects of labour and capital market imperfections*

Labour market frictions reduce the demand for training and increase the supply. With a perfect capital market the demand effect dominates. When trainees are credit constrained the effect on demand is smaller, so that labour market imperfections may increase training and the welfare of both workers and firms.

Credit constraints reduce the demand for training. In the presence of labour market frictions they can have a positive effect on supply; however the supply effect is likely to be small, and the overall effect of credit constraints is therefore to reduce training and welfare.

Finally in this section, note that although increases in η or r can sometimes increase training, the equilibrium total quantity $m^* T^*$ is always lower than first-best in the presence of either type of imperfection. An outline proof is given in the appendix.

3. Policy

Consider a policy-maker who wishes to mitigate the effects on training of labour and capital market imperfections. His objective is to raise the welfare of firms and/or workers. In this section, we use the model developed in Section 2 to look first at the effects of regulating the training offered by firms, and then at the use of subsidies; finally, we examine the impact of a training levy scheme.

3.1. *Regulation of Firms' Training*

Suppose that the policy-maker can set the amount of training in each firm that enters the market for skilled labour. We will assume that he does not regulate skilled or trainee wages: these will be determined in the markets. He sets T subject to the training demand function (16) and the entry condition for firms (17), over-riding the firm's supply function (15). Eliminating price from (16) and (17), the policy-maker's constraint is therefore:

$$E(m) + \frac{TD(mT)}{1+r} = f(T) - C(T) - WT\left(1 - \frac{1}{1+r}\right) \text{ where } W = \frac{f'(T)}{1+\eta}.$$
(24)

From (18) and (19):

$$\frac{d\Omega_f}{dT} = mE'(m)\frac{dm}{dT} \text{ and } \frac{d\Omega_w}{dT} = mTD'(m)\left(m + T\frac{dm}{dT}\right),$$
(25)

from which it is clear that the optimal level of T for workers is higher than the optimal level for firms. Differentiating (24) gives:

$$\frac{1}{m}\frac{d\Omega_f}{dT} + \frac{1}{m(1+r)}\frac{d\Omega_w}{dT} = f'(T) - C'(T)$$

$$- \left(W + T\frac{dW}{dT}\right)\left(1 - \frac{1}{1+r}\right) - \frac{D(mT)}{1+r}$$
(26)

which represents the constraint on the policy-maker's ability to raise welfare by setting T. Evaluating the right-hand side of (26) at the private optimum (T^*, m^*) we obtain:

$$\frac{1}{m}\left(\frac{d\Omega_f}{dT} + \frac{1}{1+r}\frac{d\Omega_w}{dT}\right)\Bigg|_{\substack{T=T^* \\ m=m^*}} = \frac{\eta f'(T^*)}{(1+\eta)^2} + \frac{\eta^3 f'(T^*)}{(1+\eta)^3(1+r)(1+\eta|\varepsilon|)}$$

$$- T\frac{dW}{dT}\left(1 - \frac{1}{1+r}\right).$$
(27)

The three terms in (27) represent three positive effects on welfare of raising training above the firms' private choice. The first term represents the gain, when there are labour market frictions, from internalising the benefits of training to other firms. This is the difference between wage and marginal product, multiplied by the probability that the worker will move to a different firm. The second term is the gain from preventing firms from trying to raise their own training price by reducing training relative to other firms. This term is most significant when η is high and r is low.

The third term is a price effect. When the number of trainees rises the skilled wage falls, benefiting firms. With a perfect capital market this would be exactly offset by a fall in the price trainees are prepared to pay. But when trainees are credit-constrained there is a smaller effect on the price, leading to a net increase in welfare.

Clearly the distribution of welfare gains between firms and workers depends on the elasticity of supply of firms and trainees to the market, E' and D' respectively. In the case of a perfectly elastic supply of trainees, for example, trainees obtain no surplus, and the firms obtain all of the benefit of the policy.

From (25) we can see that if firm welfare rises, worker welfare does so too. Hence a rise in Ω_f is necessary and sufficient for a Pareto improvement. Rewriting (27):

$$\frac{d\Omega_f}{dT}\bigg|_{\substack{T=T^* \\ m=m^*}} \overset{\text{sgn}}{=} \frac{\eta f'(T^*)}{(1+\eta)^2} + \frac{\eta^3 f'(T^*)}{(1+\eta)^3(1+r)(1+\eta|\varepsilon|)}$$

$$- T\frac{dW}{dT}\left(1 - \frac{1}{1+r}\right) - \frac{mTD'(mT)}{1+r}. \tag{28}$$

Firm welfare rises provided that the three gains identified above are not offset by the last term in (28), which is the increase in utility that is required to attract further trainees into the market. If r is high and/or the disutility of training does not increase much at the margin, then this term is small and we have a Pareto improvement.

The last two terms of (28) may be combined as follows:

$$\frac{d\Omega_f}{dT}\bigg|_{\substack{T=T^* \\ m=m^*}} \overset{\text{sgn}}{=} \frac{\eta f'(T^*)}{(1+\eta)^2} + \frac{\eta^3 f'(T^*)}{(1+\eta)^3(1+r)(1+\eta|\varepsilon|)} + T\left(\frac{dP}{dT} - \frac{dW}{dT}\right) \tag{29}$$

where P is the demand price of training defined by (16). From this formulation, we can say that a sufficient condition for a Pareto improvement is that the fall in the skilled wage is greater than the rise in the trainee wage.

Note that firms may gain from being required to increase the supply of training above their private choice, even when the cause of the problem is in the capital market – when it is the trainees who are investing too little. The intuition is as follows. Credit constraints flatten the training demand function. Trainees will not pay a high price for training, but when the price is low many workers are willing to train without the need for further price reductions. Hence, firms can gain collectively from raising training if the improvement in the supply of skilled labour (the fall in the wage) outweighs the fall in the price of training along the demand function. Firms cannot act individually to increase training because they would lose trainees to other firms.

Clearly this policy cannot achieve the first-best outcome (T_f, m_f) when $r > 0$ – it cannot prevent some dissipation of welfare in the imperfectly competitive capital market. When $r = 0$, the first-best outcome does lie on the policy-maker's constraint (24) and maximises the sum of worker and firm welfare; however, the policy optimum depends on the relative weight assigned to the welfare of firms and workers.

In summary, if there is significant under-investment due to labour and/or capital market imperfections, a policy of requiring firms to finance an increase in training will produce a Pareto improvement, provided that the supply of trainees is not too steeply sloping. If the supply of trainees is inelastic, there may be a transfer of welfare from firms to workers.

3.2. *Subsidy*

3.2.1. *A subsidy financed by taxing firms' profits*

It is straightforward to see that this is exactly equivalent to the policy of regulation analysed in the previous section. The policy-maker can over-ride the firm's supply decision either directly, by regulating the quantity, or indirectly by manipulating the incentive to train.

3.2.2. *A subsidy financed by taxing wages*

Suppose that the policy-maker gives a subsidy sP, where P is the price paid to firms, so that $(1 - s)P$ is paid by trainees, and sets a tax on skilled wages sufficient to raise the required revenue at the new equilibrium. This changes the demand function (16) to:

$$\frac{f'(T)}{1 + \eta} - [1 + r(1 - s)]P = D(mT) \qquad (30)$$

(provided that $0 \leqslant s \leqslant 1$) with no effect on the supply equations (15) and (17). Clearly this is equivalent to reducing the interest rate on loans to workers; with $s = 1$, the policy-maker can fully release the credit constraints. With the very simple model of capital market imperfections used here, this policy mimics the operation of a perfect capital market.

However, it can do nothing to mitigate under-investment due to labour market imperfections. This result is not model-specific: a training subsidy financed by a tax on skilled wages simply redistributes the worker's income across periods. With a perfect capital market this would have no effect at all, since the worker could redistribute income costlessly himself by borrowing or saving. In general, the best that can be done via such a policy is to boost demand to the level that would occur with a perfect capital market. A higher tax and subsidy would simply induce workers to save.

From the comparative statics results of 2.3.3 we can see that, at the private equilibrium, reducing the effective interest rate r facing workers would increase the welfare of both firms and workers, except possibly when η is high and r is already low.

3.3. *A Training Levy Scheme*

In a training levy scheme the policy-maker sets the level of resources that the firm is required to spend on training. At first sight this appears to be equivalent to regulating training. However (in the schemes instituted in the United

Kingdom, France, and other countries) the firm's liability to spend on training is assessed as a proportion of its total wage bill. Assuming that all employees are affected equally, the effect is that each employee receives some subsidised training, financed by a proportional tax on his own wages spread over the whole period of employment. We have analysed this policy in Section 3.2.2: a subsidy financed by taxing wages affects the demand function and not the supply function, and alleviates under-investment due to capital market imperfections only. Thus, if operated in this way, a levy scheme does not address the problem of external benefits to other firms arising from labour market frictions; for this, training liability should depend on profits, not wages.

3.4. *Policy Conclusions*

The above analysis clarifies the important distinction between two types of policy: *demand-side policies* (such as loans to trainees, and training subsidies financed through wage taxation) which affect the demand function only, and *supply-side policies* (taxation of profits, or regulation) affecting the training supplied by firms. Demand-side policies can only alleviate capital market problems, in which case they will normally increase the welfare of both workers and firms. Supply-side policies are first-best only for problems arising in the labour market, but can raise welfare irrespective of the source of under-investment. They deliver a Pareto improvement if the supply of potential trainees is sufficiently elastic; otherwise there may be a transfer of welfare from firms to workers.

Perhaps surprisingly, training levy schemes (as normally operated) are a demand-side policy, effective only against capital market problems. Previous discussion of training levies in the economics literature has supposed precisely the opposite: that they are an inappropriate intervention if capital market imperfections are the main source of training market failure (Lees and Chiplin, 1970; Layard *et al.*, 1995) but can be justified when there are externalities between firms (Jones, 1988; Chapman, 1993; Booth and Snower, 1996; Stevens, 1996).

The present model does not allow us to make distinctions between different types of demand-side and supply-side policy. To go further, we would need a more detailed model of the source of capital market imperfections: for example, if trainees' decisions are affected by risk and uncertainty loans may not be equivalent to a subsidy financed through wage taxation. Perhaps more importantly, we should allow for the limited information available in practice to the policy-maker, which will affect his ability to redress capital market problems, and his choice between taxation and regulation of firms.[10] When implementing *any* policy designed to raise the level of training the policy-maker faces a monitoring problem to ensure that the resultant training is of an appropriate quantity and quality.

---

[10] Here, the issues are similar to those arising in environmental policy, as in the classic treatment of Weitzman (1974).

Should firms be required to pay for vocational training? The model allows us to draw the following conclusions. First, if, due to labour market imperfections, training allows firms to earn significant rents from the employment of skilled workers, it is appropriate to make firms bear higher training costs (by, for example, taxing profits). Second, imposing training costs on firms could be a second-best policy, raising the welfare of firms and workers, even when the cause of underinvestment lies in the capital market. Third, contrary to appearances, training levy schemes do not 'make firms pay' – they affect the decisions of trainees, not firms. But if, in spite of this, the question is interpreted as meaning 'Are levy schemes a good idea?' we can say that they could be an appropriate response to under-investment arising from capital market imperfections, whose effectiveness in practice should be compared with other demand-side policies such as loans.

Nuffield College, Oxford

Date of receipt of first submission: March 1999
Date of receipt of final typescript: November 2000

Appendix

A.1. *Derivation of (9):*
Equation (8) can be written:

$$\frac{U_k^e}{W} = w_k \iint\limits_{w_k x > y} x g_n(y) g_1(x) \, dy \, dx + \iint\limits_{w_k x < y} y g(y) \, dy \, dx.$$

When $w_k \leqslant 1$ this is:

$$\frac{U_k^e}{W} = w_k \int_0^h x g_1(x) \left[\int_0^{w_k x} g_n(y) \, dy \right] dx + \int_0^h g_1(x) \left[\int_{w_k x}^h y g_n(y) \, dy \right] dx$$

$$= \frac{n}{h^{n+1}} \int_0^h \left(w_k x \int_0^{w_k x} y^{n-1} \, dy + \int_{w_k x}^h y^n \, dy \right) dx.$$

Evaluating this, using $h = (n+2)/(n+1)$, gives the first line of (9). For $w_k \geqslant 1$ the calculation is similar, but we integrate in reverse order (with respect to x first, then y).

A.2. *Comparative statics for η*
Equilibrium is determined by (15), (16) and (17). Using (15) define the supply price:

$$P_s(T, r, \eta) \equiv C'(T) - \left(\frac{\eta}{1+\eta}\right)^2 f'(T) \left[1 - \frac{\alpha}{(1+r)} \right] \quad \text{where} \quad \alpha(\eta) \equiv \frac{\eta}{(1+\eta)(1+\eta|\varepsilon|)}.$$

Differentiating (16) and (17), after substituting $P = P_s$, gives:

$$A\frac{\partial T}{\partial \eta} + T^2 D' \frac{\partial m}{\partial \eta} = -\frac{Tf'(T)}{(1+\eta)^2}[1 - (1+r)\gamma]$$

$$B\frac{\partial T}{\partial \eta} - E'(m)\frac{\partial m}{\partial \eta} = -\frac{Tf'(T)}{(1+\eta)^2}(1-\gamma)$$

where:

$$A \equiv (1+r)T\frac{\partial P_s}{\partial T} - \frac{Tf''(T)}{1+\eta} + mTD' > 0$$

and

$$B \equiv T\frac{\partial P_s}{\partial T} - \frac{Tf''(T)}{1+\eta} + \beta f'(T) > 0;$$

$$\beta(\eta, r) > 0; \quad \gamma(\eta, r) = \frac{a}{1+r}\{[2(1+r) - 3a](1+\eta|\varepsilon|) + a\eta|\varepsilon|(1+\eta)\}.$$

Solving:

$$\frac{\partial m}{\partial \eta} \overset{\text{sgn}}{=} A(1-\gamma) - B[1-(1+r)\gamma],$$

$$\frac{\partial(mT)}{\partial \eta} \overset{\text{sgn}}{=} (A - mTD')T(1-\gamma) - (BT + mE')[1-(1+r)\gamma].$$

It can be verified that $0 < \gamma < 1$, and that for r sufficiently large, $1 - (1+r)\gamma < 0$. These expressions can then be signed for the cases $r = 0$ and high r.

A.3. *Comparative Statics for r*
Similarly:

$$A\frac{\partial T}{\partial r} + T^2 D'\frac{\partial m}{\partial r} = -KT$$

where

$$K(T, \eta) \equiv C'(T) - \left(\frac{\eta}{1+\eta}\right)^2 f'(T),$$

and

$$B\frac{\partial T}{\partial r} - E'(m)\frac{\partial m}{\partial r} = -T\frac{\partial P_s}{\partial r} > 0.$$

Solving:

$$\frac{\partial m}{\partial r} \overset{\text{sgn}}{=} A\frac{\partial P_s}{\partial r} - BK$$

and

$$\frac{\partial(mT)}{\partial r} \overset{\text{sgn}}{=} (A - mTD')T\frac{\partial P_s}{\partial r} - (BT + mE')K$$

and $K > 0$ is sufficient for both derivatives to be negative.

A.4. *To prove that* $m^* T^* < m_f T_f$

Introduce another parameter, $t \in [0, 1]$, into the supply function:

$$P_s(T, r, \eta) \equiv C'(T) - \left(\frac{\eta}{1+\eta}\right)^2 f'(T) \left[1 - \frac{t\alpha}{(1+r)}\right]$$

and consider the equilibrium $m^* T^*(r, \eta, t)$. As in A.2., it is straightforward to show that

$$\frac{\partial(mT)}{\partial t} < 0 \; \forall r, \eta.$$

Also, when $t = 0$, A.2. and A.3. can be modified to show

$$\frac{\partial(mT)}{\partial r} < 0 \; \forall \eta,$$

and when $r = 0$,

$$\frac{\partial(mT)}{\partial \eta} < 0.$$

Applying these results:

$$m^* T^* = m^* T^*(r, \eta, 1) < m^* T^*(r, \eta, 0) < m^* T^*(0, \eta, 0) < m^* T^*(0, 0, 0) = m_f T_f.$$

References

Acemoglu, D. (1996). 'Credit constraints, investment externalities and growth'. In Booth and Snower (1996).

Acemoglu, D. (1997) 'Training and innovation in an imperfect labour market'. *Review of Economic Studies*, vol. 64, pp. 445–64.

Acemoglu, D. and Pischke, J.-S. (1998). 'Why do firms train? Theory and evidence'. *Quarterly Journal of Economics*, vol. 113, no. 1, pp.79–120.

Acemoglu, D. and Pischke, J.-S. (1999*a*). 'The structure of wages and investment in general training'. *Journal of Political Economy*, vol.107, no. 3, pp. 539–72.

Acemoglu, D. and Pischke, J.-S. (1999*b*). 'Beyond Becker: training in imperfect labour markets'. ECONOMIC JOURNAL, vol. 109, no. 453, pp. F112–42.

Becker, G. (1962). 'Investment in human capital: a theoretical analysis'. *Journal of Political Economy*, vol. 70, no. 5, part 2, pp. 9–49.

Bishop, J. H. (1997). 'What we know about employer-provided training'. *Research in Labor Economics*, vol. 16, pp.19–87.

Booth, A. L. and Snower, D. J. (1996). *Acquiring Skills.* Cambridge: Cambridge University Press.

Booth, A. L. and Zoega, G. (1999). 'Do quits cause under-training?'. *Oxford Economic Papers*, vol. 51, no. 2, pp. 374–86.

Card, D. E. and Krueger, A. B. (1995). *Myth and Measurement: The New Economics of the Minimum Wage.* Princeton University Press.

Chang, C. and Wang, Y. (1996). 'Human capital investment under asymmetric information: the Pigouvian conjecture revisited'. *Journal of Labour Economics*, vol. 14, no. 3, pp. 505–19.

Chapman, P. (1993). *The Economics of Training.* Hemel Hempstead: Harvester Wheatsheaf.

Confederation of British Industry (1997). *The Meaning of Training.* CBI Human Resources Brief, September.

Employment Department, Scottish Office and Welsh Office (1992). *People, Jobs and Opportunity.* Command Paper 1810, London: HMSO.

Finegold, D. and Crouch, C. (1994). 'A comparison of national institutions'. In (R. Layard, K. Mayhew and G. Owen, eds) *Britain's Training Deficit.* Aldershot: Avebury.

Green, F., Ashton, D., James, D. and Sung, J. (1999). 'The role of the state in skill formation: evidence from the Republic of Korea, Singapore, and Taiwan'. *Oxford Review of Economic Policy*, vol. 15, no. 1, pp. 82–96.

Greenhalgh, C. (1999). 'Adult vocational training policy in Britain and France'. *Oxford Review of Economic Policy*, vol. 15, no. 1, pp. 97–113.

Hamilton, J. H. (1987). 'Optimal wage and income taxation with wage uncertainty'. *International Economic Review*, vol. 28, no. 2, pp. 373–88.

Jones, I. (1988). 'An evaluation of YTS'. *Oxford Review of Economic Policy*, vol. 4, no. 3, pp. 54–71.

Layard, R., Robinson, P. and Steedman, H. (1995). 'Lifelong learning'. *Occasional Paper* No. 9, London School of Economics and Political Science, Centre for Economic Performance.

Lees, D. and Chiplin, B. (1970). 'The economics of industrial training', *Lloyds Bank Review*, vol. 96, pp. 29–41.

Stevens, M. (1994). 'A theoretical model of on-the-job training with imperfect competition'. *Oxford Economic Papers*, vol. 46, pp. 537–62.

Stevens, M. (1996). 'Transferable training and poaching externalities'. In Booth and Snower (1996).

Stevens, M. (1999). 'Human capital theory and UK vocational training policy'. *Oxford Review of Economic Policy*, vol. 15, no. 1, pp. 16–32.

Weitzman, M. (1974). 'Prices vs quantities'. *Review of Economic Studies*, vol. 41, pp. 477–91.

[7]

ELSEVIER

European Economic Review 47 (2003) 197–227

EUROPEAN
ECONOMIC
REVIEW

www.elsevier.com/locate/econbase

General training by firms, apprentice contracts, and public policy

James M. Malcomson[a],*, James W. Maw[b], Barry McCormick[c]

[a]*Department of Economics, University of Oxford, Manor Road Building, Oxford OX1 3UQ, UK*
[b]*Department of Economics, University of Wales Swansea, Swansea SA2 8PP, UK*
[c]*Department of Economics, University of Southampton, Southampton SO17 1BJ, UK*

Received 1 May 2001; accepted 12 February 2002

Abstract

Workers will not pay for general on-the-job training if contracts are not enforceable. Firms may if there are mobility frictions. Private information about worker productivities, however, prevents workers who quit receiving their marginal products elsewhere. Their new employers then receive external benefits from their training. In this paper, training firms increase profits by offering apprenticeships which commit firms to high wages for those trainees retained on completion. At these high wages, only good workers are retained. This signals their productivity and reduces the external benefits if they subsequently quit. Regulation of apprenticeship length (a historically important feature) enhances efficiency. Appropriate subsidies enhance it further. © 2002 Elsevier Science B.V. All rights reserved.

JEL classification: J24; J38

Keywords: General training; Contract enforceability; Apprenticeships; Regulation

1. Introduction

Certain transferable skills are most efficiently acquired in the workplace and many policy makers view this general training as potentially crucial for enhancing labour productivity. However, there is little consensus about whether market provision of such general training is efficient.[1] Becker (1964) showed how, in a competitive economy without distortions, workers invest in, and firms supply, efficient levels of general training. His analysis provides an intellectual underpinning for the absence in the US of

---

* Corresponding author. Tel.: +44 1865 271073; fax: +44 1865 271094.

E-mail address: james.malcomson@economics.ox.ac.uk (J.M. Malcomson).

[1] See, for example, US Department of Labor (1989) and Finegold and Soskice (1988).

198   *J.M. Malcomson et al. / European Economic Review 47 (2003) 197–227*

a national system of accreditation for post-high school training and was used to justify dismantling the UK system of trade apprenticeships. [2] Subsequent analysis of policy intervention has focused on the consequences of imperfect capital markets in which workers do not have access to funds to pay for general training. If, in a frictionless market, workers do not purchase transferable skills, firms will not supply them because trained workers can earn a wage equal to their trained marginal product at other firms and will quit unless this wage is matched by the training firm. The training firm will, as a result, be unable to recoup any return on the training provided. Consistent with this, Lynch (1992) finds that most on-the-job training in the US outside formal apprenticeships is firm-specific. Arguments of this type have prompted calls to facilitate workers' access to funds to pay for general training.

There are, however, reasons to think that workers' lack of access to capital to buy training is not the only reason for inefficient general training. The present paper explores other reasons, reasons that arise because training is a complex commodity provided by heterogeneous firms for heterogeneous trainees, and argues that these reasons are more consistent with the long history over several centuries of regulation of labour training provisions and the entitlements of employer and employee – see Earle (1989, Chapter 3). The complexity of training means that specifying the training to be provided in a way that is enforceable using a contract is problematic. We show that, as a result, trainees may not pay directly for general training even if they have the funds (or loans) to do so. Firms may pay for some general training if there are mobility frictions in skilled labour markets, as an extensive recent literature (discussed below) has shown. However, this leaves two crucial questions, which are the central concerns of our paper: How should the economic relationship between the training firm and its trainees be structured? What is the role of policy given that there is a potential for market failure in the provision of both training levels and the number of workers trained that a policy of providing loans will not overcome.

We analyse two forms of economic relationship between a general training firm and its trainees. In the first, a firm trains a worker and then sets a wage schedule that just persuades that worker not to quit given other firms' imperfect information about the worker's productivity. In the second, the firm again provides general training but offers a contract in which a worker accepts a low "apprentice" wage for a specified duration in return for a guaranteed high wage if retained after the end of the apprenticeship that ensures that the worker's productivity is revealed to the market. Apprentice contracts deliver higher profits to training firms and more trained workers.

Apprenticeship is a contractual arrangement for general training that has been common in many countries since at least medieval times, see Pirenne (1936), and is still widely used in Germany. Common features of many apprenticeships are that they last for a duration specified at the start, not just until the apprentice has demonstrated satisfactory acquisition of the appropriate skills, and that the apprentice receives a substantial pay increase at the end. Apprenticeships have, moreover, been subject to extensive

---

[2] Thus, for example, Lees and Chiplin (1970) base their criticism of the UK grant-levy system to support training in the Industrial Training Act (1964) on the Becker human capital model. The system was subsequently abolished.

J.M. Malcomson et al. / European Economic Review 47 (2003) 197–227   199

regulation by guilds and by governments. Particularly important historically has been regulation of their length. Regulation is regarded by some as improving the provision of training compared to what an unregulated market would provide, though policy differs considerably between countries – see, for example, Soskice (1994) and other chapters in Lynch (1994). This paper shows that regulation to increase apprenticeship length, coupled with a subsidy for each completed apprenticeship if the deadweight loss from raising taxes is not too high, can reduce the inefficiency in training levels and number of trainees. It is not, therefore, surprising that employers' organisations (guilds) and governments have sought to regulate the length of apprenticeships. Importantly, these conclusions apply even if training under an apprenticeship is no more effective at preventing trainees quitting than training without one. Thus, the difficulty of preventing premature quits by apprentices that historians such as Elbaum (1989) discuss in the context of the decline of apprenticeships in the US from the end of the 18th century is not sufficient reason to abandon their use even though, in our model, premature quitting will reduce both training levels and the numbers of apprentices trained.

The essential reasons for these conclusions are as follows. Because of the problems of specifying the training to be provided in a contract, workers will pay upfront only the expected value to them of the training that it is in firms' own interests to provide. As long as there are firms for which the cost of providing training is too high to be worthwhile, workers will not pay upfront for the full benefit they receive from the training by firms that actually train. With a large enough number of high cost training firms, they will not pay anything upfront.

While labour market frictions may result in firms providing some general training even if workers do not pay directly for it, there are two reasons recognised in the literature why the amount of such training may be inefficient. The first is that, when workers are free to quit without penalty, market frictions typically cannot prevent trainees using that freedom to capture some of the returns to training in the form of a higher wage even if they do not actually quit. Those returns are social returns to training that do not accrue to the training firm and so, as in the analysis of hold-up discussed extensively by Williamson (1985), firms invest too little in training. To the extent that formal apprenticeship contracts reduce the ability of trainees to capture returns from training, they reduce inefficiency by reducing hold-up. However, this role for apprenticeship contracts disappears if, as discussed by Elbaum (1989) for the US from the late 18th century on, apprenticeships cease to be effective in imposing additional penalties for premature quits.

The second reason why firm-supplied general training may be inefficient arises from asymmetric information about workers' productivities, see Chang and Wang (1996). When workers quit for jobs at other firms, that asymmetric information results in their wages being, on average, less than their marginal products. Thus part of the return to their general training goes to the new employers, an external benefit of training that is captured by neither trained workers nor training firms. Apprenticeship contracts mitigate this external effect. A contract commits at least one party to do something at some time in the future that it might not otherwise do when that time arrives. A practice well-documented for Germany, see Soskice (1994) and Acemoglu and Pischke

(1998), is that training firms retain some trainees as skilled workers at the end of their apprenticeships. By committing in advance to a high wage for these retained trainees, a training firm ensures that it retains only the better workers with marginal product at least as great as that wage. Retention at the end of the apprenticeship then reveals information about the productivity of those retained and thus increases the wage of those who subsequently quit. That both reduces the externality to the workers' new employers and makes trainees willing to work for a lower wage during the training period. As a result, training firms make higher profits from training than they would if they made no commitment to future wages but merely determined them on a period by period basis. The shorter the contract length, the sooner a training firm reveals its information about a trainee's productivity and thus the sooner quitting workers capture the returns to their training that accrue after they quit, rather than those returns being an external benefit to their new employers. However, the shorter the contract length, the sooner retained workers receive a wage equal to their full trained marginal product and thus the less time the training firm has in which to recoup the costs of training. The profit maximising contract length trades off these two effects. Although modelled here in the context of asymmetric information about workers' types, a similar phenomenon may arise with other market frictions that result in workers' current wages influencing (through, for example, bargaining as in Acemoglu (1997)) the wages they obtain when quitting. This role for apprenticeship contracts, unlike that of reducing hold-up, exists even when apprenticeships do not reduce the ability of trainees to capture returns from training.

Apprenticeship contracts cannot, however, in general prevent some of the return to general training being captured by trainees and, if they quit, by their new employers. As a result, even with apprenticeship contracts, trainees receive less training than is efficient. Moreover, when firms vary in the cost of providing training places, too few workers are trained. These two inefficiencies provide a natural role for regulation. We show that, by increasing the length of the training contract, regulation can increase the amount of training towards the efficient level. That is consistent with the historical tradition of regulation of the length of apprenticeships. Of course, regulating the length of a contract reduces the profits from training and thus the number of firms that train. Even so, it is socially worthwhile. The essential reason is that, at the profit maximising level of training, a small change in that level has only a second-order effect on profit and, hence, only a second-order effect on the number of workers trained. But, it has a first-order effect on the amount of training received by each trainee and, because of the externalities, this has a first-order effect on social welfare.

The adverse effect of regulation on the number of workers trained can be mitigated by a subsidy to firms for each completed apprenticeship. We show that, while it is worth providing some subsidy to increase the number of trainees if the deadweight loss of raising tax revenue is not too high, there are limits to what such subsidies can achieve. The difficulty of enforcing training by contract may, if the subsidy is large enough, result in firms using subsidised "trainees" simply as cheap labour without in fact providing training, an issue of serious concern with UK training policy, see Lee et al. (1990). That constrains the use of subsidies to enhance training, a constraint that can be important for policy.

J.M. Malcomson et al. / European Economic Review 47 (2003) 197–227   201

A number of recent papers have studied mobility frictions that result in firms investing in some general training for their employees when workers do not pay for it. These papers fall into four broad categories. Katz and Ziderman (1990), Chang and Wang (1996), and Acemoglu and Pischke (1998) analyse asymmetric information between training firms and other potential employers. Stevens (1994a, 1996), Acemoglu (1996), Acemoglu (1997), and Booth and Chatterji (1998) consider imperfect competition in skilled labour markets. Burdett and Smith (1996) and Loewenstein and Spletzer (1998) study matching frictions. Booth and Chatterji (1995) and Schlicht (1996) discuss general training that is a joint product with specific training. Acemoglu and Pischke (1999b) point to the common element. All these, like the model studied here, imply a worker's marginal product increasing with general training by more than the wage the firm pays, which enables the firm to capture some returns to general training. For a review, see Acemoglu and Pischke (1999a). Consistent with such frictions, Loewenstein and Spletzer (1998) conclude that firms in the US do indeed extract some of the returns to general training.

The present paper adds to this literature in a number of important respects. First, unlike most (but not all) of it, the paper does not start from an *assumption* that workers do not pay directly for general training but derives that as a conclusion. Second, it shows how contracts, and in particular traditional apprenticeship contracts, are more profitable for training firms than simply determining wages optimally at each date in response to the quit behaviour of trainees. And third, it shows the role for regulation, and in particular the historically important regulation of apprenticeship length, in improving on the market provision of general training. Finally, it addresses how policy towards both the level of training and the number of trainees should be formulated in a model in which the training level is not itself directly enforceable by contract.

Of recent papers on training, only Cantor (1990) and Hermalin (1990) share our focus on contract length. Contract length in Cantor reflects a trade-off between the firm's preference for a long pay-back period and the mitigation of a moral hazard problem – workers' unobserved effort influences the effectiveness of training but has a value to the worker that diminishes with training contract length. Cantor's analysis is directed at firm-specific training, not general training as here. Hermalin's concern with contract length is as a selection device in the face of worker adverse selection and the possible non-existence of equilibrium, again a very different issue from any discussed here. Neither paper analyses the role for policy.

The next section of the paper sets out the model of general training. Section 3 analyses the benchmark case with training provided without a contract in an unregulated market. Section 4 shows that firms make greater profits by using an apprenticeship type arrangement. Regulation is discussed in Section 5. In Section 6 we discuss historical evidence for the approach adopted here.

2. The model

Firms can each employ any number of workers with constant returns to scale. All untrained workers have productivity w^0 per period of time. A single worker can be

202   J.M. Malcomson et al. / European Economic Review 47 (2003) 197–227

trained on the job at each date if the firm sets up a training programme for that date at a fixed cost $k \in [0, \bar{k}]$. With training, a worker's productivity working for any firm increases to $w^0 + \hat{\gamma}g(c)$, where $c \geqslant 0$ is the variable cost incurred in training and $g(c)$ is strictly concave and continuously differentiable with $g(0) = 0$, $g'(c) \to \infty$ as $c \to 0$, and $g'(c) \to 0$ as $c \to \infty$. The value of $\hat{\gamma} \in \{\gamma, \bar{\gamma}\}$, with $0 < \gamma < 1 < \bar{\gamma}$, is the realisation of a random variable determining whether the worker is type γ or $\bar{\gamma}$ that is independently distributed across workers with mean 1. This realisation is unknown to firms and workers at the time of initial hiring and observed by only the training firm during training. The amount of training c is observed by trainees and by other firms once it has been provided but training is assumed to be too complex to specify its level in advance in an enforceable contract.

Firms differ only in the fixed cost k. Each knows its own fixed cost but this is unknown to anybody else and we assume that it is not possible for firms to establish a reputation for the value of k. The conditions on $g(c)$ ensure that some training is always worthwhile conditional on the fixed cost being incurred and so allow us to ignore the non-negativity constraint on c. There are $F(k)$ firms with fixed cost less than or equal to k, so the total number of *potential* training places is $F(\bar{k})$. We normalise the number of workers to 1 and assume both that $F(k)$ is twice continuously differentiable and that $F(\bar{k})$ is large (formally, $F(k) \to \infty$ as $k \to \bar{k}$).

For simplicity, we assume firms and workers are risk neutral and discount the future at the same rate r. Workers enter the labour force at age 0 and have working lifetime T. Since job turnover is important in practice, we generate that in a relatively simple way by workers of both types deciding at the rate ρ that they wish to leave their current employer for a new one for exogenous reasons independent of pay – for example, family circumstances dictating a move to another location. This can be viewed as a simple way of capturing that some turnover is efficient. The effective discount rate that a firm applies to the future profits from a particular worker is thus $r + \rho$. Firms are infinitely lived. To avoid over-complicating the analysis, we assume training takes place instantaneously at the start of employment and explain in the conclusion why, if the timing of training were endogenous, firms would be likely to provide training throughout an apprenticeship.

For what follows, it is convenient to treat time as continuous and to define

$$\beta(t) \equiv \frac{1 - e^{-rt}}{r}, \tag{1}$$

$$\delta(t) \equiv \frac{1 - e^{-(r+\rho)t}}{r + \rho}. \tag{2}$$

The function $\beta(t)$ is the capitalisation factor for turning a constant flow over a period of length t into a present discounted value, $\delta(t)$ the effective capitalisation factor for firms whose workers quit at the rate ρ. For notational simplicity, let $\beta \equiv \beta(T)$ and $\delta \equiv \delta(T)$, the capitalisation factors for the whole working lifetime T.

Training is general and thus valuable even if a worker quits, so the expected lifetime value of the output of a worker trained to the level c is $\beta[w^0 + g(c)]$, that of an untrained worker βw^0. Conditional on a worker being trained, the efficient level of training maximises the difference between the expected lifetime gain in output, $\beta g(c)$,

J.M. Malcomson et al. / European Economic Review 47 (2003) 197–227   203

and the cost. It is the solution to

$$\max_{c \geqslant 0} \beta g(c) - c, \tag{3}$$

that is, c^* uniquely defined by the first-order condition

$$\beta g'(c^*) = 1. \tag{4}$$

It is, however, efficient to train only sufficient workers for the gains from training $\beta g(c^*) - c^*$ to exceed the fixed cost k. Define k_1^* by

$$k_1^* = \beta g(c^*) - c^*. \tag{5}$$

It is never efficient to train more than $F(k_1^*)$ workers. That may, however, be more workers than there are to train. Define k_2^* by $F(k_2^*) = 1$, the highest k required to train all workers. Then the efficient number of workers to train is such that the fixed cost of the highest cost firms that train is k^* defined by

$$k^* = \min\{k_1^*, k_2^*\}. \tag{6}$$

There are, however, three reasons in the model why achieving efficient training may be problematic. One is that a contract to provide a specified level of training is unenforceable. The second is that, if low wages during training or upfront payments (bonds) are used to get workers to pay for training, firms with high values of k may take on workers in order to get cheap labour or the upfront payment without having any intention of actually providing the training. Indeed, since such firms make zero profits from employing an untrained worker, they would always do better by agreeing to train a worker, taking the upfront payment, and then going out of business. With a large number of high training cost firms that would cheat on any upfront payment by workers, workers are never prepared to offer such payments. While this conclusion follows straightforwardly from the assumptions about non-contractability and heterogeneity of firms, we emphasise it here because of its important implications for general training.[3]

The third reason why achieving efficient training may be problematic is that workers, even when apprenticed, can quit at any time without having to compensate the training firm for doing so.[4] That limits the extent to which a firm can recoup costs of training

---

[3] If workers know each firm's fixed costs of training (for example, when fixed costs are the same for all firms as in Acemoglu and Pischke (1998)), they know which firms will actually train and so, even with the amount of training non-contractable, are prepared to pay upfront for the full benefit they receive from training by those firms. In that case, an appropriately chosen contract can overcome the hold-up problem. If fixed costs of training are unknown to workers but there are only a finite number of high training cost firms, workers are prepared to pay upfront an amount that depends inversely on the probability that a randomly selected firm will fail to train. Thus this variation of the model is consistent with payment of initial fees for apprenticeships that were historically common in England, see Hamilton (1996). Incorporating this variation into the analysis complicates the exposition because the maximum upfront fee is endogenous but does not alter the result below that an unregulated market provides less than the efficient amount of training, see footnote 8. Thus, the basic conclusions of the paper apply even where limited upfront fees are paid.

[4] Hamilton (1995) argues that relatively few apprentices in her sample from Montreal actually deserted. That is, of course, entirely consistent with training firms designing contracts to induce them not to do so. Her sample provides substantial evidence of contracts being drawn up with precisely this purpose in mind.

204   *J.M. Malcomson et al. / European Economic Review 47 (2003) 197–227*

by employing trained workers at a wage below their marginal product once training has been completed. To see the implications of this, it is helpful to think of time periods being discrete and firms incurring a hiring cost to hire a new worker, and then to analyse the implications of having both the length of each period and the hiring cost go to zero. Consider the payoff to a worker whose type is known only to the current employer and who contemplates quitting for an alternative firm for the last period before stopping work at age T. The alternative firm can observe how much training c the worker has actually received once it has taken place – the lack of enforceability arises because of the problem of describing the appropriate training in a contract beforehand. It does not, however, know the worker's type. By the usual adverse selection argument (see, for example, Greenwald, 1986), the incumbent employer, who knows the worker's type, matches any outside offer no greater than the worker's productivity. Thus the expected profit to an alternative firm from any offer above the productivity of a less productive worker (with $\hat{\gamma}=\gamma$) is negative unless that worker is quitting for exogenous reasons – the *winner's curse*. As the length of the time periods goes to zero, however, the flow of workers quitting for exogenous reasons is negligible relative to the stock of less productive workers. (Formally, the flow is of order dt relative to the stock.) Thus, given the hiring cost, it is never profitable for an alternative firm to offer a wage higher than the wage the incumbent employer would pay to retain a less productive worker. It is, however, worth offering a wage equal to the lesser of that and of the average of the productivities of the two types of worker less the hiring cost. The reason is that such an offer may attract workers quitting for exogenous reasons, who consist of both types in the same proportions as in the population of workers. Competition between alternative employers ensures that they offer exactly that wage. As the hiring cost goes to zero, the wage available to a worker who quits thus approaches the productivity of a less productive type $w^0 + \gamma g(c)$.[5] Whichever type the worker is, it is worthwhile for the current employer to match that offer, so the worker stays and the worker's type remains known only to the current employer. With this outcome in the final period, the argument can be repeated for earlier periods to establish that the present discounted value of the remaining lifetime earnings that a training firm has to match at age $t \leqslant T$ to retain a trainee is

$$\beta(T-t)[w^0 + \gamma g(c)] \quad \text{for } 0 \leqslant t \leqslant T. \tag{7}$$

(It applies from $t = 0$ because we have assumed training is instantaneous.) A formal model underpinning this result is in Appendix A in the discussion paper version, Malcomson et al. (2002).[6]

---

[5] Formally, the argument involves taking the limit as the time interval goes to zero before taking the limit as the hiring cost goes to zero so that the hiring cost remains large enough to ensure that the expected productivity, less the hiring cost, of a worker hired at random from among the pool of less good workers plus those quitting for exogenous reasons is no greater than the wage the incumbent employer would pay to retain a less productive worker. The conclusion is different if limits are taken in the opposite order because that property no longer holds.

[6] Daron Acemoglu has pointed out that this model is not the only way of deriving a value less than 1 for γ in an expression like that in (7) for the present discounted value of the remaining lifetime earnings of a worker who quits.

J.M. Malcomson et al. / European Economic Review 47 (2003) 197–227   205

3. Training without contracts

In this section we analyse the benchmark case in which, as in Acemoglu and Pischke (1998), training firms do not offer training contracts but merely hire trainees, train them, and then determine each period what wage to offer them. Let $w(t)$ denote the wage paid by the firm at age t. Then the present discounted value of expected future wages received from the firm is $W(t,T)$ given by

$$W(t,T) = \int_t^T w(\theta) e^{-(r+\rho)(\theta-t)} \, d\theta. \tag{8}$$

In addition to this, the worker receives the wage $w^0 + \gamma g(c)$ at any date subsequent to quitting for exogenous reasons. By the standard calculation, the probability a worker employed at t has quit for exogenous reasons by θ is $1 - e^{-\rho(\theta-t)}$. Thus the expected future utility of a worker who does not quit at t is

$$W(t,T) + [w^0 + \gamma g(c)] \int_t^T e^{-r(\theta-t)}[1 - e^{-\rho(\theta-t)}] \, d\theta$$

$$= W(t,T) + [w^0 + \gamma g(c)][\beta(T-t) - \delta(T-t)]. \tag{9}$$

For the worker not to quit for other than exogenous reasons, this expected future utility must be at least as great as that in (7) for all t, which implies

$$W(t,T) \geqslant \delta(T-t)[w^0 + \gamma g(c)] \quad \text{for } 0 \leqslant t \leqslant T. \tag{10}$$

The expected profit $\Pi(k,c,W,T,S)$ of a firm with fixed training cost k from training a worker to the level c when the worker quits only for exogenous reasons is its expected revenue $\delta[w^0 + g(c)]$, less its training costs $k + c$ and its expected wage costs denoted by W, plus the expected present value S of any subsidy received for training paid at date T, that is,

$$\Pi(k,c,W,T,S) = \delta[w^0 + g(c)] - (k+c) - W + S. \tag{11}$$

Subsidies play a role in our discussion of regulation in Section 5.[7] We consider here the case in which it is not efficient to train all employees entering the market, that is $k_1^* < k_2^*$. Stevens (1994b, pp. 561–562) discusses the evidence for this being the relevant case for UK engineering during 1966–1988. Other cases are discussed in Appendix C in the discussion paper version, Malcomson et al. (2002). When $k_1^* < k_2^*$, an unregulated market will never train all workers entering the workforce. Thus, there will always be more employees entering the market than will be trained. Moreover, because of the finite lifetimes of workers, it is never efficient to start training workers who are not new entrants to the market because they have a shorter remaining working lifetime to generate returns on that training. New entrants not starting training straightaway, therefore, remain untrained for ever and earn market wage w^0 for

---

[7] The government could offer a subsidy to take on a trainee that is paid at the start of training but such a subsidy provides no advantage and exacerbates the gains to firms from promising to train and taking the subsidy but not actually training.

their remaining working lifetime. Untrained workers who quit for exogenous reasons can always get another job at the wage w^0. Thus the present discounted utility of a worker not successful in obtaining a training place on entering the market is βw^0 and the lifetime value of wages that equates the demand for workers with the supply of workers, denoted $\bar{W}$, is also βw^0. Thus to hire a trainee, a training firm must ensure that the utility from taking a training place, given by (9) for $t=0$, is no less than βw^0, which implies

$$W(0,T) \geqslant \delta[w^0 + \gamma g(c)] - \beta \gamma g(c). \tag{12}$$

But to prevent a trainee quitting immediately after being trained, the present discounted value of wages offered by the firm must satisfy the higher value given by (10) for $t=0$. Thus (10) for $t = 0$ is a binding constraint on the lifetime wages that firms must pay to retain trainees. A wage of $w^0 + \gamma g(c)$ at each t satisfies this constraint with equality both for $t=0$ and for all subsequent t so, with this wage, trained employees quit for an alternative employer only for exogenous reasons. Substitution of this wage into (11) gives expected profit from training without a contract when there is no subsidy:

$$\Pi^0(k,c) = \delta[w^0 + g(c)] - (k + c) - \delta[w^0 + \gamma g(c)], \tag{13}$$

$$= (1 - \gamma)\delta g(c) - (k + c). \tag{14}$$

Proposition 1. (i) *The level of training c^0 that maximises the expected profit of a training firm in the absence of a contract is given by*

$$\delta g'(c^0) = \frac{1}{1 - \gamma}. \tag{15}$$

Moreover, $c^0 < c^*$, the efficient level of training, and decreases with ρ, the exogenous quit rate, and with γ. (ii) *Training is carried out by only those firms with $k \leqslant k^0$ defined by*

$$k^0 = (1 - \gamma)\delta g(c^0) - c^0. \tag{16}$$

Moreover, $k^0 < k_1^*$ defined in (5), so fewer workers are trained than is efficient.

Proof. (i) It follows from (14) that, because $g(c)$ is differentiable and strictly concave, $\Pi^0(k,c)$ is a differentiable and strictly concave function of c. Thus the level of training that maximises expected profit is given uniquely by the first-order condition that corresponds to (15). Given $g(c)$ strictly concave, that $c^0 < c^*$ follows directly from comparison of (15) with (4) and $0 < \gamma < 1$, that c^0 is decreasing in ρ follows from (15) and the definition of δ in (2), and that c^0 is decreasing in γ follows from (15). (ii) It follows from (14) that k^0 defined in (16) is the highest fixed cost of training for which $\Pi^0(k, c^0) \geqslant 0$, so only firms with $k \leqslant k^0$ train. Note that c^* maximises $\beta g(c) - c$, whereas c^0 maximises $(1 - \gamma)\delta g(c) - c$, and that $\beta > (1 - \gamma)\delta$. It thus follows directly from comparison of (16) with (5) that $k^0 < k_1^*$. $\square$

J.M. Malcomson et al. / European Economic Review 47 (2003) 197–227   207

The intuition for these results is as follows. The level of training c^0 is less than c^*, the efficient level of training defined in (4) both because $\gamma > 0$ and because $\delta < \beta$. As long as $\gamma > 0$, the wage the worker can get by quitting increases with the amount of training the firm provides. Thus, the worker captures part of the return on the firm's investment, a form of Williamson's hold-up, and the firm under invests in training. In the extreme case as γ (and so also $\bar{\gamma}$) approaches 1, the firm is unable to earn any return on its investment in training and thus the amount of training approaches zero. At the other extreme, as γ approaches 0, the amount of training does not, however, approach the efficient level c^* because $\delta < \beta$. The reason for $\delta < \beta$, as is clear from (1) and (2), is that $\rho > 0$, that is, some employees quit for exogenous reasons. Because the training is general, it is valuable even when workers quit and so still generates a social return. However, the training firm does not capture any of the return arising after a worker quits for exogenous reasons. That return is received by the worker's new employer, who acquires an employee with expected productivity $w^0 + g(c)$ at a wage $w^0 + \gamma g(c)$. Only if both γ and ρ are zero do training firms invest efficiently. Moreover, the number of workers trained is then also efficient because the highest fixed cost that firms will incur in order to train is k^* defined in (6). [8]

4. Training contracts

In the analysis of the preceding section, training firms do not offer training contracts. They merely hire trainees, train them, and pay them a wage high enough to induce them not to quit. Alternatively, training firms may offer an apprenticeship contract with the following characteristics even if (by, for example, reducing the payoff to quitting below that in (7)) the contract does not itself reduce the ability of trainees to capture returns from training. Trainees undertake to work for a wage lower than if they were

---

[8] In the text, we have treated the case in which no worker makes an upfront payment because of the high probability that a randomly chosen firm will default on training by going out of business. (Formally, that probability approaches 1 because we have assumed $F(k) \rightarrow \infty$ as $k \rightarrow \bar{k}$.) If, however, $F(\bar{k})$ is finite, the probability that a randomly chosen firm trains is $F(k)/F(\bar{k})$ when k is the highest fixed cost at which it is profitable to train. In the absence of upfront payments, a worker receives a gain from joining a firm that trains of $\beta\gamma g(c)$, the difference between the expression in (7) at $t = 0$ and βw^0. The maximum upfront payment that would be made by a worker not knowing a firm's type, and so whether it will actually train, is thus $B = \beta\gamma g(c)F(k)/F(\bar{k})$. To a training firm, this payment is a lump sum independent of the training it actually chooses. (This is where the analysis differs crucially from the case where the level of training is contractable.) Thus training firms choose the same amount of training c^0 as without an upfront payment, which we already know to be below the efficient level c^*. The upfront payment, however, increases the highest fixed cost for which it is worth training to k^B given by

$$k^B = (1 - \gamma)\delta g(c^0) - c^0 + \frac{F(k^B)}{F(\bar{k})} \beta\gamma g(c^0),$$

which is greater than k^0. However, $k^B < k_1^* \equiv \beta g(c^*) - c^*$ because, by definition, c^* maximises $\beta g(c) - c$, so $\beta g(c^*) - c^* > \beta g(c^0) - c^0$, and $\beta > (1 - \gamma)\delta + \gamma\beta F(k^B)/F(\bar{k})$. Thus the number of workers trained is also still below the efficient level.

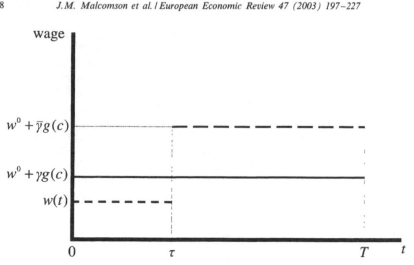

Fig. 1. Effect of training contract on wages.

hired without a contract for a specified period in return for an assurance of a higher (skilled) wage if the firm continues to employ them after that period. The higher wage is set so that the training firm offers to continue the employment of more able trainees but not of less able ones. The information contained in that offer ensures that more able trained workers can earn their marginal product with any other employer and hence, by competition, with their training firm. A training firm's incentives to train are then unaffected if a trained worker quits after this stage because that worker's wage equals the marginal product. We shall show that this contract is more profitable, and that as a result more workers are trained.

In analysing the implications of such a contract, we again consider the case in which it is not efficient to train all workers ($k_1^* < k_2^*$). Formally, the training contract specifies a period of length τ (which we call *contract length*) after which the training firm is committed, if it subsequently employs the trained worker, to pay a specified wage w strictly between the productivity of a worker of type γ trained to whatever level c the firm wishes to commit itself to provide, namely $w^0 + \gamma g(c)$, and the productivity of a worker of type $\bar{\gamma}$ trained to that level, namely $w^0 + \bar{\gamma} g(c)$. The firm is not *required* to employ the worker after τ – it merely commits itself to the wage w if it does so. The contract also specifies $w(t)$, for $0 \leqslant t \leqslant \tau$, the wage paid at time $t \leqslant \tau$ after its start. [9]

---

[9] This contract is similar to the "up-or-out" contracts analysed in Kahn and Huberman (1988), Waldman (1990) and Prendergast (1993) for specific investments. Other important differences are that here the contract induces firms, rather than employees, to invest in training and the date at which the "up-or-out" decision is made (τ) is agreed as part of the contract, not given exogenously, which enables us to study the role of contract length.

J.M. Malcomson et al. / European Economic Review 47 (2003) 197–227   209

The effect of this contract on the wage of workers trained to a given level c is illustrated in Fig. 1. With no contract as in the previous section, the winner's curse ensures all workers earn wage $w^0 + \gamma g(c)$ throughout their lifetime T, just enough to induce them not to quit. With a contract of length τ, more able workers are retained at the end of the contract and earn their marginal product $w^0 + \bar{\gamma} g(c)$ from τ on. Less able workers are not retained and obtain another job with wage equal to their marginal product $w^0 + \gamma g(c)$ from τ on. Because workers do not know their own type until it is revealed by the firm, their expected wage from τ on if they stay until the end of their contract is greater than $w^0 + \gamma g(c)$, so the wage $w(t)$ during the period up to τ can be reduced below $w^0 + \gamma g(c)$ without inducing them to quit. Thus, by using a contract that makes it credible to reveal workers' types at the end of the contract period, a training firm induces trainees to accept lower wages during the contract period.

4.1. Incentive compatibility for training firms

Revelation will, of course, occur only if the amount of training actually provided by the firm makes it profitable to retain more able trained workers and unprofitable to retain less able ones. There are three possibilities to consider. The first is that the training c actually provided is such that $w^0 + \gamma g(c) \geqslant w$. In this case, the wage w is no higher than the wage $w^0 + \gamma g(c)$ a trained worker can obtain elsewhere, so the firm has to pay $w^0 + \gamma g(c)$ to retain the worker. This reduces to the case of the previous section for which we already know it is optimal for the firm to set $c = c^0$ and receive profit $\Pi^0(k, c^0)$. As long as the firm can make greater profits by setting w at some level such that it actually trains to $c \neq c^0$, it is optimal for the firm to offer a training contract.

The second possibility is that the training c actually provided by the firm is such that $w^0 + \gamma g(c) < w < w^0 + \bar{\gamma} g(c)$. We show in Appendix B in the discussion paper version, Malcomson et al. (2002), that the training wage can be selected so that the firm wishes to retain even a less good trainee (of type γ) during the period up to date τ. The essential reason is that, as the apprenticeship progresses, the expected gains to a trainee from staying to the end loom closer, so returns to quitting early decrease. Thus, during that period the training firm receives the expected output of the trained worker, $\delta(\tau)[w^0 + g(c)]$. On completion of the contract, a trained worker is either retained by the training firm at wage w or seeks a job in another firm. It is never in the firm's interest to retain a less good worker (type γ) since such a worker has productivity less than w. It is always in the training firm's interest to retain a better worker (type $\bar{\gamma}$) since such a worker has productivity greater than w. [10] By retaining a worker, therefore, the firm signals that the worker is a good type. Outside firms will then be prepared to offer such a worker a wage of $w^0 + \bar{\gamma} g(c)$ and the firm will have

---

[10] Many trainees are in fact retained. For Germany, Acemoglu and Pischke (1998) report that 84% of apprentices stay on, at least initially, with their training firm. Soskice (1994, p. 56) argues that "the postapprentices which a non-training company will be likely to hire are those whom their training companies have chosen not to keep".

to match that offer to retain the worker. The firm's profits from training are zero from τ on and thus overall are given by (11) with δ replaced by $\delta(\tau)$: [11]

$$\Pi(k, c, W, \tau, S) \equiv \delta(\tau)[w^0 + g(c)] - (k + c) - W + S, \tag{17}$$

where W is the total expected wage payment up to τ and S is the present value of any subsidy to training paid at the end of the contract period.

The third possibility is that the training c actually provided by the firm is such that $w^0 + \bar{\gamma}g(c) \leqslant w$. In this case it is not profitable to retain a less productive trainee (type γ) and, even if the firm retains a more productive trainee (type $\bar{\gamma}$), it cannot make positive profits from doing this, so its profits from training are the same as in (17). Thus the analysis for the previous case applies to this case too. [12]

Lemma 1. *With an apprentice contract that specifies τ, w and W, the optimal training level c for a firm that trains is given by*

$$\delta(\tau)g'(c) = 1. \tag{18}$$

The optimal apprentice training level is increasing in τ.

Proof. Given a training contract that specifies τ, w and W, the firm chooses the amount of training c to maximise $\Pi(k, c, W, \tau, S)$ given by (17). [13] It follows from (17) that, because $g(c)$ is differentiable and strictly concave, $\Pi(k, c, W, \tau, S)$ is a differentiable and strictly concave function of c. Thus the level of training that maximises expected profit is given uniquely by the first-order condition that corresponds to (18). Moreover, from (2), $\delta(\tau)$ is increasing in τ. Thus, given $g(c)$ strictly concave, it follows from (18) that training c is an increasing function of contract length τ. $\square$

The intuition for this result is simply that the longer τ, the longer is the period for which the firm receives returns to training and thus the more training it provides. This

---

[11] A training firm receives profits from retaining a good worker at the end of the apprenticeship for the period until outside firms make that worker an offer of $w^0 + \bar{\gamma}g(\tilde{c})$. Formally, we consider the limit as this period goes to zero. If the period is longer, the optimal contract length is reduced and the training firm will, as Soskice (1994) argues for Germany, continue to make profits from retaining the better trained workers after the end of their training contract. The same applies if there is a continuum of trainee types. Keeping a trainee on at the end of the apprenticeship then reveals only that the trainee's type is above a threshold and firms continue to make profits because of adverse selection among those types retained. Competition between firms in initial hiring will then ensure that firms do not recoup all the training costs by the end of the apprenticeship, again as Soskice (1994) argues for Germany. We do not pursue this issue here.

[12] Because the wage available from other firms is $w^0 + \gamma g(c)$, there is potential for a profitable renegotiation between the training firm and a more productive trainee to reduce the wage to a level at which both gain by having the firm retain the employee. The trainee can, however, ensure that the renegotiated wage is strictly above $w^0 + \gamma g(c)$ because, for $w^0 + \gamma g(c)$, a threat to quit is credible. Moreover, once the firm agrees to a wage strictly above $w^0 + \gamma g(c)$, it reveals the worker to be of the more productive type so that, by the argument for the previous case, outside firms bid the wage up to $w^0 + \bar{\gamma}g(c)$. Thus the firm still makes no profits from retaining the trainee.

[13] Strictly, this maximisation is subject to the inequality constraint that c is not so large that, given W, the trainee quits. The choice of optimal contract, however, ensures that W is always such that this constraint does not bind.

J.M. Malcomson et al. / European Economic Review 47 (2003) 197–227   211

relationship is independent of worker type because worker types are unknown at the time of training though, as shown below, τ depends on γ in equilibrium. The contract cannot, however, be longer than $\tau = T$, so the highest level of training that can be induced in this way is $\bar{c}$ defined by

$$\delta g'(\bar{c}) = 1. \tag{19}$$

The firm can therefore be induced to provide any amount of training $c \in [0, \bar{c}]$ by a contract of length $\tau(c)$ that satisfies (18) for that c. The definition of $\delta(\tau)$ in (2) can be used to write

$$\tau(c) \equiv -\frac{1}{r + \rho} \ln \left[1 - \frac{r + \rho}{g'(c)} \right] \quad \text{for } c \in [0, \bar{c}]. \tag{20}$$

4.2. Incentive compatibility for trainees

We next determine the constraints imposed by workers' incentives to join, and remain in, an apprenticeship. For this, we derive the implied relationship between the amount of training, c, and the total wages paid during the contract period, W. The expected remaining lifetime utility at $t < \tau$ from a trainee staying with the training firm can be derived as follows. Let $W(t, \tau)$ denote the expected present discounted value of wages over the remainder of the contract. Given training to level c, a worker who quits for exogenous reasons before the end of the contract receives wage $w^0 + \gamma g(c)$ from the date of quitting. A worker who has not quit for exogenous reasons before the end of the contract receives the wage $w^0 + \bar{\gamma} g(c)$ from τ on if of type $\bar{\gamma}$ and $w^0 + \gamma g(c)$ if of type γ, with expected value $w^0 + g(c)$. As in the case without a contract, the probability a worker employed at t has quit for exogenous reasons by θ is $1 - e^{-\rho(\theta - t)}$. The expected value of all these components for $\tau \leqslant T$ is

$$W(t, \tau) + [w^0 + \gamma g(c)] \int_t^\tau e^{-r(\theta - t)} [1 - e^{-\rho(\theta - t)}] \, d\theta$$

$$+ \{[w^0 + \gamma g(c)][1 - e^{-\rho(\tau - t)}] + [w^0 + g(c)] e^{-\rho(\tau - t)}\} \int_\tau^T e^{-r(\theta - t)} \, d\theta$$

$$= W(t, \tau) + [w^0 + \gamma g(c)][\beta(\tau - t) - \delta(\tau - t)]$$

$$+ \{[w^0 + \gamma g(c)] + (1 - \gamma) g(c) e^{-\rho(\tau - t)}\}[\beta(T - t) - \beta(\tau - t)], \tag{21}$$

$$= W(t, \tau) + [w^0 + \gamma g(c)][\beta(T - t) - \delta(\tau - t)]$$

$$+ (1 - \gamma) g(c) e^{-\rho(\tau - t)}[\beta(T - t) - \beta(\tau - t)]. \tag{22}$$

To induce a trainee to complete the contract, therefore, the expected value of wages paid during the contract period must ensure that this expression is at least as great as that in (7) for all $0 \leqslant t < \tau$, which gives the following incentive compatibility condition

212   J.M. Malcomson et al. / European Economic Review 47 (2003) 197–227

for a worker to complete the contract:

$$W(t,\tau) \geqslant \delta(\tau - t)[w^0 + \gamma g(c)]$$

$$- (1 - \gamma)g(c)e^{-\rho(\tau - t)}[\beta(T - t) - \beta(\tau - t)] \quad \text{for all } 0 \leqslant t < \tau. \quad (23)$$

Condition (23) has an intuitive interpretation: The apprentice expects to be paid a sum equal to the discounted value of potential outside earnings up to the end of the apprenticeship less the present value of the increase in earnings from completing the apprenticeship. When it is not efficient to train all workers, (23) is a binding constraint at $t = 0$ on wages during the contract because the expected utility from quitting immediately after being trained, given by (7) for $t = 0$, is strictly greater than βw^0. The lowest present discounted value of wages W for which this constraint is satisfied at $t = 0$ for a contract of length $\tau(c)$ is

$$W = \delta[\tau(c)][w^0 + \gamma g(c)] - (1 - \gamma)g(c)e^{-\rho\tau(c)}\{\beta - \beta[\tau(c)]\}. \quad (24)$$

Of course, because potential trainees do not know a firm's fixed cost of training, they cannot rule out the possibility that a firm with a high fixed cost of training will agree to a training contract without intending actually to train if trainee wages are low enough for it to be profitable to do so. Because, however, workers can observe whether they have in fact been trained, such behaviour can be prevented by an initial training wage greater than w^0. The reason is as follows. An untrained worker can always quit to earn w^0 and will do so, thus ensuring the firm makes a loss from offering the training contract, unless the remainder of the training contract provides utility higher than provided by the wage w^0. But if the remainder of the training contract provides that higher utility, a firm that promises to train but does not do so will make a loss from a training contract if the initial wage is greater than w^0. [14] Moreover, for any W satisfying (24), there exists a wage path $w(t)$ with $w(0) > w^0$ that ensures (23) is satisfied for all $0 \leqslant t < \tau(c)$, so the trainee will not quit before $\tau(c)$, without inducing the firm to dismiss a less good trainee before $\tau(c)$. This is shown formally in Appendix B in the discussion paper version, Malcomson et al. (2002). The basic intuition is that, as the apprenticeship proceeds, the gains from staying to the end become closer and increasingly dominate any short-term gains from quitting early. Thus the incentive constraints become weaker over time.

---

[14] If trainees do not observe whether they have actually been trained, they can be sure that a firm will not agree to a training contract unless it intends to train only if expected wages over the whole training contract are no less than the untrained wage, that is, $W \geqslant \delta[\tau(c)]w^0$. The reason is as follows. Untrained workers will not be kept on at the end of the training contract and will be paid only w^0 in the market thereafter. Because there are lots of high cost training firms which will never train (formally, $F(\bar{k}) \to \infty$), the probability of being trained in a randomly chosen firm is negligible unless there is self selection of firms. Thus, one of two conditions needs to be satisfied for potential trainees to agree to a contract. One of these is that trainees receive higher utility even if the firm does not train than they would by not taking on a training contract. The other is that a firm makes less profit by signing a training contract if it does not in fact intend to train than if it simply paid the wage w^0. Both of these are equivalent to the condition specified. Substitution for W from (24) allows that condition to be written as the constraint $\gamma\delta[\tau(c)] - (1 - \gamma)e^{-\rho\tau(c)}[\beta - \beta(\tau(c))] \geqslant 0$. In this case, it turns out that the additional constraint is always binding with the optimum contract, which implies an optimal contract length that is independent of the function $g(c)$. The length of the apprenticeship is then the same for different trades for which γ, ρ and r are the same even if the function $g(c)$ is different.

J.M. Malcomson et al. / European Economic Review 47 (2003) 197–227   213

4.3. Optimal training contracts

We next determine the optimal training contract. Substitution from (24) into (17) gives the expected profit from choosing τ such that training is to level c:

$$\tilde{\Pi}(k,c,S) = (1-\gamma)g(c)\{\delta[\tau(c)] + e^{-\rho\tau(c)}[\beta - \beta(\tau(c))]\} - (k+c) + S. \qquad (25)$$

To compare the outcomes with and without training contracts, it is convenient to define

$$\tilde{\delta}(\tau) \equiv \delta(\tau) + e^{-\rho\tau}[\beta - \beta(\tau)]. \qquad (26)$$

This corresponds to an adjusted discount factor that can be interpreted in the following way. The actual discount rate of both firm and worker is r, corresponding to the discount factor $\beta(\tau)$. Trainees quit at the rate ρ. If a trainee quits during the contract period, the firm receives no more return on its investment, so the effective discount rate during the contract period becomes $r + \rho$, corresponding to the discount factor $\delta(\tau)$. Once the contract period has ended, however, workers receive all the returns to training whether or not they quit, so the quit rate ρ no longer influences the effective discount rate after the end of the contract. Moreover, these returns are passed back to firms in the form of lower wages during the contract period. The present discounted value of an increase in the post-contract wage that gets passed back to the firm is $\beta - \beta(\tau)$, which increases with the length of the post-contract period. But this accrues only if the trainee does not quit before the end of the contract period, so it is multiplied by the probability $e^{-\rho\tau}$. The discount factor $\tilde{\delta}(\tau)$ adjusts $\delta(\tau)$ for this. From the definitions of $\beta(t)$ and $\delta(t)$ in (1) and (2), note that $\tilde{\delta}(0) = \beta$ and $\tilde{\delta}(T) = \delta$. Thus, if the contract lasts the whole lifetime T so there is no post-contract period, the effective discount factor is δ whereas, if the contract has zero length so the post-contract period consists of the whole working lifetime, the effective discount rate becomes β. Moreover,

$$\tilde{\delta}'(\tau) = \delta'(\tau) - \rho e^{-\rho\tau}[\beta - \beta(\tau)] - e^{-\rho\tau}\beta'(\tau)$$

$$= -\rho e^{-\rho\tau}[\beta - \beta(\tau)] < 0 \quad \text{for } \tau < T. \qquad (27)$$

We thus have

$$\tilde{\delta}(0) = \beta,$$

$$\beta > \tilde{\delta}(\tau) > \delta \quad \text{for } 0 < \tau < T,$$

$$\tilde{\delta}(T) = \delta. \qquad (28)$$

Profit $\tilde{\Pi}(k,c,S)$ defined in (25) can then be written in terms of $\tilde{\delta}[\tau(c)]$ as

$$\tilde{\Pi}(k,c,S) = (1-\gamma)\tilde{\delta}[\tau(c)]g(c) - (k+c) + S. \qquad (29)$$

Proposition 2. *Use of an apprentice contract increases the profit a firm receives from training. It is profitable for more firms to train, and more workers are trained, with an apprentice contract than without.*

Proof. Consider the optimal training c^0 when no contract is used given by (15). It follows from comparison of (15) with (18) in Lemma 1 that to induce training of c^0

214   J.M. Malcomson et al. / European Economic Review 47 (2003) 197–227

with an apprentice contract would require a contract of length τ^0 satisfying $\delta(\tau^0) = (1 - \gamma)\delta$, which implies $\tau^0 < T$ since, by definition, $\delta(T) = \delta$. It follows from (28) that $\tilde{\delta}(\tau^0) > \delta$. It then follows from comparison of (14) with (29) that, when there is no subsidy, profit is greater when c^0 is achieved with an apprentice contract than with no contract. Since c^0 maximises expected profit when there is no contract, it follows that a training firm always makes greater expected profit with a contract than without. The highest fixed cost of training for which profits are non-negative is

$$k(c,S) \equiv (1 - \gamma)\tilde{\delta}[\tau(c)]g(c) - c + S. \tag{30}$$

Because profits for any given k are higher with an apprentice contract than without, more firms train and the number of workers trained is higher. □

Proposition 3. *The level of training and the number of trainees under apprentice contracts are lower than is efficient. The length of the apprentice contract is strictly less than the whole working lifetime T.*

Proof. The optimal training $\tilde{c}$ with a training contract ensures that the derivative of expected profit with respect to c, namely

$$\frac{\partial \tilde{\Pi}(k,\tilde{c},S)}{\partial c} = (1 - \gamma)\{\tilde{\delta}[\tau(\tilde{c})]g'(\tilde{c}) + \tilde{\delta}'[\tau(\tilde{c})]\tau'(\tilde{c})g(\tilde{c})\} - 1, \tag{31}$$

is either zero, or positive but with $\tau(\tilde{c}) = T$, the longest possible contract length. (Note that $\tau'(c) > 0$.) However, from (27) and (28), $\tilde{\delta}(T) = \delta$ and $\tilde{\delta}'(T) = 0$. It thus follows from (18) in Lemma 1 that the derivative in (31) is negative for $\tau(c) = T$, which implies that $\tau(\tilde{c}) < T$. Thus the optimal training contract certainly lasts less than the trainee's whole working lifetime T. It also follows from (18) that $\tilde{c} < \bar{c}$ defined in (19). Moreover, since $\bar{c}$ is less than the efficient level c^* whenever $\rho > 0$, training is below the efficient level. It thus follows from (30) that, in the absence of a subsidy, $k(\tilde{c},0) < k_1^*$ defined in (5), so the number of workers trained is also below the efficient level. □

The intuition for these results is as follows. As explained in the previous section, one reason for training being inefficiently low when there is no training contract is that the training firm does not capture any of the return to training arising after the trainee quits for exogenous reasons. That return is received by the worker's new employer, who acquires an employee with expected productivity $w^0 + g(c)$ at a wage $w^0 + \gamma g(c)$. A training contract provides a mechanism for the training firm to commit to ensuring its trainee receives a wage equal to marginal product after the end of the training contract, the period from τ to T in Fig. 1. Thus, when an exogenous quit occurs after the end of the training contract, the worker's new employer does not capture any of the return to training. That return goes to the worker who, in turn, passes it to the training firm in the form of lower wages during the training contract. So the training firm captures more of the return to training. To see this more formally, consider the limiting case of no exogenous quits, $\rho = 0$. Then, from (1) and (2), $\delta(t) = \beta(t)$ and thus, from (26), $\tilde{\delta}(t) = \beta$. In that case, expected profits from any given level of training

J.M. Malcomson et al. / European Economic Review 47 (2003) 197–227   215

Table 1
Market apprenticeship length (years)

r	$T = 25$		$T = 40$	
	γ: 0.5	0.9	0.5	0.9
5% pa	8.8	1.5	11.3	1.8
10% pa	6.1	1.0	6.8	1.0
20% pa	3.4	0.5	3.5	0.5

with a contract, $\tilde{\Pi}(k, c, 0)$ in (29), are identical to those without a contract, $\Pi^0(k, c)$ in (13), for any given k and c, so the optimal training level must also be the same.

By reducing the length of the contract, the training firm reduces the amount of the return to training that goes as an external benefit to the new employers of quitting workers because that increases the length of the post-contract period (τ to T in Fig. 1). However, it also reduces the length of time during which the training firm receives returns to training, the period from 0 to τ in Fig. 1. That, via (18), reduces the amount of training the firm provides. The optimal length of contract trades off these two effects. The optimal length depends in general on the form of the function $g(c)$ about which we have little information. There is, however, one case, the limiting one with no exogenous quits ($\rho = 0$), in which the optimal length of the contract is independent of the form of the function $g(c)$ and this case may be a useful guide for cases in which efficient turnover is low. For $\rho = 0$, recall that $\tilde{\delta}(t) = \beta$. Then $\tilde{\delta}'(t) = 0$ and, from (31), the first-order condition derived from setting $\partial \tilde{\Pi}(k, \tilde{c}, S)/\partial c = 0$ can be written

$$\beta g'(\tilde{c}) = \frac{1}{1 - \gamma}. \tag{32}$$

Use of this in (20) with $\rho = 0$ gives

$$\tau(\tilde{c}) \equiv -\frac{1}{r}\ln[1 - r\beta(1 - \gamma)]. \tag{33}$$

Thus values of $\tau(\tilde{c})$ can be calculated directly for given values of r, γ and T. (β is determined by r and T.)

Some sample values are given in Table 1. For the calculations, we have used working lifetimes of 25 and 40 years, which span what would seem reasonable historically given mortality rates and the fact that people may change occupations, thus reducing the useful life of skills. We have used real discount rates of 5%, 10% and 20% per year, since these need to allow for depreciation of skills that we have not incorporated explicitly into the model. There is little evidence on what would be reasonable values for γ, the proportion of the average value of acquired skills a trainee can earn by quitting before the end of the contract. Acemoglu and Pischke (1998, Table III) give point (but not very precise) estimates for Germany that completing an apprenticeship, but not staying with the training firm afterwards, adds between 0.024 and 0.041 to log wages. These can be interpreted as estimates of $\gamma g(c)/w^0$. Staying with the training firm for the initial period after training adds another 0.012 to log wages, which gives a point estimate for $\bar{\gamma}g(c)/w^0$ of between 0.036 and 0.053. These figures suggest point estimates for $\gamma/\bar{\gamma}$ of between 2/3 and 3/4. Since $\bar{\gamma} > 1$, $\gamma/\bar{\gamma}$ is a lower bound for γ. Because these estimates are not very precise, we use values of 0.5 and 0.9 for γ in the table. It is clear from the table that the calculations are not very sensitive to the working lifetime, particularly with the higher discount rates, but differ a lot between the two values of γ. It is, however, reassuring that the contract lengths given in Table 1 encompass the lengths of apprenticeships typically experienced historically. [15]

5. Regulation of training contracts

The previous section has shown that, even with a training contract, the amount of training $\tilde{c}$ and the number of workers trained in an unregulated market are less than the efficient levels whenever ρ and/or $\gamma > 0$. This section discusses appropriate policies of regulation and subsidy of training contracts under these circumstances. An obvious role for regulation is to monitor training by, for example, regulating the curriculum of training programmes and setting tests of competence. If this were 100% effective, it would make the amount of training verifiable and the issues discussed here would go away. Since, however, there are in practice many dimensions to quantity and quality of training, the cost of full monitoring may well be prohibitively high. The issues discussed here then continue to apply to any aspect of training that is not fully monitored by the regulator.

One role for regulation is in trying to ensure that trainees lose out by quitting early, which is analytically equivalent to reducing γ. The strict rules imposed by the medieval guilds against working as a journeyman before completion of an apprenticeship would have served this purpose by preventing competitors competing away apprentices. For regulation of this type, apprenticeships have the advantage that the rules need to be imposed only for the length of the apprenticeship τ, not for the worker's whole working life as in the case without a training contract. But even if γ can be reduced to zero, this will still not achieve the efficient level of training as long as $\rho > 0$.

Other policies that might be considered by government are regulation of the length of the apprentice contract and a subsidy for some observable measure of training. There are two margins of concern to a regulator. The first is the amount of training for each employee trained. The second is the total number of employees trained. The regulator can affect the latter by offering a lump sum subsidy per trainee that increases the profits from training (29) and so, as can be seen from (30), induce firms with higher fixed costs of training to take on trainees. However, a lump sum subsidy does not affect the training received by each trainee because it does not affect the first-order

---

[15] There are a number of ways in which apprenticed workers traditionally suffered greater penalties from quitting than other workers, see Hamilton (1995). To the extent that these penalties reduce trainees' ability to capture returns from training, they can be incorporated into the model by a lower value of γ for apprenticed than for other workers. In that case, firms make higher profits with an apprenticeship than without one even with $\rho = 0$. There is then an additional reason for the use of apprenticeships which reinforces that discussed here. Since the value of γ in the period after the apprenticeship ends affects only wage differentials, not the amount of training or the length of the apprenticeship, the optimal apprenticeship length is then given by the length in the table that corresponds to the value of γ *during* the apprenticeship.

J.M. Malcomson et al. / European Economic Review 47 (2003) 197–227   217

condition derived from differentiating profits in (29) with respect to c. The regulator cannot observe training but can indirectly influence the training each trainee receives by regulating the length of training contract because there is a direct relationship between the length of the contract and the amount of training via (18). [16] However, the longest possible length of contract is the whole working lifetime T and thus the highest amount of training consistent with (18) is $\bar{c}$ defined in (19). So $\bar{c}$ is an upper bound on the amount of training that can be attained with these regulatory instruments.

Regulation of contract length is ineffective without at least some regulation of the wage. Without wage regulation, the firm and the trainee could effectively evade regulation of contract length because the firm could make the privately optimal contract nominally satisfy the regulation by extending its length by the required amount, but with a wage in this extension equal to the expected trained marginal product, and guaranteeing not to dismiss less good trainees. Such evasion can be prevented by regulating the total discounted wage payment over the whole contract to the value of W given by (24) for the given regulated length and the value of c that satisfies (18). [17] The formal regulation would then be that any firm wishing to pay more than the untrained wage w^0 to a worker who has not had a previous training contract must offer the regulated training contract. [18]

There are also limitations on the amount of subsidy that can be paid. If the subsidy is large enough, it will be worth firms with high training costs offering a training contract in order to attract the subsidy even though they do not intend to train. To prevent that requires the amount of the subsidy to be less than the difference between expected wages under a training contract and expected wages to an untrained worker over the length of the training contract. That gives a constraint on the maximum subsidy of

$$S \leqslant W - \delta[t(c)]w^0 \quad \text{for } S > 0. \tag{34}$$

(Recall that S is defined as the expected present discounted value at the start of a contract of the subsidy paid at the end.) [19] Substitution for W from (24) and use of the definition of $\tilde{\delta}(\tau)$ in (26) allows that constraint to be written

$$S \leqslant g(c)\{\delta[\tau(c)] - (1 - \gamma)\tilde{\delta}[\tau(c)]\} \quad \text{for } S > 0. \tag{35}$$

With W fixed, the firm chooses c to maximise its expected revenue less the training costs over the regulated length of contract. That is the same c that maximises expected

---

[16] Alternatively, it can do so by offering a subsidy that increases with the length of training. It turns out that this has no advantages over regulation of the contract length, so we do not pursue it here.

[17] In Germany, unions regulate pay of apprentices which can serve equally well. We are grateful to Daron Acemoglu for pointing this out.

[18] If the regulation were limited to those offering training contracts, firms could choose to train without a training contract if that were more profitable. To avoid that would require another constraint on regulation that we do not explore here.

[19] Regulating a wage W above that determined by the market would relax this constraint but not in a way that is helpful to the regulator. The only reason to offer a subsidy is to induce firms with higher fixed costs of training to train. Raising the wage has the opposite effect. It is the difference between S and W that determines the highest fixed cost for which it is profitable to train. Thus raising W does not relax the constraint in a way that enables the regulator to increase the number of workers trained.

profits given in (25) for given τ and W and thus the relationship between the regulated length τ and the amount of training c is simply the first-order condition (18). Given this, we can think in terms of the regulator choosing c rather than τ and then use (18) to determine the contract length that must be regulated in order to achieve that c. For any $c \in [0, \bar{c}]$, there is always a τ that implements that c.

We assume the regulator wishes to maximise the social gains from training but, in the conventional way, allowing for a proportional cost α of subsidies to account for distortions arising from having to raise revenue from taxation. These gains can be represented in the following way. The highest fixed cost of training that it is profitable for firms to incur when training to level c with subsidy S is $k(c, S)$ defined in (30). The number of firms with fixed cost below this, and hence the number of workers trained, is $F[k(c, S)]$. The total social benefit from each worker trained consists of the additional lifetime value of output per trainee $\beta g(c)$, less the training cost $c + k$ and the deadweight loss from the subsidy αS. Thus, the optimal regulatory policy is $(\hat{c}, \hat{S})$ given by the solution to

$$\max_{S,\, c \in [0,\bar{c}]} F[k(c,S)][\beta g(c) - c - \alpha S] - \int_0^{k(c,S)} k\, \mathrm{d}F(k) \quad \text{subject to (35),} \qquad (36)$$

where the integral term is the total fixed cost of training $F[k(c, S)]$ workers.

For the moment, suppose constraint (35) is not binding and note from (30) that $\partial k(c, S)/\partial S = 1$. The first-order conditions for an interior solution to this problem, with $k_1(c, S)$ denoting the derivative of $k(c, S)$ with respect c, are then

$$- \alpha F[k(\hat{c}, \hat{S})] + \mathrm{d}F[k(\hat{c}, \hat{S})][\beta g(\hat{c}) - \hat{c} - \alpha \hat{S} - k(\hat{c}, \hat{S})] = 0, \qquad (37)$$

$$[\beta g'(\hat{c}) - 1]F[k(\hat{c}, \hat{S})] + k_1(\hat{c}, \hat{S})\, \mathrm{d}F[k(\hat{c}, \hat{S})][\beta g(\hat{c}) - \hat{c} - \alpha \hat{S} - k(\hat{c}, \hat{S})] = 0. \qquad (38)$$

Sufficient (but not necessary) conditions for the second-order conditions for a maximum to be satisfied are that $k_1(\hat{c}, \hat{S}) < 0$ and $\mathrm{d}^2 F[k(\hat{c}, \hat{S})] \leqslant 0$.

The intuition behind (37) is as follows. The marginal cost to a subsidy for given training $\hat{c}$ is the welfare loss α from the additional subsidy for each of the $F[k(\hat{c}, \hat{S})]$ workers trained. The marginal benefit is that $\mathrm{d}F[k(\hat{c}, \hat{S})]$ more firms find it profitable to train, which increases welfare by the difference between the returns to training, $\beta g(\hat{c})$, and the cost of the training both in resources $\hat{c} + k(\hat{c}, \hat{S})$ and in the deadweight loss from the subsidy, $\alpha \hat{S}$. The optimal subsidy balances these two. The marginal benefit of the training received by each trainee for given $\hat{S}$ is the difference between the marginal returns to expenditure on training $\beta g'(\hat{c})$ and its cost of 1, multiplied by the number of workers trained $F[k(\hat{c}, \hat{S})]$. That is the first term in (38). The marginal cost is that increasing training above the profit maximising level reduces the profits from training, so $\mathrm{d}F[k(\hat{c}, \hat{S})]k_1(\hat{c}, \hat{S})$ fewer firms train and there is a welfare loss of the difference between the returns to training, $\beta g(\hat{c})$, and the cost of the training both in resources

J.M. Malcomson et al. / European Economic Review 47 (2003) 197–227   219

$\hat{c} + k(\hat{c}, \hat{S})$ and in the deadweight loss from the subsidy, $\alpha \hat{S}$. The optimal amount of training balances these two effects. Our first result on regulation follows directly from (38).

Proposition 4. *For any given subsidy S (including $S = 0$) that with unregulated contracts satisfies the constraint (35), social welfare is increased by regulating a longer contract, and thereby achieving a higher training per worker, than would be set without such regulation.*

Proof. Suppose contract length is not regulated. Then firms choose a contract length that results in training c that maximises $\tilde{\Pi}(k, c, S)$ in (29) for any given S. It follows from (29) and (30) that $k_1(c, S) = \partial \tilde{\Pi}(k, c, S)/\partial c$. Thus, in the absence of regulation of contract length, training is at a level $\tilde{c}$ for which $k_1(\tilde{c}, S) = 0$. (We know from Proposition 3 that the contract is for less than the whole lifetime so that the optimum is interior with $\tilde{c} < \bar{c}$. Note that $\tilde{c}$ is actually independent of S.) At any such $\tilde{c}$, therefore, the second term in (38) is zero. However, the first term would be strictly positive – it would be zero only for the first best level of training c^* defined in (4) and we showed in Proposition 3 that training without regulation $\tilde{c}$ is less than c^*. Thus, no such $\tilde{c}$ can satisfy the first-order condition (38). Moreover, the left-hand side of (38) is the effect on welfare of an increase in c. That this left-hand side is strictly positive implies that social welfare is increased by increasing c from any $\tilde{c}$ that results in the absence of regulation.

Given $\tilde{c} < \bar{c}$, such an increase in c is feasible as long as it does not violate the maximum subsidy constraint (35). For $S = 0$, that constraint does not apply. For $S > 0$, that constraint can be satisfied at the unregulated contract length only if the right-hand side is strictly positive at $\tilde{c}$. When, however, the right-hand side of (35) is positive, its derivative with respect to c is also positive. Thus the constraint cannot become binding as regulated contract length is increased above the unregulated contract length. □

The intuition for this result is as follows. The number of workers trained is determined by the expected profit from training. At the profit maximising amount of training, a small change in that amount has only a second-order effect on expected profit and, hence, only a second-order effect on the number trained. But it has a first-order effect on the training received by each trainee and, because of the externalities, this has a first-order effect on social welfare.[20]

This result has an interesting implication. In practice, there are administrative costs in setting up a subsidy system that may have been too high to be worthwhile to, for example, medieval and Tudor government authorities. A government with no mechanism for paying subsidies, or a regulator who has no tax raising powers, will nevertheless wish to regulate the length of training. The model is, therefore, consistent with

---

[20] Although social welfare is increased by increasing contract length from the unregulated level, we have not been able to show that the global regulated optimum always has a longer contract than an unregulated market for the general form of the function $g(c)$ used here. However, it certainly does if $g(c)$ takes a constant elasticity form or if ρ is sufficiently small. We have not found examples in which it does not.

the historically widespread regulation of apprenticeships even when training is not subsidised. [21]

When there is a subsidy to training, (37) and (38) together imply

$$\beta g'(\hat{c}) - 1 + \alpha k_1(\hat{c}, \hat{S}) = 0, \tag{39}$$

which, since $k_1(c, S)$ is actually independent of S, determines $\hat{c}$, though not necessarily uniquely if $k_1(c, S)$ is not monotone decreasing in c. The corresponding subsidy $\hat{S}$ can then be calculated for any distribution $F(k)$ from (37) which, with substitution for $k(\hat{c}, \hat{S})$ from (30), can be written in the form

$$\frac{\mathrm{d}F[k(\hat{c}, \hat{S})]}{F[k(\hat{c}, \hat{S})]} \{g(\hat{c})[\beta - (1 - \gamma)\tilde{\delta}(\tau(\hat{c}))] - (1 + \alpha)\hat{S}\} = \alpha. \tag{40}$$

For given $\hat{c}$ and any distribution of k for which $\mathrm{d}F(k)/F(k)$ is monotone decreasing (a hazard rate assumption that is standard in contract theory, see Laffont and Tirole (1993, p. 66), and is satisfied by most of the standard distributions), there is a unique value of $\hat{S}$ that satisfies (40). In other cases, if there is more than one value of $\hat{S}$ that satisfies (40) or $\hat{c}$ that satisfies (39), a further check must be used to establish which is a global maximum. [22]

When the deadweight cost of taxation gets large ($\alpha \to \infty$), (40) cannot be satisfied with equality and we have the corner solution with $\hat{S} = 0$. The maximum subsidy constraint (35) does not apply when $S = 0$, so this solution is optimal. The other extreme is no deadweight cost to raising funds via taxation ($\alpha = 0$). To satisfy (39) would then require $\hat{c} = c^*$, the efficient level defined by (4). But that is not possible whenever there are exogenous quits ($\rho > 0$) because the maximum training the regulator can induce (corresponding to $\tau = T$) is $\bar{c} < c^*$. Thus we have the corner solution with $\hat{c} = \bar{c}$, corresponding to a lifetime training contract. In this case, however, the maximum subsidy condition (35) always binds. This can be seen as follows. From (28) we know that $\tilde{\delta}(T) = \delta(T) \equiv \delta$. Thus, for $\hat{c} = \bar{c}$ and hence $\tau = T$, (35) is satisfied only if $S \leqslant \delta\gamma g(\bar{c})$. But then, with $\alpha = 0$, (40) implies $\hat{S} = g(\bar{c})[\beta - (1 - \gamma)\delta]$ which, since $\beta > \delta$ when $\rho > 0$, does not satisfy the maximum subsidy constraint. Because, however, that constraint cannot be relaxed by reducing c and because c cannot be increased above $\bar{c}$, it is nevertheless optimal to set $\hat{c} = \bar{c}$ and $\hat{S} = \delta\gamma g(\bar{c})$. From (30) we then have $k(\hat{c}, \hat{S}) = \delta g(\bar{c}) - \bar{c}$. This is less than the efficient level k_1^* defined in (5). Thus, despite there being no deadweight cost to taxation, both the number of workers trained and the amount of training received by each trainee are below the efficient levels.

---

[21] The same conclusion applies even if the regulator is controlled by firms and thus wishes to maximise the total expected profits of all firms. The reason is that, because of the externality derived by non-training firms when trained workers quit for exogenous reasons, an unregulated market does not maximise total expected profits of all firms. The model is thus also consistent with medieval guilds regulating the length of apprenticeships even before government authorities did so.

[22] This argument has ignored the maximum subsidy constraint (35). As shown in the proof of Proposition 4, however, when the right-hand side of (35) is positive (a necessary condition for the constraint to be satisfied), its derivative with respect to c is also positive. Thus one cannot relax the constraint by reducing c. The implication is that the optimal level $\hat{c}$ is at least as large as that implied by (39).

J.M. Malcomson et al. / European Economic Review 47 (2003) 197–227   221

Table 2
Optimal regulated apprenticeship length (years), working lifetime 40 years

r	$\alpha = 0.5$		$\alpha = 1$		$\alpha = 2$	
γ:	0.5	0.9	0.5	0.9	0.5	0.9
5% pa	25.5	18.6	20.9	12.9	17.2	8.5
10% pa	17.0	11.6	13.3	7.8	10.6	5.0
20% pa	9.0	6.0	6.9	4.0	5.5	2.6

This raises the obvious question of whether the regulator could do better with some other kind of regulation of training contracts. It is not, however, obvious what regulation would do better. It is clear from (25) that a wage bill W that is decreasing in c for given τ would induce more investment for a given contract length. However, because c is non-contractable, it is not clear how such an arrangement could be implemented.

In the limiting case with no exogenous quits ($\rho = 0$), the optimal regulatory solution has a particularly simple form that may be a useful guide for cases in which efficient turnover is low. For $\rho = 0$, (39) reduces to

$$\beta g'(\hat{c}) = \frac{1}{1 - (\alpha/(1 + \alpha))\gamma}, \tag{41}$$

which determines $\hat{c}$ uniquely. The regulated length of apprenticeship $\hat{\tau}$ that corresponds to $\hat{c}$ is given by use of (41) in (20),

$$\hat{\tau} = -\frac{1}{r}\ln\left[1 - r\beta\left(1 - \frac{\alpha}{1 + \alpha}\gamma\right)\right]. \tag{42}$$

Moreover, in this case the maximum subsidy constraint (35) is never binding at an optimum. To see this, note that, from (40),

$$\hat{S} \leqslant \frac{\gamma\beta g(\hat{c})}{1 + \alpha}. \tag{43}$$

Thus (35) is satisfied as long as

$$\frac{\beta[\tau(\hat{c})]}{\beta} - (1 - \gamma) \geqslant \frac{\gamma}{1 + \alpha}. \tag{44}$$

But (18) and (39) imply that this condition holds with equality and hence the optimal solution always satisfies (35).

In this case, the optimal regulated length of training $\hat{\tau}$ in (42) is independent of the form of the training function $g(.)$ and the distribution function $F(.)$. Some sample values of $\hat{\tau}$ for $T = 40$ years, r and γ as in Table 1, and values for α of 0.5, 1, and 2 are given in Table 2. For the low values of all the parameters in the table, the contract lengths look on the high side but for higher values are of orders of magnitude observed historically. The Elizabethan Statute of Artificers of 1563 regulated apprenticeships to 7 years in England, see Bindoff (1950, p. 201). In modern day Germany apprenticeships for a wide variety of occupations last 3–4 years, see Soskice (1994).

222   *J.M. Malcomson et al. / European Economic Review 47 (2003) 197–227*

The general conclusion from this section is that regulation of contract length is always optimal even if subsidising training has too high a deadweight cost, or is otherwise too difficult, to be worthwhile. An unregulated market provides too little training because both trainees and the new employers of trainees who quit capture some part of the returns to the training firm's investment in training. This part of the returns is still a social benefit from training even though not a private benefit to the training firm. Regulation takes account of that.

6. Alternative views and historical evidence

This section considers the extent to which different theories of apprenticeships, including the one in this paper based on the *non-contractability of training*, fit with historical evidence. We consider three alternatives: (1) apprenticeship simply as a *label* attached to a period of general, on-the-job training for which the wage at each date is equal to the marginal product at that date but, as in Becker (1964), is low because that marginal product is net of the costs of training; (2) apprenticeship as a device for overcoming *capital constraints* that limit trainees' access to capital to pay for general training; and (3) apprenticeship as a device by which organised craftsmen can *limit supply* of competing workers, as argued by Smith (1887, Book 1, Chapter 8).

Historically, there have been a number of features typical of apprenticeships that provide general training in the workplace. One is a duration specified contractually in advance and independent of competence. Historically, this applied to the métier in France, arte in Italy, Amt, Innung, Zunft or Handwerk in Germany, and craft guild in England. Contemporary training of lawyers, doctors and accountants also typically involves a specified duration of on-the-job training that is not reduced just because a trainee is quicker than average at acquiring the appropriate skills. A second is that there has been a long history of regulation of apprenticeships. In medieval times, apprenticeships were regulated by guilds, see Pirenne (1936). In England, regulation was put on a nationwide statutory basis by the Elizabethan Statute of Artificers in 1563, see Bindoff (1950, p. 201). This regulation has typically taken the form not only of specifying a minimum duration of apprenticeship, as in the Elizabethan Statute, but also of attempting to control the adequacy of training. The craft guilds of the middle ages had supervisory functions that included the right of search to ensure that good materials and appropriate processes of manufacture were employed, and that masters "took measure to secure that workmen should be properly trained by serving a regular apprenticeship, and they made rules affecting the hours of labour and well-being of those employed" (Cunningham and McArthur, 1920, p. 61). Moreover, in modern Germany a range of institutions funded collectively by firms oversee the working of the apprentice system (Steedman, 1993; Soskice, 1994; Harhoff and Kane, 1995); and in the UK the Industrial Training Boards monitor industrial training.

The *label theory* of apprenticeship provides no role for regulation. As Becker (1964) observed, having trainees pay for their training is an efficient outcome that will be produced by a competitive market. Moreover, the apprenticeship lasts just as long as required to train that particular trainee – those who learn faster finish sooner, so there is no reason to specify the duration in advance. The label theory also implies that the wage during training is equal to net marginal product. The capital constraint and non-contractability of training theories imply a wage less than marginal product in the closing stages of an apprenticeship (in order to enable the training firm to recoup the costs of training) and the limiting supply theory is certainly consistent with this. Elbaum (1989) argues on the basis of statements from contemporaries, estimates of training costs, and the "extraordinarily large pay increases" on completion of apprenticeship, that the later stages of apprenticeship in early 20th century Britain were indeed playing the role of enabling firms to recoup costs of training.

The *capital constraint theory* is consistent with the length of apprenticeship being specified in advance if the contract is agreed before the training firm knows what the marginal product of a particular trainee will be, in which case the terms will allow it to on average recoup the training costs. It clearly requires courts to enforce the privately agreed terms of an apprenticeship. It may also provide a role for government financial inducements for training if workers have higher discount rates than firms, with the result that the enforced low consumption during training at low wages implies a significant utility loss. But, the natural policy under these circumstances is not regulation of length or adequacy of training. It is to make loans available to employees for on-the-job training because that policy addresses the capital market failure directly. Such loans have not, however, been the typical form of financial support for on-the-job training used in practice, see Dolton (1993) for the UK (where subsidies have been more common) and Lynch (1993) for the US. Apprenticeships were, moreover, used historically not only for artisan professions but also in the medical, legal and accounting professions for the younger offspring of middle class and wealthy families who were often wealthy enough to pay for general training directly, see Earle (1989, Chapter 3). For all these reasons, it seems unlikely that trainees' limited access to capital was the primary reason for the use of apprenticeships.

The theory that apprenticeships are intended to *limit supply of skilled workers* is certainly consistent with craft guilds, representing skilled workers, regulating apprenticeship duration longer than would be agreed privately by trainers and trainees. Two other characteristics one would expect with this theory are: (1) apprenticeships would decline in importance once skilled workers lost control of apprenticeships and of the numbers admitted to them; and (2) regulation should be designed to maximise rent extraction by skilled workers. While apprenticeship certainly declined in Britain after the repeal of the Statute of Artificers in 1814, the diminished institution in fact continued into the mid-20th century, long after an apprenticeship was required to sell skilled labour services. Indeed, not only did apprenticeship survive, but it expanded into the new 20th century industries that had not existed in 1814 and were not, apparently at least, controlled by their skilled workers. Moreover, efficient rent extraction would be served by a long period of training at low wages to deter, and control of numbers to limit, entry. It is not clear that it would be additionally served by incurring the costs of extensive regulation of the adequacy of training.

The problem of ensuring that firms deliver on training promises, which lies at the heart of the *non-contractability of training* model developed here, is explicit in Elbaum

(1989, p. 344): "youths who sacrificed current wages in return for the promise of training were generally vulnerable to exploitation by employers who failed to live up to their training commitments." That non-contracted considerations were important is, moreover, indicated by the extensive evidence that potential apprentices and their parents placed central emphasis on the moral character of the master, resorting where possible to a relative, see Earle (1989). The extensive use of institutions to set and monitor standards of training is also indicative that contractual enforcement of standards by individual trainees appealing to courts is not straightforward. Within the context of the model, regulation of both the length of training contracts and the adequacy of training makes sense. The more that efficient standards can be enforced either by the latter or by the direct regulation of the curriculum as in modern Germany, the less the welfare loss in the model from underprovision of training by the market. Regulation of length of apprenticeships is a welfare enhancing way to move market provision of training closer to the efficient level. Thus both these dimensions of regulation have an obvious role within the model developed here.

In addition to being consistent with the institutional structures accompanying training, the non-contractability of training theory predicts that wages of trainees staying with their training firm after the end of their apprenticeship (a) increase to the value of their marginal product from a level below marginal product during the final stage of their apprenticeship, and (b) are, ceteris paribus, higher than wages of those who change employer. There is considerable evidence supporting point (a), for example, the extraordinarily large pay increases on completion of apprenticeship documented by Elbaum (1989). Careful evidence on point (b) is rare and made problematic by the heterogeneity in types of skills and observable characteristics of those completing apprenticeships. However, in their regression study of German apprentices, Acemoglu and Pischke (1998) find that, within occupations, retained workers earn more than those leaving for another non-military job.

7. Concluding remarks

When the amount of training is not contractable and firms have costs of training that are unknown to workers, workers will not pay directly for the full cost of general training even if they have access to funds to do so. We have shown that, when in addition workers are free to quit without penalty and some do so, apprenticeships are an institution that enables firms to capture more of the returns to the general training they provide. This applies even if training with an apprenticeship is no more effective at preventing employees quitting than training without one. Thus there remains a case for using apprenticeships even where they confer no advantage in preventing rival firms bidding away trainees. The model developed here captures many of the salient characteristics of traditional on-the-job general training. Moreover, it has implications for the analysis of policy. We have shown that it is in general efficient to regulate the length of apprenticeships and, if the deadweight loss from raising funds through taxation is sufficiently low, to subsidise their completion.

J.M. Malcomson et al. / European Economic Review 47 (2003) 197–227   225

The model has been kept simple for expositional reasons. There are, for example, many ways to model worker and firm heterogeneity. Workers could differ in productivity even if not trained, not just in the returns to training. Firms could differ in the marginal, as well as the fixed, cost of training. The formulations used here are chosen for tractability. What is important for the underlying ideas is that other potential employers do not learn anything that fully reveals a trainee's productivity and that potential trainees do not observe anything that directly reveals which firms will in fact provide training.

Another obvious simplification concerns the timing of training during the apprenticeship period. In the model developed here, all training takes place straightaway at the start of the training contract. The rest of the training contract is to enable the firm to recoup the cost of training. There are, however, two reasons why firms may not wish to provide all training straightaway. The first follows from the standard assumption in human capital theory that a given amount of training is more effective if spread out over a longer period of time. The second follows from the result in the model that the binding constraint for trainee quitting is at the start of the training period. Thus firms could provide some training later in the training period without making this crucial constraint tighter. Delaying training for either reason, of course, reduces the period over which the firm can recoup the cost of training and the optimal timing would have to balance the two effects, but one would expect at least some training to occur after the start of the training period.

Other obvious simplifications are that we have assumed the environment is stationary with no uncertainty except about the types of trainees, and that firms do not build reputations for providing levels of training beyond their immediate short-term interest. These are not, however, crucial to the underlying insights. If labour productivity grew at a constant proportional rate for exogenous reasons unrelated to training, that would enter the model like a reduction in the discount rate. Moreover, if there were uncertainty about the return to training for a given type of trainee, one could simply interpret the return to training as the expected return at the time the training was given. Finally, even if information flows are sufficient to enable firms to develop reputations for providing good training, such reputations are worth maintaining only for those with fixed costs of training sufficiently low that their profits from training in the future are high enough to keep them honest in the short term. In particular, reputations will never keep marginally profitable firms honest, so the market will still provide too little training and the role for government policy remains.

It thus seems that the underlying insights in the model presented here are reasonably robust to these types of generalisation of the model. Those insights are also consistent with much of the historical evidence on general training provided by firms. They therefore seem a promising basis for further analysis.

Acknowledgements

We are grateful to Daron Acemoglu, Sujoy Mukerji and Margaret Stevens for very helpful comments on a previous version of this paper.

References

Acemoglu, D., 1996. Credit constraints, investment externalities and growth. In: Booth, A.L., Snower, D.J. (Eds.), Acquiring Skills. Cambridge University Press, Cambridge, pp. 43–62.

Acemoglu, D., 1997. Training and innovation in an imperfect labour market. Review of Economic Studies 64, 445–464.

Acemoglu, D., Pischke, J.-S., 1998. Why do firms train? Theory and evidence. Quarterly Journal of Economics 113, 79–119.

Acemoglu, D., Pischke, J.-S., 1999a. Beyond Becker: Training in imperfect labour markets. Economic Journal 106, F112–F142.

Acemoglu, D., Pischke, J.-S., 1999b. The structure of wages and investment in general training. Journal of Political Economy 107, 539–572.

Becker, G., 1964. Human Capital. Columbia University Press, New York.

Bindoff, S.T., 1950. Tudor England. Penguin, Harmondsworth.

Booth, A.L., Chatterji, M., 1995. Training and contracts. Working Paper 95-15, Research Centre on Micro-Social Change, University of Essex.

Booth, A.L., Chatterji, M., 1998. Unions and efficient training. Economic Journal 108, 328–343.

Burdett, K., Smith, E., 1996. Education and matching externalities. In: Booth, A.L., Snower, D.J. (Eds.), Acquiring Skills. Cambridge University Press, Cambridge, MA, pp. 65–80.

Cantor, R., 1990. Firm specific training and contract length. Econometrica 57, 1–14.

Chang, C., Wang, Y., 1996. Human capital investment under asymmetric information: The Pigovian conjecture revisited. Journal of Labor Economics 14, 505–519.

Cunningham, W., McArthur, E.A., 1920. Outlines of English Industrial History. Cambridge University Press, Cambridge.

Dolton, P.J., 1993. The economics of youth training in Britain. Economic Journal 103, 1261–1278.

Earle, P., 1989. The Making of the English Middle Class 1660–1730. Methuen, London.

Elbaum, B., 1989. Why apprenticeship persisted in Britain but not in the United States. Journal of Economic History 49, 337–349.

Finegold, D., Soskice, D., 1988. The failure of British training: Analysis and prescription. Oxford Review of Economic Policy 4, 21–53.

Greenwald, B.C., 1986. Adverse selection in the labour market. Review of Economic Studies 53, 325–347.

Hamilton, G., 1995. Enforcement in apprenticeship contracts: Were runaways a serious problem? Evidence from Montreal. Journal of Economic History 55, 551–574.

Hamilton, G., 1996. The market for Montreal apprentices: Contract length and information. Explorations in Economic History 33, 496–523.

Harhoff, D., Kane, T.J., 1995. Financing apprenticeship training: Evidence from Germany. In: Stacey, N. (Ed.), School-to-Work: What Does Research Say About It? Office of Educational Research and Improvement (ED), Washington, DC.

Hermalin, B., 1990. Adverse selection, short-term contracting, and the underprovision of on-the-job training. Working Paper No. 90–139. Department of Economics, University of California, Berkeley.

Kahn, C., Huberman, G., 1988. Two-sided uncertainty and "up-or-out" contracts. Journal of Labor Economics 6, 423–444.

Katz, E., Ziderman, A., 1990. Investment in general training: The role of information and labour mobility. Economic Journal 100, 1147–1158.

Laffont, J.-J., Tirole, J., 1993. A Theory of Incentives in Procurement and Regulation. MIT Press, Cambridge, MA.

Lees, D., Chiplin, B., 1970. The economics of industrial training. Lloyds Bank Review 96, 29–41.

Lee, D., Marsden, D., Rickman, P., Duncombe, J., 1990. Scheming for Youth: A Study of YTS in the Enterprise Culture. Open University Press, Buckingham.

Loewenstein, M.A., Spletzer, J.R., 1998. Dividing the costs and returns to general training. Journal of Labor Economics 16, 142–171.

Lynch, L.M., 1992. Private-sector training and the earnings of young workers. American Economic Review 82, 299–312.

Lynch, L.M., 1993. The economics of youth training in the US. Economic Journal 103, 1292–1302.

Lynch, L.M. (Ed.), 1994. Training and the Private Sector: International Comparisons. University of Chicago Press, Chicago.

Malcomson, J.M., Maw, J., McCormick, B., 2002. General Training by Firms, Apprenticeship Contracts, and Public Policy. CESifo Working Paper No. 696.

Pirenne, H., 1936. Economic and Social History of Medieval Europe. Kegan Paul, Trench, Trubner, London.

Prendergast, C., 1993. The role of promotion in inducing specific human capital acquisition. Quarterly Journal of Economics 108, 523–534.

Schlicht, E., 1996. Endogenous on-the-job training with moral hazard. Labour Economics 3, 81–92.

Smith, A., 1887. An Inquiry into the Nature and Causes of the Wealth of Nations. Bell, London.

Soskice, D., 1994. Reconciling markets and institutions: The German apprenticeship system. In: Lynch, L.M. (Ed.), Training and the Private Sector: International Comparisons. University of Chicago Press, Chicago, pp. 25–60.

Steedman, H., 1993. The economics of youth training in Germany. Economic Journal 103, 1279–1291.

Stevens, M., 1994a. Labour contracts and efficiency in on-the-job training. Economic Journal 104, 408–419.

Stevens, M., 1994b. An investment model for the supply of training by employers. Economic Journal 104, 556–570.

Stevens, M., 1996. Transferable training and poaching externalities. In: Booth, A.L., Snower, D.J. (Eds.), Acquiring Skills. Cambridge University Press, Cambridge, pp. 21–40.

US Department of Labor, 1989. Report of the Commission on Workplace Quality and Labor Market Efficiency. US GPO, Washington.

Waldman, M., 1990. "Up-or-out" contracts: A signaling perspective. Journal of Labor Economics 8, 230–250.

Williamson, O.E., 1985. The Economic Institutions of Capitalism. The Free Press, New York.

[8]

The Economic Journal, **108** (*March*), 328–343. © Royal Economic Society 1998. Published by Blackwell Publishers, 108 Cowley Road, Oxford OX4 1JF, UK and 350 Main Street, Malden, MA 02148, USA.

UNIONS AND EFFICIENT TRAINING*

Alison L. Booth and Monojit Chatterji

The paper examines the optimal level of training investment when trained workers are mobile, wage contracts are time-consistent, and training comprises both specific and general skills. The firm has *ex post* monopsonistic power that drives trained workers' wages below the social optimum. The emergence of a trade union bargaining at the firm-level can increase social welfare, by counterbalancing the firm's *ex post* monopsonistic power in wage determination. Local union-firm wage bargaining ensures that the post-training wage is set sufficiently high to deter at least some quits, so that the number of workers the firm trains is nearer the social optimum.

Does the free market provide workers and firms with the right incentives to invest in training? Is government intervention required when training investment is inefficient or can other institutions replicate the first-best training outcome? We address these issues in this paper in a two-period model of hiring, training and production, in which training comprises both specific and general elements.

Over the past decade, there has been increasing emphasis by governments on the importance of employer-led training in providing the skilled workforce necessary for improving competitiveness, adaptability and economic growth (OECD, 1995). It has also been suggested that skills acquisition will reduce the growing earnings inequality observed in some OECD countries since the 1980s.[1] But at the same time as governments have been emphasising the importance of private sector training, there has been growing concern amongst economists about the implications of imperfect competition for skills acquisition. The conventional wisdom that the free market will, unassisted, produce efficient training outcomes has been questioned by a number of recent papers, which have in common the prediction that training may confer market power upon firms, and consequently workers' wages will be less than their marginal product.[2] As a result there will be an inefficient investment in training.

At least three types of distortion may arise with training investment. First, for a given level and mix of skills, firms may train too few workers. Second, for a given number of workers, too low a level of skill may be chosen. Finally, firms

* We should like to thank Michael Burda, Melvyn Coles, Ed Lazear and an anonymous referee for helpful comments on an earlier draft. This research is produced as part of a Centre for Economic Policy Research (CEPR) programme on 'The UK Labour Market: Microeconomic Imperfections and Institutional Features', which is co-sponsored by the UK Departments for Education and Employment and the Department of Trade and Industry (Research Grant No. 4RP-154-90). Financial assistance was also provided by the Leverhulme Trust and the Economic and Social Research Council. The usual disclaimer applies. An earlier version of this paper appeared as 'Unions and Efficient Training', ESRC Research Centre on Micro-social Change, University of Essex Working Paper No. 96-13.
[1] See for example Freeman and Katz (1995).
[2] See *inter alia* Acemoglu and Pischke (1996), Askilden and Ireland (1993), Black (1994), Booth and Chatterji (1995), Burdett and Smith (1995), Snower (1996) and Stevens (1994, 1996).

may choose their mix of specific and general training to reduce quits or for other strategic purposes, thereby distorting the mix of skills. Much of the recent British theoretical work on training has focused on the first problem (Stevens, 1994, 1996; Booth and Chatterji, 1995), while recent US studies have focused on the second problem (Acemoglu, 1996; Acemoglu and Pischke, 1996; Chang and Wang, 1996). For an example of the final problem, see Askilden and Ireland (1993). In this paper, we examine training distortion of the first type, whereby too few workers may be trained for a given level and mix of skills.

If there is under-investment in training, it is not clear that government intervention will necessarily always produce the desired level of investment in human capital. Government failures may be such that intervention is costly, and can be justified only where the costs of market failure exceed those of government failure. And in practice it is hard, if not impossible, to quantify market and government failures. In this paper we adopt a different approach to the problem of inefficient training investment, and investigate the issue of whether or not non-governmental institutions such as trade unions may produce a second-best solution to the problem of inefficiency in training investment.

The impact of trade unions on the acquisition of skills has been largely ignored in the literature. We find that, with time-consistent contracts, union-bargaining at the local level can counter-balance firms' *ex post* monopsonistic power; unions may therefore be associated with outcomes that are welfare-improving. In adopting this approach, we are also able to shed some light on the stylised facts characterising some OECD countries of a positive correlation between firm-provided training and trade union presence (see for example Tan *et al.* (1992), Booth (1991) and Green *et al.* (1996)), and a negative correlation between union presence and quits (Freeman, 1980; Blau and Kahn, 1983; Freeman and Medoff, 1984; and Miller and Mulvey, 1993).

The remainder of this paper is set out as follows. The basic assumptions are described in Section 1. Section 2 analyses the socially optimal training levels in an economy in which workers are mobile and there are no trade unions. Section 3 shows that, in the absence of a social planner, the firm has *ex post* monopsonistic power associated with the specific element of training; this power drives trained workers' time-consistent wages below the socially optimal wage. Section 4 shows how the emergence of a decentralised trade union at the firm-level can reduce firms' monopsonistic power, leading to an improve-.ment in social welfare. The final section summarises the main results.

1. Model Assumptions

Suppose there are two sectors in the economy, each comprising a large number of firms. One sector employs only unskilled workers and the other employs only skilled workers. The model covers two periods, and training occurs only in the initial period. All workers enter the labour market unskilled, but training firms in the skilled sector recruit and train unskilled trainees at the start of period 1. After workers have been trained, they qualify for skilled jobs in period 2, and may choose to stay with the training firm or move to another firm in the skilled sector. Both firms and workers are risk-neutral, there is no discounting and no layoffs.

1.1 *Training Technology*

In the skilled sector of the economy, firm-provided training comprises both specific and general elements. This assumption reflects the view often advanced in the literature that training in practice combines both specific and general skills (see *inter alia* Soskice (1990), Chapman (1991), OECD (1991) and Stevens (1994, 1996)). However, the mix of skills is exogenously determined by each firm's technology: some of the skills can be used only in the firm providing the training (and reflect the idiosyncratic nature of a particular firm's production and management structure). Other skills learnt at the firm are general to the skilled sector (in which each firm produces a variation of a common product that is unique to the firm). Thus while training is provided at the level of the individual firm in our model, it has value not only to the training firm but also to other firms in the sector. However the average productivity of trained workers in the inside firm is greater than the best they can do with an outside firm in the skilled sector. This assumption captures in a simple fashion the notion that part of the training is specific to the training firm while the remaining part of the training improves the workers transferable skills - which are of value to all firms in the skilled sector including the training firm.

1.2 *Timing in the Model*

Unskilled workers are trained in period 1, during which time no production occurs but workers acquire the skills necessary to work in the skilled sector. In period 2 newly trained skilled workers either remain with the training firm and produce output, or quit to work in another firm. Workers choose to quit the training firm in period 2 if they receive an outside offer (matching their outside productivity) higher than the post-training wage offered by the training firm. The timing is shown in Fig. 1.

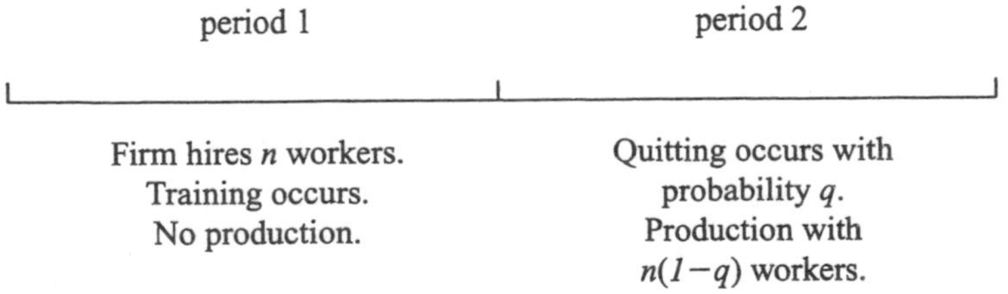

period 1	period 2
Firm hires n workers. Training occurs. No production.	Quitting occurs with probability q. Production with $n(1-q)$ workers.

Fig. 1. *The Ordering of Decisions in the 2-period Framework*

1.3 *Remuneration*

Unskilled workers who remain in the unskilled sector receive a wage b with certainty in both periods.[3] Unskilled workers recruited to the training sector receive a training wage t during their training in period 1, while in period 2 they receive a skilled wage which is uncertain. If skilled workers stay with their training firm they receive w, but if they quit the training firm at the start of period 2 in order to work in another firm in the skilled sector, they receive x.

The 'outside' productivity of trained workers varies across firms: the idiosyncratic 'risk' for outside jobs is modelled as a drawing from a common distribution of productivities.[4] While neither firms nor workers know *ex ante* which individuals will be vulnerable to outside offers post-training, the distribution of *ex post* outside productivities is common knowledge. Heterogeneity in the *ex post* value of firm-provided training to other firms in the skilled sector may arise for several reasons. First, idiosyncrasies in firms' production methods and management styles may mean that the value of transferable training varies across firms in the same industry in accordance with their production and management techniques. Moreover, firm-specific shocks may mean that the value of training varies across firms in period 2 even if workers were all identical in the initial period. Second, the transferable component of training may vary across individuals in accordance with their preferences which, while unknown prior to training, develop over the training period and which affect their productivity in outside firms. The source of the heterogeneity is not at issue here: we simply assume a known *exogenous* distribution of *ex post* outside productivities and corresponding wage offers which are equal to marginal and average productivity. This is tantamount to assuming that competitive forces prevail in the outside labour market.

The outside marginal productivity and wage x is distributed according to a twice differentiable distribution function $F(x)$ with support $[a, \lambda]$, where $a > b$, $F(a) = 0$, $F(\lambda) = 1$, and $F(x)$ is strictly log-concave in x.[5] In period 1, the outside wage is not known, although its distribution $F(x)$ is. A useful way of thinking of this is that, for a given number of workers trained in the initial period, the training firm faces an upward sloping labour retention function in the second period. Thus the training firm is uncertain about whether or not trained workers will remain once their training is complete. A high wage increases retentions of skilled labour but adds to labour costs. A low wage does the opposite. The firm resolves this potential conflict by setting an 'efficiency wage'.

---

[3] For simplicity we do not consider training learnt while performing a job; thus unskilled workers are unskilled in both time periods.

[4] This assumption is similar to that in Mortenson and Pissarides (1994), and reflects the importance of idiosyncratic factors in the determination of job creation and job destruction reported in Davis *et al.* (1995).

[5] Log concavity is widely used in the literature, and ensures well-behaved second-order conditions and comparative static results. Log-concave distributions include the normal, exponential, gamma and Weibull distributions (see Caplin and Nalebuff, 1991).

The training firm pays the same wage to all its internally trained workers, who have identical productivity in the training firm. A perfectly discriminating monopsonist could prevent any of its trained workforce from quitting by paying each worker a wage rate equal to his or her outside productivity. However such behaviour is rarely observed in practice for a number of reasons. If workers performing the same job in a given firm were paid different wage rates, morale might be adversely affected and lower paid workers might reduce their effort. Transactions and monitoring costs may also preclude payment of such differential. Moreover, asymmetric information may mitigate against perfectly discriminating monopsony. Since firms are unable to verify outside offers easily, workers may cheat in getting fraudulent outside offers to boost their insider wage.

1.4 *The Production Function*

The second period production functions of both training and poaching firms are characterised by constant returns to scale. Period 2 output in the training firm is given by $an(1-q)$, where $n(1-q)$ denotes effective labour, given by the number of trainees n less the number of quits nq, and a is a constant denoting average (and marginal) product. The assumption of constant returns for skilled workers in 'outside firms' implies that x is a measure of marginal and average productivity of skilled workers in outside firms. The constant value of average 'insider' productivity is greater than the maximum outsider productivity:

$$b < a < \lambda < a. \tag{1}$$

This is because a component of productivity in the training firm is specific. Since $a > b$ by assumption, skilled workers will always receive a higher wage than b and will thus never return to the unskilled sector.

1.5 *Direct Costs of Training*

The direct costs of training n trainees in period 1 are given by a continuous twice differentiable function $c = c(n)$, where $c(0) = 0$, $c'(n) > 0$, $c''(n) > 0$. This assumption reflects diseconomies of scale in teaching, not least because firms run into constraints of capital equipment required for training as the number of trainees is increased.

1.6 *The Quitting Probability*

Workers quit at the end of the first period if and only if $x > w$. Given $x \in [a, \lambda]$, the quit rate q is given by

$$q = P(x > w) = [1 - F(w)], \quad a \leq w < \lambda \tag{2a}$$

$$= 0, \quad w \geq \lambda. \tag{2b}$$

The retention rate is given by

$$(1 - q) = P(x \leqslant w) = F(w), \quad a \leqslant w < \lambda \tag{3a}$$

$$= 1, \quad w \geqslant \lambda. \tag{3b}$$

To ensure that $0 \leqslant q \leqslant 1 \Leftrightarrow 0 \leqslant (1 - q) \leqslant 1$, the following inequality must hold:

$$b < a \leqslant w \leqslant \lambda < a. \tag{4}$$

1.7 *Expected Return of Skilled Workers*

The worker's *ex ante* two-period expected return $E(R)$ from training is

$$E(R) = t + (1 - q)w + qE(x|x > w) \geqslant 2b \tag{5a}$$

$$= t + wF(w) + \int_w^\lambda xf(x)\, dx, \tag{5b}$$

$E(R) \geqslant 2b$, otherwise no workers would want to train. We assume that in period 1, there is an infinitely elastic supply of unskilled workers at the two period wage $2b$; thus the constraint is binding (since workers have no bargaining power at the start of period 1). Integrating $(5b)$ by parts, and rearranging, gives

$$E(R) = t + w + \int_w^\lambda [1 - F(x)]\, dx = 2b. \tag{6}$$

$E(R)$ is increasing because $\partial E(R)/\partial w = F(w) > 0$. Equation (6) shows all combinations of t and w that induce workers to train. Note from (4) and (6) that $t < b$. Since $E(R)$ is increasing in w and t, t and w are *negatively* related. This is the fundamental trade-off the firm faces: to recruit trainees it can either pay a high skilled wage or a high training wage.

2. First-best Training and Wages

This Section determines the efficient number of trainees in period 1 and their period 2 allocation between the training firm and outside 'poaching' firms in the skilled sector. This amounts to the social planner choosing the number of period 1 trainees $\hat{n}$ and period 2 quits $\hat{q}$ in order to maximise the social ·returns from training, S. S is the sum of the value of the training firm's output from its retained workforce in period 2, plus the value of output produced by trained workers who quit to work in other firms in the skilled sector in period 2, less the costs to society of training (the training firm's direct expenditure on training $c(n)$ in period 1 and the opportunity cost of labour over the two periods, given by $2bn$). Thus S can be written as:

$$S = an(1 - q) + \beta qn - c(n) - 2bn \tag{7}$$

where β is the average productivity of trained workers in outside firms. Since

$\beta < \alpha$, $S_q = (\beta - \alpha) n < 0$. It pays society to reduce quits to zero for any n, thereby not losing any of the gains from specific training. Thus $\hat{q} = 0$. Substitution of $\hat{q} = 0$ in (7) yields:

$$S = \alpha n - c(n) - 2bn. \tag{8}$$

The first order condition for maximisation with respect to n is:

$$S_n = \alpha - 2b - c'(n) = 0, \tag{9}$$

which simply states that social returns from training are largest when the marginal social benefit from training $(\alpha - 2b)$ equals the marginal social cost $c'(n)$. The second order conditions for a maximum are satisfied, since $S_{nn} = -c''(n) < 0$.

PROPOSITION 1. *If and only if $(\alpha - 2b) > c'(0)$, a unique equilibrium exists, and is characterised by $\hat{S} > 0$, $\hat{q} = 0$, $c'(\hat{n}) = \alpha - 2b$.*

The proof is in the Appendix, and illustrated in Fig. 2. A first-best training outcome is one which satisfies (9) and in which $\hat{q} = 0$. In effect, the first best situation requires all returns to first period training to be fully recouped and, given the presence of some specific skills, this implies the necessity of zero quits.

In a command economy, the social planner could enforce these decisions. However, in a decentralised economy, the planner's instrument is the second period wage. To ensure zero quits, the social planner would set $\hat{w} = \lambda$ thus inducing the training firm to select the efficient number of trainees. This can be seen by noting that over the two periods the training firm pays each worker $2b$ and incurs training costs $c(n)$; hence its *ex-ante* profits when $q = 0$ are the same as the social surplus, given by (8). Thus the social planner can fully decentralise the efficient allocation by guaranteeing a long term contract with

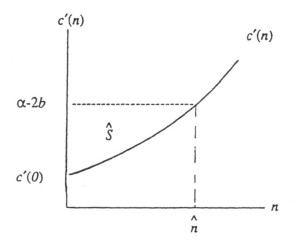

Fig. 2. *The Social Optimum*

a second period wage of λ in the training firm. It should be noted that this decentralising mechanism involves those workers whose alternative wage is below λ earning rents in the insider firm.[6]

3. Training and Wages in the Absence of a Social Planner

Now suppose it is impossible to enforce long term contracts of the sort adopted by the social planner in the previous section. As a result, there may be a 'poaching' or 'quitting' externality. At the start of period 1, each firm determines the number of workers to train n and the first period training wage t. The credible wage w^* is set by the firm at the start of period 2 to maximise its second period profits *given* the earlier choices of n and t.[7] We first examine the optimum values in the final period, which ensures that the private optimum is calculated in a time-consistent manner.

3.1 *The Firm's Ex Post Profits*

At the start of period 2 the training firm, for its expected workforce of $n(1 - q)$ workers, sets w^* to maximise its expected *ex post* profits $\bar{\pi}$, where

$$\max_{w} \bar{\pi} = n(1 - q)(a - w) = nF(w)(a - w). \tag{10}$$

Note from (4) that $\bar{\pi} \geqslant 0$ because $w \leqslant a$. The second order conditions for the maximisation problem hold, since maximising $\bar{\pi}$ produces the same result as maximising $\log \bar{\pi}$, and $\log \bar{\pi}$ is strictly concave given the strict log concavity of $F(x)$. The first and second order conditions are:

$$\bar{\pi}_w = n[(a - w)F'(w) - F(w)] = 0 \tag{11}$$

$$\bar{\pi}_{ww} = n[(a - w)F''(w) - 2F'(w)] < 0. \tag{12}$$

The first order conditions simply state that the marginal revenue from raising the wage equals the marginal cost. The marginal revenue from raising the wage consists of the extra output sold by the additional workers retained as a result, given by $aF'(w)$. The marginal cost has two elements: the addition to total cost because of additional retentions given by $wF'(w)$, and the addition to total cost because the higher wage has to be paid to all retained workers, given by $F(w)$. Thus the total marginal cost is given by $(wF'(w) + F(w))$. Solving (11) we obtain:

$$w^* + \frac{F(w^*)}{F'(w^*)} = a. \tag{13}$$

---

[6] If perfect discrimination were possible, these rents could be eliminated by the social planner paying each worker his/her alternative wage. From a narrow efficiency point of view, the issue of rents is not material.

[7] Suppose firms were to announce at the start of period 1 a wage $w > w^*$. Workers, having rational expectations, will know that firms will renege on this *ex post*, and hence $w > w^*$ is not credible.

In the Appendix we prove that, provided insider productivity a is sufficiently low, (13) has a unique solution. This is summarised in:

PROPOSITION 2. *In a decentralised economy with low enough insider productivity, specifically* $a < \lambda + [1/F'(\lambda)]$, *there exists a unique wage* $w^*(a)$ *which maximises the firm's second period profits. It is characterised by (13).*

3.2 The Firm's Ex Ante Profits

In period 1, the firm's profits are uncertain, since some trained workers may quit before period 2 production occurs. The training firm's *ex ante* expected profits, denoted by π, are:

$$\pi = a n(1 - q^*) - w^* n(1 - q^*) - c(n) - tn. \tag{14}$$

This characterisation of profits relates only to profits generated by internally trained workers. The training firm may also 'poach' skilled workers from other training firms but these 'poachees' are paid their average product; consequently their net contribution to profits is zero and is not included in (14). Equation (14) can be simplified by substituting out the last term on the RHS, using the participation constraint of (6), yielding the following:

$$\max_{n} \pi = a n(1 - q^*) + w^* n q^* + n \int_{w^*}^{\lambda} [1 - F(x)]\, dx - 2bn - c(n) \tag{15a}$$

$$= n\mu^* - 2bn - c(n) \tag{15b}$$

where μ^* is a weighted average of the productivity of skilled labour, given by:

$$\mu^* \equiv \mu[w^*(a), a] = a(1 - q^*) + w^* q^* + \int_{w^*}^{\lambda} [1 - F(x)]\, dx. \tag{16}$$

Thus μ^* may also be thought of as the private marginal benefit from training to the training firm. Once w^* is obtained from (13), the value of μ^* is completely determined and depends only on the exogenous parameters a and λ. From (13) w^* is continuous, and increasing in a, and hence μ^* is continuous also.

The first order condition from maximisation of (15) is:

$$\pi_n = \mu^* - c'(n^*) - 2b = 0 \tag{17}$$

which states that the firm chooses trainees in period 1 so that the private marginal benefit from training μ^* equals the private marginal cost of training $c'(n^*) + 2b$. The second order condition is:

$$\pi_{nn} = -c''(n) < 0. \tag{18}$$

PROPOSITION 3. *For* $\mu^* - 2b > c'(0)$, *an equilibrium exists, and is characterised by the firm training a unique number of workers* n^*, *given by (17), and* $n^* < \hat{n}$ *(the social optimum).*

The proof is in the Appendix, and illustrated in Fig. 3. Given that marginal training costs are rising and private marginal benefits are less than social marginal benefits, the firm trains two few workers ($n^* < \hat{n}$). Because the firm pays too low a post-training wage it suffers too many quits. Since the worker's two-period return in both cases is $2b$, $\hat{w} > w^*$ implies $t^* > \hat{t}$. The private wage profile is too flat relative to the efficient profile. The problem is that, in the absence of legally binding long term contracts, the firm has no credible mechanism for persuading workers that it will pay the appropriate second period wage. It is also clear from Fig. 3 that the social surplus S^* is smaller than $\hat{S}$. The shaded area shows the welfare loss relative to first best.

4. Unions and Wages

The previous section showed that the training firm has monopsony power in *ex post* wage determination. This allows it to set trained wages below the social optimum and thus obtain rents. Consequently, there is a clear incentive for trained workers to unionise at the start of period 2, to reduce firms' power. Firms will also be made better off, as their *ex ante* expected profits are higher. Since firms will have rational expectations about the gains to trained workers from unionisation, how will the training outcome be affected?

Suppose a local union forms at the start of period 2 to bargain with the

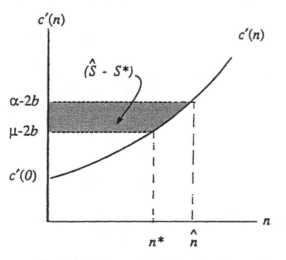

Fig. 3. *The Private and Social Optimum Compared*

training firm about period 2 wages for internally trained workers.[8] The optimal value of the bargained wage is denoted by $\tilde{w}$. The union bargains on behalf of workers who stay with the training firm, and maximises the expected utility of the median retained worker. The median retained worker is defined by that value of x, denoted by w^m, which separates workers who do not quit into two equal groups:

$$F(w^m) = \tfrac{1}{2}F(\tilde{w}). \tag{19}$$

Notice that w^m is increasing in the insider wage $\tilde{w}$, since $dw^m/d\tilde{w} = f(\tilde{w})/2f(w^m)$. This is because a higher inside wage reduces quits, expanding the pool of stayers, and the new median worker is characterised by a higher level of outside opportunities. Denote by $W = \tilde{w} - w^m$ the period 2 *gain to the union* from reaching an agreement. Hence $W_w = 1 - dw^m/d\tilde{w} > 0$.[9] The period 2 *gain to the firm* from reaching an agreement is $\bar{\pi}$ as defined in (10) (since the fall-back position for the firm if no agreement is reached is zero). The solution concept is the generalised Nash bargain, which involves maximisation of the product of each agent's gains from reaching an agreement weighted by their respective bargaining strengths. Thus the maximand is

$$\max_w B = W^\theta \bar{\pi}^{1-\theta} \tag{20}$$

where θ is the bargaining strength of the union. The first and second order conditions are given by (21) and (22) respectively:[10]

$$B_w = \theta \frac{W_w}{W} + (1-\theta)\frac{\bar{\pi}_w}{\bar{\pi}} = 0 \tag{21}$$

$$B_{ww} = \theta[W_{ww}W - (W_w)^2]/W^2 + (1-\theta)[(\bar{\pi}_{ww}\bar{\pi}) - (\bar{\pi}_w)^2]/\bar{\pi}^2 < 0. \tag{22}$$

PROPOSITION 4. *(i) Local union-firm bargaining results in a higher wage, more training and a higher social surplus as compared to a situation with no local union. (ii) There exists a critical value of union power, $\hat{\theta}$, which is the minimum level of union power necessary to induce first best.*

The proof is in the Appendix. To show that $\tilde{w} > w^*$, (where $\tilde{w}$ is the wage set by union-firm bargaining, and w^* is the wage set by the firm where the

---

[8] Thus we have a form of 'insider-outsider' model, in which the insiders are the internally trained workers who are represented by an in-house trade union, while the outsiders are the externally trained 'poachees' who are unrepresented by the union.

[9] From (19) $\log F(w^m) = \log(\tfrac{1}{2}) + \log F(\tilde{w}) \Rightarrow G(w^m) = \log\tfrac{1}{2} + G(\tilde{w})$, where $G \equiv \log F$, is strictly concave. Hence $dw^m/d\tilde{w} = G'(\tilde{w})/G'(w^m)$. But through strict concavity of G and $\tilde{w} > w^m$, $G'(\tilde{w}) < G'(w^m) \Rightarrow dw^m/d\tilde{w} < 1$.

[10] The weakest sufficient condition for $B_{ww} < 0$ is as follows (where $\log F \equiv G$):

$$d^2 w^m/d\tilde{w}^2 = -\left\{ G''[w^m(\tilde{w})]G'(\tilde{w})\frac{dw^m}{dw} - G'[w^m(\tilde{w})]G''(\tilde{w}) \right\} \Big/ G'[w^m(\tilde{w})]$$

and $W_{ww} = -(d^2 w^m/d\tilde{w}^2)$. A sufficient condition for $W_{ww} \leqslant 0$ is

$$G''[w^m(\tilde{w})] \leqslant \left[\frac{G'(\tilde{w})}{G'(w^m)}\right]^2 G''(\tilde{w})$$

where the term in square brackets on the right hand side of this inequality is a fraction, from concavity of G.

© Royal Economic Society 1998.

workforce has no bargaining power), note that $\bar{\pi}_w(\tilde{w}) < 0$. In the previous equilibrium where the firm set wages unilaterally, $\bar{\pi}_w(w^*) = 0$. Since $\bar{\pi}_{ww} < 0$, then $\tilde{w} > w^*$. We now show that $\tilde{\mu} > \mu^*$, that is, the marginal private benefit from training is greater with union bargaining than it is without. Write $\tilde{\mu}$ as:

$$\tilde{\mu} = a + \tilde{q}(\tilde{\beta} - a) \tag{23}$$

where $\tilde{\beta} \equiv E(x|x > \tilde{w})$. Since $\tilde{w} > w^*$ for given a, then $\tilde{\beta} > \beta^*$ and $\tilde{q} < q^*$. We can also write $\tilde{\mu} - \mu^* = (a - \beta^*)(q^* - \tilde{q}) + \tilde{q}(\tilde{\beta} - \beta^*) > 0$. Hence the marginal private benefit from training is greater with union bargaining than without. Since the union forces up the period 2 wage, fewer internally trained workers quit to work in outside firms. Thus the average wage of internally trained workers rises, increasing μ. Hence the social surplus also rises. Fig. 4 illustrates.

Note from (17) that $\tilde{w}$ depends on θ and $B_{\tilde{w}\theta} > 0$. Hence, $d\tilde{w}/d\theta = -B_{\tilde{w}\theta}/B_{ww} > 0$; an increase in union power increases the bargained wage and hence reduces quits. If θ is at its maximal value of 1, the solution to the bargaining problem (20) involves setting $\tilde{w}$ to its maximum value a, which exceeds λ, the wage necessary to induce the efficient quit rate of zero. By continuity, there exists some level of union power $\hat{\theta}$ just sufficient to induce a wage of λ and reduce quits to zero. But if $q = 0$, then $\mu = a$ and the marginal benefit from training is maximal at $a - 2b$. Hence for all $\theta \geqslant \hat{\theta}$, first best outcomes are achieved. This discussion is summarised in Proposition 4.[11]

Thus the emergence of a trade union bargaining at the firm-level can

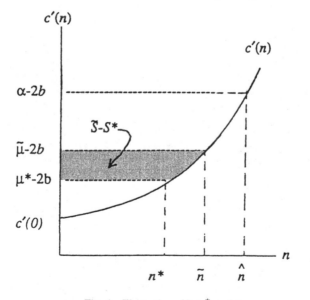

Fig. 4. *Illustration of $\tilde{n}$, n^* and $\hat{n}$*

[11] Note that, since $\hat{w} \geqslant \tilde{w} > w^*$, $\hat{t} \leqslant \tilde{t} < t^*$. The amount of the training costs actually borne by the firm depends on the relative magnitude of insider and outsider productivity. Since this is not germane to our analysis in the present paper, we do not pursue it further.

increase social welfare, by counterbalancing the firm's period 2 monopsonistic power in wage determination. The training firm's *ex ante* profits are also increased (although its *ex post* profits are not).[12] Local union-firm wage bargaining ensures that the period 2 wage is set sufficiently high to deter quits, and to ensure that the firm trains the efficient number of workers. It should be noted that local unions achieve this result only by widening earnings differentials between skill groups. Industry-level union bargaining is unlikely to lead to an increase in social welfare, since the outside wage distribution $F(x)$ would also shift up, and quits from the training firm may therefore be unaffected.

5. Conclusions

The paper investigates investment efficiency when training comprises both specific and transferable skills. By increasing the bargaining power of skilled workers, a local union increases wages in the training firm, thereby reducing quits. In effect, this overcomes the weakness of an institutional structure that prevents firms offering workers credible long term contracts. Thus the emergence of a trade union at the establishment level can increase social welfare, by counterbalancing the firm's *ex post* monopsonistic power in wage determination. Union-firm wage bargaining ensures that the post-training wage is set sufficiently high to deter quits, and to ensure that the firm trains the socially optimal number of workers. Therefore in any empirical work we would expect to see that local union presence is associated with fewer quits and longer job tenure, higher post-training wages, and more trained workers, than in firms where there is no trade union. Stylised facts from the existing empirical literature are consistent with the predictions of our model. For example, empirical studies have found, first, that unions reduce quits (Freeman, 1980; Blau and Kahn, 1983; Freeman and Medoff, 1984; Miller and Mulvey, 1993); and secondly, that there is a positive correlation between firm-provided training and union presence (see *inter alia* Tan *et al.* (1992), Booth (1991) and Green *et al.* (1996)). Legally binding long-term contracts would have the same effect. Of course, the model developed in this paper is partial equilibrium. It would be of interest in future work to extend this to a more general equilibrium framework wherein wage setting in other skilled sector firms is also endogenous.

University of Essex

University of Dundee

Appendix: Proofs of Propositions

Proof of Proposition 1.
Rewrite the first-order condition of (9) as

$$\phi(n) = a - 2b - c'(n) \tag{A1}$$

---

[12] This is because, when $q = 0$, *ex ante* profits for the firm are the same as for the social planner, given by (8).

Notice that ϕ is continuous from continuity of $c'(n)$, and monotonically decreasing because $\phi'(n) = -c''(n) < 0$. Moreover, since $\phi(0) = a - 2b - c'(0) > 0$, there exists $\hat{n} > 0$ such that $\phi(\hat{n}) = 0$. It follows from monotonicity that this $\hat{n}$ is unique (see Fig. 2). To demonstrate that the social surplus is actually positive at $(\hat{q} = 0, \hat{n})$, note that the maximised value of S is given by:

$$\hat{S} = \int_0^{\hat{n}} [a - 2b - c'(n)] \, dn. \tag{A2}$$

Since the integrand is positive over the range of integration, $\hat{S}$ is strictly positive.

Proof of Proposition 2.

For convenience, we rewrite (13) in the text as (A3):

$$w^* + \frac{F(w^*)}{F'(w^*)} = a. \tag{A3}$$

From equation (A3), $w^* < a$ unless $F(w^*) = 0 \Rightarrow w^* = a$. But if $F(w^*) = 0$, from (A3) $w^* = a$ which is a contradiction since, from inequality (4), $a < a$. Hence $w^* < a$; that is, there is a wedge between the optimal period 2 wage for the training firm w^* and the worker's inside marginal productivity a, where the wedge is given by $F(w^*)/F'(w^*)$. Uniqueness of w^* follows from log-concavity, as noted in the text. We now consider existence of w^*.

Define $\phi(w)$ as follows:

$$\phi(w) = w^* + \frac{F(w^*)}{F'(w^*)} - a \tag{A4}$$

Since $F(w)$ has the support $[a, \lambda]$, then $\phi(a) = a - a < 0$, and $\phi(\lambda) = \lambda + [1/F'(\lambda)] - a$, which we assume is positive. (That is, we assume that $F'(\lambda)(a - \lambda) < 1$.) Hence there exists some $w^* \in (a, \lambda)$ such that $\phi(w^*) = 0$, and existence is proved. Uniqueness of w^* follows directly from the fact that $\log \bar{\pi}$ is strictly concave. Note that $dw^*/da > 0$, from direct differentiation of (13) and the log concavity of F.

Proof of Proposition 3.

For convenience, we rewrite (16) in the text as (A5):

$$\mu^* \equiv \mu[w^*(a), a] = a(1 - q^*) + w^* q^* + \int_{w^*}^{\lambda} [1 - F(x)] \, dx. \tag{A5}$$

Total differentiation of (A5) with respect to a (noting that both w^* and q^* are functions of a), and use of Leibnitz' rule, yields:

$$d\mu/da = (1 - q^*) + (w - a) \, dq^*/da > 0. \tag{A6}$$

Since $dq^*/da = (dq^*/dw^*)(dw^*/da) < 0$, then $d\mu/da > 0$. We now show that $\mu^* < a$. From (5a) and (6) if follows that:

$$\int_{w^*}^{\lambda} [1 - F(x)] \, dx = qE(x|x > w) - qw. \tag{A7}$$

Substitute RHS of (A7) into the last term on RHS of (A5) to obtain:

$$\mu^* = a(1 - q^*) + q^* E(x|x > w) = a + q^* (\beta^* - a) \tag{A8}$$

where $\beta^* \equiv E(x|x > w^*)$. Since $\beta^* < \alpha$, then $\mu^* < \alpha$ also. As noted, μ^* is simply the weighted average of the productivity of skilled labour; at the social optimum $\hat{\mu} = \alpha$, because there are no quits. However, at the private optimum, there are quits, and hence the weighted average of the productivity of skilled labour $\mu^* < \alpha$. The proof of existence is as follows. Rewrite (17) in the text as:

$$\pi_n = \mu^* - c'(n^*) - 2b = 0. \tag{A9}$$

Note that π_n is continuous from continuity of $c'(n)$ and monotonically decreasing, since $\pi_{nn} = c''(n) < 0$. Moreover, since $\pi_n(0) = \mu^* - 2b - c'(0) > 0$, there must be some $n^* > 0$ such that $\pi_n(n^*) = 0$. Monotonically decreasing π_n implies that n^* is unique. Since $\mu^* < \alpha$ and $c''(n) > 0$, then $n^* < \hat{n}$. Fig. 3 illustrates.

References

Acemoglu, D. (1996). 'Credit constraints, investment externalities and growth', in Booth, A. L. and D. J. Snower (eds), *Acquiring Skills: Market Failures, their Symptoms and Policy Responses*, Cambridge: Cambridge University Press, ch. 3.

Acemoglu, D. and Pischke, J.-S. (1996). 'Why do firms train? Theory and evidence', mimeo, Department of Economics MIT.

Askildsen, J. A. and Ireland, N. J. (1993). 'Human capital, property rights and labour managed firms', *Oxford Economic Papers*, vol. 45, pp. 229–42.

Black, J. (1994). 'Training, poaching and wage contracts', mimeo Department of Economics, University of Exeter.

Blau, F. D. and Kahn, L. M. (1983). 'Unionism, seniority and turnover', *Industrial Relations*, vol. 22(3), pp. 362–73.

Booth, A. L. (1991). 'Job-related formal training: who receives it and what is it worth?', *Oxford Bulletin of Economics and Statistics*, vol. 53(3), pp. 281–94.

Booth, A. L. and Chatterji, M. (1995). 'Training and contracts' Working Paper no. 95–15, Research Centre on Micro-social Change, University of Essex.

Burdett, K. and Smith, E. (1995). 'The low skill trap', mimeo, Department of Economics, University of Essex.

Caplin, A. and Nalebuff, B. (1991). 'Aggregation and social choice: a mean voter theorem' *Econometrica*, vol. 59(1), pp. 1–23.

Chang, C. and Wang, Y. (1996). 'Human capital investment under asymmetric information: the Pigovian conjecture revisited' *Journal of Labor Economics*, vol. 14(3), pp. 505–19.

Chapman, P. G. (1991). 'Institutional aspects of youth employment and training policy in Britain: a comment', *British Journal of Industrial Relations*, vol. 29, pp. 491–5.

Chatterji, M. (1995). 'Training subsidies, technical progress and economic growth', *The Manchester School*, vol. 63(3), pp. 274–82.

Davis, S. J., Haltiwanger, J. C. and Schuh, S. (1995). *Job Creation and Job Destruction*, Cambridge, MA: MIT Press.

Freeman, R. B. (1980). 'The exit-voice tradeoff in the labor market: unionism, job tenure, quits and separations' *Quarterly Journal of Economics*, vol. 94(4), pp. 643–74.

Freeman, R. B. and Medoff, J. L. (1984). *What Do Unions Do?* New York: Basic Books.

Freeman, R. B. and Katz, L. F. (1995). *Differences and Changes in Wage Structures*, NBER Comparative Labour Markets Series, University of Chicago Press.

Green, F., Machin, S. and Wilkinson, D. (1996). 'Trade unions and training practices in British workplaces', mimeo, University College London.

Hashimoto, M. (1981). 'Firm-specific human capital as a shared investment' *American Economic Review*, vol. 71, pp. 475–82.

Miller, P. and Mulvey, C. (1993). 'What do Australian trade unions do?' *Economic Record*, vol. 69, pp. 315–42.

Mortenson, D. T. and Pissarides, C. A. (1994). 'Job creation and job destruction in the theory of unemployment' *Review of Economic Studies*, vol. 61, pp. 397–415.

OECD (1991). 'Enterprise-related training', *OECD Employment Outlook*, July, Paris: OECD.

OECD (1995). *The Jobs Study*, Paris.

Snower, D. J. (1996). 'The low skill, bad job trap', in Booth, A. L. and Snower, D. J. (eds), *Acquiring Skills: Market Failures, their Symptoms and Policy Responses*, Cambridge: Cambridge University Press, ch. 6.

Soskice, D. (1990). 'Reinterpreting corporatism and explaining unemployment: coordinated and uncoordinated market economies' in (R. Brunetta and C. Dell' Aringa, eds.) *Labour Relations and Economic Performance*, Basingstoke: Macmillan.

Stevens, M. (1994). 'A theoretical model of on-the-job training with imperfect competition' *Oxford Economic Papers*, vol. 46(4) (October), pp. 537–62.

Stevens, M. (1996). 'Transferable training and poaching externalities', in Booth, A. L. and Snower, D. J. (eds), *Acquiring Skills: Market Failures, their Symptoms and Policy Responses*, Cambridge: Cambridge University Press, ch. 2.

Tan, H. W., Chapman, B., Peterson, C. and Booth, A. L. (1992). 'Youth training in the US, Great Britain and Australia', *Research in Labor Economics*, vol. 13, pp. 63–100.

Part II
Empirical Evidence on the
Determinants of Training

[9]

Do U.S. Firms Invest Less in
Human Resources?
Training in the World Auto Industry

JOHN PAUL MACDUFFIE and THOMAS A. KOCHAN*

We investigate the common assertion that U.S. firms invest less in human resources than key international competitors, testing four alternative explanations for differences in training effort found in survey data from an international sample of fifty-seven automobile assembly plants. We find the strongest support for the view that the level of training is derived from the requirements of the business/production strategy and the overall "bundle" of human resource policies—beyond training—adopted by the firm.

IN THIS PAPER, we investigate the often asserted but untested argument that U.S. firms invest less in human resource development of workers relative to their key international competitors (Dertouzos, Solow, and Lester, 1989). We do so by testing four alternative explanations for differences in cross-firm and cross-national training investments observed in an international sample of fifty-seven automobile assembly plants: (1) national-level comparative advantage with respect to human resources; (2) national-level cultural and/or institutional proclivities; (3) new or advanced technologies that require training for new skills; and (4) firm-level strategic choices about how to organize technical and human capabilities within the overall production system.

The macrolevel competitiveness debates have done a good job of stating the basic comparative advantage proposition. Training is important to firms in the United States and other advanced economies because they

---

* The authors' affiliations are, respectively, Wharton School, University of Pennsylvania, and Sloan School, Massachusetts Institute of Technology. The authors gratefully acknowledge the financial support of the International Motor Vehicle Program and the Leaders for Manufacturing Program at MIT. We are also appreciative of helpful comments from Peter Cappelli, Paul Osterman, and Mari Sako.

INDUSTRIAL RELATIONS, Vol. 34, No. 2 (April 1995). © 1995 Regents of the University of California Published by Blackwell Publishers, 238 Main Street, Cambridge, MA 02142, USA, and 108 Cowley Road, Oxford, OX4 1JF, UK.

148 / John Paul MacDuffie and Thomas A. Kochan

cannot compete successfully with low-wage countries on labor costs. There-fore, they must seek comparative advantage from product quality, flexibil-ity, innovation, and product differentiation (Piore and Sabel, 1984), which requires a high-quality labor force. The first hypothesis, therefore, is that firms in advanced industrial economies such as the United States, Japan, and the countries of Western Europe would be expected to train more than firms in low-wage, newly industrialized countries. Since the required skills are often firm-specific, this hypothesis would hold even if one assumes that a higher base of skills is provided by the educational system in these countries than in the low-wage countries.[1]

But among advanced economies, why do we believe there is variation, and particularly variation that reveals low levels of training for U.S. firms? The second hypothesis focuses on macrolevel differences either in national culture or in the industrial relations system that emerge from a country's history and institutional context. Japan, for example, is argued to invest more because "lifetime employment" policies for core employees make labor a fixed rather than a variable cost, thus increasing the value of investments in firm-specific skills (Koike, 1988; Shimada, 1983). Germany is said to invest more because of a national industrial and educational policy that provides apprenticeship training during the secondary school years to facilitate the school-to-work transition (Casey, 1986; Wever, Kochan, and Berg, 1992).

The third hypothesis operates at the industrial or firm level, and takes a "technological upgrading" view—that the implementation of advanced technology will require more highly skilled "knowledge workers" who will need high levels of training (Adler, 1986). The opposite hypothesis—that technological change leads to a net *reduction* in skills and hence a reduced need for training—has also been advanced, as part of the "upskilling vs. downskilling" debate. Empirical evidence to date is inconclusive; automa-tion results in some upskilling and some downskilling, across occupations and different industry contexts (Cappelli, 1993; Attewell, 1992; Kelley, 1989). These findings have stimulated various contingency versions of the "upgrading" hypothesis that emphasize the firm's strategic choices about how technology is used.

---

[1] From this perspective, one should expect the educational system of the advanced industrialized countries to produce graduates with a high level of basic skills that can be further developed through firm training. Given the current furor about the problems of the U.S. educational system, it is clear that this hypothesis does not always hold. Nevertheless, this hypothesis would anticipate an even higher level of training in order to compensate for any deficits in the educational system. This leaves unresolved the claim by some U.S. companies that the poor educational system prevents them from finding the skilled employees necessary for the high value-added strategy.

Do U.S. Firms Invest Less in Training? / 149

The fourth hypothesis operates at the level of the firm and suggests that training investments are dependent on firm-level strategic choices rather than exogenous factors such as macroeconomic context, national culture, or new technologies. This hypothesis draws on what strategy researchers call the "resource-based view of the firm" (Barney, 1986) for its view that business and production strategies emerge from a firm's "core capabilities"—the knowledge of products and processes and relationships with suppliers and customers that convey sustainable competitive advantage. These capabilities are grounded in the firm-specific skills of employees, which provides an incentive for both on-the-job and off-the-job training (Cappelli and Singh, 1993).

This hypothesis also draws on two themes found in recent literature on the link between human resource (HR) practices and economic performance: (1) that "bundles" of interdependent HR practices, rather than individual practices, are the appropriate level of analysis for understanding the link to performance (Ichniowski, Shaw, and Prennushi, 1993; Arthur, 1992; Cutcher-Gershenfeld, 1991; MacDuffie, 1995); and (2) that these HR bundles or systems must be integrated with the firm's business strategy to be effective (Majchrzak, 1988; Kochan, Cutcher-Gershenfeld, and MacDuffie, 1991).

From this perspective, the level of training is derived from the requirements of the overall business strategy and the bundle of HR policies—beyond training—adopted by the firm. In the context of the automotive industry, we argue that firms using flexible production systems require more skill and motivation from employees than those using traditional mass production. As such, they have a strong incentive to invest in a bundle of innovative HR practices—including a high level of training—that yield the desired work force capabilities, irrespective of national context or level of technology. We develop this hypothesis further below, in the context of flexible production.[2]

In the studies cited above, training is treated as one item in the bundle of HR policies and the whole bundle is used as the relevant dependent or independent variable. Here we need to separate out training from the

---

[2] These hypotheses do not address the issue of how training affects economic performance. Another paper based on these data (MacDuffie, 1995) finds that flexible production plants, which combine low levels of buffers with bundles of HR policies promoting worker motivation and skill development, achieve higher productivity and quality than traditional mass production plants. The role of training in performance is subsumed under the broader question of how the overall HR system affects performance. This is consistent with the "flexible production systems" hypothesis, and suggests a related (although untested) hypothesis—that high training levels alone, in the context of a traditional mass production system, would not lead to better economic performance.

150 / John Paul MacDuffie and Thomas A. Kochan

overall bundle to test the influence of firm choices about production system and HR policies relative to the larger forces captured by the national-level and technology hypotheses. Support for the fourth hypothesis will indicate that flexible production systems do have high levels of training, as the "bundling" perspective implies. However, some plants with mass production systems may very well train at high levels because of the national industrial relations system or the level of advanced technology.

Sorting out the relative importance of these explanations should have implications for public policy. If the comparative advantage explanation dominates, then natural market forces should lead firms operating in advanced industrial countries to invest in training since it will be the only way to sustain their high-skill advantage. If the national culture/institutions hypothesis dominates, then public policy needs to focus on national strategies and structures for requiring or encouraging firms and workers to invest in training. If technology drives training, then strategies that encourage investments in automation should suffice. If transforming production and human resource systems increases training, then policies that encourage these organizational transformations are called for.

The "Organizational Logic" of Flexible Production

Flexible production organizes both technical capabilities and human capabilities differently than mass production, with direct implications for training. The "organizational logic" of flexible production *reduces* the technical system's ability to function in the face of contingencies (problem conditions) through the minimization of buffers of all kinds—thus reducing slack, increasing task interdependence, and raising the visibility of problems—and *expands* human capabilities, so that people can deal effectively with these problem conditions and achieve improvements in the production system.

Under mass production, the realization of economies of scale is paramount, so buffers (e.g., extra inventories or repair space) are added to the production system to protect against potential disruptions, such as sales fluctuations, supply interruptions, and equipment breakdowns. Such buffers are seen as costly under flexible production because they hide production problems. As long as inventory stocks are high, a defective part has no impact on production, because it can simply be scrapped and replaced. But when inventories are very low, as with a Just-in-Time inventory system, a bad part can bring the production system to a halt. The minimization of buffers serves a cybernetic or feedback function, providing valuable information about production problems (Schonberger, 1982).

Do U.S. Firms Invest Less in Training? / 151

Under flexible production's philosophy of continuous improvement, problems identified through the minimization of buffers are seen as opportunities for organizational learning (Ono, 1988; Imai, 1986). Ongoing problem-solving processes on the shop floor, alternating between experimentation with procedural change and the careful standardization of each improved method, yield a steady stream of incremental improvements (Tyre and Orlikowski, 1993). In a sense, the "buffering" capability to cope with change shifts from the technical system to the human system (Adler, 1992; Cole, 1992; MacDuffie, 1991).

In order to identify and resolve quality problems as they appear, workers must have both a conceptual grasp of the production process and the analytical skills to identify the root cause of problems.[3] To develop such skills and knowledge, flexible production utilizes a variety of multiskilling practices, including work teams, quality circles, job rotation within a few broad job classifications, and the decentralization of quality responsibilities from specialized inspectors to production workers. Furthermore, to insure that workers contribute the attentiveness and analytical perspective necessary for effective problem-solving, flexible production is characterized by such "high commitment" human resource policies as employment security, compensation that is partially contingent on performance, and a reduction of status barriers between managers and workers (Shimada and MacDuffie, 1986).

This account of flexible production is challenged by various observers (e.g., Parker and Slaughter, 1988; Huxley, Robertson, and Rinehart, 1991) who claim that such a system is based on "management by stress." The reduction of buffers is said to increase work pace and to create stress among workers by focusing blame on them when mistakes are found. Related changes in work organization (e.g., teams) and human resource

---

[3] For example, there are many possible reasons why a worker might have difficulty installing a component on the assembly line. The component could have quality problems as delivered by the supplier that must be fixed before it can be installed. The attachment holes on the body may not be drilled or may be in the wrong location due to problems in the welding department, or blocked with sealer because of improper application in the paint department. A misinstalled part from an upstream operation on the assembly line could be the problem. A tool with the wrong torque could strip the threads on a bolt during the fastening process. The immediate decision for a worker is whether or not to stop the assembly line, in order to remedy the situation quickly (e.g., scraping off the sealer blocking an attachment hole). The next step is to find out whether the problem is recurrent and, if so, to develop a short-term "countermeasure" to prevent defects from continuing to be produced. The team leader and support staff would help here by communicating information about the defect to the supplier or the appropriate upstream department or work station. Finally, in a "off-line" quality circle or other form of problem-solving group, workers would seek a "permanent" countermeasure, applying various analytical techniques (e.g., Statistical Process Control, Pareto analysis, "fishbone" analysis, using the "five whys" to track each problem back to its "root cause").

152 / JOHN PAUL MACDUFFIE AND THOMAS A. KOCHAN

policies (e.g., performance-linked pay) are seen as efforts to increase management influence and weaken worker solidarity. High levels of training under flexible production are similarly seen as efforts to exert cultural control over workers, socializing them to accept the demands of the production system, rather than to impart necessary skills. While the data available for this paper do not allow these issues to be addressed directly, this view of flexible production will be considered in the closing discussion.

Training under Flexible Production

Unlike mass production, which is premised on the assumption that production work involves little skill and requires little training, flexible production sees production workers as skilled problem solvers who must be adequately prepared for their task through effective training. One consequence is that flexible production requires a high level of competency in reading, math, reasoning, and communication skills. If the existence of these skills is not reliably guaranteed by the public educational system, flexible production plants are likely to screen carefully for these skills or to provide remedial training.

Under flexible production, the majority of training in technical skills is carried out by the firm, through a lengthy period of on-the-job training (OJT) (Koike, 1988). In contrast, mass production firms tend to provide limited off-the-job technical training in classroom settings, which they view as superior to OJT. Under mass production, OJT has had a connotation of brief, informal training—for example, a new hire who is given a few hours of instruction from a co-worker and then "learns the ropes" through unstructured observation and imitation. By comparison, OJT in flexible production plants involves trainers who work intensively with new hires, at first demonstrating, then coaching, and who stay on the shop floor after initial training to show workers how to handle non-routine problem conditions (Ford, 1986). This is a very effective way to convey tacit knowledge about jobs and leads to high retention of what is learned, both because of its experiential approach and because individuals acquire skills very close to the time when they will need to use them.

Finally, training in these flexible production plants aims to teach not only substantive knowledge but also processes of problem-solving and learning (Imai, 1986; Lillrank and Kano, 1989). This training, combined with employment continuity policies, reinforces the willingness of the firm to invest heavily in its employees, thus bolstering the cultural norms of reciprocal obligation that help maintain employee commitment and motivation under flexible production (Dore, 1992).

Do U.S. Firms Invest Less in Training? / 153

Thus, having a work force that is multiskilled, adaptable to rapidly changing circumstances, and with broad conceptual knowledge about the production system is critical to the operation of a flexible production system. The learning process that generates these human capabilities is an integral part of how the production system functions, not a separate training activity. The demand for training is a function of the extent to which a flexible production system is deployed (Sako, 1992).

Hypotheses

The four competing hypotheses on training we are testing can be summarized as follows:

H1: Comparative advantage. Investments in training result from national comparative advantage with respect to human resources. Specifically, firms in the advanced industrial economies (U.S., Japan, and Western Europe) that cannot compete on the basis of low labor costs will invest more in training than "low wage" newly industrialized countries.

H2: National institutions. Investments in training result from the education/training institutional infrastructure that exists in different countries for cultural and/or historical reasons. Specifically, firms located in Japan and Germany (among other European countries) will invest more in training than firms located in the U.S. and newly industrialized countries.

H3: Technology. Investments in training result from the extent to which the firm has implemented advanced automation. Specifically, firms with higher levels of robotics will invest more in training than firms with fewer or no robots.

H4: Flexible production. Investments in training are an interrelated part of the firm's choices about business/production strategy and the overall human resource system. Specifically, firms that utilize a flexible production system will invest more in training than firms utilizing a mass production system.

Empirical Evidence

Sample. Our data are from the International Assembly Plant Study, carried out through the International Motor Vehicle Program (IMVP) at M.I.T.[4] Ninety assembly plants were contacted, representing twenty-four

---

[4] The International Motor Vehicle Program (IMVP) was a five-year research program (1985–90) sponsored by virtually every automotive company in the world (Womack, Jones, and Roos, 1990). IMVP continues now as one of the Sloan Foundation-funded centers for the study of industrial competitiveness.

154 / John Paul MacDuffie and Thomas A. Kochan

producers in sixteen countries, and approximately 60 percent of total assembly plant capacity worldwide. Survey responses were received from seventy plants during 1989 and early 1990. The proportion of plants in different regions is closely related to the proportion of worldwide production volume, with some underrepresentation of Japanese plants in Japan and overrepresentation of Newly Industrialized Countries (NIC) and Australian plants, whose volumes are low. Plants were chosen to achieve a balanced distribution across regions and companies, and to reflect a range of performance within each participating company, minimizing the potential for selectivity bias.

Questionnaire Administration. Questionnaires were sent to a contact person who distributed different sections to the appropriate departmental manager or staff group. Plants and companies were guaranteed complete confidentiality and, in return for their participation, received a feedback report comparing their responses with mean scores for different regions. All ninety plants that were contacted were visited by one of the two primary researchers between 1987 and 1990. Early visits provided the field observations that became the foundation of the assembly plant questionnaire. For the seventy plants that returned a questionnaire, the visit often followed receipt of the questionnaire, providing an opportunity to fill in missing data, clarify responses that were unclear or not internally consistent, and carry out interviews to aid the later interpretation of data analyses.

Variables. Methodological details for variables in the Assembly Plant Study, including the control variables used here, can be found in Krafcik (1988), MacDuffie (1991), and MacDuffie and Krafcik (1992). Here only the main dependent and independent variables are described in detail. For these variables, we have complete data from fifty-seven plants.

In comparison with other studies, the data used here have a number of advantages, particularly in the measurement of HR practices. Many studies of HR practices look across industries and must therefore specify those practices in broad, general terms. Furthermore, many such studies measure practices at the firm level, with little indication of within-company variation (e.g., Ichniowski, 1991; Lawler, Mohrman, and Ledford, 1992). In comparison, these data come from one context, thus controlling for industry and technology/task complexity. Questions are customized to auto assembly plants, boosting their reliability and allowing intracompany variation to be captured.

Training Effort. This dependent variable is based on the number of hours of off-the-job and on-the-job training received by new and experi-

Do U.S. Firms Invest Less in Training? / 155

enced (over one year of employment) production workers.[5] They are the employees most likely to receive different training treatment in the situations captured by the four hypotheses—particularly in auto assembly, where production work has traditionally been seen as unskilled (or marginally semi-skilled) work requiring little training.[6] Since new hires typically receive many more hours of training than experienced production workers do annually,[7] training hours for these two groups are standardized by conversion to z-scores before being added together to form the Training Effort measure. To aid interpretability when presenting regional means, the summed z-scores are rescaled so that 0 represents the plant with the lowest training effort in the sample, and 100 the plant with the highest effort. Table 1 contains regional means for actual training hours for these two groups of employees, as well as means and standard deviations for the Training Effort index and t-tests for statistically significant differences in the regional scores.

One caveat with an effort-based measure of training is that more training is not always better than less training. The Training Effort measure does not distinguish between different topics or different methods of training. As such, it cannot address questions about what kinds of training in what areas are most effective.

---

[5] The questions on training asked for hours of training per employee provided in the first six months of employment (for new hires) or in the past calendar year (for employees with more than one year of previous experience) for three groups of employees: production workers, first-line supervisors, and plant engineers. These total hours are divided between the percentage provided on-the-job and the percentage provided off-the-job. Other training questions asked about whether off-the-job training was provided by plant staff, corporate staff, outside consultants/educational institutions, or vendors. Open-ended questions asking for the "five most important training topics" proved difficult to evaluate because of the wide diversity of topics that were listed and the difficulty in interpreting the content of topics in an international sample.

[6] Training hours for maintenance/skilled trades workers were not measured. This raises the question of whether the training of production workers allows them to do tasks once performed by skilled maintenance workers, with a consequent reduction in training for this latter group. While there is evidence that the *number* of indirect employees (who perform maintenance, material handling, and quality control tasks) is lower in flexible production plants (Ittner and MacDuffie, 1994), there is little reason to expect that the *skill level* of maintenance workers (and hence their need for training) in flexible production plants would be lower because of higher levels of training for production workers. Presumably well-trained production workers would take over simple maintenance tasks requiring relatively little technical skill, thus boosting the skill content of tasks performed by maintenance workers.

[7] One might expect the level of training to vary as a function of the educational level of employees, both new hires and experienced workers, and in relation to whether the plant is new and hiring lots of employees or old and hiring few (or no) employees. Both of these factors were investigated as variables added to the regression analyses reported below, but neither helped explain any of the variation in training.

156 / JOHN PAUL MACDUFFIE AND THOMAS A. KOCHAN

TABLE 1

REGIONAL MEANS
TRAINING HOURS AND TRAINING EFFORT INDEX FOR PRODUCTION WORKERS

	Jpn/Jpn	Jpn/NA	US/NA	US/Eur	Eur/Eur	NIC	Aust
Newly Hired Production Workers (hours in first 6 months)	364	225	42	43	178	260	40
Experienced Production Workers (hours per year for those with over 1 year of experience)	76	52	31	34	52	46	15
Training Effort Index[a]	49.1[b]	31.5[c]	12.5[d]	13.6[e]	28.5[f]	31.0[g]	6.0[h]
S.D. for Training Effort Index	28.6	8.2	8.0	12.7	20.8	31.8	3.9
n	8	4	14	4	10	11	6

[a] Index is the sum of z-scores for training hours for new and experienced production workers, rescaled from 0 to 100. Significance level for all t-tests is $p < .05$.
[b] Mean significantly different from US/NA, US/Eur, Aust.
[c] Mean significantly different from US/NA, US/Eur, Aust.
[d] Mean significantly different from Jpn/Jpn, Jpn/NA, Eur/Eur, NIC.
[e] Mean significantly different from Jpn/Jpn, Jpn/NA.
[f] Mean significantly different from US/NA, Aust.
[g] Mean significantly different from US/NA, Aust.
[h] Mean significantly different from Jpn/Jpn, Jpn/NA, Eur/Eur, NIC.

Jpn/Jpn = Japanese-owned plants in Japan
Jpn/NA   = Japanese-owned plants in North America
US/NA   = U.S.-owned plants in North America
US/Eur   = U.S.-owned plants in Europe
Eur/Eur = European-owned plants in Europe
NIC   = Newly industrialized countries (Korea, Mexico, Taiwan, Brazil)
Aust   = Australia

Production Organization Measures. To operationalize the "organizational logic" of flexible and mass production systems, two measures related to a plant's production organization are developed: Use of Buffers and HR System. Each is an index made up of multiple variables, described below, that are standardized by conversion to z-scores before being additively combined. Each index is then transformed for easier interpretability, on a scale from 0 to 100 where 0 is the plant with the lowest score in the sample and 100 the plant with the highest score. Reliability tests for each index show a Cronbach's alpha score of .63 for Use of Buffers and .80 for HR System. Table 2 contains the means of individual variables making up these two indices and the indices themselves, for the whole sample and for three clusters of plants—mass production and flexible production plants at the ends of the continuum and a group of "transition" plants in between.[8]

---

[8] Previous analyses comparing various clustering methods (not reported here) found that the Euclidean measure for distance between cluster centroids and the Within Group Average method of forming clusters produced the most statistically distinct clusters. These methods were used to derive two, three, and four cluster solutions. Means from the three-cluster solution are presented here, since they can be readily interpreted.

Do U.S. Firms Invest Less in Training? / 157

TABLE 2
MEANS OF PRODUCTION ORGANIZATION VARIABLES AND INDICES ACROSS CLUSTERS OF PLANTS

Variable	Sample (n = 57)	MassProd (n = 29)	Transition (n = 14)	FlexProd (n = 14)	F
Repair Area (Sq. feet as % Assembly Area)	10.4	13.7	9.1	4.8	15.8***
Paint-Ass'y Buffer (% of 1-shift production)	23.3	29.7	18.7	14.6	3.9**
Inventory Level (Days supply for 8 parts)	2.1	2.8	2.1	0.63	18.7***
% Work Force in Teams	22.4	5.0	10.4	70.2	38.6***
% Work Force in EI, QC Groups	32.5	16.5	20.9	77.4	17.8***
Suggestions per Employee	9.2	0.24	0.33	36.5	15.3***
% Suggestions Implemented	36.3	25.5	23.8	72.0	16.8***
Job Rotation Index (0 = none, 4 = extensive)	1.8	1.2	1.9	3.0	20.8***
Quality Control at Shop Floor (0 = none, 4 = extensive)	3.1	2.6	2.9	4.5	2.8*
Hiring Criteria (Low = match past experience to job, High = interpersonal skills, willingness to learn new skills)	35.1	32.7	35.8	39.4	12.7***
Training New Hires (0 = low, 3 = high)	1.6	1.0	1.9	2.4	13.1***
Training Experienced Employees (0 = low, 3 = high)	1.4	0.9	1.6	2.1	7.9***
Contingent Compensation (0 = none, 4 = based on plant performance)	1.6	0.72	2.2	3.0	20.0***
Status Differentiation (0 = extensive, 4 = little)	1.9	1.1	2.0	3.4	17.7***
Use of Buffers Index	58.7	44.7	62.7	83.5	28.3***
Human Resource System Index	33.6	16.1	30.1	73.2	59.4***

* Statistically significant at .10 level; ** statistically significant at .05 level; *** statistically significant at .01 level.

Use of Buffers: This index measures a set of production practices that are indicative of overall production philosophy with respect to buffers (e.g., incoming and work-in-process inventory), with a low score signifying a "buffered" system and a high score signifying a "lean" system. It consists of three items:

- the space (in square feet) dedicated to final assembly repair, as a percentage of total assembly area square footage;
- the average number of vehicles held in the work-in-process buffer between the paint and assembly areas, as a percentage of one shift production; and
- the average level of inventory stocks, in days for a sample of eight key parts, weighted by the cost of each part.

158 / JOHN PAUL MACDUFFIE AND THOMAS A. KOCHAN

HR System: This index captures how work is organized, in terms of both formal work structures and the allocation of work responsibilities, the participation of employees in production-related problem-solving activity, and HR policies that affect the "psychological contract" between the employee and the organization, and hence employee motivation and commitment. A low score for this index indicates an HR system that is "low-skill" and "low-commitment" in orientation, while a high score indicates a "multiskilling," "high-commitment" orientation. It consists of seven different items:

- the percentage of the work force involved in "on-line" work teams and "off-line" employee involvement groups;
- the number of production-related suggestions received per employee and the percentage implemented;
- the extent of job rotation within and across teams (0 = no job rotation, 1 = infrequent rotation within teams, 2 = frequent rotation within teams, 3 = frequent rotation within teams and across teams of the same department, 4 = frequent rotation within teams, across teams and across departments);
- the degree to which production workers carry out quality tasks (0 = functional specialists responsible for all quality responsibilities; 1, 2, 3, 4 = production workers responsible for 1, 2, 3 or 4 of the following tasks: inspection of incoming parts, work-in-process, finished products, gathering Statistical Process Control data);
- the hiring criteria used to select employees in three categories: production workers, first line supervisors, and engineers (the sum of rankings of the importance of various hiring criteria for these three groups of employees, with low scores for criteria that emphasize the fit between an applicant's existing skills and job requirements ("previous experience in a similar job") and high scores for criteria that emphasize openness to learning and interpersonal skills ("a willingness to learn new skills" and "ability to work with others");
- the extent to which a compensation system is contingent upon performance (0 = no contingent compensation; 1 = compensation contingent on corporate performance; 2 = compensation contingent on plant performance, for managers only; 3 = compensation contingent on plant performance or skills acquired, production employees only; and 4 = compensation contingent on plant performance, all employees);
- the extent to which status barriers between managers and workers are present (0 = no implementation of policies that break down status barriers and 1, 2, 3, 4 = implementation of 1, 2, 3, or 4 of

Do U.S. Firms Invest Less in Training? / 159

these policies: common uniform, common cafeteria, common park-
ing, no ties).

Robotic Index. This variable indicates the extent to which advanced technology is used in a plant. It measures the number of robots, defined as programmable equipment with at least three axes of movement, in the weld,
paint, and assembly departments of an assembly plant, adjusted for plant
scale. This is one of two alternate technology variables used in the larger
study. The other, Total Automation, covers the entire automation stock of a
plant, measuring the percentage of direct production steps in the welding,
paint, and assembly areas that are automated. While Total Automation is
more comprehensive, it does not distinguish the age or type (e.g., programmable vs. dedicated) of automation. Thus the Robotic Index is more appropriate for testing the technology hypothesis, given that training needs are
said to increase most when new, programmable technology is implemented.[9]

Control Variables. Four other measures of the plant's production system
are used here as controls. **Plant Scale** is defined as the average number of
vehicles built during a standard, non-overtime day, adjusted for capacity
utilization. **Model Mix Complexity** measures the mix of different products
and product variants produced in the plant. It includes the number of distinct platforms, models, body styles, drive train configurations (front-wheel
vs. rear-wheel drive), and export variations (right-hand vs. left-hand steer-
ing). The **Parts Complexity** index includes three measures of parts
variation—the number of engine/transmission combinations, wire har-
nesses, and exterior paint colors—that affect the sequencing of vehicles, the
task variability facing production workers, and material handling requirements; and three measures—the number of total parts to the assembly area,
the percentage of common parts across models, and the number of suppliers
to the assembly area—that affect the administrative/coordination requirements for dealing with suppliers. **Product Design Age** is the weighted average number of years since a major model change introduction for each of the
products currently being built at each plant, and serves as a partial proxy for
manufacturability in the assembly area, under the assumption that products
designed more recently are more likely to have been conceived with ease of
assembly in mind than older products.

---

[9] The two measures are very highly correlated ($r = .81$), since plants with above-average scores for
Total Automation have generally directed most of their recent technology investment toward robotic
technology. The results reported below, using the Robotic Index variable, are nearly identical when the
Total Automation measure is used.

160 / John Paul MacDuffie and Thomas A. Kochan

Regional Differences in Training Effort. The regional means in Table 1 provide the initial basis for evaluating the "comparative advantage" and "national institutions" hypotheses concerning national-level training differentials.[10] Plants in the newly industrialized countries (NIC) train *more* than U.S.-owned plants in North America and plants in Australia, suggesting that the hypothesis linking higher levels of training to advanced industrialized economies is not supported. The very high differentials in training effort among the three most industrialized groups of plants (in the United States, Europe, and Japan) call both the first and second hypotheses into question.[11] This variation suggests that the determinants of training go well beyond wage rates, since wage differentials among the United States, Japan, and Europe are much smaller than the training differentials.

Examination of Japanese-owned plants in North America (J/NA) and U.S.-owned plants in Europe (US/Eur) also challenges the hypothesis that the national infrastructure for education and training determines training levels, since both sets of "transplants" offer different amounts of training than locally owned plants—the J/NA plants train more than US/NA plants, and US/Eur plants train less than Eur/Eur plants. Another sign that training differentials reflect firm-level rather than national-level factors is the lack of significant differences in training effort between J/J and J/NA plants and between US/NA and US/Eur plants. These findings suggest that the "comparative advantage" and "national institutions" hypotheses are not supported, although a full test of national-level factors requires controls for other variables, as below.

Regression Analyses. Table 3 contains descriptive statistics and Table 4 reports the results of regression analyses with the Training Effort index as the dependent variable.

Equation (1) includes dummy variables for the regional groups in Table

---

[10] Examination of the distribution of the Training Effort variable shows that five plants are outliers above the sample mean—two Japanese-owned plants in Japan, one European-owned plant in Europe, and two plants in newly industrialized countries. These outliers account for the high standard deviation for these three regional groupings, and undoubtedly affect the regional means as well. Since we have no reason to believe that the data from these plants are incorrect, we judged that it was better to include them when calculating the sample mean, rather than excluding them. To test the impact of these outliers, all regression analyses (reported below) were repeated using log training effort as the dependent variable. The results were unchanged.

[11] While there is variation within the group of plants in Europe, which come from seven countries, it appears to be based on the company rather than the country. This is particularly striking with respect to Germany, which is often described as having very high levels of training. The two German plants in the sample train less than some plants in France, Belgium, Sweden, and Italy, although more than plants in Britain and Spain. Indeed, the level of variation within many of the regional groupings is impressively high.

Do U.S. Firms Invest Less in Training? / 161

TABLE 3
DESCRIPTIVE STATISTICS FOR REGRESSION ANALYSES
(n = 57)

Variable	Mean	S.D.
Training Effort	24.7	23.7
Scale	936	651
Model Mix Complexity	30.6	21.2
Parts Complexity	56.5	23.5
Product Design Age	4.7	3.3
Robotic Index	2.2	2.0
Use of Buffers	58.7	22.4
HR System	33.6	26.3
Buffers by HR System	371.3	626.4
Jpn/Jpn Dummy	0.14	0.35
Jpn/NA Dummy	0.07	0.26
US/Eur Dummy	0.07	0.26
Eur/Eur Dummy	0.17	0.38
NIC Dummy	0.19	0.40
Australia Dummy	0.10	0.31

1 to test the two national-level hypotheses, with the dummy for U.S.-owned plants in North America omitted to make it the comparison group. The results echo the comparison of means, with statistically significant differences in training level from the comparison group for Japanese-owned plants in Japan, European-owned plants in Europe, and plants in newly industrialized countries. Contrary to Table 1, the "Japanese transplant" dummy was not statistically significant, with a T-value of 1.62 (p = .11), but the sign of the coefficient for this and the other regional dummies (U.S.-owned plants in Europe and Australian plants) is in the right direction. Again, the "comparative advantage" and "national institutions" hypotheses are not supported. However, with an adjusted R^2 of .243, this equation does suggest that national/regional differences in training are pronounced.

Equation (2) tests the "technology" hypothesis by including the Robotic Index and the four control variables, and is also the "base case" for testing the other firm-level hypotheses. With a non-significant adjusted R^2 of .029 and coefficients for all variables that are indistinguishable from zero, the hypothesis about the relationship between advanced automation and training effort is disconfirmed. Clearly, plants with similar levels of robotics have very different training policies.

Equations (3)–(5) test the "flexible production systems" hypothesis, in three stages. In each case, an F-test is applied to the change in R^2 from the preceding equation, to see if the added variables boost predictive power.

162 / John Paul MacDuffie and Thomas A. Kochan

TABLE 4

REGRESSION MODEL FOR TRAINING IN THE AUTOMOBILE INDUSTRY
(standard error in parentheses)

Variable	(1)	(2)	(3)	(4)	(5)	(6)
Jpn/Jpn Dum	36.7***	—	—	—	—	1.53
	(9.15)					(22.9)
Jpn/NA Dum	18.99	—	—	—	—	−2.03
	(11.7)					(14.8)
US/Eur Dum	1.14	—	—	—	—	11.6
	(11.7)					(12.4)
Eur/Eur Dum	16.1*	—	—	—	—	26.7***
	(8.55)					(9.70)
NIC Dum	18.5**	—	—	—	—	21.9***
	(8.31)					(9.27)
Aust Dum	−6.47	—	—	—	—	−11.9
	(10.1)					(10.5)
Scale	—	.008	.005	.007	.007	.002
		(.006)	(.006)	(.005)	(.006)	(.005)
Model Mix Complexity	—	.129	.021	.018	.034	.066
		(.170)	(.171)	(.161)	(.157)	(.158)
Parts Complexity		−.124	−.077	−.151	−.204	−0.369**
		(.176)	(.171)	(.163)	(.162)	(.173)
AgeCar	—	−1.46	.004	−.318	−.545	−1.89
		(1.13)	(1.28)	(1.21)	(1.18)	(1.21)
Robotic Index	—	.432	.536	−1.50	−1.58	−1.18
		(2.01)	(1.94)	(1.97)	(1.92)·	(2.08)
Use of Buffers	—	—	.384***	.076	.112	.231
			(.176)	(.199)	(.196)	(.202)
HR System	—	—	—	.422***	.206	.105
				(.154)	(.191)	(.220)
Buffers by HRSys	—	—	—	—	.012**	.016**
					(.006)	(.008)
Adj. R^2	.243	.029	.095	.199	.237	.380
F for equation	4.0***	1.3	2.0*	2.9***	3.2***	3.5***
F for Change in R^2 from Preceding Equation	—	—	4.8**	7.5***	3.4*	2.9**

* = Statistically significant at .10 level; ** = statistically significant at .05 level; *** = statistically significant at .01 level.

Equation (3) adds the Use of Buffers index to the control variables, has an adjusted R^2 of .095 and is statistically significant. The Buffers index is significant at the 99 percent confidence level and has the expected sign, with more training associated with smaller buffers of inventory and repair space, consistent with the hypothesis about flexible production.

Equation (4), which adds the other production organization index, HR System, has an adjusted R^2 of .199, a significant increase from equation (3). With HR System and Use of Buffers both in the equation, only the

Do U.S. Firms Invest Less in Training? / 163

former is significant, at the 99 percent confidence level. This is not surprising, given the high correlation ($r = .65$) between the two indices. This finding is also consistent with evidence from other analyses (not presented here) that some plants begin the transition to flexible production by reducing buffers but do not make corresponding changes in their HR policies (at least initially).

Equation (5) includes the interaction term, Buffers by HR System, to test whether the hypothesized integration of production policies and HR policies helps explain training levels better than the individual indices. The adjusted R^2 of this equation is .237, which represents a statistically significant increase over equation (4). Here only the interaction term is statistically significant (at the 95 percent significance level) and the individual indices are not. This is strongly supportive of the idea that training is linked to the overall "organization logic" of flexible production (and not just its bundle of HR practices) and provides the strongest evidence for this hypothesis.

Finally, equation (6) reintroduces the regional dummy variables from equation (1) to assess the relative explanatory power of different variables when all are included. The adjusted R^2 of .38 is a statistically significant increase over equation (5). The Buffers by HR System interaction term retains the same significance level. Of the regional dummy variables, those for European-owned plants in Europe and for newly industrialized countries are significant, as in equation (1), with positive coefficients. In fact, their coefficients are higher in equation (6), with greater statistical significance, than in equation (1). In other words, both of these regional groups provide higher levels of training than their approach to the production system (which is closer to mass production than flexible production) would predict.

But the regional dummy for Japanese-owned plants in Japan is not significant once the production system variables are included. Furthermore, the coefficient for the "Japanese transplant" dummy variable, which is not significant in either equation (1) or (6), drops dramatically in equation (6). The Japanese-owned plants appear to train a lot because they rely heavily on flexible production, while the U.S.-owned plants in Europe and the Australian plants appear to train very little because they follow traditional mass production practices and philosophies.

These results provide limited support for the view that differences in national practices affect the level of training, even aside from differences in production systems. In Europe, in particular, many countries have strong public policy support for extensive training, with the German apprenticeship model as the most notable example. But plants in Europe

164 / John Paul MacDuffie and Thomas A. Kochan

(whether European-owned or U.S.-owned) have not, for the most part, implemented flexible production. One explanation is that the volume producers in Europe (Volkswagen, Fiat, Renault) have used the past fifteen years to move closer to the high volume, standard product approach of mass production—a goal that proved elusive in earlier years, when production volumes were low and craft methods more strongly entrenched (Womack, Jones, and Roos, 1990). As a result, the *demand* for worker skills in European auto plants may be limited because mass production principles are used, even though the education and training infrastructure has produced an ample *supply* of those skills. On the other hand, U.S.-owned plants in Europe appear bound by U.S.-set policies and exempt from (or resistant to) host-country institutional pressures to boost training.

The case of the newly industrialized countries is equally intriguing. Plants in these low-wage countries, where absenteeism and turnover are typically high, are not expected to offer much training. Nevertheless, some auto assembly plants in these countries have achieved quality (if not productivity) levels comparable to those in the advanced industrialized countries, and they have been willing to make unusually high investments in training (if not wages) to achieve these results.

Discussion

These results support the popular hypothesis that U.S. firms tend to invest less in the development of human resources than their Japanese and European competitors. Moreover, this gap will not be automatically closed by greater investments in high technology. Training levels have virtually no relationship with the level of technology in these assembly plants, nor with a plant's scale, product mix, or parts complexity. Instead, these results suggest that two factors drive investments in training—the production strategy employed by the organization and some characteristics of the national environment of the parent firm.

The significance of the production organization indices, both separately and in interaction, suggests that one way to encourage training in U.S. firms is to support the diffusion of flexible production models that demand greater training. This raises a variety of issues about supply vs. demand for skills and training. The case of Europe shows that the presence of relatively high levels of training is not automatically associated with the adoption of flexible production systems. So public policies that boost the supply of skills through mandated training, in the absence of action by firms to adopt new approaches to organizing work, may not improve the demand

Do U.S. Firms Invest Less in Training? / 165

(and hence utilization) of skills.[12] On the other hand, if firms move toward flexible production and are not able to find an adequate supply of workers with the necessary skills in reading, math, and analytical problem-solving, the implementation of new work structures may be slowed or firms may have to assume the cost of remedial training.

This analysis implies that firm choices about production strategy will still be the primary determinant of training effort. The examples of Japanese-owned plants in North America and U.S.-owned plants in Europe, both of which train at very different levels than other plants located in the same region,[13] reveal how strong the influence of corporate-wide training policies is, compared with national-level institutional pressures.[14] Thus the role for public policy may lie primarily in encouraging the demand for skills by the firm. Policies that promote the adoption and diffusion of flexible production and new approaches to organizing work (often labeled "high performance" work systems) should have a positive byproduct of increasing the level of training.

While not addressed by these data, the *content* of training under flexible production has important implications for both firm-level and national-level training policy. Training prompted by national government policies or institutionalized throughout the national industrial relations system is more likely to emphasize the development of technical skills that are porta-

---

[12] As European companies move toward flexible production, their highly trained workers may prove to be an important asset in the transition. However, this will depend on whether the skills of European workers are well-suited to the requirements of flexible production. The German apprenticeship-based approach to training and certification arguably produces excellent functional specialists, whereas flexible production appears to require multiskilled generalists.

[13] To test for a possible "ownership" effect on training, the regression analyses in Table 5 were repeated using dummy variables signifying the home region of the company that owns each assembly plant. For example, this categorization would group together plants from a U.S.-owned multinational (e.g., General Motors) located in the United States, Europe, Central and Latin America, and Australia. With U.S. company-owned plants as the comparison category, only the Japanese-owned dummy variable was significant in equation (1) and only the European-owned dummy variable was significant in equation (6). We concluded that the regional dummies used in Table 5 are preferable because the within-group variation among the U.S.-owned, European-owned, Japanese-owned, and Korean-owned groups is quite high. For example, the standard deviation for all U.S.-owned plants is 16.7, vs. 8.0 for U.S.-owned plants in North America and 12.7 for U.S.-owned plants in Europe.

[14] Ownership of a plant will only correspond to the nationality of a firm's management if expatriate managers are sent to run the plant—something that appears to be true for Japanese-owned plants in the U.S. but may not be true for U.S.-owned plants in Europe. The dummy variable for the Japanese transplants already captures the "nationality of management" effect for this group. At most other plants located out of the home region of their parent company, local managers feature more prominently in the plant management. A full test of the "nationality of management" hypothesis would require some threshold level that identifies when expatriates can be said to be managing the plant, or precise data on the mix of local and expatriate managers—not available in this data set.

166 / John Paul MacDuffie and Thomas A. Kochan

ble across jobs and therefore taught, evaluated, and certified according to national standards. Training carried out entirely by the firm is likely to emphasize motivation as well as technical skill, and focus on firm-specific skills.

Flexible production plants appear to require some mix of general skills necessary for effective problem-solving (reading, math, and reasoning skills) and firm-specific skills related to the firm's technology and production system. Furthermore, because of their reliance on work teams, these plants are likely to emphasize interpersonal and communication skills as well.

Thus the training provided by firms using flexible production may yield some general skills that can be valuable in any job (e.g., those related to problem solving and functioning in a team) but will also develop firm-specific skills that are not portable. This is one reason critics of flexible production argue that extensive training may bring more benefits to management than to workers. Yet earning a portable certificate for technical skills based on national standards may be less valuable for workers, given the rapid pace of technical change and the firm specificity of much technical knowledge, than general skills in problem solving, working in teams, and communication. This suggests that public policy focused on training standards should emphasize not only technical skills but also the more broadly applicable cognitive and interpersonal skills that are commonly taught in flexible production settings.

We expect that the training effort differentials reported in this paper will narrow in the future, depending on the rate at which flexible production diffuses worldwide and whether public policy changes in various countries. In the United States, training has risen since 1989–90, when these data were collected, as an industry resurgence has allowed joint training funds between each of the Big Three companies and the UAW (Ferman et al., 1990) to be replenished and expanded. The test of whether or not this reflects a permanent increase in training effort by the Big Three will come in the next industry downturn, when training budgets are often cut.

If U.S. auto companies do act to boost training levels, as part of a gradual transition to flexible production, the biggest training gap to be filled by public policy will be in the area of basic skills—literacy and math. These skills form the foundation for training (both technical and non-technical) that firms will provide in support of flexible production. With the Big Three anticipating extensive hiring of young workers to replace retirees in the next ten years, their training decisions—and potentially the extent of their transition to flexible production—will be critically affected by whether or not they are able to find a sufficient supply of these skills.

Do U.S. Firms Invest Less in Training? / 167

Only the countries where the public education system provides these basic skills in ample quantity will be able to follow the desirable high-quality, high-variety, high-wage strategy in more than a few exemplar companies.

REFERENCES

Adler, Paul S. 1986. "New Technologies, New Skills." *California Management Review* 29:9–28.
——. 1992. "The 'Learning Bureaucracy': New United Motor Manufacturing, Inc." In *Research in Organizational Behavior,* edited by Barry M. Staw and Larry L. Cummings, pp. 111–94. Greenwich, CT: JAI Press.
Attewell, Paul. 1992. "Skill and Occupational Changes in U.S. Manufacturing." In *Technology and the Future of Work,* edited by Paul S. Adler, pp. 46–88. New York: Oxford University Press.
Arthur, Jeffrey B. 1992. "The Link Between Business Strategy and Industrial Relations Systems in American Steel Minimills." *Industrial and Labor Relations Review* 45:488–506.
Barney, Jay. 1986. "Strategic Factor Markets: Expectations, Luck, and Business Strategy." *Management Science* 32:1231–41.
Cappelli, Peter. 1993. "Are Skill Requirements Rising? Evidence from Production and Clerical Jobs." *Industrial and Labor Relations Review* 46:515–30.
Cappelli, Peter, and Harbir Singh. 1992. "Integrating Strategic Human Resources and Strategic Management." In *Research Frontiers in Industrial Relations,* edited by Peter Sherer, David Lewin, and Olivia Mitchell, pp. 165–92. Madison, WI: Industrial Relations Research Association series.
Casey, Bernard. 1986. "The Dual Apprenticeship System and the Recruitment and Retention of Young Persons in West Germany." *British Journal of Industrial Relations* 24(1) (March):63–82.
Cole, Robert A. 1992. "Issues in Skill Formation and Training in Japanese Manufacturing." In *Technology and the Future of Work,* edited by Paul S. Adler, pp. 187–209. New York: Oxford University Press.
Cutcher-Gershenfeld, Joel. 1991. "The Impact on Economic Performance of a Transformation in Workplace Relations." *Industrial and Labor Relations Review* 44:241–60.
Dertouzos, Michael, Robert Solow, and Richard Lester. 1989. *Made in America.* Cambridge, MA: MIT Press.
Dore, Ronald P. 1992. "Japan's Version of Managerial Capitalism." In *Transforming Organizations,* edited by Thomas A. Kochan and Michael Useem, pp. 17–27. New York: Oxford University Press.
Ferman, Louis A., Michele Hoyman, Joel Cutcher-Gershenfeld, and Ernest J. Savoie, eds. 1990. *New Developments in Worker Training: A Legacy for the 1990s.* Madison, WI: IRRA.
Ford, G. W. 1986. "Learning from Japan: The Concept of Skill Formation." *Australian Bulletin of Labor* 12(2):119–127.
Huxley, Christopher, David Robertson, and Jim Rinehart. 1991. "Team Concept: A Case Study of Japanese Management in a Unionized Canadian Auto Plant." Unpublished paper, Canadian Auto Workers Research Group.
Ichniowski, Casey. 1991. "Human Resource Management Systems and the Performance of U.S. Manufacturing Businesses." *NBER Working Paper Series #3449.* Cambridge, MA: National Bureau of Economic Research.
Ichniowski, Casey, Kathryn Shaw, and Giovanni Prennushi. 1993. "The Effect of Human Resource Management Practices on Productivity." Unpublished paper, Columbia University.
Imai, Kenichi. 1986. *Kaizen.* New York: Free Press.
Ittner, Christopher, and John Paul MacDuffie. 1994. "Exploring the Sources in International Differences in Manufacturing Overhead." Unpublished paper, Wharton School, University of Pennsylvania.
Kelley, Mary Ellen. 1989. "Unionization and Job Design under Programmable Automation." *Industrial Relations* 28(2) (Spring):174–87.
Kochan, Thomas A., Joel Cutcher-Gershenfeld, and John Paul MacDuffie. 1991. "Employee Participa-

168 / JOHN PAUL MACDUFFIE AND THOMAS A. KOCHAN

tion, Work Redesign, and New Technology: Implications for Manufacturing and Engineering Practice." In *Handbook of Industrial Engineering*, 2d ed., edited by Gavriel Salvendy, pp. 798–814. New York: John Wiley.

Koike, Kazuo. 1988. *Understanding Industrial Relations in Modern Japan*. London: Macmillan Press.

Krafcik, John F. 1988. "Comparative Analysis of Performance Indicators at World Auto Assembly Plants." Unpublished master's thesis, Sloan School of Management, MIT.

Lawler, Edward E. III, Susan Mohrman, and Gerald E. Ledford, Jr. 1992. *Employee Involvement and TQM: Practice and Results in Fortune 1000 Companies*. San Francisco, CA: Jossey-Bass.

Lillrank, Paul, and Noriaki Kano. 1989. *Continuous Improvement: Quality Control Circles in Japanese Industry*. Ann Arbor, MI: Center for Japanese Studies, University of Michigan.

MacDuffie, John Paul. 1991. "Beyond Mass Production: Flexible Production Systems and Manufacturing Performance in the World Auto Industry." Unpublished doctoral dissertation, Sloan School of Management, MIT.

———. 1995. "Human Resource Bundles and Manufacturing Performance: Organizational Logic and Flexible Production Systems in the World Auto Industry." *Industrial and Labor Relations Review* 48(2) (January):197–221.

MacDuffie, John Paul, and John F. Krafcik. 1992. "Integrating Technology and Human Resources for High Performance Manufacturing." In *Transforming Organizations*, edited by Thomas A. Kochan and Michael Useem, pp. 209–25. New York: Oxford University Press.

Majchrzak, Ann. 1988. *The Human Side of Factory Automation*. San Francisco, CA: Jossey-Bass.

Ono, Taiichi. 1988. *Workplace Management*. Cambridge, MA: Productivity Press.

Parker, Mike, and Jane Slaughter. 1988. *Choosing Sides: Unions and the Team Concept*. Boston, MA: South End Press.

Piore, Michael, and Charles Sabel. 1984. *The Second Industrial Divide*. New York: Basic Books.

Sako, Mari. 1992. "Training, Productivity, and Quality Control in Japanese Multinational Companies: Preliminary Studies in Britain and Germany." Unpublished manuscript, London School of Economics.

Schonberger, Richard. 1982. *Japanese Manufacturing Techniques*. New York: Free Press.

Shimada, Haruo. 1983. "Japanese Industrial Relations—A New General Model?" In *Contemporary Industrial Relations in Japan*, edited by Taishiro Shirai, pp. 5–23. Madison, WI: University of Wisconsin Press.

Shimada, Haruo, and John Paul MacDuffie. 1986. "Industrial Relations and 'Humanware': Japanese Investments in Automobile Manufacturing in the United States." Working paper, Sloan School of Management, MIT.

Tyre, Marcie, and Wanda Orlikowski. 1993. "Exploiting Opportunities for Technological Improvement in Organizations." *Sloan Management Review* 35:13–26.

Wever, Kirsten, Thomas A. Kochan, and Peter Berg. 1992. "Labor, Business, Government, and Skills in the U.S. and Germany: The Role of Institutions." Unpublished paper.

Womack, James P., Daniel Jones, and Daniel Roos. 1990. *The Machine That Changed the World*. New York: Rawson-Macmillan.

[10]

Technological Change and the Skill Acquisition of Young Workers

Ann P. Bartel, *Columbia University and National Bureau of Economic Research*

Nachum Sicherman, *Columbia University and National Bureau of Economic Research*

Since technological change influences the rate at which human capital obsolesces and also increases the uncertainty associated with human capital investments, training may increase or decrease at higher rates of technological change. Using the National Longitudinal Survey of Youth, we find that production workers in manufacturing industries with higher rates of technological change are more likely to receive formal company training. At higher rates of technological change, the training gap between the more and less educated narrows, low-skilled nonproduction workers receive significantly more training than higher-skilled nonproduction workers, and the proportion of individuals receiving training increases.

I. Introduction

Economists have been long interested in the effect of technological change on the labor market. In the 1950s, the Bureau of Labor Statistics

This research was supported by a grant from the U.S. Department of Labor, Office of Economic Research of the Bureau of Labor Statistics, National Longitudinal Survey Small Purchase Order Program. An earlier version of this article was presented at the C. V. Starr Center Conference on Technologies and Skills, New York University, December 1994. We thank Eric Bartelsman, Charles Himmelberg, Boyan Jovanovic, Chris Paxson, Wilbert van der Klaauw, and seminar participants at the National Bureau of Economic Research, Hebrew University, and Tel Aviv University for useful suggestions and comments. We also thank Steve Davis, Barbara Fraumeni, Christopher Furgiuele, John Haltiwanger, Barry Hirsch, Saul Lach, and Sam Kortum for providing us with various data sets used in this article.

[*Journal of Labor Economics*, 1998, vol. 16, no. 4]

began its case studies of the effect of "automation" on employment. More recently, researchers' attention has focused on the effect of technological change on the wage structure (Lillard and Tan 1986; Mincer 1989; Allen 1992; Krueger 1993; Berman, Bound, and Griliches 1994; Bartel and Sicherman 1997), the demand for educated workers (Bartel and Lichtenberg 1987, 1991), intercountry differences in wage structures (Mincer and Higuchi 1988), and retirement decisions of older workers (Bartel and Sicherman 1993). The observed increase in wage inequality between college and high school graduates in the 1980s might be interpreted to imply that the status of less educated workers will deteriorate with the pace of technological change. But this prediction ignores other adjustments that may occur in the marketplace, one of which is a change in the postschooling investment of different education groups. In this article, we utilize a cross-sectional framework to investigate the effect of industry rates of technological change on young workers' investments in on-the-job training. While two earlier studies, Lillard and Tan (1986) and Mincer (1989), did consider the effect of technological change on the training of young workers, both of these papers have limitations which our article overcomes.[1]

Economic theory does not provide a clear prediction on the sign of the relationship between technological change and investments in training. Observed investments in training are the outcome of a supply and demand interaction of employers and workers, and technological change will influence the incentives of both parties. One argument is that technological change makes formal education and previously acquired skills obsolete. As a result, both workers and firms will find it optimal to invest in on-the-job training in order to match the specific requirements of each wave of innovation.[2] In accordance with this view, technological change should spread investment in human capital, thus increasing investment in training and reducing investment in formal education. The alternative view is that general education enables workers to adjust to and benefit from technological change (Welch 1970). Workers who expect to experience higher rates of technological change on the job should, therefore, invest more in schooling and rely less on acquiring specific training on the job. This prediction is based on the assumption that differences in expected rates of technological change do affect educational choices. For the young workers whom we study, differences in the rates of technological change

---

[1] Lillard and Tan (1986) used the Current Population Survey and the National Longitudinal Survey Samples of Young Men and Young Women, while Mincer (1989) analyzed the young workers in the Panel Study of Income Dynamics. Unlike this study, they use limited information on training and rely on only one measure of technological change.

[2] This is the argument underlying the model developed by Tan (1989).

across industries are likely to reflect differences in expectations faced by young workers that chose different careers.[3]

Higher rates of technological change are also likely to increase the uncertainty associated with investments in human capital in the sense that the output from a given level and type of human capital is more uncertain. Levhari and Weiss (1974) have shown, however, that uncertainty has an ambiguous effect on human capital investments. If increased uncertainty implies an increase in the variance of the returns to human capital, investments will decrease (under standard assumptions such as risk aversion of workers.) But some types of human capital (e.g., general education) may facilitate adjustment to future shocks, which would lead to a decrease in the variance of returns. Investments in this type of human capital would increase, while investments in more specific types of human capital would decrease.

We can also derive implications for the way in which technological change is likely to affect the relationship between education and training. In general, more educated workers train more, either because human capital is an input in the production of new human capital (Mincer 1962; Rosen 1976) or because individuals who are better "learners" will invest more in both schooling and training. They will train less, however, the greater the substitutability is between schooling and training in performing job tasks. As we later show, in general, the complementarity between training and schooling dominates the substitutability.[4] However, if the general skills of the more educated enable them to adapt faster to new technologies, the substitutability between schooling and training will be greater at higher rates of technological change. If this is true, then, at higher rates of technological change, we will observe a narrowing of the postschool-training gap between the less and more educated workers.

In sum, there are a number of avenues by which technological change influences training decisions, and as we have shown, unambiguous predictions do not exist. We conduct a detailed empirical analysis that can assess the relative importance of the competing effects. Our work improves on previous research in this area in a number of ways.

One problem with earlier work on training and technological change was the limited available information on training. We use the National Longitudinal Survey of Youth (NLSY), which is unique in terms of the comprehensiveness of the training information that is reported. Unlike

---

[3] For older workers, these same differences may reflect unexpected changes that cannot affect schooling decisions and will, therefore, be more likely to increase training as part of the existing human capital is destroyed. In Bartel and Sicherman (1993), we also studied the effects of expected and unexpected technological change on the retirement decisions of older workers.

[4] Sicherman (1991) provides evidence of the substitutability between schooling and training.

other data sets, it includes detailed information on all formal training spells experienced by the individual, including the duration of the training.[5] With this data set, we conduct a more comprehensive and reliable study of the training effects of technological change. The NLSY has the added advantage of providing data through 1992, enabling us to conduct a more current analysis than previous studies.

The second way in which we improve on previous research is by utilizing a variety of measures of technological change. Estimating the rate of technological change faced by the worker in his job is very difficult. Since the measurement of technological change outside the manufacturing sector is very problematic (Griliches 1994), our analysis is restricted to workers in manufacturing. Even within this sector, however, no single proxy is likely to be perfect. We, therefore, link the NLSY with several alternative data sets that contain proxies for industries' rates of technological change. Specifically, our analysis uses the Jorgenson productivity growth series, the National Bureau of Economic Research (NBER) productivity data, the Census of Manufactures series on investment in computers, the R&D-to-sales ratio in the industry, and the industry's use of patents. Previous studies on training and technological change relied primarily on the Jorgenson productivity growth series. Our analysis enables us to examine the robustness of alternative measures of technological change, thereby increasing confidence in the results.

Third, unlike the earlier research, we carefully dissect the relationship between technological change and training in order to answer the following questions: (1) How does technological change affect training investments for workers with different levels of education? (2) Does technological change increase both entry-level training and training of more experienced workers? (3) Does the pool of trainees increase in response to technological change, or is it mainly the previously trained workers who train more intensively? To our knowledge, this is the first article to address these important questions.

In Section II, we discuss the data sources for our study, explain the various measures of training and technological change, and present the basic equations that we estimate. Regression results are discussed in Section III, and a summary is given in Section IV.

II. Empirical Framework

A. Microdata

We use the main file and the work-history file of the 1987–92 National Longitudinal Survey of Youth ages 14–21 in 1979 and restrict our analysis

---

[5] Although Lynch (1991, 1992a) used the National Longitudinal Survey of Youth (NLSY) data to study the determinants of private-sector training, her

to males in manufacturing (see app. A). The main file is the source of information on personal characteristics such as main activity during the survey week, education, age, race, marital status, health status, and so forth. An individual enters our sample when he first reports that his main activity during the survey week was "in the labor force." The work-history file contains employment-related spell data, such as wages, tenure, and separations, constructed from the main NLSY file. For each respondent, employment information is reported for a maximum of five jobs in each survey year. The work-history file enables us to distinguish information for each job, especially the reasons for and timing of job transitions. One of these jobs is designated as a "CPS job," and it is the most recent or current job at the time of the interview. Typically it is also the main job. There are a host of important questions that are asked for the CPS job only, such as industry, occupation, and firm size. Hence, our analysis is restricted to CPS jobs.

The NLSY is particularly well suited for a study of employee training because of the vast amount of information on the subject that is recorded.[6] Data on a maximum of seven different training programs taken at any time since the last interview are included. Beginning with the 1988 survey, data on the following items are available for each of the seven training programs, excluding government programs: starting and ending dates of the training program, the number of weeks that the individual attended the program, what type of program it was,[7] and how many hours he usually devoted per week to this program. In the NLSY, company training encompasses three types of training: (1) training run by the employer; (2) training run at work, not by employer; and (3) company training outside of work.

Prior to 1988, detailed information on type of private-sector training, as well as the weeks and hours per week spent in training, were only recorded if the training spell lasted at least 4 weeks. In other words, for the 1979–86 time period, the researcher can measure incidence of private-sector and government training, but it is impossible to determine if the private-sector training was company-provided training, an apprenticeship program, or obtained in other ways, such as a vocational or technical institute, business college, or correspondence course. In addition, even if the training spell lasted at least 4 weeks, the measure of training duration

---

work did not analyze the role played by technological change. In addition, as we discuss in Section IIA, we use a more accurate estimate of training duration.

[6] Like most other data sets, the NLSY provides information only on formal training. Ignoring informal training, a major portion of on-the-job training, is a drawback (see Sicherman 1990).

[7] Types of training programs are apprenticeships, company training, technical or vocational training off the job (such as business college, vocational and technical institutes, and correspondence courses), and government training.

provided in the pre-1988 surveys is extremely unreliable because it is based on the starting and ending dates of the training program.[8] In 1987, no training questions were asked. However, training information for 1987 can be imputed from the 1988 data, thereby enabling us to add 1 more year of data to our analysis; the regressions we report cover the time period 1987–92.

Table 1 reports the incidence and duration of private-sector training, by education and size of firm, for the manufacturing sector for the 1988–92 time period. In panel I, the production and nonproduction workers are combined, while panels II and III show the separate results for each of the occupation groups. Incidence and duration are calculated on an annual basis. On average, 17% of the individuals reported receiving private-sector training during the "12"-month period between consecutive surveys.[9] For production workers, the incidence is 13%, while it is 25% for nonproduction workers. Median duration of training (for workers with positive hours) was 40 hours, that is, approximately 1 week, and the mean duration was 137 hours, or approximately $3\frac{1}{2}$ weeks. The results in panels II and III show that, while the incidence of training is lower for production workers, duration of training is higher. Production workers have a median duration of 48 hours and a mean duration of 180 hours, while nonproduction workers have a median of 40 hours and a mean of only 101 hours. The probability of receiving private-sector training increases monotonically with education, with the exception of nonproduction workers with 13–15 years of education. The relationship between training duration and education is not monotonic; as we show below, this occurs because of the association between type of private-sector training and education level.

The detailed data from the 1988–92 surveys can be used to calculate the distribution of private-sector training across three categories: (1) company, or in-house, training; (2) apprenticeships; and (3) other training, such as training received in a business college, a vocational or technical institute, or a correspondence course. For the entire sample, approximately 76% of private-sector training is provided by the company. This percentage ranges from a low of 55% for the lowest education group to a high of 95% for the highest education group. For production workers, 64% of private-sector training is provided by the company, while nonproduction workers receive 88% of their private training through the company. In panel I, we see that company training has a median duration of

---

[8] For example, if an individual reported starting a training program in January of the survey year and finishing it in December of that year, training duration would be recorded as 52 weeks, even if the individual had only received 1 day of training per month.

[9] Fifty-six weeks is the average length of time between survey dates.

Table 1
Annual Incidence and Duration of Private-Sector Training, by Type of Training and Schooling Level, for Males in Manufacturing Industries, 1988–92

	All Workers			Schooling < 12			Schooling = 12			Schooling 13–15			Schooling 16+		
	% Trained	M	Median	% Trained	M	Median	% Trained	M	Median	% Trained	M	Median	% Trained	M	Median
I. Production and nonproduction workers:															
All firms:															
All training	17.4 [4,045]	137 (319)	40	10.1 [929]	122 (176)	48	15.7 [1,722]	194 (424)	40	17.6 [607]	111 (230)	40	30.6 [723]	93 (240)	40
Company	13.2	102 (260)	40	5.6	77 (104)	40	10.5	130 (322)	40	14.2	95 (219)	40	28.9	87 (240)	36
Apprenticeship	1.1	482 (686)	290	1.1	500 (316)	400	1.5	552 (893)	174	1.0	52† (219)	52	.1	560* (240)	N.A.
Other	3.6	215 (377)	80	3.8	100 (116)	48	4.2	286 (476)	80	3.4	168 (260)	55	1.9	140 (133)	98
Large firms:															
All training	23.2 [1,842]	129 (311)	40	10.2 [284]	126 (205)	48	18.7 [796]	176 (408)	40	22.8 [302]	102 (225)	40	39.2 [460]	106 (265)	40
Company	19.8	99 (247)	40	7.4	73 (94)	40	14.7	111 (257)	32	18.9	88 (208)	32	36.7	98 (266)	40
Apprenticeship	1.1	758 (886)	525	.7	600† (94)	600	1.6	1,012 (1,115)	525	1.6	3.2* (208)	3.2*	.2	560* (266)	N.A.
Other	3.1	181 (322)	54	2.8	103 (104)	48	3.0	253 (441)	70	4.0	142 (282)	40	3.0	140 (133)	98
Small firms:															
All training	12.5 [2,198]	152 (333)	40	10.1 [641]	120 (155)	52	13.2 [975]	219 (448)	50	12.4 [305]	131 (241)	52	15.2 [263]	44 (80)	24
Company	7.7	107 (289)	36	4.8	82 (116)	44	7.0	164 (416)	40	9.5	109 (244)	40	15.2	44 (80)	24
Apprenticeship	1.0	206 (211)	100	1.2	433‡ (116)	400	1.3	91‖ (416)	40	.3	100* (244)	N.A.	0	0 (80)	
Other	4.0	243 (419)	80	4.2	99 (125)	68	5.2	304 (498)	80	2.9	240§	192	0	0	

continued overleaf

	1a	1b	1c	2a	2b	2c	3a	3b	3c	4a	4b	4c	5a	5b	5c
II. Production workers:															
All firms:															
All training	13.3 [2,635]	180 (357)	48	9.8 [802]	122 (182)	44	13.8 [1,417]	210 (424)	40	16.6 [325]	194 (323)	84	.248 [77]	75 (94)	50
Company	8.5	133 (317)	40	5.5	70 (82)	40	8.6	151 (376)	39	12.0	174 (326)	50	.234	53 (38)	50
Apprenticeship	1.4	386 (403)	290	1.2	500 (316)	400	1.5	333 (470)	167	1.5	100*	N.A.	0	0	N.A.
Other	3.8	239 (399)	80	3.5	90 (120)	36	4.0	313 (484)	80	4.3	204 (311)	84	.013	400*	N.A.
Large firms:															
All training	16.8 [1,052]	160 (305)	42	9.9 [232]	135 (225)	44	16.2 [634]	169 (338)	40	23.8 [151]	181 (319)	72	.428 [35]	91 (104)	65
Company	13.3	123 (267)	40	7.3	83 (101)	40	12.8	131 (298)	31	18.5	159 (305)	40	.410	63 (38)	50
Apprenticeship	1.5	681 (509)	525	.9	600*	600	1.6	735‡	525	2.6	...		0	0*	N.A.
Other	2.9	179 (279)	48	2.6	68 (98)	32	2.5	209 (304)	80	5.3	172 (329)	44	.028	400*	N.A.
Small firms:															
All training	10.9 [1,578]	208 (417)	50	9.9 [566]	113 (150)	44	11.8 [782]	268 (519)	52	10.3 [174]	222 (345)	109	.095 [42]	26 (22)	26
Company	5.3	153 (402)	40	4.8	58 (60)	40	5.1	202 (518)	40	6.3	211 (387)	60	.095	26 (22)	26
Apprenticeship	1.3	206 (211)	100	1.4	433‡	400	1.5	91 (138)	40	.6	100*	N.A.	0	0	
Other	4.4	279 (460)	96	3.9	99 (130)	40	5.2	365 (550)	88	3.4	332†	332	0	0	
III. Nonproduction workers:															
All firms:															
All training	25.1 [1,407]	101 (278)	40	12.0 [126]	127 (151)	80	23.4 [355]	158 (426)	45	18.9 [281]	46 (56)	28	.313 [645]	94 (249)	36
Company	22.0	82 (214)	36	6.3	111 (183)	43	18.0	87 (169)	40	16.7	40 (39)	32	.296	90 (250)	32
Apprenticeship	.4	855 (1,313)	314	0	0		1.1	1,429*	N.A.	.3	32*		.001	560*	
Other	3.2	155 (316)	72	5.5	159‡	140	5.1	205 (459)	36	2.5	96 (95)	55	.020	103 (89)	96

Table 1 (Continued)

	All Workers			Schooling < 12			Schooling = 12			Schooling 13–15			Schooling 16+		
	% Trained	Hours Trained		% Trained	Hours Trained		% Trained	Hours Trained		% Trained	Hours Trained		% Trained	Hours Trained	
		M	Median		M	Median		M	Median		M	Median		M	Median
Large firms:															
All training	31.8 [190]	109 (314)	40	11.5 [52]	91 (99)	56	28.4 [162]	191 (547)	40	21.8 [151]	37 (43)	15	.390 [425]	107 (275)	40
Company	28.3	85 (234)	36	7.7	25‡	10	22.2	62 (67)	36	19.2	35 (40)	14	.365	101 (276)	39
Apprenticeship	.6	855 (1,313)	314	0	0	N.A.	1.8	1,429*	N.A.	.7	3.2*		.002	560*	
Other	3.4	184 (399)	96	3.8	190†	N.A.	4.9	367 (726)	36	2.6	61‡	25	.030	103 (89)	96
Small firms:															
All training	16.5 [617]	81 (330)	33	12.2 [74]	171 (208)	88	19.2 [193]	120 (224)	50	15.4 [130]	63 (74)	40	.164 [220]	46 (85)	24
Company	13.9	73 (152)	31	5.4	197‡	80	14.5	115 (236)	40	13.8	48 (38)	40	.164	46 (86)	24
Apprenticeship	.2	0		0	0		.5	0		0	0		0	0	
Other	2.9	111 (150)	64	6.7	96*	N.A.	5.2	104 (171)	49	2.3	147†		0	0	

NOTE.—N.A. = not applicable. Numbers in square brackets are *N*. Numbers in parentheses are SDs for hours trained. *M* and median hours are calculated for positive hours only.

* 1 observation.
† 2 observations.
‡ 3 observations.
§ 4 observations.
‖ 5 observations.

40 hours for all education groups. This is considerably shorter than the median duration of apprenticeships and somewhat shorter than the duration of other private-sector training. Thus, although more educated individuals are more likely to receive private-sector training, their training duration is shorter because their skills are acquired in company training programs rather than apprenticeships or other outside programs.[10]

We distinguished large from small firms on the basis of whether the number of employees in the individual's firm was at least 1,000. Panel I shows that the incidence of company-provided training in large firms is 20% compared with only 7.7% in small firms, confirming the earlier findings of Barron, Black, and Loewenstein (1987). The positive effect of firm size on the incidence of training holds for all education groups.

B. Measures of Technological Change

In the absence of a direct measure of the rate of technological change faced by the individual in his place of work, we link the NLSY with several alternative data sets that contain proxies for the industry's rate of technological change.[11] Below we describe each of these measures and analyze their strengths and weaknesses. Since no single proxy is a perfect measure, we feel it is important to use several alternative measures in our analysis. If similar results are obtained with different measures, we can have more confidence in the reliability of the findings.[12]

The five measures of technological change that we use are (1) the total factor productivity growth series calculated by Jorgenson, Gollop, and Fraumeni (1987) and updated through 1989; (2) the NBER total factor productivity growth series; (3) 1987 Census of Manufactures' data on investment in computers; (4) the R&D-to-sales ratio in the industry as reported by the National Science Foundation, and (5) the number of patents used in the industry. Each of these measures has advantages and disadvantages as we describe below.

The Jorgenson total factor productivity series has been used extensively in previous research (e.g., Lillard and Tan 1986; Mincer and Higuchi

---

[10] This also explains why training duration is longer for production workers than nonproduction workers. Production workers receive a greater share of their training outside the firm where average durations are longer.

[11] An alternative approach would be to collect data from a small sample of firms that are undergoing technological change and analyze the effect on their employees. The disadvantage of this approach is that the findings may not hold for individuals who work in other firms. See Siegel (1994) for a study restricted to high-tech firms on Long Island.

[12] Another approach is to create a composite index of technological change similar to the one used by Lichtenberg and Griliches (1989). Because of the different levels of aggregation in our measures of technological change, we do not employ this method here.

1988; Tan 1989; Gill 1990; and Bartel and Sicherman 1993). Technological change is measured as the rate of change in output that is not accounted for by the growth in the quantity and quality of physical and human capital.[13] One problem with this approach is that, in addition to technological change, other factors, such as fluctuations in capacity utilization and nonconstant returns to scale, are also likely to affect productivity growth. In order to account for such effects, the empirical analysis will include controls for the industry unemployment rate, the rates of entry and exit of firms in the industry, and the capacity utilization rate. The Jorgenson series is currently available for the time period 1947–89. The main advantage of the Jorgenson series is that changes in the quality of labor input are carefully used to correctly measure net productivity growth. Also, the new Jorgenson series utilizes the Bureau of Economic Analysis constant-quality price deflator; the earlier series underestimated productivity growth in high-tech industries (e.g., the computer industry) since quality improvements were not incorporated into the output price index. The major disadvantage of the Jorgenson series is that it is a residual (rather than a direct) measure of technological change. In addition, the data are reported for only 22 broad industry categories in the manufacturing sector, equivalent to 2-digit standard industrial classifications.

The NBER manufacturing-productivity database, described in Bartelsman and Gray (1996), contains annual information on total factor productivity growth for 450 (4-digit) manufacturing industries for the time period 1958–89. The advantage of the NBER database over the Jorgenson database is its narrow industry categories yielding data on 83 3-digit industries in manufacturing. Like the Jorgenson data, the NBER variable also has the disadvantage of being a residual measure of technological change. Another limitation of the NBER data is that the productivity growth measure was not adjusted for changes in labor quality.

The third measure that we use is investment in computers. During the 1980s, there was an enormous growth in the amount of computer resources used in the workplace. Indeed, it has been argued (see Bound and Johnson 1992) that the most concrete example of technological change in the 1980s was the "computer revolution."[14] Hence the extent to which

---

[13] There is some evidence that total factor productivity growth is a good indicator of innovative activity in an industry. For example, using data on 28 sectors from the Census-Penn-Stanford Research Institute data set, Griliches and Lichtenberg (1984) found that, for the time period 1959–76, there was a significant relationship between an industry's intensity of private R&D expenditures and subsequent growth in productivity. Lichtenberg and Siegel (1991) also found that this relationship existed at the company level in the 1970s and 1980s.

[14] Krueger (1993) used data from the October 1984 and 1989 Current Population Surveys to show that workers who use computers on their job earn 10%– 15% higher wages.

firms invest in information technology can serve as a good proxy for the rate of technological change at the workplace. Using data from the 1987 Census of Manufacturers, we calculate the ratio of investment in computers to total investments. The advantages of this measure are that (1) unlike data on R&D expenditures, it measures use (not production) of an innovation, and (2) it is available for several hundred 4-digit industries in the manufacturing sector, which reduces to approximately 100 3-digit industries for the NLSY sample. A disadvantage of this measure is that it may not capture other types of innovations.

A fourth proxy for technological change is the ratio of company R&D funds to net sales reported by the National Science Foundation (1993) for industries in the manufacturing sector. The advantage of this variable is that it is a direct measure of innovative activity in the industry, but as indicated above, the innovative activity refers only to the industry in which the innovation originates, not the industry where the innovation is actually used. Another limitation is that some R&D is an input to innovation, not an output.

A fifth indicator of technological change is the number of patents used in 2-digit manufacturing industries.[15] Patent data are generally collected by technology field and have not been available at the industry level. Kortum and Putnam (1995) present a method for predicting patents by "industry of use" in the United States, using the information on the distribution of patents across technological fields and industries of use in the Canadian patent system. The data actually used here are the number of patents used by 2-digit manufacturing industries analyzed by Lach (1995). For the 1957–83 period, Lach (1995) found that this measure is highly correlated with total factor productivity (TFP) growth. Because the likelihood of an innovation being patented has differed historically across technology fields, and, hence, across industries, we control for these systematic differences by constructing the following variable for each 2-digit manufacturing industry: the number of patents used during the years 1980–83 (which are closest to our starting year, 1987) divided by the number of patents used during the 1970s. The main advantage of proxying technological change by "industry of use" is that, like the computer-investment variable discussed earlier, it measures the direct use of innovations. However, as usual with patent data, because many innovations are not patented, and many patented innovations are not used, patents could still be a noisy proxy for innovations. Another concern is that the patent data are only reported for 20 manufacturing industries.

We have examined the rankings of the various industries on the basis of

---

[15] See Griliches (1990) for evidence of the link between patent statistics and technological change.

Table 2
Correlations between the Different Measures of Technological Change

	Jorgenson TFP	NBER TFP	R&D-to-Sales Ratio	Patents
NBER TFP	.31			
R&D-to-sales ratio	.47	.65		
Use of patents	.35	.65	.71	
Investment in computers	.40	.52	.65	.65

NOTE.—NBER = National Bureau of Economic Research. TFP = total factor productivity. These correlations are calculated by using the individual-level data that contain the five technological change proxies for each individual's industry.

the five different measures of technological change in order to determine whether the five proxies produce similar patterns regarding high and low technological change industries in the manufacturing sector. The listings, not reported here to conserve space,[16] showed that some industries consistently appear at or near the top of each measure's list. When 2-digit industry classifications were used, nonelectrical and electrical machinery ranked at the top. When a more detailed classification was used, the top-ranking industries were electronic computing equipment; radio, television, and communication equipment; and office and accounting machines—all subcategories of the broader nonelectrical machinery and electrical machinery categories.

A closer look at the five measures indicated, however, that they are different enough so that they each capture a facet of the industry rate of technological change. For example, according to the computer-investment measure, the leather-product industry has a relatively high rate of technological change, but this is not captured by the other proxies. By comparison, petroleum refining ranks high for the Jorgenson and NBER productivity measures and the patent variable but not for the other three proxies. Additional comparisons of the five listings also demonstrated that, in many cases, the rankings are dissimilar.

The correlations among the five measures, given in table 2, show that no two measures are perfectly correlated, and, therefore, there is no redundancy in using all of them in our analysis. The correlations between the different measures range from .3 to .7, which is consistent with our argument that each proxy is likely to capture a different aspect of technological change.[17] If all proxies produce similar results about the effect of

[16] See Bartel and Sicherman (1995) for the complete listings.

[17] One factor that affects the correlations is the different levels of aggregation used to construct the different measures. We calculated the correlations by using the individual-level data that contains the five technological change proxies for each individual's industry.

technological change on training, confidence in our conclusions will be significantly enhanced.

C. Matching the Microdata and Industry Measures of Technological Change

Since there is a high degree of randomness in annual changes in the measures that are available on an annual basis and the true variation is likely to be greater across industries than within industries, our analysis relies on cross-sectional variations in technological change, where the effects of measurement errors will be less severe.[18] All of the measures that we use have a common trait, that is, they are proxies for the industry rate of technological change. We recognize that an industry measure of technological change may not have the same effect for all of the occupations in that industry. For example, an innovation in the industry's production processes may have little or no effect on clerical employees. Since, in most cases, production workers are more likely to be affected by technological change in the manufacturing sector, we conduct separate analyses for production and nonproduction workers.

In order to match the different measures of technological change to the industrial classification used in the NLSY (the Census of Population classification), we use industry employment levels as weights whenever aggregation is required. When we utilize the Jorgenson and NBER productivity growth measures, we characterize industry differences in the rate of technological change by using the mean rate of productivity growth over the most recent 10-year time period, that is, 1977–87. In the case of investment in computers, we use data from 1987 as described earlier. The R&D-to-sales ratio for each industry is calculated as a 3-year moving average for the 3-year period prior to the year of analysis, for example, averaging data for 1984–86 for the 1987 NLSY, and so forth. For the patent data, we calculate the number of patents used during the time period 1980–83 divided by the number used during the 1970s. Hence, with the exception of the R&D variable, we use a fixed time-period measure of technological change that may act like a fixed effect for each industry, capturing other fixed attributes of the industry. We deal with this problem by including several industry characteristics in the regressions that may influence the relationship between training and our measures of technological change. They are the annual industry unemployment rate obtained from Employment and Earnings, annual measures of percent unionized in the industry compiled from the CPS by Hirsch and MacPherson (1993), and the annual rates of job creation and job

---

[18] Griliches and Hausman (1986) show that, when first differences or deviations from means are used, measurement errors are magnified.

destruction for both start-up and continuing establishments in the industry constructed by Davis and Haltiwanger (1992).[19]

Another issue is that the standard errors of our estimated coefficients
may be biased downward because industry-level shocks may be correlated
across individuals within a given industry. In order to deal with this
issue, we reestimated all the models reported in this article, using linear-
probability random-effect models. None of the findings reported here
were changed in a significant way. We chose to present the logit estimates
because a linear model is an inappropriate specification in the case of a
discrete-choice model, even though the estimation results are often similar
to those obtained by maximum-likelihood estimation (see Dhrymes 1978,
pp. 331–34).

D. Econometric Model

Our econometric analysis is restricted to company training because, as
was shown in table 1, three-quarters of private-sector training is provided
by the firm. We do provide some evidence of the effect of technological
change on other forms of private-sector training and contrast these effects
with those for company training.

In order to estimate the effect of technological change on the likelihood
of company training, we adopt a simple logit framework.[20] In each period,
between two surveys, an individual will face one of the following two
alternatives described by m: engage in company training ($m = 1$), or not
($m = 0$).

The choice m occurs when the latent variable $Y_{it}^* > 0$, where

$$Y_{it}^* = X_{it}\alpha + \delta T_{it} + \varepsilon_{it}, \tag{1}$$

where i is the individual index, t is time, m is the alternative, and X_{it} is a
vector of individual, job, and industry characteristics that may vary over
time. The vector X includes the following variables: marital status, race,
years of education, residence in a standard metropolitan statistical area,

---

[19] We also added annual measures of capacity utilization by 2-digit industry,
constructed by the Federal Reserve Board. Adding this variable serves two purposes. First, it makes the Jorgenson and NBER productivity growth variables
cleaner proxies for technological change. Second, it enables us to test whether
firms provide more training during recessionary periods. We found that the capacity utilization variable was insignificant and its inclusion did not affect any of
our results.

[20] In Bartel and Sicherman (1995), we also utilized a standard Tobit model to
estimate the effects of technological change on the amount of time spent in
company training. We found that technological change had no effect on the
duration of training.

years of experience and its square, tenure and its square, union membership, whether or not the individual is employed by a large firm, the
industry unemployment rate, union coverage in the industry, and job
creation and destruction in the industry. The variable T_{it} is the rate of
technological change in the industry in which the individual is working
at time t. In order to test whether the effect of technological change varies
by education or occupation group, in some of our specifications
we interact the proxies for technological change with education or occupation group.

This specification treats technological change as an exogenous variable.
It is possible that the decision to adopt a technology will depend on
the trainability of a firm's workforce, making technological change an
endogenous variable. However, since we measure the rate of technological
change at the industry level, using multiyear means, it is reasonable to
assume that firms and workers treat these measures of technological
change as exogenous.[21]

As the discussion in Section I demonstrated, the sign on T_{it} is indeter-
minate. If high rates of technological change make previously acquired
skills obsolete, workers and employers have an incentive to invest
in on-the-job training to match the specific requirements of the new
technology. Alternatively, investments in general training (education)
may be substituted for specific on-the-job training if such investments
enable the worker to more easily adapt to change. Similarly, viewing
technological change as contributing to increased uncertainty about
the payoffs from investments leads to an ambiguous prediction that
depends on the way in which such investments enable the worker to
adjust to future shocks.

Assuming that ε is logistically distributed gives rise to a logit model in
which the underlying probabilities are

$$P_m = \frac{\exp(Z\beta_m)}{\sum_{k=0}^{1} \exp(Z\beta_k)}, \quad m = 0, 1, \tag{2}$$

where $Z = X$ and T, from equation (1).

In order to identify the parameters, the normalization $\beta_0 = 0$ is imposed,
and the estimated parameters are obtained by maximum likelihood.

III. Results

A. Incidence of Company Training

Table 3 reports the mean differences in the incidence of company training for workers in industries with high and low rates of technological

---

[21] In addition, the simultaneity problem is also minimized by the fact that our
technological change proxies are dated prior to the training variables.

Table 3
Annual Incidence of Private-Sector Company Training by Schooling Level, for Males in Manufacturing Industries, 1988–92: "High-Tech" and "Low-Tech" Industries

	All Schooling Groups	Years of Schooling			
		<12	12	13–15	16+
I. All workers:					
A. All firms:					
High	.173	.059	.142	.181	.330
	(2,041)	(388)	(850)	(364)	(436)
Low	.090	.054	.070	.082	.226
	(2,004)	(541)	(922)	(243)	(287)
B. Large firms:					
High	.235	.084	.176	.228	.389
	(1,075)	(131)	(426)	(215)	(303)
Low	.145	.065	.113	.092	.325
	(767)	(153)	(370)	(87)	(157)
C. Small firms:					
High	.104	.047	.106	.114	.195
	(963)	(255)	(423)	(149)	(133)
Low	.057	.049	.042	.077	.108
	(1,235)	(386)	(552)	(156)	(130)
II. Production workers:					
A. All firms:					
High	.103	.060	.106	.138	.250
	(1,392)	(381)	(760)	(203)	(44)
Low	.066	.050	.062	.090	.212
	(1,243)	(421)	(657)	(122)	(33)
B. Large firms:					
High	.157	.099	.151	.191	.421
	(597)	(111)	(357)	(110)	(19)
Low	.101	.050	.097	.171	.375
	(455)	(121)	(277)	(41)	(16)
C. Small firms:					
High	.061	.045	.065	.075	.120
	(792)	(268)	(402)	(93)	(25)
Low	.046	.050	.037	.049	.059
	(786)	(298)	(380)	(81)	(17)
III. Nonproduction workers:					
A. All firms:					
High	.303	.064	.292	.248	.352
	(682)	(31)	(137)	(153)	(361)
Low	.142	.063	.110	.070	.225
	(725)	(95)	(218)	(128)	(284)
B. Large firms:					
High	.343	.062	.301	.292	.389
	(460)	(16)	(73)	(96)	(275)
Low	.200	.083	.157	.018	.320
	(330)	(36)	(89)	(55)	(150)
C. Small firms:					
High	.221	.067	.281	.175	.232
	(222)	(15)	(64)	(57)	(86)
Low	.094	.051	.077	.109	.119
	(395)	(59)	(129)	(73)	(134)

NOTE.—We use R&D-to-sales ratio and define "high" and "low" using the median rate of technological change for the sample. We distinguished large from small firms on the basis of whether the number of employees in the individual's firm was at least 1,000. The same table, using other indicators, is available on request from us. *N*s are in parentheses.

Technological Change and Skill   735

Table 4
The Effects of Technological Change on the Likelihood of Company
Training in the Manufacturing Sector: Maximum Likelihood Logit
Estimation Results

	All		Production		Nonproduction	
	Coefficient (1)	Derivative (2)	Coefficient (3)	Derivative (4)	Coefficient (5)	Derivative (6)
I. Jorgenson TFP	25.26 (8.18)	.021	32.95 (11.5)	.018	9.56 (12.8)	.013
II. Share of investment in computers	2.11 (1.25)	.010	3.90 (2.06)	.012	−.02 (1.67)	−.0002
III. NBER TFP	2.36 (1.45)	.006	5.99 (2.62)	.01	.002 (1.82)	.00001
IV. R&D-to-sales ratio	.0805 (.024)	.021	.1622 (.039)	.026	.0289 (.033)	.012
V. Use of patents	6.13 (2.18)	.016	10.85 (3.59)	.018	1.267 (2.89)	.005
N	3,856		2,541		1,312	

NOTE.—The sample is limited to males in the manufacturing sectors who work in the private sector and have been working at least half of the weeks since the previous survey. The time period is 1987–92. In parentheses, below the logit coefficients, are SEs. To the right of each estimated coefficient is the derivative (dP/dX) multiplied by the SD of the measure of technological change. The derivative is calculated as $\beta\bar{P}(1 - \bar{P})$, where $\bar{P}$ is the mean incidence of training in the sample. NBER = National Bureau of Economic Research. TFP = total factor productivity. The values for the SDs are .0086 for Jorgenson's TFP, .05 for investment in computers, .027 for the NBER TFP, 2.57 for the R&D-to-sales ratio, and .027 for use of patents. The mean rates of training for the subsamples in the regressions are .111 for all workers in manufacturing, .067 for production workers, and .196 for nonproduction workers. The other variables in the regressions are marital status, race, educational dummies, a dummy for standard metropolitan statistical area, labor-market experience (and its square), tenure with employer (and its square), union membership, a dummy for large firm (more than 1,000 workers), industry unemployment rate, industry level of unionization, industry rate of job creation (M over 1980–88), industry rate of job destruction (M over 1980–88), and year dummies.

change.[22] In general, the incidence of training is higher at higher rates of technological change. With a few exceptions, this is true for all schooling groups, in small and large firms, and for production and nonproduction workers.

Table 4 reports a summary of the estimates from our logit models on the incidence of company training in the manufacturing sector.[23] Columns 1–2 report the effects of each of the five technological indicators on the incidence of training for all workers in the manufacturing sector, while columns 3–6 show separate results for production and nonproduction workers. We present the logit coefficient and its standard error (shown

[22] See the table for the definition of high and low rates of technological change.
[23] Complete regression results for one model are given in app. B, where we see the typical patterns regarding the effect of education, firm size, and other characteristics on the incidence of training, using the R&D-to-sales ratio. When other proxies for technological change are used, the coefficients on the nontechnological change variables are very similar to those shown in app. B.

in parentheses beneath the coefficient). To the right of each coefficient, we show the derivative (dP/dX) multiplied by the standard deviation of the measure of technological change. This estimate enables us to compare the magnitudes of the effects of the various technological change measures. The results in columns 1–2 show that all five proxies for technological change have a positive and significant effect on the incidence of training in the manufacturing sector. The robustness of these results is an important finding given our earlier discussion about the limitations of the various technological change measures.

The positive and significant effects of technological change on the incidence of training are consistent with the notion that technological change makes previously acquired skills obsolete, thereby inducing workers and firms to invest in training to match the specific requirements of the latest innovation. It is also consistent with Levhari and Weiss's (1974) argument that an increase in uncertainty will lead to an increase in investments in human capital that facilitate adjustments to future shocks. The largest effects are observed for the Jorgenson TFP measure, the R&D-to-sales ratio and use of patents, where a 1 standard deviation increase in the rate of technological change is associated with a 2 percentage point increase in the incidence of training. Comparing the results in column 3–4 with those in column 5–6 shows that the effect of technological change on the incidence of training is larger for production workers than nonproduction workers, as anticipated. In fact, the estimated coefficients for nonproduction workers are not statistically significant.

B. Incidence of Noncompany Training

Although three-quarters of private-sector training is provided by the firm, young workers do receive some training outside the firm. In table 5, we consider whether technological change also has a positive effect on noncompany training. In columns 1–6, the dependent variable is the likelihood of any type of private-sector training (company or noncompany), and in columns 7–12, we show results for the likelihood of noncompany training. Since the vast majority of private-sector training is company provided, the results in columns 1–6 are quite similar to those reported in table 4. The analysis of noncompany training alone shows that, with the exception of the Jorgenson TFP measure, technological change does not have a significant effect. This is consistent with the notion that the type of human capital investments that will increase with technological change are those that are more firm specific. Hence, the remainder of our analysis is confined to company training.

C. Education and Training

As we discussed in the introduction, the effect of technological change on the incidence of training may vary by education. More

Table 5
The Effects of Technological Change on the Likelihood of All Types of Training and Noncompany Training in the Manufacturing Sector

	Any Training						Noncompany Training					
	All		Production		Nonproduction		All		Production		Nonproduction	
	Coefficient (1)	Derivative (2)	Coefficient (3)	Derivative (4)	Coefficient (5)	Derivative (6)	Coefficient (7)	Derivative (8)	Coefficient (9)	Derivative (10)	Coefficient (11)	Derivative (12)
I. Jorgenson TFP	24.76 (6.88)	.027	36.43 (9.11)	.031	−.93 (11.8)	.001	25.61 (13.4)	.007	41.62 (16.2)	.012	−40.85 (28.3)	.01
II. Share of investment in computers	1.88 (1.10)	.012	3.41 (1.67)	.017	.21 (1.58)	.002	−.081 (2.23)	.0001	.444 (2.84)	.001	−.284 (4.04)	.0004
III. NBER TFP	1.08 (1.33)	.004	1.89 (2.35)	.005	.64 (1.76)	.003	−3.26 (3.23)	.003	−4.98 (5.08)	.005	.300 (4.84)	.0002
IV. R&D-to-sales ratio	.033 (.02)	.01	.072 (.03)	.018	.020 (.03)	.008	−.079 (.05)	.006	−.069 (.066)	.006	−.062 (.084)	.004
V. Use of patents	3.13 (1.94)	.011	4.76 (2.99)	.013	.657 (2.74)	.003	−3.51 (4.07)	.003	−5.32 (5.16)	.005	.101 (7.06)	.0001
N	3,856		2,541		1,312		3,812		2,524		1,286	

NOTE.—NBER = National Bureau of Economic Research. TFP = total factor productivity. In parentheses, below the logit coefficients, are SEs. To the right of each estimated coefficient is the derivative (dP/dX) multiplied by the SD of the measure of technological change. See table 4 for more details and for a list of variables that are included in the regressions.

Table 6
Interaction Effects of Technological Change and Education on the
Likelihood of Company Training in the Manufacturing Sector

	All	Production	Nonproduction
I. Jorgenson TFP:	58.68	−3.92	122.8
	(36.2)	(65.6)	(61.6)
A. Years of education	.26	.09	.31
	(.044)	(.08)	(.07)
B. Jorgenson × Educ	−2.54	3.10	−8.10
	(2.60)	(5.38)	(4.05)
II. Investment in computers:	25.76	49.61	24.76
	(5.86)	(13.1)	(9.22)
A. Years of education	.347	.393	.332
	(.04)	(.09)	(.07)
B. Computers × education	−1.62	−3.74	−1.58
	(.40)	(1.06)	(.59)
III. NBER TFP:	24.45	20.78	28.39
	(8.23)	(18.7)	(12.5)
A. Years of education	.25	.14	.24
	(.03)	(.05)	(.04)
B. NBER × education	−1.52	−1.25	−1.86
	(.56)	(1.51)	(.81)
IV. R&D-to-sales ratio:	.436	.340	.508
	(.10)	(.20)	(.16)
A. Years of education	.291	.147	.303
	(.036)	(.07)	(.06)
B. R&D × education	−.025	−.015	−.031
	(.007)	(.016)	(.01)
V. Use of patents:	37.56	41.68	36.09
	(10.2)	(21.0)	(15.8)
A. Years of education	.987	1.029	1.00
	(.25)	(.60)	(.37)
B. Patents × education	−2.197	−2.59	−2.28
	(.71)	(1.71)	(1.03)
N	3,812	2,524	1,286

NOTE.—NBER = National Bureau of Economic Research. TFP = total factor productivity. Standard errors are in parentheses. See table 4 for a list of variables that are included in the regressions.

educated individuals may require less training in response to technological change if their general skills enable them to learn the new technology and adapt to the changed environment, that is, the substitutability between training and education increases at higher rates of technological change. We test this hypothesis in table 6, where the regressions include an interaction effect between education and the proxy for technological change.

The results in table 6 show that for all workers, production and nonproduction workers alike, the more educated are more likely to receive company training.[24] The interaction effects show, however, that

---

[24] See app. B for separate coefficients on education groups. The results show a monotonic relationship between years of education and training.

technological change attenuates the effect of education on training. This implies that, at higher rates of technological change, the training gap between the highly educated and the less educated narrows. The separate results for the production and nonproduction workers generally support this conclusion; with the exception of one measure, whenever the technological change indicator has a positive and significant effect on the incidence of training, the education-technological change interaction effect is negative and usually significant. The result is consistent with the model presented in Heckman, Lochner, and Taber (1998), where in a second and longer phase of a technological transition, the narrowing of the training gap acts to widen the wage gap between high- and low-skilled workers.

In order to more fully understand the relationship between technological change and the incidence of training for different education groups, we estimated the regressions in table 6 using a set of dummies for education groups (1–8, 9–11, 12, 13–15, 16, and 17+ years of schooling), in place of the continuous measure, and interacted the dummy variable with the technological change indicator. We used these coefficients to create plots (see figs. 1 and 2) that depict the effect of technological change on the incidence of training for a worker of given characteristics in each education group.[25] Whenever a slope is significantly different from zero, we indicate it with the letter *S*.

Although the education interactions are not monotonic and significant effects are observed for only one or two educational groups, figures 1 and 2 generally support the conclusion that, at higher rates of technological change, the gap between the training incidence of the highly educated and the less educated narrows. In the case of production workers, with the exception of the Jorgenson measure, we find that workers with some high school (9–11) and high school graduates train significantly more at higher rates of technological change, in some cases overtaking the training received by the 13–15 education group. For nonproduction workers, again with the exception of the Jorgenson measure, we find that the 13–15 group trains more at higher rates of technological change, overtaking those with at least 16 years of schooling.

Bartel and Lichtenberg (1987) have argued that highly educated workers have a comparative advantage with respect to learning and implementing new technologies and, hence, that the demand for these workers relative to the demand for less educated workers is a declining function

---

[25] For these plots, we assumed that the individual had the following characteristics: married, lives in a standard metropolitan statistical area, works in a large firm, has 10 years of market experience, and has 4 years of tenure with his employer. All other variables are the mean values, and the year is 1992.

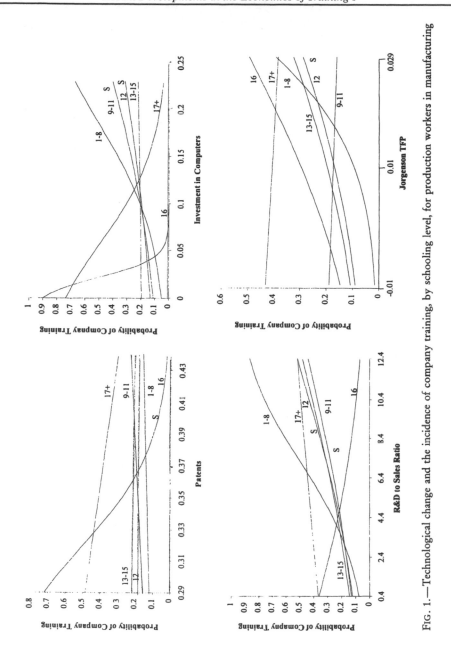

FIG. 1.—Technological change and the incidence of company training, by schooling level, for production workers in manufacturing

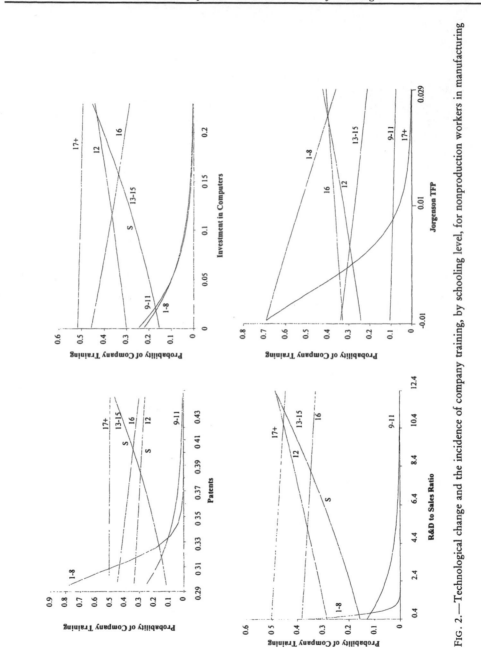

FIG. 2.—Technological change and the incidence of company training, by schooling level, for nonproduction workers in manufacturing

of experience with the technology. When a new technology is first introduced, there is a great deal of uncertainty about job tasks, and highly educated workers are needed to help the firm through this difficult implementation stage. The general skills of the highly educated workforce serve as a substitute for company training. As experience with the new technology is gained, however, it is possible to train the less educated employees to perform the new tasks. In our empirical analysis, we measure "long-term" differences across industries in the rate of technological change, and our finding that the training gap between the more and less educated narrows is consistent with the idea of the firm utilizing training to enable the less educated to work with the new technology.[26] Thus it appears that technological change has acted to reduce the gap in the stocks of human capital accumulated by different education groups through formal company training.

We recognize that one reason for the observed narrowing of the formal training gap between education groups could be selectivity. At higher rates of technological change, firms are less likely to employ or retain the less able employees within each education group. This bias is likely to be more pronounced for the less educated workers, resulting in an overestimate of the effect of technological change on the training of the less educated. We attempted to correct for this bias by including a set of ability test scores (not reported here), and our results on the effect of technological change were virtually unchanged. We did find, however, a positive and significant correlation between ability (holding schooling constant) and the likelihood of training and a smaller coefficient on education.

D. Occupations and Training

It is possible that our findings regarding the effect of technological change on education groups may reflect the fact that, within the categories of production and nonproduction workers, individuals with different amounts of education perform distinct job tasks, some of which are more sensitive to technological change. We, therefore, reestimated the regressions in table 6, adding 1-digit occupation dummies. The estimated coefficients of the interactions between the technological change measures and the education dummies were virtually unchanged.[27]

The question of whether the effect of technological change varies across

---

[26] If job training is more likely to be informal at higher levels of education, it could bias our results. Notice, however, that we do find a monotonic increase of formal training with the level of schooling. See tables 1, 3, and the complete regression results in app. B.

[27] The occupation dummies were also added to the regressions in table 4, and the coefficients on the technological change variables were unaffected.

occupation groups can be considered directly. We estimated a regression that includes the 1-digit occupation dummies and a set of interactions of these dummies with technological change. The results are shown in table 7. In the case of production workers, we find that, at very low levels of technological change, there are no occupational differences in training incidence. But, at higher rates of technological change, craftsmen receive significantly more training than other production workers.[28] For nonproduction workers, a very different pattern emerges. We find that, at low levels of technological change, clerical and unskilled workers receive the least amount of training among nonproduction workers. However, at high rates of technological change, they receive more training than the other nonproduction workers.[29] It is interesting to note that this group includes occupations such as clerks, computer and peripheral equipment operators, secretaries, and office-machine operators, occupations where the introduction of computers is likely to have had a strong effect on job tasks.[30]

E. Initial Training versus Retraining

We have interpreted our findings as indicating that the observed differences in training are due to higher rates of technological change. Alternatively, one could argue that our results are due to differences in the nature of technology across industries. Perhaps industries that we rank higher using different indicators are simply industries that use more sophisticated technologies. These technologies may require more initial training in order for the worker to learn how to use them. If this hypothesis is correct, we would expect to see more training (especially formal training) when workers join the firm and much less training of more senior workers.

In order to distinguish these two possible effects, we interact the measures of technological change with two dummies, one indicating that the worker has tenure of 1 year or less with the employer and the other indicating tenure of more than 1 year.[31] Our assumption is that the effect of the technological change measure on longer-tenured workers is more likely to reflect the response to technological change.

---

[28] When the technological change/occupation interaction terms are deleted, we find that craftsmen on average receive more training than other production workers. This result is not reported in the table.

[29] These two findings do not hold for the Jorgenson measure.

[30] A Canadian survey of employers (McMullen 1996) found that the introduction of computer-based technology led to an increase in skill requirements primarily for low-skilled workers. Presumably, these workers would then receive more training.

[31] A more accurate distinction would be based on tenure in job assignment, which we do not observe.

Table 7
The Effects of Technological Change on the Likelihood of Training
by Occupational Category

	Jorgenson TFP	Investment in Computers	NBER TFP	Use of Patents	R&D-to-Sales Ratio
I. Production workers (N = 2,541): Occupational dummies (omitted: operatives, except transport):					
Craftsmen and kindred workers	−.021 (.31)	.218 (.30)	.209 (.20)	−1.72 (2.16)	−.113 (.26)
Transport equipment operatives	−.480 (.66)	.385 (.56)	−.047 (.44)	5.40 (6.87)	−.110 (.44)
Laborers, except farm laborers	−.349 (.60)	−.324 (.66)	−.813 (.58)	−2.13 (6.23)	−.427 (.62)
Interaction with technological change:					
Craftsmen and kindred workers	44.97 (14.7)	3.86 (2.46)	7.592 (3.12)	12.53 (4.27)	.224 (.05)
Operatives, except transport	19.21 (16.0)	3.178 (2.94)	2.243 (4.65)	6.82 (5.49)	.073 (.06)
Transport equipment operatives	44.41 (43.7)	−12.83 (14.3)	−15.05 (37.4)	−10.23 (20.9)	−.017 (.26)
Laborers, except farm laborers	−32.33 (53.2)	−9.51 (15.0)	.322 (39.7)	10.63 (18.0)	−.250 (.40)
II. Nonproduction workers (N = 1,312): Occupational dummies (omitted: professional, technical and kindred workers):					
Managers and administrators	−.603 (.36)	−.751 (.32)	−.430 (.22)	−2.82 (1.87)	−.600 (.27)
Sales workers	−.156 (.41)	.089 (.41)	−.115 (.28)	.144 (2.22)	−.320 (.34)
Clerical and unskilled workers	−.484 (.39)	−1.65 (.47)	−.620 (.28)	−7.89 (2.50)	−1.23 (.36)
Farm laborers, laborers and foremen, and service workers	−.845 (.78)	−.680 (.60)	−.350 (.61)	−.926 (5.13)	−.744 (.55)
Interaction with technological change:					
Professional, technical and kindred workers	−2.41 (16.7)	−2.46 (1.94)	−1.761 (2.21)	−2.627 (3.51)	−.015 (.04)

continued overleaf

Table 7 (*Continued*)

	Jorgenson TFP	Investment in Computers	NBER TFP	Use of Patents	R&D-to-Sales Ratio
Managers and administrators	22.21	3.02	4.715	4.50	.0581
	(20.0)	(2.90)	(3.66)	(4.87)	(.05)
Sales workers	−5.85	−6.16	−4.956	−3.72	.004
	(23.2)	(3.66)	(3.98)	(5.96)	(.06)
Clerical and unskilled workers	7.435	11.86	10.06	18.34	.233
	(21.8)	(3.90)	(4.68)	(6.53)	(.06)
Farm laborers, laborers & foremen, and service workers	57.29	7.45	13.226	−.727	.239
	(49.8)	(8.76)	(39.2)	(15.1)	(.19)

NOTE.—Standard errors are in parentheses. See table 4 for a list of variables that are included in the regressions. NBER = National Bureau of Economic Research. TFP = total factor productivity.

Table 8 reports the estimated coefficients on the technological change variables on the likelihood of training, separated for tenure levels below and above 1 year. If our earlier results were due simply to the cross-sectional differences in the nature of technology, we would not expect to observe significant coefficients for workers beyond their first year of tenure. The results in table 8 show that, although the measured effects of the technological change variables are larger for individuals with less than 1 year of tenure, all of the technological change proxies have positive and significant effects on longer-tenured production workers. Hence these results indicate that what we are indeed measuring is the effect of technological change, not only the nature of technology, and ongoing technological change results in training of workers beyond their first year of tenure.

F. The Effects of Prior Training

The increased likelihood of training at higher rates of technological change could be due to workers training more frequently (intensive margin) or to more workers being trained (extensive margin). In an earlier version of this article (Bartel and Sicherman 1995), we estimated a standard Tobit model, the results of which showed that technological change does not increase the number of hours of training, conditional on participation. In this section, we exploit the panel nature of the NLSY data and examine whether higher rates of technological change induce firms to provide training to individuals who have already received training or to those who did not receive training in the prior period. If the latter is true, then technological change serves an important function; it acts to increase the proportion of workers who

Table 8
First Year and Beyond: Is the Effect of Technological Change Different
in the First Year of Tenure?

	Production		Nonproduction	
	Coefficient	Derivative	Coefficient	Derivative
I. Jorgenson TFP:				
Low tenure	39.48	.021	.726	.001
	(17.8)		(17.4)	
High tenure	31.69	.017	11.572	.016
	(11.8)		(13.1)	
II. Investment in computers:				
Low tenure	4.79	.015	−2.38	.019
	(3.12)		(2.44)	
High tenure	3.645	.011	.578	.005
	(2.17)		(1.72)	
III. NBER TFP:				
Low tenure	8.31	.014	−4.74	.02
	(5.00)		(3.81)	
High tenure	5.39	.009	.962	.004
	(2.87)		(1.92)	
IV. R&D-to-sales ratio:				
Low tenure	.165	.027	−.016	.006
	(.06)		(.05)	
High tenure	.162	.026	.038	.015
	(.04)		(.03)	
V. Use of patents:				
Low tenure	10.5	.018	.860	.004
	(3.66)		(2.95)	
High tenure	10.95	.019	1.40	.006
	(3.60)		(2.90)	
N	2,541		1,312	

NOTE.—In parentheses, below the logit coefficients, are SEs. To the right of each estimated coefficient is the derivative (dP/dX) multiplied by the SD of the measure of technological change. See table 4 for more details and for a list of variables that are included in the regressions. NBER = National Bureau of Economic Research. TFP = total factor productivity.

receive training. We test this hypothesis in table 9 by interacting the various measures of technological change with two dummy variables, one indicating that the individual received training in the prior year (i.e., between t-2 and t-1, since the dependent variable is training between t-1 and t) and the other indicating no training in the prior year. In columns 1 and 2, the sample is restricted to individuals who did not change industries between time periods t-2 and t, and in columns 3 and 4, we restrict the analysis to individuals who did not change employers between the 2 time periods. The results show insignificant effects of technological change for previously trained workers and significant effects for most of the technological change indicators for individuals who did not receive training in the prior year. A test of equality of coefficients for the two groups rejects the hypothesis that they are equal. The higher incidence of training at higher rates of

Technological Change and Skill   747

Table 9
**Past Training, Technological Change, and Current Training: Interacting
Technological Change with Past-Training Dummies**

	Did Not Change Industry (2 Digit)		Did Not Change Employer	
	Production (1)	Nonproduction (2)	Production (3)	Nonproduction (4)
I. Jorgenson TFP:				
Past training	2.42	−6.61	−19.2	−10.6
	(30.3)	(25.23)	(27.9)	(24.6)
No past training	31.55	−.53	26.5	−8.7
	(18.1)	(20.0)	(17.3)	(18.7)
II. Investment in computers:				
Past training	6.12	−3.02	.679	−2.67
	(4.92)	(3.36)	(4.19)	(3.32)
No past training	5.57	.431	4.73	3.61
	(3.28)	(2.79)	(3.19)	(2.54)
IV. NBER TFP:				
Past training	8.38	−.81	−1.72	−1.40
	(7.08)	(3.79)	(5.42)	(3.79)
No past training	9.60	−1.78	6.54	−.58
	(4.23)	(3.15)	(4.20)	(2.82)
V. R&D-to-sales ratio:				
Past training	.151	−.026	.048	−.024
	(.09)	(.06)	(.07)	(.06)
No past training	.206	−.002	.179	.028
	(.06)	(.05)	(.06)	(.05)
IV. Use of patents:				
Past training	11.33	−2.43	2.17	−6.47
	(9.35)	(5.79)	(7.30)	(5.62)
No past training	14.35	4.45	12.26	4.48
	(5.14)	(4.88)	(5.66)	(4.30)
N	1,285	684	1,354	749

NOTE.—NBER = National Bureau of Economic Research. TFP = total factor productivity. The dummies are "past training" = 1 if the person received company training between t-2 and t-1 (the dependent variable is training between t-1 and t); "no past training" = 1 if the person did not train between t-2 and t-1. In the first two columns, the sample is limited to workers who did not change industry since t-2. In the last two columns, the sample is limited to workers who did not change employer since t-2. Standard errors in parentheses. See table 4 for a list of variables that are included in the regressions.

technological change occurs mainly because more individuals are receiving training.[32]

IV. Summary and Implications

The effect of technological change on young workers' investments in on-the-job training is theoretically ambiguous. Technological change

---

[32] This finding is consistent with the model of Galor and Tsiddon (1997), which postulates that there are two stages of the technological change process: invention and innovation. During the innovation phase, the technology becomes more accessible to a greater number of employees, which would lead to our observation of an increased pool of trainees.

influences the rate at which various types of human capital obsolesce and also increases the uncertainty associated with human capital investments. As we discussed in the introduction, these mechanisms can cause training to increase or decrease at higher rates of technological change. The relationship between education and training will also be affected by technological change. If the general skills of the more educated enable them to more easily adapt to new technologies, we will observe a narrowing of the postschool-training gap between more and less educated workers.

We linked a sample of male workers in manufacturing industries from the 1987–92 waves of the NLSY to five different measures of industry rates of technological change in order to empirically resolve the ambiguous theoretical predictions and found essentially similar results for all five measures. In particular, we found the following. (1) Production workers in industries with higher rates of technological change are more likely to receive formal company training than those working in industries with lower rates of technological change, controlling for a set of worker, job, and industry characteristics. (2) While more educated workers are more likely to receive training, at higher rates of technological change, the training gap between the highly educated and the less educated narrows. (3) The relationship between training and technological change is insignificant for the aggregate group of nonproduction workers (only after controlling for various characteristics). Disaggregating the group, we find that, at higher rates of technological change, the lower-skilled nonproduction workers, that is, clerical and unskilled workers, receive significantly more training compared with the more highly skilled nonproduction workers, such as professionals, technical employees, managers, and sales workers. (4) Technological change acts to increase the extensive margin of training, increasing the pool of trainees. At higher rates of technological change, firms are more likely to train individuals who have not received training in the prior period rather than those who were previously trained.

We remind the reader that these findings pertain to young workers only, do not include informal training, and may not generalize to other time periods. With these limitations in mind, we can conclude from our analysis that, at higher rates of technological change, firms employ more educated workers and provide more formal training to their workforces. At the same time, however, higher rates of technological change induce employers to provide more formal training to their less educated employees; although the more educated still receive more training, technological change shifts the balance in favor of the less educated. This happens because the general skills of the more educated facilitate their adaptation to the new technologies. It is not clear a priori how these effects will impact the wage structure, a topic that we reserve for future research.

Appendix A
Data
I. General

The data are from the 1979–92 NLSY of youth ages 14–21 in 1979. Additional data are obtained from the NLSY work-history file. The NLSY work-history file contains primarily employment-related spell data constructed from the main NLSY file. Both files are available in CD-ROM format. Many questions are asked with regard to the time since the last survey. For the first survey (1979), the questions, in most cases, are with regard to the time period since January 1, 1978.

In addition to the NLSY, we use information from variety of sources. These are industry measures of technological change and other industry-level variables. They are described in the text.

II. The Sample

The number of men interviewed in 1979 is 6,403. Not all individuals are interviewed each year. The first observation for an individual (to be included in our sample) is the first survey in which the main activity reported for the week prior to the survey is working "1," with a job but not working "2," or looking for a job "3." Following that, an individual is included in the sample as long as he is interviewed (even if leaving the labor market). Other restrictions apply only for specific analyses. The panel is unbalanced, and the number of observations per individual varies.

III. CPS Job

For each respondent, employment information on up to a maximum of five jobs is recorded in each survey year. One of these jobs is designated as a "CPS" job, and it is the most recent or current job at the time of interview. Typically it is also the main job. Each job is identified by a number (1–5), and job 1 in most cases is also the "CPS" job. For only this so-called "CPS" job, there are a host of additional employer/employee related questions that are asked in the NLSY surveys. Our analysis is restricted to CPS jobs.

IV. The Work-History File

We use the work-history file to construct the tenure, separation, and reason for separation variables.

Tracing jobs and tenure with employer. — The tenure variable is already constructed in the work-history file. The major difficulty is tracing CPS jobs over the interview years. A variable called PREV allows matching of employers between consecutive interview years. For each job in a particular survey year, it gives the job number that was assigned to that job in the previous year (assuming of course that the current job existed in the previous year). Our programming strategy was to pick CPS jobs in which the respondents are actually employed at the time of interview and to trace these jobs to the next survey year via the PREV variable in the succeeding survey year. There are, however, a few cases where we cannot trace the current CPS job in the succeeding interview year with PREV. The current tenure value is the total number of weeks worked up to the interview date. A shortcoming of PREV is that it allows for matching employers between consecutive interview years only. If, therefore, a respondent worked for a particular employer say in 1980 but not in 1981 and started working for the same employer in survey year 1982, then there is no way of knowing the total years of tenure with that employer since employer numbers are followed only in contiguous interviews. This may not be a problem for turnover analysis since reemployment with the same employer after an absence of that length (i.e., a period longer than that between 2 successive interview years) may be considered a new job.

V. Weeks between Surveys

The number of weeks between surveys ranges between 26 and 552 weeks. The large numbers are the results of individuals not being surveyed for several years. In all our analyses, we included (when it made sense) the variable WKSSINCE (weeks since last survey). The variable was excluded if it made no difference.

VI. Training

A variety of formal training questions were asked in all survey years, except 1987. Individuals were asked to report on several vocational or technical programs in which they were enrolled since the previous survey. Until 1986, the maximum was two programs, and in 1988 it was increased to four. In addition, individuals were asked to report up to two government programs in which they were enrolled.

Up until 1986, further questions were asked, in particular the type of program and the dates it started and ended, only if the program lasted more than 4 weeks. Starting in 1988, these questions were asked about all programs, regardless of length. The 4 weeks condition up to 1986 is a major shortcoming of the data set. Any analysis that focuses on a specific type of training (e.g., company training) has to be limited to post-1986. The following example illustrates the problem: the percentage of workers in our sample that reported enrollment in company training is 4.7% over the period 1976–90. Limiting the sample to 1988–90, the rate increases to 11%.

In certain years (1980–86, 1989–90), a distinction was made between programs in which the individual was enrolled at the time of the previous interview and programs that started after the previous interview. When such a distinction is made, up to two programs at the time of the last interview can be reported. A person was asked about training that took place at the time of the last interview only if the interviewer had a record indicating so. Therefore, for 1980–86, such a record did not exist if training took less than a month.

For all programs, the starting and ending month and year are reported. Also reported are the average number of hours per week spent in training.

In our programming, we number all programs in the following order: the four vocational or technical programs are numbered 1–4, the two programs at time of last interview are numbered 5–6, and the government programs are numbered 7–8.

Type of training.—Up to 1986, the following categories are reported: 1 = business college, 2 = nurses program, 3 = apprenticeship, 4 = vocational or technical institution, 5 = barber or beauty school, 6 = flight school, 7 = correspondence, 8 = company or military, and 9 = other. We aggregate them into company training (8), apprenticeship (3), and "other" (1, 2, 4, 5, 6, 7, 9). Starting in 1988, the breakdown is more detailed: 1–7 are unchanged; 8 = a formal company training run by employer or military training (excluding basic training); 9 = seminars or training programs at work run by someone other than employer; 10 = seminars or training programs outside of work; 11 = vocational rehabilitation center; and 12 = other. We now aggregate 8–10 as company training and 11–12 as "other."

Below are additional descriptions of some of the variables used.

Any technical or vocational training dummy.—Designates whether the worker received any technical or vocational training since (or at the time of) the last interview.

Any training dummy (TANYD).—Like the above, but TANYD also includes government training.

Company training dummy (TCOMD).—Designates if any of the training programs were 8 up to 1985 or 8, 9, or 10 after 1986. Notice that only after 1986 the type of program was asked of all workers who reported training. Prior to 1988, the program-type question was asked only for those who spent more than 4 weeks on training (see above for more discussion of this problem).

Length of training.—Starting in 1988, in addition to asking when (month and year) different training programs start and end, individuals were also asked, "Altogether, for how many weeks did you attend this training?" The question was not asked of government training. If the answer was zero (less than a week), we recoded it to half a week. For each of the eight programs, individuals were asked for the average hours per week spent training. Multiplying the hours per week in each program with the weeks in each program, we get the total hours in each program.

Imputing training data for 1987.—In 1987, no training questions were asked. We utilize the answers to the 1988 survey to construct training information for the 1987 survey. We do so by using information on the starting and ending dates of training programs. If employees reported in 1988 that they were still in training (end month = 0 and endyr = 0 or 1), we set the end date to the interview date. For some individuals the answer for the beginning date indicates "still in training." This is an error.

Appendix B

Table B1
The Likelihood of Company Training: Estimated Logit Results for Male Workers in Manufacturing

Variable	All Workers		Production Workers		Nonproduction	
	Coefficient	Derivative	Coefficient	Derivative	Coefficient	Derivative
Intercept	−4.889	−.482	−3.649	−.2291	−5.971	−.9406
	(.802)		(1.185)		(1.14)	
If married	.2304	.023	.2986	.0187	.1440	.0227
	(.121)		(.184)		(.165)	
If nonwhite	−.2447	−.024	−.2201	−.0138	−.2487	−.0392
	(.145)		(.196)		(.224)	
1–8 years of schooling	−.6689	−.066	−.2832	−.0178	−1.391	−.2191
	(.429)		(.478)		(1.05)	
9–11 years of schooling	−.4227	−.042	.0103	.0006	−1.677	−.2642
	(.199)		(.225)		(.543)	
13–15 years of schooling	.0807	.008	.1088	.0068	−.3944	−.0621
	(.166)		(.244)		(.241)	
16 years of schooling	.7376	.073	.7315	.0459	.1695	.0267
	(.157)		(.419)		(.207)	
17+ years of schooling	1.212	.120	.8223	.0516	.6579	.1036
	(.209)		(.652)		(.254)	
Lives in SMSA	.0350	.003	−.00371	−.0002	−.1554	−.0245
	(.136)		(.188)		(.209)	
Experience	.1660	.016	.0513	.0032	.3109	.0490
	(.113)		(.160)		(.164)	
Experience^2	−.0076	−.001	−.0040	−.0002	−.0133	−.0021
	(.006)		(.008)		(.008)	
Tenure	.0332	.003	.0671	.0042	.0190	.0030
	(.054)		(.080)		(.078)	
Tenure^2	−.0026	−.000	−.0035	−.0002	−.0043	−.0007
	(.005)		(.006)		(.007)	
Union member	−.1168	−.012	.2006	.0126	−.4278	−.0674
	(.154)		(.189)		(.316)	
Large firm	.8422	.083	.7805	.0490	.8311	.1309
	(.119)		(.176)		(1.66)	
Durables	−.1183	−.012	−.0710	−.0045	−.0331	−.0052
	(.156)		(.240)		(.209)	
Industry unemployment	−.1188	−.012	−.0695	−.0044	−.1696	−.0267
	(.050)		(.073)		(.074)	
Industry union coverage	.0016	.000	.0037	.0002	.0025	.0004
	(.006)		(.008)		(.009)	
Industry jobs creation	−.0751	−.007	−.1598	−.0100	.0143	.0023
	(.084)		(.121)		(.123)	
Industry jobs destruction	.0965	.010	−.0084	−.0005	.1956	.0308
	(.068)		(.097)		(.101)	
Industry R&D/sales	.0805	.008	.1622	.0102	.0289	.0045
	(.024)		(.039)		(.033)	
1988	1.317	.130	1.386	.0870	1.331	.2096
	(.275)		(.443)		(.357)	
1989	1.401	.138	1.479	.0928	1.395	.2198
	(.273)		(.441)		(.352)	
1990	1.630	.161	1.866	.1171	1.548	.2439
	(.272)		(.430)		(.358)	
1991	1.608	.159	1.947	.1222	1.408	.2217
	(.285)		(.447)		(.379)	
1992	1.627	.161	1.954	.1226	1.474	.2321
	(.302)		(.472)		(.403)	
N	3,856		2,541		1,312	

NOTE.—Standard errors are in parentheses. SMSA = standard metropolitan statistical area.

References

Allen, Steven G. "Technology and the Wage Structure." Photocopied. Paper presented at National Bureau of Economic Research (NBER) Summer Institute in Labor Economics. Cambridge, MA: NBER, July 1992.

Barron, John M.; Black, Dan A.; and Loewenstein, Mark A. "Employer Size: The Implications for Search, Training, Capital Investment, Starting Wages and Wage Growth." *Journal of Labor Economics* 5 (January 1987): 76–89.

Bartel, Ann P., and Lichtenberg, Frank R. "The Comparative Advantage of Educated Workers in Implementing New Technology." *Review of Economics and Statistics* 69 (February 1987): 1–11.

———. "The Age of Technology and Its Impact on Employee Wages." *Economics of Innovation and New Technology* 1 (1991): 215–31.

Bartel, Ann P., and Sicherman, Nachum. "Technological Change and Retirement Decisions." *Journal of Labor Economics* 11 (January 1993): 162–83.

———. "Technological Change and the Skill Acquisition of Young Workers." Working Paper no. 5107. Cambridge, MA: NBER, May 1995.

———. "Technological Change and Wages: An Inter-industry Analysis." Working Paper no. 5941. Cambridge, MA: NBER, February 1997.

Bartlesman, Eric J., and Gray, Wayne. "The NBER Manufacturing Productivity Database." Technical Working Paper no. 205. Cambridge, MA: NBER, October 1996.

Berman, Eli; Bound, John; and Griliches, Zvi. "Changes in the Demand for Skilled Labor within U.S. Manufacturing Industries: Evidence from the Annual Survey of Manufacturing." *Quarterly Journal of Economics* 109 (May 1994): 367–98.

Bound, John, and Johnson, George. "Changes in the Structure of Wages during the 1980s: An Evaluation of Alternative Explanations." *American Economic Review* 82 (June 1992): 371–92.

Davis, Steve, and Haltiwanger, John. "Gross Job Creation, Gross Job Destruction, and Employment Reallocation." *Quarterly Journal of Economics* 107 (August 1992): 819–63.

Dhrymes, Phoebus J. *Introductory Economics.* New York: Springer-Verlag, 1978.

Galor, Oded, and Tsiddon, Daniel. "Technological Progress, Mobility and Growth." *American Economic Review* 87, no. 2 (June 1997): 363–82.

Gill, Indermit. "Technological Change, Education, and the Obsolescence of Human Capital: Some Evidence for the U.S." Unpublished manuscript. Buffalo: State University of New York at Buffalo, May 1990.

Griliches, Zvi. "Patent Statistics as Economic Indicators: A Survey." *Journal of Economic Literature* 28 (December 1990): 1661–1707.

———. "Productivity, R&D, and the Data Constraint." *American Economic Review* 84 (March 1994): 1–23.

Griliches, Zvi, and Hausman, Jerry A. "Errors in Variables in Panel Data." *Journal of Econometrics* 31 (1986): 93–118.

Griliches, Zvi, and Lichtenberg, Frank. "R&D and Productivity Growth at the Industry Level: Is There Still a Relationship?" In *R&D, Patents, and Productivity,* edited by Zvi Griliches. Cambridge, MA: NBER, 1984.

Heckman, James J.; Lochner, Lance; and Taber, Chris. "Explaining Rising Wage Inequality Explorations with a Dynamic General Equilibrium Model of Labor Earnings with Heterogeneous Agents." *Review of Economic Dynamics* 1, no. 1 (May 1998): 1–58.

Hirsch, Barry, and MacPherson, David A. "Union Membership and Coverage Files from the Current Population Surveys: Note." *Industrial and Labor Relations Review* 46 (April 1993): 574–78.

Jorgenson, Dale W.; Gollop, Frank M.; and Fraumeni, Barbara M. *Productivity and U.S. Economic Growth.* Cambridge, MA: Harvard University Press, 1987.

Kortum, Samuel, and Putnam, Jonathan. "Predicting Patents by Industry: Tests of the Yale-Canada Concordance." Photocopied. Boston: Boston University, 1995.

Krueger, Alan B. "How Computers Have Changed the Wage Structure: Evidence from Microdata, 1984–1989." *Quarterly Journal of Economics* 108 (February 1993): 33–60.

Lach, Saul. "Patents and Productivity Growth at the Industry Level: A First Look." *Economics Letters* 49 (1995): 101–8.

Levhari, David, and Weiss, Yoram. "The Effects of Risk on the Investment in Human Capital." *American Economic Review* 64 (December 1974): 950–63.

Lichtenberg, Frank R., and Griliches, Zvi. "Errors of Measurement in Output Deflators." *Journal of Business and Economic Statistics* 7, no. 1 (January 1989): 1–9.

Lichtenberg, Frank R., and Siegel, Donald. "The Impact of R&D Investment on Productivity: New Evidence Using Linked R&D-LRD Data." *Economic Inquiry* 29 (April 1991): 203–28.

Lillard, Lee A., and Tan, Hong W. "Training: Who Gets It and What Are Its Effects on Employment and Earnings?" Report R-3331-DOL/RC. Santa Monica, CA: RAND, 1986.

Lynch, Lisa M. "The Role of Off-the-Job and On-the-Job Training for the Mobility of Young Workers." *American Economic Review* 81 (May 1991): 151–56.

———. "Differential Effects of Post-school Training on Early Career Mobility." Working Paper no. 4034. Cambridge, MA: NBER, March 1992. (*a*)

———. "Private-Sector Training and the Earnings of Young Workers." *American Economic Review* 82 (March 1992): 299–312. (*b*)

McMullen, Kathryn. "Skill and Employment Effects of Computer-Based Technology: The Results of the Working with Technology Survey III." Working paper. Ottawa: Canadian Policy Research Networks, April 1996.

Mincer, Jacob. "On the Job Training: Costs, Returns, and Some Implications." _Journal of Political Economy_ 70, pt. 2 (October 1962): 50–79.

——. "Human Capital Responses to Technological Change in the Labor Market." Working Paper no. 3207. Cambridge, MA: NBER, December 1989.

Mincer, Jacob, and Higuchi, Yoshio. "Wage Structures and Labor Turnover in the United States and Japan." _Journal of the Japanese and International Economies_ 2 (June 1988): 97–133.

National Science Foundation. "Research and Development in Industry: 1990." Report no. 94-304. Arlington, VA: National Science Foundation, 1993.

Rosen, Sherwin. "A Theory of Life Earnings." _Journal of Political Economy_ 84, pt. 2 (August 1976): S45–S68.

Sicherman, Nachum. "The Measurement of On-the-Job Training." _Journal of Economic and Social Measurement_ 16 (1990): 221–30.

——. "Over-education in the Labor Market." _Journal of Labor Economics_ 9, no. 2 (April 1991): 101–22.

Siegel, Donald. "The Impact of Technological Change on Employment and Wages: Evidence from a Panel of Long Island Manufacturers." Paper presented at C.V. Starr Conference on Technologies and Skills, New York University, New York, December 2–3, 1994.

Tan, Hong W. "Technical Change and Its Consequences for Training and Earnings." Unpublished manuscript. Santa Monica, CA: RAND, 1989.

Welch, Finis. "Education in Production." _Journal of Political Economy_ 78, no. 1 (January 1970): 35–59.

[11]

Skill, Training, and Work Organization in American Establishments

PAUL OSTERMAN*

This paper examines the relationship between skill, training, and work organization in American firms. It is based on results from an original survey of a representative sample of private-sector establishments with fifty or more employees. The paper begins by briefly reviewing the literature regarding skill, training, and work organization. The empirical work is then presented in three sections: the first two describe skill and training patterns and trends, and the third estimates a regression model explaining variation in training across establishments. This model examines a number of the hypotheses found in the literature as well as question the impact of work organization upon the level of training provided by firms. Strong evidence is found that establishments that introduce so-called high performance work organizations provide more training than do other establishments. However, this effect tends to decay over time. In addition the paper finds a clear trend toward upskilling in work but one that is more pronounced for technical/professional than for blue-collar jobs. Hiring criteria for technical/professional jobs tended to focus more on skill, whereas behavioral traits were emphasized more heavily (but by no means exclusively) in blue-collar work. Finally, the regressions show that there is a clear make or buy choice, firms with more "humanistic" values train more, and the presence of a union increases training as does the payment of efficiency wages and links to a larger organization.

THE LONG-RUNNING DEBATE in labor economics and sociology regarding skill and training has taken a new turn. In the 1970s and 1980s an ex-

* Sloan School, Massachusetts Institute of Technology. This research was supported by the Spencer Foundation. I am grateful to Peter Cappelli, Harry Katz, Richard Murnane, Jim Rebitzer, and three referees for their comments.

INDUSTRIAL RELATIONS, Vol. 34, No. 2 (April 1995). © 1995 Regents of the University of California
Published by Blackwell Publishers, 238 Main Street, Cambridge, MA 02142, USA, and 108 Cowley
Road, Oxford, OX4 1JF, UK.

126 / PAUL OSTERMAN

plosion of literature debated the merits of Braverman's (1974) deskilling hypothesis. The driving question was whether the technological trajectory of modern industrial development brought about a secular decline in skill. However, this hypothesis has been turned on its head. Growing evidence that flexible work systems carry with them productivity gains (McDuffie, 1991; Kaufman, 1992; Applebaum and Batt, 1993; Ichniowski, Shaw, and Prennushi, 1993) has raised the ancillary question of whether firms and schools are providing enough training to enable effective use of these systems. Hence the presumed tendency is now in the direction of upskilling and the question is under what circumstances it is occurring and whether the pace is fast enough. This perspective is given additional weight by data that seem to show a substantial twist in the wage structure in the direction of increased demand for skill (Levy and Murnane, 1992; Katz and Murphy, 1992).

These discussions can be characterized as centering around two factual questions and a hypothesized relationship. The first question concerns the use of skill in American firms. What can we say about changes in the distribution of high- and low-skill work? The second, and obviously related, question, concerns training. How much training is occurring in American enterprises and where and for whom is it found? The hypothesized relationship, which ties the skill and training themes together, concerns work organization. Is it true that organizations that are adopting High Performance Work Organizations[1] are demanding greater skill and are providing more training? If true then this has important implications for understanding the trajectory of skill, for explaining recent wage developments, and for pointing to directions for public policy.

This paper is based on results from an original survey that collected work organization and training data from a representative sample of private-sector establishments with fifty or more employees. The paper begins by briefly reviewing the literature regarding skill, training, and work organization. The empirical work is then presented in three sections: the first two describe skill and training patterns and trends and the third estimates a regression model explaining variation in training across establishments. This model examines a number of the hypotheses found in the literature and questions the impact of work organization.

The Discussion Regarding Skill

Until recently the scholarly discussion of skills has centered on whether the technological trajectory of modern industry leads to higher or lower

---

[1] This term is not very well defined. For a review of the literature and an effort to distinguish among the various ways in which the term is used see Applebaum and Batt (1994).

Skill, Training, and Work Organization / 127

skill demands (Braverman, 1974; Bell, 1973; Blauner, 1964). The debate between these perspectives led to a proliferation of case study research. The verdict from this line of work is mixed. As Flynn (1988) shows in her review of 197 studies, one can find cases that support either of the extreme positions or virtually any point in the middle. Furthermore, and perhaps most unfortunately, it has proved difficult to generalize about any relationship between context and the impact of technical change on skill.

If case studies tie down one end of the research spectrum the other is represented by studies that employ large national data sets. These most typically use the *Dictionary of Occupational Titles* to measure occupational skill levels. Some analysts have examined trends in the DOT itself (Spenner, 1983) while others have linked the DOT to census data and have used the changing distribution of census job titles as input to their analysis of skill change (Howell and Wolff, 1991). The findings from this line of work are more uniform than those from the case studies: most research finds evidence of mild skill upgrading although Howell and Wolff argue that this trend began to level off in the 1980s.[2]

If the case studies suffer from problems of generalizability, the DOT/census studies lack adequate detail. In particular they are typically unable to examine changes within occupational titles (i.e., the duties of the same job title shifting) and instead rely on changes in the distribution of occupations. In addition, these studies contain no information on the characteristics of firms (i.e., the context) and hence we cannot understand what explains variation.

More recently a third line of research has emerged at an intermediate point. For example, Kelley (1989) examined trends in the machine tool industry using an original survey and Keefe (1991) studied the same industry by combining the DOT with Industry Wage Surveys. Cappelli (1993) studied 94 job titles in 93 manufacturing firms as well as clerical jobs in 211 firms with data from the Hay Associates consulting firm. These studies capture much more contextual detail than do the census studies and also contain rich information on skill. However, the findings remain mixed. For example, Keefe found very weak, if any, net upgrading from numerically controlled equipment and Cappelli found strong evidence of upskilling in manufacturing jobs and no clear trend for clerical work.

---

[2] Howell and Wolff find upgrading (i.e., higher levels of demand) for interactive and cognitive skills and a declining trend for motor skills. In addition, they find that the service sector has a higher average demand for skill than does the goods-producing sector but that there is greater dispersion across different elements of the service sector.

The Discussion Regarding Training

A new element in the discussion regarding skills has been added by recent concerns with international competitiveness. The point is twofold: first, that American firms do not train their employees as extensively as do employers in our main trading partners and, second, that this failure is related to the slow adoption of more flexible work systems. This view is present in scholarly publications, particularly those that have collected matched firm data in a common industry (McDuffie, 1991; Womack, Jones, and Roos, 1990; Jaikumar, 1986) as well as in reports of various national commissions (Cuomo Commission on Trade and Competitiveness, 1988; Commission on the Skills of the American Workforce, 1990; Dertouzos, Lester, and Solow, 1989). The evidence is also based on broad comparisons of national systems: the German dual apprenticeship system in contrast with the rather weak vocational training offered American high school youth (Osterman, 1988) and the extensive training provided to Japanese blue-collar employees contrasted with the tendency of American firms to devote most training resources to white-collar workers and managers (Lynch, 1990; Cairncross and Dore, 1989).

Empirical evidence from several representative national surveys—a supplement to the Current Population Survey (CPS) and the National Longitudinal Survey (NLS) of Youth—have been brought to bear on these issues. In addition, business organizations such as the American Society of Training and Development (Carnevale, Gainer, and Villet, 1990), The Conference Board (Lusterman, 1985), and *Training Magazine* have also conducted surveys although the technical quality is somewhat mixed.[3] These surveys tend to show that the aggregate volume of training expenditure is quite high and that the distribution of training is very much biased toward managers and white-collar workers and away from blue-collar employees (Lynch, 1990; Lynch, 1991; Kochan and Osterman, 1993; Brown, 1990). However, these studies, like the earlier research with the DOT and the census, typically contain little contextual information on firms and so we cannot understand which kinds of employers do what.

It is unfortunate that the best quality nationally representative training data (e.g., the CPS and the NLS) are on individuals and provide little information on the employer since at the heart of this recent discussion is the linkage of training with work organization. What produces productivity improvements, so the argument goes, is adoption of High Performance

---

[3] The response rate to the widely cited *Training Magazine* survey was 15.8 percent.

Skill, Training, and Work Organization / 129

Work Organization (HPWO) and improved training is a necessary part of this process. In this sense emerging conventional wisdom has "resolved" the earlier discussion of skilling versus deskilling: the most productive firms of the future will be those who adopt HPWOs and this entails considerable increases in worker skill.

The emphasis on work organization and productivity has also added a slightly different twist to the skills debate. The discussion of the skill trajectory of new technology often carried with it the implicit assumption that once the technology was in place how it was used was foreordained. This "technological determinism" view left little space for choice. The more recent discussion, with its emphasis on international comparisons, shows quite clearly that the same technology can be deployed in different ways and with different impacts on skill. This is the central lesson of the international automobile industry research (McDuffie, 1991; Womack, Jones, and Roos, 1991; Brown, Reich, and Stern, 1991; Adler, 1993; Milkman and Pullman, 1991). This finding in turn transforms the older question—"what is the impact of technology on skill"—into the issue now more commonly debated in policy circles—"how much training is there and why do some employers train more than others?" In other words, skill has come to be seen as the outcome variable that in turn is determined by choices that vary across employers.

The foregoing review of the literature suggests that the survey employed here can be utilized to understand two questions:

- What is the distribution of training patterns, skill requirements, and hiring criteria across American firms?
- How can the training practices of establishments be related to the nature of their work organization and other aspects of establishment structure? This includes, but is not limited to, the more narrow but important question of whether it is true that establishments that adopt elements of HPWO tend to provide more training to their employees than do other enterprises.

More Detail on the Survey

The survey was conducted in 1992 and contains 875 observations on American establishments. An establishment is defined as a business address and is distinct from a company. The survey was a telephone interview and had a response rate of 65.5 percent. The sampling universe was the Dun and Bradstreet establishment file. The sampling was limited to estab-

130 / Paul Osterman

lishments with fifty or more employees in nonagricultural industries. More detail regarding the sampling procedure and response rates can be found in Osterman (1994).

A final point regarding the survey procedure concerns the unit of analysis within the establishment. Many variables were collected for the entire establishment. However, detailed information on training and work organization was obtained only for CORE employees. This is because no single answer regarding say, job training, is likely to be applicable to all occupational groups within a firm since firms have distinctive internal labor market systems for different families of jobs (Osterman, 1987). It was not practical to collect ILM data on all job families and so the notion of a CORE job was developed. The CORE job was defined in the survey as[4]

> The largest group of non-supervisory, non-managerial workers at this location who are directly involved in making the product or in providing the service at your location. We want you to think of the various groups directly involved in making the product or providing the service and then focus on the largest group. For example, these might be assembly-line workers at a factory or computer programmers in a software company, or sales or service representatives in an insurance company.

Descriptive Data on Skill, Hiring Criteria, and Training

A useful way to begin is to simply describe what the survey tells us about skill and training in the establishments. Table 1 describes the respondents' assessment of the skill distribution of the CORE jobs and their description of how the skill content of the jobs are changing.[5] The table includes data for the entire sample and distinguishes between blue-collar employees and professional/technical employees[6] (these two categories were selected both because of their intrinsic interest and also because together they accounted for 77 percent of the unweighted observations).

---

[4] The distribution of CORE jobs in the survey was professional/technical, 14.1 percent; sales, 18.4 percent; clerical, 5.9 percent; service, 19.0 percent; and blue-collar, 42.4 percent.

[5] The respondents were asked, "Which best characterizes the skill level of CORE employees?" and were asked to respond on a five-point scale ranging from not skilled to extremely skilled. They were also asked, "Have the skills involved in doing the CORE job changed in the past few years?" and if the answer was yes then they were asked how and the responses were "more complex," "less complex," or "equally complex, different skills." They were also asked an open-ended question: "briefly describe how the skills are different now," and this response was coded as described in the text.

[6] Recall that the definition of CORE jobs excluded managers and supervisors.

Skill, Training, and Work Organization / 131

TABLE 1
SKILL LEVEL AND SKILL TRENDS

	All	Blue-Collar	Professional/ Technical
Skill Level			
Not Skilled	1.8%	4.1%	0.0%
Slight Skill	19.5	19.6	0.0
Moderate Skill	43.2	46.5	14.5
Very Skilled	28.1	22.0	63.9
Extremely Skilled	7.2	7.5	21.5
Change in Skill			
No Change	38.1%	46.6%	29.1%
Less Complex	3.5	0.6	0.0
More Complex	39.9	39.7	51.1
Same Level, Different Skill	17.7	12.9	19.7

It comes as no surprise to learn that professional/technical jobs are considered higher skill on average than are blue-collar jobs. Of perhaps greater note is the substantial fraction of blue-collar CORE jobs that are at the lower end of the skill spectrum. It is, however, not entirely clear how to interpret these data since they are not anchored in a common metric (in the sense that the DOT purports to measure months required to learn a job or years of education a job requires). The information on skill change in the second panel are less subject to this criticism.

For professional/technical employees the trend is clearly toward more complex work. While for blue-collar employees the trend is also upward (in the sense that a larger fraction indicates an increase in complexity rather than a decrease) the upskilling is less pronounced than is true for professional/technical workers. There is also a relationship between the level of skill and the direction of change. For example, among blue-collar workers whose jobs were very or extremely skilled 56.1 percent were reported to experience an increase in complexity whereas among the not skilled, slightly skilled, and moderately skilled the figure was 33.0 percent. This pattern, along with the stronger upgrading of professional/technical compared to blue-collar employment, suggests that there is a growing inequality in the skill distribution.[7]

Table 2 provides information on the nature of the changes in job content in those cases in which the jobs became more complex. These data were

---

[7] Whether this is related to the growing inequality in wages is the subject of a separate investigation.

132 / Paul Osterman

TABLE 2

Nature of Skill Change When Jobs Are Becoming More Complex

	Professional/Technical	Blue-Collar
Interpersonal Skills/Responsibility	8.1%	14.4%
Cognitive	3.7	9.2
Job Characteristics	59.1	55.9
Computer Usage	28.8	20.3

elicited via an open-ended question in which the respondent was asked to indicate how the job had changed. These responses were then coded into these categories.[8]

For both blue-collar and professional/technical jobs it is apparent that the shifts involved changes in job content more than shifts in the personal qualities required for the job. Beyond this, however, there is a significant difference for the two occupational groups. While for both groupings shifts in technology and heightened use of computers are important, they are relatively less so for blue-collar workers. By contrast, general behavioral changes are more important for blue-collar employees. This lends some support to the hypothesis that innovations such as teamwork and quality programs are transforming the nature of blue-collar work. This conclusion receives more support below when we examine the relationship between skill and work organization.

Hiring

A different angle on the skill question is to ask what firms look for when they hire employees. Do they seek skills, trainability, or behavioral traits such as capacity for teamwork or ability to get along with fellow employees?

The survey tried to get at the relative importance of employee characteristics by asking respondents to indicate the first and second most important qualities they sought in new hires for CORE jobs. I recoded the open-ended responses into three broad groups: skills, behavior, and ability to learn.[9]

---

[8] The underlying responses are taken directly from responses to an open-ended question and I then recoded these into the categories that appear in this paper. An appendix describing the coding scheme is available from the author. Examples of responses coded as interpersonal skills/responsibility are "more independence is required," and "ability to exercise discretion"; examples of responses coded as cognitive are "need to be smarter/more analytical," and "more math/numeracy"; and examples of job characteristics are "more variety," and "faster paced machinery."

[9] An appendix describing the coding scheme is available from the author. Examples of qualities coded as skill are "reading comprehension," and "technical capacity"; examples coded as behavior are "get along/ambition," and "no absenteeism"; and examples coded as learn are "ability to learn job," and "willingness to learn."

Skill, Training, and Work Organization / 133

TABLE 3

HIRING CRITERIA

1st/2nd Criteria	All Prof./Tech.	All Blue-Collar	Prof./Tech. Job More Complex	Blue-Collar Job More Complex
Skill/Skill	29.5%	13.4%	23.0%	10.6%
Behavior/Behavior	15.4	25.0	19.1	27.5
Skill/Behavior	42.5	26.0	40.8	24.1
Behavior/Skill	7.8	19.0	12.3	14.6
Learn/Learn	0.0	0.03	0.0	0.08
Learn/Behavior in Either Order	0.8	11.5	.09	16.0
Learn/Skill in Either Order	3.5	4.6	4.4	6.7

Table 3 shows the distribution of hiring characteristics for four groups: all blue-collar CORE employees, all CORE professional/technical employees, and then for the same two groups but limited to those enterprises that reported that the CORE job was becoming more complex.

It is apparent that for all groups hiring criteria represent a mixture of skill and behavioral concerns (ability to learn plays a surprisingly weak role). It is quite striking, however, that skill is relatively much more important for professional/technical employees while behavioral traits are more important for blue-collar workers.[10] Recall, however, the earlier caution that behavioral skills may be fully legitimate skills related to work organization and not simply "getting along." There is also a hint in the data that for those jobs that are becoming more complex, behavior is relatively more important. However, this effect is not very pronounced.

Training

It is quite difficult to devise questions that accurately capture the training effort of firms. Firms do not keep good or standardized data on their training expenditures. When asked to estimate the amount spent on training, some firms will estimate their actual program costs while others will compute program costs plus the costs of the employee's time spent in the program while still others will impute an overhead rate to cover fixed costs (facilities, training staff, etc.).

---

[10] Although, as both Peter Cappelli and Richard Murnane pointed out to me, the interpretation may depend on what employers assume new hires bring to the job. They might, for example, assume that white-collar candidates all possess good interpersonal skills (the educational process either taught these or screened for them) and hence employers select on the basis of the more scarce technical skills. By contrast, blue-collar employees are assumed to have more variance in interpersonal skills and hence these are an important consideration in hiring.

134 / PAUL OSTERMAN

To complicate the measurement problem further, a great deal of employee development or "training" occurs informally on the job. Supervisors, co-workers, mentors, etc., all are important "trainers" for employees as they improve their proficiency.

In order to obtain estimates of training effort consistent across establishments, the questionnaire asked about a relatively narrow, but still important, form of training: the fraction of the CORE employees who attended formal off-the-job training (which could occur in vestibules, rooms at the work site, or in educational institutions). In addition, we asked about the number of days per year spent in such training.

The first panel of Table 4 shows the distribution of off-the-job training effort for all CORE employees. It is apparent that the distribution is bimodal with the weight of the distribution at the two tails. The second panel confirms two broadly held views. Blue-collar employees receive less training (in the sense that a smaller percent receive it) than do professional/technical workers. In addition, for blue-collar workers, training increases with establishment size. The latter finding, however, is not true for technical/professional employees for whom the relationship between establishment size and training is the inverse of what we would expect. For those employees who do receive formal off-the-job training,

TABLE 4

TRAINING EFFORT FOR CORE EMPLOYEES

A. Distribution of Off-the-Job Training

Fraction of CORE Employees Who Receive Formal Off-the-Job Training	Percentage of Establishments
0%	31.9%
1–24%	31.1%
25–49%	6.5%
50–74%	4.8%
75–79%	6.5%
100%	18.9%

B.

	All	All Prof./Tech.	All Blue-Collar	All in Estabs. > 500	Prof./Tech. in Estabs. > 500	Blue-Collar in Estabs. > 500
Percent of CORE Employees Who Receive Any Off-the-Job Training	32.0%	51.0%	27.0%	38.6%	40.2%	35.9%
Annual Days of Training for Those Who Receive Any	8.0	7.8	10.1	8.2	7.1	7.9

Skill, Training, and Work Organization / 135

the training time spent does not seem to vary a great deal by occupation or establishment size.

Explaining the Variation in Firm Training Practices

Why do some firms provide more training than do others? In this section, I will test a number of explanations commonly found in the literature. In the discussion that follows, I will describe hypotheses as they have emerged in the discussion to date and will also indicate how the relevant variables will be operationalized. I will also indicate which variables refer only to CORE employees (in general these are the variables dealing with work organization and employee characteristics) and which refer to the establishment as a whole. The dependent variable in the models that follow is the percent of the establishment's CORE employees who receive formal off-the-job training.

Work Organization. The key issue in the current debate, as I have already noted, is whether newer "transformed" forms of work organization require more skills and training. The range of actual practices that appear in the literature and in field studies suggests that no single measure or question is likely to be appropriate in all establishments. Therefore the survey asked about five practices (all with respect to the CORE job family): self-directed work teams, job rotation, use of employee problem-solving groups (or quality circles), Statistical Process Control, and use of Total Quality Management. For each of these, the respondent was asked whether or not the practice was employed in the establishment and if so what percentage of CORE employees were involved.[11]

I will enter these variables in three ways into models explaining training effort. Initially I will use a scale based on the first principal component of the five penetration variables.[12] (In an earlier draft I used an index that simply counted the number of the practices that the establishment had implemented at the fifty percent or higher level of penetration. With the exception, noted below, of a coefficient on a variable measuring workforce gender, the results are the same regardless of which index is employed.)

In addition to this variable, I also directly enter the percent involvement in each practice as independent variables. Finally, I will examine whether it

---

[11] The precise definitions for each practice can be found in Osterman (1994).

[12] The first principal component accounted for 39 percent of the variance and had an eigenvalue of 1.96.

136 / PAUL OSTERMAN

makes a difference how recently the practices were introduced as well as the importance of each practice separately.

Make or Buy. Firms have a choice between training their own employees or hiring employees who already possess the requisite skills. Driving this choice is the extent of available external supply, the extent to which the needed skills are highly firm specific, the importance of socialization in firm procedures and culture, and the cost of internal training. In the models that follow I include a dummy variable which takes the value of 1 if prior skill was both the first and the second most important hiring criterion for CORE jobs.[13]

Employee Characteristics. Previous literature on training (e.g., Lynch, 1991) has demonstrated that women tend to receive less on-the-job training than do men and that training is positively correlated with level of education. I include variables measuring the percent of the CORE employees who are women and the average educational attainment of CORE employees.[14]

Internal Labor-Market Structure. The risk inherent in substantial training investments is that employees will leave and take the training investment with them. Internal labor-market structures that create incentives to remain are a solution to this problem. Three variables capture several alternative policies along these lines. The establishments were asked how much preference was given to internal versus external candidates in filling vacancies, and they were also asked how much weight was given to seniority in choosing among internal candidates for promotion. These are two measures of job ladders and are included in the models.[15]

In addition to job ladders, another commonly cited strategy for retaining employees is to pay above-market wages. This strategy, sometimes termed "efficiency wages," can pay for itself provided that the gains, in this case reduced turnover and retention of workers in whom the firm has invested,

---

[13] Recall the earlier discussion of hiring criteria. The dummy variable used here takes on the value of 1 if skill is cited as both the first and the second most important hiring standard.

[14] The respondent was asked to characterize the education level of CORE employees as being "mostly dropouts," "about equal high school dropouts and graduates (with no further education)," "mostly high school graduates," "about equal high school graduates and at least some college," "mostly at least some college." In this model the dummy variable takes on the value 1 if the response was in the first three categories (mostly high school graduates or less) and 0 otherwise.

[15] Two variables were created to measure ladders: one if the respondent said that when a vacancy occurred it was very or extremely important to fill it with insiders (versus not important, slightly important, or moderately important), and one that used the same scale to measure whether seniority was used as a criterion for choosing which insiders to promote.

Skill, Training, and Work Organization / 137

exceeds the cost. The survey asked whether the establishment paid CORE workers a wage higher than that paid to comparable employees in local firms, and a variable measuring the response is included.[16]

Skill and Technology. The amount of training should obviously be related to the level of skill required in the job. This is measured by the variable SKLEV which takes on the value of 1 if the production process requires high levels of skill and 0 otherwise.[17] In addition, standard human capital theory predicts that when skills are enterprise specific, training provided by the firm will be more extensive (because the fear of turnover will be lessened). The variable SPECIFIC measures the extent of skill specificity.[18]

Institutional Considerations. There are several characteristics of the establishment that might be expected to influence the extent of training. One consideration is size. Most of the training literature has found that small firms provide less formal training than do large ones (Baron, Black, and Lowenstein, 1987). This may be due to greater fears of turnover among small firms (who are less able to develop lengthy job ladders) or fewer resources or less managerial slack to devote to training.

A second institutional consideration concerns the values of the enterprises' managers. The strategic-choice literature in industrial relations (Kochan, Katz, and McKersie, 1986) suggests that managerial values may be important in selection of work organization and this may also be true with respect to the degree of investment in the work force.

About 50 percent of the survey instrument contained a long series of questions about benefits, particularly work-family benefits, and with enterprise values regarding these benefits. This portion of the questionnaire was administered prior to the work organization questions. In the context of asking about benefits the respondent was asked, "In general, what is your establishment's philosophy about how appropriate it is to help increase the well-being of employees with respect to their personal or family situations?" Establishments that responded (on a five-point scale) that it was

---

[16] The question asked whether for the establishment's CORE employees there was a policy in place to pay wages that were higher, the same as, or lower than employees in comparable occupations in the same industry in the same geographic area. The variable is coded 1 if the policy was to pay a higher wage.

[17] Respondents were asked to characterize the skill level of the CORE jobs on a scale from 1 to 5, and SKLEV is coded 1 if the reply was very skilled or extremely skilled.

[18] Respondents were asked whether the skills in the CORE job were easy to transfer, moderately difficult to transfer, or very difficult to transfer to firms in other industries. A dummy variable was coded 1 if the skills were very difficult to transfer.

138 / Paul Osterman

"very" or "extremely" appropriate are assigned 1 on a dummy variable (called VALUE).[19]

The presence or absence of a union may be important. Unions can be expected to serve as a pressure group, or voice mechanism, pushing for increased investment in employees, and hence one would expect a positive association between unionism and training effort. On the other hand, unions sometimes may act as protectors of traditional job rights and this may diminish the extent of training.

The sociological literature on institutions suggests that certain "non-market" considerations may influence. the extent of training programs (Scott and Meyer, 1991). The survey asked whether or not the establishment was part of a larger organization. If it is then pressures for organizational conformity and legitimation within the context of bureaucratic structures may lead to more extensive training (DiMaggio and Powell, 1983; Pfeffer and Cohen, 1984; Baron, Jennings, and Dobbin, 1988). In addition, establishments that are part of larger organizations (e.g., a branch plant) may receive greater resources, information, and technical assistance. A dummy variable LARGER takes on the value of 1 if the establishment is part of a larger organization.

In general, it is reasonable to expect that the greater importance an establishment gives to human resources as part of its competitive strategy the greater the effort devoted to training. The survey asked, "When senior management makes important decisions regarding long-run competitiveness how important are human resource considerations?" If the reply was very or extremely important the variable HRROLE was coded 1.[20]

Finally, controls are included for the occupational group of the CORE job. As already noted, most prior research suggests that, all else constant, blue-collar workers receive less training than do higher level professional/technical employees.

Results

Variable means and definitions are provided in Table 5, and Table 6 contains the estimated model. Because the dependent variable— percentage of the CORE employees who receive formal off-the-job

---

[19] The distribution of responses on the five-point scale was 1.7 percent, "not appropriate," 9.4 percent, "a little appropriate," 33.0 percent "moderately appropriate," 42.8 percent "very appropriate," and 12.8 percent "extremely appropriate."

[20] One might be concerned that this variable is tautological in that it is simply another way of asking whether the establishment trains its work force. However, the question was asked in a section dealing with general strategic issues (i.e., not in the section on work organization and training) and asked about the overall importance of HR as a strategic consideration.

Skill, Training, and Work Organization / 139

TABLE 5
VARIABLE DEFINITIONS AND MEANS

Variable	Definition	Mean
Trnper	Percent of CORE employees who receive formal off-the-job training	.320
Edu	1 if most CORE employees have a high school degree or less education; 0 otherwise	.61
Per Fem	Percentage of CORE employees who are women	.435
Wage	1 if establishment pays CORE employees more than comparable workers in the same occupation in the same industry in the local area; 0 otherwise	.365
Specific	1 if it is very or extremely difficult to use the skills of the CORE job elsewhere; 0 otherwise	.139
Ladder1	1 if it is very or extremely important to give preference to insiders in filling vacancies; 0 otherwise	.708
Ladder2	1 if it is very or extremely important to use seniority to determine which incumbents are promoted to vacancies; 0 otherwise	.303
Hpwo	Score based on principal components analysis of the penetration of the five work practices	.000000009
Hire Skill	1 if skills are the first and second most important hiring criteria for the CORE job; 0 otherwise	.133
Union	1 = a union is present; 0 = no union	.237
SkLev	1 = CORE job very or extremely skilled; 0 = not	.369
Larger	1 = establishment part of a larger organization; 0 = not	.660
Values	1 = it is very or extremely appropriate for establishment to accept responsibility for personal and family well-being of employees; 0 = otherwise	.552
Size1	1 = establishment has 50–99 employees	.509
Size3	1 = establishment has 500–999 employees	.048
Size4	1 = establishment has 1000–2499 employees	.026
Size5	1 = 2500+ employees	.006
HRROLE	1 if Human Resources Department involved in major strategic decisions; 0 otherwise	.541
Blue-Collar	1 if CORE job blue-collar	.423
Sales	1 if CORE job sales	.190
Clerical	1 if CORE job clerical	.060
Service	1 if CORE job service	.183
Prof	1 if CORE job professional/technical	.143
Recent Index	Number of innovative work practices that have been introduced in the past five years	.885
Old Index	Number of innovative work practices that are more than five years old	.420
Percent in Teams	Average percent of CORE employees in teams (including zeros)	.390
Percent in Rotation	Average percent of CORE employees in job rotation (including zeros)	.264
Percent in TQM	Average percent of CORE employees in TQM (including zeros)	.252
Percent in QC	Average percent of CORE employees in quality circles (including zeros)	.277
Percent in SPC	Average percent of CORE employees in statistical process control (including zeros)	.114

140 / Paul Osterman

TABLE 6

Tobit Estimate of Off-the-Job
Training
(t-statistics)

Edu	−.012
	(−.195)
Per Fem	−.148
	(−1.585)
Union	.143**
	(2.006)
Values	.221**
	(4.012)
Larger	.168**
	(2.780)
Wage	.113**
	(2.046)
Size 1	−.331
	(−2.749)
Size 2	−.047
	(−.400)
Size 4	−.041
	(−.183)
Size 5	−.399
	(−1.199)
Specific	−.181**
	(−2.243)
Hire Skill	−.225**
	(−2.809)
Blue-Collar	−.276**
	(−2.857)
Service	−.294**
	(−2.992)
Clerical	−.119
	(−.903)
Sales	−.113
	(−1.122)
Ladder 1	.012
	(.203)
Ladder 2	.095
	(1.529)
Sklev	.184**
	(2.913)
Hrrole	.209**
	(3.844)
HPWO	.055**
	(2.879)
Constant	.220
	(1.291)
Log Likelihood	−595.965
N	693

** Significant at .05 level.

Skill, Training, and Work Organization / 141

training—is truncated both at zero and one hundred the appropriate estimation technique is the Tobit model.

The central findings are as follows:

1. Use of high performance work systems are positively associated with increased training effort.

2. There is, indeed, a trade-off between make or buy. Firms that place heavy emphasis on hiring employees with previously acquired skills are less likely to provide training.[21]

3. There is no relationship between education level and training nor between the fraction of the CORE labor force that is female and training.[22]

4. The higher skill the CORE job the more training provided. However, contrary to expectations, jobs with specific skills have a lower rate of employer provided training. This is the only coefficient in the model that is directly inconsistent with prior expectations.

5. Jobs ladders do not seem to be related to training. However, payment of efficiency wages is associated with higher levels of training.

6. Values are strongly related to training propensity. Two additional institutional variables are also important: the importance of human resource considerations and whether or not the establishment is part of a larger organization. In addition, unionism is also significantly related to training effort by establishments.

7. Blue-collar employees are, all else equal, less likely to be the recipients of formal off-the-job training than are professional/technical workers. The same is true for service employees.

In summary this equation performs very well. It is clear that the new "conventional wisdom" is correct: techniques associated with high-performance work systems are associated with heightened training. It is also apparent that the training effort of a given establishment is determined by a mix of standard economic as well as institutional considerations.

---

[21] Richard Murnane points out to me that this finding may be inconsistent with the common observation that more educated employees (who receive higher pay offers) also receive more training by firms. However, the finding in this paper is best interpreted as referring to particular skills, not general education.

[22] This latter point, regarding the impact of gender on training, is sensitive to the particular specification that is used. In only slightly different specifications, the Percent Female variable is significant (and negative).

142 / PAUL OSTERMAN

TABLE 7

COEFFICIENTS FOR ALTERNATIVE
WORK PRACTICE VARIABLES[a]
(t-statistics)

A. Separate Practices	
Percent in Teams	−.032
	(−.509)
Percent in Rotation	−.237**
	(−3.380)
Percent in TQM	.147**
	(2.048)
Percent in QC	.178**
	(2.411)
Percent in SPC	.200**
	(2.158)
B. Impact of Date of Introduction	
1. Recent Index	.065**
	(2.991)
2. Old Index	−.013
	(−.382)

** Significant at .05 level.
[a] Each panel refers to a Tobit equation that includes the additional variables, except for the HPWO index, shown in the preceding table. The New Index includes only the work place innovations that had been put in place within five years of the survey and the Old Index includes only the innovations that had been put in place earlier than five years before the survey. The variables Percent in Teams and so on are the percent of CORE workers involved in each of the practices.

Returning to the theme of the relationship of work organization to training, two additional questions can be addressed. The first concerns whether the impact of flexible work organization on skill and training is permanent or rather associated with the recency of the innovation. The second issue is whether particular forms of "transformed" work systems require more training than do others. Table 7 presents the coefficients of the work organization variables using alternative specifications that address these questions (the rest of the equations are the same as the earlier one).

The first panel examines each work organization practice separately. Each practice is entered as the percent of CORE employees involved in the particular practice (these variables were entered together in the standard equation with the scale omitted).[23] It is apparent that it is quality

---

[23] The results are not sensitive to this specification. Similar results are achieved when the variables are simply entered as dummy variables that take the value of 1 if penetration of the practice is above the fifty percent threshold.

Skill, Training, and Work Organization / 143

practices that are positively associated with heightened training. Evidently work organization such as teams and rotation do not lead to additional formal training although they may well be associated with heightened levels of informal OJT.

The survey asked establishments the date at which they introduced each of the five work organizational innovations. The second panel reports results for an index that is the count of innovations at the 50 percent level of penetration based on the date of introduction. In the first part the index is the number of innovations that had been in existence for five years or less at the time of the survey while in the second panel only those innovations that are older than five years are included. It is clear that the positive impact of innovative practices, specifically quality practices, on training holds true only for the more recently introduced innovations.

Because we have just seen that the impact of quality practices on training is different than the impact of teams and job rotation, it is natural to worry (as a referee suggested) that the index regarding when the innovations were introduced may simply reflect different mixes in practices across different time periods. However, when each practice is entered separately in two equations, one that contains dummy variables for recent practices and one that contains dummies for old practices, the conclusion that only recent innovations increase training is unchanged.[24]

The most natural interpretation of this pattern is that once the innovation has been in place for a length of time, it becomes sufficiently routinized so that additional formal off-the-job training is not necessary (beyond that provided by establishments that are otherwise statistically identical but have not introduced the work organization changes). This, however, is speculative and alternative interpretations are also possible.

Conclusion

There has been considerable prior work on training and skill in American firms and this paper builds on that by bringing to bear a new source of data that compensates for some of the gaps in previous work. Specifically, these data are able to link skill and training patterns with extensive contextual data on the character of the establishments. These characteristics include how work is organized, and hence the paper can address a central

---

[24] In the equation with dummy variables for recent practices (at the fifty percent level or more of penetration), the three quality programs each had positive and significant coefficients while rotation had a negative and significant coefficient and teams was insignificant. By contrast, in the equation that included dummy variables for practices that had been in place for more than five years, no practice had a positive and significant impact on training and in fact both TQM and rotation had significantly negative impacts.

144 / Paul Osterman

question in current discussions: whether new "flexible" forms of work organization require more skill. However, the paper goes beyond this theme to also examine a range of factors including technology, firm values, size, internal labor-market structure, make or buy decisions, and links to larger organizations.

The paper found a clear trend toward upskilling in work but one that was more pronounced for technical/professional than for blue-collar jobs. In addition, hiring criteria for technical/professional jobs tended to focus more on skill whereas behavioral traits were emphasized more heavily (but by no means exclusively) in blue-collar work. The regressions showed that new forms of work organization are associated with higher levels of training. In addition, there is a clear make or buy choice, firms with more "humanistic" values train more, and the presence of a union increases training as does the payment of efficiency wages and links to a larger organization.

The descriptive data on skill levels, trends in skill, and hiring strategies should add to our understanding of these issues, and the regression models do quite well in sorting among a range of hypotheses regarding training. There is, however, one large puzzle that remains. When the work organization practices were examined separately, it emerged that quality practices led to more training (relative to the baseline level that all of the other considerations generated) while the more direct work practices of team production and job rotation did not. The explanation that immediately comes to mind is that training for teams and rotation is done more via informal on-the-job training whereas this survey measures formal off-the-job training. This makes sense if one believes that quality activities are in general sufficiently new and distanced from direct production that they are best taught outside the flow of daily work. While perhaps sensible, this explanation clearly needs to be tested in future work.

An important additional issue that was not satisfactorily resolved concerns the nature of the relationship between training and work organization. A critic of the foregoing analysis might well argue that the estimated model suffers from simultaneity bias. The model treats work organization as an independent variable that drives training yet it is plausibly the case that firms that, for other reasons, engage in more training find it easier to adopt new work systems.

It is difficult to resolve this question with cross-sectional data; however, the evidence on timing provides some reassurance. The fact that some years after the introduction of new work systems training effort plateaus suggests that work systems drive training rather than the other way around. Nonetheless, this difficulty of interpretation points to the need for

Skill, Training, and Work Organization / 145

longitudinal data to track the evolution of employment systems in firms and establishments.

REFERENCES

Adler, Paul. 1993. "The New 'Learning Bureaucracy': New United Motor Manufacturing, Inc." *Research in Organizational Behavior* 15:111–94.
Applebaum, Eileen, and Rose Batt. 1994. *The New American Workplace.* Ithaca: Cornell University Press.
Baron, James, P. Devereau Jennings, and Frank Dobbin. 1988. "Mission Control? The Development of Personnel Systems in U.S. Industry." *American Sociological Review* 53 (August): 497–514.
Baron, John, Dan Black, and Mark Lowenstein. 1987. "Employer Size: The Implications for Search, Capital Investment, Starting Wages, and Wage Growth." *Journal of Labor Economics* 5:76–89.
Bell, Daniel. 1973. *The Coming of Post-Industrial Society.* New York: Basic Books.
Blauner, Robert. 1964. *Alienation and Freedom.* Chicago: University of Chicago Press.
Braverman, Harry. 1974. *Labor and Monopoly Capital.* New York: Monthly Review Press.
Brown, Charles. 1990. "Empirical Evidence on Private Sector Training." In *Research in Labor Economics*, edited by Ronald Ehrenberg, pp. 97–113. Greenwich: JAI Press.
Brown, Clair, Michael Reich, and David Stern. 1991. "Skills and Security in Evolving Employment Systems: Observations from Case Studies," mimeo, Institute of Industrial Relations, U.C. Berkeley.
Cairncross, David, and Ronald Dore. 1989. "Employee Training in Japan." Washington, DC: Office of Technology Assessment.
Cappelli, Peter. 1993. "Are Skill Requirements Rising? Evidence from Production and Clerical Jobs." *Industrial and Labor Relations Review* 46(3):515–30.
Carnevale, Anthony, Leik Gainer, and Janice Villet. 1990. *Training in America.* San Francisco: Jossey-Bass.
Commission on the Skills of the American Workforce. 1990. *America's Choice: High Skills or Low Wages.* Washington, DC: National Center on Education and the Economy.
Cuomo Commission on Trade and Competitiveness. 1988. *The Cuomo Commission Report.* New York: Simon & Schuster.
Dertouzos, Michael, Richard Lester, and Robert Solow. 1989. *Made in America.* Cambridge: MIT Press.
DiMaggio, Paul, and Walter Powell. 1983. "The Iron Cage Revisited: Institutional Isomorphism and Collective Rationality in Organizational Fields." *American Sociological Review* 48:147–60.
Doeringer, Peter, and Michael Piore. 1972. *Internal Labor Markets and Manpower Analysis.* Lexington, MA: D. C. Heath.
Flynn, Patricia. 1988. *Facilitating Technological Change.* Cambridge: Ballinger.
Howell, David, and Edward Wolff. 1991. "Trends in the Growth and Distribution of Skill in the U.S. Workplace, 1960–1985." *Industrial and Labor Relations Review* 44(3) (April): 481–501.
Ichniowski, Casey, Kathryn Shaw, and Giovanna Prennushi. 1993. "The Effects of Human Resource Management Practices on Productivity." Draft manuscript, Carnegie Mellon University, June.
Jaikumar, R. 1986. "Postindustrial Manufacturing." *Harvard Business Review* (November–December): 69–76.
Johnston, W. B., and A. Packer. 1987. *Workforce 2000: Work and Workers for the 21st Century.* Indianapolis: Hudson Institute.
Katz, Larry, and Kevin Murphy. 1992. "Changes in Relative Wages, 1963–1987: Supply and Demand Factors." *Quarterly Journal of Economics* 107 (February):35–78.
Kaufman, Roger T. 1992. "The Effects of IMPROSHARE on Productivity." *Industrial and Labor Relations Review* 45 (January):311–22.

146 / PAUL OSTERMAN

Keefe, Jeffrey. 1991. "Numerically Controlled Machine Tools and Worker Skills." *Industrial and Labor Relations Review* 44:503–19.

Kelley, Mary-Ellen. 1989. "Unionization and Job Design Under Programmable Automation." *Industrial Relations* 28 (Spring):174–87.

Kochan, Thomas, Harry Katz, and Robert McKersie. 1986. *The Transformation of American Industrial Relations.* New York: Basic Books.

Kochan, Thomas, and Paul Osterman. "Human Resource Development: Does the United States Do Too Little?" Paper prepared for the American Council on Competitiveness.

Levy, Frank, and Richard Murnane. 1992. "U.S. Earnings Levels and Earnings Inequality." *Journal of Economic Literature* 5(3) (September):1333–81.

Lynch, Lisa. 1990. "The Private Sector and Skill Formation in the United States: A Survey." Working Paper #3125 90 BPS, MIT.

Lynch, Lisa. 1991. "The Role of Off-the-Job Training for the Mobility of Women Workers." *American Economic Review* 81(2):151–56.

Lusterman, Seymour. 1985. *Trends in Corporate Education and Training.* New York: The Conference Board.

McDuffie, John Paul. 1991. *Beyond Mass Production, Flexible Production Systems and Manufacturing Performance in the World Auto Industry.* Unpublished Ph.D. diss. Sloan School of Management, MIT.

Milkman, Ruth, and Cydney Pullman. 1991. "Technological Change in the Auto Assembly Plant: The Impact on Workers' Skills and Tasks." *Work and Occupations* 18(2) (May):123–47.

Osterman, Paul. 1987. "Choice among Alternative Internal Labor Market Systems." *Industrial Relations* 26(1) (February):46–67.

Osterman, Paul. 1988. *Employment Futures: Reorganization, Dislocation, and Public Policy.* New York: Oxford University Press.

Osterman, Paul. 1994. "How Common Is Workplace Transformation and Who Adopts It?" *Industrial and Labor Relations Review* 47(2) (January):173–88.

Pfeffer, Jeffrey, and Yinon Cohen. 1984. "Determinants of Internal Labor Markets in Organizations." *Administrative Science Quarterly* 29:550–72.

Scott, Richard, and John Meyer. 1991. "The Rise of Training Programs in Firms and Agencies: An Institutional Approach." In *Research in Organizational Behavior,* pp. 297–326. Greenwich, CT: JAI Press.

Spenner, Kenneth. 1983. "Deciphering Prometheus: Temporal Changes in Work Content." *American Sociological Review* 48 (December):824–37.

Womack, James, Daniel Jones, and Daniel Roos. 1991. *The Machine that Changed the World.* New York: Rawson-Macmillan.

[12]

TRADE UNIONS AND TRAINING PRACTICES IN BRITISH WORKPLACES

FRANCIS GREEN, STEPHEN MACHIN, and DAVID WILKINSON*

The authors use British establishment-level data from the 1991 Employers' Manpower and Skills Practices Survey (EMSPS) and individual-level data from the Autumn 1993 Quarterly Labour Force Survey (QLFS) to investigate the links between training provision and workplace unionization. Both the probability of receiving training and the amount of training received are found to have been substantially higher in unionized than in nonunion workplaces. The authors view these results as showing that trade unions can play an important role in developing and boosting skill formation in Britain.

Many authors have emphasized the role that effective employee training can play in influencing worker productivity, wages, and individual career development. Among the subjects examined by the extensive research on training have been effects on individual performance, workplace and company performance, and macroeco-nomic performance.[1] Many governments now give high priority to policies thought to stimulate skill formation, either through

*Francis Green is Professor in the Department of Economics at the University of Kent; Stephen Machin is Professor in the Department of Economics at University College London and Director of the Industrial Relations Programme in the Centre for Economic Performance at the London School of Economics; and David Wilkinson is a Senior Research Officer in the Office for National Statistics. Part of this paper draws on a report the authors produced in April 1995 for the Department of Employment entitled "Unions and Training: An Analysis of Training Practices in Unionized and Non-Unionized Workplaces." They are grateful to the Department of Employment for financial support and to Louise Corcoran, Andrew Wareing, and participants in a Centre for Economic Performance (LSE) seminar for useful comments. They also thank Steve Woodland for help with the EMSPS and WIRS data.

Additional results referred to in the paper can be obtained from David Wilkinson, Office for National Statistics, B3/08, 1 Drummond Gate, London SW1V 2QQ, UK. Social and Community Planning Research is the depositor of the Employers' Manpower and Skills Practices Survey; the Employment Department, the Economic and Social Research Council, the Policy Studies Institute, and the Advisory, Conciliation and Arbitration Service are joint depositors of the Workplace Industrial Relations Survey data; the Employment Department is the depositor of the Quarterly Labour Force Survey data. All data sets are deposited at the ESRC Data Archive, from which the data sets and documentation were obtained.

[1]Much of the research looking at the effects of training on individual performance has focused on wages (for example, Lynch 1992; Veum 1995; Blundell, Dearden, and Meghir 1995) or job mobility (Veum 1997; Dearden et al. 1997). A recent example of a matched plant study examining the effects of training on workplace and company performance is Mason, Prais, and van Ark (1992). Finegold and Soskice (1988) and Crouch (1992) are two of many studies highlighting international training differences and relating them to macroeconomic outcomes.

Industrial and Labor Relations Review, Vol. 52, No. 2 (January 1999). © by Cornell University.
0019-7939/99/5202 $01.00

direct intervention and subsidies of company training or through support for a "training market" via loan provision, dissemination of information about good practice, and other measures.

Given the importance of skills for economic performance, it seems important to understand what kinds of workplaces provide training for their workers (Green 1993b). In particular, a variety of studies in many countries have demonstrated that the institutional environment in which businesses operate affects the process of skill formation in firms, and may interact with government policies (for example, Streeck 1989; CEDEFOP 1987; Koike and Inoke 1990; Osterman 1995). An important aspect of that environment is the character of employee relations in the organization.

In this paper we provide evidence on this issue using two British data sources: the establishment-level Employers' Manpower and Skills Practices Survey (EMSPS) of 1991 and the individual-level Quarterly Labour Force Survey (QLFS) of autumn 1993. Specifically, we consider the role unions play in skill formation, both on their own and in conjunction with other employee relations features, by examining the link between unions and training. Other studies have revealed a union-training link, but usually as a by-product of the analysis. For example, in a number of studies a union variable has been included in a training equation, but the union link has not been the main focus of the analysis. In this paper, the union-training link is the center of attention.

Unions and Training: Theory and Existing Work

Training and Union Bargaining

In looking for an empirical association between training provision and unionization, the first question one might reasonably ask is the extent to which unions are actually able to bargain about training. Following the major upheavals of the 1980s, British trade unions have been attempting to develop a new agenda for bargaining

and consultation. Because of the trend toward the decentralization of bargaining, there has been an especially strong effort to bring within the ambit of bargaining those issues negotiated at the company or establishment level. One key subject in this new agenda is training. By 1990 a number of union officials claimed to be either bargaining or consulting over training matters (Labour Research Department 1990). The late 1980s saw major unions, such as the Transport and General Workers' Union, the National Association of Local Government Officers, and Manufacturing, Science, and Finance, develop their own training initiatives in attempts to encourage their negotiators to discuss training agreements with employers.

Influenced by these major players, and by the belief that improved training and consequent improved productive efficiency were crucial to raising union members' living standards, the Trades Union Congress announced that training should be an important aspect of a new bargaining agenda for trade unions in the 1990s (Trades Union Congress 1991). The strategy involved negotiating minimum levels and standards of training, equal opportunities, and close involvement in training decisions, if possible through workplace training committees. In the absence of favorable legislation, negotiators were to aim for voluntary agreements along the lines of proposed training models.

It is probably too early to tell whether trade unions will successfully place training on the bargaining agenda widely across British industry. Whether unions succeed probably depends on many factors outside their direct control, in particular the attitudes taken by companies themselves and the public policy environment. But through the first half of the present decade, unions did *not* make large inroads. For the most part, managers continued to regard training as an area for their own decision-making, independent of collective bargaining. Evidence of this comes from responses to the third Workplace Industrial Relations Survey of 1990 (Millward et al. 1992:255), which indicated that few managers had conceded training as a bargaining issue. A subsequent analysis of agreements reached during the 30 months following January 1991 showed that relatively few such agreements contained a provision for formal consultation over training and even fewer provided for bargaining over training levels or content (Claydon and Green 1994).

There is, however, some contrasting evidence that unions may be having an informal role in training matters in some workplaces, and that this role may not always be recognized by management (Heyes 1993; Stuart 1994). While trade unions' direct influence on the extent and nature of training is likely to have been relatively limited in recent years, this does not mean that their impact can be ignored. Potentially as important as unions' direct influence on training is their indirect influence. Even where unions do not bargain directly over training, their presence could condition the whole character of employee relationships in establishments, thereby affecting the extent of training.

In the simplest case, unions could have a negative impact on training through their influence on pay. Empirical evidence for Britain shows that unions raise wages relative to the nonunion sector, especially for manual workers (for example, Blanchflower 1986; Stewart 1987, 1995), which may discourage employers from paying for training courses. One reason unions might push harder for wage gains than for increased training for younger workers, Ryan (1991) argued, is that they cannot easily monitor the quality of training provided, especially when much of the training is on-the-job and uncertified. In addition, Mincer (1983) has argued that the seniority rules imposed by many U.S. unions, which affect promotions to higher grades, reduce workers' incentives to invest in training.

Moreover, recent aggregate patterns in the extent of training and unionization in Britain move in opposite directions. Training participation became more widespread during the 1980s, while unionization fell sharply over the same time period (see, for example, Disney, Gosling, and Machin 1995; Millward et al. 1992). Could these opposing trends be related, with the weakening of unions relieving a constraint on skill formation?

On the other hand, not all plausible theoretical approaches unambiguously predict a negative union impact on training; indeed, some predict the opposite. Unions could positively affect training through their influence on channels of communication, managerial behavior, and job tenure, and, through those effects, on the level of employee turnover. Unions provide a "voice" for individual grievances and for contributions toward productive efficiency that would often be unavailable to individual employees (Freeman and Medoff 1984). Insofar as this reduces labor turnover (and there is empirical evidence for such an effect in Britain; for example, see Elias 1994), there is likely to be a longer period to reap the benefits of investments in training, and therefore a larger return. Where unions have an influence in an establishment, employees may also feel more secure, and therefore less threatened by the changes in work practices that often accompany training courses. Furthermore, the formality a union presence engenders may encourage managers to set up more formal procedures for identifying training needs and defining skill levels as required by pay formulas. From all these points of view, it is arguable that the presence of active trade unions in the workplace may lead both to a greater level of training and to a more developed training infrastructure within the establishment and the company. (For more detail, see Claydon and Green 1994; Kennedy et al. 1994.)

Whether positive or negative, any link between trade unions and training is a potentially important one, and future changes in the level of unionization in Britain may have an appreciable impact on skill formation at the workplace.

Existing Work

Existing empirical evidence is, rather like the predictions of different theoretical models, somewhat mixed. Some U.S work (see, *inter alia*, Duncan and Stafford 1980;

Mincer 1983) points to a negative union impact on training. However, even in the United States some more recent work challenges this finding. Lynch (1992), for example, reported a positive coefficient on union variables in probit models of on-the-job training and a negative (and statistically insignificant) union coefficient in an off-the-job training probit; Veum (1995) considered seven different forms of training (two on-the-job, five off-the-job) and obtained positive (and statistically significant) coefficients on a union variable in probit models of the determinants of on-the-job training (company training and apprenticeships)[2] and statistically insignificant (one positive, four negative) coefficients on the union variable in the off-the-job training equations. In establishment-level studies, both Osterman (1995) and Frazis et al. (1995) found a statistically significant positive effect of union presence on formal training; however, Lynch and Black (1995) found no statistically significant impact of unionization on either the provision of formal training or the proportion of workers receiving it.

Existing research for Britain in this area is limited. Green (1993a) reported a positive, statistically significant coefficient for union membership in a training participation equation for workers in small workplaces (those with fewer than 25 employees) and a statistically insignificant coefficient in an equation for workers in larger workplaces. Some other studies that have focused on different or broader issues (for example, Booth 1991; Greenhalgh and Mavrotas 1994; Arulampalam et al. 1995) also have reported positive union effects using individual-level data, but they have not focused in any detail on the union effect.[3]

However, the existing studies have a number of shortcomings in terms of this issue, mainly due to data limitations. The data sources we use allow us to avoid a number of these drawbacks. First, as most existing research concentrates on individual-based data, there is limited information about the nature of industrial relations at workplaces, including what type of union is active (if at all) and whether a closed shop is operating. Moreover, it is also known that some forms of training, in particular apprenticeship, are interpreted differently by employees and employers, so that it will be of interest in our establishment-level work to see whether training, as defined by the employers who actually provide it, is influenced by employee relations systems.

The second shortcoming of previous analyses (with the exception of Booth 1991, Frazis et al. 1995, and Lynch and Black 1995) is that they have taken union membership as their measure of unionism. Membership is only an imperfect measure of the extent and impact of union activity (Disney, Gosling, and Machin 1995). There are many employees for whom pay and conditions are effectively negotiated by a union, but who choose not to become members. Thus a measure of whether a union is recognized for some bargaining purposes is likely to be a superior measure of unionism.

Another limitation of previous studies is that while they have examined union effects on the probability of receiving any training, they have not looked at length of training for those who receive training. Unionism could, for example, reduce the probability of receiving training but increase the quantity of training received.

Data Description

Our first data source, the Employers' Manpower and Skills Practices Survey (EMSPS), was set up to examine aspects of

----

[2]In some later work (Veum 1997), the positive and significant union coefficient is confined to on-the-job training, which is paid for by the company.

[3]See also Arulampalam and Booth (1997), who used the same data source (the National Child Development Study) as Arulampalam et al. (1995). They reported four models of the determinants of receipt of work-related training (two for men, two for women)

----

in which the estimated coefficients on a union membership variable were all positive but only statistically significant for one of the female specifications.

TRADE UNIONS AND TRAINING PRACTICES   183

employers' skill formation, including their skill needs, recruitment practices, and training. It was conducted as a follow-up to the 1990 Workplace Industrial Relations Survey (WIRS3), which is a nationally representative survey of 2,061 British establishments with 25 or more employees in all sectors except agriculture, forestry and fishing, and coal mining. Once establishments with unproductive and out-of-scope responses were excluded, the EMSPS sample consisted of 1,693 establishments, for a response rate of 89%. Face-to-face interviews were conducted by experienced interviewers employed by Social and Community Planning Research (SCPR) between November 1990 and October 1991 using a structured questionnaire. The training we analyze is defined as that provided to employees apart from any initial job training.

The second data set we use is the autumn 1993 Quarterly Labour Force Survey (QLFS). For the first time in that quarter, respondents were asked a set of questions about whether they worked at an establishment where a union was recognized for bargaining purposes (Corcoran and Wareing 1994). The QLFS covers individuals in a sample of about 60,000 responding households in Great Britain. We restrict our analysis to employees only and exclude the armed forces. Training incidence refers to the standard Labour Force Survey measure, which is any experience of education or training that is deemed by the respondent to be related to the current job (or a potential future job) in the four weeks preceding the survey interview date. More details, including descriptions and means of all the variables used from both surveys, are given in the appendix (see also Green, Machin, and Wilkinson 1995).

Econometric Methodology

Our analysis is at both the establishment level and the individual level. At each level we use both the incidence and intensity of training as dependent variables.

Training incidence. We model the probability that an economic agent (i = establishment, j = individual) provides or re-

ceives training with a simple discrete choice framework and estimate probit models of training provision or receipt. Let P_i and π_j be dummy variable indicators of training, U_i be a 0–1 indicator of whether unions are recognized in the workplace, X_i and Z_j be vectors of establishment- and individual-level controls, respectively, and Φ denote the standard normal distribution function. We can define $\Pr[P_i = 1] = -[X_i'\beta + \gamma U_i]$ as the probability that establishment i trains its workers and $\Pr[\pi_j = 1] = -[Z_j'\delta + \lambda U_i]$ as the probability that individual j receives training, and we can obtain the union impact on training (the marginal effect) as follows:

$$(1) \quad \Pr[P_i = 1 \mid U_i = 1] - \Pr[P_i = 1 \mid U_i = 0] = \Phi[X_i'\beta + \gamma] - \Phi[X_i'\beta]$$

$$\Pr[\pi_j = 1 \mid U_i = 1] - \Pr[\pi_j = 1 \mid U_i = 0] = \Phi[Z_j'\delta + \lambda] - \Phi[Z_j'\delta]$$

As we are interested in a *ceteris paribus* union/nonunion comparison, we evaluate at union means.[4] The control variables included in X and Z are conventional ones found in the literature relating to both individual and job characteristics.

Training intensity. We compute training intensity measures as

$$(2) \quad \text{Establishment-level intensity} = P_i D_i$$

$$\text{Individual-level intensity} = l_j h_j,$$

where D_i is the average number of days of training received over the last year for workers in establishment i, l_j is whether an indi-

---

[4]In practice we could choose any values for X_i or Z_j (that is, we face the usual index number issue in comparisons of this kind). We have also considered overall sample means and nonunion means to evaluate these differences, and we find that the overall results are largely unaffected by this choice. Evaluating these probabilities at the mean for unionized establishments provides a simple interpretation of any union/nonunion difference. It can be thought of as the effect of taking away union recognition from a typical establishment that has a recognized union, while holding constant all other factors.

Table 1. Descriptive Statistics.

| | EMSPS | | | | QLFS | | | |
| | | | | Union/
Nonunion
Gap | | | | Union/
Nonunion
Gap |
Statistic	Variable Definition	Union Mean	Nonunion Mean	(Standard Error)	Variable Definition	Union Mean	Nonunion Mean	(Standard Error)
Manual Workers								
Incidence	P_i	0.755	0.499	.255 (.026)	π_j	.079	.065	.015 (.0001)
Sample Size		822	558			8,568	8,407	
Intensity	$P_i.D_i$	2.318	1.895	.423 (.447)	$l_j.h_j$	.700	.595	.105 (.003)
Sample Size		589	386			8,578	8,503	
Intensity for Trainers	$[P_i.D_i]|P_i=1$	3.376	3.458	−.083 (.664)	$[l_j.h_j]|l_j=1$	16.428	14.810	1.617 (.057)
Sample Size		460	213			359	335	
Non-Manual Workers								
Incidence	P_i	0.907	0.721	.185 (.021)	π_j	.217	.125	.091 (.0001)
Sample Size		834	559			17,004	16,954	
Intensity	$P_i.D_i$	3.909	1.973	1.936 (.332)	h_j	1.451	.989	.461 (.003)
Sample Size		594	418			17,056	17,157	
Intensity for Trainers	$[P_i.D_i]|P_i=1$	4.480	3.196	1.284 (.408)	$[l_j.h_j]|l_j=1$	12.291	13.365	−1.074 (.025)
Sample Size		529	301			2,004	1,258	

Notes: i denotes establishment, j denotes individual. $P_i = 1$ if provided training in last 12 months, 0 otherwise; $\pi_j = 1$ if received training in the last 4 weeks, 0 otherwise; $l_j = 1$ if received training in the last week, 0 otherwise; D_i = average number of days training received in the last 12 months; h_j = average number of hours training received in the last week. The reported statistics are weighted means across establishments/individuals, using WIRS/QLFS weights. Precise questions from the relevant surveys are reproduced in the appendix.

vidual received training in the last week, and h_j is the hours of training received in that time.[5]

Since some establishments do not provide any training for particular employees and some individuals have zero hours of training, these training intensity measures are censored. We use a Tobit estimator to deal with the censoring. The same set of control variables was used as for the analysis of training incidence, and marginal

union/nonunion differences were calculated in a similar manner.[6]

Descriptive Statistics

Table 1 reports a set of descriptive statis-

---

[5]One should note that, owing to the QLFS question structure, the individual intensity measure is a weekly measure, while the incidence measure described above corresponds to the last four weeks.

[6]For a Tobit model of training intensity (I) defined (dropping the subscripts for convenience) as $I^* = X'b + cU + v$, where $I^* = I$ for $I > 0$ and $I^* = 0$ for $I = 0$, the marginal union effect is computed as $\Phi((X'b+c)/\sigma)[X'b+c+\sigma M^u] - \Phi(X'b)/\sigma)[X'b+\sigma M^n]$, where σ is the estimated standard error of the Tobit regression, Φ is the standard normal distribution function, ϕ is the normal density function, and M^k ($k = u, n$) is the appropriate Mills ratio term (u = union, n = nonunion) defined as $M^u = \phi((X'b+c/\sigma)/\Phi((X'b+c/\sigma)$ and $M^n = \phi((X'b)/\sigma)/\Phi((X'b/\sigma)$.

TRADE UNIONS AND TRAINING PRACTICES   185

tics on training incidence and intensity from EMSPS and QLFS, broken down by union recognition status in all cases, and reported separately for manual and non-manual employees. Average training incidence is described by P, the mean of P_j, which gives the proportion of establishments that trained any of their (manual or non-manual) workers in the last twelve months; and by π, the mean of π_j, which gives the proportion of individuals who received training in the last four weeks. In the raw data both P and π are higher, at statistically significant levels, in unionized workplaces than in nonunion workplaces: in EMSPS, 76% of unionized workplaces provided training for manual workers, as compared to 50% of nonunion workplaces (comparable percentages for non-manuals are 91% and 72%); in the QLFS, 8% of manual workers in unionized workplaces received training in the last four weeks, as compared to 6.5% in nonunion workplaces (for non-manuals the percentages were 22% and 13%, respectively).

Training intensity, too, is higher (and the gap is statistically significant) in unionized than in nonunion workplaces. Average training intensity in EMSPS, defined as average days trained per worker (the mean of PD_j), is 2.3 days for manuals and 3.9 days for non-manuals in the union sector and 1.9 days for manuals and 2.0 days for non-manuals in the nonunion sector. In the QLFS, where training intensity is defined as average hours of training received in the last week, intensity is also higher in the union sector, for both manuals and non-manuals. In sum, these simple descriptive statistics indicate that there is a substantially greater amount of training participation and training intensity in the union sector than in the nonunion sector.

Estimated Models of the Determinants of Training

The Incidence of Training

Estimates of probit models of the determinants of training are reported for manual and non-manual workers separately in models (1) and (2) of Table 2a and models (5) and (6) of Table 2b. The marginal union effect, calculated as described in equation (1) above, is reported in the bottom row of each table. In all the reported models the coefficient on the union recognition variable is estimated to be positive and statistically significant at the 1% level.[7] The establishment-level EMSPS data in Table 2a suggest that unionized establishments are some 17% more likely to provide training for manual workers in the year preceding the survey; they are about 7% more likely to have provided training for non-manual workers. In the individual-level QLFS equations of Table 2b, manual workers in unionized workplaces are about 1.6% more likely than their nonunion counterparts to have received training in the four weeks preceding the survey, and non-manual workers about 5.1% more likely.

In each case we have included as control variables a range of workplace and individual characteristics likely to affect training incidence or intensity.[8] According to the establishment data, training incidence is greater for manual (non-manual) workers where manual (non-manual) workers form a larger proportion of the establishment's work force, greater if managers reported a skill shortage, and greater in larger establishments. For manual workers only, an increase in the proportion of female workers is associated with a lower

---

[7]This conclusion withstands variations in the specification of the control variables, as well as a more detailed occupational disaggregation of the sample. See Green, Machin, and Wilkinson (1995, 1996). For the QLFS models we also estimated a probit model of training receipt in the week preceding the survey (including the same controls as in models 5 and 6 of Table 2b) and obtained qualitatively similar results. For manual workers, the estimated coefficient (standard error) on the union recognition variable was .150 (.047), with an associated marginal effect of .009; for non-manual workers the coefficient estimate (standard error) was .153 (.025) and the marginal effect was .026.

[8]A full set of descriptive statistics is available from the authors on request.

incidence of training. For non-manual workers, there is evidence of greater training incidence where there were at least five competitors, and where the establishment is part of a multi-site organization. Neither race nor location in the public sector appears to have had a statistically significant effect on training incidence. According to the individual-level data, individuals were more likely to receive training if they had less work experience, if they worked in larger workplaces or in the public sector, if they had higher educational qualifications, and if they were skilled (for manuals) or professionals (for non-manuals). For non-manuals only, training was greater if they worked full-time, if they had less job tenure, and if they were married. These findings are broadly consistent with earlier research on training determinants in Britain (Green 1993b). Indeed, the positive influence of establishment size and of an individual's prior human capital on training incidence appears to be a general finding (see, for example, Lynch and Black 1995).

While the estimated equations have plausible coefficients, there remains a possibility that union effects may be biased due to unobserved heterogeneity. It is possible that an unobserved variable, such as management "style," is correlated both with higher levels of training and with more formal employee relations and hence unionization. Unfortunately, because there are no variables in either of these cross-sectional data sets that could plausibly be argued to have direct effects on unionization but not on training, we cannot use a Heckman-type procedure to separately *identify* the union impact on training in such a context. Thus, here, as in most of the literature on training determinants, the possible endogeneity of the right-hand-side variables qualifies the findings. The assertion we defend is that unionization is associated with greater training incidence after we control for a rich array of other establishment and individual characteristics, and that the estimated union effect is robust, withstanding many variations in the precise specification used.

The Intensity of Training

Models (3) and (4) in Table 2a and models (7) and (8) in Table 2b are Tobit estimates of training intensity equations for manual and non-manual workers, with the appropriate marginal union effects reported in the last row. The estimated coefficient on the union recognition variable is always positive and statistically significant (at the 1% level). In the EMSPS models, unionized establishments provide about 0.9 days more training than do nonunion establishments over the year before the survey for both manual and non-manual workers. In the QLFS models, manual workers employed in unionized workplaces received about 0.17 hours' more training in the previous week, and non-manuals about 0.34 more hours, than did their counterparts in nonunion workplaces.

The estimated coefficients on the control variables follow a pattern broadly similar to that shown in the analysis of training incidence, but there are two differences of some interest. First, while establishment size is positively related to training incidence according to the probit estimator, it has no statistically significant impact on training intensity. Second, training intensity is greater, at statistically significant levels, for temporary non-manual workers than for workers with "permanent" contracts. A likely explanation is that these temporary workers especially need to acquire more human capital because they have lower job security.

More Detailed Estimated Union Effects

The models of Tables 2a and 2b provide strong evidence that unions are associated with both a higher frequency and greater intensity of training in British workplaces. Table 3 reports a set of further tests based on the employer survey that re-specify the training equations in a number of ways, enabling us to consider the nature of the estimated union effects in more detail. The first row of the upper panel of the table simply reproduces the basic union recognition effect from Tables 2a and 2b. We use

TRADE UNIONS AND TRAINING PRACTICES   187

Table 2a. Statistical Models of the Incidence and
Intensity of Training, from the Employer Survey.
(Standard Errors in Parentheses)

Indep. Var.	Probit Models of the Incidence of Training		Tobit Models of the Intensity of Training	
	(1)	(2)	(3)	(4)
	Manual	Non-Manual	Manual	Non-Manual
Constant	−0.814 (0.277)***	−0.476 (0.285)	−1.373 (1.504)	0.489 (1.325)
Union Recognition	0.488 (0.106)***	0.376 (0.132)***	1.968 (0.599)***	1.378 (0.527)***
Proportion Manual/ Non-Manual	1.650 (0.172)***	1.934 (0.253)***	1.712 (0.938)***	0.647 (0.869)
Public Sector	−0.064 (0.165)	0.175 (0.178)	−1.535 (0.855)	−0.439 (0.741)
Proportion Female	−0.751 (0.259)***	−0.252 (0.290)	−2.224 (1.453)**	0.976 (1.268)
Proportion Part-Time	0.146 (0.224)	0.222 (0.256)	1.399 (1.154)	1.794 (1.065)*
Proportion-Ethnic Minorities	0.080 (0.109)	−0.166 (0.126)	1.501 (0.601)**	0.356 (0.525)
Skill Shortage in Establishment	0.193 (0.094)**	0.282 (0.118)**	0.743 (0.500)	0.928 (0.440)**
Fewer Than Five Competitors	0.064 (0.109)	−0.202 (0.119)*	−0.372 (0.564)	−0.113 (0.502)
Single Site Establishment	−0.056 (0.137)	−0.480 (0.144)***	−0.129 (0.758)	−1.992 (0.700)***
Establishment Size (Omitted Category: 25–49 Employees)				
50–99 Employees	0.244 (0.140)*	0.127 (0.154)	−0.738 (0.813)	0.976 (0.695)
100–199 Employees	0.266 (0.140)*	0.268 (0.162)	−0.832 (0.822)	−0.014 (0.709)
200–499 Employees	0.378 (0.154)**	0.494 (0.179)***	−0.410 (0.860)	0.946 (0.739)
500–999 Employees	0.621 (0.179)***	0.635 (0.212)***	0.775 (0.931)	−0.329 (0.829)
1,000+ Employees	1.145 (0.191)***	1.385 (0.285)***	−0.211 (0.943)	0.001 (0.814)
Industry and Region Dummies[a]	Included	Included	Included	Included
Log-Likelihood	−553.3	−380.8	−2,111.8	−2,418.5
Sample Size	1,217	1,219	869	893
Mean of Dependent Variable	0.612	0.799	2.134	2.747
Marginal Union Effect	0.168	0.070	0.911	0.860

Notes: The dependent variables are: in models (1) and (2)—whether any training was provided for the relevant group of employees in the last year; models (3) and (4)—the proportion of the relevant group of employees receiving training in the last year multiplied by the average number of days training received. Except where stated, all covariates are 0–1 dummy variables.

[a]All models include eight one-digit industry and ten regional dummies.

*Statistically significant at the .10 level; **at the .05 level; ***at the .01 level (two-tailed tests).

these numbers as the benchmark for comparison purposes in the remainder of Table 3.

We considered two ways of specifying more detailed union effects. Following the theoretical arguments outlined earlier, the first focuses on situations in which one expects the union wage gain to be larger, and the second considers a possibility for union voice effects. Considering the first of these, existing evidence suggests that British unions raise wages by more (that is, achieve a higher union-nonunion wage dif-

ferential) in the presence of closed shop arrangements (Stewart 1987, 1995) or where there are multiple unions that bargain separately (Machin, Stewart, and Van Reenen 1993). The simple union monopoly approaches discussed above (under "Unions and Training") predict lower training activity in conjunction with higher wage gains; hence, we should expect less training where union recognition is accompanied by a closed shop agreement and where there are multiple unions.

We investigated these possibilities in turn.

Table 2b. Statistical Models of the Incidence and
Intensity of Training, from the Individual Survey.
(Standard Errors in Parentheses)

Indep. Var.	Probit Models of the Incidence of Training		Tobit Models of the Intensity of Training	
	(5)	(6)	(7)	(8)
	Manual	*Non-Manual*	*Manual*	*Non-Manual*
Constant	−1.402 (0.093)***	−1.171 (0.060)***	−51.810 (4.206)***	−34.074 (1.921)***
Union Recognition	0.140 (0.039)***	0.197 (0.022)***	6.505 (1.628)***	3.619 (0.659)***
Skilled Manual / Professional	0.203 (0.037)***	0.057 (0.020)***	6.232 (1.535)***	1.131 (0.623)*
Public Sector	0.085 (0.051)*	0.111 (0.029)***	0.243 (2.148)	2.752 (0.896)***
Female	−0.033 (0.046)	0.010 (0.020)	−2.015 (1.846)	−1.012 (0.590)*
Work Part-Time	−0.005 (0.053)	−0.152 (0.024)***	3.483 (2.084)*	−0.104 (0.707)
Not White	−0.088 (0.095)	−0.060 (0.047)	−4.341 (4.095)	−0.410 (1.393)
Married	−0.061 (0.039)	−0.090 (0.021)***	−1.325 (1.635)	−2.781 (0.621)***
Potential Experience (years)	−0.040 (0.005)***	−0.013 (0.003)***	−1.762 (0.198)***	−0.640 (0.081)***
Potential Experience (years) Squared	0.0005 (0.0001)***	0.0000 (0.0001)	0.022 (0.004)***	0.005 (0.002)***
Temporary Employment	0.041 (0.063)	−0.005 (0.035)	1.370 (2.463)	2.742 (0.974)***
Job Tenure (months)	0.0001 (0.0002)	−0.0004 (0.0001)***	−0.010 (0.009)	−0.010 (0.004)***
Workplace Size > 25 employees	0.073 (0.039)*	0.048 (0.020)**	2.182 (1.601)	0.751 (0.612)
Highest Qualification(Omitted Category is "No Qualifications")				
Degree	0.686 (0.124)***	0.530 (0.042)***	16.357 (5.105)***	10.354 (1.314)***
Further Education	0.766 (0.079)***	0.615 (0.041)***	18.681 (3.384)***	13.126 (1.311)***
A Level	0.524 (0.060)***	0.471 (0.041)***	14.845 (2.503)***	10.210 (1.302)***
Apprenticeship	0.349 (0.050)***	0.253 (0.045)***	9.612 (2.183)***	4.750 (1.428)***
O Level	0.508 (0.054)***	0.323 (0.040)***	14.845 (2.503)***	6.873 (1.249)***
CSE	0.274 (0.063)***	0.120 (0.052)**	7.509 (2.634)***	1.295 (1.651)
Other Qualification	0.251 (0.063)***	0.322 (0.052)***	6.832 (2.766)**	6.608 (1.664)***
Industry and Region Dummies[a]	Included	Included	Included	Included
Log-Likelihood	−3,904.7	−14,329.8	−5,117.6	−21,558.0
Sample Size	16,790	33,306	16,893	33,557
Mean of Dependent Variable	0.071	0.173	0.629	1.222
Marginal Union Effect	0.016	0.051	0.169	0.339

Notes: The dependent variables are: in models (5) and (6)—whether any training was received in the last four weeks; models (7) and (8)—the number of hours training received in the last week. Except where stated, all covariates are 0–1 dummy variables.

[a]All models include nine one-digit industry and ten regional dummies.

*Statistically significant at the .10 level; **at the .05 level; ***at the .01 level (two-tailed tests).

We entered in the equations a term interacting union recognition with a dummy variable indicating whether there were multiple unions present. Then, separately, we entered a term interacting union recognition with a dummy variable indicating a "union membership arrangement" (UMA), where a UMA is defined as the presence of closed shop arrangements or, given the outlawing of the closed shop by 1990, where management recommends union member-ship.[9] There is no evidence for a reduced training impact in either case. In none of the models can we reject the null hypothesis of equal coefficients for single or multiple union and UMA or no UMA establish-

[9]We view the "management recommends membership" group as *de facto* closed shops: see Machin and Stewart (1996) for more discussion.

Table 3. More Detailed Union Effects on Training
Participation and Training Intensity from Employer Survey.

| | Probit Models of the Incidence of Training | | | | Tobit Models of the Intensity of Training | | | |
| | Manual | | Non-Manual | | Manual | | Non-Manual | |
Description	Coefficient (Standard Error)	Marginal Effect	Coefficient (Standard Error)	Marginal Effect	Coefficient (Standard Error)	Marginal Effect	Coefficient (Standard Error)	Marginal Effect
Recognition	0.488*** (0.106)	0.168	0.376*** (0.132)	0.070	1.968*** (0.599)	0.911	1.378*** (0.527)	0.860
Single / Multiple Union								
Single Union	0.474*** (0.117)	0.165	0.311** (0.143)	0.065	1.950*** (0.650)	0.907	1.580*** (0.589)	0.964
Multiple Union	0.511*** (0.133)	0.176	0.496*** (0.171)	0.093	1.998*** (0.734)	0.933	1.123* (0.623)	0.668
χ^2 Test of Equality of Coefficients (p-value)[a]	0.08 (0.773)		1.25 (0.264)		0.01 (0.943)		0.59 (0.443)	
Union Membership Arrangements								
No UMA	0.512*** (0.118)	0.173	0.307** (0.143)	0.062	1.864*** (0.651)	0.873	1.122** (0.568)	0.665
UMA	0.413*** (0.132)	0.144	0.491*** (0.172)	0.090	1.786** (0.702)	0.832	1.862*** (0.649)	1.149
χ^2 Test of Equality of Coefficients (p-value)[a]	0.63 (.428)		1.26 (.262)		0.02 (0.899)		1.66 (0.198)	
Joint Consultative Committee (JCC) and Employee Involvement (EI)								
No Recognition, but either JCC or EI	0.432*** (0.140)	0.169	0.236 (0.150)	0.057	2.789*** (0.870)	1.031	2.349*** (0.683)	1.265
Recognition, but neither JCC nor EI	0.514*** (0.182)	0.199	0.423* (0.223)	0.093	2.761*** (1.042)	1.018	3.099*** (0.926)	1.748
Recognition and either JCC or EI	0.868*** (0.151)	0.316	0.573*** (0.173)	0.116	4.381*** (0.900)	1.836	2.985*** (0.719)	1.672
χ^2 Test of Equality of Recognition Coefficients (p-value)[a]	5.30 (.021)		0.58 (.447)		4.43 (0.036)		0.02 (0.877)	

Notes: See notes to Table 2a.

[a]In each case the tests of equality were Wald tests, in which the number reported is the χ^2 value followed by the p-value in parentheses. In the case of JCC and EI, the test compared the impact of recognition without either a JCC or an EI with the impact of recognition accompanied by either a JCC or an EI (or both).

ments, as indicated by the χ^2 statistics shown in the table.

Second, we investigated whether there was any interaction between union presence and two other plant characteristics: the presence of employee involvement schemes (EI), and the presence of a joint consultative committee (JCC). We view these as indicating improved communication channels and, as such, as a measure of collective voice within the workplace. If collective voice is a means through which unions have an impact on establishments, one would expect any impact of unions on training to be greater where such channels are also present.

Table 4. Measures of Training Infrastructure.

Type of Training Infrastructure	Sample Size	Proportion of Establishments with Training Center/ Budget/Plan	Recognition Coefficient (Standard Error)[a]		Marginal Effect[a]
Training Center or School Covering Employees at Establishment	1,225	0.562	0.456	(0.104)	0.178
Training Budget That Covers the Establishment	1,432	0.543	−0.021	(0.099)	−0.008
Training Plan That Covers the Establishment	1,432	0.539	0.215	(0.095)	0.085

Notes:

[a]The coefficient attaches to the recognition dummy in a probit analysis using the same control variables that were used in Table 2a. See the notes to that table. The marginal effects are calculated from the estimated probit equations, as evaluated at the union means.

Union and nonunion weighted means for the three measures of training infrastructure are: Training Center, .636 (union recognized), .445 (union not recognized); Training Budget, .599 (union recognized), .479 (union not recognized); Training Plan, .590 (union recognized), .479 (union not recognized).

According to the specifications in the lower panel of Table 3, for manual workers the union impact on training is higher (p < .01) where a union is recognized and there is a JCC or EI. We view this as important evidence of an indirect positive union influence on training via collective voice–type mechanisms. For non-manual workers the impact of recognition is not altered at a statistically significant level by whether there is or is not a JCC or EI.

Finally, a further possibility is that the impact of union recognition interacts with the other variables in our model. To investigate whether such interactions may be affecting our results, we first split the samples, using both data sets, into union and nonunion segments and tested whether the coefficients of the models in each segment were different using standard likelihood ratio tests. Using the EMSPS data, for both probit models and, in the case of manual workers, for the Tobit model, we could not reject the hypothesis that the coefficients for the union and nonunion segments were equal. However, for the non-manual Tobit model of training intensity, and for all the models in the case of the QLFS models, the likelihood ratio χ^2 value indicated that the coefficients in the two segments were different.

To examine whether our results for the mean impact of unions are affected by this interaction, we first included terms interacting recognition with all the other control variables in the models. We then excluded interactions that were not statistically significant, and estimated the models with just statistically significant terms included. Finally, we calculated the marginal impact of union recognition from the coefficients in this parsimonious model. With the EMSPS data, the result for the model of training intensity for non-manual workers was a marginal union impact of 0.82 days, which is not much lower than the estimate of 0.86 from the basic model without interactions as given in Table 2a. In the case of the individual-level data, we carried out the same procedure for all the models. The estimated marginal effects of unions on training incidence were 0.019 (for manuals) and 0.059 (for non-manuals), while the estimated marginal impact on training intensity was 0.169 (for manuals) and 0.369 (for non-manuals). These figures are relatively close to those shown in Table 2b, again suggesting that our conclusions are little affected by the inclusion of interaction terms in the models.

Other Training Measures

Do unions' positive effects on training

stem from their provision of collective voice? A finding that unionization is also positively related to formal training strategies and infrastructures would be consistent with that hypothesis. We are fortunate that the EMSPS survey contains details regarding training practices in British workplaces (see Dench [1993a, 1993b, 1993c] or Green, Machin, and Wilkinson [1995] for more details). We used these rich data in an analysis examining the relationship between unionization and three measures of the degree of formality of the training infrastructure in the establishments. Table 4 reports the basic results from probit models of whether the organization of which the establishment is part has a training center, a training budget, or a training plan covering the establishment. The models, not shown in full here,[10] all include the same controls as are used in the EMSPS equations of Table 2a.

The results provide more evidence for a positive association between the extent of training practices and unionization. The estimated coefficients on the union variable are all positive and differ from zero at statistically significant levels in the training center and training plan equations. The marginal effects suggest that unionized workplaces are 18% and 9% more likely than nonunion workplaces to have a training center and a training plan, respectively.

Concluding Remarks

Using data from the establishment-level Employers' Manpower and Skills Practices Survey of 1991 and the individual-level Autumn 1993 Quarterly Labour Force Survey, we have investigated the relationship between union presence and the incidence and extent of training in Britain. The analysis, which controls for numerous other determinants of training, yields strong evidence that unionized workers, both manual and non-manual, were more likely than

nonunionized workers to participate in training, and that among those who received training, the amount of training was higher for workers in unionized establishments than for those in nonunion establishments.

These effects are of large magnitude. Our point estimates suggest that the impact of unionization on average days of training is 0.17 (manual) and 0.34 (non-manual) hours per week, based on the individual-level data, and just under 1 day per year, based on the establishment-level data. These are not inconsiderable effects when compared to existing averages, namely 0.6 (manual) and 1.3 (non-manual) hours per week, or 2.1 (manual) and 2.7 (non-manual) days per year. These findings suggest that the rise in training in Britain beginning in the early 1980s occurred *despite*, not *because of*, the downward trend in unionization.

Given that the direct role of unions in training matters appears to have been quite limited at the time of the surveys, our results should be interpreted largely as reflecting the indirect influence of unions. The presence of unions is likely to influence channels of communication and management behavior by providing a "voice" both for individual grievances and for contributions to productive efficiency. Unions' presence may also make employees feel more secure and less threatened by changes in work practices that sometimes accompany training. Labor turnover will then be lower in such workplaces, allowing for a longer period over which the benefits of training may be reaped. There may also be a more formal environment in unionized workplaces, allowing for better identification of training needs.

An interesting question that remains is whether the continuing decline in union presence will have an impact on training participation and volume in future years and whether the skills problems regularly cited by British employers will be exacerbated by this decline. The results in this paper suggest that, despite past declines in aggregate membership, unions still have a potentially important role to play in the skill formation process in British work-

---

[10]These can be obtained from the authors by request.

places. This role could be enlarged if unions succeed in their objectives of playing a more direct role in bargaining over training. As we have seen, the extent of the direct role that unions play in training strategy is unclear. It remains the case that British managers tend to regard training as an area for their own decision-making, but there is some evidence that unions have a direct, though informal, role in training matters in some workplaces (Heyes 1993; Stuart 1994). It is possible that the direct role of unions in training matters will increase in the future, and this is clearly an aim of the Trades Union Congress and several large unions. The findings here suggest that the size of the union sector in the future could potentially have an important influence on the extent of human capital formation in the British economy.

APPENDIX

Variable Definitions and Sources

Variable	Definition	Source
	Employer Survey Variables (taken from both the 1990 Workplace Industrial Relations Survey [WIRS] and the 1991 Employers' Manpower and Skills Practices Survey [EMSPS])	
Training Receipt	= 1 if a positive percentage of employees in any of the manual/non-manual groups have received training in the past 12 months. Relevant question: "Thinking now about employees who have *completed* an initial job training, about what percentage of them have received any (other) training in the last 12 months?"	EMSPS
Training Intensity	Proportion of manual/non-manual employees receiving training in the past twelve months (as indicated by the answer to the *Training Receipt* question) multiplied by the average number of days they spent receiving training in this period (relevant question: "Among that per cent, how many working days on average did they spend receiving training over the last 12 months?").	EMSPS
Training Center	= 1 if the answer to the following question is yes: "Does your organization have a training center or school which covers employees at this establishment?"	EMSPS
Training Budget	= 1 if the answer to the following question is yes: "Is there a training budget which covers this establishment?"	EMSPS
Training Plan	= 1 if the answer to the following question is yes: "Is there a training plan which covers this establishment?"	EMSPS
Union Recognition	= 1 if the answer to the following question is yes: "Are any unions/staff associations recognized by management for negotiating pay and conditions for any section of the workforce in the establishment?" This question is asked separately for manual and non-manual workers.	WIRS
Single Union	= 1 if there is one union or staff association that has members among the manual/non-manual work force.	WIRS
Multiple Union	=1 if the number of unions/staff associations is greater than one.	WIRS
Union Membership Arrangements	=1 if one of the following is true: (i) all manual/non-manual workers have to be members of unions in order to get or keep their jobs; (ii) some groups of manual/non-manual workers have to be members of unions in order to get or keep their jobs; (iii) management strongly recommends that all manual/non-manual workers become union members; (iv) management strongly recommends, for some groups of manual/non-manual workers, that they become union members.	WIRS

Continued

TRADE UNIONS AND TRAINING PRACTICES   193

APPENDIX
Continued

Variable	Definition	Source
Employer Size	Dummy variables for whether the establishment has 25–49 employees, 50–99 employees, 100–199 employees, 200–499 employees, 500–999 employees, and 1,000 or more employees. (WIRS and EMSPS only cover establishments with 25 or more employees.) In the multivariate analysis the omitted category is 25–49 employees.	EMSPS
Employment Shares	Proportions of employees in the establishment who are manual, non-manual, female, and part-time.	EMSPS
Ethnic Minorities	= 1 if some ethnic minorities are employed at the establishment.	WIRS
Public Sector	= 1 if the establishment operates in the public sector.	WIRS
Fewer Than Five Competitors	= 1 if the establishment is in a market with fewer than five competitors.	WIRS
Skill Shortage	= 1 if the establishment has experienced a "skill shortage" in the last 12 months.	EMSPS
Single Site Establishment	= 1 if the establishment is a single independent establishment and not one of a number of different establishments belonging to the same organization.	WIRS
Industry and Region	Dummy variables for one-digit industries and the standard regions.	WIRS

Individual Survey Variables
(taken from the Sept.–Nov. 1993 Quarterly Labour Force Survey [QLFS])

Variable	Definition	Source
Training Receipt	= 1 if in the previous 4 weeks the individual had taken part in any education or any training connected with his or her job, or a job that he or she might be able to do in the future.	
Training Intensity	Number of hours spent on education or training connected with the job, including private study time, in the week prior to the survey.	
Union Recognition	= 1 if unions, staff associations, or groups of unions are present at the workplace and any of them are recognized by management for negotiating pay and conditions of employment.	
Public Sector	= 1 if the individual works in the public sector.	
Female, Part-time, Temporary, Not White, and Married	Dummy variables equal to one if the individual is female, works part-time, works in a temporary job, is not white, and is married.	
Potential Experience	Current age in years of the individual minus the age of the individual when he or she left full-time education.	
Job Tenure	Number of months the individual has worked with his or her current employer.	
Workplace Size	= 1 if the individual works in a workplace that employs 25 or more employees.	
Highest Qualification	Dummy variables equal to one for a range of levels of the highest qualification of the individual. In reverse order by rank, these qualifications are Degree, Further Education, 'A' Level, Apprenticeship, 'O' Level, CSE, Other Qualification, and No Qualification. In all the models estimated, the omitted highest qualification category is No Qualification.	
Industry and Region	Dummy variables for one-digit industries and the standard regions.	

REFERENCES

Arulampalam, Wiji, and Alison Booth. 1997. "Who Gets over the Training Hurdle? A Study of the Training Experiences of Young Men and Women in Britain." *Journal of Population Economics,* Vol. 10, pp. 197–218.

Arulampalam, Wiji, Alison Booth, and Peter Elias. 1995. "Count Data Models of Work-Related Training: A Study of Young Men in Britain." Mimeo, University of Essex.

Blanchflower, David. 1986. "What Effect Do Unions Have on Relative Wages in Great Britain?" *British Journal of Industrial Relations,* Vol. 24, pp. 195–204.

Blundell, Richard, Lorraine Dearden, and Costas Meghir. 1995. "The Determinants and Effects of Work-Related Training in Britain." Mimeo, Institute for Fiscal Studies.

Booth, Alison. 1991. "Job-Related Formal Training: Who Receives It and What Is It Worth?" *Oxford Bulletin of Economics and Statistics,* Vol. 53, pp. 281–94.

CEDEFOP. 1987a. "The Role of the Social Partners in Vocational Training and Further Training in the Federal Republic of Germany." Berlin.

____. 1987b. "The Role of Unions and Management in Vocational Training in France." Berlin.

Claydon, Tim, and Francis Green. 1994. "Can Trade Unions Improve Training in Britain?" *Personnel Review,* Vol. 23, pp. 37–51.

Corcoran, Louise, and Andrew Wareing. 1994. "Trade Union Recognition: Data from the 1993 Labour Force Survey." *Department of Employment, Employment Gazette,* December, pp. 441–51.

Crouch, Colin. 1992. "The Dilemmas of Vocational Training Policy: Some Comparative Lessons." *Policy Studies,* Vol. 13, pp. 33–48.

Dearden, Lorraine, Stephen Machin, Howard Reed, and David Wilkinson. 1997. "Labour Turnover and Work-Related Training." Institute for Fiscal Studies Report, May.

Dench, Sally. 1993a. "What Types of Employer Train?" Employment Department, Social Science Research Branch Working Paper No. 3.

____. 1993b. "Employers' Training: Its Infrastructure and Organisation." Employment Department, Social Science Research Branch Working Paper No. 4.

____. 1993c. "Employers' Provision of Continuous Training." Employment Department, Social Science Research Branch Working Paper No. 6.

Disney, Richard, Amanda Gosling, and Stephen Machin. 1995. "British Unions in Decline: Determinants of the 1980s Fall in Trade Union Recognition." *Industrial and Labor Relations Review,* Vol. 48, pp. 403–19.

Duncan, Greg, and Frank Stafford. 1980. "Do Union Members Receive Compensating Differentials?" *American Economic Review,* Vol. 70, pp. 355–71.

Elias, Peter. 1994. "Job-Related Training, Trade Union Membership, and Labour Mobility: A Longitudinal Study." *Oxford Economic Papers,* Vol. 46, pp. 563–78.

Finegold, David, and David Soskice. 1988. "Britain's Failure to Train: Explanations and Possible Strategies." *Oxford Review of Economic Policy,* Vol. 4, pp. 21–53.

Frazis, Harley J., Diane E. Herz, and Michael W. Horrigan. 1995. "Employer-Provided Training: Results from a New Survey." *Monthly Labor Review,* May, pp. 3–17.

Freeman, Richard, and James Medoff. 1984. *What Do Unions Do?* New York: Basic Books.

Green, Francis. 1993a. "The Impact of Trade Union Membership on Training in Britain." *Applied Economics,* Vol. 25, pp. 1033–43.

____. 1993b. "The Determinants of Training of Male and Female Employees in Britain." *Oxford Bulletin of Economics and Statistics,* Vol. 55, No. 1, pp. 103–22.

Green, Francis, Stephen Machin, and David Wilkinson. 1995. "Unions and Training: An Analysis of Training Practices in Unionized and Non-Unionized Workplaces." Discussion Paper E95/08, School of Business and Economic Studies, University of Leeds.

____. 1996. "Trade Unions and Training Practices in British Workplaces." Discussion Paper, Centre for Economic Performance, London School of Economics.

Greenhalgh, Christine, and George Mavrotas. 1994. "The Role of Career Aspirations and Financial Constraints in Individual Access to Vocational Training." *Oxford Economic Papers,* Vol. 46, pp. 579–604.

Heyes, Jason. 1993. "Training Provision and Workplace Institutions: An Investigation." *Industrial Relations Journal,* Vol. 24, pp. 296–307.

Kennedy, S., R. Drago, J. Sloan, and M. Wooden. 1994. "The Effect of Trade Unions on the Provision of Training: Australian Evidence." *British Journal of Industrial Relations,* Vol. 32, pp. 565–80.

Koike, K., and T. Inoki, eds. 1990. *Skill Formation in Japan and Southeast Asia.* Tokyo: University of Tokyo Press.

Labour Research Department. 1990. "Bargaining Report." January.

Lynch, Lisa. 1992. "Private Sector Training and the Earnings of Young Workers." *American Economic Review,* Vol. 82, pp. 299–312.

Lynch, Lisa, and Sandra E. Black. 1998. "Beyond the Incidence of Employer-Provided Training." *Industrial and Labor Relations Review,* Vol. 52, No. 1 (October), pp. 64–81.

Machin, Stephen, and Mark Stewart. 1996. "Trade Unions and Financial Performance." *Oxford Economic Papers,* Vol. 48, pp. 213–41.

Machin, Stephen, Mark Stewart, and John Van Reenen. 1993. "The Economic Effects of Multiple Unionism: Evidence from the 1984 Workplace Industrial Relations Survey." *Scandinavian Journal of Economics,* Vol. 95, pp. 279–96.

Mason, Geoff, Sig Prais, and Bart van Ark. 1992. "Vocational Education and Productivity in the Netherlands and Britain." *National Institute Economic Review,* Vol. 140, pp. 45–63.

Millward, Neil, Mark Stevens, David Smart, and W. R.

TRADE UNIONS AND TRAINING PRACTICES 195

Hawes. 1992. "Workplace Industrial Relations in Transition: The ED/ESRC/PSI/ACAS Surveys." Aldershot: Dartmouth.

Mincer, Jacob. 1983. "Union Effects: Wages, Turnover, and Job Training." In *New Approaches to Labor Unions.* Greenwich, Conn.: JAI Press.

Osterman, Paul. 1995. "Skill, Training, and Work Organization in American Establishments." *Industrial Relations,* Vol. 34, No. 2, pp. 125–46.

Ryan, Paul. 1991. "Information Costs, Training Quality, and Trainee Exploitation." Mimeo, Cambridge University, July.

Stewart, Mark. 1987. "Collective Bargaining Arrangements, Closed Shops, and Relative Pay." *Economic Journal,* Vol. 97, pp. 140–56.

Stewart, Mark. 1995. "Union Wage Differentials in an Era of Declining Unionisation." *Oxford Bulletin of Economics and Statistics,* Vol. 57, pp. 143–66.

Streeck, Wolfgang. 1989. "Skills and the Limits of Neo-Liberalism: The Enterprise of the Future as a Place of Learning." *Work, Employment and Society,* Vol. 3, No. 1, pp. 89–104.

Stuart, Mark. 1994. "Training in the Printing Industry: An Investigation into the Recruitment, Training, and Retraining Agreement." *Human Resource Management Journal,* Vol. 4, No. 3, pp. 62–78.

Trades Union Congress. 1991. "Collective Bargaining Strategy for the 1990s." London.

Veum, Jonathan. 1995. "Sources of Training and Their Impact on Wages." *Industrial and Labor Relations Review,* Vol. 48, pp. 812–26.

_____. 1997. "Training and Job Mobility among Young Workers in the United States." *Journal of Population Economics,* Vol. 10, pp. 219–34.

[13]

Trade Union Presence and Employer-Provided Training in Great Britain

RENÉ BÖHEIM and ALISON L. BOOTH*

Using linked employer-employee data from the British 1998 Workplace Employee Relations Survey, we find a positive correlation between workplace union recognition and private-sector employer-provided training. We explore the avenues through which union recognition might affect training by interacting recognition with the closed shop, the level at which pay bargaining takes place, and multiunionism. For non-manual-labor men and women, only union recognition matters. The various types of collective-bargaining institutions have no separate effect. However, the male manual training probability is significantly increased by union presence only through multiple unionism with joint negotiation. In contrast, for women manual workers, union recognition at the workplace has no effect on the training probability.

USING NEW LINKED EMPLOYER-EMPLOYEE DATA FROM THE 1998 Workplace Employee Relations Survey, we investigate the correlation between union presence and private-sector employer-provided training in Great Britain. Our measure of union presence is workplace union recognition. We find that this is positively correlated with the individual training probability for non-manual-labor men and women and manual-labor men (but not for manual-labor women), and we offer some explanations for this correlation. We then investigate various avenues through which union recognition might affect training by interacting recognition with three types of bargaining institutions: the closed shop, the level at which pay bargaining

* The authors' affiliations are, respectively, Department of Economics, Johannes Kepler Universität Linz, Linz, Austria, and Economics Program, RSSS, Australian National University, Canberra, Australia. E-mail: *alison.booth@anu.edu.au* and *Rene.Boheim@jku.at*. We would like to thank Mark Bryan, Gordon Kemp, the anonymous referees, and participants in seminars at the Universities of Essex and Munich for helpful suggestions on an earlier draft. The support of the ESRC, the University of Essex, and the Leverhulme Trust (under Award F/00213C, "Work-Related Training and Wages of Union and Nonunion Workers in Britain") is gratefully acknowledged. We acknowledge the Department of Trade and Industry (1999), the Advisory, Conciliation and Arbitration Service, and the Policy Studies Institute as the originators of the 1998 Workplace Employee Relations Survey data and the Data Archive at the University of Essex as the distributor. None of these organizations bears any responsibility for the authors' analysis and interpretations.

INDUSTRIAL RELATIONS, Vol. 43, No. 3 (July 2004). © 2004 Regents of the University of California Published by Blackwell Publishing, Inc., 350 Main Street, Malden, MA 02148, USA, and 9600 Garsington Road, Oxford, OX4 2DQ, UK.

Trade Union Presence and Employer-Provided Training   / 521

takes place, and multiunionism. We also investigate whether or not training is increased by direct negotiation between management and worker representatives.

A number of studies have estimated the correlation between union coverage or union status and work-related training. However, to our knowledge, none has explored the degree to which other institutions associated with collective bargaining are correlated with training provision, no doubt owing to lack of suitable data. U.S. studies provide conflicting evidence about the impact of trade unions on training. For example, Lynch (1992) reported a significant positive impact of unions on on-the-job training, whereas Lynch and Black (1998) reported a typically insignificant association between union status and training. Mincer (1983) and Frazis, Gittleman, and Joyce (2000) found a significantly negative impact of unions on training. In contrast, British studies consistently report a significant positive impact of unions on on-the-job training (Arulampalam and Booth 1998; Booth 1991; Green, Machin, and Wilkinson 1999; Harris 1999; Heyes and Stuart 1998), but none has used linked employer-employee data.

In this article we use a new British data source—the 1998 linked employer-employee Workplace Employee Relations Survey (WERS98)— that facilitates such an investigation. WERS98 is the first comprehensive survey of its kind for Great Britain. It differs from the earlier Workplace Industrial Relations Surveys through a new component, the linked employee questionnaires, distributed randomly to 25 employees at each workplace and generating over 28,000 responses [see Cully et al. (1999) for further details]. These data allow us to investigate in detail union influence on skill formation using linked employer-employee characteristics.

The channels through which unionization can affect training are potentially quite complex, and it is not immediately obvious *a priori* that unionization will be associated with a higher or lower training incidence. According to human capital theory, wage flexibility is a necessary condition for efficient training investment in competitive labor markets (Becker 1964). Some studies therefore argue that where wages are set collectively by trade unions, wage dispersion is reduced, and individual incentives to invest in general training at the workplace are distorted (see, e.g., Mincer 1983). Consequently, individuals and firms will not invest efficiently in such training (Barron, Fuess, and Loewenstein 1987), and there will be a negative correlation between union presence and training.

However, Stevens (1996) and Acemoglu and Pischke (1999) showed that the "wage compression" associated with imperfectly competitive labor markets actually may increase the incentives for *firms* to finance general training whenever training-augmented productivity increases at a faster rate than do wages. Thus some of the returns to training accrue to the training firm, providing an incentive for the firm to invest in general training, although the amount of training provided will not necessarily be optimal from the viewpoint of society. Stevens (1996:36) also showed that the number of firms operating in a skilled labor market is important because if there are few firms, then training is transferable rather than general, and wages will diverge from marginal product.

Recent theory thus suggests that the impact of unions on training is not as clearcut as predicted by orthodox human capital theory and that it is ultimately an empirical issue as to whether union recognition per se increases or decreases the individual probability of receiving training.

There are, of course, other avenues through which unions can affect training. For example, if unions are instrumental in improving worker morale and organization at the work place, labor turnover may be reduced and firms' incentives to train increased because they are less likely to lose trained workers (Freeman and Medoff 1984). Indeed, higher union-set wages actually may increase the incentives for employers to invest in training in order to improve the productivity of their workforce.[1]

Conversely, union restrictive work practices and resistance to the introduction of new skill-intensive technologies may be expected to reduce employer incentives to provide training. Restrictive practices in Great Britain are less common than they used to be following the Thatcher reforms of the 1980s, and union power in Great Britain, moreover, has been declining (Machin 2000). The decline in union power means not only that restrictive practices have been further eroded but also that unions are less able to affect the bargaining agenda. The net outcome of these changes on any union-training link is uncertain, and owing to the cross-sectional nature of our data, we are unable to explore changes over time. However, we can use other proxies for union power in a cross-sectional context, as we demonstrate later in this article.

The Data

The 1998 Workplace Employee Relations Survey is a nationally representative survey of workplaces with 10 or more employees covering full- and

---

[1] Streeck (1989) points out the potential for unions and employers to cooperate to exploit mutual gains in training provision. It is interesting that at the beginning of the 1990s the Trades Union Congress (1991) in Great Britain introduced a "new bargaining agenda" that included training as way to a more "integrative" bargaining strategy. [For evaluations, see Claydon and Green (1994) and Munro and Rainbird (2000).]

Trade Union Presence and Employer-Provided Training   / 523

part-time workers in the private and public sectors and excluding agriculture and coal mining.[2] We use linked components of the 1998 survey: the management interview questionnaire and the individual self-completion questionnaire of 25 employees randomly selected at each workplace (or all employees in smaller workplaces). The management interview was carried out face to face with the most senior workplace manager responsible for personnel or employee relations. Interviews were conducted in 2191 workplaces over the period from October 1997 to June 1998, with a response rate of 80 percent. The Survey of Employees was distributed to the 1880 workplaces where management permitted it, and there was a response rate of 64 percent.[3]

Because of the nature of the sampling procedure, we weight the data as recommended by Forth and Kirby (2000). Our estimating subsample is 17,378 private-sector men and women who are employed in workplaces with at least 10 employees and with complete information on the variables of interest. Summary statistics are provided in the Appendix in Table A.1. We focus only on the private sector. Our preliminary testing showed that it is inappropriate to pool private- and public-sector workers because the coefficients across the subgroups differ significantly, as might be expected given that public- and private-sector employers typically have different objective functions.

Training. Training incidence is obtained from the employee questionnaire in response to the question, "During the last 12 months, how much training have you had, either paid for or organized by your employer? (Include only training away from your normal place or work, but it could be on or off the premises.)" We define *training incidence* to take the value 1 if the employee received any such training and zero otherwise. The framing of this question, emphasizing as it does "only training away from your normal place or work," suggests that the training responses should be interpreted as more formal courses of instruction rather than informal on-the-job training.

Barron, Berger, and Black (1997) use U.S. data from a matched survey to compare the employer's response about training with the response of the

---

[2] The sample of workplaces was obtained through a process of stratified random sampling using variable sampling fractions and with overrepresentation of larger firms, necessitating the use of weights in analysis of these data [for details, see Forth and Kirby (2000) and *http://www.niesr.ac.uk/niesr/wers98/*].

[3] Forth and Millward (2000:14) note that the "survey results can be generalised with confidence to the population of workplaces in Great Britain employing 10 or more employees in 1998. These 340,000 or so establishments employed roughly 18.6 million employees, 82 per cent of employees in England, Scotland and Wales."

524 / René Böheim and Alison L. Booth

worker who received the training.[4] They find substantial measurement error in the training variables and that firms tend to report more training than workers. We are unable to do such a comparison with the WERS data because the training question asked of the employer's representative is different from that asked of employees. In particular, employers report training at the workplace if at least one worker has received training. For this reason, the vast majority of workplaces surveyed in WERS report that they provide training. However, these responses give no indication of the proportion of workers covered, and we therefore use only the worker responses to the training question given earlier.

Trade Union Recognition. Information on union activity is provided in both the management and employee questionnaires. We use whether or not a union is recognized at the workplace for bargaining as our broad measure of trade unionism and construct union recognition from the managers' responses on how many unions are recognized for negotiating pay and conditions.[5] The variable means show that about 50 percent of men work in establishments where at least one union is recognized for bargaining purposes. For women, the corresponding figure is 37 percent. This measure of union influence applies to all workers at an establishment; consequently, it has no within-establishment heterogeneity, and we therefore cannot estimate fixed-effects models using it.[6]

---

[4] Campanelli et al. (1994) note, from a study of linguistic and survey data, that interpretation of the term *training* varies across groups in the population, in particular employers, employees, and training researchers. They emphasize that individuals typically interpret training as referring to "that which happens in formal courses" (1994:92).

[5] Union recognition is a good proxy for union influence at the workplace. Cully et al. (1999), who designed WERS 98, discuss alternative measures of union presence—union recognition or collective bargaining. They argue (1999:96) that union recognition is of fundamental importance in British workplaces, a view reinforced by the support of the Trades Union Congress and the Labour Party for the new union-recognition machinery of the 1999 Employment Relations Act. In an earlier version of this article we carried out analyses based on collective bargaining as well as on union recognition and found that union recognition typically produced the most robust correlations. Most other British studies of training incidence use union coverage or recognition based on individual-level responses. However, it is sometimes suggested (e.g., Jones 1982) that union coverage in individual-level surveys will be measured with more error than membership. This is so because employees will be aware of their membership status if they belong to the union but will be less aware of whether or not there is indeed a recognized union at their workplace, particularly if they are not members. Therefore, union-coverage effects estimated using individual-level data may be biased toward zero. This is not a problem for our study, which uses managers' responses on union recognition matched with individual data.

[6] This is so because the union-recognition dummy variable would be absorbed into the establishment-level fixed effect. Moreover, the Chamberlain conditional logit model cannot be used to estimate the union-recognition effect because there is, by definition, no within-establishment variation in union recognition. Similarly, there is no within-establishment variation in two other variables of interest: the closed shop and multiple unionism.

Trade Union Presence and Employer-Provided Training   / 525

TABLE 1

TRAINING INCIDENCE BY UNION RECOGNITION AND SEX

	Men		Women		
	Union Recognized	No Union Recognized	Union Recognized	No Union Recognized	N
Panel A					
All					
Incidence (proportion)	0.553	0.528	0.558	0.558	
N	4,578	4,790	3,035	4,975	17,378
Panel B					
Non-manual-labor workers					
Incidence (proportion)	0.746	0.612	0.691	0.591	
N	2,123	2,545	1,870	2,851	9,389
Panel C					
Manual-labor workers					
Incidence (proportion)	0.464	0.467	0.453	0.532	
N	2,455	2,245	1,165	2,124	7,989

NOTE: Sampling weights used; *N* are unweighted observations. WERS 1998 linked employer-employee data, private sector employees. Training incidence provided by employees; trade union recognition, by managers.

Table 1 gives the incidence of training as reported by employees by whether or not any union is recognized for bargaining (as reported by the manager) in that workplace.[7] We distinguish between manual and non-manual workers because these represent two distinct labor markets. Moreover, some of the questions in WERS98, such as the level at which pay bargaining occurs, are disaggregated by occupational group. The first row of Table 1 reveals only small differences between unionized and nonunionized workers with respect to training incidence. About 55 percent of private-sector employees obtained training over the last 12 months, as shown in panel A of Table 1, and there is little difference in training incidence for workers in the union and non-union-recognized establishments when manual and non-manual groups are pooled. However, when the data are stratified on the basis of the white-collar/blue-collar distinction (see panels B and C), some interesting differences emerge. Union-covered non-manual-labor men and women are significantly more likely to receive training than nonunion non-manual-labor men and women, whereas *nonunion* manual-labor women are significantly more likely to be trained than union manual-labor women.

---

[7] All analyses use Stata 7. We control for the complex sampling scheme, as laid out in Forth and Kirby (2000), using the weights provided with the data.

526 / René Böheim and Alison L. Booth

There is no significant difference in training incidence for union and non-union manual-labor men.

The incidence of training from the WERS98 data is quite high, even for Great Britain, and considerably higher than for the United States, where formal training incidence in a year is typically about 15 percent (Loewenstein and Spletzer 1999). A recent British comparison is provided by Booth, Francesconi, and Zoega (2003), who used waves 1 to 6 of the British Household Panel Survey (BHPS) for the period 1991–1996. The BHPS makes a useful comparison because it employs the same time frame for the training question (12 months) and is focused on more formal training. Booth, Francesconi, and Zoega (2003) reported, for waves 2 to 6, that between 36 and 40 percent of employed public- and private-sector men received formal training to increase or improve their skills in the current job over the previous 12 months. However, they found that training incidence was significantly higher in the first wave of the BHPS in 1991, when 45 percent of respondents reported having received skill-enhancing training. It seems likely that respondents in a single cross section—such as the WERS98 or the first wave of the BHPS—might have reported higher training incidence due to recall bias. For example, they may include in their responses not only training events that occurred in the last 12 months but also those received prior to the last 12 months, and this might explain the higher reported incidence levels.[8] Nonetheless, the main substance of our results should not be affected unless union-recognized workers differ significantly from non-union workers and manual-labor workers from non-manual-labor workers in their probability of suffering from recall bias. This seems unlikely.

It is also possible that the higher training incidence reported by WERS98 as compared with the BHPS reflects a greater reporting of informal training by WERS98 respondents. The BHPS question explicitly asks for details of

---

[8] The OECD (1999:Table 3.2, p. 142) reports a training incidence for the United Kingdom of 45 percent of the workforce aged 25 to 54 years in the mid-1990s. However, using British data from the 1993 Quarterly Labour Force Survey (QLFS), Green, Machin, and Wilkinson (1999) found that approximately 7 percent of manual workers and 17 percent of nonmanual workers received formal training in the 4 weeks that preceded their interview. Using the same data source between 1983 and 1996, Dearden, Reed, and Van Reenen (2000) found that the proportion of workers receiving training during the last 4 weeks grew from about 5 to 15 percent. It is hard to see how these figures differ from ours because the definition of training receipt in the QLFS is different [for example, in Green, Machin, and Wilkinson (1999), training receipt is equal to unity if, in the previous 4 weeks, the worker had taken part in any education or any training connected with the job or a job that he or she might be able to do in the future], and the time frame over which training is measured is also different (the last 4 weeks rather than the last year or so). The incidence of work-related training in Germany also appears to be lower than the WERS and BHPS figures, at about 31 percent for men aged 16 to 64 between 1986 and 1989 (Pischke 2001). The training incidence is even lower in the United States, as noted in Lynch (1992) and Loewenstein and Spletzer (1999).

Trade Union Presence and Employer-Provided Training / 527

"training schemes or courses," and hence it is probably less likely to include the more informal types of training that WERS98 respondents may be reporting—even though the WERS question explicitly excludes on-the-job training. This possibility should be kept in mind when interpreting our results. It also should be borne in mind that much training is informal and workplace-based, and hence our estimates may be picking up only some aspects of work-related training. Our cross-tabulations reported in Table 1 show that non-manual-labor workers receive more formal training than manual-labor workers. However, it is possible that manual-labor workers receive more *informal* training that is not measured with our data. We do not investigate union influence over such informal training in this article.

Estimation

We estimate determinants of the probability that a worker participated in employer-provided formal training over the last 12 months using a discrete choice model where the dependent variable takes the value 1 if the worker received training and 0 otherwise. While the structure is essentially a probit model, the observations are not independent within a given workplace, and we therefore need to control for different sampling probabilities. We do this by using the sampling weights provided with WERS98 and estimating via pseudolikelihood methods.[9]

Our testing showed that it is inappropriate to pool manual-labor and non-manual-labor workers because the coefficients across the subgroups differ significantly. Separate tests also showed that it is inappropriate to pool men and women. We therefore present separate estimates of the impact of union recognition on the training probability for manual-labor and non-manual-labor men and women.

Union Recognition and Training

In the top panel of Table 2 we present the estimated coefficient to union recognition for a baseline specification similar to that reported in studies using individual cross-sectional surveys (see, e.g., Green, Machin, and Wilkinson 1999). Explanatory variables are detailed in the footnote to

---

[9] We use svyprobt with Stata 7.0. We use the weights to control for the stratified sampling, and we correct the standard errors to allow for nonindependence within units.

528 / René Böheim and Alison L. Booth

TABLE 2

Incidence of Training Estimates (Survey Probit Regression), Private-Sector Workers
(Specifications 1 and 2)

	Male Manual		Male Nonmanual		Female Manual		Female Nonmanual	
	Coeff.	SE	Coeff.	SE	Coeff.	SE	Coeff.	SE
Specification 1								
TU recognized	0.266**	(0.085)	0.275**	(0.091)	−0.064	(0.105)	0.263**	(0.085)
Part time	−0.134	(0.108)	−0.422**	(0.160)	−0.102	(0.076)	−0.201**	(0.081)
Part time *	−0.556**	(0.181)	0.487	(0.332)	−0.131	(0.135)	−0.231*	(0.133)
TU recognition								
Multisite establishment	0.303**	(0.162)	−0.143	(0.195)	0.572**	(0.160)	0.386**	(0.152)
Specification 2								
TU recognized	0.230**	(0.084)	0.264**	(0.089)	−0.032	(0.104)	0.303**	(0.084)
Part time	−0.154	(0.109)	−0.418**	(0.159)	−0.090	(0.076)	−0.201**	(0.082)
Part time *	−0.510**	(0.182)	0.492	(0.335)	−0.144	(0.133)	−0.224*	(0.133)
TU recognition								
Multisite establishment	0.303**	(0.162)	−0.133	(0.197)	0.529**	(0.158)	0.342**	(0.140)
Difficulties filling	0.038	(0.067)	0.119	(0.074)	−0.043	(0.074)	0.131*	(0.076)
vacancies								
EU work's	−0.043	(0.092)	0.161	(0.095)	−0.188	(0.119)	0.101	(0.111)
council (EWC)								
Few competitors	−0.091	(0.097)	−0.045	(0.102)	−0.131	(0.129)	−0.095	(0.102)
Many competitors	−0.142	(0.090)	−0.050	(0.088)	0.003	(0.121)	−0.037	(0.088)
N	4,679		4,666		3,267		4,718	

NOTE: "Closed shop" is 1 if either "TU member to get job," "TU member to keep job," or "Ought to be TU member" is equal to 1, and zero otherwise. Specification 1 also includes age, education, race, occupation, job tenure, size of the workplace and of the organization, whether fixed-term contract, SIC codes, unemployment rate, and vacancy rate as covariates. Specification 2 as specification 1 plus time at current address, whether franchise, whether company is foreign-owned, financial performance, and whether workplace is the headquarters of the company. Employees in establishments with 10 or more employees. Estimations are weighted.
**(*)Indicates significance at the 5% (10%) level.

Table 2, and their means are given in Appendix Table A.1.[10] The effect of local demand-side factors is captured by regional unemployment and vacancy rates. The full set of estimates is available from the authors on request. The marginal effects are reported in Appendix Table A.2.

Our estimates show that union recognition significantly increases the individual training probability for manual-labor and non-manual-labor men and for non-manual-labor women. This observed positive coefficient to union recognition may arise because unions reduce labor turnover, making it less likely that training investments are lost to the firm, or because unions

---

[10] The propensity to train varies across industries because some industries use more specialized equipment than others and have more stringent safety requirements, e.g., nuclear fuel (Dearden, Reed, and Van Reenen 2000). We therefore include 49 industry dummy variables on a two-digit standard industrial classification (SIC) level in our regressions to control for such differences.

Trade Union Presence and Employer-Provided Training / 529

reduce wage dispersion, making it more likely that firms will provide training (as suggested by the "new training" theory outlined earlier). However, for manual-labor women, the coefficient is negative and statistically insignificant.

We include in all specifications a variable for part-time status (self-defined as working fewer than 30 hours per week). Part-time workers have a shorter period over which any training investment can be amortized, and for this reason, we would expect them to receive less training. This hypothesis is confirmed across all specifications for non-manual-labor men and women. We also include the interaction of part-time status and union recognition. Here we wish to test whether or not unions are able to look after the interests of part-time workers in successfully negotiating training for these workers.[11] The coefficient on this interaction variable—while not statistically significant at conventional levels except for manual-labor men—is positive for non-manual-labor men and negative for all other subsamples. The union–part-time status interaction coefficient must be read in conjunction with the recognition coefficient. For example, the total union recognition effect for part-time manual-labor men is given by $0.266 - 0.556 = -0.290$, and this difference is statistically significant at the 1 percent level. Part-time manual-labor men who work in establishments with a recognized union are significantly less likely to be trained.

We include in our specifications the variable *multisite*, which takes the value 1 if the establishment is one of a number of different workplaces within a larger organization and 0 otherwise. We wished to establish if—after controlling for both workplace and organization size—multisite establishments are associated with more training. To the extent that workers might be obliged to transfer between sites, multisite establishments might necessitate more training because of diversity of production techniques or health and safety procedures. We find that the training probability is significantly higher for manual-labor and non-manual-labor women working in multisite establishments, but there is no effect for non-manual-labor men.

The bottom panel of Table 2 presents estimates from an augmented specification that includes all the controls in Specification 1 plus some additional variables from the management questionnaire. We are particularly interested in how the probability of being trained is affected by skilled labor shortages ("difficulties filling vacancies"), the presence of European Union works councils, and the degree of product market competition (proxied by

---

[11] Note that we also experimented in preliminary regressions for both men and women with interactions of part-time status with union recognition and with all the other collective-bargaining institutional measures. Since these were insignificant except for part-time status interacted with union recognition for women, we report in our tables only the interaction of part-time status with union recognition.

530 / René Böheim and Alison L. Booth

the variables *many competitors* and *few competitors*, with the base being *no competitors*).[12] We therefore report the coefficients on these and the union-recognition variables only. (The full set of controls is listed in the notes under each table, and the estimates are available from the authors on request.)

The first thing to note about Specification 2 is that the magnitude of the statistically significant union-recognition estimates is little altered by the inclusion of the extra controls. Union recognition significantly increases the individual training probability for manual-labor and non-manual-labor men and for non-manual-labor women but has no significant impact on the training probability for manual-labor women. It is interesting that typically "difficulties in filling vacancies" have no significant impact on the training probability, suggesting that firms are not training up their current workers when they cannot fill skilled vacancies. This is the case even though nearly two-thirds of men and over half of women are employed in workplaces where management reports such difficulties (see Appendix Table A.1). This finding is consistent with (although it does not prove) the hypothesis that there may be a "quitting" or "poaching" externality: Firms may not train sought-after workers because they may leave [and in that sense there might be undertraining, as noted in Stevens (1996)].

European works councils (EWCs) are the outcome of the European Commission Directive of 1994, which requires multinational firms within the European Union above a minimum size to establish EWCs either according to a statutory model or through a negotiated agreement with unions in firms. Most EWC agreements cover consultation and information only (Marginson and Sisson 1998). Works councils can be viewed as representing greater control by employees over management issues, and to this extent, they may be associated with a higher training probability, However, across all subsamples, the estimated coefficient to the works council variable is insignificantly different from zero.

Also of interest is the relationship between the individual training probability and the degree of product market competition faced by an individual's employer. The degree of product market competition is included to investigate the hypothesis that oligopolists choose to spend some of their rents on training or that firms are less willing to pay for training if it is anticipated that trained workers may be poached elsewhere—the fewer the

---

[12] The European Union works council is a requirement for informing and consulting employees at the European level for employers with at least 1000 employees across the member states and at least 150 employees in each of two or more of those member states (Department of Trade and Industry 1999b). Other employers, however, may wish to implement the stipulated regulations voluntarily.

competitors, the lower the poaching probability. For both these reasons, we would expect there to be a negative correlation between the training probability and a competitive product market.[13] We therefore included two dummy variables—the employer has many competitors or has few competitors—where the base is no competitors. However, although we do indeed find a negative coefficient to each of these variables as expected, neither is statistically significant. Finally, note that the *multisite* coefficients remain similar across specifications and are statistically significant for manual-labor and non-manual-labor women.

In summary, our union-recognition estimates are robust to the inclusion of the additional workplace controls. We now turn to the second goal of this article—to see if we can further unravel the mechanism through which union presence at the workplace affects individual training outcomes. To do this, we exploit the additional information provided in the management questionnaires about other features of the collective-bargaining environment.

Collective-Bargaining Institutions and Training

It is widely recognized that union objective functions include wages and employment, and one way for powerful unions to ensure that union workers receive high wages and greater job security is by ensuring that their skills are deepened and/or kept up to date.[14] In this section we investigate whether or not workers covered by more powerful unions have a higher training probability, as well as some other hypotheses that we outline below.

Union presence at the workplace is felt not only through union recognition but also through closed shops, the degree of centralization of pay bargaining, and whether or not there are multiple unions at the establishment. We briefly describe our construction of these variables before turning to our estimates of their effects on training in Table 3. We also have information about whether or not training is negotiated with employee representatives.

---

[13] The training question asks individuals for information about "training either paid for or organized by the employer." This does not necessarily exclude training that is paid for by the individual but organized by the employer. However, the firm presumably would be involved with some costs even in organizing training.

[14] Nickell, Jones, and Quintini (2002) point to a rise in the job insecurity of British men over the past two decades. While the probability of becoming unemployed has not risen, there has been an increase in the costs of becoming unemployed in terms of real wage losses. There also has been a growth in the probability of experiencing real wage losses for the continuously employed. We would suggest that one way in which unions might have provided insurance against these expected losses is to increase the human capital of union-covered workers through more training.

532 / René Böheim and Alison L. Booth

The Closed Shop. An important measure of union power is the extent to which the union can control the available supply of labor to a firm. This depends in part on a worker's right to remain outside a union, as opposed to the right of the union to require all workers to be union members in a *union*, or *closed, shop.*[15] Vestiges of the closed shop remain in a small proportion of workplaces in Great Britain (see Wright 1996). We combine into a single indicator labeled *closed shop* the variables for the presence at the workplace of preentry or postentry closed shops and whether or not management recommends union membership for some employees. About 5 percent of employees work in an establishment in which there is a closed shop of this form for at least some of the workforce.[16] Since this information is provided only where an establishment has a recognized union, the variable can be thought of as the interaction between union recognition and closed shop. Our first hypothesis is that individuals in workplaces with more powerful recognized unions—as proxied by the closed shop—have a higher training probability than those with weaker unions.

Bargaining Structure. Although Great Britain is perceived as having a decentralized bargaining structure relative to the rest of Europe, there is still considerable variation in the form that pay bargaining takes (Forth and Millward 2000). Moreover, the location of collective bargaining often varies for different bargaining topics (Katz 1993), and it is possible that wages and training are bargained at different levels. Since the level at which pay bargaining occurs also affects union power, as emphasized by the contributions in Boeri, Brugavini, and Calmfors (2001), the type of bargaining structure may well have an impact on the incidence of training in Great Britain. On

---

[15] Stewart (1987) showed that the preentry closed shop increased the capacity of the union to raise wages above noncompetitive levels; the postentry closed shop much less so. Metcalf and Stewart (1992) further showed that abolition of the closed shop under the Thatcher administration accounted for much of the reduction in the capacity of British unions to influence wages over that period. In the United Kingdom there were until the mid-1980s two forms of closed-shop arrangements under which unions could require workers to be union members. The preentry closed shop gave the union more power over labor supply because it enabled the union to dictate to firms the pool of workers (the set of registered union members) from which the firm could recruit. In contrast, the postentry closed shop merely enabled the union to require all employed workers (not the entire pool of all possible workers) to become union members ex post, after they had been hired by the firm. In the 1980s, the Thatcher government instituted a number of legislative changes that had the effect of effectively outlawing the closed shop and reducing union bargaining power.

[16] About 1 percent of employees work in establishments where management states that some of the workforce has to be union members to keep the job. About 0.5 percent of employees work in a preentry closed shop and 4 percent in establishments where management recommends union membership for at least some employees.

Trade Union Presence and Employer-Provided Training   / 533

the one hand, coordinated unions bargaining nationally or at the industry level may be able to negotiate more training, thereby raising the amount of embodied human capital of union employees and increasing their welfare. On the other hand, where bargaining is decentralized, firms and unions may be more responsive to product demand fluctuations and individual workers' needs and therefore be more willing to negotiate training. Moreover, if the firm's cost centers are decentralized, decentralized bargaining can confer advantages to the firm (Marginson and Sisson 1998), which might take the form of more training. Ultimately, it is an empirical issue as to which effect—if any—dominates. Our second hypothesis is therefore that individuals in workplaces with recognized union(s) and decentralized bargaining will have a different probability of being trained than individuals with more centralized bargaining.

To shed light on the relationship between collective-bargaining processes and employer-provided training, we use information from the managers' responses on how pay is determined and match it to each worker's characteristics. For each occupational group (managers, professionals, technicians, clerks, crafts, personal services, sales, operators, other) we have information about how pay is usually set.[17] Pay determination can be (1) the result of collective bargaining (either multiemployer, single employer, or workplace), (2) set by management (at the workplace or at a higher level), (3) the outcome of individual negotiations, or (4) set by some other method, e.g., by a pay review body. The categories are not mutually exclusive and sum to more than 1.

After preliminary estimation, we created five variables to cover various methods of pay determination. The first three variables represent the interaction between union recognition at the establishment and whether or not the individual's occupational group has its pay determined by collective bargaining that is either multiemployer, single employer, or workplace. The fourth pay-determination variable captures the fact that some individuals work at establishments without a recognized union, but nonetheless management stated that pay for their occupational group was determined by some form of collective bargaining. For these individuals, we create a variable *no recognition but collective bargaining at some level.* The final variable takes the value 1 for individuals whose pay is determined by some other method that is unrelated to collective bargaining. This is the base group, and therefore it is omitted from the estimation.

---

[17] Thus for each individual we map in workplace data on how pay is usually set for that individual's occupational group.

534 / RENÉ BÖHEIM AND ALISON L. BOOTH

Multiple Unionism. Historically, union organization in Great Britain developed initially on a craft or occupational basis and only later along industrial lines. The evolution of craft unions in the United Kingdom provides a partial explanation of the widespread—though diminishing—incidence of multiunionism, which occurs when a heterogeneous workforce at a single workplace is represented by more than one union. The traditional strategy of occupational unions was not only to restrict access to training (typically youth access to apprenticeships) as a means of controlling the supply of labor but also to control the quality of training (Webb and Webb 1897; Ryan 1994).[18] Thus multiple unionism potentially may pick up the influence of separate bargaining by what remains in Great Britain of occupational unionism among manual-labor workers. In particular, according to this hypothesis, we might expect that multiple unions with separate bargaining may be associated with lower training incidence for manual-labor workers, *ceteris paribus.* Our third hypothesis is therefore that manual-labor workers in plants with a single recognized union or with multiple unionism and joint bargaining will have a higher training probability than those with multiple recognized unions with separate bargaining.

Multiunionism with separate bargaining may reduce efficiency if each union protects its members' jobs by adhering to inefficient working practices and resisting the introduction of new technology. However, such multiunionism also can be thought of as increasing rather than reducing competitiveness to the extent that it allows the consideration of separate issues for each union. Multiunionism with separate bargaining also may allow employers to operate a "divide and rule" strategy, as suggested in Machin, Stewart, and Van Reenen (1993), making it easier for management to introduce technological change. Therefore, it is not unambiguously clear a priori as to what effect multiunionism will have on the training probability.

For workers in establishments where more than one union is recognized, we use information on whether negotiations between management and unions are conducted jointly with all recognized unions or separately with each recognized union or with groups of recognized unions. More men than women are employed in workplaces where more than one trade union is recognized (the percentages are 29 and 14 percent). About 17 percent of men and 6 percent of women work in establishments where negotiations are carried out jointly with all recognized unions. For 12 percent of men and 7 percent of women, negotiations are undertaken separately, either with separate trade unions or with separate groups of unions. The two

---

[18] Our data do not provide information on training quality or actual productivity, and so we are unable to investigate the potential impact of unions on training quality as compared with quantity.

Trade Union Presence and Employer-Provided Training / 535

multiunionism variables reported in Table 3 represent the interaction of union recognition and joint negotiations and union recognition and separate negotiations. The base group is the union-recognition variable in the first row of the table. This represents a single recognized union at the workplace with no closed shop and workplace-level collective bargaining.

Training Negotiated. The *training negotiated* variable takes the value 1 if management reports that, at this workplace, it normally negotiates with employee representatives over the training of employees. (The base group is no training negotiated.) The hypothesis to be tested through the inclusion of this variable is whether or not there is any direct influence of worker representatives on training, as well as the indirect influence already picked up by the union-recognition variable.

One percent of workers in each of our subsamples falls into this category. Although two-thirds of workers whose management reports that it normally negotiates with employee representatives who are union-recognized, this unfortunately represents too few observations to allow us to interact *union recognition* with *training negotiated* in our regressions.[19]

The Estimates. Table 3 reports estimates of our expanded model—Specification 3—including all the variables discussed above in addition to those of Specification 2. The marginal effects are reported in Appendix Table A.3. We first consider the impact of union recognition.[20] The first row of Table 3 reports the union-recognition coefficient for each of the four subsamples.[21] This represents the union-recognition base, consisting of individuals at establishments with a single union bargaining at the workplace level and no closed shop. Non-manual-labor men and women in such a situation have a significantly higher probability of being trained relative to no recognition. Now suppose that one of these non-manual-labor union-covered men is transferred into a workplace that is identical in all respects except that there

---

[19] Inclusion of the interaction term introduces collinearity into the regressions. The results are typically an insignificant coefficient for the interaction terms and a greatly inflated coefficient for *training negotiated.*

[20] Although we cannot use log-likelihood tests to discriminate between specifications due to the estimation technique, we obtained log-likelihoods by estimating maximum-likelihood probit models using the appropriate weights. The log-likelihood ratio tests on these models reveal that Specification 3 is the preferred model. We also tested the joint significance of the added variables by a Wald test (svytest), and our conclusions remain the same.

[21] In an earlier draft of this article we experimented with replacing union recognition by an alternative measure of union presence, namely, collective bargaining. The estimates using collective bargaining were less precisely determined compared with those using union recognition reported in Table 3.

TABLE 3
INCIDENCE OF TRAINING ESTIMATES (SURVEY PROBIT REGRESSION), PRIVATE-SECTOR WORKERS (SPECIFICATION 3)

	Male Manual		Male Nonmanual		Female Manual		Female Nonmanual	
	Coeff.	SE	Coeff.	SE	Coeff.	SE	Coeff.	SE
TU recognized	0.096	(0.100)	0.270**	(0.101)	−0.176	(0.121)	0.238**	(0.095)
Bargaining level * TU recognition								
Employers	−0.220*	(0.124)	0.045	(0.182)	−0.051	(0.183)	0.209	(0.151)
Organization	0.174*	(0.091)	−0.189	(0.115)	0.181	(0.124)	0.068	(0.125)
No recognition, but collective bargaining at workplace	−0.224	(0.160)	−0.158	(0.198)	−0.102	(0.204)	−0.140	(0.191)
Multiunionism * TU recognition								
Joint negotiations	0.337**	(0.124)	0.2068	(0.124)	0.267	(0.241)	0.018	(0.128)
Separate negotiations	0.124	(0.118)	−0.149	(0.131)	0.324*	(0.181)	0.151	(0.168)
Closed shop * TU recognition	−0.61	(0.118)	0.043	(0.209)	−0.045	(0.183)	−0.025	(0.173)
Part time	−0.151	(0.110)	−0.437**	(0.160)	−0.090	(0.076)	−0.203**	(0.082)
Part time * TU recognition	−0.475**	(0.186)	0.508	(0.333)	−0.143	(0.131)	−0.218	(0.135)
Difficulties filling vacancies	0.029	(0.067)	0.086	(0.071)	−0.058	(0.073)	0.127*	(0.077)
EU work's council (EWC)	−0.060	(0.091)	0.157*	(0.093)	−0.177	(0.124)	0.120	(0.112)
Training negotiated	0.311	(0.196)	0.470**	(0.198)	0.173	(0.400)	0.534**	(0.222)
Few competitors	−0.075	(0.094)	−0.064	(0.097)	−0.117	(0.132)	−0.091	(0.101)
Many competitors	−0.104	(0.088)	−0.052	(0.085)	0.016	(0.123)	−0.033	(0.088)
Multisite establishment	0.334**	(0.163)	−0.111	(0.196)	0.518**	(0.157)	0.353**	(0.138)
N	4,679		4,666		3,267		4,718	

NOTE: "Closed shop" is 1 if either "TU member to get job," "TU member to keep job," or "Ought to be TU member" is equal to 1, and zero otherwise. The specification also includes age, education, race, occupation, job tenure, size of the workplace and of the organization, whether fixed-term contract, SIC codes, unemployment rate, vacancy rate, time at current address, whether franchise, whether company is foreign-owned, financial performance, and whether or not the workplace is the headquarters of the company. Employees in establishments with 10 or more employees. Estimations are weighted.
**(*)Indicates significance at the 5% (10%) level.

Trade Union Presence and Employer-Provided Training   /   537

is now more than one recognized union. Suppose further that this multi-unionism is associated with separate bargaining. The total training effect of union recognition now becomes $0.270 - 0.149 = 0.121$. However, this difference is not statistically significant, and thus this effect is not significantly different from the estimated effect for a man in a single-union workplace.

Indeed, for non-manual-labor men and women, none of the additional variables interacting union recognition with other collective-bargaining characteristics is statistically significant. Thus for non-manual-labor workers we can reject the hypotheses that (1) individuals in workplaces with more powerful recognized unions—as proxied by the closed shop—have a higher training probability than those with weaker unions, (2) individuals in workplaces with recognized union(s) and decentralized bargaining are more likely to be trained than those with more centralized bargaining, and (3) individuals in workplaces with a single recognized union have a higher training probability than those with multiple recognized unions. The rejection of the last hypothesis is not surprising, given that it was formulated with manual-labor men in mind.

Nonetheless, for non-manual-labor men and women we do find that union recognition is associated with a significantly greater training probability. These results have proved to be remarkably robust across different specifications. Our interpretation is that the presence of a recognized union at the workplace is likely to be associated with features well documented elsewhere [for surveys, see Freeman and Medoff (1984) and Booth (1995)] and that are conducive to training. These features include reduced labor turnover (making it less likely that training investments are lost to the firm) and/or reduced wage dispersion (making it more likely that firms will provide training, as suggested by the "new training" theory outlined earlier).

Now consider the impact of the *training negotiated* variable for non-manual-labor men and women (fourth last line of Table 3). The training probability is significantly higher for non-manual-labor men and women if their management normally negotiates with employee representatives over the training of employees (*training negotiated*). In summary, we cannot reject the hypothesis that there is a direct positive association between training negotiation between management and worker representatives on the one hand and the individual training probability on the other. This direct effect is in addition to the indirect influence of unions on training already picked up by the union-recognition variable. With a cross-sectional survey such as WERS98, we are unable to establish causation. It may be that workplaces investing in the human capital of their workforce are more likely to set up procedures for negotiation about the type of investment or that in workplaces with a high level of cooperation between management and worker

538 /   René Böheim and Alison L. Booth

representatives—as proxied by *training negotiated*—more care and resources are devoted to training.

We now turn to the results for manual-labor men. The coefficient reported in the first cell is 0.096. It represents the union-recognition base, consisting of manual-labor men at establishments with a single union bargaining at the workplace level and no closed shop. Now suppose that this union-covered manual-labor man is transferred to a workplace that is identical in all respects except that there is now multiunionism with joint bargaining. The total training effect of union recognition becomes 0.096 + 0.337 = 0.433. The difference between the two estimated coefficients is statistically significant at the 5 percent level. None of the other interacted collective-bargaining variables has a statistically significant effect. Thus the positive union-recognition effect on training for manual-labor men works through multiunionism with *joint* negotiations. This provides partial support for our third hypothesis (that manual-labor workers in plants with a single recognized union or with multiple unionism and joint bargaining will have a higher training probability than those with multiple recognized unions with separate bargaining). Our interpretation is that multiunionism and *separate* bargaining for manual-labor men pick up the effect of what remains in Great Britain of occupational unionism with its restrictions over training labor.

Now consider manual-labor women. In the specifications reported in Table 2, we found that union recognition had no statistically significant impact on the training probability for manual-labor women. It comes as no surprise that further disaggregation of this union-recognition effect does not affect our earlier finding. Union presence in its various guises does not affect the incidence of work-related training of manual-labor women. Therefore, manual-labor women are unlikely to join union-recognized workplaces to improve their human capital—at least as measured by work-related training.

Finally, note that the magnitude and statistical significance of the other controls reported in the tables remain broadly similar across specifications.

Conclusions

Using linked employer-employee data from the 1998 Workplace Employee Relations Survey (WERS98), we investigate the impact of union presence on the incidence of formal training provided by private-sector employers to employees. Our measure of union presence is union recognition. We find that this is positively correlated with the individual training probability for non-manual-labor men and women and manual-labor men

Trade Union Presence and Employer-Provided Training / 539

but not for manual-labor women. Our interpretation is that the presence of a recognized union at the workplace is likely to be associated with features that are conducive to training. These include reduced labor turnover (making it less likely that training investments are lost to the firm) and/or reduced wage dispersion (making it more likely that firms will provide training, as suggested by the "new training" theory).

We then explored the potential avenues through which union recognition affects training by interacting recognition with three types of bargaining institutions: the closed shop, the level at which pay bargaining takes place, and multiunionism. We find that for non-manual-labor men and women only union recognition matters. The various types of collective-bargaining institutions have no separate effect. However, the results differ for manual-labor workers. The male manual-labor training probability is significantly increased by union presence only through multiple unionism with joint negotiation. In contrast, for women manual-labor workers, union recognition at the workplace has no effect on the training probability.

Finally, we note the possibility that individual training and union status may be determined jointly. For example, in firms in which there is union presence, management may vet new hires and train their workforce more carefully, or better workers may self-select into unionized firms.[22] To the extent that management or worker quality are unobservable with our data but are correlated with union recognition and the dependent variable, the estimated coefficient to union recognition may suffer from omitted variable bias. Since our data are cross-sectional, we were unable to control for individual unobserved heterogeneity using panel data methods. We also were unable to exploit the within-establishment variation in training as a function of union recognition because there is no within-establishment variation in union recognition. However, relative to other studies on this topic, we do have a particularly rich set of controls that should mitigate potential selectivity bias in our estimates. And our results across all specifications consistently show, for non-manual-labor men and women, a statistically significant positive association between union recognition at the workplace and the individual training probability.

REFERENCES

Acemoglu, Daron, and Jörn-Steffen Pischke. 1999. "The Structure of Wages and Investment in General Training." *Journal of Political Economy* 107(3):539–72.

---

[22] As another example, firms that enjoy product market rents will be more likely to be unionized and more likely to offer training (because they have a greater surplus to share with their workers). For this reason, among others, we control for product market rents and industry in our estimation.

540 / René Böheim and Alison L. Booth

Arulampalam, Wiji, and Alison L. Booth. 1998. "Training and Labour Market Flexibility: Is There a Trade-off?" *British Journal of Industrial Relations* 36(4):521–36.

Barron, John M., Mark C. Berger, and Dan A. Black. 1997. *On-the-Job Training*. Kalamazoo, MI: W. E. Upjohn Institute for Employment Research.

Barron, Scott M., Fuess, Jr., and Mark A. Loewenstein. 1987. "Further Analysis of the Effect of Unions on Training (Union Wages, Temporary Layoffs, and Seniority)." *Journal of Political Economy* 95(3):632–40.

Becker, Gary. 1964. *Human Capital*. Chicago: University of Chicago Press.

Boeri, Tito, Agar Brugiavini, and Lars Calmfors, eds. 2001. *The Role of the Unions in the Twenty-first Century*. Oxford, UK: Oxford University Press.

Booth, Alison L. 1991. "Job-Related Formal Training: Who Receives It and What Is It Worth?" *Oxford Bulletin of Economics and Statistics* 53:281–294; reprinted in *The Economics of Training*, edited by O. Ashenfelter, and R. J. Lalonde. Cheltenham, UK: Edward Elgar, 1996.

———. 1995. *The Economics of the Trade Union*. Cambridge, UK: Cambridge University Press.

———, Marco Francesconi, and Gylfi Zoega. 2003. "Unions, Work-Related Training, and Wages: Evidence for British Men." *Industrial and Labor Relations Review* 57(1):68–91.

Campanelli, Pamela, and Joanna Channell with contributions from Liz McAulay, Antoinette Renouf, and Roger Thomas. 1994. *Training: An Exploration of the Word and the Concept*. Employment Department Research Series No. 30. London: The Stationery Office.

Claydon, T., and F. Green. 1994. "Can Trade Unions Improve Training in Britain?" *Personnel Review* 23:37–51.

Cully, Mark, Stephen Woodland, Andrew O'Reilly, and Gill Dix. 1999. *Britain at Work, as Depicted by the 1998 Workplace Employee Relations Survey*. London: Routledge.

Dearden, Lorraine, Howard Reed, and John Van Reenen. 2000. "Who Gains When Workers Train? Training and Corporate Productivity in a Panel of British Industries," Institute for Fiscal Studies Working Paper No. 00/04, London, March.

Department of Trade and Industry. 1999a. *Workplace Employee Relations Survey: Cross-Section, 1998*, 4th ed. Colchester, UK: Data Archive (computer file).

———. 1999b. *The Transnational Information and Consultation of Employees Regulations 1999*. Statutory Instrument 1999 No. 3323. London: The Stationery Office; *http://www.legislation.hmso.gov.uk/si/si1999/19993323.htm*.

Forth, John, and Simon Kirby. 2000. "Guide to the Analysis of the Workplace Employee Relations Survey 1998," Version 1.1, National Institute of Economic and Social Research, London, April.

——— and Neil Millward. 2000. "The Determinants of Pay Levels and Fringe Benefit Provision in Britain." National Institute for Economic and Social Research Discussion Paper No. 171, November, London.

Frazis, Harley, Maury Gittleman, and Mary Joyce. 2000. "Correlates of Training: An Analysis Using Both Employer and Employee Characteristics." *Industrial and Labor Relations Review* 53(3):443–62.

Freeman, Richard B., and James L. Medoff. 1984. *What Do Unions Do?* New York: Basic Books.

Green, Francis, Stephen Machin, and David Wilkinson. 1999. "Trade Unions and Training. Practices in British Workplaces." *Industrial and Labor Relations Review* 52(2):177–95.

Harris, Richard I. D. 1999. "The Determinants of Work-Related Training in Britain in 1995 and the Implications of Employer Size." *Applied Economics* 31:451–63.

Heyes, Jason, and Mark Stuart. 1998. "Bargaining for Skills: Trade Unions and Training at the Workplace." *British Journal of Industrial Relations* 36(3):459–67.

Jones, Ethel. 1982. "Union/Nonunion Differentials: Membership or Coverage?" *Journal of Human Resources* 17(2):276–85.

Katz, Harry C. 1993. "The Decentralization of Collective Bargaining: A Literature Review and Comparative Analysis." *Industrial and Labor Relations Review* 47:3–22.

Loewenstein, Mark A., and James R. Spletzer. 1999. "Formal and Informal Training: Evidence from the NLSY," in *Research in Labor Economics*, Vol. 18, edited by Solomon Polachek, pp. 403–38. Greenwich, CT: JAI Press.

Trade Union Presence and Employer-Provided Training   / 541

Lynch, Lisa M. 1992. "Private Sector Training and the Earnings of Young Workers." *American Economic Review* 82:299–312.

———— and Sandra E. Black. 1998. "Beyond the Incidence of Employer-provided Training." *Industrial and Labor Relations Review* 52(1):64–81.

Machin, Stephen. 2000. "Union Decline in Britain." *British Journal of Industrial Relations* 38:631–45.

————, Mark B. Stewart, and John Van Reenen. 1993. "The Economic Effects of Multiple Unionism." *Scandinavian Journal of Economics* 95(3):279–96.

Marginson, Paul, and Keith Sisson. 1998. "European Collective Bargaining: A Virtual Prospect?" *Journal of Common Market Studies* 36(4):505–28.

Metcalf, David, and Mark B. Stewart. 1992. "Closed Shops and Relative Pay: Institutional Arrangement or High Density?" *Oxford Bulletin of Economics and Statistics* 54(4):503–16.

Mincer, Jacob. 1983. "Union Effects: Wages, Turnover, and Job Training," in *New Approaches to Labor Unions.* Greenwich, CT: JAI Press.

Munro, Anne, and Helen Rainbird. 2000. "The New Unionism and the New Bargaining Agenda: UNISON—Employer Partnerships on Workplace Learning in Britain." *British Journal of Industrial Relations* 38(2):223–40.

Nickell, Stephen, Patricia Jones, and Glenda Quintini. 2002. "A Picture of Job Insecurity Facing British Men." *Economic Journal* 112(January):1–27.

Organisation for Economic Cooperation and Development (OECD). 1999. *Employment Outlook.* Paris: OECD, June.

Pischke, Jörn-Steffen. 2001. "Continuous Training in Germany." *Journal of Population Economics* 14(September):523–48.

Ryan, Paul. 1980. "The Cost of Job Training for a Transferable Skill." *British Journal of Industrial Relations* 8:334–52.

————. 1994. "Training Quality and Training Exploitation," in *Britain's Training Deficit*, edited by R. Layard, K. Mayhew, and G. Owen, CEP Report, pp. 92–124. Avebury, UK: Ashgate Publishing Company.

Stevens, Margaret. 1996. "Transferable Training and Poaching Externalities," in *Acquiring Skills: Market Failures, Their Symptoms and Policy Responses*, edited by Alison L. Booth, and Dennis J. Snower, pp. 21–40. Cambridge, UK: Cambridge University Press.

Stewart, Mark B. 1987. "Collective Bargaining Arrangements, Closed Shops and Relative Pay." *Economic Journal* 97:140–56.

Streeck, Wolfgang 1989. "Skills and the Limits of Neo-Liberalism: The Enterprise of the Future as a Place of Learning." *Work, Employment and Society* 3(1):89–104.

Trades Union Congress. 1991. *Collective Bargaining Strategy for the 1990s.* London: Trades Union Congress.

Webb, Sidney, and Beatrice Webb. 1897. *Industrial Democracy.* London: Longmans and Green.

Wright, Martyn. 1996. "The Collapse of Compulsory Unionism." *British Journal of Industrial Relations* 34(4):497–513.

542 / René Böheim and Alison L. Booth

APPENDIX

TABLE A.1

Summary Statistics

	Male Manual		Male Nonmanual		Female Manual		Female Nonmanual	
	Mean	SD	Mean	SD	Mean	SD	Mean	SD
TU recognized	0.541		0.425		0.374		0.359	
Bargaining level * TU recognition								
Employers	0.112		0.033		0.120		0.028	
Organization	0.193		0.144		0.171		0.156	
Workplace	0.225		0.102		0.119		0.068	
No recognition, but collective bargaining at workplace	0.117		0.019		0.173		0.014	
Multiunionism * TU recognition								
Joint negotiations	0.183		0.161		0.041		0.090	
Separate negotiations	0.125		0.095		0.064		0.067	
Closed shop * TU recognition	0.053		0.033		0.033		0.032	
Part time	0.140		0.047		0.599		0.275	
Part time * TU recognition	0.045		0.013		0.211		0.108	
Difficulties filling vacancies	0.611		0.606		0.548		0.544	
EU work's council (EWC)	0.137		0.177		0.095		0.130	
Training negotiated	0.010		0.010		0.010		0.010	
Few competitors	0.331		0.303		0.290		0.230	
Many competitors	0.500		0.465		0.566		0.520	
Multisite establishment	0.713		0.734		0.723		0.660	
Age								
<20	0.083		0.017		0.119		0.027	
20–24	0.081		0.066		0.103		0.100	
25–29	0.120		0.152		0.112		0.180	
40–49	0.205		0.244		0.220		0.220	
50–59	0.176		0.163		0.179		0.174	
>60	0.071		0.039		0.035		0.020	
Education								
Less than O levels	0.196		0.056		0.162		0.103	
O levels	0.261		0.204		0.279		0.342	
A levels	0.106		0.200		0.114		0.177	
Degree	0.042		0.422		0.046		0.249	
Race								
White	0.968		0.955		0.957		0.956	
Black Caribbean	0.005		0.005		0.004		0.008	
Black African	0.004		0.004		0.002		0.004	
Black other	0.001		0.000		0.004		0.003	
Indian	0.009		0.014		0.018		0.009	
Pakistani/Bangladeshi	0.004		0.003		0.002		0.001	
Chinese	0.000		0.002		0.001		0.003	
Other	0.005		0.013		0.010		0.013	
Occupation								
Manager	0.000		0.331		0.000		0.139	
Professional	0.000		0.285		0.000		0.126	

Trade Union Presence and Employer-Provided Training   / 543

TABLE A.1 (cont.)

SUMMARY STATISTICS

	Male Manual		Male Nonmanual		Female Manual		Female Nonmanual	
	Mean	SD	Mean	SD	Mean	SD	Mean	SD
Associate professional	0.000		0.204		0.000		0.129	
Clerical	0.000		0.128		0.000		0.569	
Craft and skilled service	0.318		0.000		0.075		0.000	
Personal and protective service	0.049		0.000		0.125		0.000	
Sales	0.107		0.000		0.397		0.000	
Operative and assembly	0.374		0.000		0.174		0.000	
Other	0.152		0.000		0.229		0.000	
Tenure								
Less than 1 year	0.184		0.150		0.219		0.182	
1 to less than 2 years	0.112		0.138		0.162		0.134	
2 to less than 5 years	0.213		0.218		0.230		0.252	
5 to less than 10 years	0.203		0.218		0.200		0.238	
10 years or more	0.284		0.275		0.188		0.191	
Size of workplace								
10–499 employees	0.680		0.634		0.700		0.651	
500 1499 employees	0.136		0.174		0.075		0.121	
More than 1500 employees	0.080		0.076		0.030		0.050	
Number of employees in U.K.								
1–49	0.005		0.003		0.012		0.006	
50–99	0.016		0.014		0.015		0.017	
100–499	0.076		0.110		0.050		0.085	
500 999	0.052		0.064		0.019		0.058	
1000–9999	0.255		0.267		0.206		0.230	
More than 10,000	0.267		0.242		0.373		0.223	
Time at current address								
1–4 years	0.118		0.169		0.133		0.175	
5–9 years	0.146		0.187		0.202		0.200	
10–24 years	0.225		0.233		0.317		0.291	
More than 25 years	0.509		0.409		0.342		0.330	
Financial performance								
Above average	0.510		0.517		0.571		0.555	
Below average	0.077		0.065		0.074		0.046	
Fixed-term contract	0.064		0.045		0.063		0.045	
Franchise business	0.044		0.025		0.016		0.017	
Under foreign ownership	0.235		0.236		0.099		0.139	
Headquarters of company	0.076		0.146		0.067		0.149	
Unemployment rate	4.823	(0.07)	4.700	(0.06)	4.852	(0.08)	4.721	(0.06)
Vacancy rate	1.078	(0.01)	1.033	(0.01)	1.075	(0.01)	1.020	(0.01)
N	4,679		4,666		3,267		4,718	

TABLE A.2

INCIDENCE OF TRAINING ESTIMATES (SURVEY PROBIT REGRESSION), PRIVATE-SECTOR WORKERS (SPECIFICATIONS 1 AND 2, ESTIMATED MARGINAL EFFECTS)

	Male manual		Male Nonmanual		Female manual		Female Nonmanual	
	Marginal Effects	SE	MEs	SE	MEs	SE	MEs	SE
Specification 1								
TU recognized	0.105*	(0.033)	0.104*	(0.035)	−0.024	(0.041)	0.096*	(0.032)
Part time	−0.053	(0.043)	−0.164*	(0.064)	−0.040	(0.030)	−0.079*	(0.032)
Part time * TU recognition	−0.219*	(0.068)	0.172	(0.105)	−0.053	(0.053)	−0.085	(0.053)
Multisite establishment	0.120**	(0.063)	−0.052	(0.073)	0.217	(0.060)	0.154*	(0.057)
Specification 2								
TU recognized	0.090*	(0.033)	0.101*	(0.034)	−0.013	(0.041)	0.114*	(0.031)
Part time	−0.061	(0.043)	−0.162*	(0.062)	−0.036	(0.030)	−0.077*	(0.031)
Part time * TU recognition	−0.201*	(0.070)	0.174**	(0.105)	−0.057	(0.052)	−0.086**	(0.052)
Multisite establishment	0.117**	(0.062)	−0.050	(0.073)	0.203*	(0.057)	0.131*	(0.053)
Difficulties filling vacancies	0.015	(0.026)	0.045	(0.028)	−0.017	(0.029)	0.049**	(0.029)
EU work's council (EWC)	−0.017	(0.037)	0.060**	(0.035)	−0.073	(0.046)	0.038	(0.040)
Few competitors	−0.036	(0.038)	−0.017	(0.039)	−0.051	(0.051)	−0.036	(0.039)
Many competitors	−0.056	(0.035)	−0.019	(0.033)	0.001	(0.048)	−0.014	(0.033)
N	4,679		4,666		3,267		4,718	

NOTE: "Closed shop" is 1 if either "TU member to get job," "TU member to keep job," or "Ought to be TU member" is equal to 1, and zero otherwise. Specification 1 also includes age, education, race, occupation, job tenure, size of the workplace and of the organization, whether fixed-term contract, SIC codes, unemployment rate, and vacancy rate as covariates. Specification 2 as specification 1 plus time at current address, whether franchise, whether company is foreign-owned, financial performance, and whether workplace is the headquarters of the company. Employees in establishments with 10 or more employees. Estimations are weighted.
**(*)Indicates significance at the 5% (10%) level.

TABLE A.3

INCIDENCE OF TRAINING ESTIMATES (SURVEY PROBIT REGRESSION), PRIVATE-SECTOR WORKERS (SPECIFICATION 3, ESTIMATED MARGINAL EFFECTS)

	Male Manual		Male Nonmanual		Female Manual		Female Nonmanual	
	Marginal Effects	SE	MEs	SE	MEs	SE	MEs	SE
TU recognized	0.038	0.040	0.103*	0.039	−0.070	0.048	0.089*	0.036
Bargaining level * TU recognition								
Employers	−0.088**	0.050	0.009	0.069	−0.020	0.072	0.076	0.053
Organization	0.069**	0.036	−0.073	0.045	0.072	0.050	0.025	0.046
No recognition, but collective bargaining at workplace	−0.089	0.063	−0.061	0.078	−0.040	0.080	−0.053	0.074
Multiunionism * TU recognition								
Joint negotiations	0.133*	0.048	0.077**	0.045	0.106	0.096	0.007	0.047
Separate negotiations	0.049	0.047	−0.057	0.052	0.129**	0.071	0.055	0.060
Closed shop * TU recognition	−0.024	0.047	0.016	0.079	−0.018	0.072	−0.009	0.065
Part time	−0.060	0.044	−0.169*	0.062	−0.036	0.030	−0.076*	0.031
Part time * TU recognition	−0.186*	0.069	0.179**	0.104	−0.056	0.052	−0.083	0.053
Difficulties filling vacancies	0.012	0.027	0.033	0.027	−0.023	0.029	0.047**	0.029
EU work's council (EWC)	−0.024	0.036	0.059**	0.034	−0.070	0.048	0.044	0.040
Training negotiated	0.122	0.074	0.162*	0.060	0.069	0.159	0.173*	0.060
Few competitors	−0.030	0.037	−0.024	0.037	−0.046	0.052	−0.034	0.038
Many competitors	−0.042	0.035	−0.020	0.033	0.006	0.049	−0.012	0.033
Multisite establishment	0.132*	0.065	−0.042	0.073	0.199*	0.060	0.134*	0.052
N	4,679		4,666		3,267		4,718	

NOTE: "Closed shop" is 1 if either "TU member to get job," "TU member to keep job," or "Ought to be TU member" is equal to 1, and zero otherwise. The specification also includes age, education, race, occupation, job tenure, size of the workplace and of the organization, whether fixed-term contract, SIC codes, unemployment rate, vacancy rate, time at current address, whether franchise, whether company is foreign-owned, financial performance, and whether or not the workplace is the headquarters of the company. Employees in establishments with 10 or more employees. Estimations are weighted.
**(*)Indicates significance at the 5% (10%) level.

[14]

Southern Economic Journal 2004, 70(3), 566–583

The Impact of Minimum Wages on Job Training: An Empirical Exploration with Establishment Data

David Fairris* and Roberto Pedace†

Human capital theory suggests that workers may finance on-the-job training by accepting lower wages during the training period. Minimum wage laws could reduce job training, then, to the extent they prevent low-wage workers from offering sufficient wage cuts to finance training. Empirical findings on the relationship between minimum wages and job training have failed to reach a consensus. Previous research has relied primarily on survey data from individual workers that typically lack both detailed measures of job training and important information about the characteristics of firms. This study addresses the issue of minimum wages and on-the-job training with a unique employer survey. We find no evidence indicating that minimum wages reduce the average hours of training of trained employees and little to suggest that minimum wages reduce the percentage of workers receiving training.

1. Introduction

Human capital theory suggests that workers must contribute toward investments in job training and that one way in which they might do so is through reduced wages (Becker 1964). Minimum wage laws might be expected to reduce on-the-job training, then, to the extent they prevent workers from accepting lower wages (Rosen 1972).[1] Existing empirical studies of the relationship between minimum wages and job training yield divergent results. However, most of these studies utilize worker survey data that lack detailed measures of job training and establishment-level variables that are important

---

* Department of Economics, University of California, Riverside, CA 92521, USA; E-mail dfairris@ucrac1.ucr.edu.

† Department of Economics, University of Redlands, Redlands, CA 92373, USA; E-mail roberto_pedace@redlands.edu; corresponding author.

The authors thank Bill Carter, David Merrell, Mark Mildorf, Arnie Reznek, and Mary Streitwieser for their help in acquiring and creating the data. Robert Breunig, Craig Gundersen, David Neumark, Paul Sicilian, Jeffrey Wooldridge, participants of the Claremont McKenna College and UC-Riverside seminar series, and two anonymous referees provided valuable comments and suggestions on previous drafts of this paper. Financial support was provided by the UC Institute for Labor and Employment. The data used are confidential under Title 13 and 26, United States Code. Access was obtained through the Center for Economic Studies (CES) at the U.S. Census Bureau. Researchers can access this version of the National Employer Survey with a CES-approved proposal (see http://www.ces.census.gov/ces.php/home). A public-use version of the data is available (see http://www.irhe.upenn.edu/research/research-main.html). The findings and opinions expressed do not reflect the position of the institutions represented by the authors, the National Center for Postsecondary Improvement, the Consortium for Policy Research in Education, the National School-to-Work Office, or the U.S. Census Bureau.

Received March 2002; accepted February 2003.

[1] Workers and employers are likely to share in the costs of training, but the relative contributions depend on the type of training acquired. Typically, workers' relative contributions will be greater with general training because the rewards to these skills can be reaped with numerous employers. Firm-specific training, on the other hand, usually requires a smaller relative investment from workers. Minimum wages should therefore have a larger effect on general training, where the cost/wage contributions by workers are the greatest.

determinants of training. In this paper, we overcome these problems by using an establishment data set that possesses both good measures of job training and good establishment-level control variables.

The decision to offer training is ultimately made by the firm. Even if workers pay for some or all of their training through the acceptance of lower wages, their decision to undertake training is made largely by the choice of which firm to join. Thus, we believe the firm is the logical unit of analysis for exploring the issue of job training and minimum wages.

In the first section of the paper, we review the empirical literature on the impact of minimum wages on job training. The second and third sections discuss the empirical specification and data to be used in the analysis. The fourth section discusses the empirical results. We find little evidence linking minimum wages to reductions in the percentage of the establishment workforce receiving training and absolutely no evidence linking them to reduced hours of training per trained worker.

2. Review of the Literature

The empirical literature on the impact of minimum wages on job training is not voluminous. The earliest efforts focused primarily on wage growth as a proxy for training, producing mixed results. Two studies found age-earnings profiles to be significantly flatter for workers whose wages were bound to the minimum (Leighton and Mincer 1981; Hashimoto 1982), while a third study (Lazear and Miller 1981) found no statistically significant relationship between minimum wages and the slope of age-earnings profiles. Recent evidence has cast serious doubt on the validity of this entire approach.

Grossberg and Sicilian (1999) find that while minimum wages are indeed associated with reduced wage growth, they appear to have no significant impact on job training. Acemoglu and Pischke (1999) offer an insightful interpretation of these results. They claim that minimum wages eliminate part of the lower tail of the wage distribution, bunching workers around the wage minimum and thereby lowering the age-earnings profile quite independently of their impact on training. Thus, it seems clear that valid tests of the relationship between minimum wages and job training must be conducted with information on worker training and not simply wage growth.

There are only five empirical studies offering evidence on the impact of minimum wages directly on job training. The basic approach is to regress a measure of job training on a set of explanatory variables and a variable capturing the degree to which minimum wages act as a constraint on wage reductions. The hypothesis is that the more binding the minimum wage constraint, the less job training the worker and firm will undertake. There exist two levels of analysis in the literature, one operating at the state or regional level and the other operating at the level of the individual worker. Both have flaws.

Leighton and Mincer (1981) and Neumark and Wascher (2001) exploit variation in state wage minimums to explore the relationship between minimum wages and training. Both use data on individual workers, but their measures of the minimum wage exist at the state level. For example, Neumark and Wascher use the extent to which the state minimum wage exceeded the federal minimum over the previous three years. The results of both studies suggest that the higher the state minimum wage, the less likely it is that workers will receive on-the-job training.

However, there are several econometric problems plaguing this approach. First, these studies use state-level measures of minimum wages with individual-level data. Because the minimum wage variable exists at a higher level of aggregation than the unit of observation, the estimated standard error may understate the inaccuracy of the estimated coefficient (Moulton 1986), leading the researcher to perhaps mistakenly conclude that minimum wages reduce training when in fact they do not. A second concern is that the minimum wage variable may capture unobserved state effects on training that are correlated with minimum wages.[2]

Another approach to analyzing the impact of minimum wages on job training utilizes individual-level data only. Schiller (1994) and Grossberg and Sicilian (1999) adopt measures of the degree to which wages are bound by the minimum wage that vary at the level of the individual worker. Grossberg and Sicilian, for example, compare the impact on training of workers who are paid the minimum wage with those who earn both below the minimum and slightly more than the minimum. Schiller finds evidence that minimum wages reduce training, whereas Grossberg and Sicilian do not.

The problem with using minimum wage measures that vary at the level of the individual worker is that omitted determinants of training are likely to be correlated with the wage, which itself is used to assess the degree to which the minimum wage is binding. The estimated impact of minimum wages on training may well be biased as a result, the nature of the bias depending on the exact specification employed. For example, while it is possible that binding minimum wages reduce training, it is most probable that job training raises wages and thereby makes workers' wages less bound by the minimum wage. The wage component of the minimum wage measure is, therefore, likely to be correlated with left-out determinants of training, biasing the estimated impact of minimum wages on training. And here, the bias is likely to be upward.[3]

Acemoglu and Pischke (1999) conduct a first-difference analysis of the individual worker training equation using panel data. Fixed components of the error term will be eliminated in this approach, thereby reducing the possible bias found in cross-sectional levels regressions. Acemoglu and Pischke find no evidence of a training effect of minimum wages in their results. However, their measure of on-the-job training is also a particularly blunt one—namely, the change in whether the worker received job training at the current firm.

Indeed, poor measures of job training plague this literature more generally. Probably the most common measure of training is a dichotomous variable indicating its existence or lack thereof. An important exception is the Grossberg and Sicilian (1999) study, which utilizes data from establishments. The job training information they use refers to the amount of job training given to the last-hired worker. Specifically, their training measure is the number of hours devoted to training over the first three months of tenure of the most recently hired worker. However, Grossberg and Sicilian are unable to account for many important establishment-level determinants of training.

In this paper, we utilize a unique data set on establishments that offers an interesting alternative to the data used in most of the existing literature. First, we have good measures of job training—the percentage of the workforce receiving training and the average hours of training conditional on receiving training. Second, we possess good measures of a number of establishment-level control variables, including labor turnover and employee fringe benefits levels, that are absent from most existing studies.

Efficiency wage theory suggests that firms may reduce costly turnover by paying higher wages (Akerlof and Yellen 1986). Thus, wages (and therefore the extent to which wages are bound by the minimum wage) may be negatively correlated with turnover. But turnover reduction may also be a prerequisite for on-the-job training (Prendergast 1993) and so an important determinant in the training equation. If turnover is related to both the measure of the minimum wage and to job training in the way we have claimed, the failure to control for turnover may bias upward the estimated impact of minimum

---

[2] Neumark and Wascher (2001) use a difference-in-difference approach that allows them to add state controls. We employ this technique in some of our empirical results later and discuss more fully at that time our concerns with this specification of the training equation.

[3] The Grossberg and Sicilian (1999) results are not subject to this type of bias because they use the starting wage of the worker.

wages on training. It is important to control for fringe benefits in an analysis of the minimum wage impact on training because training could be financed by accepting lower benefits levels rather than by accepting lower wages.

Economies of scale in training and a host of other considerations suggest to us that job training is likely to exist as a matter of policy at the establishment or firm level, thereby making the establishment the appropriate unit of analysis for any investigation of job training. Workers receive training by virtue of the firm to which they attach themselves. Focusing on the determinants of training solely from the worker's point of view might make sense in a world of costless mobility, where the public-good nature of training poses no real problem for individual choice (Tiebout 1956). However, the very mention of job training typically suggests a context in which there is greater attachment between worker and firm than ideal microeconomics models posit and therefore in which firm policy and firm-level variables matter.

3. Econometric Specification

The empirical approach we take resembles that of the existing literature, but we use two different measures of job training and incorporate a wide range of establishment-level control variables into the analysis. We begin with a simple training equation of the following form:

$$t_{js} = \alpha + \mathbf{x}'_{js}\beta + m_s\psi + \varepsilon_{js}, \tag{1}$$

where t_{js} is a measure of the job training provided by establishment j in state s, $\mathbf{x}_{js}$ is a vector of establishment characteristics (e.g., industry, workforce size, percentage of female workers, percentage of workers with a high school diploma, turnover, fringe benefits, and so on), and m_s is the difference between the state minimum wage and the federal minimum wage.[4]

In order to employ this measure of the minimum wage, we identify states with minimum wages above the federal minimum and assign to establishments in those states the value of the difference between the state and federal minimums; all remaining establishments receive a zero for this variable. In this specification, the minimum wage variable is measured at a higher level of aggregation (the state level) than is the unit of observation (the establishment level). Under such circumstances, the standard assumption of uncorrelated errors across the observations is violated, and the error structure will have the following form:

$$\varepsilon_{js} = \lambda_s + \varphi_{js}. \tag{2}$$

This may lead to possible downward bias in the standard errors of the estimated minimum wage effect, thereby allowing one to mistakenly find in favor of a statistically significant effect on training when no such effect exists. We therefore correct, in all of our results here, the standard errors for this "clustering" of observations at the state level using the technique recommended by Moulton (1986).

Another concern with this approach is that the minimum wage measure may capture state effects on training that are correlated with minimum wages. Suppose, for example, that states with higher minimum wages also possess policies—such as training subsidies or employment programs that yield better job matches—that lead to greater incentives for training by firms. In this case, the absence of state controls will tend to result in an underestimation of the negative effect of minimum wages on training.

---

[4] Aside from the minimum wage measure, the specification of the training equation closely resembles that of Lynch and Black (1998), who utilize an earlier version of the NES data.

To address this concern, we estimate the training equation utilizing a difference-in-difference estimation technique, similar to that of Neumark and Wascher (2001), that allows for the inclusion of state controls. Thus, the training equation becomes

$$t_{ijs} = \alpha + \mathbf{x}'_{js}\beta + \mathbf{s}'_s\gamma + \mathbf{d}'_{ijs}\delta + \mathbf{i}'_{ijs}\psi + \varepsilon_{ijs}, \qquad (3)$$

where t_{ijs} is a measure of training for occupation group i at establishment j in state s, $\mathbf{x}_{js}$ is a vector of establishment characteristics as in Equation 1, $\mathbf{s}_s$ is a vector of state dummy variables, $\mathbf{d}_{ijs}$ is a vector of dummy variables representing the occupation from which the observation was drawn, and $\mathbf{i}_{ijs}$ is a vector of interactions between the occupation dummies and the minimum wage measure used in Equation 1. Assuming that the training of managerial workers is unlikely to be affected by the minimum wage, they can be used as the base category in the vector of interactions. Controlling for state fixed effects, the causal effect of the minimum wage is captured by ψ, which reports the differential impact of the minimum wage on occupational categories that are more likely to be affected relative to an occupational category—namely, managerial workers—that is unlikely to be affected.

One drawback to this approach is that it assumes that the unobservables—state policy, for example—that are correlated with both the minimum wage and training have the same effect on all the occupational estimates of the minimum wage impact on training. This might be a quite restrictive assumption given that states with high minimum wages are also arguably more likely to possess active labor market policies that disproportionately affect the training needs of low-skill workers. In addition, we must also restrict all the establishment characteristics to have the same effect on training for all occupational groups.

Another drawback, one that the difference-in-difference approach shares with the specification in Equation 1, is that the minimum wage variable is a rather blunt measure of the extent to which minimum wages are binding on establishments. This measure varies only at the state level and indeed only among those states with minimum wages greater than the federal minimum.

Thus, in a final specification of the training equation, we utilize a measure of minimum wages that operates at the establishment and occupation level rather than the state level. This training equation is as follows:

$$t_{ijs} = \alpha_i + \mathbf{x}'_{js}\beta_i + \mathbf{s}'_s\gamma_i + \frac{m_s}{w_{ijs}}\psi_i + \varepsilon_{ijs} \qquad (4)$$

where t_{ijs} is a measure of training for occupation group i at establishment j in state s, $\mathbf{x}_{js}$ is a vector of establishment characteristics as in Equations 1 and 3, $\mathbf{s}_s$ is a vector of state dummies as in Equation 3, m_s is the applicable state minimum wage, and w_{ijs} is the average wage for the occupation in each establishment.[5] The i subscripts on the parameters indicate that the training equation is estimated individually for each occupational category.

This approach identifies the minimum wage impact on training by exploring whether establishments whose average establishment or occupation wage is closer to the state minimum wage offer less training. Unfortunately, this approach raises a number of challenging specification issues. Most important, it is plagued by the presence of the establishment wage on the right-hand side of the training equation. While the extent of job training may be related to how bound wages are to the minimum wage, it

---

[5] Acemoglu and Pischke (1999) construct a similar variable that measures the ratio of the minimum wage to the average wage in the MSA (Metropolitan Statistical Area). However, since wages can vary considerably within MSAs, even less aggregation may be appropriate. We construct a minimum wage measure that captures the extent to which workers in given occupational groups are, on average, bound by the minimum wage at their place of employment.

is also true that training affects wages. Thus, left-out determinants of training may be correlated with the establishment average wage. Where necessary, then, we must correct for endogeneity bias by instrumenting the average wage variable, raising all the attendant problems and pitfalls such a correction entails.

A final concern we have with all the estimated training equations stems from the high incidence of censoring among the establishment responses to the survey questions on training. Roughly 17% of the establishments in our sample report that they offer no training at all to their workers, and approximately 16% report that they train all their workers. This clustering of values for the dependent variable raises the possibility of censored regression bias in our results. To correct for this, we estimate both training equations with a Tobit maximum likelihood estimation technique and report these results as well.[6] The "hours of training" regressions are estimated with lower-limit censoring, and the "percentage trained" regressions are estimated with both lower- and upper-limit censoring.

4. Data

This study utilizes the 1997 National Employer Survey (NES), supplemented with Standard Statistical Establishment List (SSEL) data. The SSEL is the U.S. Census Bureau's master list of all establishments and enterprises in the United States. It provides the sampling frame for the Census Bureau's economic censuses and surveys, including the NES. We use the SSEL to establish the geographical location of firms in our survey, without which we would be unable to assign the relevant minimum wage level to each surveyed firm. The 1995 SSEL serves as the sampling frame for the 1997 NES.

Survey data were collected with a computer-assisted telephone interview (CATI). The sample was evenly divided between manufacturers and nonmanufacturers, with explicit oversampling of establishments that have 100 or more employees and implicit oversampling of manufacturers because they are greatly outnumbered by nonmanufacturers in the SSEL universe. Establishments in California, Kentucky, Maryland, Michigan, and Pennsylvania were also oversampled in order to support in-depth analysis of school reforms of interest to the survey sponsors (the National Center for Postsecondary Improvement, the Consortium for Policy Research in Education, and the National School-to-Work Office).

The survey was administered by the Census Bureau in the summer of 1997 and asked establishments about conditions in 1996.[7] It represents the responses of approximately 5400 establishments for a 78% overall response rate. This is higher than the response rate for other establishment surveys but is similar to that of the 1994 NES (Lynch and Black 1998). After deleting observations with missing values on the variables of interest, we were left with 1098 valid observations. All our descriptive statistics and regression results are calculated from this sample of firms. The

---

[6] Papke and Wooldridge (1996) suggest the use of a quasi–maximum likelihood logit estimator (QMLE) for fractional response–dependent variables. In the case of our "percentage trained" variable, both the Tobit and QMLE provide different but reasonable functional forms for the conditional mean. The advantage of the QMLE is that it requires specification only of the conditional mean, while the Tobit requires the specification of the entire distribution and, therefore, relies heavily on the normality (and joint normality) assumptions. The Tobit estimates can be sensitive to specification, but the QMLE provides consistent estimates even in the presence of functional form misspecification (Papke and Wooldridge 1996; Johnston and DiNardo 1997). We check the robustness of our Tobit estimates by also estimating Equations 3 and 4 with a QMLE.

[7] In October 1996 the federal minimum wage increased from \$4.25 to \$4.75, so we assign a weighted average to represent the minimum wage for that year.

Table 1. States with Minimum Wages That Exceeded the Federal Minimum Wage

	Minimum Wage in 1996	Weighted Gap
Federal	4.25/4.75	
Alaska	4.75	0.375
Connecticut	4.27	0.000
Delaware	4.65	0.275
District of Columbia	5.25	0.875
Hawaii	5.25	0.875
Iowa	4.65	0.275
New Jersey	5.05	0.675
Oregon	4.75	0.375
Rhode Island	4.45	0.075
Vermont	4.75	0.375
Washington	4.90	0.525

In 1996, the federal minimum wage was not implemented until October 1. All other minimum wages were implemented at the beginning of the calendar year. The minimum wage gaps are calculated using a weighted average of the federal minimum wage (i.e., $4.375).

presence of oversampled establishments requires the use of the provided weights in order to produce representative statistics and parameter estimates. Table 1 displays the minimum wage in cases where the state minimum exceeded the federal minimum. Table 2A provides descriptive statistics for the variables used in the analysis.

While previous studies often rely on dichotomous measures of training (e.g., whether the individual received training), the NES offers two detailed measures of job training: the "percentage of workers trained" and the "average number of hours devoted to training" in the establishment. The survey questions regarding job training begin with the following statement:

> I am now going to ask you some questions about structured or formal training that your employees experience. This training may be offered at your establishment or at another location, and may occur during working hours or at other times. Structured training includes all types of training activities that have a pre-defined objective. Examples of structured or formal training include seminars, lectures, workshops, audio-visual presentations, apprenticeships, and structured on-the-job training.

This is followed by specific questions regarding training:

> In the past year, how many workers received formal instruction, and what was the approximate average number of hours of training per employee?

The responses to this question are used to construct our dependent training measures.

Tables 2B and 2C provide descriptive measures of training by occupation and firm size, respectively.[8] While the support staff in the average establishment receives markedly less training than do supervisors, in general there is less variation across occupational categories in both the percentage of workers trained and the average hours of training than was expected. Training investments vary by establishment size in the expected way—namely, there exists more training in larger establishments.

The data set contains measures of labor turnover and a host of other variables that affect the firm's decision to offer training. Some, such as the gender and racial composition and average level of schooling of the workforce, mirror the kinds of variables one finds in estimated training regressions using worker-level survey data. Others, such as the quality of the local high school, are important

---

[8] Note, however, that we do not have the ability to distinguish general training from firm-specific training.

Table 2A. Descriptive Statistics for the Explanatory Variables

Variable	Mean	Standard Deviation
Employment and sales		
50–99 employees	0.1430	0.3502
100–249 employees	0.2240	0.4171
250–999 employees	0.3752	0.4844
1000 or more employees	0.1494	0.3566
Multiple-establishment firm	0.7031	0.4571
Employment increased in past three years	0.4827	0.4999
Employment decreased in past three years	0.2140	0.4103
Turnover rate	19.0276	185.7143
Average number of weeks to fill a position	3.3342	3.0289
Natural log of total sales	17.4848	1.7816
Region		
Establishment located in West	0.1639	0.3704
Establishment located in Midwest	0.2996	0.4583
Establishment located in South	0.3770	0.4849
Workforce characteristics		
% 18+ with a high school diploma	31.2046	6.5922
% 18+ with a bachelor's degree	12.5718	4.9626
Number of permanent part-time workers	25.8315	143.4752
Number of temporary workers	18.1521	105.4377
% of female workers	38.5591	23.5415
% of minority workers	25.9598	24.3694
% of frontline workers	58.6984	23.9328
% of support staff workers	12.7694	12.4860
% of technician workers	10.5807	12.9012
% of supervisory workers	7.6821	5.0851
% of nonsupervisors unionized	23.2995	37.6262
Quality of local high school unacceptable	0.0219	0.1463
Quality of local high school barely acceptable	0.1658	0.3720
Quality of local high school acceptable	0.5692	0.4954
Quality of local high school more than adequate	0.1821	0.3861
Quality of local high school outstanding	0.0146	0.1199
Workplace organization		
% of nonmanagement in self-managed teams	17.7716	29.5405
% of nonsupervisors in job rotation	22.4222	30.6450
Benefits		
Establishment contributes to pension or severance	0.8707	0.3357
Establishment contributes to medical or dental	0.9927	0.0851
Establishment contributes to child care or family leave	0.7514	0.4324
Establishment contributes to life insurance	0.9517	0.2144
Establishment contributes to sick pay or vacation	0.9945	0.0738
Minimum wage		
State minimum wage	4.4115	0.1381
State minimum wage minus federal minimum wage	0.0365	0.1381

This table includes all the explanatory variables in the regressions except the categorical industry and the establishment- and occupation-specific minimum wage variables.

Table 2B. Descriptive Statistics for Training and Wage Variables by Occupation

Variable	Mean	Standard Deviation
All		
% of workers receiving training	58.0761	36.9062
Average number of hours trained	27.6146	43.8773
Average wage	14.1039	4.2221
Front line		
% of workers receiving training	59.2058	40.8478
Average number of hours trained	28.1876	48.9843
Average wage	12.7150	7.2125
Support staff		
% of workers receiving training	54.2217	39.3727
Average number of hours trained	20.4044	30.1949
Average wage	12.2880	3.5758
Technical		
% of workers receiving training	61.7915	39.5289
Average number of hours trained	30.9882	48.9026
Average wage	16.0765	4.9419
Supervisory		
% of workers receiving training	65.0735	39.9918
Average number of hours trained	27.5455	38.1044
Average wage	16.7594	4.8256
Managerial		
% of workers receiving training	59.8867	40.1285
Average number of hours trained	27.8470	49.2504
Average wage	23.1587	7.8222

worker-related determinants of job training that are rarely found in individual survey data.[9] And still others, such as whether the establishment has recently increased employment or is experimenting with new forms of workplace organization (e.g., self-managed teams or job rotation), are establishment-level variables that clearly impact training but are virtually impossible to obtain from worker survey data.

5. Results

In Table 3, we present the results of ordinary least squares (OLS) training regressions using the specification in Equation 1.[10] In Table 4, the results from the difference-in-difference specification in Equation 3 are presented, with managerial workers as the base occupation. The estimated coefficients for the various control variables are omitted in order to conserve space (see the Appendix for estimated coefficients of the other explanatory variables from the column 1, Table 4, results).

---

[9] The quality of the local high school may affect how much firms rely on in-house training programs for the transmission of basic skills. This effect will be less significant to the degree that workers migrate across district boundaries.

[10] Given Royalty's (1996) and Grossberg's (2000) results, we were concerned about possible endogeneity bias in the estimated coefficient on labor turnover. However, Hausman–Wu tests (Greene 2000) failed to reject the null hypothesis of exogeneity in any of the results we present here. Turnover was instrumented with the "percentage of workers unionized" as the identifying variable.

Table 2C. Descriptive Statistics for Training and Wage Variables by Firm Size

Variable	Mean	Standard Deviation
1–49 employees		
% of workers receiving training	48.8899	42.3634
Average number of hours trained	27.2904	72.7526
Average wage	14.6345	4.2177
50–99 employees		
% of workers receiving training	44.3509	39.6647
Average number of hours trained	18.1832	24.6551
Average wage	13.6102	3.6745
100–249 employees		
% of workers receiving training	55.2653	37.2239
Average number of hours trained	25.0227	31.8413
Average wage	13.6613	4.3466
250–999 employees		
% of workers receiving training	63.6000	33.9529
Average number of hours trained	31.3155	43.2826
Average wage	13.7479	3.9130
1000+ employees		
% of workers receiving training	68.2201	30.6076
Average number of hours trained	31.4688	46.3714
Average wage	15.7495	4.8356

The results in the first row of column 1, Table 3, suggest that establishments in states with minimum wages that exceed the federal minimum train a smaller percentage of their workforce. The estimated effect is not only statistically significant but quantitatively significant as well. A 50-cent increase in the state minimum wage, holding the federal minimum wage constant, reduces the fraction of workers receiving training by over 15 percentage points. Evaluated at the mean, this translates into roughly a 25% reduction in the fraction of workers receiving training.

In the first row of column 2, we present the results for the "average hours of training" regression. In this regression, the estimated coefficient on the minimum wage variable is not statistically significantly different from zero. Thus, while minimum wages reduce the percentage of the workforce receiving training in this specification, they appear to have no impact on the average hours of training among trained employees.

Greater insight into these results may be achieved through an analysis of the job training impact of minimum wages on specific occupational groups. In the column 2 results, although average hours of training for the trained workforce as a whole do not appear to change in response to the minimum wage, it is possible that some occupational groups receive fewer hours of training while other occupational groups receive more hours of training as the minimum wage becomes more binding in a plant. This is entirely consistent with theory, which predicts that, in response to a minimum wage, employers may upgrade their technology of production and invest greater amounts of job training in fewer, more highly skilled workers. The lost training for those low-skilled workers who are finance constrained by the existence of minimum wages are merely transferred to more highly skilled, less-finance-constrained workers. While our occupational categories are rather broad and so may disguise training substitution effects of this sort within occupations, we find no evidence in the

Table 3. The Effect of Minimum Wages on Percentage of Workers Trained and Hours of Training Using a State-Level Minimum Wage Measure

Occupational Group	Dependent Variable: Percentage of Workers Trained	Average Hours of Training per Worker
All		
Estimate	−33.2047	−6.4543
Standard error	(11.9402)	(12.3958)
R^2	0.4296	0.1924
Front line		
Estimate	−38.5873	−6.1059
Standard error	(13.5612)	(14.3963)
R^2	0.4153	0.1985
Support staff		
Estimate	−11.3607	−14.5429
Standard error	(12.1278)	(10.9801)
R^2	0.4161	0.2447
Technical		
Estimate	−40.0778	−0.0762
Standard error	(15.2753)	(15.3427)
R^2	0.3602	0.1691
Supervisory		
Estimate	−19.8936	−9.2563
Standard error	(13.0260)	(9.0628)
R^2	0.4138	0.2027
Managerial		
Estimate	−28.6259	−3.6990
Standard error	(13.2516)	(8.4537)
R^2	0.3958	0.2288

The sample size is 1098 for all regressions. All equations include the remaining variables in the table of descriptive statistics in addition to 20 industry dummies. Standard errors, which are adjusted for state group effects, are in parentheses.

occupation-specific results of column 2 to suggest that some workers receive greater training as the result of more binding minimum wages.

Turning to the column 1 results, we see that the reduction in the percentage of workers trained as a result of greater minimum wages takes place across the occupational distribution: among frontline workers and technical workers but also among management, the highest paid of the occupational categories. Because we expect that minimum wages are unlikely to affect the training of managerial workers, this finding seems to us an indication that the results of this specification are tainted by omitted-variable bias.

In Table 4 we present the results of the difference-in-difference approach, which, because it focuses on relative training effects, allows us to net out the effect of unobservables that may be producing bias in the results of Table 3 by adding state effects. The results from column 1 of Table 4 suggest that the relative percentage of workers trained is not affected for any of the included occupational groups by a difference between the state and the federal minimum wage. In column 2, the results are presented for the "average hours of training" regression. In this regression, the estimated relative minimum wage effects are also insignificantly different from zero, and the quantitative impacts on training are extremely

Table 4. Difference-in-Difference Estimates of the Effects of Minimum Wages on the Percentage of Workers Trained and Hours of Training

Occupational Group	Dependent Variable: Percentage of Workers Trained	Average Hours of Training per Worker
Front line		
Estimate	−2.3420	0.2407
Standard error	(14.9700)	(13.1012)
Support staff		
Estimate	6.5899	−4.7185
Standard error	(15.4666)	(9.8664)
Technical		
Estimate	−12.5184	8.7051
Standard error	(15.4672)	(14.1721)
Supervisory		
Estimate	6.4784	−1.4752
Standard error	(16.3385)	(9.3511)
R^2	0.4338	0.2143
Hausman–Wu	0.29	0.50

The base category is managerial workers. All equations include the remaining variables in the table of descriptive statistics in addition to 20 industry dummies and state fixed effects. Standard errors, which are adjusted for group effects, are in parentheses.

small. Possessing a state minimum wage that is higher than the federal minimum by 50 cents decreases the training of frontline workers relative to managers by roughly one percentage point.

While none of the estimated coefficients in Table 4 is statistically significant, the alternating negative/positive pattern is interesting and perhaps suggestive of substitution effects of the minimum wage on training. Interestingly, the alternating positive/negative pattern is exactly the opposite in the "percentage trained" and "average hours of training" regressions, which suggests that when the minimum wage causes firms to train fewer workers, firms increase the average hours of training of those workers who continue to receive training.

Ultimately, though, these results suggest that minimum wages have absolutely no effect on either the extensive (percentage of workers trained) or the intensive (hours of training per trained employee) margins. Thus, the difference-in-difference results offer considerable evidence to suggest that the Table 3 results are biased.

The integrity of the difference-in-difference results rests on the assumption that unobservables such as state policy affect the impact of minimum wages on training similarly for every occupational group. However, there are reasons to believe this assumption may be in error, suggesting that we attempt to identify the minimum wage impact on training separately for each occupation. Moreover, both the difference-in-difference specification and the simple state-level specification of Equation 1 utilize a minimum wage measure that is especially blunt in that it varies at the state level only and indeed only for states that have enacted a minimum wage higher than the federal minimum.

The results reported in Table 5 utilize an alternative minimum wage variable, one that measures the extent to which state minimum wages are binding for workers in a given firm and occupation and that incorporates state fixed effects whose impacts vary across occupational categories. The challenge posed by estimating this specification of the training equation is that the average wage variable must be instrumented in order to avoid endogeneity bias. We have used the "percentage of workers unionized" and the "natural log of total sales" in the establishment as identifying variables in this

Table 5. The Effect of Minimum Wages on Percentage of Workers Trained and Hours of Training Using Establishment- and Occupation-Level Minimum Wage Measures

Occupational Group	Dependent Variable: Percentage of Workers Trained	Average Hours of Training per Worker
All		
Estimate	−41.0771	10.7036
Standard error	(22.9898)	(43.4677)
R^2	0.5336	0.2649
Hausman–Wu	2.01	0.01
Front line		
Estimate	−7.1464	−19.5497
Standard error	(16.6077)	(14.8701)
R^2	0.5390	0.2805
Hausman–Wu	1.68	0.96
Support staff		
Estimate	−211.4745	10.7424
Standard error	(58.2997)	(21.3342)
Corrected standard error	(77.1454)	
R^2	0.5197	0.3945
Hausman–Wu	3.63**	0.40
Technical		
Estimate	7.2278	22.7799
Standard error	(27.0670)	(31.5805)
R^2	0.4720	0.2253
Hausman–Wu	0.63	1.78
Supervisory		
Estimate	−117.6360	71.2078
Standard error	(50.4879)	(41.4297)
Corrected standard error	(58.8394)	
R^2	0.5449	0.2848
Hausman–Wu	2.34*	1.37
Managerial		
Estimate	−1.5424	50.9651
Standard error	(29.6088)	(36.1476)
R^2	0.5451	0.2806
Hausman–Wu	0.97	0.07

All equations include the remaining variables in the table of descriptive statistics in addition to 20 industry dummies and state fixed effects. Standard errors, which are adjusted for state group effects, are in parentheses. * and ** indicate that the Hausman–Wu test statistic is large enough to reject the null hypothesis of exogeneity at the 5% and 1% level of significance, respectively. In those cases, the two-stage results are reported.

instrumental variables (IV) procedure. While unions affect wages and thereby training levels indirectly, they seldom have direct effects on training through collective bargaining agreements. Higher sales may affect wages through rent sharing but should not affect training directly.

Results from Generalized Method of Moments specification tests suggest that these are indeed valid identifying variables in the overall system of structural equations (Hausman 1978; Newey 1985). They are statistically significant determinants of average wages across establishments but have no independent effect on training other than through their impact on average wages. We have utilized the instrumental variables procedure only when a Hausman test revealed statistically significant evidence of endogeneity bias in the OLS regression results.[11]

The results in column 1 indicate that there are negative minimum wage effects on training for the workforce as a whole and that these negative effects are restricted to two of the occupational groups. Specifically, support staff and supervisory workers appear to witness statistically significant reductions in the percentage of workers trained as a result of higher minimum wages. A 50-cent increase in the minimum wage, *ceteris paribus*, reduces the fraction of support staff and supervisory workers receiving training by roughly eight and three percentage points, respectively. Evaluated at the mean, this translates into a 15% reduction for support staff workers and a 5% reduction for supervisory workers. The results in column 2 lend support to earlier findings suggesting that minimum wages have no effect on the hours that workers are trained.

The largest of the estimated minimum wage effects on training is for support staff workers, which is consistent with their economic position in the firm. Of the five occupational categories that can be identified with our data, this occupation has the lowest average wage and therefore should be most bound by the minimum wage. However, the negative estimated effect for supervisory workers, although smaller, is not as easily explained. The average wage of supervisory workers is significantly larger than that of either support staff or frontline workers.

While we believe this specification has several virtues that the other specifications lack, we are also less than fully satisfied with the IV procedures employed and with the robustness of our findings. The establishment unionization rate, for example, is an important determinant of frontline or technical workers' pay but less so of manager or supervisor pay, yet the minimum wage bindingness variable exhibited no signs of endogeneity bias in either of the former two occupational training regressions but did so in the supervisor training regression.

More important, the only two instances in which we find evidence of a negative training effect of minimum wages among the occupation regressions are the two cases in which Hausman tests revealed the need for an IV procedure. The OLS estimated coefficients on the bindingness variables in these two cases are far from statistically significant, and their magnitudes are smaller by 10-fold than the IV results. While we have followed strict statistical procedures in arriving at these estimates, the dramatic change in magnitudes when IVs are used, coupled with the fact that negative and statistically significant training effects are found only in those instances where instrumental variables are employed, leaves us with some concern for the integrity of these results.

In Tables 6 and 7, we replicate the regressions of Tables 4 and 5 but correct for the censored nature of the dependent variable using a Tobit estimation procedure.[12] Qualitatively, the results are entirely consistent with the regressions that ignore the censored nature of the dependent variable. As in Table 4, the Table 6 results suggest that minimum wages do not alter the percentage of the establishment workforce receiving training or the hours of training per employee.[13]

For the Table 7 regressions, in cases where the average wage must be instrumented, the non-linear nature of the Tobit estimates requires that we give special attention to the standard errors. There are two instances where a two-stage estimation is required—the "percentage trained" regressions for

---

[11] We reject the null hypothesis of exogeneity in only 2 of the 10 regressions. In all but these two cases, then, we are able to treat the average wage as exogenous.

[12] In order to compare the Tobit results to the uncensored estimates, they must be multiplied by an adjustment factor. The estimated effect is given by $\frac{\delta E[t|\cdot]}{\delta m} = \Phi(\frac{i}{\sigma})\psi$, where Φ is the standard normal cumulative distribution function and i is calculated using the mean values for the explanatory variables. For ease of interpretation, this adjustment factor is included in each of the relevant tables.

[13] Our QMLE results yield the same conclusions—there are no significant minimum wage effects on training.

Table 6. Tobit Difference-in-Difference Estimates of the Effects of Minimum Wages on the Percentage of Workers Trained and Hours of Training

Occupational Group	Dependent Variable: Percentage of Workers Trained	Average Hours of Training per Worker
Front line		
Estimate	−12.5407	0.4814
Standard error	(39.5420)	(18.7843)
Support staff		
Estimate	6.4306	−5.7485
Standard error	(42.4360)	(15.5504)
Technical		
Estimate	−35.4213	10.3315
Standard error	(43.2113)	(19.2656)
Supervisory		
Estimate	16.1544	−1.6631
Standard error	(46.4181)	(15.3457)
$\Phi(\hat{t}/\sigma)$	0.7764	0.7224
Wald chi-squared	605.36	622.63

The base category is managerial workers. All equations include the remaining variables in the table of descriptive statistics in addition to 20 industry dummies and state fixed effects. Standard errors, which are adjusted for group effects, are in parentheses. The degrees of freedom for the Wald chi-squared statistics are 61 for the percentage of workers trained regression and 104 for the average hours of training per worker regression.

support staff and supervisory workers. Murphy and Topel (1985) define a covariance matrix for the nonlinear least squares estimator that accounts for the variability in the explanatory variable that is introduced through the two-step procedure.[14] However, our first-stage regressions are used to obtain predicted values for the average establishment wage, which are then used to construct our establishment-level minimum wage measure. Consequently, the Murphy–Topel correction is not directly applicable in this case. In the two instances in which we utilize a two-stage Tobit estimation, we account for the variation in the first stage and correct the standard errors using a bootstrap procedure. This has been shown to produce reliable standard error estimates when these cannot be derived analytically (Johnston and DiNardo 1997).[15]

Nevertheless, we continue to find statistically significant negative minimum wage effects for support staff and supervisory workers. Moreover, quantitatively, the estimated impacts of minimum wages on training using the Tobit specification are larger. In the Table 5 results, for example, a 50-cent difference between the state and federal minimum wages reduces the fraction of support staff workers receiving training by eight percentage points. This compares with a 17-percentage-point reduction in Table 7. Once again, there are no significant minimum wage effects on hours of training.[16]

---

[14] Generally, this adjustment leads to an increase in the computed standard errors.

[15] Jeong and Maddala (1993) have argued that most applications using standard errors for the purpose of hypothesis testing are useless because of unreliable distributional assumptions and should, therefore, use the bootstrap method directly.

[16] The QMLE results also indicate negative minimum wage effects only on the percentage of support staff and supervisors trained. Moreover, the QMLE magnitudes are nearly identical to those using the Tobit procedure.

Table 7. Tobit Estimates of the Effect of Minimum Wages on Percentage of Workers Trained and Hours of Training Using Establishment- and Occupation-Level Minimum Wage Measure

Occupational Group	Dependent Variable: Percentage of Workers Trained	Average Hours of Training per Worker
All		
Estimate	−95.6686	−10.0012
Standard error	(40.7012)	(61.1640)
Wald chi-squared	898.99	572.79
$\Phi(\hat{t}/\sigma)$	0.9049	0.7291
N left-censored	189	189
N right-censored	172	0
Front line		
Estimate	−24.7889	−26.5001
Standard error	(38.1088)	(20.8376)
Wald chi-squared	369.25	694.70
$\Phi(\hat{t}/\sigma)$	0.8289	0.7357
N left-censored	189	189
N right-censored	423	0
Support staff		
Estimate	−531.5070	11.1665
Standard error	(133.4764)	(29.3706)
Corrected standard error	(174.2821)	
Wald chi-squared	466.90	2528.92
$\Phi(\hat{t}/\sigma)$	0.8238	0.7157
N left-censored	189	189
N right-censored	340	0
Technical		
Estimate	−34.7793	32.1258
Standard error	(90.7214)	(43.1963)
Wald chi-squared	22.84	193.62
$\Phi(\hat{t}/\sigma)$	0.7324	0.7054
N left-censored	189	189
N right-censored	430	0
Supervisory		
Estimate	−281.2885	94.8657
Standard error	(141.6928)	(53.5086)
Corrected standard error	(180.6712)	
Wald chi-squared	257.30	357.38
$\Phi(\hat{t}/\sigma)$	0.8106	0.7486
N left-censored	189	189
N right-censored	491	0
Managerial		
Estimate	−36.1474	45.3279
Standard error	(121.9013)	(44.2573)
Wald chi-squared	223.60	196.23
$\Phi(\hat{t}/\sigma)$	0.8289	0.7454
N left-censored	189	189
N right-censored	399	0

All equations include the remaining variables in the table of descriptive statistics in addition to 20 industry dummies and state fixed effects. Standard errors, which are adjusted for state group effects, are in parentheses. The degrees of freedom for the Wald chi-squared statistics are 54 for the percentage of workers trained regression and 95 for the average hours of training per worker regression.

6. Conclusions

This study utilizes establishment-level data to explore the impact of minimum wages on job training. The decision to offer training ultimately rests with firms, and so we believe the firm is the logical unit of analysis for exploring this issue. Using establishment data provides the opportunity to control for establishment-level variables, such as turnover and the provision of fringe benefits, which have been absent from previous analyses of training because of the reliance on individual worker data.

In our view, problematic specification issues plague all existing approaches to the estimation of the impact of minimum wages on job training, ours included. Nonetheless, one finding that is consistent across all specifications of the training equation is that minimum wage policies have no significant impact on the average hours of training for workers who receive training. The evidence on whether minimum wages reduce the percentage of the workforce receiving training is more mixed. Among occupations for which it is plausible to expect a negative minimum wage impact on training, only support staff workers exhibited such an effect, and only in one of the three specifications of the training equation we estimated. Therefore, we think the most prudent conclusion to draw from this set of findings is that there is little evidence to suggest that minimum wages affect the percentage of the workforce receiving training.

Appendix
OLS Coefficient Estimates for "Percentage Trained" Regression of Equation 3

Variable	Estimate	Standard Error
Employment and sales		
50–99 employees	−1.5261	2.7524
100–249 employees	−0.0845	2.8994
250–999 employees	0.7913	3.2128
1000 or more employees	11.3054	3.7528
Multiple-establishment firm	6.7397	2.0466
Employment increased in past three years	3.4842	1.9556
Employment decreased in past three years	8.3347	3.1884
Turnover rate	−0.1212	0.0423
Workforce characteristics		
% 18+ with a high school diploma	1.8782	0.3428
% 18+ with a bachelors degree	1.1346	0.3512
Number of permanent part-time workers	−0.0244	0.0025
Number of temporary workers	0.0047	0.0087
% of female workers	0.1829	0.0561
% of minority workers	−0.0350	0.0498
% of frontline workers	0.1094	0.1129
% of support staff workers	0.2222	0.1397
% of technician workers	0.1455	0.1272
% of supervisory workers	−0.1280	0.2258
Quality of local high school unacceptable	−9.6451	7.4622
Quality of local high school barely acceptable	26.5028	4.6127
Quality of local high school acceptable	10.7400	3.9521
Quality of local high school more than adequate	12.2541	4.1207
Quality of local high school outstanding	−2.4334	6.4764
Workplace organization		
% of nonmanagement in self-managed teams	0.2791	0.0315
% of nonsupervisors in job rotation	0.0400	0.0346

Appendix
Continued

Variable	Estimate	Standard Error
Benefits		
Establishment contributes to pension or severance	6.8975	2.4343
Establishment contributes to medical or dental	−32.4541	11.9500
Establishment contributes to child care or family leave	13.6998	2.1177
Establishment contributes to life insurance	5.5753	4.3566
Establishment contributes to sick pay or vacation	−4.8653	7.4043
Occupation dummies		
Front line	0.4813	3.7696
Support staff	−5.1791	3.2538
Technical	9.4531	4.1630
Supervisory	3.0989	3.7876

This table excludes industry and state dummies.

References

Acemoglu, Daron, and Jorn-Steffen Pischke. 1999. Minimum wages and on-the-job training. NBER Working Paper No. 7184.

Akerlof, George A., and Janet L. Yellen. 1986. *Efficiency wage models of the labor market.* Cambridge, UK: Cambridge University Press.

Becker, Gary S. 1964. *Human capital: A theoretical and empirical analysis, with special reference to education.* New York: Columbia University Press.

Greene, William H. 2000. *Econometric analysis.* 4th edition. Englewood Cliffs, NJ: Prentice Hall.

Grossberg, Adam J. 2000. The effect of formal training on employment duration. *Industrial Relations* 39:578–99.

Grossberg, Adam J., and Paul Sicilian. 1999. Minimum wages, on-the-job training, and wage growth. *Southern Economic Journal* 65:539–56.

Hashimoto, Masanori. 1982. Minimum wage effects on training on the job. *American Economic Review* 72:1070–87.

Hausman, Jerry A. 1978. Specification tests in econometrics. *Econometrica* 46:1251–71.

Jeong, Jinook, and G. S. Maddala. 1993. A perspective on application of bootstrap methods in econometrics. In *Handbook of statistics,* edited by G. S. Maddala, C. R. Rao, and H. D. Vinod. Amsterdam: Elsevier, pp. 573–610.

Johnston, Jack, and John DiNardo. 1997. *Econometric methods.* 4th edition. New York: McGraw-Hill.

Lazear, Edward P., and Frederick H. Miller. 1981. Minimum wage versus minimum compensation. In *Report of the minimum wage study commission, 5.* Washington, DC: U.S. Government Printing Office, pp. 347–80.

Leighton, Linda, and Jacob Mincer. 1981. The effects of minimum wages on human capital formation. In *The economics of legal minimum wages,* edited by Simon Rottenberg. Washington, DC: American Enterprise Institute, pp. 155–73.

Lynch, Lisa M., and Sandra E. Black. 1998. Beyond the incidence of employer-provided training. *Industrial and Labor Relations Review* 52:64–81.

Moulton, Brent R. 1986. Random group effects and the precision of regression estimates. *Journal of Econometrics* 32:385–97.

Murphy, Kevin, and Robert Topel. 1985. Estimation and inference in two step econometric models. *Journal of Business and Economic Statistics* 3:370–9.

Neumark, David, and William Wascher. 2001. Minimum wages and training revisited. *Journal of Labor Economics* 19:563–95.

Newey, Whitney K. 1985. Generalized method of moments specification testing. *Journal of Econometrics* 29:229–56.

Papke, Lelie E., and Jeffrey M. Wooldridge. 1996. Econometric methods for fractional response variables with and application to 401(k) plan participation rates. *Journal of Applied Econometrics* 11:619–32.

Prendergast, Canice. 1993. The role of promotion in inducing specific human capital acquisition. *Quarterly Journal of Economics* 108:523–34.

Rosen, Sherwin. 1972. Learning and experience in the labor market. *Journal of Human Resources* 7:326–42.

Royalty, Anne Beeson. 1996. The effects of job turnover on the training of men and women. *Industrial and Labor Relation Review* 49:506–21.

Schiller, Bradley R. 1994. Moving up: The training and wage gains of minimum-wage entrants. *Social Science Quarterly* 75:622–36.

Tiebout, Charles. 1956. A pure theory of local expenditures. *Journal of Political Economy* 64:416–24.

[15]

Minimum Wages and Training Revisited

David Neumark, *Michigan State University and National Bureau of Economic Research*

William Wascher, *Board of Governors of the Federal Reserve System*

Theory predicts that minimum wages will reduce employer-provided on-the-job training designed to improve workers' skills on the current job, but it is ambiguous regarding training that workers obtain to qualify for a job. We estimate the effects of minimum wages on both types of training received by young workers, exploiting cross-state variation in minimum wage increases. Much of the evidence supports the hypothesis that higher minimum wages reduce formal training to improve skills on the current job. But there is little or no evidence of offsetting increases in training undertaken to qualify for or obtain jobs.

I. Introduction

The existing research on the economic consequences of minimum wage laws has focused disproportionately on the disemployment effects of such laws on younger and lesser-skilled workers. One drawback of this focus is that it provides too narrow a basis for policy evaluation; that is, there

We are grateful to Scott Adams and David Wetzell for outstanding research assistance, to Jim Heckman, Steven Pischke, and Aloysius Siow for helpful comments, and to Yoram Barzel for suggesting this line of inquiry. The views expressed are ours only and do not necessarily reflect those of the Federal Reserve Board or its staff.

[*Journal of Labor Economics*, 2001, vol. 19, no. 3]

may be other channels through which minimum wages influence the well-being of the population.[1] In this article, we address what we perceive as one shortcoming along these lines—the near absence of evidence on the effects of minimum wages on skill formation associated with on-the-job training. Of course, lost opportunities for on-the-job training are a cost of the disemployment effects of minimum wages. But if there are also reductions in on-the-job training for individuals who remain employed, the overall effect of minimum wages on skill formation could be considerably larger.

The possibility that minimum wages reduce on-the-job training was initially raised by Rosen (1972), Feldstein (1973), and Welch (1978). In the simplest arrangement, training is financed out of workers' wages. Because the Fair Labor Standards Act (FLSA) specifies that the minimum wage applies to the wage net of any deducted training costs, however, a higher minimum wage raises the floor below which the net wage cannot fall and, hence, may deter training. Alternatively, an arrangement could be structured such that the worker receives a wage above the minimum but pays the employer for training. In this case, however, the employer must still pay the worker for time spent in training required for the job, which raises the cost of training to the employer without raising its value to the employee. Thus, regardless of the arrangement, the FLSA is likely to reduce on-the-job training paid for by the worker. Of course, to the extent that training is firm-specific rather than general, the employer should bear more of the cost. In this case, a higher minimum wage makes it less likely that employers will find it profitable to hire a worker and pay for on-the-job training.

The best-known empirical test of the prediction that minimum wages reduce on-the-job training is Hashimoto (1982), who finds evidence consistent with this hypothesis for white men.[2] However, there are several reasons to question this evidence. First, Hashimoto uses an indirect test based on empirical observations on wage growth taken from panel data. This test is potentially problematic because other factors—such as relative demand shifts induced by minimum wages—could also affect wage pro-

---

[1] For example, this research ignores the effects of minimum wages on family incomes (e.g., Neumark and Wascher, in press [a]).

[2] Hashimoto also reports evidence suggesting that the higher wages attributable to minimum wage increases are unlikely to offset the higher wage growth (and eventual higher wages) that training would have produced in the absence of the minimum wage hike. In Hashimoto's model, the theoretical prediction regarding the effects of minimum wages on training is unambiguous, while the prediction regarding disemployment effects is ambiguous. The ambiguity surrounding the direction of the employment effect stems from the possibility of decreasing returns to scale in the provision of training by the firm, so that hiring an additional worker can raise the cost of all labor. As in the standard monopsony model (Stigler 1946), this can lead to positive employment effects of minimum wages.

files. In addition, if wage profiles slope upward because of long-term incentive contracts (Lazear 1979), then a higher minimum wage can lead to flatter wage profiles by creating rents for employed workers and therefore reducing their incentive to shirk (Lazear and Miller 1981). Thus, evidence that minimum wage increases are associated with flatter wage profiles may not speak to the relationship between minimum wages and training, and indeed the existence of incentive contracts can generate spurious evidence that minimum wages reduce training. For these reasons, direct evidence on on-the-job training would be more convincing. Second, Hashimoto uses only time-series variation in minimum wages, stemming from the 1967 amendments to the FLSA. In contrast, the standard approach in the "new" minimum wage research has been to exploit cross-state variation in minimum wages to avoid attributing to minimum wages influences from unmeasured variables common to all observations in particular years. In this article, we attempt to remedy both of these problems by utilizing cross-state variation in minimum wage increases coupled with direct information on on-the-job training available in the 1983 and 1991 Current Population Survey (CPS) supplements.

Hashimoto's work, and the discussion so far, focuses on the effects of minimum wages on on-the-job training. As emphasized by Leighton and Mincer (1981), however, minimum wages may encourage low-skilled individuals to obtain more schooling if the additional education raises their marginal product above the minimum wage floor. Whether or not minimum wages provide an incentive for schooling depends on the extent to which education increases an individual's market wage above the minimum and on the opportunity cost of the additional schooling; the latter, in turn, depends on the minimum wage and on the probability of finding employment if one searches for work instead of going to school.[3]

This raises the possibility that even if higher minimum wages reduce on-the-job training, they need not reduce skill formation if they provide an incentive for individuals to obtain additional schooling. This point is perhaps most relevant to the argument, made by some advocates of minimum wages in policy circles and the media, that higher minimum wages lead to a "high-wage" economy by increasing training. To a large extent, this argument is based on flawed reasoning regarding the effects of minimum wages on on-the-job training. For example, Levin-Waldman (1996)

---

[3] See also Welch (1974), Ehrenberg and Marcus (1979), Gustman and Steinmeier (1982), Lang (1987), and Agell and Lommerud (1997) for additional discussion of the effects of minimum wages on enrollment or education decisions. There is a sizable empirical literature on the effects of minimum wages on schooling; in addition to Leighton and Mincer, Mattila (1978), Cunningham (1981), Ehrenberg and Marcus (1982), and Neumark and Wascher (1996, in press [b]) have studied this issue. No clear consensus is evident from these papers, although our own previous work suggests that minimum wages reduce school enrollments.

argues that "if raising the minimum wage might increase the demand for skilled labor, employers might consequently be induced to provide the type of on-the-job training necessary to make so-called low-skilled workers more productive workers" (p. 27). As we just illustrated, however, in terms of standard human capital theory, coupled with the constraints imposed by the FLSA, this argument is incorrect. Nonetheless, insofar as minimum wages could increase schooling or other training acquired by workers in order to qualify for jobs, this so-called high-wage strategy cannot be dismissed.

In the present article, we do not revisit the entire issue of schooling decisions and minimum wages. We do, however, consider evidence concerning the effects of minimum wages on the proportion of workers who undertook training to qualify for their present jobs, including training received in school. We use this evidence to assess whether, consistent with the arguments made about schooling, such training provides an offset to the effects of minimum wages on on-the-job training. Much of the evidence indicates that minimum wages reduce on-the-job training, as predicted by the basic human capital model. Moreover, we do not find evidence that minimum wages induce additional training intended to help workers qualify for their current job, although the ability of our data to detect very general skill accumulation is somewhat limited.

Of course, because the skills acquired in school that helped a worker qualify for his or her present job may not reflect the total investment content of schooling, the evidence presented here is not sufficient to draw firm conclusions regarding the net effect of minimum wages on skill formation. If minimum wages also reduce schooling generally (as we have reported in Neumark and Wascher [1996]), then the results presented here would suggest that minimum wages reduce skill accumulation among young and relatively unskilled workers. But even if minimum wages increase schooling levels, reductions in on-the-job training can still lead to a net decline in skill formation.

II. Previous Work on the Effects of Minimum Wages on Training

Despite the potential effects of minimum wages on training, and the voluminous literature on other issues relating to training, there is remarkably little empirical work on this topic beyond Hashimoto's original research. For a long time the only other detailed published study was by Leighton and Mincer (1981), who examined the relationship using a minimum wage variable based on state coverage and a "standardized state wage." The latter is the estimated state dummy variable coefficient from a regression of wages on personal and job characteristics and is presumed to capture the idea that the federal minimum wage has more of a "bite" in states with lower wages. Specifically, Leighton and Mincer define their minimum wage variable as the state coverage ratio divided by one plus this standardized wage; the predicted effect of this variable on measures of on-the-job training is therefore negative.

Using data from the Panel Study of Income Dynamics (PSID) for 1973–75 and from the National Longitudinal Survey (NLS) for Young Men for 1967–69, Leighton and Mincer first report evidence that wage growth was lower in states with higher values of the minimum wage variable. This finding holds for both white men and black men, although the evidence is generally significant only for white men.[4] Second, they examine the relationship between the minimum wage variable and direct training measures in the two data sets.[5] In general, the estimated minimum wage effects on on-the-job training are negative and significant, at least for those with a high school education or less. Finally, the authors report some evidence from the NLS using a measure of off-the-job training (excluding schooling), which might increase as a result of a higher minimum wage. The evidence is in this direction but is generally not statistically significant. Overall, Leighton and Mincer conclude that "the hypothesis that minimum wages tend to discourage on-the-job training is largely supported by our empirical analysis" (p. 171).

We attempt to improve on this analysis in two ways. First, as was the case with Hashimoto's analysis, Leighton and Mincer do not use any information on variation in minimum wages across states, probably because there was very little variation in the 1967–75 period that they examine. The identifying information they use comes mainly from variation in state wages, which may itself be related to training (which is not included as a regressor in constructing the standardized state wage). In particular, because training is likely to be positively related to wages at the state level, and because the wage variable appears in the denominator of the dependent variable, there is the potential for negative bias in the estimated coefficient. This bias would increase the likelihood of finding evidence consistent with the theoretical prediction. This is particularly troubling because in separate estimates of the coefficients of coverage and the standardized wage in a set of appendix tables, Leighton and Mincer report that much of the effect of the minimum wage variable comes from

---

[4] They also report results for turnover, arguing that if training has a firm-specific component, more training should be associated with lower turnover. They find evidence in the PSID data that higher coverage is associated with shorter job tenure, but in the NLS find this only for black males.

[5] In the PSID, one question asks whether the respondent is learning things on his job that could lead to a better job or a promotion, while a second administered to those with at most a high school education asks whether the respondent received any training other than schooling. The NLS has a question on training on the current job, which, according to the authors, appears to refer to more formal training.

this standardized wage rather than from coverage. Second (and related), although the data come from multiple years, there is no attempt to control for state-specific differences by including state dummies or data on some other group whose training is unlikely to be affected by minimum wages. Again, the empirical analysis in this study aims to remedy these deficiencies.

Finally, Grossberg and Sicilian (1999) report that in the Employment Opportunities Pilot Project (EOPP) data set, men and women in minimum wage jobs experienced lower wage growth than workers in other low-wage jobs. Using the direct measures of training available in the EOPP, however, only for men do they find evidence that workers in minimum wage jobs receive significantly less training than these comparison groups (workers earning either less than the minimum or earning just above the minimum). Thus, their results are consistent with Hashimoto's finding that minimum wages lower wage growth, but the evidence of a relationship between the minimum wage and direct measures of training is more ambiguous.

However, we view their evidence and interpretation as suspect for a number of reasons. First, those workers in jobs paying less than the minimum are presumably in the uncovered sector, where training may be less frequent. If so, there will be a systematic upward bias in a comparison of training of minimum wage workers to training of workers earning less than the minimum wage; this bias could explain their results for women. Second, the authors define their treatment groups based on a worker's starting wage; however, this wage is likely to be jointly endogenous with training, making it difficult to interpret these estimates.[6] Third, the authors include as a control variable a measure of job complexity, which refers to the number of weeks it takes a new employee in the position surveyed to become fully trained and qualified; clearly this variable may pick up much of the variation in training.

Thus, there is relatively little evidence on the effects of minimum wages on training, and the evidence that exists has some potentially serious limitations. Consequently, we think that an empirical analysis revisiting this question is of considerable interest.

III. The Data

The data we use to measure training are taken from supplements to the January 1983 and January 1991 CPS surveys. The 1983 survey included an Occupational Mobility, Training, and Job Tenure Supplement, and the

---

[6] The authors attempt to address this endogeneity in the wage growth estimates, but not in the training estimates.

Minimum Wages and Training Revisited   569

1991 survey included a Training Supplement.[7] The measures of training available in these supplements appear to dovetail nicely with the two types of training for which the effects of minimum wages may differ: training to improve skills on the current job and training to obtain (qualify for) the current job. The two supplements are very similar, with nearly identical questions on many aspects of training.[8] As explained below, some of our statistical experiments rely only on the 1991 data, in which case comparability of the questions over time is not an issue. But others require both surveys, making this relevant.

The first set of questions we use concerns training to improve skills on the current job, which we interpret as measuring on-the-job training, and which theory predicts will decline in response to a higher minimum wage. The relevant questions are identical in 1983 and 1991, and are as follows:

> 1. Since you obtained your present job, did you take any training to improve your skills?
>
>   Did you take the training in: A formal company training program? Informal on-the-job training?

In general, we expect that minimum wages are more likely to affect formal than informal training, as informal training may be considerably less costly to employers.

The second set of questions concerns training for skills needed to obtain the current job.[9] We interpret these questions as indicators of training to qualify for the job. There are some slight differences in these questions in the two years, as follows:

> 2. Did you need specific skills or training to obtain your current (last) job?
>
>   1983: Did you obtain those skills or training through one or more of the following: A training program in high school or post-secondary school? A formal company training program such as apprenticeship training or other type of training having an instructor and a planned program? Informal on-the-job training or

[7] These surveys are used by Constantine and Neumark (1996) and Bowers and Swaim (1994) to study changes in training over time, the contribution of these changes to the growth in wage inequality, and changes in returns to training.

[8] There are more differences between the surveys in detailed questions regarding financing of training, length of training, etc.

[9] The question actually refers to the current or last job, but as the first training question pertains only to those currently with a job, we restrict the analysis to those currently with jobs in order to keep the samples the same.

experience in previously held job or jobs?

1991: Did you obtain those skills or training through one or more of the following: A training program in high school or post-secondary school, including colleges and universities? A formal company training program, including apprenticeships? Informal on-the-job training?

These training variables are undoubtedly imperfect measures of training. But as documented in appendix table A1, they are strongly (and significantly) associated with higher wages, when added to standard human capital earnings equations.[10] A more specific problem, however, is that the type of training that people might undertake to raise their productivity in order to obtain a job, in the face of a minimum wage increase, may refer to any sort of general skill improvement. In contrast, a respondent could interpret question 2 more narrowly to refer to the specific skills used on the current job, so some skill accumulation could be missed. In this sense, there is some ambiguity regarding our empirical measure, although we think that the examination of in-school training mitigates this concern at least partially, since such training seems likely to be quite general.

We supplement these data on training with information from the CPS on race, sex, schooling, age, marital status, industry, occupation, and state of residence. We also retain the CPS individual weights to construct weighted estimates, since the estimated means play a role in some of the subsequent analysis.[11] To be included in our extract, respondents must be currently working (according to the labor force status recode) and not self-employed. Finally, we appended to the CPS records information on the state and federal minimum wage in January of each year from 1979 to 1991.[12]

IV. Empirical Analysis

Minimum Wages

The exogenous variation that we exploit to infer the effects of minimum wages on training comes from increases in state and federal minimum

---

[10] Constantine and Neumark (1996) also review evidence suggesting that these regressions reflect, at least in part, causal effects of training.

[11] This weight adjusts for overall nonresponse, using information on location and race. We do not correct for nonresponse to these supplements, as discussed in Diebold, Neumark, and Polsky (1997). In that paper, this latter nonresponse was critical because the estimation involved ratios of counts from different supplement years.

[12] Observations from Washington, DC, are dropped because minimum wages there differ by occupation, making it more difficult to measure annual increases in the minimum wage (see Neumark and Wascher 1992).

wages. Thus, we initially focus on the evidence from the January 1991 CPS, a period that followed numerous increases in state minimum wages in the late 1980s and an increase in the federal minimum wage in 1990. Table 1 presents the legislated minimum wages by state (the higher of the state or federal minimum) as of January of each year from 1983 through 1991, along with the federal minimum.[13] The second-to-last column indicates that 12 states had minimum wages above the federal minimum in 1991, while the column for 1983 shows only two states above the federal minimum in that year.

We could, in principle, use the state-level increase in the minimum wage between 1983 and 1991 as our exogenous source of variation. However, there is additional variation associated with differences in the timing of state-level minimum wage increases that may also be relevant. That is, because the questions in the CPS are not limited to training received in the current year, the minimum wage effect on training may be related to how binding the minimum was over a worker's early years in the labor market, rather than just in 1991. For example, although the legislated minimum wage was $4.25 in 1991 in both California and Iowa, California's increased to $4.25 in 1989, while Iowa's increased to $3.85 in 1990 and $4.25 in 1991. In this case, we might expect to find a bigger impact of the minimum wage on the 1991 incidence of training in California than in Iowa. To capture these differences in timing, in most of our specifications we use as the explanatory variable the percent by which the state minimum exceeded the federal minimum over the previous 3 years. The last column of table 1 reports this gap for each state; it ranges from 0 to a high of 21.86% for California and Connecticut.[14]

Training to Improve Skills on the Current Job

Table 2 reports descriptive statistics from the 1991 CPS for the variables measuring training obtained to improve skills on the current job. We show results both for the overall age group of 16–24-year-olds, as well as for the 16–19 (teenager) and 20–24 (young adult) subgroups. Although a higher proportion of 16–19-year-olds are paid the minimum wage, the

[13] For workers covered under state and federal laws, the higher minimum wage prevails. Because the differences in coverage are minor, we simply take the higher of the two minimum wages as the prevailing one.

[14] These gaps obviously would change if we were to use a different "window," such as 2 or 4 years instead of 3 years. Below, we report results using alternative windows to explore the robustness of our results, and find that they are generally insensitive to such changes.

As table 1 shows, state minimum wages were above the federal minimum wage in 1983 only in Connecticut and Alaska. As explained below, when we use data from the 1983 survey as well as the 1991 survey, we define a similar minimum wage gap variable that exceeds zero for these two states.

Table 1
Effective Minimum Wage by State and the Average Percentage Difference between State and Federal Minimums over the Last 3 Years

	1983	1984	1985	1986	1987	1988	1989	1990	1991	Gap (%)
AK	3.85	3.85	3.85	3.85	3.85	3.85	3.85	3.85	4.30	14.34
AL	3.35	3.35	3.35	3.35	3.35	3.35	3.35	3.35	3.80	0
AR	3.35	3.35	3.35	3.35	3.35	3.35	3.35	3.35	3.80	0
AZ	3.35	3.35	3.35	3.35	3.35	3.35	3.35	3.35	3.80	0
CA	3.35	3.35	3.35	3.35	3.35	3.35	4.25	4.25	4.25	21.86
CO	3.35	3.35	3.35	3.35	3.35	3.35	3.35	3.35	3.80	0
CT	3.37	3.37	3.37	3.37	3.37	3.75	4.25	4.25	4.25	21.86
DE	3.35	3.35	3.35	3.35	3.35	3.35	3.35	3.35	3.80	0
FL	3.35	3.35	3.35	3.35	3.35	3.35	3.35	3.35	3.80	0
GA	3.35	3.35	3.35	3.35	3.35	3.35	3.35	3.35	3.80	0
HI	3.35	3.35	3.35	3.35	3.35	3.85	3.85	3.85	3.85	10.39
IA	3.35	3.35	3.35	3.35	3.35	3.35	3.35	3.85	4.25	8.92
ID	3.35	3.35	3.35	3.35	3.35	3.35	3.35	3.35	3.80	0
IL	3.35	3.35	3.35	3.35	3.35	3.35	3.35	3.35	3.80	0
IN	3.35	3.35	3.35	3.35	3.35	3.35	3.35	3.35	3.80	0
KS	3.35	3.35	3.35	3.35	3.35	3.35	3.35	3.35	3.80	0
KY	3.35	3.35	3.35	3.35	3.35	3.35	3.35	3.35	3.80	0
LA	3.35	3.35	3.35	3.35	3.35	3.35	3.35	3.35	3.80	0
MA	3.35	3.35	3.35	3.35	3.55	3.65	3.75	3.75	3.80	7.96
MD	3.35	3.35	3.35	3.35	3.35	3.35	3.35	3.35	3.80	0
ME	3.35	3.35	3.45	3.55	3.65	3.65	3.75	3.85	3.85	9.39
MI	3.35	3.35	3.35	3.35	3.35	3.35	3.35	3.35	3.80	0
MN	3.35	3.35	3.35	3.35	3.35	3.55	3.85	3.95	4.25	14.89
MO	3.35	3.35	3.35	3.35	3.35	3.35	3.35	3.35	3.80	0
MS	3.35	3.35	3.35	3.35	3.35	3.35	3.35	3.35	3.80	0
MT	3.35	3.35	3.35	3.35	3.35	3.35	3.35	3.35	3.80	0
NC	3.35	3.35	3.35	3.35	3.35	3.35	3.35	3.35	3.80	0
ND	3.35	3.35	3.35	3.35	3.35	3.35	3.35	3.35	3.80	0
NE	3.35	3.35	3.35	3.35	3.35	3.35	3.35	3.35	3.80	0
NH	3.35	3.35	3.35	3.35	3.45	3.55	3.65	3.75	3.85	7.40
NJ	3.35	3.35	3.35	3.35	3.35	3.35	3.35	3.35	3.80	0
NM	3.35	3.35	3.35	3.35	3.35	3.35	3.35	3.35	3.80	0
NV	3.35	3.35	3.35	3.35	3.35	3.35	3.35	3.35	3.80	0
NY	3.35	3.35	3.35	3.35	3.35	3.35	3.35	3.35	3.80	0
OH	3.35	3.35	3.35	3.35	3.35	3.35	3.35	3.35	3.80	0
OK	3.35	3.35	3.35	3.35	3.35	3.35	3.35	3.35	3.80	0
OR	3.35	3.35	3.35	3.35	3.35	3.35	3.35	4.25	4.75	17.29
PA	3.35	3.35	3.35	3.35	3.35	3.35	3.70	3.70	3.80	6.97
RI	3.35	3.35	3.35	3.35	3.55	3.65	4.00	4.25	4.25	19.37
SC	3.35	3.35	3.35	3.35	3.35	3.35	3.35	3.35	3.80	0
SD	3.35	3.35	3.35	3.35	3.35	3.35	3.35	3.35	3.80	0
TN	3.35	3.35	3.35	3.35	3.35	3.35	3.35	3.35	3.80	0
TX	3.35	3.35	3.35	3.35	3.35	3.35	3.35	3.35	3.80	0
UT	3.35	3.35	3.35	3.35	3.35	3.35	3.35	3.35	3.80	0
VA	3.35	3.35	3.35	3.35	3.35	3.35	3.35	3.35	3.80	0
VT	3.35	3.35	3.35	3.35	3.45	3.55	3.65	3.75	3.85	7.40
WA	3.35	3.35	3.35	3.35	3.35	3.35	3.85	4.25	4.25	17.88
WI	3.35	3.35	3.35	3.35	3.35	3.35	3.35	3.65	3.80	2.99
WV	3.35	3.35	3.35	3.35	3.35	3.35	3.35	3.35	3.80	0
WY	3.35	3.35	3.35	3.35	3.35	3.35	3.35	3.35	3.80	0
Federal	3.35	3.35	3.35	3.35	3.35	3.35	3.35	3.35	3.80	...

NOTE.—The effective minimum wage is the state's own legislated minimum unless the federal minimum is greater, in which case the federal minimum wage becomes the state's effective minimum wage. The gap column indicates the average percentage by which a state's effective minimum wage exceeds the federal minimum wage. For the 1979–83 period, the federal minimum was $2.90 in 1979, $3.10 in 1980, and then fixed at $3.35 beginning in 1981. (All of these minimum wages were effective as of January 1 of each year.) Of the 50 states, only Alaska and Connecticut had higher minimum wages. Alaska's was $.50 higher than the federal minimum in each year, while Connecticut's was one to two cents higher in each year.

Table 2
Descriptive Statistics for Training to Improve Skills on Current Job,
1991 CPS

	Any Training to Improve Skills on Current Job (1)	Formal (2)	Informal (3)	N (4)
Overall proportions:				
Ages 16–24	.2687	.0780	.1448	6,745
Ages 16–19	.1829	.0253	.1315	2,057
Ages 20–24	.3044	.0999	.1504	4,688
Ages 35–54	.4768	.1941	.1675	22,941
Proportions by average minimum wage levels in last 3 years:				
State minimum = federal minimum (35 states):				
Ages 16–24	.2746	.0811	.1468	4,757
Ages 16–19	.1815	.0212	.1315	1,457
Ages 20–24	.3131	.1058	.1531	3,300
State minimum > federal minimum (15 states):				
Ages 16–24	.2557	.0712	.1404	1,988
Ages 16–19	.1860	.0342	.1313	600
Ages 20–24	.2853	.0868	.1442	1,388

incidence of training is higher among 20–24-year-olds. In particular, the proportions for the whole sample shown in the top panel of table 2 indicate that the reported incidence of any training to improve skills on the current job is .27 among 16–24-year-olds, quite a bit lower (.18) for teenagers, and correspondingly higher (.30) for young adults. As a result, although teenagers have been the focus of most work on disemployment effects of minimum wages, the influence of minimum wages on training may be greater for 20–24-year-olds. That is, the effects of minimum wages on training need not be strongest for those with a wage right at the minimum. Rather, the effects will be most evident among workers having a combination of wages that are sufficiently low and training costs that are sufficiently high to cause the minimum wage to be a binding constraint. The workers for whom this holds are not necessarily the lowest-wage workers, as the training costs for these workers may be minimal; for example, because of higher turnover teenagers may be in jobs that require little if any training. The table also reports estimates for 35–54-year-olds, who, as explained below, are used as a control sample in some of the estimations.

Turning to the types of training, the reported incidence of formal training to improve skills is .08 for 16–24-year-olds, while the reported incidence of informal training is .14.[15] In both cases, the estimates are higher for the older workers and lower for the younger workers. In particular, the incidence of formal training among teenagers is extremely low (.025 vs. .100 for 20–24-year-olds), suggesting that minimum wages (or anything else) are likely to have relatively little detectable impact on formal training among teenagers.[16]

To provide a rough sense of the relationship between training and minimum wage increases, the bottom panels of table 2 report means for these training variables disaggregated by whether the minimum wage in the state was above or equal to the federal minimum wage over the 3-year window we use—that is, whether the state minimum wage gap was positive or zero. The estimates indicate that the incidence of any training among 16–24-year-olds and among 20–24-year-olds was lower in the subset of states in which minimum wages were higher. The same is true of formal and informal training.

Of course, this simple comparison of means masks a number of other possible sources of variation in training that may generate a spurious negative relationship with minimum wages. For example, in principle, at least, the states with a relatively high minimum wage may have had persistently high minimum wages in the past and (for some unrelated reason) a persistently lower incidence of training. In this case, we would not want to draw any causal inference from the relationship between training reported in 1991 and minimum wages over the last few years. As we showed in table 1, however, virtually no states had minimum wages exceeding the federal level between 1983 and 1987, so that our minimum wage gap variable essentially captures state-level changes in the 3 years prior to the data we have on the incidence of training.

In addition, a simple comparison between states that did and did not increase their minimum wages takes no account of differences in training across states that may arise as a result of technological change, economic conditions, government policy, etc. and which may also be correlated with minimum wage increases. For example, if firms in states in which market wages are relatively higher, perhaps due to a higher incidence of training, are less constrained by an increase in the minimum wage, then a simple

---

[15] Formal training and informal training are not exhaustive. The survey also asks about training via correspondence courses, armed forces, and friends or relatives. These are included in the "any training" measure.

[16] The low incidence of reported formal training among teenagers in the 1991 data is not attributable solely to higher minimum wages in some states in 1991. In the 1983 data, the proportions are similar, with .076 of 20–24-year-olds and .019 of 16–19-year-olds reporting formal training of this type. Of course, we cannot rule out the possibility that the federal minimum wage in both years was sufficiently high to deter training among teenagers.

Minimum Wages and Training Revisited   575

comparison of means would generate a bias against finding that minimum wages reduce training. Alternatively, if those states with relatively less training in every year were those in which minimum wages rose relatively more, the bias would be in the other direction. To address this problem, we need to identify a control sample for which the minimum wage in 1991 (and the immediately preceding years) should not have an influence on the incidence of training. We could then use the differences between the minimum wage-training relationship in our treatment and control samples to identify the effects of minimum wages.

In particular, we recast the simple comparisons shown in table 2 as regressions of the form:

$$T_{ij} = \alpha + \beta I_j + \epsilon_{ij}, \tag{1}$$

where T_{ij} is the training measure (a dummy variable) for individual i in state j in 1991, and I_j is a dummy variable for states with increases in the minimum wage exceeding the federal increase. Estimated as a linear probability model, this regression model would give us precisely the same estimate as the comparison between the two subsamples in table 2. Of course, once we get beyond a simple comparison of means, we can also substitute our minimum wage gap variable (denoted MW_j) for I_j.

We then construct a difference-in-difference estimator using two alternative control samples. The first comprises workers aged 35–54. Because this group has higher average wage levels and because any training they did receive was likely in the more distant past, the incidence of training they report is likely to be associated with longer-run state-specific differences in training levels rather than with recent cross-state variation in minimum wage increases. Specifically, we estimate the regression:

$$T_{ij} = \alpha + S_j\beta + \gamma Y_{ij} + \delta MW_j \cdot Y_{ij} + \epsilon_{ij}, \tag{2}$$

where 35–54-year-olds are now added to the sample, Y_{ij} is a dummy variable indicating that the individual is in the younger age group (either 16–24, 16–19, or 20–24, depending on the specification), and S_j is a vector of state dummy variables.[17] In this specification, the vector of coefficients β captures the cross-state variation in training common to the workers in all age groups, while γ picks up the average difference in training between the age groups. Finally, δ picks up the differences in the incidence of training between younger and older workers associated with variation

[17] Because the data for this specification are for a single year, the state dummy variables (S_j) pick up the state-level variation in the minimum wage variable (MW_j).

in the state minimum wage gap; this is interpreted as the causal effect of the minimum wage.[18]

As a second control sample, we use respondents to the 1983 CPS training supplement who are in the same younger age groups as our 1991 treatment sample. Unlike in equation (2), once we introduce the data from 1983, the minimum wage variable is not the same for all observations in a state (i.e., it is not the same for 1983 and 1991). Thus, we can simply introduce this variable along with state dummy variables to identify the minimum wage effects.[19] In this case, we estimate the following regression using the data for 1983 and 1991:

$$T_{ijt} = \alpha + S_j\beta + \gamma Z_t + \delta MW_{jt} + \epsilon_{ijt},   (3)$$

where Z_t is a dummy variable indicating that the observation comes from 1991. In this regression, β again captures the cross-state variation in training, while γ now picks up the average difference in training between 1983 and 1991. Finally, δ captures the extent to which training has changed more (or less) in states with larger minimum wage increases, which again is interpreted as the causal effect of the minimum wage.

These alternative control samples each have their own advantages and disadvantages. The advantage of using the 35–54-year-olds in 1991 is that, because the control sample comes from the same year as the treatment sample, we capture state effects even if they vary over time. The disadvantage is that if the incidence of training among 16–24-year-olds is affected by minimum wages, then the incidence of training among 35–54-year-olds may be affected indirectly. For example, employers training fewer 16–24-year-olds because of higher minimum wages may substitute toward training 35–54-year-olds if they need to increase workforce skills. Alternatively, if higher skills among older and younger workers are complementary in production, training could fall for the older group. Al-

[18] Note that in contrast to specifications for the employment effects of minimum wages (e.g., Neumark and Wascher 1992), we do not use a minimum wage variable defined relative to an average wage. In employment studies, the relevant factor is the relative price of unskilled to more-skilled labor, leading naturally to specifying the minimum wage variable relative to an average for all workers. In studying training, however, we are most interested in the minimum wage relative to what the market wage for young, unskilled workers would be in the absence of the minimum. This is unobserved, and the observed average for these workers clearly will be affected by the minimum wage. Thus, we specify our models in terms of the difference between the state minimum wage and the federal minimum wage, and allow the state and year dummy variables to capture variation in market wages.

[19] Because there was essentially no variation in minimum wage increases across states in 1983, the earlier data largely control for state differences in training due to other sources.

though the direction of bias is therefore ambiguous, the point is that in neither of these scenarios would the older group be a valid control sample.

Using the 16–24-year-olds from 1983 essentially reverses these advantages and disadvantages. On the one hand, because the data are from 8 years earlier, the control sample is much more plausibly unaffected by the treatment. On the other hand, using the earlier sample may be inadequate for controlling for state variation in training, since the unmeasured state effects may not be completely invariant over this time period. As a consequence, we report results using both control samples to explore the robustness of our estimates. Our confidence in the results is bolstered by the fact that both control samples yield quite similar conclusions.

In addition to the problems addressed by the alternative control samples, training may also vary with individual characteristics. We thus include in the regression models a vector of individual-level controls for race, sex, schooling, age, and marital status.[20] We estimate each model as a linear probability model, with heteroscedasticity-consistent standard errors.[21]

In both specifications, there is also the potential for bias associated with a positive correlation between training and unobserved ability or productivity. In the training literature, this correlation is apparent in comparisons of cross-sectional and longitudinal estimates of the returns to training (Bartel 1992; Lynch 1992), and in comparisons of cross-sectional estimates of the returns to training with and without controls for ability (Gardecki and Neumark 1998). By raising the cost of the lowest-ability workers, minimum wage increases may lead employers to hire relatively more higher-ability workers. If higher-ability workers are more likely to receive training, then variation in the average unobserved productivity or quality of employed young workers across states may generate a positive bias in estimates of the effects of minimum wage increases on training,

---

[20] Because the industry and occupation in which young individuals find work may be related to the ease with which they can be trained, we do not include them as control variables here; however, the results were little changed when these variables were added.

[21] The results were very similar using probit models. There were, however, two exceptions, for formal and in-school training for teenagers using older workers as a control group, in which we obtained large positive estimates with much higher standard errors (and hence insignificant coefficient estimates). Because this was true even for specifications without control variables, and because the estimates from these latter specifications were much different from what was implied by the means, we attribute these exceptions to problems with the distributional assumption. We therefore chose to present the results from the linear probability model, which provides consistent estimates of the conditional mean of the dependent variable without strong distributional assumptions. The linear probability and probit estimates were very similar for all other types of training, and for all of the specifications using younger workers in 1983 as the control sample.

                                  Neumark and Wascher

Table 3
Difference-in-Difference Estimates of Minimum Wage Effects on Training to Improve Skills on Current Job, 1983 and 1991 CPS

	Any Training to Improve Skills on Current Job		Formal		Informal	
	(1)	(1′)	(2)	(2′)	(3)	(3′)
Older workers in 1991 as control sample:						
Ages 16–24	−.1651	−.0825	−.1198	−.0947	−.0397	−.0288
	(.0957)	(.0943)	(.0630)	(.0625)	(.0769)	(.0769)
Ages 16–19	−.1068	−.0593	.0172	.0219	−.0479	−.0434
	(.1447)	(.1469)	(.0774)	(.0784)	(.1263)	(.1264)
Ages 20–24	−.1986	−.0909	−.1792	−.1450	−.0395	−.0252
	(.1112)	(.1100)	(.0736)	(.0730)	(.0884)	(.0884)
Workers of same age in 1983 as control sample:						
Ages 16–24	−.2274	−.2112	−.1276	−.1197	−.0478	−.0481
	(.1023)	(.1008)	(.0587)	(.0580)	(.0834)	(.0834)
Ages 16–19	−.1338	−.1255	.0505	.0529	−.1068	−.1072
	(.1675)	(.1677)	(.0751)	(.0754)	(.1482)	(.1485)
Ages 20–24	−.2706	−.2431	−.1993	−.1832	−.0271	−.0278
	(.1255)	(.1240)	(.0762)	(.0752)	(.1003)	(.1003)
Demographic controls	No	Yes	No	Yes	No	Yes

NOTE.—Estimated coefficients from linear probability models are reported. Heteroscedasticity-consistent standard errors are reported in parentheses. The demographic control variables include race, gender, schooling, age (within-group), and marital status. The first panel reports estimates of eq. (2), while the second panel reports estimates of eq. (3).

weakening any negative effect of minimum wages on training to improve skills on the current job and strengthening any positive effect of minimum wages on training to qualify for the current job. Given that we find evidence of negative effects of minimum wages on training to improve skills and no evidence of positive effects on training to qualify, the existence of this bias only strengthens our conclusions.

The results from the two alternative difference-in-difference regressions are reported in table 3. Focusing first on the estimates using older workers as a control sample (col. 1 in the top panel), we find that minimum wages reduce the incidence of on-the-job training among 16–24-year-olds, with the estimated effect significant at the 10% level. The point estimate for 16–19-year-olds is also negative, but not significant, while the point estimate for 20–24-year-olds is negative (−.199) and significant at the 10% level. This coefficient estimate indicates that a 10% higher minimum wage reduces the proportion receiving training by 2 percentage points. Since 30.4% of this age group reports receiving any training (table 2), this estimate implies an elasticity of about $-.65$, indicative of a large deterrent effect from minimum wages. However, when the individual-level control variables are included (col. 1'), the estimated effect becomes insignificant for all age groups, with t-statistics around one for 16–24- and 20–24-year-olds.

The results for separate estimates of the effects of minimum wages on formal and informal training are reported in table 3, columns 2–3'. For informal training, we find small and insignificant effects of minimum wages for all age groups. For formal training, however, the effects on the 16–24-year-old age group are negative and significant or nearly so at the 10% level, and the negative effects on 20–24-year-olds are negative and significant at the 5% level; the estimated magnitudes of the effect for 20–24-year-olds imply that a 10% rise in the minimum wage reduces the incidence of formal training by 1.5 to 1.8 percentage points. Given that about 10% of workers in this age group report formal training, the implied elasticities are as high as -1.8.

The bottom panel of table 3 reports results using young workers from 1983 as the control sample. These estimates provide even stronger evidence that minimum wages deter on-the-job training. In column 1, where we look at overall training, the effects on training for 16–24- and 20–24-year-olds are negative and significant at the 5% level, whether or not we include the individual-level controls. In this case, there is still no evidence that minimum wages deter informal training or that minimum wages have significant adverse effects for teenagers. On the other hand, the evidence that minimum wages deter formal training among 16–24- or 20–24-year-olds is stronger, with the estimated effects negative and significant at the 5% level whether or not the individual-level controls are included.[22]

Taken as a whole, the evidence generally supports the hypothesis that minimum wages reduce the incidence of training aimed at improving skills on the current job, as theory suggests. The effects are strongest for formal training, which would be expected if formal training entails higher direct and indirect costs, while informal training is a joint product with output. Because the descriptive statistics in table 2 indicate that formal training is less prevalent for young workers than is informal training, these results also indicate that an important component of training does not appear to be reduced by minimum wages. However, the wage regression estimates reported in appendix table A1 suggest that the returns to the incidence of formal training are much higher (possibly because of greater intensity

---

[22] Given that theory makes an unambiguous prediction about training to improve skills on the current job, one could argue that our hypothesis tests should be one-sided. In that case, the estimates reported in the above paragraphs as significant at the 10% level would instead be significant at the 5% level.

or duration), so the consequences of reduced formal training may be much more severe.

The evidence also indicates that the reductions in training associated with higher minimum wages are largest among 20–24-year-olds; indeed, we find little evidence that minimum wages reduce the incidence of training among 16–19-year-olds. This presumably reflects the near absence of formal training among the younger group in the first place, so that there is little scope for minimum wages to have much impact despite the lower average wage for teens. In addition, the training that teenagers do receive appears to be low cost, and thus a higher minimum wage may not be much of a constraint. For example, among teenagers who reported receiving formal training in the 1991 CPS, 58% reported receiving 1 week of training or less, 28.7% reported 2–12 weeks, and 13.5% reported 13 or more weeks. In contrast, the corresponding percentages for 20–24-year-olds were 41.8, 42.3, and 16.0. Thus, training for 20–24-year-olds is both more prevalent and more lengthy. As we suggested earlier, if the impact of minimum wages depends both on the amount of training these workers would otherwise receive and its cost, it will not necessarily be the lowest-wage workers whose training is most adversely affected by minimum wage increases, and thus it should not be surprising that the negative effects of minimum wages on training are strongest among 20–24-year-olds.

Training to Obtain the Current Job

While theory predicts that minimum wages will reduce training to improve skills on the current job, the possibility exists that this effect will be offset by an increase in training to qualify for a job. Tables 4 and 5 lay out exactly the same analyses of training to obtain the current job as were done for training to improve skills in tables 2 and 3. The only difference is that in-school training is also considered. Given the similarities of the analyses, the results can be summarized briefly.

The descriptive statistics in table 4 indicate that the incidence of this type of training is somewhat higher than the incidence of training on the current job. Although the incidence of formal training is similar here to that in table 2, there is both more informal training and more in-school training (which was very rare for training to improve skills on the current job and hence was not reported in that table). Simple difference estimates based on the lower panels of table 4 are suggestive of positive effects of minimum wages on this type of training, as the incidence of training is higher in states with a positive minimum wage gap for any training (all age groups), formal training (16–24- and 16–19-year-olds), and informal and in-school training (all age groups). However, in the difference-in-difference estimates reported in table 5, the evidence for positive effects

Minimum Wages and Training Revisited   581

Table 4
Descriptive Statistics for Training to Obtain Current Job, 1991 CPS

	Any Training to Obtain Current Job (1)	Formal (2)	Informal (3)	School (4)	N (5)
Overall proportions:					
Ages 16–24	.3945	.0681	.2081	.1973	6,745
Ages 16–19	.2515	.0359	.1552	.0818	2,057
Ages 20–24	.4540	.0815	.2302	.2454	4,688
Ages 35–54	.6248	.1354	.2959	.3714	22,941
Proportions by average minimum wage levels in last 3 years:					
State minimum = federal minimum (35 states):					
Ages 16–24	.3875	.0673	.2032	.1961	4,757
Ages 16–19	.2377	.0273	.1443	.0778	1,457
Ages 20–24	.4493	.0838	.2275	.2450	3,300
State minimum > federal minimum (15 states):					
Ages 16–24	.4099	.0698	.2190	.1999	1,988
Ages 16–19	.2816	.0545	.1787	.0905	600
Ages 20–24	.4642	.0762	.2361	.2463	1,388

evaporates. The only consistently positive coefficient estimates on the minimum wage variable are for 16–19-year-olds, but none of these are statistically significant.[23] Moreover, for 16–24-year-olds as a whole and 20–24-year-olds separately, the coefficient estimates are nearly always negative, and they are significant at the 5% or 10% level for some types of training when older workers in 1991 are used as the control sample.

Thus, the available evidence does not support the hypothesis that minimum wages increase the incidence of training to qualify for the current job; if anything, minimum wages may reduce the incidence of the types of such training reported by respondents. Recall, though, that our measure of training to qualify for a job may miss some general skill acquisition that occurs in response to minimum wage increases, suggesting some caution in interpreting these results.

Robustness and Sensitivity Analysis

In this subsection, we report on some additional analyses that we conducted to explore the robustness and sensitivity of the estimated rela-

---

[23] Because the theoretical prediction is ambiguous, two-sided tests are appropriate in this case.

Table 5
Difference-in-Difference Estimates of Minimum Wage Effects on Training to Obtain Current Job, 1983 and 1991 CPS

	Any Training to Obtain Current Job		Formal		Informal		School	
	(1)	(1')	(2)	(2')	(3)	(3')	(4)	(4')
Older workers in 1991 as control sample:								
Ages 16–24	−.1011	−.0009	−.0802	−.0760	−.1582	−.1616	−.1404	.0147
	(.1014)	(.0978)	(.0600)	(.0598)	(.0886)	(.0885)	(.0852)	(.0810)
Ages 16–19	−.0043	.0457	.0478	.0364	−.1051	−.1190	.0616	.1583
	(.1604)	(.1583)	(.0833)	(.0848)	(.1359)	(.1375)	(.1161)	(.1164)
Ages 20–24	−.1575	−.0260	−.1352	−.1267	−.1878	−.1931	−.2350	−.0365
	(.1171)	(.1143)	(.0698)	(.0695)	(.1027)	(.1025)	(.0999)	(.0959)
Workers of same age in 1983 as control sample:								
Ages 16–24	−.0880	.0119	−.0522	−.0451	−.0760	−.0712	−.0342	.0318
	(.0978)	(.1086)	(.0589)	(.0586)	(.0950)	(.0947)	(.0884)	(.0840)
Ages 16–19	.0909	.1360	−.0057	.0043	.0856	.1038	.1345	.1668
	(.1909)	(.1872)	(.0929)	(.0925)	(.1577)	(.1570)	(.1259)	(.1236)
Ages 20–24	−.0882	−.0158	−.0719	−.0617	−.1446	−.1397	−.0987	−.0026
	(.1357)	(.1325)	(.0735)	(.0732)	(.1167)	(.1167)	(.1118)	(.1064)
Demographic controls	No	Yes	No	Yes	No	Yes	No	Yes

NOTE.—Estimated coefficients from linear probability models are reported. Heteroscedasticity-consistent standard errors are reported in parentheses. The demographic control variables include race, gender, schooling, age (within-group), and marital status. The first panel reports estimates of eq. (2), while the second panel reports estimates of eq. (3).

tionships between minimum wages and training. First, as we noted earlier, we have used a 3-year window to define the percentage gap between the state minimum wage and the federal minimum wage. This is a somewhat arbitrary choice, and there are arguments for using both shorter and longer windows. For example, because mean current job tenure is closer to 1 year than to 3 years (especially for teenagers), a shorter window might be desirable for the analysis of training to improve skills on the current job.[24] Alternatively, for the analysis of training to obtain skills, a longer window spanning multiple jobs may be more relevant, especially for the 20–24-year-olds. In addition, because employers may not make year-to-year changes in the provision of training, a longer-run view of the level of minimum wages in a state may be most pertinent to how much training young workers receive.

To assess the robustness of the results to using different windows, table 6 presents difference-in-difference estimates corresponding to those in the earlier tables for windows of 5, 4, 2, and 1 years.[25] Only specifications including the demographic controls are reported, so these estimates are most comparable to those in the columns with a prime superscript in tables 3 and 5. Focusing first on the results for training to improve skills on the current job, the estimates of the minimum wage effect are very robust to using different windows to define the minimum wage variable. Regardless of the control sample used, the estimated effects are always negative for any training, formal training, and informal training among 16–24- and 20–24-year-olds, and for any training and informal training among teenagers. The estimated coefficients for informal training are not significant, whereas the estimated coefficients for any training and especially for formal training are often significant at the 5% or 10% level for 16–24- and 20–24-year-olds. In general, the negative effects of the minimum wage are strongest and most significant for 20–24-year-olds, for formal training, and when using workers of the same age in 1983 as the control sample. The findings for training to obtain the current job are similarly robust. Thus, the results in table 6 indicate that our conclusions are not sensitive to the precise window used to define the level of the state minimum wage relative to the federal minimum wage and confirm our finding that the principal effect of minimum wages on training is to reduce training to improve skills on the current job, without apparent

---

[24] In the 1991 CPS supplement, mean tenure is 1.34 years for 16–24-year-olds, .67 for 16–19-year-olds, 1.62 for 20–24-year-olds, and 8.84 for 35–54-year-olds.
[25] When we use a window of 1 year, we are simply using the percentage gap between the minimum wage prevailing in January 1991 and the federal minimum wage.

Table 6
Alternative Difference-in-Difference Estimates of Minimum Wage Effects, 1983 and 1991 CPS, Based on Cumulative Minimum Wage Changes over the Last 5 Years, 4 Years, 2 Years, and 1 Year

	Training to Improve Skills on Current Job			Training Received to Obtain Current Job			
	Any	Formal	Informal	Any	Formal	Informal	In-School
For minimum wage changes over the last 5 years:							
Older workers in 1991 as control sample:							
Ages 16–24	−.1382 (.1480)	−.1583 (.0980)	−.0382 (.1208)	.0067 (.1536)	−.1198 (.0940)	−.2276 (.1386)	.0365 (.1276)
Ages 16–19	−.0585 (.1848)	.0248 (.1212)	−.0255 (.2009)	.0751 (.2467)	.0609 (.1333)	−.1701 (.2133)	.2566 (.1843)
Ages 20–24	−.1628 (.1731)	−.2377 (.1150)	−.0471 (.1388)	−.0343 (.1803)	−.2021 (.1097)	−.2730 (.1614)	−.0436 (.1516)
Workers of same age in 1983 as control sample:							
Ages 16–24	−.3154 (.1590)	−.1949 (.0913)	−.0588 (.1315)	.0314 (.1714)	−.0598 (.0925)	−.0708 (.1490)	.0614 (.1336)
Ages 16–19	−.1636 (.2635)	.0844 (.1161)	−.1325 (.2347)	.2641 (.2929)	.0210 (.1449)	.1981 (.2447)	.2983 (.1958)
Ages 20–24	−.3720 (.1961)	−.2981 (.1191)	−.0342 (.1582)	−.0312 (.2101)	−.0878 (.1159)	−.1792 (.1847)	−.0057 (.1704)
For minimum wage changes over the last 4 years:							
Older workers in 1991 as control sample:							
Ages 16–24	−.1083 (.1206)	−.1288 (.0798)	−.0295 (.0985)	−.0038 (.1252)	−.0971 (.0766)	−.1924 (.1129)	.0303 (.1040)
Ages 16–19	−.0591 (.1884)	.0212 (.0992)	−.0273 (.1637)	.0683 (.2014)	.0523 (.1090)	−.1388 (.1742)	.2189 (.1505)
Ages 20–24	−.1268 (.1409)	−.1939 (.0936)	−.0334 (.1131)	−.0332 (.1468)	−.1648 (.0892)	−.2321 (.1313)	−.0386 (.1233)
Workers of same age in 1983 as control sample:							
Ages 16–24	−.2624 (.1292)	−.1565 (.0741)	−.0507 (.1069)	.0173 (.1392)	−.0504 (.0751)	−.0711 (.1210)	.0446 (.1084)
Ages 16–19	−.1381 (.2144)	.0708 (.0947)	−.1147 (.1909)	.2102 (.2384)	.0169 (.1182)	.1535 (.1992)	.2421 (.1596)
Ages 20–24	−.3091 (.1591)	−.2409 (.0966)	−.0292 (.1285)	−.0344 (.1705)	−.0739 (.0940)	−.1611 (.1498)	−.0012 (.1378)

continued overleaf

For minimum wage changes over the last 2 years:						
Older workers in 1991 as control sample:						
Ages 16–24	−.1275 (.0977)	−.0926 (.0650)	−.0467 (.0792)	−.0036 (.1017)	−.0771 (.0615)	−.1625 (.0921)	−.0107 (.0841)
Ages 16–19	−.0906 (.1513)	.0181 (.0793)	−.0421 (.1305)	.0743 (.1644)	.0445 (.0879)	−.1002 (.1433)	.1387 (.1176)
Ages 20–24	−.1402 (.1143)	−.1397 (.0765)	−.0502 (.0910)	−.0304 (.1191)	−.1305 (.0714)	−.1999 (.1068)	−.0342 (.1005)
Workers of same age in 1983 as control sample:						
Ages 16–24	−.2409 (.1048)	−.1274 (.0610)	−.0676 (.0864)	.0368 (.1130)	−.0358 (.0600)	−.0485 (.0985)	.0313 (.0876)
Ages 16–19	−.1417 (.1729)	.0449 (.0768)	−.1095 (.1533)	.1865 (.1940)	.0094 (.0951)	.1567 (.1627)	.1542 (.1253)
Ages 20–24	−.2792 (.1293)	−.1909 (.0795)	−.0545 (.1041)	−.0010 (.1381)	−.0504 (.0749)	−.1285 (.1216)	.0012 (.1117)
For minimum wage changes over the last year:						
Older workers in 1991 as control sample:						
Ages 16–24	−.2140 (.1365)	−.1194 (.0918)	−.0741 (.1093)	−.0325 (.1431)	−.1234 (.0844)	−.2571 (.1287)	−.0147 (.1188)
Ages 16–19	−.1776 (.2108)	−.0116 (.1067)	−.0445 (.1827)	.0937 (.2300)	.0338 (.1250)	−.1685 (.2000)	.1960 (.1595)
Ages 20–24	−.2251 (.1600)	−.1675 (.1094)	−.0875 (.1248)	−.0903 (.1680)	−.1928 (.0970)	−.3098 (.1494)	−.0898 (.1436)
Workers of same age in 1983 as control sample:						
Ages 16–24	−.3493 (.1481)	−.1415 (.0878)	−.0999 (.1208)	.0511 (.1598)	−.0325 (.0819)	−.0674 (.1383)	−.0092 (.1251)
Ages 16–19	−.2043 (.2418)	.0729 (.1024)	−.1087 (.2152)	.2501 (.2724)	−.0098 (.1351)	.2362 (.2263)	.1667 (.1717)
Ages 20–24	−.4078 (.1830)	−.2241 (.1155)	−.0992 (.1455)	−.0067 (.1956)	−.0380 (.1010)	−.1860 (.1710)	−.0653 (.1606)

NOTE.—Estimated coefficients from linear probability models are reported. Heteroscedasticity-consistent standard errors are reported in parentheses. All models include race, gender, schooling, age (within-group), and marital status as demographic control variables.

offsetting benefits in the form of additional training to qualify for the current job.[26]

In table 7, we examine whether our estimated minimum wage effects might reflect spurious correlations between minimum wages and the incidence of training. In particular, although we have used young workers in 1983 and older workers in 1991 as control samples to compare with the treatment sample of young workers in 1991, it is possible that reported training fell relatively more for both young and older workers in states in which minimum wages rose. Given our stated reasons for choosing older workers as a control sample in the first place, we would tend to interpret such evidence as indicative of a spurious relationship between minimum wages and training, because minimum wages are expected to have little effect on training reported by older workers.[27] To address this concern, table 7 reports estimates of equation (3) for workers aged 35–54. In this estimation, we use 35–54-year-olds in 1991 as the treatment sample, and 35–54-year-olds in 1983 as the control sample. We report results with windows of 1–5 years for defining the minimum wage variable.

A failure to find any evidence of minimum wage effects in the 35–54-

[26] The only possible exception is the estimated positive effect of minimum wages on in-school training to obtain the current job among 16–19-year-olds, which is sometimes marginally significant in table 6.

We also attempted to use information on the duration of training to verify whether the evidence of negative effects on the incidence of training to improve skills carried over to the data on length of training. The 1991 survey includes some very broad measures of the duration of training, although they do not measure its intensity (i.e., hours per day). Specifically, data are available for formal training to improve skills on the current job, and for formal and in-school training to obtain the job, in intervals of: no training; 1 week or less; 2–12 weeks; 13–25 weeks; or 26+ weeks. For 1983 there are no data on the duration of formal training to improve skills on the current job, but there are data on duration of formal and in-school training to obtain the current job. Because we were most interested in exploring the robustness of our findings on training to improve skills on the current job, we restricted attention to the 1991 data, using the older workers as a control sample. We estimated models similar to those described above, but exploiting the information on duration (using multinomial logit and ordered logit models). Qualitatively, the evidence on duration pointed in the same direction as that for the incidence of training, with the probability of longer training spells to improve skills on the current job lower in states that had raised their minimum relatively more; however, the estimates were generally not statistically significant, probably due to the crude measurement of training with these data. We also found no evidence of positive effects of minimum wages on the duration of training to qualify for the job. Thus, although the duration data are noisier, they are consistent with the main findings we report.

[27] Alternatively, as suggested earlier, minimum wages could deter training among younger workers but increase training among older workers, which would lead to an overly strong estimate of the effect of minimum wages on training received by younger workers.

Table 7
Difference-in-Difference Estimates of Minimum Wage Effects on Training for Older Workers (Ages 35–54), Using Workers of the Same Age in 1983 as the Control Sample

	Training to Improve Skills on Current Job			Training to Obtain Current Job			
	Any	Formal	Informal	Any	Formal	Informal	In-School
For minimum wage changes over the last:							
1 year	−.0004	.0068	.1034	−.0264	.0858	−.0366	−.0866
	(.0972)	(.0776)	(.0747)	(.0915)	(.0700)	(.0964)	(.0853)
2 years	−.0207	−.0041	.0489	−.0510	.0640	−.0421	−.0711
	(.0686)	(.0548)	(.0533)	(.0640)	(.0493)	(.0680)	(.0610)
3 years	−.0277	.0108	.0317	−.0554	.0714	−.0443	−.0690
	(.0660)	(.0525)	(.0517)	(.0615)	(.0474)	(.0654)	(.0580)
4 years	−.0272	.0211	.0432	−.0683	.1002	−.0491	−.0946
	(.0843)	(.0670)	(.0657)	(.0785)	(.0603)	(.0833)	(.0739)
5 years	−.0196	.0282	.0599	−.0719	.1305	−.0484	−.1136
	(.1037)	(.0824)	(.0808)	(.0966)	(.0742)	(.1024)	(.0909)

NOTE.—Estimated coefficients from linear probability models are reported. Heteroscedasticity-consistent standard errors are reported in parentheses. All models include race, gender, schooling, age (within-group), and marital status as demographic control variables.

year-old treatment sample would bolster our confidence that our findings for young workers reflect causal effects of minimum wages, and this is exactly what table 7 shows. For training to obtain the current job, we found little evidence of minimum wage effects for young workers, and we find little evidence of any effect here. Of course, the more important analysis is for training to improve skills on the current job, for which we found negative and significant effects of minimum wages for young workers. As can be seen in the first three columns of table 7, however, all of the point estimates are close to zero and insignificant for the older workers. Thus, there is no indication of a negative relationship between minimum wages and training for older workers that would call into question a causal interpretation of the negative relationship we found for younger workers.

Plausibility of the Estimates

A rough assessment of the plausibility of our estimates can be obtained by comparing the implied reduction in the incidence of training from a "typical" minimum wage increase with the reported incidence in our data. Such an assessment was suggested in a very recent paper by Acemoglu and Pischke (1999), who argue that our estimates of the effects of minimum wages on training are implausibly large. Using our estimate for

20–24-year-olds in column 2′ of table 3 (−.1450), and the value of the minimum wage gap for California in 1991 of 21.86%, they note that the implication of our coefficient estimate is that the incidence of formal training among workers in this age group is 3.2 percentage points (21.86 × .1450) lower than in states subject to the lower federal minimum. They then take two steps to reach their conclusion that our estimated effect is implausibly large. First, they assume that minimum wages affect training propensities only among workers earning 160% of the minimum wage or less, which they report constitutes 30% of workers aged 20–24. Form- ing the ratio 3.2/.30, this implies that the reduction in training among "affected" workers in California would be 10.7 percentage points. Second, they note that the average incidence of training among workers aged 20–24 earning 160% of the minimum wage or less in states at the federal min- imum is 2.7%. As the ratio 10.7/2.7 = 4.0, they claim that our estimate "implies that introducing California's minimum wage to low minimum wage states should have wiped out all training *four times* among affected workers in these states" (p. 6).

It turns out, though, that Acemoglu and Pischke's claim rests on several suspect assumptions and a couple of miscalculations, and a more credible version of this same calculation indicates that our estimates are in a plau- sible range. First, their figures are actually based on a cutoff of 150% of the minimum rather than the 160% cutoff they cite. Second, these per- centages are incorrectly applied to a minimum wage of $3.35 rather than the $3.80 minimum that prevailed as of January 1991, the date to which the incidence estimates apply. If we instead use the cutoff of 160% that they suggest is appropriate for identifying affected workers and use the $3.80 minimum wage, we end up with 49% of workers presumed to be affected by the minimum wage rather than the 30% figure that Acemoglu and Pischke use. This higher cutoff also affects the estimated average incidence of training among workers aged 20–24 earning 160% of the minimum wage or less in states at the federal minimum, raising it from 2.7% to 4.5%.

Third, Acemoglu and Pischke's counterfactual entails introducing Cal- ifornia's minimum wage to low minimum wage states. As the federal minimum was $3.80 in January 1991, this implies an increase in the min- imum from $3.80 to $4.25, or an 11.84% increase, and not the 21.86% increase that Acemoglu and Pischke use. Repeating their calculation with these changes yields the following: (1) the implied reduction in training for this group overall is .017 (.1184 × .1450) instead of .032; (2) dividing this figure by .49 instead of .30 to get the reduction in training among the "affected" workers in California yields a figure of 3.5 percentage points instead of 10.7 percentage points; and (3) given that the correct average incidence of training among workers aged 20–24 earning 160% of the prevailing minimum wage or less in states at the federal minimum is 4.5%,

Minimum Wages and Training Revisited   589

when we divide the 3.5 percentage point reduction by the 4.5% incidence
figure, the implication of Acemoglu and Pischke's calculation is that the
implied effect of introducing California's minimum wage to low minimum
wage states would be to reduce training by .78 times its incidence rather
than by the outsized figure of 4 reported by Acemoglu and Pischke.

Even aside from these specific problems with their calculation, we
would question their reasoning. In particular, we see no compelling reason
to believe that the effects of minimum wages on training fall exclusively
on low-wage workers. If training costs are high and workers receive wages
net of training costs, the minimum wage can reduce training for some
higher-wage workers as well; that is, in the absence of a minimum wage
some of these higher-wage workers would receive lower wages plus training. Training of higher-wage workers could be more adversely affected
than that of low-wage workers if fixed costs of training are greater for
higher-wage workers. Such considerations would reduce even further the
implied reduction in training suggested by our estimates, as the effects
would not be concentrated exclusively among those earning 160% of the
minimum or below.

Some evidence on this question is reported in table 8. Column 1 repeats
the estimates for 16–24-year-olds and 20–24-year-olds (on which Acemoglu and Pischke have focused) from table 3. We then go on to explore
whether there is any evidence that minimum wage effects on training are
weaker for higher-wage workers, although we reiterate our earlier concerns with using wages in this way, as they presumably are jointly endogenous with training. To do this, we have to restrict attention to the
outgoing rotation groups in the CPS, for whom wages are available; column 2 reports estimates of the same specifications as in column 1 for this
subsample. The point estimates rise somewhat in absolute value in the
upper panel but fall in the lower panel. Given the large increases in the
standard errors (caused by dropping about three-fourths of the sample),
the estimated minimum wage effects are no longer significant. Finally, in
columns 3 and 4 we report estimates of specifications that include interactions of the minimum wage variable with a dummy variable indicating
high-wage workers (greater than or equal to 160% of the $3.80 federal
minimum wage); as explained in the notes to the table, the specifications
are also augmented to include all of the other main and interactive effects
that are needed to estimate the correct difference-in-difference. In all four
cases, the estimated coefficient of the minimum wage–high wage interaction is negative (although insignificant). That is, Acemoglu and Pischke's
key assumption that minimum wage effects on training occur exclusively
among workers near the minimum, implying a positive interactive effect,
is not supported by the data.

The consequence of this for the calculations described above is that we
should divide by a number larger than .49 in computing the implied

Table 8
Difference-in-Difference Estimates of Minimum Wage Effects on Formal Training to Improve Skills on the Current Job, High-Wage versus Low-Wage Workers, 1983 and 1991 CPS

	Full Sample, Minimum Wage Effect Estimates (1)	Outgoing Rotation Groups, Minimum Wage Effect Estimates (2)	Outgoing Rotation Groups, Minimum Wage Effect Estimates		Sample Size for Outgoing Rotation Groups (5)
			Overall Effect (3)	Differential Effect for High-Wage Workers (4)	
Older workers in 1991 as control sample:					
Ages 16–24	−.0947	−.1790	−.1224	−.1404	6,772
	(.0625)	(.1487)	(.1524)	(.2244)	
Ages 20–24	−.1450	−.1784	−.0969	−.1886	6,263
	(.0730)	(.1762)	(.1922)	(.2698)	
Workers of same age in 1983 as control sample:					
Ages 16–24	−.1197	−.0646	−.0694	−.0313	4,326
	(.0580)	(.1349)	(.1353)	(.1997)	
Ages 20–24	−.1832	−.0808	−.0888	−.0311	2,965
	(.0752)	(.1738)	(.1817)	(.2428)	

NOTE.—Estimated coefficients from linear probability models are reported. Heteroscedasticity-consistent standard errors are reported in parentheses. All models include race, gender, schooling, age (within-group), and marital status as demographic control variables. Column 1 replicates col. 2′ of table 3. Columns 2–4 report estimates for the outgoing rotation group files, for which wages are available. For the results reported in cols. 3 and 4, let HW_{ij} be a dummy variable indicating high-wage workers (those earning at least 160% of the federal minimum). Then, the specification estimated in the top panel is an augmented version of eq. (2), which can be written $T_{ij} = \alpha + S_j\beta + \gamma Y_j + \delta MW_j \cdot Y_j + \omega HW_{ij} + \omega' HW_{ij} \cdot Y_j + \delta' HW_{ij} \cdot MW_j \cdot Y_j + \varepsilon_{ij}$. The specification estimated in the bottom panel is an augmented version of eq. (3), which can be written $T_{ijt} = \alpha + S_j\beta + \gamma Z_t + \delta MW_{jt} + \omega HW_{ijt} + \delta' HW_{jt} \cdot MW_{jt} + \varepsilon_{ijt}$. Estimates of δ are reported in col. 3, and estimates of δ' are reported in col. 4.

reduction for affected workers. For example, if we simply assume that minimum wage effects fall equally on all workers, we would divide by 1.0 instead of .49. And, rather than scaling the estimated reduction by .045—the incidence of training among "low-wage" workers—we would divide by the overall training incidence for this age group (about .1). The resulting estimate would imply that increasing the minimum wage to California's minimum wage level would wipe out 17% (or .17) of training in the states in which the federal minimum wage prevailed, a much smaller figure than the 400% figure that Acemoglu and Pischke assert is implied by our estimates.[28]

[28] Interestingly, the incidence of formal training in California for 20–24-year-olds in the 1991 CPS is .0799, compared with .1058 in the states in which the

V. Conclusion

Theory predicts that minimum wages will reduce on-the-job training intended to improve skills on the current job but may increase training to qualify for a job. If the former effect is larger, the influence of minimum wages on training may represent an additional cost of minimum wage increases that is not captured by traditional estimates of the disemployment effects, because reductions in on-the-job training potentially affect a greater number of persons. If the latter effect dominates, then part of the costs of minimum wages may be offset by an increase in human capital accumulation associated with individuals raising their skills sufficiently to compete for minimum wage jobs. Either way, understanding the effects of minimum wages on training is essential in evaluating the wisdom of minimum wage increases. Surprisingly, there is very little evidence on this question, except with respect to the effects of minimum wages on schooling.

We estimate the effects of minimum wages on the incidence of training among young workers, focusing both on on-the-job training used to improve skills on the current job and on training that helped workers obtain or qualify for their current job. We exploit cross-state variation in minimum wage increases to assess the effects of minimum wages on the training received by young workers, using either older workers contemporaneously, or young workers from an earlier period, as a control sample.

The evidence generally supports the hypothesis that minimum wages reduce training aimed at improving skills on the current job, especially formal training. For young workers in their early 20s, the estimated effects indicate elasticities of the incidence of formal training with respect to the minimum wage ranging from about -1 to -2, implying sizable deleterious effects of minimum wages. Moreover, there is little or no evidence that minimum wages raise the amount of training obtained by workers to

---

federal minimum prevailed (see table 2). Thus, the incidence of training is 24% lower in California, in line with the 17% reduction attributable to California's higher minimum wage by the above calculation.

Acemoglu and Pischke also present some new evidence based on NLSY data indicating for the most part no effect of minimum wages on training. There are numerous factors that make the data sources and specifications noncomparable. One important difference is the measurement of training; the CPS data measure training ever received, while the NLSY measures training in the past year. More important, Acemoglu and Pischke's sample is much older. The NLSY respondents were aged 14–21 in 1979. Since their data set covers 1987–92, the age range in their sample extends from 22 to 34. In contrast, our most comparable sample covers ages 20–24. When we use workers in the CPS of the same ages as in Acemoglu and Pischke's sample (weighted to reflect the representation of each age group that would be expected in the NLSY given the age ranges and years covered) we obtain a very small (.03) and insignificant estimate of the minimum wage effect on training. (More details are available from the authors on request.)

qualify for their current job (and indeed there is some evidence that minimum wages reduce this type of training). We would add two potential qualifications to this evidence. First, the evidence on formal training to improve skills on the job does not point to stronger effects for workers most likely to be bound by the minimum, although we have argued that theory does not make a firm prediction that this should be the case. Second, regarding training to obtain the current job, it is possible that our data do not detect some general skill accumulation that responds positively to minimum wage increases, although given other research suggesting that minimum wages reduce school enrollments, and the evidence in this article on in-school training, we are relatively confident that any positive effects of minimum wages on general training to qualify for jobs would not be large. Consequently, we interpret the evidence as indicating that the principal effect of minimum wages on training is to substantially reduce formal training to improve skills on the current job, with no apparent offset from other types of human capital accumulation. Among other implications, this evidence undermines the case for using minimum wages to encourage a "high-wage" path for the economy.

Appendix

Table A1
Log Wage Regressions for 16–24-Year-Olds, 1991 CPS

	Any Training to Improve Skills on the Current Job		Formal or Informal Training to Improve Skills on the Current Job		Any Training That Was Needed to Obtain the Current Job		Formal or Informal Training That Was Needed to Obtain the Current Job	
	(1)	(1′)	(2)	(2′)	(3)	(3′)	(4)	(4′)
Any training to improve skills on the current job	.1955 (.0294)	.1144 (.0296)	. . .	. . .	. . .	. . .	. . .	. . .
Formal training to improve skills on the current job	. . .	. . .	.3075 (.0429)	.1771 (.0392)	. . .	. . .	. . .	. . .
Informal training to improve skills on the current job	. . .	. . .	.0439 (.0378)	.0367 (.0372)	. . .	. . .	. . .	. . .
Any training received to obtain current job	. . .	. . .	. . .	. . .	.2278 (.0253)	.1170 (.0248)	. . .	. . .
Formal training received to obtain current job	. . .	. . .	. . .	. . .	. . .	. . .	.2301 (.0534)	.1391 (.0478)

Minimum Wages and Training Revisited   593

Table A1 (Continued)

	Any Training to Improve Skills on the Current Job		Formal or Informal Training to Improve Skills on the Current Job		Any Training That Was Needed to Obtain the Current Job		Formal or Informal Training That Was Needed to Obtain the Current Job	
	(1)	(1′)	(2)	(2′)	(3)	(3′)	(4)	(4′)
Informal training received to obtain current job	...	...	...	...	...	...	.0715 (.0339)	.0289 (.0298)
Age	...	.0175 (.0828)	...	.0429 (.0832)	...	.0432 (.0844)	...	.0237 (.0836)
Age squared	...	.0011 (.0020)	...	.0005 (.0020)	...	.0004 (.0020)	...	.0010 (.0020)
Male	...	.0504 (.0224)	...	.0511 (.0226)	...	.0478 (.0225)	...	.0461 (.0226)
White	...	.0369 (.0306)	...	.0296 (.0304)	...	.0323 (.0297)	...	.0311 (.0305)
Married	...	.0082 (.0303)	...	.0074 (.0304)	...	.0073 (.0304)	...	.0055 (.0308)
Highest grade completed	...	.0428 (.0140)	...	.0423 (.0140)	...	.0392 (.0145)	...	.0441 (.0141)

NOTE.—Estimated coefficients are reported for each independent variable included in a specification, with standard errors in parentheses.

References

Acemoglu, Daron, and Pischke, Jorn-Steffen. "Minimum Wages and On-the-Job Training." Photocopied. Cambridge, MA: MIT, 1999.

Agell, Jonas, and Lommerud, Kjell Erik. "Minimum Wages and the Incentive for Skill Formation." *Journal of Public Economics* 64 (April 1997): 25–40.

Bartel, Ann P. "Training, Wage Growth and Job Performance: Evidence from a Company Database." Working Paper no. 4027. Cambridge, MA: National Bureau of Economic Research, 1992.

Bowers, Norman, and Swaim, Paul. "Recent Trends in Job Training." *Contemporary Economic Policy* 12 (January 1994): 79–88.

Constantine, Jill, and Neumark, David. "Training and the Growth of Wage Inequality." *Industrial Relations* 35 (October 1996): 491–510.

Cunningham, James. "The Impact of Minimum Wages on Youth Employment, Hours of Work, and School Attendance: Cross-Sectional Evidence from the 1960 and 1970 Censuses." In *The Economics of Legal Minimum Wages*, edited by Simon Rottenberg, pp. 88–123. Washington, DC: American Enterprise Institute, 1981.

Diebold, Francis X.; Neumark, David; and Polsky, Daniel. "Job Stability in the United States." *Journal of Labor Economics* 15 (April 1997): 206–33.

Ehrenberg, Ronald G., and Marcus, Alan. "Minimum Wage Legislation

594   Neumark and Wascher

and the Educational Decisions of Youths." *Research in Labor Economics* 3 (1979): 61–93.

———. "Minimum Wages and Teenagers' Enrollment-Employment Outcomes." *Journal of Human Resources* 17 (Winter 1982): 39–58.

Feldstein, Martin. "The Economics of the New Unemployment." *Public Interest* 33 (Fall 1973): 3–42.

Gardecki, Rosella, and Neumark, David. "Order from Chaos? The Effects of Early Labor Market Experiences on Adult Labor Market Outcomes." *Industrial and Labor Relations Review* 51 (January 1998): 299–322.

Grossberg, Adam J., and Sicilian, Paul. "Minimum Wages, On-the-Job Training and Wage Growth." *Southern Economic Journal* 65 (January 1999): 539–56.

Gustman, Alan L., and Steinmeier, Thomas L. "Labor Markets and Evaluations of Vocational Training Programs in the Public High Schools: Toward a Framework for Analysis." *Southern Economic Journal* 49 (July 1982): 185–200.

Hashimoto, Masanori. "Minimum Wage Effects on Training on the Job." *American Economic Review* 72 (December 1982): 1070–87.

Lang, Kevin. "Pareto Improving Minimum Wage Laws." *Economic Inquiry* 25 (January 1987): 145–58.

Lazear, Edward P. "Why Is There Mandatory Retirement?" *Journal of Political Economy* 87 (December 1979): 1261–84.

Lazear, Edward P., and Miller, Frederick H. "Minimum Wage versus Minimum Compensation." In *Report of the Minimum Wage Study Commission*, vol. 5, pp. 347–81. Washington, DC: U.S. Government Printing Office, 1981.

Leighton, Linda, and Mincer, Jacob. "The Effects of Minimum Wages on Human Capital Formation." In *The Economics of Legal Minimum Wages*, edited by Simon Rottenberg, pp. 155–73. Washington, DC: American Enterprise Institute, 1981.

Levin-Waldman, Oren M. "The Minimum Wage and the Path towards a High Wage Economy." Working Paper no. 166. Annandale-on-Hudson, NY: Jerome Levy Economics Institute, 1996.

Lynch, Lisa M. "Private Sector Training and the Earnings of Young Workers." *American Economic Review* 81 (March 1992): 299–312.

Mattila, J. Peter. "Youth Labor Markets, Enrollments, and Minimum Wages." *Proceedings of the Thirty-First Annual Meeting*, Industrial Relations Research Association Series, 1978, pp. 134–40.

Neumark, David, and Wascher, William. "Employment Effects of Minimum and Subminimum Wages: Panel Data on State Minimum Wage Laws." *Industrial and Labor Relations Review* 46 (October 1992): 55–81.

———. "The Effects of Minimum Wages on Teenage Employment and Enrollment: Evidence from Matched CPS Surveys." *Research in Labor Economics* 15 (1996): 25–63.

———. "Do Minimum Wages Fight Poverty?" *Economic Inquiry* (in press). (*a*)

———. "Minimum Wages and Skill Acquisition: Another Look at Schooling Effects." *Economics of Education Review* (in press). (*b*)

Rosen, Sherwin. "Learning and Experience in the Labor Market." *Journal of Human Resources* 7 (Summer 1972): 326–42.

Stigler, George J. "The Economics of Minimum Wage Legislation." *American Economic Review* 36 (June 1946): 358–65.

Welch, Finis. 1974. "Minimum Wage Legislation in the United States." *Economic Inquiry* 12 (September 1974): 285–318.

———. "The Rising Impact of Minimum Wages." *Regulation* 2 (November/December 1978): 28–37.

[16]

The Economic Journal, 114 (*March*), C87–C94. © Royal Economic Society 2004. Published by Blackwell Publishing, 9600 Garsington Road, Oxford OX4 2DQ, UK and 350 Main Street, Malden, MA 02148, USA.

TRAINING AND THE NEW MINIMUM WAGE*

Wiji Arulampalam, Alison L. Booth and Mark L. Bryan

Using the British Household Panel Survey, we estimate the impact of the national minimum wage, introduced in April 1999, on the work-related training of low-wage workers. We use two 'treatment groups'– those workers who explicitly stated they were affected by the new minimum and those workers whose derived 1998 wages were below the minimum. Using difference-in-differences techniques for the period 1998 to 2000, we find no evidence that the introduction of the minimum wage reduced the training of affected workers and some evidence that it increased it.

Human capital theory predicts that the introduction of a minimum wage in competitive labour markets will reduce general training investment by covered workers who can no longer finance such training through lower wages (Rosen, 1972). However if the low-paid labour market is imperfectly competitive, firms will be more likely to pay for general training, although under-provision may result; see *inter alia* Stevens (1994); Acemoglu and Pischke (1999). Intuitively, the monopsonistic character of the labour market compresses workers' returns to human capital, allowing the firm to keep some of the surplus. By compressing wages further the introduction of a minimum wage can increase training.

Early empirical studies that looked at the effect of training on wage growth found minimum wages to lower wage growth (Leighton and Mincer, 1981; Hashimoto, 1982). However more recent studies – all using US microdata – perform more direct tests with better data but with mixed results. While Schiller (1994) and Neumark and Wascher (2001) found that workers subject to a minimum wage received less training, Grossberg and Sicilian (1999) and Acemoglu and Pischke (2003) found no clear evidence either way.

A UK National Minimum Wage (NMW) was introduced on 1st April 1999. It followed a period of 6 years, from the abolition of the Wages Councils, during which there was no statutory wage-floor in any sector but agriculture. The Government views the NMW as an 'important cornerstone of Government strategy aimed at providing employees with decent minimum standards and fairness in the workplace' [http://www.dti.gov.uk/er/nmw/index.htm]. At the same time it emphasises the development of workforce skills – 'particularly the basic skills of some adults' [http://www.dfes.gov.uk/research/]. Our analysis empirically investigates if the two goals are compatible.

Our study provides the only investigation of the training effects of minimum wages in Britain. Moreover it utilises important new data from the British Household Panel Survey (BHPS) – on both training and whether or not individuals' wages were increased to comply with the NMW – facilitating a comparison of

* This research was supported by the Leverhulme Trust Award F/00213C 'Work-related Training and Wages of Union and Non-union Workers in Britain'. For helpful comments, we thank an anonymous referee, Mark Stewart and seminar participants at the University of Essex, the Australian National University, the Policy Studies Institute and the Centre for Economic Performance.

training evolution across various groups. We use individuals' responses as to whether or not they were affected by the NMW to identify groups 'affected' and 'not affected'. We compare these results to those derived using an alternative definition based on hourly wages. Our methodology is similar to that of Stewart (2003), who uses the BHPS to analyse the employment effect for low-wage workers of the NMW.

1. Empirical Framework

We estimate the mean impact of the NMW on training for those affected by this policy intervention using the difference-in-differences estimator in the context of a Linear Probability Model (LPM).

Let $T_{it} = 1$ if individual i received any training (to increase or improve skills in the current job during the past 12 months) in period t and zero otherwise. Then

$$\Delta T_{it} = \Delta \mathbf{X}_{it} \boldsymbol{\beta} + \alpha + \gamma A_i + \Delta \varepsilon_{it} \tag{1}$$

where $A_i = 1$ if individual i is in the affected group and zero otherwise; $\mathbf{X}_{it}$ is a vector of individual and job characteristics influencing the outcome variable; and γ is our parameter of interest. Differences in training experiences common across individuals due to, say, business cycle effects, are captured by α. The equation implicitly allows for individual-specific unobservable effects that may be correlated with some of the regressors. $\Delta \varepsilon_{it}$ is allowed to have arbitrary heteroscedastic covariance matrix in the LPM estimation. We stress that all our analysis is conditional on employment.[1]

2. The Data

Our data are from Waves 8 to 10 of the BHPS. The pre-NMW data are from Wave 8 and the post-NMW data are from Wave 10, conducted in 1998 and 2000 respectively.[2]

The BHPS is a nationally representative panel survey of private households in Britain. From Wave 8, a new format was introduced for work-related training. The new questions cover up to three training events since September of the previous year, and provide information on where training occurred, how it was financed, its duration, and if it led to qualifications. Our sample of individuals was interviewed in Wave 8 between August 1998 and March 1999 about training received since 1st September 1997. In Wave 10 they were interviewed between September 2000

---

[1] Stewart (2003), using the BHPS, finds no statistically significant evidence of employment effects of the NMW. It should anyway be emphasised that our estimated model accounts for selection biases arising from correlation with unobserved individual-specific characteristics.
[2] We use the data from 1998 onwards because major changes to the training questions were introduced in 1998. See Booth and Bryan (2002) for discussion about the differences in the questionnaires and training responses before and after this change. Bryan (2002) analysed training changes over 1995–7, when no minimum wage was in place, finding no significant differential effect for workers who would have been covered by the minimum wage. The government introducing the NMW came to power in May 1997, so one might have expected to see any 'announcement effect' reflected in reported training in 1997.

and May 2001 about training experienced since 1st September 1999. Reported training therefore falls unambiguously before and after the introduction of the NMW. We do not use training data from Wave 9 since we cannot determine if reported training occurred before or after the NMW was introduced.

The NMW was introduced at three levels: a main rate of £3.60 per hour, a youth rate of £3.00 for 18–21 year olds, and a special development rate of £3.20 for workers over 21 years old undertaking specific types of approved training. The existence of the development rate potentially distorts the training decision since employers can pay a lower wage in return for providing training. Although we are unable to identify explicitly individuals covered by this provision, in principle we can identify them indirectly by using a reported hourly wage measure which was introduced to the BHPS in Wave 9 (for hourly paid employees only). We found no such cases.

Our analysis covers employees aged between 18 and 60 years in Wave 8, who are not in the army, farming or fisheries, and with valid training information. Individuals reporting over 100 working hours per week (hours are used to derive hourly wages) were dropped. Where there were many missing observations on control variables, we created dummy variables indicating their status, to maintain reasonable sample sizes. Individuals must satisfy the selection criteria in at least Waves 8 and 10. For one of the treatment-control groups discussed below, they must also be present in Wave 9.

2.1. *The Outcome Variables and the Treatment/Control Groups*

We use two outcome variables: changes in training incidence ΔT_{it} and training intensity ΔT^*_{it} . These are identical unless training incidence is positive in both periods; then $\Delta T^*_{it} = 1$ if intensity increases, $\Delta T^*_{it} = -1$ if intensity decreases and $\Delta T^*_{it} = 0$ if intensity remains the same.

We define two alternative treatment and control groups, summarised in Table 1. *Treatment group 1* contains individuals whose derived hourly wage was below the NMW for their age in wave 8. These individuals' wages should have been raised to the NMW in April 1999 (assuming their derived wages are free of measurement error and would anyway not have increased in real terms between Waves 8 and 9). *Control group 1* comprises individuals earning between the NMW and 15% more than the NMW in Wave 8. To investigate spill-over effects, we include the group of individuals ('high-wage') from the rest of the wage distribution above 115% minimum wage in 1998.

Individuals replying positively to the new question, 'Has your pay or hourly rate in your current job been *increased* to bring you up to the National Minimum Wage or has it remained the same?' were categorised as belonging to *treatment group* 2. Since this question was only asked of individuals who did not change jobs between 1st April 1999 and the date of interview (from August 1998 to March 1999), this definition will exclude some workers who were subject to the NMW in a new job.[3]

---

[3] The treatment group will therefore tend to over-represent job stayers. However, insofar as individuals remain in their jobs because of characteristics, which are constant over time, the differencing estimator will eliminate potential selection bias.

Table 1

Means of Training Incidence, Training Intensity and the Derived Wage

Treatment/ control group definition	Wave	Treatment group				Control group				High-wage group§			
		Training incidence	Training intensity	Derived wage	N	Training incidence	Training intensity	Derived wage	N	Training incidence	Training intensity	Derived wage	N
		Derived wage† < NMW				NMW ≤ Derived Wage < 1.15 NMW				Derived Wage ≥ 1.15 NMW			
1 (based on derived wage in wave 8)*	8	0.160	2.551	2.818	259	0.189	6.465	3.818	221	0.290	5.212	8.942	2,777
	9			3.947				4.452				9.274	
	10	0.243	4.779	4.422	259	0.180	2.824	4.814	221	0.317	5.310	9.555	2,777
2 (based on whether wage increased to NMW)‡	8	0.101	2.257	3.837	99	0.280	4.951	8.451	2,405				
	9			4.353				8.833					
	10	0.172	6.508	4.583	99	0.303	4.882	9.109	2,405				

Notes:
*Wave 8 refers to pre-NMW period and Wave 10 to post-NMW period.
†Wave 8 derived wage calculated as: (12/52) [*PAYGU* / (*JBHRS* + 1.5*PDOT*)], where *PAYGU* is usual gross pay per month, *JBHRS* is usual standard weekly hours and *PDOT* is usual paid overtime weekly hours.
‡'Has your pay or hourly rate in your current job been *increased* to bring you up to the National Minimum Wage or has it remained the same?' Variable *INMWPACH* (wave 9 only), asked if respondent did not change jobs between 1/4/99 and interview);
§Since the second definition of what constitutes a treatment group and a control group is *not* based on information on wages, we do not define a 'high-wage' group here;
Of the 189 individuals in Treatment Group 1 who did not change jobs between 1/4/99 and interview, 53 were also in Treatment Group 2.

However, the question provides a treatment group that is arguably less prone to measurement error than the derived wage used for treatment group 1. Our *control group 2* is corresponding individuals who were job-stayers and who answered no to the above question. Since the question was only asked in Wave 9, this selection requires individuals to be present in all three waves (8, 9, and 10). The sample size is therefore smaller than for treatment group 1. Since the definition is based entirely on a question that does not use the wage information, we do not include any other groups in this specification.

Table 1 reports mean training for the pre and post NMW periods. Training incidence typically increased in all groups, with a particularly marked proportionate increase in the treatment groups. For example, incidence in treatment group 2 increased from 0.10 in wave 8 to 0.17 in wave 10; in control group 2, incidence went from 0.28 to 0.30. Despite the increases, training is much less prevalent amongst workers earning close to the minimum wage than in the higher-paid groups.

The pattern is less clear when we consider (unconditional) training intensity. In treatment group 1, mean intensity rose from 2.6 days in wave 8 to 4.8 days in wave 10. In control group 1, intensity fell sharply from 6.5 days to 2.8 days. An increase over the period, from 2.3 days to 6.5 days is observed in treatment group 2. In the two groups of higher paid workers ('high-wage' group 1 and control group 2), intensity, like incidence, is quite stable at around 5 days a year. The volatility in the smaller groups is possibly caused by their sizes, or by the noisiness of training intensity. If so, incidence change ΔT may be the preferred dependent variable. In the next Section we present results for both ΔT and ΔT^* and highlight the differences in the model estimates.

3. Results

The *raw difference-in-differences estimates* of (1) with no additional controls are reported in Table 2, columns (1)–(4). Columns (1) and (2) show the results for ΔT (incidence-changes) and columns (3)–(4) the results for ΔT^* (intensity-changes). Column (1) indicates that the training probability in treatment group 1 increased by about 9 percentage points more than it did in the control group. This increase is statistically significant at the 5% level. The training probability also increased in the high wage group relative to the control group but the coefficient is not statistically significant. This suggests no spill-over effect of the NMW into this group. From column (2) where we use treatment and control groups 2, we see that, although training incidence increased more in the treatment group (by 5.0 percentage points) than in the control group, the estimate of the effect of the NMW on the training probability is not statistically significant at conventional levels. In this equation, however, the constant, capturing the trend increase in incidence, is significant at 10%. The differences between columns (1) and (2) may be because control group 1 comprises workers just above the NMW, whereas control group 2 contains higher paid workers as well.

However, the results in columns (3) and (4) show that a similar result is obtained when information on changes in intensity is incorporated into the definition of training. More specifically, affected workers appear to be 10 percentage

Table 2

The Effect of the NMW on Training

	Raw difference-in-differences				Regression adjusted			
	ΔT		ΔT*		ΔT		ΔT*	
	Treatment/control group		Treatment/control group		Treatment/control group		Treatment/control group	
	1 (1)	2 (2)	1 (3)	2 (4)	1 (5)	2 (6)	1 (7)	2 (8)
Treatment group	0.0901 (1.98)**	0.0503 (1.18)	0.1004 (1.97)**	0.1046 (2.19)**	0.0785 (1.72)*	0.0422 (1.00)	0.0876 (1.71)*	0.0984 (2.02)**
High-wage group	0.0343 (0.98)		0.0187 (0.47)		0.0392 (1.12)		0.0242 (0.61)	
Intercept	−0.0090 (0.27)	0.0204 (1.83)*	−0.0000 (0.00)†	0.0166 (1.24)	−0.0706 (1.41)	−0.0418 (0.94)	−0.0790 (1.36)	−0.0663 (1.26)
Observations	3,257	2,504	3,257	2,504	3,257	2,504	3,257	2,504

Notes:

Absolute robust t statistics in parentheses; *significant at 10%; **significant at 5%.

Regression-adjusted estimates have the following first-differences controls: age-squared, part-time status, whether the job is fixed-term or temporary, whether the worker changed employers, marital status, union-coverage, sector, firm size, 1-digit industry, local unemployment rate, and dummies for missing values.

Table 1 defines dependent variables ΔT and ΔT*.

†The estimated standard error for this coefficient is 0.04.

points more likely to experience an increase in training than workers in the control group. The increases are statistically significant. These results suggest that the NMW may have resulted in increased training.[4]

Columns (5)–(8) of Table 2 show the *regression-adjusted difference-in-differences estimates* of equation (1) incorporating individual and job characteristics. We exclude potentially endogenous variables like tenure and occupation. Insofar as the additional variables change significantly over time, they help control for individual differences in training growth. Regression-adjusted estimates of the treatment effect are slightly lower than the estimates in columns (1)–(4). Thus for treatment group 1, the NMW increases the training probability by 8.0 percentage points *ceteris paribus*, significant at the 10% level. The training probability in the high-wage group increases by 4.0 percentage points but this is not significant at conventional levels. Both figures are relative to the base of control group 1. When the dependent variable is redefined to incorporate the information on intensity, the estimate, shown in column (7), is slightly higher at 8.8 percentage points.

In the specifications comparing treatment group 2 with control group 2 (columns (6) and (8)), the estimates are again similar to those without additional control variables (columns (2) and (4)). The NMW does not appear to significant affect the training incidence probability (the coefficient is positive), while it significantly increases intensity by 9.8 percentage points.

Overall, we interpret these results as providing support for the hypothesis that the NMW increased work-related training against the null hypothesis of no effect.[5]

4. Conclusions

We estimated the impact of the new national minimum wage on the work-related training of low-wage workers using two 'treatment groups'. These were first, those workers whose derived 1998 wages were below the minimum and, secondly, those workers explicitly stating they were affected by the new minimum. Using difference-in-differences techniques and information on training incidence and intensity, we found no evidence that the minimum wage introduction reduced the training of affected workers and some evidence that it increased it. In particular we found that the training probability increased by 8 to 11 percentage points for affected workers. Our findings provide little evidence supporting the human capital model as it applies to training and weak evidence of new theories based on imperfectly-competitive labour markets. Finally, our estimates suggest that two of the UK government's goals – improving wages of the low-paid and developing their skills – have been compatible, at least for the introductory rates of the minimum wage.

---

[4] We model the sign of changes in training intensity rather than the magnitude, since this relates directly to relevant theory. Modelling the exact change in training intensity would require us to address the issue that a change from 8 to 10 days is not necessarily the same as a change from 4 to 2 days or even a change from 2 to 0 days. Such analysis is beyond the scope of our current study.

[5] In companion papers, we describe extensions of the analysis (Bryan, 2002; Arulampalam *et al.* 2003). These alternative models (that also investigate the sensitivity of our estimates to changes in the definitions of treatment group 1 and its control group) produced similar results to those reported here and our conclusions are unchanged.

C94   THE ECONOMIC JOURNAL   [MARCH 2004]

University of Warwick
Australian National University and University of Essex
University of Essex

References

Acemoglu, D. and Pischke, J.-S. (1999). 'The structure of wages and investment in general training', *Journal of Political Economy*, vol. 107 (3), (June), pp. 539–72.

Acemoglu, D. and Pischke, J.-S. (2003). 'Minimum wages and on-the-job training', *Research in Labor Economics*, vol. 22, pp. 159–202.

Arulampalam, W., Booth, A. L. and Bryan, M. L. (2003). 'Work-related training and the new national minimum wage in Britain', Working Papers of the Institute for Social and Economic Research, No. 2003-5, University of Essex.

Booth, A. L. and Bryan, M. L. (2002). 'Who pays for general training? Testing some predictions of human capital theory', mimeo, Australian National University, (June).

Bryan, M. L. (2002), 'The effect of the national minimum wage on training', ch. 3 of thesis in preparation for PhD Examination, University of Essex.

Grossberg, A. J. and Sicilian, P. (1999). 'Minimum wages, on-the-job training and wage growth', *Southern Economic Journal*, vol. 65 (1), pp. 539–56.

Hashimoto, M. (1982). 'Minimum wage effects on training on the job', *American Economic Review*, vol. 72, pp. 1070–87.

Leighton, L. and Mincer, J. (1981). 'The effects of minimum wages on human capital formation', in (S. Rottenberg, ed.) *The Economics of Legal Minimum Wages*, pp. 155–73, Washington DC: American Enterprise Institute.

Neumark, D. and Wascher, W. (2001). 'Minimum wages and training revisited', *Journal of Labor Economics*, vol. 19 (3), pp. 563–95.

Rosen, S. (1972). 'Learning and experience in the labor market', *Journal of Human Resources*, vol. 7, pp. 326–42.

Schiller, B. R. (1994). 'Moving up: the training and wage gains of minimum wage entrants', *Social Science Quarterly*, vol. 75 (3), (September), pp. 622–36.

Stevens, M. (1994), 'A theoretical model of on-the-job training with imperfect competition', *Oxford Economic Papers*, vol. 46, pp. 537–62.

Stewart, M. B. (2003). 'The impact of the introduction of the UK minimum wage on the employment probabilities of low wage workers', mimeo, University of Warwick, (February).

[17]

OXFORD BULLETIN OF ECONOMICS AND STATISTICS, 55, 1 (1993)
0305-9049 $3.00

THE DETERMINANTS OF TRAINING OF MALE AND FEMALE EMPLOYEES IN BRITAIN*

Francis Green

I. INTRODUCTION

For some time now, the reform and expansion of training and education in Britain has been placed high on the political agenda. This imperative derives from the recognition that skill levels are relatively low overall in the British workforce and that this is a probable contributory factor to Britain's poor long-term economic performance. There is, accordingly, increasing interest in knowing who gains access to training and education, and in estimating how much is the economic reward to them and to society. Where large amounts of public funding are at stake, it is more than useful to know where it should best be spent.

We have at hand, in human capital theory, a ready-made model of who is likely to demand and to be provided with training. This model suggests that training decisions are like other investments: they respond to economic incentives. Training would thus be expanded up until the point where the net present value of training projects is zero. Hence it is predicted that, *ceteris paribus*, training is more likely to occur (a) where an individual is young (since this gives a greater expected post-training period of working life); (b) where the individual already has good educational qualifications (this may be interpreted plausibly as raising 'trainability' or, alternatively, as lowering the 'psychic' costs of training); (c) in expanding industries or industries with greater technological change; (d) where the individual is regarded, rightly or wrongly, as more committed to paid labour (bereft, for example, of family caring responsibilities); (e) in larger firms, where the company can both reap economies of scale in training provision and be more certain of retaining the trainee; (f) in occupations where the labour process is more subject to change, mainly higher-level occupations; (g) in the public sector, since private profit-

*This research was supported by ESRC Grant Number R000232636. The author is extremely grateful to Johnny Sung for his excellent research assistance. Material from the 1987 General Household Survey made available through the OPCS and the ESRC Data Archive has been used by permission of the Controller of HM Stationary Office. An earlier version of the paper was presented to the International Conference on the Economics of Training, Cardiff Business School, September 1989.

maximizing firms are more likely than public employers to be inhibited by the fear of poaching; (h) for individuals who have been recently recruited to a new job.

Earlier empirical studies have thrown some light on some of these matters (see Table 1). There is, to start with, a consensus that training decreases, *ceteris paribus*, with age. Other predictions of the human capital model also

TABLE 1
British Studies of the Determinants of Training

Hypothesis	*Studies confirming it*
(a) Training decreases with age	For males or for both sexes together: all For females: (1) and (4) confirm; (3) and (5) show insignificant effect
(b) Higher-level qualifications raise training probability	(1), (2), (4), (5) and (6)
(c) Growing or changing technology industries raise training	(6). Others show no consistent pattern
(d) Caring for children reduces training probability	(1), (4), (5). (3) shows no effect
(e) Larger establishments do more training	(2), (3), (4) and (5)
(f) Higher-level occupations require more retraining	(1), (2) and (5)
(g) Training is greater in the public sector	(4)
(h) Recent recruits to new jobs need training	(2) and (5)
(i) Sex discrimination over training access	(1), (3), (4) and (5)

Studies	*Data set*
(1) Greenhalgh and Stewart (1987)	National Training Survey (1975)
(2) Rigg (1989)	Training in Britain, Survey of Individuals, Summer (1987)
(3) Booth (1990)	Survey of Graduates and Diplomats (1980)
(4) Booth (1991)	British Social Attitudes Survey (1987)
(5) Green (1991a)	Labour Force Survey (1984)
(6) Allen, McCormick and O'Brien (1991)	Sample of unemployed in Sunderland (1986)

DETERMINANTS OF TRAINING OF MALE AND FEMALE EMPLOYEES   105

receive support, with the exception that the independent effect of industry shows little consistency in its pattern. While the construction industry tends to have a negative impact on training, only one study (this of the unemployed) claimed to find a pattern predicted by the human capital theory model.

There can be little pretence, however, that training decisions are taken solely on the basis of a rational individualistic calculus. For example, that the bulk of training activity is concentrated in the first years of working life is an institutional feature with historical origins in the apprenticeship system and in traditional sluggish attitudes to retraining for older workers, rather than an implicit or explicit cost-benefit calculation. As a second example, it is widely held that British companies have under-invested in training activities because they underestimated their value (Ashton, Green and Hoskins, 1989): this is the rationale for considerable governmental effort being devoted to high-lighting the benefits of training through the conferring of National Training Awards for good practice.

Another important institutional factor forms the focus of this paper. Given the changing sex composition of the workforce, the differential stance taken by and towards men and women as regards training is of considerable interest. The differential impact of sex on training participation is evident, either explicitly or implicitly, in some previous studies. The aim here is to investigate the separate determinants of participation in 'job-related' training for male and female employees and to derive explicit quantitative measures of employer discrimination. The study utilizes a new source of training data, the 1987 General Household Survey (GHS). This survey is nationally representative, and identifies any 'education, training or self-instruction that would help with (your job or) a job that you might do in the future' that happened in the four weeks prior to interview.[1] Section II develops some basic statistical models to investigate the determinants of the level and type of employee training, and uses these to define indices of discrimination analogous to conventional measures of wage discrimination. Section III presents the results, and Section IV summarizes and concludes the argument with a brief discussion of policy implications.

II. INDICES OF DISCRIMINATION IN A MODEL OF THE DETERMINANTS
OF TRAINING

It should first be emphasized that the observation that an employee is being trained is the joint outcome of two decisions, those of employer and employee. It is possible for either party to be frustrated. Some 43 percent of

---

[1] The survey also has the advantage of including motivational data that helps to distinguish between specific and general training. The survey includes, too, comprehensive information about participation in educational programmes. For an analysis of these aspects of the data, and for a picture which dovetails the stylized facts of training with those of education, see Green (1991b).

individuals from the Training in Britain survey (Rigg, 1989) recalled occasions when they wanted to but were unable to get some training. Not all of these would have been employees, but the figure suggests a considerable unmet training demand. Conversely, the General Household Survey data shows a quarter of individuals doing training that was a compulsory part of a job: presumably some of these individuals might have preferred not to train. Employers may also, at times, have difficulty in finding employees for training, as for example when YTS schemes became more difficult to fill in the South during the 1988–89 boom years. Since we cannot separately analyse employer and employee demands for training in individual cross-section data, the ensuing models must be regarded as reduced form equations.

In order to focus also on the different training determinants for males and females separate analyses were performed for each sex. I define 'market discrimination' as occurring when male and female employees, having the same personal characteristics (including the same existing human capital), have an unequal chance of receiving training. This, of course, is only a limited measure of the extent to which the societal opportunities for males and females to acquire skills are differently circumscribed. It excludes forms of 'pre-market discrimination' and, by concentrating on the extent of training, sets aside the widely recognized problem that much training reinforces the existing segregation of labour into male and female jobs, thereby reproducing pay differentials.[2] The definition also cannot be taken unequivocally to mean 'involuntary' discrimination, in the sense that women who apply for training are more likely than men to be denied it by discriminatory employers. It may well be the case that the attitudes of men and women towards training differ, as a result of pre-market experiences. Yet this distinction between voluntary and involuntary is not ultimately helpful, because the attitudes and choices of people are liable to be affected by the opportunities they perceive. If women see less opportunity for training and career advancement, they will be less likely than men to apply to their employers for training. Finally, the definition makes no reference to the motivation for employers' discrimination, whether it be sheer prejudice, or whether it be related to a possibly rational fear that women are more likely than men to quit their jobs. Such 'statistical discrimination' may or may not be a profit-maximizing strategy. To the extent, therefore, that discrimination is revealed, the conclusion points to the gains to be had from a policy of state intervention to internalize the externality associated with high turnover of female labour, and from better enforcement of anti-discriminatory legislation.

Let Y^* be the net unobserved present value of training, to be shared by employee and employer. Assuming an efficient bargain is struck, training will

---

[2] For discussion of wider discriminatory processes over training in society, see Green (1991a), Mallier and Rosser (1987), Bennett and Carter (1943), Cockburn (1987) or the overview by Clarke (1991).

DETERMINANTS OF TRAINING OF MALE AND FEMALE EMPLOYEES   107

take place if Y^* is positive. Hence our model is:

$$Y^{*F} = a^F X^F + u^F \tag{1}$$

$$Y^{*M} = a^M X^M + u^M \tag{2}$$

$$\left. \begin{array}{ll} Y^k = 1 & \text{iff} \quad Y^{*k} > 0 \\ Y^k = 0 & \text{iff} \quad Y^{*k} \leq 0 \end{array} \right\} \quad \text{for } k = \text{M, F}$$

where Y is a dummy variable indicating training participation, X a vector of firm and individual characteristics, u the error term, and superscripts M and F refer to males and females respectively. I assume the error terms have a logistic distribution, and hence (1) and (2) may be estimated by a standard logit procedure.

Separate estimation for the male and female samples allows the impact of independent variables to differ from males to females, but it also means there is no single measure of discrimination. Four possible measures may be obtained. Let $P(\bar{X}^k, a^j)$ (where $k, j = \text{M or F}$) be the predicted probability of training for an individual with average characteristics. The first definition considers an individual with average female characteristics $\bar{X}^F$, and contrasts the probabilities of training using female and male coefficients:

$$D_{F1} = \frac{P(\bar{X}^F, a^M)}{P(\bar{X}^F, a^F)} - 1$$

Inserting the logistic distibution, this gives:

$$D_{F1} = \frac{e^{-a^F \bar{X}^F} + 1}{e^{-a^M \bar{X}^F} + 1} - 1 \tag{3}$$

Alternatively, we may calculate the mean probability of training obtained by applying the male coefficients to the female sample, and compare this to the mean probability of training by applying the female coefficients to the female sample:

$$D_{F2} = \frac{\overline{P(X^F, a^M)}}{\overline{P(X^F, a^F)}} - 1 \tag{4}$$

By virtue of the maximum likelihood first order conditions,[3] the denominator of the first term is simply the sample frequency for females training (this assumes X includes an intercept term). However, owing to the non-linearity of the logistic function, in general $D_{F1} \neq D_{F2}$.

We may, of course, equally choose the male sample as the base for comparisons and ask what happens if their training is determined according to the

[3] Maddala (1983), p. 26.

female coefficients. This produces two more discrimination measures:

$$D_{M1} = 1 - \frac{e^{-\alpha^F \bar{X}^M} + 1}{e^{-\alpha^M \bar{X}^M} + 1} \tag{5}$$

and

$$D_{M2} = 1 - \frac{\overline{P(X^M, \alpha^F)}}{\overline{P(X^M, \alpha^M)}} \tag{6}$$

That $D_{M1} \neq D_{F1}$, $D_{M2} \neq D_{F2}$ is the familiar index number problem.

Unfortunately, none of these measures lends itself to an interpretation analogous to the Oaxaca method of separating pay differentials into a component due to discrimination and a component due to differences in characteristics (Oaxaca, 1973). To see this, we may write the difference in actual training participation rates of males and females as:

$$\overline{P(X^M, \alpha^M)} - \overline{P(X^F, \alpha^F)}$$
$$= [\overline{P(X^M, \alpha^M)} - \overline{P(X^M, \alpha^F)}] + [\overline{P(X^M, \alpha^F)} - \overline{P(X^F, \alpha^F)}] \tag{7}$$

While the first term in square brackets relates to definition D_{M2}, the second term cannot be expressed in terms of the differences between male and female characteristics, again due to the non-linear nature of the logistic function.[4]

Finally, analogous expressions may also be calculated in the context of models to explain participation in different types of training, and to explain the length of time spent in training.

III. DATA AND RESULTS

Participation in Training

These models were estimated using training participation data on 7,969 employees drawn from the 1987 GHS. It is first necessary and instructive to compare this training data to that which is more commonly used and quoted from the Labour Force Surveys (LFS) of 1984 onwards. The General House-hold Survey questionnaire is designed specifically to identify training, separately from education, and as such participation in certain types of further education are not counted here as training, including some day or block release education. Despite this, the GHS records noticeably wider training participation over a four-week period than does the Labour Force Survey. Three reasons contribute towards this difference. First, the GHS explicitly

---

[4] Note also that the second term in square brackets could just as likely be negative as positive, there being no reason to expect male characteristics necessarily to favour higher training.

DETERMINANTS OF TRAINING OF MALE AND FEMALE EMPLOYEES   109

includes 'self-instruction' (an example given to interviewers is 'teaching your-self to use a word processor over a period of time'); therefore it may pick up more instances of learning than the LFS which does not ask about self-instruction. Second, a prompt card with many examples of types of training was handed to respondents of the GHS but not to respondents of the LFS; such cards may help to jog memories. Finally, more than a third of LFS respondents are interviewed in any case by proxy. It seems likely that, in at least a few instances of short training, the family member responding may be unaware or may not recall that they ever happened. Some confirmation of this was obtained by an examination of LFS 1989 data, which showed that the recorded training participation rate of those who responded directly was 2.8 percentage points higher than that of those responding by proxy.[5] For these reasons the 1987 GHS, despite having a sample size smaller than the LFS, is a valuable addition to the available training data for Britain.[6]

The independent variables to be used, as suggested by theory and earlier work, are shown in Table 2. Table 3 presents the maximum likelihood esti-mates of equations (1) and (2) from the samples of all male and female employees aged 16 to 59. These reveal some notable differences between the processes determining male and female training participation.

There are different age profiles, in that for males the probability of training declines sharply with age, levelling off to a minimum at 68 (beyond the sample span), while for females there is but a gentle and statistically insignifi-cant decline with age. This finding is consistent with the hypothesis that employers are relatively more reluctant to train younger women than older women for fear that they will quit for child rearing, and confirms previous findings (Green, 1991a). There are also differences in the impact of previous qualifications and of occupation: being in a higher level occupation and having higher qualifications raises the chances of training, as previous work has found, but the effects are notably more pronounced for females. There is, also, a large and significant negative impact for females of being part-time. As an illustration of the effect of these factors, Table 4 presents the predicted probability for a basic case and a few variations.

There is also, as expected from theory, an impact from size of establish-ment: *ceteris paribus*, smaller establishments are likely to find unit training costs higher and to be less sure of reaping the benefits of training. Training also tends to decrease with job tenure, more sharply so in the case of females. The explanation for this is that training is more likely for those relatively new to a job. Training may be particularly important for women returning to jobs after spending time out of the labour force. As expected, too, family caring responsibilities (as represented by DEPCHLD and MARRIED) tended to decrease the likelihood of training, significantly for women. The explanation

[5] Author's own calculation.
[6] The training questions were more limited in the 1988 and 1989 GHS, and dropped altogether thereafter, a matter of some regret.

110 BULLETIN

TABLE 2

The Determinants of Training for Male and Female Employees:
Independent Variable Means

		Males	Females
AGE		36.6	36.7
AGE²		1475	1484
MARRIED		0.73	0.70
DEPCHILD	Under 5 child present	0.19	0.10
PAY	Gross hourly pay (£)	5.43	3.57
PT	Part-time = 1; full-time = 0	0.03	0.44
PUB	Public sector dummy	0.27	0.33
Establishment size (No. of employees):			
SIZE1	1–2	0.03	0.06
SIZE3	100–199	0.34	0.27
SIZE4	1,000 and over	0.14	0.09
Job tenure:			
JOBTEN1	Less than 3 months	0.05	0.07
JOBTEN3	6 months but less than 12 months	0.09	0.10
JOBTEN4	12 months but less than 5 years	0.26	0.36
JOBTEN5	5 years or more	0.56	0.41
MAN_PROF	Managers and professionals	0.27	0.10
INTNONMA	Intermediate non-manual	0.11	0.21
JUNNONMA	Junior non-manual	0.10	0.46
SKMA	Skilled and semi-skilled manual	0.45	0.15
Highest qualifications:			
HIGH_DEG	Degree and other higher qualifications	0.25	0.12
VOCAT	Nursing, commercial, apprenticeships	0.07	0.15
A_LEVEL	At least one GCE A-level	0.13	0.07
O_LEVEL	CSE and GCE O-levels	0.23	0.28
OTH_QUAL	Other and foreign qualifications	0.03	0.02

may be either that employers judge women with family responsibilities to be less worth investing in, or that the women themselves feel obliged to sacrifice training opportunities owing to the putative priority of their husbands' jobs or of their children's needs. Among the included industry dummies, only 'Energy and Water Supplies' and 'Other Services' showed a significant (positive) effect on training compared to the construction industry, and this only for males: there is, therefore, little support for the thesis that training is especially important in certain faster-growing industries, but it should be added that the data were only disaggregated at the level of division. There was also no significant effect of being in the public sector, a result which thereby fails to confirm that of Booth (1991), who found on her different data

DETERMINANTS OF TRAINING OF MALE AND FEMALE EMPLOYEES   111

TABLE 3
The Determinants of Training for Male and Female Employees:
Logit Estimates

	Males		Females	
AGE	−0.079	(−2.73)	0.01	(0.33)
AGE²	0.00058	(1.58)	−0.00031	(−0.76)
MARRIED	0.10	(0.86)	−0.28	(−2.55)
DEPCHLD	−0.18	(−1.60)	−0.45	(−2.65)
PAY	0.0023	(0.19)	0.0082	(1.17)
PT	0.09	(0.37)	−0.49	(−4.23)
PUB	0.11	(0.88)	0.02	(0.14)
SIZE1	−0.11	(−0.4)	−0.13	(−0.57)
SIZE3	0.25	(2.71)	0.05	(0.44)
SIZE4	0.12	(0.96)	0.21	(1.35)
JOBTEN1	0.12	(0.54)	0.28	(1.26)
JOBTEN3	−0.54	(−2.58)	−0.38	(−1.77)
JOBTEN4	−0.57	(−3.10)	−0.84	(−4.56)
JOBTEN5	−0.63	(−3.38)	−0.88	(−4.57)
MAN_PROF	1.16	(5.04)	1.81	(4.54)
INTNONMA	1.24	(5.23)	1.86	(4.83)
JUNNONMA	0.82	(3.40)	1.44	(3.82)
SKMA	0.44	(2.00)	0.76	(1.86)
HIGH_DEG	0.96	(7.10)	1.21	(7.13)
VOCAT	0.33	(1.60)	0.59	(3.65)
A_LEVEL	0.70	(4.71)	0.80	(4.17)
O_LEVEL	0.52	(3.99)	0.54	(3.69)
OTH_QUAL	0.44	(1.53)	0.82	(2.66)
CONSTANT	−0.45	(−0.82)	−2.28	(−3.09)
INDUSTRY DUMMIES	Included		Included	
Mean of dependent variables	0.219		0.185	
Likelihood ratio index	0.10		0.14	
Sample size	4,125		3,844	

t-Statistics in parentheses

set that training was less likely to occur in the private sector. Finally, hourly pay was included, principally for comparison with earlier work which found that higher pay raised the probability of training (Rigg, 1989). There is no *a priori* reason for entering this variable, since what is relevant for the individuals is the future pay deriving from current training. Current pay has no clear relation to future pay, nor to current training costs. In the event the

112						BULLETIN

TABLE 4
Predicted Probabilities for Employees of Receiving Training

	Male	Female
Basic case*: Single childless person on £3 an hour, full-time, unskilled, private-sector manual worker with no qualifications, 3 to 12 months in establishment of 100 to 999 workers, in financial and business services	23.0	10.5
As basic, but part-time*	26.5	5.2
As basic, but aged 40, on £4 an hour	11.1	9.1
As basic, but a junior non-manual worker with O-levels	48.0	48.7
Person with average female characteristics*	20.1	13.8
Person with average male characteristics*	18.8	16.0

Source: Estimates from Table 3.
*Male/female difference significant at the 5% level.

TABLE 5
Discrimination Coefficients

Female data as base	D_{F1}	45.5
	D_{F2}	26.4
Male data as base	D_{M1}	15.3
	D_{M2}	8.4

Source: Estimates from Table 3.
For definitions, see text.

coefficient is small and insignificant, which suggests that Rigg's conclusion derives from the omission of key variables (of which the full-time/part-time dummy seems an obvious candidate).

These results may now be drawn together with the estimates of overall discrimination. The coefficients defined in (3) to (6) are presented in Table 5, indicating a considerable degree of discrimination.[7] For example, they suggest that the females in the sample would have had 26.4 percent greater training participation if they had all been treated as or acted as males; the average female would have had been 45 percent more likely to participate in training if she had been treated like a male. As to which measure is the 'correct' one there is no single answer: it depends, of course, on the question asked.

[7] D_{F1} and D_{M1} were both significantly above zero at the 5 percent level; it was not possible, using LIMDEP, to obtain standard errors for D_{F2} and D_{M2}.

DETERMINANTS OF TRAINING OF MALE AND FEMALE EMPLOYEES   113

The measure appears to be heavily dependent on whether a female or male base is used. The chief reason is that males and females differ considerably in the proportions working part-time (3 percent compared to 44 percent) and this variable has a substantial negative impact for females, while not for males. This suggests that, taking only full-timers, the extent of discrimination will be lower. To investigate this, further estimates were obtained that compared males with full-time females. Two resulting discrimination coefficients were obtained, giving $D_{F1} = 14.7$ percent and $D_{M1} = 13.3$ percent. These being close to the estimate for the whole sample using the male data as base, it is confirmed that the higher discrimination coefficients calculated from the whole female data base derive from the substantial impact of the 44 percent part-time females being treated like part-time males.[8]

Before concluding the discussion of this model, a caveat needs briefly to be mentioned. Where coefficients are estimated for special samples, there is often a possibility of sample selectivity which can bias coefficient estimates. It is perhaps plausible that attitudes towards and aptitude for training could affect individuals' decisions to seek employment, or of firms to employ them. This effect may be different for males and females. By restricting the above analyses to samples of employees, there may be an unobserved missing variable causing $E(u_F) \neq 0$. Taking, first, older women, it is possible that their employment, and hence inclusion in the sample, would be promoted by any unobserved positive attitudes towards training or by employers' perceptions of their 'trainability'. To this extent the measure of discrimination is likely to be understated, since the above argument is far less likely to affect males, and so the conclusion earlier, that discrimination against older women is reduced or removed, must be qualified. On the other hand, for young people aged 16 to 18 there is a major choice to be made between schooling and college education and employment. For this group, participation in employment could reflect a negative attitude to the acquisition of human capital. This may differ for males and females, and it is possible that those young women in employment may have greater unobserved negative attitudes towards training: if so, the measure of discrimination would be an overstatement.

This argument suggests that the analysis might be improved by incorporating a sample selection correction procedure, which estimates the training probabilities conditioned on individuals' employment. There are, however, two difficulties with such a course of action, one practical the other theoretical. First, the employment decision would need to be modelled in a sophisticated manner, taking into account the various alternative states which include unemployment, full-time education and other forms of being 'econo-

---

[8] A further comparison was made by separating males and part-time females. Unsurprisingly, the discrimination coefficients were much higher ($D_{F1} = 154$ percent, $D_{M1} = 69$ percent). However, the part-timer sample was relatively small, and the equation was not very well defined; consequently the variance of the predicted logit for an average part-time female was high, and the resulting estimate of discrimination subject to such a large margin of error that it was not significantly different from zero.

TABLE 6

The Determinants of On-the-Job or Off-the-Job Training for Males and Female Employees: Multinominal Logit Estimates

| | On-the-Job Training Involved | | Only Off-the-Job Training | |
	M	F	M	F
AGE	-0.113 (-3.15)	-0.041 (-1.1)	0.021 (0.47)	0.104 (2.30)
AGE^2	0.00094 (1.99)	0.00028 (0.57)	-0.00053 (-0.97)	-0.00143 (-2.39)
MARRIED	0.07 (0.52)	-0.26 (-1.9)	0.16 (0.97)	-0.29 (-1.92)
DEPCHLD	-0.12 (-0.85)	-0.40 (-1.84)	-0.22 (-1.41)	-0.50 (-2.09)
PAY	-0.00026 (-1.25)	0.00008 (0.96)	0.00015 (1.01)	0.00008 (0.82)
PT	-0.02 (-0.08)	-0.55 (-3.70)	0.31 (0.80)	-0.41 (-2.5)
PUB	0.06 (0.39)	0.16 (0.87)	0.18 (1.00)	-0.16 (-0.85)
SIZE1	-0.24 (-0.7)	-0.19 (-0.6)	0.05 (0.14)	-0.05 (-0.14)
SIZE3	0.37 (3.2)	0.03 (0.24)	0.11 (0.86)	0.09 (0.59)
SIZE4	0.19 (1.2)	0.33 (1.8)	0.05 (0.32)	0.05 (0.24)
JOBTEN1	0.22 (0.92)	0.53 (2.09)	-0.47 (-0.98)	-0.28 (-0.83)

DETERMINANTS OF TRAINING OF MALE AND FEMALE EMPLOYEES 115

JOBTEN3	-0.62	(-2.66)	-0.24	(-0.94)	-0.30	(-0.81)	-0.62	(-1.98)
JOBTEN4	-0.81	(-3.94)	-0.88	(-4.0)	-0.004	(-0.17)	-0.79	(-3.07)
JOBTEN5	-0.91	(-4.33)	-0.94	(-4.0)	-0.05	(-0.17)	-0.82	(-3.1)
MAN_PROF	1.09	(3.87)	1.91	(3.50)	1.21	(3.38)	1.74	(3.08)
INTNONMA	1.34	(4.65)	1.83	(3.44)	1.12	(3.05)	1.92	(3.51)
JUNNONMA	0.96	(3.36)	1.53	(2.94)	0.52	(1.33)	1.33	(2.47)
SKMA	0.49	(1.86)	0.70	(1.26)	0.37	(1.05)	0.86	(1.46)
HIGH_DEG	0.82	(4.72)	0.91	(4.11)	1.16	(5.81)	1.49	(6.31)
VOCAT	0.25	(0.92)	0.64	(3.15)	0.45	(1.55)	0.52	(2.20)
A_LEVEL	0.69	(3.77)	0.62	(2.60)	0.75	(3.32)	1.06	(3.89)
O_LEVEL	0.49	(3.05)	0.58	(3.20)	0.60	(2.90)	0.43	(1.93)
OTH_LEVEL	0.41	(1.13)	0.71	(1.73)	0.48	(1.17)	0.92	(2.22)
CONSTANT	0.17	(0.26)	-1.84	(-1.99)	-4.09	(-4.64)	-5.0	(-4.5)
INDUSTRY DUMMIES	Included		Included		Included		Included	
Mean of dependent variable	0.125		0.109		0.094		0.078	
Likelihood ratio index	Males: 0.10 Females: 0.13							

mically inactive'; the determinants of which state the individual rests in will vary with age. But second, it is doubtful whether such a modelling procedure would improve further the reliability of the interpretation we may place upon the estimates of discrimination, because the employment decision itself may be subject to the very discriminatory process herein examined. Discrimination against females for jobs with training associated amounts also, of course, to discrimination over the training.

Participation in On-the-Job and Off-the-Job Training

While the previous analysis has examined all training for employees, it is of some interest to split the experience of training according to whether it involved at least some on-the-job training ('learning by practice and example while actually doing the job') or whether it involved exclusively off-the-job training. Nearly three-fifths of trainees (male or female) were involved in on-the-job training.

These outcomes are analysed by a straightforward generalization of the previous section using a trinomial logit procedure, and the results are presented in Table 6.

The fairly remarkable finding is that for the most part the conclusions with regard to training determinants, discussed in the previous analysis, apply to both types of training separately. They will not therefore be repeated here. There are two main exceptions. First, for women, the estimated probability of receiving off-the-job training actually increases to a peak at age 35 then falls off, while for men the probability falls from age 19 onwards. This is no less consistent, however, with human capital theory, since it is common practice for women to leave the workforce and return later in need of some retraining. Second, the effect of size is important and significant only where the training involves on-the-job learning.

The third column of Table 7 presents some coefficients of discrimination, calculated by predicting, with each type of training, the average probability of training with male or female coefficients (columns 1 and 2), for the members of the female (or male) data set.[9] These coefficients may be compared with their equivalents, D_{F2} and D_{M2} in Table 5. The conclusion is that, using the female data as the base, there is much more discrimination over on-the-job training than over off-the-job training. However, this is not observed where males are used as the base.

---

[9] For example, for any individual the predicted probability of receiving on-the-job ($j=1$) or only off-the-job training ($j=2$) is given by

$$P_j = \frac{e^{\alpha_j X}}{1 + e\alpha_1^X + e\alpha_2^X} \qquad j = 1, 2$$

These probabilities are then averaged over the females or males in the sample to give the predicted probabilities and hence the discriminations coefficients in Table 7.

DETERMINANTS OF TRAINING OF MALE AND FEMALE EMPLOYEES   117

TABLE 7
Discrimination Coefficients: Types of Training

	Predicted probabilities (%)		
	[1] Male coefficient estimates	[2] Female coefficient estimates	[3] Discrimination coefficient
Female data set as base:			
Involving on-the-job training	14.73	10.89	35.2
Off-the-job training only	8.96	7.79	15.1
Male data set as base:			
Involving on-the-job training	12.51	11.57	7.5
Off-the-job training only	9.41	8.36	11.1

The Determinants of the Length of Training

Survey respondents who answered that they had received training were also asked how long each training 'episode' in the previous four weeks had lasted. It is possible to aggregate multiple episodes, where they occurred, by adding the mid-points of the hours' bands, and allocating each trainee to a band of total hours received as shown in Table 8. This method being somewhat approximate it was thought more reliable to regard these bands as an ordinal rather than a cardinal ranking. Unfortunately, only 57 percent of those participating in training gave information about how many hours and episodes of training they had received. Ideally one would want to include those with no training in the analysis. In view of the missing information, it was decided instead to examine only those who had responded on training hours, but to regard the results with some caution.

Given the ordinal ranking of training hours, an ordered probit analysis was considered appropriate,[10] and the resulting estimates, using the same independent variables as in the earlier analysis, are presented in Table 9.

A glance at the *t*-statistics reveals that the estimates are on the whole poorly determined, and the equations do not give a good fit to the data. Nonetheless, the χ^2 statistics indicate some of the variance is being explained. Of particular note is the finding that whereas for females the higher-level occupations tend to involve longer hours of training, for males the reverse is the case: the male unskilled manual worker has significantly longer training than all other groups. The effect of qualifications is also uneven. The male

[10] See, e.g. Maddala (1983), pp. 46–9.

118   BULLETIN

TABLE 8
The Length of Training for Males and Females

	% of Males	% of Females
Proportions of training workers who receive over 4 weeks:		
Less than 5 hours	20.4	25.6
5 to 9 hours	23.3	25.6
10 to 14 hours	11.0	12.3
15 to 19 hours	11.2	9.8
20 to 29 hours	12.3	11.0
30 to 39 hours	7.4	6.0
40 hours and over	14.4	9.6

Note:
   In a minority of cases, workers had more than one training spell in the four-week reference period. In such cases, the mid-point of the training hours' category was used to aggregate spell lengths, and allocate each case to the appropriate band. If one spell was of 40 hours or over the aggregate spell length was automatically also allocated to 40 hours or over.

with A-levels seems to be the one who has the longest hours of training, other things equal. Also of note is that female workers in the public sector have shorter training spells than those in the private sector. It is also worth recording that being part-time which, as the earlier analysis showed, has a substantial effect on participation in training, has no significant effect on the hours spent training by trainees.

An appropriate analogous measure of discrimination, in this context, is the difference between the predicted length of training according to whether male or female coefficients are used. This shows that (whether an average male or an average female base is used) the predicted training length is 5 to 9 hours for female coefficients and 10 to 14 hours for male coefficients.[11] However, since the estimates are poorly determined, the difference between the two was not highly significant.[12]

IV.   CONCLUSION

The analyses in this paper have confirmed a number of features of training incidence consistent with the human capital approach. The main findings which confirm the consensus of earlier studies comprise the following:

   (i)   At least for males, training (especially on-the-job training) declines significantly with age.

[11] The predicted outcome is defined as the range containing βX where β is the vector of estimated coefficients and X is the characteristics vector.
[12] For both the average male and average female bases, the t-statistic was 1.0.

DETERMINANTS OF TRAINING OF MALE AND FEMALE EMPLOYEES   119

TABLE 9

The Determinations of the Length of Training: Ordered Probit Estimates

	Male		Female	
AGE	−0.02	(−0.62)	0.02	(0.48)
AGE^2	0.00016	(0.34)	−0.00027	(−0.46)
MARRIED	−0.18	(−1.3)	−0.23	(−1.78)
DEPCHLD	−0.01	(−0.12)	0.02	(0.1)
PAY	−0.00022	(−1.09)	−0.00021	(−1.05)
PT	0.06	(0.26)	−0.09	(−0.65)
PUB	0.15	(0.96)	−0.27	(−1.52)
SIZE1	0.09	(0.27)	0.18	(0.64)
SIZE3	0.17	(1.51)	0.18	(1.29)
SIZE4	0.13	(0.88)	0.32	(1.80)
JOBTEN1	0.54	(1.76)	0.33	(1.19)
JOBTEN3	0.30	(1.08)	0.42	(1.36)
JOBTEN4	0.29	(1.22)	0.08	(0.34)
JOBTEN5	0.45	(1.88)	0.21	(0.92)
MAN_PROF	−0.79	(−2.47)	1.15	(1.91)
INTNONMA	−1.02	(−3.13)	0.89	(1.50)
JUNNONMA	−1.07	(−3.09)	0.87	(1.48)
SKMA	−0.98	(−2.96)	0.18	(0.28)
HIGH_DEG	0.26	(1.51)	−0.33	(−1.37)
VOCAT	−0.03	(−0.12)	−0.40	(−1.59)
A_LEVEL	0.50	(2.55)	0.16	(0.59)
O_LEVEL	0.23	(1.25)	0.01	(0.06)
OTH_QUAL	0.21	(0.57)	−0.32	(−0.78)
CONSTANT	1.71	(2.29)	−0.41	(−0.41)
INDUSTRY DUMMIES	Included		Included	
Likelihood ratio index	0.029		0.035	
$\chi^2(32)$	56.4		49.1	
Sample size	539		398	

(ii) Those with higher qualifications are more likely to receive training. The explanation may be either that they are likely to benefit more from the training or that the psychic costs may be lower.

(iii) Those, especially women, with family responsibilities, are less likely to receive training.

(iv) Those working in larger establishments are more likely to receive on-the-job training.

(v) Certain occupations, particularly the higher status ones, require more participation in training.

(vi) Those who have recently started a new job tend to need and receive training.

120   BULLETIN

The main new findings that go beyond the earlier consensus are as follows:

(vii) This analysis has added support to those previous studies which showed a substantially different training–age relationship for females, in that the decline of training of females with age is but gentle and significant; moreover it has revealed that, for females, off-the-job training increases with age to a peak in the mid-30s.

(viii) A new finding is that the receipt of off-the-job training is not affected by establishment size and, accordingly, that all the establishment size effect works through on-the-job training.

(ix) As a qualification of (v) it appears that, for males, trainees in unskilled manual occupations have relatively long training hours.

(x) Finally, a result which contradicts earlier evidence is that training is not significantly greater, *ceteris paribus*, for employees working in the public sector.

None of these findings, however, necessarily lends any support to the proposition that human capital acquisition is best left to individuals and firms, given market incentives. Indeed, the paper has focused on a particular institutional determinant of training, lying largely outside the human capital approach, by developing a measure of discrimination over training. Discrimination occurs in that, through a complex of institutional mechanisms, employers systematically provide less training for their female employees than for their male employees with otherwise identical characteristics. The 1987 General Household Survey was divided into males and females and separate analyses carried out. If, then, it is asked 'by how much would the females in the sample have raised their training frequency if they had been treated as males' the answer is 26 percent. Other measures of discrimination, equally plausible, range from 8 percent to 45 percent, depending on the precise question asked.

The policy implications of these findings depend first upon accepting the proposition that more training should be encouraged. Given that, the findings support measures to raise the contribution of small establishments to training, and measures to provide childcare facilities which would enable women to participate more in training. They also call for greater efforts generally to resist discrimination, particularly against younger women. Insofar as some of this discrimination is not plain prejudice but is based on the perceived risk of losing women employees, there is a strong case both for a campaign to change employers' perceptions (in this age of continually growing female participation in the labour force), and for state intervention to fund the training of women who may otherwise suffer from moving into and out of the labour force. A recent evaluation study of the 'Training Opportunity Scheme', later the 'Old Job Training Scheme', has shown how they provided a wide range of skills training, some at high levels, and that these schemes were relatively beneficial for women, especially women returners (Payne, 1991). It is a matter of regret that these schemes were subsumed and disappeared within

DETERMINANTS OF TRAINING OF MALE AND FEMALE EMPLOYEES   121

the cheaper Employment Training Scheme, which provides very little high-level skill training and is far less use for women. On the other hand, the general expansion of training participation during the expansion period of the mid- and late-1980's, as highlighted by successive Labour Force Surveys, has raised the numbers of women participating in training (Greenhalgh and Mavrotas, 1991). Such changes suggest that discrimination against women may alter over time and over the course of the business cycle. Only further work will reveal whether the diminution of government-provided adult training opportunities for women has been counter-balanced significantly by the growth of job-related training for employees.

Department of Economics and Centre for
Labour Market Studies, University of Leicester

Date of Receipt of Final Manuscript: May 1992

REFERENCES

Allen, H. J., McCormick, B. and O'Brien, R. J. (1991). 'Unemployment and the demand for retraining: an econometric analysis', *Economic Journal*, Vol. 101, March, pp. 190–201.

Ashton, D., Green, F. and Hoskins, M. (1989). *Training in Britain: An Overview of the Evaluation of the Net Benefits of Training*, Training Agency.

Bennett, Y. and Carter, D. (1983). *Day Release For Girls*, Equal Opportunities Commission, Manchester.

Booth, A. (1990). 'Earning and Learning: What Price Firm Specific Training?', Birkbeck College, mimeo.

Booth, A. (1991). 'Job-Related Formal Training: Who Receives It and What Is It Worth?', *BULLETIN*, Vol. 53, pp. 281–94.

Clarke, K. (1991). *Women and Training: A Review of Recent Research and Policy*, Equal Opportunities Commission, Manchester.

Cockburn, C. (1987). *Two-Track Training: Sex Inequalities and the YTS*, Macmillan, London.

Green, F. (1991a). 'Sex Discrimination in Job-Related Training', *British Journal of Industrial Relations*, Vol. 29, pp. 295–304.

Green, F. (1991b). *The Determinants of Training of Male and Female Employees in Britain*, University of Leicester, Department of Economics, Discussion Paper No. 153.

Greenhalgh, C. and Mavrotas, G. (1991). 'Workforce Training in the Thatcher Era — Market Forces and Market Failures', paper presented to the International Conference on the Economics of Training, Cardiff Business School, September 1991.

Greenhalgh, C. and Stewart, M. (1987). 'The Effects and Determinants of Training', *BULLETIN*, Vol. 49, pp. 171–90.

Maddala, G. S. (1983). *Limited-dependent and Qualitative Variables in Econometrics*, Cambridge University Press, Cambridge.

Mallier, A. T. and Rosser, M. J. (1987). *Women and the Economy*, Macmillan, London.

Oaxaca, R. (1973). 'Male–Female Wage Differentials In Urban Labor Market', *International Economic Review*, Vol. 14, pp. 693–709.

Payne, J. (1991). *Women, Training and the Skills Shortage: The Case for Public Investment*, Policy Studies Institute.

Rigg, M. (1989). *Training in Britain: Individuals' Perspectives*, HMSO, London.

[18]

THE ECONOMIC RECORD, VOL. 80, SPECIAL ISSUE, SEPTEMBER, 2004, S53–S64

Employee Training in Australia: Evidence from AWIRS*

FILIPE ALMEIDA-SANTOS

[1] *Department of Economics and Related Studies, University of York, UK and Instituto Universitário de Desenvolvimento e Promoção Social, Universidade Católica Portuguesa, Viseu, Portugal*

KAREN A. MUMFORD

Department of Economics and Related Studies, University of York, York, UK and National Institute for Labour Studies, Adelaide, Australia

We use linked data for 13 991 employees and 1494 workplaces to analyse the incidence of employer-provided training in Australia. We find potential experience, current job tenure, low education levels, skilled vocational training and part-time or fixed-term employment status are all associated with a lower probability of recent training. In contrast to studies for other countries, we find no evidence of discrimination on the basis of demographic characteristics in the provision of this job-related training. Finally, and in support of recent non-competitive training models, higher levels of wage compression are found to be positively related to a greater incidence of employee training.

I Introduction

In this paper we explore the determinants of workers receiving employer-provided training in Australia. The potential for training to impact on productivity and wages has long been discussed in the economics literature, perhaps beginning in 1776 with Smith's *Wealth of Nations* (Smith 1952, p. 49). In the first half of the last century Pigou (1912, p. 12) and Rosenstein-Rodan (1943) developed and expanded many of the issues related to the provision of training, however, it is Gary Becker's contribu-

tion (1962; 1964) that decisively marks economic thought in this area. Becker emphasises the importance of training as a factor in accumulating human capital and how this can be translated into effective growth in the value of the worker's marginal productivity and, consequently, in their wage.[1] In particular, Becker argues that the impact of training on marginal productivity and wages depends on the nature of the training, that is, whether it is specific or general in nature.

More recent papers have returned to Becker and extended his work to consider training outcomes in a range of imperfectly competitive enviroments, finding that the theoretical distinction between general and specific training becomes obscured (Polachek & Siebert 1993; Stevens 1994; Leuven 2002). A dichotomy between general and specific training is also rarely observed empirically (Bishop 1997) and many authors have sought to explain the apparent sharing of general training costs between firms and employees

* We thank the AWIRS95 sponsors and providers; they are not responsible for any of the findings or claims made in the paper. We also thank participants of the ESA 2003 meetings, Sue Richardson, Miles Goodwin and the referees. Almeida-Santos is grateful for funding from the Fundacao para a Ciencia e Tecnologia – Ministerio da Ciencia e Tecnologia (Portugal) and Mumford is grateful for financial support from the Leverhulme Foundation, and for her Visiting Fellowship at the Economics Programme, RSSS, Australian National University.

Correspondence: Karen Mumford. Department of Economics and Related Studies, University of York, York YO10 5 DD, UK. Email: kam9@york.ac.uk

[1] Alternatively, Spence (1973) argues that high productivity workers merely use education as a signalling mechanism to employers (see also Autor 2000).

that occurs in the labour market. An early example is provided by Parsons (1972) who argues that the economic value of a worker is determined by the amount of their specific human capital and also by the transfer costs faced if s/he decides to move to an alternative firm. By firms and employees sharing the costs of training, the period of productivity gains from training rises since the likelihood of either party severing the employment relationship is lowered (Parsons 1972, p. 1122).

Hashimoto (1980) and Hashimoto & Yu (1980) also formally analyse how the costs of training are shared between employee and employer; arguing that the presence of costs of evaluating and agreeing on the worker's productivities in the training firm and all others firms in the post-investment period raise doubts about how secure the returns from investing in training are (Hashimoto 1981, p. 477). To avoid non-optimal separations and a possible hold-up problem, the parties define the optimal sharing level prior to initiating the investment.

More recent approaches extend on the idea that employers, in the presence of asymmetric information, may finance general training. For example, the true level of training conferred may be unobservable to other firms (Katz & Ziderman 1990; Chang & Wang 1996), or training may allow the employer to obtain information regarding the quality of its workers in an independent manner (Acemoglu & Pischke 1998, 1999a; Scoones & Bernhardt 1998).

Imperfections in job search, the presence of efficiency wages, and labour-market institutions (such as union wage setting and minimum wages) may also compress the wage structure and motivate firms to invest in general training (Acemoglu & Pischke 1998, 1999a; 1999b).

While the differences between general and specific training may be essentially notional, empirical investigation of the determinants of training (for both the firm and employee) and the potential returns from this training are still unresolved and are potentially very fruitful areas of research (Pischke 2001, p. 543; Leuven 2002, p. 34).

There have been a limited number of studies of training in Australia (Boot 1992; Smith 2001, p. 10). Many of the studies that do exist concentrate on the macroeconomic implications of government policies impacting on training and the role that institutions, such as trade unions, may play in the provision of training (recent surveys are provided in Junor 1993; Bryce 1995; Smith 2001). This emphasis in the Australian literature may have been due to a lack of suitable micro data (Boot 1992, p. 2; Karmel 2003) and/or may reflect a common research interest (Smith

2001; Dowling 2003). In general, these papers conclude that there is a positive return (often measured in terms of labour productivity) for firms who have training programs and that this return is higher when the training program is facilitated by a well-developed human resource management structure and integrated trade union involvement.

There have also been a series of studies of training in Australia using workplace level information from the Australian Workplace Industrial Relations (AWIRS) surveys. The emphasis in these papers has also been to establish productivity and innovation gains in workplaces that provide training, rather than exploring the determinants of training. Examples are found in Drago and Wooden (1992) who use data from the 1990 version of the AWIRS (AWIRS90); Laplagne and Bensted (1999), Loundes (1999) and Rogers (1999) combine workplace information from the AWIRS90 and the 1995 AWIRS (AWIRS95) data sets; and Hawke and Drago (1998) who use workplace level information from the AWIRS95 data set.

Our contribution is to build on this previous literature by using the linked employee and workplace data available in AWIRS95 to analyse the types of employees who are more likely to engage in employer-provided training, the characteristics of their workplaces, and a possible relationship between the incidence of training and wage compression.

The data are discussed in Section II, Section III presents the model of training. The econometric estimation is considered in Section IV, Section V provides results and further discussion and Section VI concludes.

II Data

AWIRS95 is the second in a series of large-scale surveys of workplaces in Australia (the first survey, AWIRS90, was carried out in 1990). Both AWIRS surveys were undertaken by what is now the Australian Department of Employment and Workplace Relations. Our study will concentrate on AWIRS95. Surveying for AWIRS95 was conducted between August 1995 and January 1996 (Morehead *et al.* 1997). The respondents were taken from 2001 workplaces, all of which employed 20 or more employees. From each of these workplaces, the general manager, employee relations manager and trade union delegate (from the union with most members at the workplace) were asked to complete separate face-to-face surveys. The results from each of these three surveys are fully linkable. Furthermore, individual employees from these workplaces were also surveyed for a range of information including their personal characteristics, individual job characteristics, work environment etc.

This survey of individual employees included 19 155 employees. It is also fully linkable to the main (workplace) surveys.

Of the workplaces considered in the main AWIRS95 surveys, 2001 returned at least one of the three surveys. However, less than 1 700 workplaces responded across all the three main surveys that we use in our analysis. We then encounter some further missing values (apparently randomly distributed) across the variables, so that 1 494 workplaces and 13 991 employees are included in our regression analysis.

III Modelling Training

We adopt the Acemoglu and Pischke (AP) model as the basis for our empirical analysis of training. We present an abridged version of their model in this section, emphasising those features that will guide our variable choice in the empirical estimation presented in Section IV below.

Following similar lines to Chang and Wang (1996) and Katz and Ziderman (1990), Acemoglu and Pischke (1998; 1999a; 1999b) construct a two-period model in which the worker is hired and receives training of τ in period 0. Workers are assumed to have two different levels of ability (φ): low ability ($\varphi = \varphi_l$) that occurs with a probability p and high ability ($\varphi = \varphi_h$) that occurs with a probability $(1 - p)$. The worker's marginal product, $y(\varphi, \tau)$, is a function of their ability (φ) and skills acquired via training (τ) and is assumed to be increasing, differentiable and concave. The costs of training, $c(\tau)$, are assumed to be increasing, differentiable and convex.

Ability is assumed to be complementary with training,[2] so that workers with high ability are more able to receive training, $y(\tau, \varphi) = \tau\varphi$. The worker's actual ability will be known only at the end of period 0, and the wage offered in the beginning of period 1 will be contingent to it: $w(\tau, \varphi)$.

The potential recruiting firm observes only the training level and offers in the beginning of the first period a wage contingent to it: $v(\tau)$. The worker will quit if $w(\tau, \varphi) < v(\tau)$ but, due to exogenous reasons the worker may quit even when $v(\tau) \le w(\tau, \varphi)$ with probability μ (where $0 \le \mu < 1$). The authors also assume that with probability q the firm will receive an adverse demand shock and the work relationship will come to an end.

The incumbent firm, in order to avoid the resignation of the worker, will offer in the beginning of the first period a wage equal to the one s/he would receive in the outside labour market: $w(\varphi, \tau) = v(\tau)$. The

internal wage structure is therefore endogenous and set according to the outside wage offer (Acemoglu & Pischke 1999a, p. 547). If the worker decides to quit after receiving the training, s/he is assumed to face mobility or transactions costs (due, e.g. to frictional costs related to job search imperfections) equal to $\Delta(\tau)$, with $\Delta'(\tau) > 0$.

For the firm, the resulting profit or surplus received will be equal to $\Delta(\tau) = y(\varphi, \tau) - w(\varphi, \tau)$, which will be greater with higher levels of τ.[3] Thus, the presence of transaction costs creates a positive surplus to the training firm if the worker stays and, consequently, some incentive for the firm to invest in general training (Acemoglu & Pischke 1999b). The worker may, however, be able to extract some share, Y, of this surplus, where $0 \le Y < 1$.

To reiterate, the wage function is increasing with the level of training but at a lower rate than is productivity, $w'(\varphi, \tau) < y'(\varphi, \tau)$. The potential rents, $\Delta(\tau)$, obtained are higher at greater levels of τ, leading to what the authors identify as a compressed wage structure. 'Wage compression arises naturally because the surplus brought to the employment relation is larger when the worker is more skilled, and the firm obtains a share of this larger pie' (Acemoglu & Pischke 1999b, footnote 3).

The recruiting firm will expect a profit in the first period of:

$$\pi = p[y(\tau, \varphi_l) - v(\tau)] + (1 - p)\mu[y(\tau, \varphi_h) - v(\tau)] \quad (1)$$

The training firm pays the cost of training for all workers in period 0 and obtains a profit of $y(\tau, \varphi_h) - v(\tau)$ for each worker with high ability who decides to stay in period 1. The fraction of high-ability workers continuing with the training firm is equal to $(1 - p)(1 - \mu)$ and expected profit is:

$$\pi(\tau) = (1 - p)(1 - \mu)(1 - Y)[y(\tau, \varphi_h) - v(\tau)] - c(\tau) \quad (2)$$

The level of training will be chosen in order to guarantee the maximum profit.[4] The first order condition for training is:

$$\pi'(\tau) = (1 - p)(1 - \mu)(1 - Y)[y'(\tau, \varphi_h) - v'(\tau)] - c'(\tau) = 0 \quad (3)$$

Indicating that the marginal return is equal to the marginal cost for a given level of training in

---

[2] This is an assumption occasionally made in the literature, for example, see Leuven (2002, p. 23).

[3] If the costs of moving between jobs $[\Delta = y(\tau) - w(\tau)]$ are independent of the level of training and $y' - w' = 0$, the firm will not receive a benefit from providing training.

[4] If the outside market is competitive, then the expected profit will be equal to zero, and the market wage is then given by: $v(\tau) = (1 - p)\mu\tau)/[p + (1 - p)\mu]$.

equilibrium. The result that $[y'(\tau, \varphi_h) - v'(\tau)]$ is greater than 0 implies the presence of wage compression,[5] since $v'(\tau) = (1 - p)\mu/p + (1 - p)\mu < 1$. Furthermore, as long as $Y > 0$ and $v'(\tau) > 0$ or $\mu > 0$, an increase in the turnover rate reduces general training investment and the equilibrium training level will be below the social optimum level.

The firm has an incentive to invest in general training since there are complementarities between firm-specific and general skills and because the bargaining share of the worker (Y) and the marginal propensity to quit (μ) are both lower than one.

We adopt an eclectic specification in the following econometric analysis, as is indicated by the range of empirical papers in the literature (Leuven 2002), although we attempt to capture some of the major predictions of the AP model. In particular, we seek variables reflecting employee's ability; the quit rate; adverse demand conditions; relative bargaining strength; the costs of training; the outside wage offer; and wage compression. Obviously, there are substantial overlaps across these categories and this needs to be taken into consideration in the following discussions.

IV Variable Definition and Interpretation

Summary statistics and variable definitions are provided in Table 1, with full sample means and standard errors presented in columns one and two (respectively) throughout the table (fuller variable definitions and descriptive statistics are available from the authors). Panel one presents the summary statistics for employees' characteristics and panel two presents those for workplaces. Column three in panel one provides means for those individual employees who have trained in the previous 12 months, and column three in panel two provides means for workplaces that have a formal training program in operation. The data throughout the paper have been weighted to allow for complex survey design (Deaton 1998) and represent the sampling population.

(i) Training

The AWIRS95 survey asked employees 'has your employer provided you (or paid for), over the last 12 months, any training to help you do your job?' The proportion of employees responding that they had received employer-provided training in Australia is substantial at 62 per cent (column 1, of Table 1).

Managers were also asked if the workplace had a formal off-the-job training program in place. The majority of workplaces are found to have a training program in operation (68 per cent), although the proportion of the workforce trained in the previous 12 months does not differ greatly across workplaces with or without a formal training program (64 per cent and 62 per cent, respectively).

(ii) Ability

To be able is not necessarily just to be clever. We select a range of variables typical of those generally associated with an individual's aptitude and opportunities (Leuven 2002): potential work experience, high or low education level (based on the highest earned education qualification); having a skilled vocational qualification, gender, being Aboriginal or Torres Strait Islander, country of birth and being a parent.

Average potential work experience is 19 years across all workers or 18 years for those with recent training. Potential work experience is expected to be negatively related to training opportunities, ceteris paribus, reflecting a shorter time horizon for collecting returns.

The expected relationship between education and training is positive if education and training are complementary and training increases ability (Bishop 1997, p. 75). Dummy variables are included in the regression analysis for education: 'low education' and 'high education' (the omitted category being completing secondary school). A binary variable is also included for having a skilled vocational qualification. The expected relationship with training is ambiguous as this qualification indicates previously being successful in work-related training but may also indicate less need to further train the employee.

On average, Australian employees have current job tenure of 6 years (Mumford & Smith 2004a). The likelihood of training will decrease with the length of current job tenure (Bishop 1997; Orrje 2000) if new hires have greater need for job-related training. The potential length of pay back period also declines with older workers (Becker 1964). This negative effect may be partially offset, however, as longer tenure reflects a quality match between firm and employee.

Of the remaining demographic measures, 45 per cent of the workforce is female, 41 per cent have a dependent child, 1 per cent are Aboriginal and 77 per cent are Australian-born. These average characteristics show little difference across individuals with or without recent training. We would expect from

---

[5] 'Intuitively, the presence of low-ability workers in the second-hand labor market implies that firms view workers in this market as lemons' (Acemoglu & Pischke 1999a, p. 558).

TABLE 1
Variable Definitions and Means, Individual Employee Characteristics (Source: Australian Workplace Relations Survey (1995; Social Science Data Archive, ANU))

Characteristics	Mean (1)	Standard Error (2)	With training Mean (3)	With training Standard Error (4)
(1) Individual employee characteristics				
Employer provided job training in previous 12 months	0.62	0.01	1.00	0.00
Potential Experience	19.01	0.19	17.95	0.22
Female	0.45	0.01	0.46	0.01
Any Dependent Children Aged 0–18	0.41	0.01	0.40	0.01
Aborigine or Torres Strait Islander	0.01	0.00	0.01	0.00
Australian Born	0.77	0.01	0.78	0.01
Low Education (below completion of secondary school)	0.32	0.01	0.28	0.01
High Education (above completion of secondary school)	0.24	0.01	0.28	0.01
Skilled Vocational Qualification	0.11	0.00	0.10	0.00
Current Job Tenure	6.04	0.10	5.61	0.11
Part-Time Employee	0.18	0.01	0.16	0.01
Fixed-Term Contract	0.08	0.00	0.09	0.01
Current Union Member	0.49	0.01	0.47	0.01
Wage Compression (10 to 90 percentile)	9.78	0.01	9.78	0.01
Occupations				
Labourer and Related Workers	0.15	0.01	0.11	0.01
Plant & Machine Operator and Drivers	0.08	0.00	0.07	0.01
Sales and Personal Service Workers	0.15	0.01	0.15	0.01
Clerical and Secretarial	0.18	0.01	0.19	0.01
Tradespersons and Apprentices	0.08	0.00	0.07	0.00
Para (associate) professional	0.11	0.01	0.12	0.01
Professionals	0.17	0.01	0.20	0.01
Managers	0.07	0.00	0.08	0.00
Other occupational groups	0.01	0.00	0.00	0.00
(2) Workplace characteristics				
Formal Training Scheme Operates from Workplace	0.68	0.02	1.00	0.00
Employer Provided Job Training in Previous 12 Months	0.62	0.01	0.64	0.01
Proportion of Workforce Resigned in Previous 12 Months	0.15	0.01	0.15	0.01
Decreasing Demand for Main Product or Service	0.10	0.01	0.10	0.01
Workplace Operates in Public Sector	0.44	0.02	0.40	0.02
Number of Employees in Workplace	280.20	29.61	333.95	41.87
Age of the Workplace	30.68	1.32	30.95	1.75
One of Multiple Workplaces in Enterprise	0.85	0.01	0.86	0.01
Workplace is Foreign Owned	0.13	0.01	0.14	0.01
Recognised Union(s) in Workplace	0.82	0.01	0.82	0.02
Workplace has a Human Resources Employee	0.40	0.02	0.44	0.02
Workplace Rewards Seniority	0.06	0.01	0.05	0.01
Workplace Rewards Ability	0.24	0.01	0.25	0.02
Index of Three Work Life Balance Practice in Workplace.	1.19	0.03	1.22	0.04
Proportion of Non-Managerial Workforce in Quality Circles	0.17	0.01	0.20	0.02
Proportion of Workforce in Formally Designated Teams	0.52	0.02	0.57	0.02
Industries				
Mining	0.01	0.00	0.02	0.00
Manufacturing	0.20	0.01	0.20	0.02
Electrical, Gas, Water and Sewerage	0.02	0.00	0.02	0.00
Construction (general and trade)	0.02	0.00	0.02	0.00

S58   ECONOMIC RECORD   SEPTEMBER

TABLE 1
Continued

Characteristics	Mean (1)	Standard Error (2)	With training Mean (3)	With training Standard Error (4)
Wholesale	0.04	0.01	0.03	0.01
Retail	0.11	0.01	0.12	0.01
Accommodation, Cafes, Restaurants	0.05	0.01	0.05	0.01
Transport and Storage	0.03	0.00	0.03	0.01
Communication Services	0.02	0.00	0.02	0.01
Finance, Insurance and Financial services.	0.05	0.01	0.06	0.01
Property and Business Services	0.07	0.01	0.07	0.01
Government Administration	0.11	0.01	0.11	0.02
Education	0.10	0.01	0.07	0.01
Health and Community Services	0.11	0.01	0.11	0.01
Sport and Recreation	0.02	0.00	0.02	0.00
Personal and Other Services	0.03	0.00	0.03	0.01
Regions				
New South Wales	0.38	0.02	0.39	0.02
Victoria	0.25	0.01	0.26	0.02
Queensland	0.16	0.01	0.16	0.02
South Australia	0.08	0.01	0.07	0.01
Western Australia	0.08	0.01	0.08	0.01
Tasmania	0.03	0.01	0.02	0.01
Northern Territory	0.005	0.002	0.005	0.003
Australian Capital Territory	0.02	0.00	0.01	0.00
Metropolitan (Urban)	0.70	0.01	0.72	0.02
Number of employees	13 991	n/a	n/a	n/a
Number of workplaces	1 494	n/a	n/a	n/a
Number of individuals trained in previous 12 months	n/a	n/a	8 706	n/a
Number of workplaces with formal training programs	n/a	n/a	1 023	n/a

The sample means and standard errors are fully weighted to account for the complex survey design. Industries classified according to the Australian and New Zealand Standard Industrial Classification (ANZIC) 1993.
n/a, not applicable.

the literature on discrimination (Cain 1986; Mumford 1988) and segmented labour markets (Doeringer & Piore 1971) that, if these demographic variables did have an impact on training, then being older, non-white or female (especially with children) would be associated with less training.

Occupational choice, is often treated in much the same way as educational outcome since they both reflect a range of variables, particularly individual ability and opportunity (Filer 1986). AWIRS only covers those currently employed so these occupational choices may be also somewhat constrained. Whilst less skilled occupations are associated with lower training levels and are expected to have lower levels of recent training, the occupational dummies are included primarily as control variables in the following regression analyses.

(iii) Quit Rate

We proxy the AP quit rate with the percentage of the workplace workforce that has voluntarily resigned in the previous 12 months. The average value of this quit rate is 15 per cent.

(iv) Bargaining strength

We recognise that relative bargaining strength is a particularly complex measure (Mumford & Dowrick 1994) and that variables impacting on this are very likely to also impact on other determinants of training (such as the quit rate and adverse demand conditions). With this in mind, we include measures of unionism as indicators of relative bargaining strength.

Union membership was still substantial in Australia in 1995 (at 49 per cent) and is slightly lower amongst recently trained workers (47 per cent). The level of union recognition in the bargaining process in workplaces is very high at 82 per cent and is also the same in workplaces with a formal training program. It is arguable that recognition is a better measure of workplace unionism than, for example, union density, impacting as it does on the union's ability to provide an aggregate voice in negotiations with management. We will explore both measures in our empirical analysis.

(v) Adverse Demand Conditions

At the time of of the survey Australia had moved out of recession and was growing at 1 per cent above its average rate for the period since 1980. This growth is reflected in only 10 per cent of the workplaces responding that the market for their main product or service was decreasing. The AP model predicts adverse demand conditions will be negatively related to training.

(vi) Costs of Training

Measuring the costs of training is difficult, especially given the heterogeneous nature of training (Leuven 2002, p. 29). We have no explicit information on training costs. Nevertheless, we believe workplaces that are larger or older are more likely to have access to capital markets, and thereby be able to fund training program with greater ease.

The organisation of the workforce may also impact on the ability of employees to cover for each other whilst in training and to share newly acquired skills. The proportion of the workforce in formally designated teams, the proportion of non-managerial workforce in quality circles, multiple workplaces (within an enterprise), operating in the public sector and the presence of a human resource manager in the workplace are included in the analysis to reflect workplace organisation that is more conducive to training.

We also include measures of whether the employee is part-time and/or fixed-term. In both cases, the firm has less potential time to reap the benefit from training and may be less prepared to pay the costs for it. More than one in six Australian employees work part-time, and 8 per cent are on fixed-term contracts.

Table 1 reveals that there is very little industry-based difference across workplaces who do and do not offer training. There may, however, be industry-based differences in the costs of training. For example, the costs of training in manufacturing may differ substantially from those in the service sectors. We do not have strong priors as to how these costs may be distributed and industry dummies are therefore included as control variables in the following regression analysis.

(vii) Outside Wage Offer

Higher outside wages are predicted to reduce employer-provided training in the AP model. We do not have a direct measure of the outside wage rate for employees, instead a series of regional dummy variables (which will control for differences in regional wage rates) are included in the regressions as control variables.

We also include a range of variables that reflect the non-pecuniary nature of the job: if the workplace rewards seniority; if the workplace rewards ability; and an index of three family-friendly work–life balance measures.[6] We believe that jobs with higher non-pecuniary rewards would, ceteris paribus, be more attractive to employees resulting in less future quits and more training (Budd & Mumford 2004).

(viii) Wage Compression

The AP model requires an increase in absolute wage compression for firms to be willing to sponsor general training.[7] We measure wage compression as the log of the absolute difference between the 90th and the 10th percentile levels of the wage distribution for full-time employees ($\log(90\text{th}-10\text{th})$).[8]

As Brunello (2001) discusses, the average wage rate has little relevance for individual employees as an alternative wage rate since earnings vary substantially by age, occupation, industrial sector and region. (Brunello's study uses data from the European Household Panel Survey and his measure of region is country based.) We similarly construct our wage compression measures by age (three bands: those aged less than 30, those aged between 30 and 49, and those aged more than 50), occupation (nine

---

[6] This index ranges in value from zero to three depending on how many of the following are available: paternity or maternity leave; workplace nursery or child care; and parental, family or carers leave.

[7] '. . . recall that what is necessary for firm sponsored training is that the wage structure is compressed in the sense that the worker does not get fully compensated for increases in his productivity due to training' Acemoglu and Pischke (1999b, footnote 7).

[8] The wage information provided in AWIRS is banded (23 categories), we set each band value to its midpoint and top-coded at the starting value of the maximum category. A continuous, non-truncated wage measure would be preferable but is rarely available; and is not available in an Australian dataset suitable for exploring training incidence. With 23 bands, however, we do not believe this categorisation will seriously affect our wage compression measure. A related issue is discussed in Mumford and Smith (2004c) which explores the gender wage gap in Britain using the sister dataset, WERS98. They found no significant difference when using interval regression techniques.

occupations) and industrial sector (16 industries). The occupations and industries used in the groupings are the standard definitions (see Table 1 for definitions and summary statistics). This wage compression measure is then linked to individual employees with the relevant (age, occupation and industry) characteristics to place them in that cell.[9]

The higher the value of our measure the lower is absolute wage compression, so we expect a negative relationship with our measure and training according to the AP model.

V Econometric Specification

The probability of the training T of worker i in workplace k is given by:

$$\Pr(T_{ik}{=}1) = \phi(\beta X_{ik}), \qquad (4)$$

$$T_{ik} = 1 \quad \text{if } T_{ik}^* > 0, \quad T_{ik} = 0 \text{ else,}$$

where X_{ik} is a vector of the explanatory variables thought to influence the decision to train, and ϕ is the standard normal distribution function (Greene 2001).

The presence of linked employee and employer workplace information also allows us to estimate models of training differentials across workplaces, conditional on characteristics of individual workers. The linked nature of the datasets to be employed can thus be used to good effect. The model to be estimated is:

$$\Pr(T_{ik}{=}1) = \phi(\beta X_i + \alpha_k) \qquad (5)$$

where the probability of training worker i in workplace k (T_{ik}) is explained by a set of individual characteristics (X_i) and a workplace specific effect (α_k). When evaluating the estimation results we compare estimates that omit the workplace specific effects (entitled 'probit' in the tables) and the full estimates (entitled 'workplace effects').[10]

---

[9] We also considered the wage compression measure constructed over the full database of 18 981 observations rather than over the actual sample (13 991 observations) used in the regressions. (The mean value for the wage compression measure over the full data set (18 981 observations) is 9.7934 with a standard error of 0.0064, the mean value of the sample used (13 991 observations) is 9.7813 with a standard error of 0.0069.) We found no significant differences in any of our results, suggesting that measurement error due to cell size is not a problem in this case.

[10] There may also be unobservable idiosyncratic individual effects, however, it is not possible to identify these in our data and we relegate them to the residual. We believe any resultant biases in our estimates to be small (Mumford & Smith 2004b) especially given the array of explanatory variables that we do include; a point we elaborate on further in discussing the results below.

Among our demographic and occupational groupings we have groups who have been identified in a variety of papers as more likely to be in a different labour market segmented from the remainder (such as females and non-whites, see Doeringer & Piore 1971). A test of this idea can be carried out by comparison of the coefficients between the probit and the workplace effects results. If a demographic identifier is significant in the probit estimates but not in the workplace effect estimates, then we can attribute the impact of membership of that demographic group to the workplace rather that to the worker's individual characteristic. This would be evidence suggesting segmentation.

VI Results

Results for the probability of an employee training in the previous 12 months are presented in Table 2. Columns 1 and 2 provide results from probit estimations using only individual characteristics as explanatory variables; columns 3 and 4 include workplace characteristics in the probit estimation; and columns 5 and 6 report results from workplace-specific effects estimations. We report marginal effects rather than raw coefficient estimates, except for binary variables where differential effects are reported. The overall test of the explanatory power of the regressors is clearly significant for all the regressions and while the measures of fit are not high they are comparable with those found in other studies of training using cross-sectional data (see Leuven 2002; Almeida-Santos & Mumford 2003). Overall, the parameter estimates are generally well defined and have the expected sign. We investigate the results in more detail by addressing the impact of the right hand side variables in turn.

The theoretically predicted declining relationship between age and training is supported as is common in the literature (Leuven 2002). Potential work experience is found to be significantly related to the incidence of training only through the level term, overall, there is a very small and (weakly) significant negative effect (at the mean) from potential work experience. The level of current job tenure is also found to be negatively and significantly associated with training as predicted, the quadratic is positive, suggesting a concave relationship between tenure and training. At the mean, the negative effect dominates. Similar results are found in Orrje (2000) and Bishop (1997).

We find limited evidence for a relationship between ability and training incidence. Workers with low education levels are significantly less likely (3–4 per cent less likely) to be recently trained, as predicted. (High education levels are generally positively related

TABLE 2
Probability That the Employee Has Recently Trained (Source: Australian Workplace Industrial Relations Survey (1995))

	Probit		Probit		Workplace Effects	
	dF/dx	z-value	dF/dx	z-value	dF/dx	z-value
Individual measures						
Potential Experience	−0.003	−1.91*	−0.005	−2.65***	−0.004	−1.87*
Potential Experience Squared (×1000)	0.012	0.33	0.036	0.93	0.045	0.99
Female	0.002	0.18	0.007	0.51	0.010	0.61
Any Dependent Children Aged 0–18	0.002	0.13	0.0003	0.03	−0.012	−1.01
Aborigine or Torres Strait Islander	0.026	0.59	0.027	0.60	0.074	1.47
Australian Born	0.018	1.53	0.016	1.34	0.011	0.90
Education Below Completed Secondary	−0.037	−2.75***	−0.028	−2.07**	−0.031	−2.09***
Education Above Completed Secondary	0.005	0.26	−0.007	−0.37	0.003	0.20
Skilled Vocational Qualification	−0.054	−2.93***	−0.050	−2.67***	−0.040	−1.97**
Current Job Tenure	−0.011	−5.49***	−0.012	−5.85***	−0.010	−4.36***
Current Job Tenure Squared (×1000)	0.298	4.14***	0.318	4.46***	0.241	2.98***
Part-time	−0.065	−4.28***	−0.062	−3.84***	−0.057	−2.98***
Fixed term Contract	−0.027	−1.44	−0.040	−2.09**	−0.051	−2.07**
Union Member	0.012	1.05	−0.016	−1.37	0.011	0.66
Wage Compression (10–90 per centile)	−0.031	−1.98**	−0.002	−0.08	−0.037	−1.85*
Constant	n/a	Yes***	n/a	Yes***	n/a	Yes***
Occupation (8)	n/a	Yes***	n/a	Yes***	n/a	Yes***
Industry (16)	n/a	n/a	n/a	Yes***	n/a	n/a
Region (8)	n/a	Yes	n/a	n/a	Yes	n/a
Workplace measures	n/a	n/a	n/a	n/a	n/a	n/a
Proportion of the Workforce Resigned in the Previous 12 Months	n/a	−0.035	−1.72*	n/a	n/a	n/a
Decreasing Demand for Main Product or Service	n/a	n/a	−0.007	−0.41	n/a	n/a
Workplace Operates in the Public Sector	n/a	n/a	0.054	3.08***	n/a	n/a
Number of Employees in Workplace	n/a	n/a	−0.049	−4.30***	n/a	n/a
Age of the Current Workplace	n/a	n/a	0.255	−1.48	n/a	n/a
One of Multiple Workplaces in Enterprise	n/a	n/a	0.033	2.02**	n/a	n/a
Workplace is foreign owned	n/a	n/a	0.080	5.29***	n/a	n/a
Recognised Union(s) in Workplace	n/a	n/a	−0.017	−1.09	n/a	n/a
Workplace has Human Resources Employee	n/a	n/a	0.023	2.18**	n/a	n/a
Workplace Rewards Seniority	n/a	n/a	0.003	0.13	n/a	n/a
Workplace Rewards Ability	n/a	n/a	−0.007	−0.52	n/a	n/a
Index of Three Work Life Balance Practices Available in Workplace	0.021	2.91***	n/a	n/a	n/a	n/a
Proportion of Non-Managerial Workforce in Quality Circles	n/a	n/a	0.013	0.96	n/a	n/a
Proportion of Workforce in Formally Designated Teams	n/a	n/a	0.048	4.56***	n/a	n/a
Number of Observations	13 991	n/a	13 991	n/a	13 991	n/a
F-test	12.02*** (31 1463)	9.86*** (61 1433)			n/a	n/a
Pseudo R squared	0.040	n/a	0.061	n/a	n/a	n/a
Predicted mean of the dependent	0.623	n/a	0.626	n/a	0.60	n/a
Wald xhi2	(31)	517***	(61)	826***	(23)	300***

* Statistically significant at 0.05 level; ** Statistically significant at 0.025 level; *** Statistically significant at 0.005 level.
Each entry in columns (1), (3) and (5) contain the marginal effect (or differential effect in the case of a binary variable). All regressions are fully weighted to allow for stratification and clustering in the sampling procedure. Industry, occupation and region tests are joint tests.
n/a, not applicable.

to training but not significantly so.) Training is also found to be strongly and negatively related to previous skilled vocational qualification. Employees with a skilled vocational qualification are 5.4 per cent less likely to have recently trained, or 4 per cent less likely when we fully allow for the characteristics of the workplaces they are employed in (column 5).

We find no consistent significant differences in the probability of training for females, parents or Aborigines. The empirical findings on the impacts of gender and parenthood on training are not clear in the literature (Frazis *et al*. 1998) and may differ according to the type of training being offered (Leuven 2002). Non-whites are, however, usually found to have less training (see also Lynch 1992; Veum 1993; Almeida-Santos & Mumford 2003). Being an Aborigine may not be a representative measure of all non-whites in Australia. We include being Australian-born as an indicator of discrimination that may be levied towards foreigners and do not find a significant relationship with this variable and the probability of recent training.

We find that both part-time and fixed-term employees are less likely to be trained as predicted by the AP model. For fixed-term employees, this relationship strengthens as we increasingly allow for their workplace characteristics (moving from column 1 to 3 to 5) suggesting that they are more likely to be working in workplaces with greater (than average) training incidence but that, as individuals, they are less likely to be trained within these workplaces. In general, however, when moving from column 1 to 5 in Table 2, the marginal effects on the demographic variables do not change significantly. This result indicates that these individuals are not being segmented into firms with disproportionate training incidences; further suggesting a lack of discrimination on the basis of demographic characteristics in the provision of employee training in Australian workplaces.

Considering bargaining strength, we found both union membership and union recognition in the bargaining process to be consistently insignificantly associated with training. The impact of unionism on training is far from uniform in the literature (Drago & Wooden 1992; Frazis *et al*. 1998; Almeida-Santos & Mumford 2003) and there is obviously much more that can be done in this area in future work.

Turning to the workplace characteristics (column 3), the quit rate is (weakly) significant and negatively related to training, as predicted. A marginal increase in the workplace resignation rate (above its mean value) is associated with 3.5 per cent less probability that the employee has recently trained.

We do not find a significant relationship between adverse demand conditions and training, however, as we only have cross sectional data and this was a year of very strong growth, we may not have information on enough workplaces to measure this effect accurately.

Organisational structures that may lower the costs of training are found to have a substantial impact on the probability of recent training: the proportion of the workforce in designated teams is associated with a 5 per cent higher probability of recent training. Similarly, workplaces that are foreign-owned and/or have a human resource manager provide more training. We do not find a strong relationship between workplace age and training and we find, contrary to many other studies (Bishop 1997; Leuven 2002), that larger workplaces are actually less likely to provide training. These results suggest that it is explicit facilitating organisational structures, rather than the simple physical attributes of the workplace, that are important predictors for the incidence of training in Australia.

Finally, in line with recent non-competitive training models, there is evidence that higher levels of wage compression are positively associated with a greater probability of training (which is revealed by negative findings for our wage compression measure, although not at uniformly high confidence levels).

VII Conclusions

We use linked data for 1494 workplaces and 13 991 employees from the Australian Workplace Industrial Relations Survey 1995 to analyse the incidence of employer provided worker training for employees. We find the probability that an employee has recently trained is negatively associated with potential experience, lower education levels, longer current job tenure and part-time or fixed-term employment status. We find no evidence of discrimination on the basis of demographic characteristics (gender, race, parenthood or being Australian-born) in the provision of this job related training. Furthermore, in line with recent non-competitive training models, higher levels of wage compression are positively associated with a greater incidence of training.

Our results are the first empirical investigation of the determinants of training for the firm and employee together in Australia and help towards filling the gap in this still unresolved area of research (Pischke 2001, p. 543; Leuven 2002, p. 34). Our results are also generally supportive of the new non-competitive training models and, in particular, the behavioural axioms presented by Acemoglu and Pischke (1998; 1999a; 1999).

REFERENCES

Acemoglu, D. and Pischke, J.S. (1998), 'Why do firms train? Theory and evidence'. *Quarterly Journal of Economics* **113**, 79–119.

Acemoglu, D. and Pischke, J.S. (1999a), 'The structure of wages and investment in general training'. *Journal of Political Economy* **107**, 539–72.

Acemoglu, D. and Pischke, J.S. (1999b), 'Beyond becker: training in imperfect labor markets'. *Economic Journal* **109**, F112–42.

Almeida-Santos, F. and Mumford, K. (2003), 'Employee Training, Wage Compression and Workplace Performance in Britain', Mimeo. September, University of York, York.

Autor, D. (2000), *Why Do Temporary Help Firms Provide Free General Skills Training? NBER Working Paper Series no. 7637*. National Bureau for Economic Research, Boston.

Becker, G.S. (1962), 'Investment in human capital: a theoretical analysis'. *Journal of Political Economy* **70**, 9–49.

Becker, G.S. (1964), *Human Capital: a Theoretical and Empirical Analysis, with Special Reference to Education*, 3rd edn. University of Chicago Press, Chicago.

Bishop, J.H. (1997), 'What we know about employer-provided training? A review of the literature'. *Research in Labor Economics* **16**, 19–87.

Boot, H.M. (1992), On-the-Job Training, Wages and the Formation of Human Capital: Some Comments on the Federal Government's Proposals on Training as Contained in the 'One Nation: The Statement', in *The Proceedings of a Conference of the H.R. Nicholls Society* **12**, 1–5.

Brunello, G. (2001), *Is Training More Frequent When Wage Compression is Higher? Evidence from 11 European Countries*. Pure Publications, The Research Institute of the Finnish Economy, Helsinki, Finland.

Bryce, M. (1995), 'Delivering Training Reform: The Critical Role of Employers and the Workplace'. ACIRRT Working Paper No. 36. ACIRRT, Sydney.

Budd, J. and Mumford, K.A. (2004), 'Trade unions and family friendly work policies in Britain'. *Industrial and Labor Relations Review* **57**, 204–22.

Cain, G.C. (1986), 'The economic analysis of labor market discrimination. A survey', in Ashenfelter, O. and Layard, Richard R. (eds). *Handbook of Labor Economics*, Vol. 1. North Holland, Amsterdam; 693–785.

Chang, C. and Wang, Y. (1996), 'Human capital investment under asymmetric information: the pigovian conjecture revisited'. *Journal of Labor Economics* **14**, 505–19.

Deaton, A. (1998), *The Analysis of Household Surveys. A Microeconometric Approach to Development Policy*. World Bank & John Hopkins University Press, Baltimore.

Doeringer, P.B. and Piore, M.J. (1971), *Internal Labor Markets and Manpower Analysis*. D.C. Heath, Massachusetts.

Dowling, P. (2003), 'Report on the Dusseldorp Skills Forum and Group Training Skills Round Table', Mimeo, July 21. [Cited 16 July, 2004.] Available from URL: http://www.grouptraining.com.au/aboutgta/gtadownloads/reports/Skills_forum.pdf

Drago, R. and Wooden, M. (1992), 'The Australian workplace industrial relations survey and workplace performance'. *Australian Bulletin of Labour* **18**, 142–67.

Filer, R. (1986), 'The role of personality and tastes in determining occupational structure'. *Industrial and Labor Relations Review* **39**, 412–24.

Frazis, H., Gittleman, M. and Joyce, W. (1998), 'Determinants of Training: An Analysis using Both Employer and Employee Characteristics', mimeo. Bureau of Labor Statistics, Washington.

Greene, W.H. (2001), *Econometric Analysis*, 4th edn. New Jersey: Prentice Hall International.

Hashimoto, M. and B.T. (1980), 'Specific capital, employment contracts, and wage rigidity'. *Bell Journal of Economics* **2**, 536–49.

Hashimoto, M. (1981), 'Firm-specific human capital as a shared investment'. *American Economic Review* **71**, 3–257.

Hawke, A. and Drago, R. (1998), 'The Impact of Enterprise Agreements: Evidence for the AWIRS'. Discussion Paper 4, the Transformation of Australian Industrial Relations Project. National Institute of Labour Studies, Adelaide.

Junor, A. (1993), 'Emerging Training Patterns: Productive, Equitable?' ACIRRT Working Paper No. 25. ACIRRT, Sydney.

Karmel, T. (2003), 'Capturing the total VET effort'. *Insight* **12**, 1–2.

Katz, E. and Ziderman, A. (1990), 'Investment in general training: the role of information and labour mobility'. *Economic Journal* **100**, 1147–58.

Laplagne, P. and Belsted, L. (1999), 'The Role of Innovation in Workplace Performance'. Staff Research Paper. Productivity Commission of Australia, Melbourne.

Leuven, E. (2002), 'The Economics of Training: A Survey of the Literature', mimeo. Available from <http://www.fee.uva.nl/scholar/mdw/leuven/reviewart.pdf>.

Loundes, J. (1999), 'Labour Productivity in Australian Workplaces: Evidence from the AWIRS', Working Paper No. 19/99. Melbourne Institute of Applied Economic and Social Research, Melbourne.

Lynch, L.M. (1992), 'Differential Effects of Post-School Training on Early Career Mobility', Working Paper NBER no. 4034. National Bureau for Economic Research, Boston.

Morehead, A., Steele, M., Alexander, M., Stephen, K. and Duffin, L. (1997), *Changes at Work: the 1995 Australian Workplace Industrial Relations Survey*. Addison Wesley Longman, Sydney.

Mumford, K. (1988), *Women Working: Economics and Reality*. Allen & Unwin, Sydney.

Mumford, K. and Dowrick, S. (1994), 'Wage bargaining with endogenous profits, overtime working and heterogenous labor'. *Review of Economics and Statistics* **76**, 329–36.

Mumford, K. and Smith, P.N. (2004a), 'Job reallocation, employment change and average job tenure: theory and workplace evidence from Australia'. *Scottish Journal of Political Economy* **51**, 402–21.

Mumford, K. and Smith, P.N. (2004b), 'Job tenure in Britain: employee characteristics versus workplace effects'. *Economica* **21**, 275–295.

Mumford, K. and Smith, P.N. (2004c), 'The Gender Earnings Gap in Britain', IZA Discussion Paper no. 1109. [Cited 16 June 2004.] Available from URL: http://www.iza.org

Orrje, H. (2000), 'The Incidence of On-the-Job Training. An Empirical Analysis using Swedish Data'. Working Paper No. 6/2000. Swedish Institute for Social Research, Stockholm.

Parsons, D. (1972), 'Specific human capital: an application to quit rates and layoff rates'. *Journal of Political Economy* **80**, 1120–43.

Pigou, A.C. (1912), *Wealth and Welfare*. Macmillan, London.

Pischke, J.S. (2001), 'Continuous training in Germany'. *Journal of Population Economics* **14**, 523–48.

Polachek, S. and Siebert, S. (1993), *The Economics of Earnings*. Cambridge University Press, Cambridge.

Rogers, M. (1999), 'Innovation in Australian Workplaces: An Empirical Analysis using AWIRS 1990 and AWIRS 1995', Working Paper No. 3/99. Melbourne Institute of Applied Economic and Social Research, Melbourne.

Rosenstein-Rodan, P. (1943), 'Problems of industrialization of eastern and southern-eastern Europe'. *Economic Journal* **53**, 202–11.

Scoones, D. and Bernhardt, D. (1998), 'Promotion, turnover, and discretionary human capital acquisition'. *Journal of Labor Economics* **16**, 122–41.

Smith, A. (1952), *An Inquiry Into the Wealth of Nations*. (Originally published in 1776.) William Benton, Chicago.

Smith, A. (2001), *Return on the Investment in Training: Research Readings*. Australian National Training Authority, Sydney.

Spence, M. (1973), 'Job market signalling'. *Quarterly Journal of Labor Economics* **87**, 355–74.

Stevens, M. (1994), 'A theoretical model of on-the-job-training with imperfect competition'. *Oxford Economic Papers* **46**, 537–63.

Veum, J.R. (1993), 'Training among young adults: who, what kind and for how long?' *Monthly Labor Review* **116**, 27–32.

[19]

The Economic Journal, 112 (*March*), C201–C219. © Royal Economic Society 2002. Published by Blackwell Publishers, 108 Cowley Road, Oxford OX4 1JF, UK and 350 Main Street, Malden, MA 02148, USA.

MATCHING THE DEMAND FOR AND SUPPLY OF TRAINING IN THE SCHOOL-TO-WORK TRANSITION*

M. J. Andrews, S. Bradley and D. Stott

This empirical paper investigates skill formation in the youth labour market. Using event-history data collected from the administrative records of Lancashire Careers Service, we model 'training preferences' formed at school by young people and 'training destinations', ie the occupation of the first job/training scheme. We also model the duration of the individual's first unemployment spell. Competing risks models with flexible piece-wise linear baseline hazards and unobserved heterogeneity are estimated. There is evidence of occupational segregation by gender and an excess demand for general training. Outcomes are mainly determined by examination performance, ethnicity and whether disadvantaged.

There is considerable concern about the quality and quantity of workforce skills in many advanced countries. This concern stems from the view that a highly skilled workforce is necessary for survival in an increasingly competitive world market, and from the view that the pace of skill-biased technological change generates a need for an adaptable and flexible workforce.[1] In Britain, the problem is even more acute, as it is well-established that Britain suffers from a so-called 'skills gap' in comparison with some of its main international competitors, such as Germany.

In Britain, the skills gap is widest at the intermediate level, where there are too few craft and technician workers. These skills are often acquired early in a worker's career, via apprenticeships, traineeships and the Youth Training (YT) programmes, the last of these having attracted considerable amounts of public funding by successive British governments.[2] A popular current view is that the problem is due to a lack of demand for vocational qualifications by young people.[3]

For some individuals, YT is a direct route to a wide range of intermediate level occupations, which provide training leading to the acquisition of certificated general transferable skills (hereafter 'general training'). For other individuals, YT acts as a bridge between school and work, by providing work experience for those who would otherwise be unemployed. This emphasises the Active Labour Market Policy role of YT. It is wrong, therefore, to regard YT as a homogeneous pro-

* The authors thank The Nuffield Foundation (under grant SFW058) for financial assistance. The data were kindly supplied by Lancashire Careers Service. The comments of Rob Crouchley, Helen Robinson, Richard Upward, the Editorial Board of this JOURNAL, and two anonymous referees are gratefully acknowledged, as are those from participants at various presentations. These include the Economics Department at Manchester and the 2001 Royal Economic Society Conference (Durham) and the 2001 EEEG Conference (Leicester).

[1] For the United States, see US Department of Labor (1999); for the European Union, see European Union (1999); and for Britain, see National Skills Task Force (2000).

[2] Throughout this paper we refer to all versions of publicly-funded training programmes as Youth Training (YT).

[3] The current Labour Government believes that there is ' . a lack of demand for vocational qualifications ...' and that '... reforms to the work-based route as a means of progression into higher education have to be considered in the context of deepseated barriers in this area.' (*Times Higher Education Supplement*, June 29, 2001.)

gramme. In fact, it comprises schemes of variable quality: some individuals will end up in occupations where they are able to acquire general skills, whereas for other individuals, YT leads to low-level, or unskilled, occupations. On the other hand, many young people will go straight from compulsory schooling to jobs where they can also acquire general skills. It is important to move away from the over-simplistic view that YT will necessarily deliver the appropriate training and to recognise that jobs in certain occupations will.

This empirical paper is about the acquisition of skills in the youth labour market. Our aim is to investigate the determinants of the demand for, and supply of, general training in the context of the school-to-work transition. The way we examine whether or not the individual will undertake general training is to examine the 3-digit occupation of his/her first job or YT scheme after compulsory schooling, and classify individuals according to whether the occupation is one where certificated general transferable skills are acquired. For both jobs and YT schemes, we also stratify by whether the occupation is manual or non-manual, one reason being that there is occupational segregation between young men and women.

We address three issues. First, we examine the demand for general training (hereafter labelled as 'training preferences') by observing a young person's preferred occupation before they leave compulsory schooling. This is modelled as a multinomial logit. Second, we examine the occupation of first job/training scheme after leaving compulsory schooling (hereafter 'training destinations'), also modelled as a multinomial logit. By comparing preferences with destinations, we can classify individuals by whether their choices 'match' or 'mismatch', and examine whether the mismatch is consistent with either excess demand for, or excess supply of, training. Third, we examine the spell of unemployment (if any) between leaving compulsory schooling and first job/training scheme, using competing risks methods. Exit states are a job or YT, but also stratified by whether or not there is (mis)match above, ie whether the transition from school to work is successful.

The data we use in this paper are event-history data on the population of young people aged 16–19 who left school between 1988 and 1991 in Lancashire, totalling 36,500 individuals. These administrative data were collected by Lancashire Careers Service (LCS). The paper represents a substantial departure from the existing empirical literature on the determinants of training and the school-to-work transition, for two reasons. First, as far as we are aware, no other dataset records an individual's preferred occupation before leaving compulsory schooling, which is why we are able to analyse supply and demand in the market for training.[4] Second, most of the existing literature on the determinants of training incidence and the school-to-work transition analyses cross-section data, and therefore ignores the impact of previous labour states, particularly unemployment. (For Britain, see, for example, Green (1993), Arulampalam and Booth (1997) and Shields (1998) on training and Rice (1999), Leslie and Drinkwater

---

[4] Moreover, with the quasi-privatisation of the Careers Service since the mid-1990s, it is unlikely that similar information has been recorded since.

2002]   MATCHING THE DEMAND FOR AND SUPPLY OF TRAINING   C203

(1999) and Andrews and Bradley (1997) on the school-to-work transition. One exception is Dolton *et al.* (1994).)

In the next section of this paper we discuss the institutional background in Britain, which describes how training preferences are formed and how the Careers Service uses them in matching demand and supply in the youth labour market. In Section 2, we discuss our econometric methodology and in Section 3 we present our results. In the Conclusion we draw together our main findings.

1. Data and Institutional Background

The data analysed in this paper are the administrative records used by LCS. In Britain, there is a Careers Service for each local education district, and each fulfills a similar role for the youth labour market as Employment Offices and Job Centres fulfill for adults. Their main responsibilities are, first, to provide vocational guidance for youths and, second, to act as a free employment service to employers and youths. Throughout the final two years of compulsory schooling, young people attend lessons in Careers Education and all young people receive individual guidance on job choice, which is provided by a professional Careers Advisor in one or more interviews. Interviews typically last 30 minutes and involve the collection of data on the young person's academic qualifications, health status, travel-to-work intentions, interests, etc. One important outcome of this guidance process is that a young person and the Careers Advisor agree the occupations she would prefer to work in, which are coded into one of 74 Occupational Training Families (OTFs).

The occupational preferences of each young person are held on a computerised matching system, together with other personal information (for example, qualifications and travel-to-work intentions), so that when vacancies are notified to the Careers Service, it can quickly pre-select the most suitable candidates for interview. Because the government's guarantee of a place on the programme for all unemployed young persons aged 16 needs to be monitored, all YT vacancies are notified to the Careers Service. In contrast, approximately one third of job vacancies are notified to the Service.[5] All young people are in regular contact with the Careers Service, which means that the data record the outcome of their search regardless of which search channel (Careers Service, informal contacts, advertisements) a young person uses. The data also record individual event histories: after leaving compulsory schooling at the age of 16, a young person is observed in one of four labour-market states: employment (J), Youth Training (Y), unemployment (U) and further education. Since our focus is on the demand for, and supply of, training in the youth labour market, we drop young persons who continue their education.

---

[5] The key difference between jobs and YT schemes is that the latter are of fixed duration, typically two years, and trainees receive an allowance rather than a wage. In our data, the hourly mean wage for jobs is £1.45 but only £0.70 for YT schemes (see Andrews, *et al.* (2001*b*, p. 340) for more details).

2. Econometric Methodology

2.1. *Dependent Variables*

Using the 'occupational preference', recorded as one of 74 OTFs, we examine each 3-digit occupation and classify it as delivering certificated general transferable skills, or not. These occupations are labelled as 'skilled' and 'unskilled' respectively. Also, because there is considerable occupational segregation by gender, we stratify each by manual or non-manual occupations. Thus, each 'occupational preference' is recoded into four 'training preferences', denoted S, as follows:

- Skilled non-manual (eg trainee bank clerk) ($S = 1$)
- Skilled manual (eg apprentice engineer) ($S = 2$)
- Unskilled non-manual (eg shop assistant) ($S = 3$)
- Unskilled manual (eg labouring) ($S = 4$).

To make clear how the richness of data allows us to model the demand for general training in a novel way, consider one specific 2-digit OTF (out of 11), 08 – food preparation and food services. Then the seven 3-digit OTFs that belong to this 2-digit occupation are recoded as follows:

08E – hotel management trainee → $S = 1$
08A – chef → $S = 2$
08C – baker → $S = 2$
08D – food and customer service → $S = 3$
08F – butcher/slaughterman → $S = 3$
08O – general food preparation → $S = 3$
08B – fast food assistant → $S = 4$.

Notice that the first three occupations involve apprenticeships or traineeships which lead to the creation of certificated general transferable skills, whereas the remaining four do not.[6] This coding should also make it clear that this paper is not about occupational choice *per se* (in which case the matching would be done at either the 2- or 3-digit level).

By definition, each young person's initial labour-market state (R_0) is a spell of unemployment (U), and, for those whose spell is not censored, this is followed by either a job (J) or Youth Training (Y), once his/her search has finished.[7] The 'occupational destination' is recorded (again one of 74 OTFs) and then recoded into one of four 'training destinations', denoted D, whose categories are the same as S above. The duration of the unemployment spell is denoted t. For those who finish their search before the end of compulsory schooling, their unemployment duration is zero.

---

[6] The majority of young persons classified under 08F worked in shops and were therefore involved in non-manual duties. There were almost no slaughterhouse (ie manual) positions in Lancashire in the sample period.

[7] A few young people are dropped from the analysis, namely those who end up in a diagnostic training scheme without specific occupational category and those who express a preference for Further Education, but end up in a job/YT.

The four exit states $R = 1, \ldots, 4$ from the unemployment spell are modelled as follows:

- Job matches (ie $R = 1$ if $R_1 = J$ and $S = D$)
- Job mismatches (ie $R = 2$ if $R_1 = J$ and $S \neq D$)
- YT matches (ie $R = 3$ if $R_1 = Y$ and $S = D$)
- YT mismatches (ie $R = 4$ if $R_1 = Y$ and $S \neq D$)

where R_1 denotes the labour-market state of the young person's post unemployment spell. Censored unemployment spells are denoted $R = 0$.

Table 1 cross-tabulates 'training destinations' with the 'training preferences'. Clearly, observations on the main diagonal represent those young people whose exit states from unemployment are $r = 1, 3$. Thus, out of 15,780 females, 8,743 (55%) end up in occupations they previously stated a preference for; similarly, 11,232 out of 20,774 males (54%) do the same. Notice that the denominator does not exclude those who are censored, because most of these young persons had the opportunity to match, but did not. In other words, a censored unemployment spell indicates a low propensity to match.

With no other comparative benchmark, it is difficult to judge whether these percentages are high or low. However, further examination of the data clearly suggests that this is due to unrealistic expectations in terms of finding occupations with general training. 77% of males prefer 'skilled' occupations (60% for females), but only 53% of males and 42% of females actually enter these occupations. A more transparent way of viewing these data is to ignore the manual/non-manual split. Now, even though 64% of females match (5,813 plus 4,124), of those who do not, there is a clear majority (more than two-to-one) for those who want occupations with training but do not enter them (2,054) rather than the reverse (884).

Table 1

Training Preferences and Training Destinations

| | Destination | | | | | | |
Preference	$d = 1$	$d = 2$	$d = 3$	$d = 4$	Censored*	Total	%
Females							
Skilled non-manual ($s = 1$)	5,412	65	1,058	665	1,340	8,540	54.1
Skilled manual ($s = 2$)	122	214	186	145	183	850	5.4
Unskilled non-manual ($s = 3$)	641	73	2,078	814	1,028	4,634	29.4
Unskilled manual ($s = 4$)	133	37	193	1,039	354	1,756	11.1
Total	6,308	389	3,515	2,663	2,905	15,780	100.0
%	40.0	2.5	22.3	16.9	18.4	100.0	
Males							
Skilled non-manual ($s = 1$)	2,114	712	490	712	921	4,949	23.8
Skilled manual ($s = 2$)	507	6,623	646	2,000	1,261	11,037	53.1
Unskilled non-manual ($s = 3$)	135	204	685	294	273	1,591	7.7
Unskilled manual ($s = 4$)	102	568	225	1,810	492	3,197	15.4
Total	2,858	8,107	2,046	4,816	2,947	20,774	100.0
%	13.8	39.0	9.8	23.2	14.2	100.0	

* Young people whose first unemployment spell is censored ($d = 0$).

The ratio for males is even more pronounced (four-to-one): 3,848 want occupations with training, but do enter them, compared with 1,009 for whom $s = 3, 4$ and $d = 1, 2$. (62% of males match.) This is clear evidence of excess demand for training and is a key finding of this paper, and is, of course, contrary to what is often thought (see Footnote 3 above).

Another noticeable feature of the data is that females overwhelmingly prefer non-manual occupations (83%) whereas 62% of females actually enter non-manual occupations (see Table 1). The equivalent numbers for males are 31% and 24%. Because of this clear occupational segregation, we model males and females separately.

Our analysis is only meaningful if true preferences are being revealed and recorded. For example, it might be that young persons are identifying occupations to which they think they will be matched, rather than ones they actually prefer. The very fact that the gap between S and D is so large and systematic suggests that this is not so. It is certainly the case that Careers Advisors are well informed about labour-market opportunities as they discuss with employers their selection criteria and they also study vacancy information on the characteristics of young people required for each type of occupation. This means that preferences are not formed in a vacuum, and will therefore take account of labour-market conditions; on the other hand it is not the Careers Service's brief to ration job or YT opportunities. We also note that, given that one performance indicator for the Careers Service is to maximise the number of successful matches, there are clear incentives that the Careers Service ensure that young persons take the careers guidance interview seriously. Thus, we conclude that the main reason why a young person's training destination might not match his/her training preference is that employers are not supplying what young people want.[8]

The exit states from the competing risks models were defined above. Of 8,743 females whose preferences matched their destination, 3,864 ended up in jobs ($r = 1$) and 4,879 ended up on a YT scheme ($r = 3$). Of those who did not match, 2,522 ended up in jobs ($r = 2$) and 1,610 ended up on a YT scheme ($r = 4$). 2,905 females are censored ($r = 0$). These are the sample sizes for the competing risks models. The equivalent numbers for males are 4,459 ($r = 1$), 6,773 ($r = 3$), 3,588 ($r = 2$), 3,007 ($r = 4$), and 2,947 ($r = 0$).

Table 2 cross-tabulates whether the first job ($r = 1, 2$) or YT scheme ($r = 3, 4$) is in an occupation which offers general training ($d = 1, 2$) or not ($d = 3, 4$). This clearly indicates that it is important to move away from the over-simplistic view that YT will necessarily deliver certificated general transferable skills and to recognise that jobs in certain occupations will. This is best seen by observing that 41% of females and 28% of males are on YT schemes in occupations that do not deliver general training, and illustrates our claim in the Introduction that YT schemes are of variable quality.

In the empirical work that follows, we estimate the following three models: (i) a multinomial logit for 'training preference' S; (ii) a multinomial logit for 'training

---

[8] We also observe subsequent preference changes, and we report in another paper that preferences are more likely to change the longer a spell of unemployment.

Table 2

Training Destinations and First Job/Training Scheme*

Destination	Jobs[a] $(r = 1, 2)$	YT $(r = 3, 4)$	Total
Females			
Skilled occupation, ie with training $(d = 1, 2)$	2,861	3,836	6,697
Unskilled occupation, ie without training $(d = 3, 4)$	3,525	2,653	6,178
Total	6,386	6,489	12,875
Males			
Skilled occupation, ie with training $(d = 1, 2)$	3,880	7,085	10,965
Unskilled occupation, ie without training $(d = 3, 4)$	4,167	2,695	6,862
Total	8,047	9,780	17,827

* Excludes young people whose first unemployment spell is censored $(d = r = 0)$.

destination' D; and (iii) a competing risks model for unemployment duration T with exit states R. The motivation behind the two sets of multinomial logits is straightforward, namely to identify variations across individuals (controlling for background etc) in these raw data discussed above. The competing risks model can also be viewed as a multinomial logit for exit states, that is, a model for whether training preferences match training outcomes, stratified by job/training scheme. But it is more general than this, because we can also observe the dynamics of the matching and sorting process as young people make the transition from school to work, and we can also control for unobserved heterogeneity. This is particularly important when we note that a substantial proportion of the sample go straight from schooling to either a job or YT scheme, ie their duration of unemployment is zero; these individuals might well be unobservably better than the rest.

2.2. *Modelling Training Preferences and Training Destinations*

As noted above, young people formulate their training preferences at school, denoted $S_i = 1, \ldots, 4$, and $i = 1, \ldots, n$ indexes individuals. These preferences are modelled as a multinomial logit, and are a function of observed characteristics, collected in a vector $\mathbf{x}_i$. To establish some notation, we write the multinomial logit as follows:

$$P_{is}^0 \equiv \Pr(S_i = s) = \frac{\exp(\mathbf{x}_i' \mathbf{c}_s^0)}{\sum_j \exp(\mathbf{x}_i' \mathbf{c}_j^0)} \qquad s = 1, \ldots, 4, \tag{1}$$

where P_{is}^0 is the probability that the s-th preference is made by the i-th young person with characteristics $\mathbf{x}_i'$. We report the estimated marginal effects, $\delta_s^0 \equiv \partial P_{is}^0 / \partial \mathbf{x}_i'$, with the normalisation that $\sum_s \delta_s^0 = 0$. The frequencies of the dependent variable and the sample sizes are given in the right-hand columns of Table 1. Table 3 provides information on the vector of covariates that are used throughout our analysis, which are individual-level variables (including ethnicity, health, disadvantage, and qualifications), school-level variables, local labour market conditions, and (ward-level) socioeconomic variables.

Table 3

Variable Means for the Most Important Covariates $\bar{\mathbf{x}}^*$

	Preference MNL		Destination MNL		Competing risks	
Definition	Females	Males	Females	Males	Females	Males
No unemployment spell	0.394	0.388	0.483	0.453	0.043	0.044
Average GCSE grades	0.327	0.357	0.336	0.370	0.301	0.307
1–3 GCSE A–C grades	0.241	0.216	0.248	0.222	0.226	0.203
4+ GCSE A–C grades	0.257	0.201	0.253	0.189	0.264	0.235
Non-white	0.053	0.039	0.042	0.023	0.084	0.090
Disadvantage	0.024	0.028	0.037	0.049	0.041	0.053
Sample size	15,780	20,774	12,875[†]	17,827[†]	143,434[‡]	183,046[‡]

[*]Other covariates used in regressions, but not reported here, are *personal*, ie year left school (1988/89/90/91), whether willing to travel only to specific parts of the local labour market/anywhere within the local labour market/other local labour markets, English and Maths GCSE, health problems; *school type*, ie co-educational/single sex school/under direct LEA control/voluntary assisted/voluntary controlled or special agreement/grant maintained/comprehensive school/grammar school/secondary modern; *local labour market*, ie log(unemployment rate), log(number of careers officers), log(number of vacancies notified), *socio-economic*, ie % of households with >1.5 persons per room, % of households with 3+ siblings, % lone parents, % professionals, % non-manual workers, % skilled manual workers.
[†] The sample sizes for the destination MNLs are less than those for the preference MNLs due to censoring.
[‡] Individual–weeks. See note ‡ in Table 6 below.

Exactly the same set of covariates are used to model training destinations

$$P_{id}^1 \equiv \Pr(D_i = d) = \frac{\exp(\mathbf{x}_i' \mathbf{c}_d^1)}{\sum_j \exp(\mathbf{x}_i' \mathbf{c}_j^1)} \qquad d = 1, \ldots, 4. \tag{2}$$

Again marginal effects, $\delta_d^1 \equiv \partial P_{id}^1 / \partial \mathbf{x}_i'$, sum to zero. The frequencies of the dependent variable are given in the bottom two rows of each panel of Table 1 (excluding those who are censored).

2.3. *Modelling the Hazard to the First Destination*[9]

The data are discrete.[9] Each young person exits in the interval $[t_i - 1, t_i)$ to either one of the four states defined above ($r_i = 1, \ldots, 4$) or the observation is censored ($r_i = 0$). Notice that everybody is observed as unemployed, even if some individuals exit before the end of compulsory schooling ($t_i = 0$).

The data are organised into 'sequential binary response' form (Prentice and Gloeckler, 1978; Han and Hausman, 1990), that is, the data form a panel of individuals with the i-th individual contributing $j = 1, 2, \ldots, t_i$ observations. For each exit state $r = 1, \ldots, 4$ in this competing risks framework, all observations y_{ij} are zero except the last, and only if the individual exits to state r is unity recorded.

The hazard for each j and for each exit state r (we suppress the r subscripts for notational clarity) is modelled as follows. We assume proportional hazards and introduce a positive-valued random variable (or mixture) v:

[9] This section draws heavily on Stewart (1996).

$$h_j(\mathbf{x}'_t, v_i) = \bar{h}_j v_i \exp(\mathbf{x}'_i \boldsymbol{\beta}),$$

where h_j is the hazard of exit, $\bar{h}_j$ is the baseline hazard, $\mathbf{x}'_i$ is the same vector of observable covariates as above, and $u \equiv \log v$ has density $f_u(u)$. The likelihood $L_i(\boldsymbol{\beta}, \gamma)$ for each individual with observed covariates $\mathbf{x}'_i$ in this 'mixed proportional hazards' model is

$$L_i(\boldsymbol{\beta}, \gamma) = \int_{-\infty}^{\infty} \left[\prod_{j=1}^{t_i} h_j(\mathbf{x}'_t, u_i)^{y_{it}} [1 - h_j(\mathbf{x}'_t, u_i)]^{1-y_{it}} \right] f_u(u_i) \, du_i, \qquad (3)$$

$$h_j(\mathbf{x}'_t, u_i) = 1 - \exp[-\exp(\mathbf{x}'_i \boldsymbol{\beta} + \gamma_j + u_i)]. \qquad (4)$$

Because of the proportional hazards assumption, the covariates affect the hazard via the complementary log-log link. The γ_js are interpreted as the log of a non-parametric piece-wise linear baseline hazard, as $\gamma_j \approx \log \bar{h}_j$ when $\mathbf{x}'_i \boldsymbol{\beta} = 0$. The γ_j are collected into a vector γ. Each interval corresponds to a week, but, because of data thinning, these are grouped into longer intervals at longer durations (by constraining the appropriate γ_js). Consequently we have 55 intervals for male regressions and 49 for female regressions.

We model the unobserved heterogeneity using Normal mixing. Details on how the likelihood function is amended are given in Stewart (1996). We also experimented with non-parametric mixing (Heckman and Singer, 1984), but the impact of the covariates and the shape of the baseline hazard are very similar.

This equation is estimated separately for each exit state. We also assume that the four u_i are uncorrelated across the risks. The vectors $\boldsymbol{\beta}_r$, $r = 1, \ldots, 4$, convey no information about the effect of a single covariate x on either the likelihood of exit via risk r (Π_r), or the expected waiting time until exit via risk r (E_r) (Lancaster, 1990; Thomas, 1996).[10] This is because Π_r (and therefore E_r) depend on all four hazards $h_{1j}, \cdots, h_{4j}$ via the overall survivor function

$$\Pi_r = \sum_{j=1}^{\infty} h_{rj} S_{j-1}, \qquad E_r = \frac{1}{\Pi_r} \sum_{j=1}^{\infty} j h_{rj} S_{j-1}, \qquad S_j = \prod_{s=1}^{J} \left(1 - \sum_{r=1}^{4} h_{rs} \right). \qquad (5)$$

However, a result provided by Thomas (1996) is particularly useful when proportional hazards are assumed. Instead of examining the effects of a single covariate x on the unconditional probability of exit, it is computationally much easier to focus on the probability of exit via state r conditional on exiting during the interval j, denoted P_{rj}:

$$P_{rj} = \frac{h_{rj}}{\sum_r h_{rj}}, \qquad r = 1, \ldots, 4. \qquad (6)$$

In order to interpret our results, we compute both E_r and P_{rj}. The baseline hazards used to compute these are

---

[10] In the rest of this subsection, we label the risks with a subscript r, but drop the i subscript for an individual. In other words, the hazard (or 'transition intensity') of exiting via risk r at time j is denoted h_{rj}.

$$\hat{h}_\eta = 1 - \exp[-\exp(\bar{\mathbf{x}}'\hat{\boldsymbol{\beta}} + \hat{\gamma}_\eta)], \qquad r = 1, \ldots, 4, \tag{7}$$

where $\bar{\mathbf{x}}$ is set at the sample mean. We report the marginal effect of a single covariate $\mathbf{x}$ on the conditional exit probability, given by

$$\delta_r \equiv \frac{\partial P_\eta}{\partial \mathbf{x}} = \frac{h_\eta \sum_{k \neq r} h_{kj}(\beta_r - \beta_k)}{\left(\sum_{r=1}^4 h_\eta\right)^2}. \tag{8}$$

Because the probabilities sum to unity, across r, the corresponding vectors of marginal effects δ_r sum to zero across r, as for a multinomial logit.

We also report the 'simulated' marginal effect of a covariate on the expected waiting time. E_r is initially computed at the sample mean, using (5) and (7) above. For dummy variables, we then re-evaluate at $x = 0$ and $x = 1$. For continuous covariates, we move each $\bar{x}$ by one standard error. We denote these simulated marginal effects as $\Delta E_r / \Delta x$ and these can be viewed as close numerical approximations to the marginal effects. To summarise, in our tables of regression results, we report $\Delta E_r / \Delta x$ and $\partial P_\eta / \partial x$, as well as the p-value for underlying parameter estimate on x.

3. Results

Table 4 reports the results of estimating a multinomial logit model of training preferences for each gender. Table 5 shows equivalent multinomial logits for training destinations. The competing risks models (hereafter 'Gaussian proportional hazards') are reported in Table 6. The particular covariates we focus on are ethnicity, qualifications and individual disadvantage, as these are the only covariates that have a significant and relatively large impact across all three sets of regressions. All the other covariates are described in a footnote in Table 3.[11]

Before discussing the baseline hazards for the competing risks models, we report our methods for dealing with those who go straight from school to either a job or YT, namely 39% of both males and females.[12] This is a form of left-censoring, and so this group creates a spike in the baseline hazards at the first discrete interval (week). We need to consider whether they should be modelled separately because they might be observably or unobservably different to the other group. In fact, the two groups have identical training preferences and training destinations – it is only for exit states R where there are differences. 71% of females match before leaving school whereas only 65% match if they do not; the same differential occurs for males (66% versus 61%). Males (but not females) are more likely to enter a job if they go straight from school, 49% compared with 42% for the other group. If they were modelled as separate groups, then one would be assuming that the unobserved heterogeneity for the two groups is being drawn from separate distributions, which would be incorrect.

---

[11] The full versions of these regressions are available from the authors on request.
[12] The earliest young persons can legally leave compulsory schooling is the Easter of Year 11 (15–16 years old). Most will stay on to May/June to take their GCSEs.

Table 4

Multinomial Logit for Training Preferences*

| | Skilled | | Unskilled | |
	Non-manual $s = 1$	Manual $s = 2$	Non-manual $s = 3$	Manual $s = 4$
Females				
Average GCSE grades	0.232 (0.000)	−0.010 (0.084)	−0.120 (0.000)	−0.103 (0.000)
1–3 GCSE A–C grades	0.385 (0.000)	−0.017 (0.005)	−0.234 (0.000)	−0.134 (0.000)
4+ GCSE A–C grades	0.568 (0.000)	−0.026 (0.000)	−0.377 (0.000)	−0.165 (0.000)
Non-white	0.075 (0.000)	−0.038 (0.001)	−0.066 (0.000)	0.028 (0.002)
Disadvantage	−0.098 (0.002)	0.025 (0.025)	0.053 (0.035)	0.021 (0.102)
Observations	15,780			
Log likelihood	−15864.115			
Males				
Average GCSE grades	0.119 (0.000)	0.016 (0.121)	−0.015 (0.003)	−0.120 (0.000)
1–3 GCSE A–C grades	0.208 (0.000)	0.000 (0.986)	−0.025 (0.000)	−0.183 (0.000)
4+ GCSE A–C grades	0.318 (0.000)	−0.060 (0.000)	−0.037 (0.000)	−0.221 (0.000)
Non-white	0.088 (0.000)	−0.125 (0.000)	0.072 (0.000)	−0.035 (0.008)
Disadvantage	−0.069 (0.009)	0.026 (0.297)	0.012 (0.285)	0.031 (0.007)
Observations	20,774			
Log likelihood	−22584.134			

* Estimates of (1). Marginal effects δ_s^0 evaluated at the sample mean and p-values in parentheses.

Table 5

Multinomial Logit for Training Destinations*

| | Skilled | | Unskilled | |
	Non-manual $d = 1$	Manual $d = 2$	Non-manual $d = 3$	Manual $d = 4$
Females				
Average GCSE grades	0.212 (0.000)	−0.015 (0.000)	−0.067 (0.000)	−0.131 (0.000)
1–3 GCSE A–C grades	0.357 (0.000)	−0.014 (0.002)	−0.132 (0.000)	−0.211 (0.000)
4+ GCSE A–C grades	0.516 (0.000)	−0.006 (0.235)	−0.203 (0.000)	−0.307 (0.000)
Non-white	−0.010 (0.716)	0.019 (0.002)	−0.122 (0.000)	0.113 (0.000)
Disadvantage	−0.127 (0.000)	0.031 (0.000)	0.033 (0.184)	0.063 (0.000)
Observations	12875			
Log likelihood	−13269.654			
Males				
Average GCSE grades	0.081 (0.000)	0.048 (0.000)	−0.003 (0.626)	−0.125 (0.000)
1–3 GCSE A–C grades	0.130 (0.000)	0.064 (0.000)	−0.013 (0.103)	−0.181 (0.000)
4+ GCSE A–C grades	0.201 (0.000)	0.055 (0.000)	0.001 (0.895)	−0.257 (0.000)
Non-white	0.057 (0.001)	−0.233 (0.000)	0.092 (0.000)	0.084 (0.000)
Disadvantage	−0.061 (0.001)	0.026 (0.206)	−0.012 (0.308)	0.048 (0.002)
Observations	17827			
Log likelihood	−20810.502			

* Estimates of (2). Marginal effects δ_d^1 evaluated at the sample mean and p-values in parentheses.

Consequently we pool both groups but allow the parameter vector to vary across the two groups. In fact, Chow-type tests indicate that the impact of the covariates is the same for both groups.

Table 6

Gaussian Proportional Hazards Competing Risks Models to First Job/Training Scheme, with/without Matching*

	Jobs		YT	
	Match $r = 1$	Mismatch $r = 2$	Match $r = 3$	Mismatch $r = 4$
Females				
Average GCSE grades	−1.644 (0.047)	−2.141 (0.005)	−1.355 (0.000)	−4.825 (0.945)
	−0.047	−0.013	0.061	−0.001
1–3 GCSE A–C grades	−2.078 (0.000)	−2.869 (0.876)	−1.741 (0.000)	−6.631 (0.000)
	0.031	−0.090	0.064	−0.006
4+ GCSE A–C grades	−1.041 (0.000)	−1.835 (0.003)	−1.255 (0.010)	−4.005 (0.000)
	0.258	−0.168	−0.076	−0.014
Non-white[‡]	1.349 (0.000)	1.742 (0.010)	1.434 (0.001)	3.001 (0.898)
	−0.032	0.052	−0.023	0.002
Disadvantage	0.517 (0.000)	0.836 (0.027)	0.767 (0.174)	1.665 (0.000)
	−0.127	0.031	0.079	0.016
Individuals[†]	3,864	2,522	4,879	1,610
Variance (σ_u^2)	0.000 (1.000)	0.000 (1.000)	9.774 (0.000)	13.444 (0.000)
Log likelihood	−13180.571	−10515.252	−15132.936	−7219.886
Males				
Average GCSE grades	−1.111 (0.371)	−1.453 (0.018)	−1.844 (0.000)	−3.429 (0.008)
	−0.073	0.003	0.067	0.003
1–3 GCSE A–C grades	−1.101 (0.123)	−1.464 (0.658)	−1.758 (0.000)	−3.534 (0.746)
	−0.069	−0.012	0.082	−0.001
4+ GCSE A–C grades	0.224 (0.479)	0.198 (0.000)	0.461 (0.087)	0.559 (0.000)
	0.057	−0.069	0.027	−0.015
Non-white[‡]	1.198 (0.000)	1.063 (0.000)	1.949 (0.000)	−1.316 (0.000)
	0.042	0.074	−0.115	−0.001
Disadvantage	−0.596 (0.000)	−0.729 (0.000)	−0.642 (0.000)	−2.737 (0.000)
	−0.148	−0.009	0.125	0.033
Individuals[†]	4,459	3,588	6,773	3,007
Variance (σ_u^2)	0.000 (1.000)	0.000 (1.000)	11.114 (0.000)	15.652 (0.000)
Log likelihood	−15625.027	−14676.321	−21947.372	−12702.004

* The 3 cells for a given covariate x are its effect on (i) the expected waiting time $\Delta E_r/\Delta x$; (ii) the conditional probability of exit $\partial P_{rj}/\partial x$; and (iii) p-value for underlying parameter estimate on x. (ii) is evaluated at $j = 4$ for females and $j = 6$ for males. The waiting times differentials (i) come from the sample mean values of 3.320, 4.641, 2.620, 12.390 for females and 4.355, 6.910, 8.217, 20.425 for males for $r = 1, 2, 3, 4$ respectively.

[†] No. of individuals exiting to state described at column head. Another 2,905 females and 2,947 males were censored, giving 15,780 females and 20,774 males in total. These totalled 143,434 female observations and 183,046 male observations. The 8,743 females and 11,232 males who match ($r = 1, 3$) correspond to those who match ($s = d$) in Table 1.

[‡] Of 834 non-white females, 291 (34.89%) were censored, compared with only 17.49% of white females. Of 811 non-white males, 406 (50.06%) were censored, compared with only 12.73% of white males.

3.1. Baseline Hazards

For females, the baseline hazards for the 'Gaussian proportional hazards' models are plotted (with solid lines) in Fig. 1.[13] Their homogeneous equivalents are also plotted with dashed lines.[14] Notice that σ_u^2 is significant for 4 out of 8 models,

---

[13] The plots for males are very similar and are available on request.
[14] The figures also report the number of exits used to estimate each linear segment at the longer durations, where the exits 'thin out'. Also, we only plot the first 40 weeks.

which is why there are clear differences between the two hazards for those who exit to training schemes, but not to jobs.

For those who go straight from school to jobs/YT there is a spike, clearly seen for all the homogeneous models. However, after controlling for unobserved heterogeneity, the spike for the hazards for YT mismatches disappears altogether ($r = 4$) and the spike for YT matches is much smaller. The hazards for all positive unemployment durations are also lower, leaving a virtually flat, or exponential, hazard. This implies that it is the unobservably 'good' youths who are able to find a YT before leaving compulsory schooling. This clear effect of heterogeneity for the YT hazards supports our view that YT is not a homogeneous programme and attracts young persons of varying unobserved 'qualities'.

We also compute the unconditional exit probabilities and note that jobs have a higher unconditional exit probability than YT ($\Pi_1 + \Pi_2$ is computed as 0.75 for females and males). However, females are more likely to match than males: $\Pi_1 + \Pi_3$ is 0.71 for females but only 0.66 for males. Also note that modelling unobserved heterogeneity has a big impact on $\Pi_1 + \Pi_2$ (but not $\Pi_1 + \Pi_3$). When the regressions are re-run with only observable covariates, $\Pi_1 + \Pi_2$ drops to 0.54 for females and 0.51 for males, and drops again to 0.50 for females and 0.49 for males if the covariates are also dropped. This clearly suggests that unobserved 'better' young people prefer jobs to YT schemes. Noting the conclusions from the previous paragraph, this also suggests that unobservably 'poorer' young people are being sorted into the 'poorer' YT schemes at longer durations.

Using the baseline hazards for each exit state, we next plot, in Fig. 2, the conditional exit probabilities P_{rj} given in (6) above. The patterns are roughly similar for men and women. The figure shows that, of those young women who go straight from school to a job/YT (P_{r0}), most are to a matching job (46%), with the remainder either finding a mismatching job (26%) or a matching YT scheme (28%). If we compare these numbers with the corresponding unconditional probabilities (Π_r), by integrating over all j, they are virtually identical. However, there are clear patterns in conditional matching probabilities. This is because, for those with an unemployment spell, in the first week, almost nobody enters a training scheme and everybody exits to a job. This is an institutional feature, with not all training schemes being available immediately (there is an annual 'recruitment cycle') and taking time to be filled. In the subsequent weeks, proportionally more young women enter matching training schemes, but fewer find jobs; eventually the unconditional probabilities coincide with those who go straight from school to job/YT.

For males a slightly different picture emerges, reflecting a bigger degree of heterogeneity across males and the fact that better males find what they want before the end of compulsory schooling. The conditional exit probabilities P_{r0} for those young men who go straight from school to a job/YT are 47% for a matching job, 28% for mismatching jobs and 23% for matching YT (and are very similar to females). Compared with all males (Π_r), these are 43%, 32% and 23% respectively. Clearly for those who have a spell of unemployment, the chance of getting a matching job is appreciably lower − 43% being a weighted average of 47% and 40% − and these young men end up taking mismatching jobs.

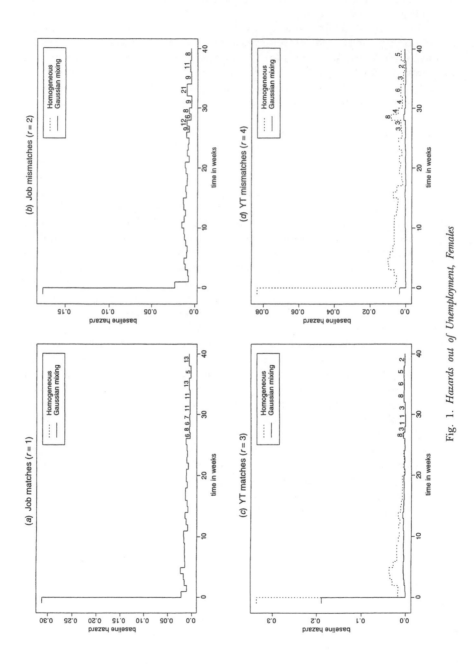

Fig. 1. *Hazards out of Unemployment, Females*

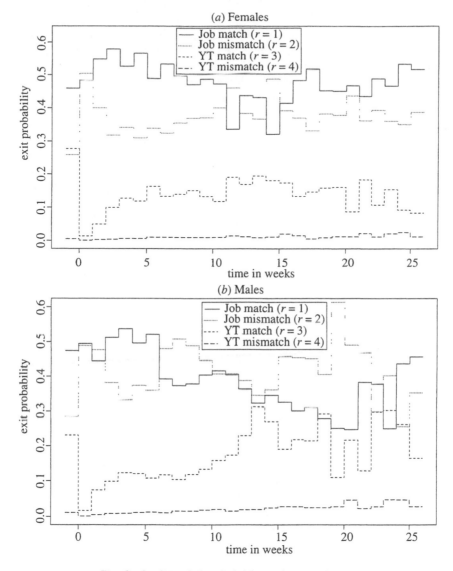

Fig. 2. *Conditional Exit Probabilities, Gaussian Mixing*

Finally, almost nobody ends up in mismatching YT. This suggests that there are no supply constraints in the provision of YT places for those young people who cannot find jobs.

3.2. Effects of Covariates

3.2.1. Disadvantage. Young people are classified by Careers Advisors according to whether they are 'disadvantaged' in some way. This is because such young people attract extra funding and support whilst they are on a YT programme. Disadvantage refers to poor home background, involvement in criminal activities etc. An almost universal finding from the existing literature is that young people from a 'disadvantaged' social background are more likely to make an unsuccessful transition from school, do not receive training and are more likely to become unemployed.

Tables 4 and 5 show that females from a disadvantaged background, compared with their base counterparts, prefer not to enter skilled non-manual occupations (-0.10 for $s = 1$) and this is confirmed once in the labour market (-0.13 for $d = 1$). In fact, disadvantaged females are more likely to enter unskilled manual occupations (0.06 for $d = 4$). As expected (Table 6), disadvantaged females are more likely to enter matching YT (0.08 for $r = 3$) and less likely to get matching jobs (-0.13 for $r = 1$). The outcomes for disadvantaged males are broadly similar, but stronger, in that they are even more likely to enter matching YT (0.13 for $r = 3$) and less likely to end up in matching jobs (-0.15 for $r = 1$). These are quite large marginal effects. Note that for both disadvantaged males and females, preferences are realistic, as marginal effects in the two multinomial logits are very similar.

3.2.2. Ethnic minorities. The results in Table 4 show that females from the ethnic minorities, relative to their 'white' counterparts, prefer skilled non-manual occupations (0.08 on 'non-white' for $s = 1$) and rank unskilled non-manual occupations lowest (-0.07 for $s = 3$). These preferences are not realised once these young people enter the labour market (Table 5), in that non-white females are more likely to end up in unskilled manual occupations (0.11 for $d = 4$) but are even less likely to end up in unskilled non-manual occupations (-0.12 for $d = 3$). This suggests the pre-labour market 'sorting' by young people and their advisors does not match the subsequent labour-market sorting by employers. This evidence of mismatching is also seen in the competing risks model (Table 6), whereby non-white females end up in mismatching jobs (0.05 for $r = 2$), rather than finding matching jobs (-0.03 for $r = 1$) or matching training schemes (-0.02 for $r = 3$).

Like non-white females, non-white males also have preferences that do not match destinations. Relative to their preferences, males are much more likely to end up in an unskilled manual occupation and less likely to end up in a skilled manual occupation. However, male occupational preferences are different to non-white females: compared with their 'white' counterparts, they clearly prefer non-manual occupations (0.09 for $s = 1$ and 0.07 for $s = 3$) at the expense of manual occupations (-0.13 for $s = 2$ and -0.04 for $s = 4$). In short, non-white males end up in jobs – most in jobs that do not match their preference (0.07 for $r = 2$) and some that do (0.04 for $r = 1$) – rather than end up in YT schemes that do match their preference (-0.12 for $r = 3$).

These results raise implications about the issue of equality of opportunity in access to YT. Government policy offers all 16 and 17 year old school leavers a guaranteed place on YT. What appears to happen is that ethnic minority school-leavers are excluded from YT and instead enter a mismatching job if female or any job if male. Note that waiting times are longer than their white counterparts. All in all, this suggests either discrimination by employers and/or unrealistic expectations by non-white young persons. It is worth noting that Andrews *et al.* (2001*b*) find direct evidence of discrimination in a two-sided search model of the matching probability, using these data.

3.2.3. *Qualifications.* By far the strongest effects of all the covariates come from the examination grade for the GCSE taken immediately prior to leaving compulsory schooling. The four categories are 'low GCSE grades' (the base category), 'average GCSE grades', '1–3 GCSE A–C grades', and '4+ GCSE A–C grades'. Basically, the better the grade, the more likely are young people to choose, and end up in, skilled non-manual occupations ($s = d = 1$). For example, females with 4+ GCSE A–C grades are more likely to choose, by 0.57 log-points, and end up in, by 0.52 log-points, these occupations. The corresponding effects for males are weaker, but strong nonetheless, namely 0.32 and 0.20 respectively.

There are two differences between male and female preferences and outcomes, both reflecting the clear occupational segregation in the labour market noted earlier. First, as females obtain better grades, they eschew all manual occupations, whereas males eschew only unskilled manual occupations. Second, males with any grades whatsoever are more likely to end up in skilled manual occupations, even though grade has no effect on preferences for these occupations. This reflects traditional apprenticeship opportunities that females do not have.

Compared with no qualifications, a young person with intermediate grades is much more likely to take up a matching training scheme: the estimates for females are 0.06 on 'average GCSE grades' for $r = 3$ and 0.06 on '1–3 GCSE A–C grades' for $r = 3$; for males they are 0.07 and 0.08 respectively. However, the best qualified males end up in matching jobs, as the coefficient increases by 0.13 going from '1–3 GCSE A–C grades' to '4+ GCSE A–C grades' for $r = 1$, offset by a change of -0.06 on matching YT ($r = 3$) and by a change of -0.06 on mismatching jobs ($r = 2$). The effect for females is much stronger, increasing by 0.23 for matching jobs and decreasing by 0.14 for matching YT and decreasing by 0.08 for mismatching jobs.

To conclude, these findings are consistent with previous research, which shows that there is a complementarity between educational qualifications and the propensity to train in occupations which offer general training. The most able are at the front of the job queue and those with intermediate qualifications are sorted into matching YT schemes, where qualifications are less important. This is expected, because the Government guarantees a place on YT for all 16 year old school leavers. The fact that those with no qualifications eschew YT is of some concern.

4. Summary and Conclusions

Our main findings in this paper are:

1. In the raw data, (a) there is clear evidence of occupational segregation (females prefer non-manual occupations; males prefer skilled occupations); (b) just under two-thirds of young persons end up in occupations which match their preference; (c) mismatch occurs because of excess demand for training; (d) two-in-five young people go straight from school to either a job or YT scheme.

2. In the regressions, once we control for unobserved heterogeneity, (a) women are more likely to match than men (also observed in the raw data); (b) the baseline hazards suggest that it is unobservably 'good' young persons who exit first, to either jobs or 'good' YT schemes; (c) there are no supply constraints in the provision of YT places, in that the unemployed are absorbed into schemes that match their original training preference; and (d) the matching probabilities for those who go straight from school to jobs or YT schemes are the same for all the sample, except for unemployed males, for whom the probability of finding a matching job is lower.

3. Variations in training preferences, training destinations, and labour-market outcomes are primarily because of examination performance, although there are substantial differences for non-whites and the disadvantaged. Specifically, (a) because of the extra funding available to employers, the disadvantaged are very clearly more likely to enter YT and less likely to end up in jobs; (b) ethnic minority school-leavers are excluded from training schemes that match their preference and instead enter a mismatching job if female or any job if male; (c) the most able are at the front of the job queue and those with intermediate qualifications are sorted into matching YT schemes. Those with no qualifications eschew YT.

These results are able to inform the issue raised in the introduction, namely is it young persons or employers who are constraining acquisition of intermediate skills? By comparing training preferences with training destinations it is possible to examine whether the (mis)match between the two is consistent with either excess demand for, or excess supply of, youth training. As far as we are aware, this has not been possible in previous research. We conclude that young persons demand more training than they are offered by employers. In other words, there is excess demand for training; this is at odds with conventional wisdom (see, for example, the Government's view quoted in footnote 3). We believe that this finding generalises, and is relevant today, even with the quasi-privatisation of YT in the early 1990s. New training programmes have been introduced, such as Modern Apprenticeships, but nonetheless they remain rooted in the 'traditional' YT scheme and it is the same 'players' who deliver the training.

The obvious question is why is there rationing of training places when training suppliers, who are future employers, have requirements for skilled workers? In fact, other research with these data concludes (Andrews, 2001a) that employers find it much harder to fill (and often withdraw) 'skilled' vacancies. There is no reason to believe that standard market-failure type arguments do not apply in the market for youth labour: training suppliers are unwilling to finance general training because of poaching, imperfect capital markets and imperfect information.

Finally, does it actually matter that mismatching occurs? We argue that it does because, quite apart from the well-established view that there is an intermediate skills gap, ongoing research suggests that those young persons with job mismatches are more likely to re-enter unemployment than those with job matches. The raw differentials of about 6% for young women and 9% for young men are large, implying that those young people who do match will have more stable careers.

University of Manchester
Lancaster University
Lancaster University

References

Andrews, M. and Bradley, S. (1997), 'Modelling the transition from school and the demand for training in the United Kingdom', *Economica*, vol. 64, pp. 387–413.

Andrews, M., Bradley, S. and Upward, R. (2001*a*), 'Employer search, vacancy duration, and skill shortages: an analysis of vacancies in the youth labour market', Discussion paper, University of Nottingham, June.

Andrews, M., Bradley, S. and Upward, R. (2001*b*), 'Estimating the probability of a match using micro-economic data for the youth labour market', *Labour Economics*, vol. 8, pp. 335–57.

Arulampalam, S. and Booth, A. (1997), 'Who gets over the training hurdle? A study of the training experiences of young men and women in Britain', *Journal of Population Economics*, vol. 10, pp. 197–217.

Dolton, P., Makepeace, G. and Treble, J. (1994), 'The Youth Training Scheme and the school-to-work transition', *Oxford Economic Papers*, vol. 46, pp. 629–57.

European Union (1999), 'Teaching and learning: towards the learning society', White Paper on Education and Training.

Green, F. (1993), 'The determinants of training of male and female employees in Britain', *Oxford Bulletin of Economics and Statistics*, vol. 55, pp. 103–22.

Han, A. and Hausman, J. (1990), 'Flexible parametric estimation of duration and competing risk models', *Journal of Applied Econometrics*, vol. 5, pp. 1–28.

Heckman, J. and Singer, B. (1984), 'Econometric duration analysis', *Journal of Econometrics*, vol. 24, pp. 63–132.

Lancaster, T. (1990), *The Econometric Analysis of Transition Data*. Cambridge: Cambridge University Press.

Leslie, D. and Drinkwater, S. (1999), 'Staying on in full-time education: reasons for higher participation rates among ethnic minority males and females', *Economica*, vol. 66, pp. 63–78.

National Skills Task Force (2000), 'Tackling the adult skills gap: upskilling adults and the role of workplace learning', Third report, Department for Education and Employment.

Prentice, R. and Gloeckler, L. (1978), 'Regression analysis of grouped survival data with application to breast cancer data', *Biometrics*, vol. 34, pp. 57–67.

Rice, P. (1999), 'The impact of local labour markets on investment in further education: evidence from the England and Wales Youth Cohort Studies', *Journal of Population Economics*, vol. 12, pp. 287–312.

Shields, M. (1998), 'Changes in the determinants of employer-funded training for full-time employees in Britain', *Oxford Bulletin of Economics and Statistics*, vol. 60, pp. 189–214.

Stewart, M. (1996), 'Heterogeneity specification in unemployment duration models', Mimeo, University of Warwick, September.

Thomas, J. (1996), 'On the interpretation of covariate estimates in independent competing-risks models', *Bulletin of Economic Research*, vol. 48, pp. 27–39.

US Department of Labor (1999), 'Futurework: trends and challenges for work in the 21st century', Economic Report, US Department of Labor.

Part III
Empirical Evidence on the Impact of Public Training Programmes

[20]

The Economic Journal, 109 (July), 313–348. © Royal Economic Society 1999. Published by Blackwell Publishers, 108 Cowley Road, Oxford OX4 1JF, UK and 350 Main Street, Malden, MA 02148, USA.

THE PRE-PROGRAMME EARNINGS DIP AND THE DETERMINANTS OF PARTICIPATION IN A SOCIAL PROGRAMME. IMPLICATIONS FOR SIMPLE PROGRAMME EVALUATION STRATEGIES*

James J. Heckman and Jeffrey A. Smith

The key to estimating the impact of a programme is constructing the counterfactual outcome representing what would have happened in its absence. This problem becomes more complicated when agents, such as individuals, firms or local governments, self-select into the programme rather than being exogenously assigned to it. This paper uses data from a major social experiment to identify what would have happened to the earnings of self-selected participants in a job training programme had they not participated in it. We investigate the implications of these earnings patterns for the validity of widely-used before-after and difference-in-differences estimators.

The key to estimating the impact of a programme is constructing the counter-factual outcomes representing what would have happened in its absence. This problem becomes more complicated when agents, such as individuals, firms or local governments, self-select into the programme rather than being exogenously assigned to it. In many cases, agents self-select on the basis of the outcome variable that the programme is designed to affect, as when trainees choose to take training when their earnings are low, or when states reform their social assistance systems in response to increases in the caseload. This can lead to selection bias in evaluating the programme.

This paper examines a prototypical job training programme into which participants self-select. It uses data from a major social experiment to identify what would have happened to the earnings of participants in a job training programme had they not participated. We investigate the implications of these earnings patterns for the validity of widely-used before-after and difference-in-differences estimators. We demonstrate that these estimators do not produce credible estimates of the impacts of training. This leads us to investigate the determinants of programme participation. We find that labour force dynamics, rather than earnings or employment dynamics, drive the participation process. For women, dynamic family processes related to marriage and childbearing are also important. Our evidence suggests that training programmes function as a form of job search for many of their participants. Evaluation methods that only control for earnings dynamics, like the conventional difference-in-differences estimator, do not adequately capture the underlying choices leading to

* This research was supported by NSF SBR 91-11-455 and SBR 93-21-048 and by grants from the Russell Sage Foundation, the American Bar Foundation and the Social Science and Humanities Research Council of Canada. We thank Jingjing Hsee for her programming work, Theresa Devine for her comments and assistance with the SIPP data, Karen Conneely and Edward Vytlacil for their excellent research assistance and seminar participants at the October 1993 NBER Labor Studies Group meeting, Carnegie-Mellon University, the University of Western Ontario, Queen's University and McMaster University for their comments.

differences in unobserved variables between participants and non-participants. Application of our findings about the participation process in either matching estimators or a conditional (on the probability of participation) nonparametric version of the difference-in-differences estimator yields large reductions in the extent of selection bias in non-experimental estimates of the effect of training on earnings.

Historically, evaluators of early U.S. job training programmes used before-after comparisons of participant earnings. The problem with this approach is that it attributes all improvements in outcomes relative to pre-programme levels to the programme being evaluated. If there are general increases in earnings due to economy-wide effects or life-cycle earnings growth, then this estimator will be biased.

To address this problem, it became common to utilise a comparison group of non-participants to eliminate common life-cycle and economy-wide factors from the before-after estimator. Such methods were widely used in the literature on evaluating educational interventions (see, for example, Campbell and Stanley, 1966). In the conventional difference-in-differences approach, the before-after earnings change for participants is compared to the before-after change for a temporally aligned group of non-participants. In the context of evaluating training programmes, Ashenfelter (1978) noted a potentially serious limitation of this procedure when he observed that the mean earnings of participants in government training programmes decline in the period prior to programme entry. Subsequent research finds this regularity, sometimes called 'Ashenfelter's dip' or the 'pre-programme dip', for participants in many other training and adult education programmes (see Ashenfelter and Card, 1985, Bassi, 1983, 1984, and the comprehensive survey by Heckman *et al.*, 1999).

Whether the pre-programme drop in earnings is permanent or transitory determines what would have happened to participants had they not participated. Knowing whether the dip is permanent or transitory has important implications for the validity of both the before-after and conventional difference-in-differences estimation methods. Furthermore, the validity of variants of the conventional difference-in-differences approach that control for earnings histories depends on the relationship between earnings in the post-programme period and the determinants of programme participation.

Analysts of training programmes using non-experimental data can only speculate about what the earnings of participants would have been had they not participated. In this paper, we use data on the control group from the National JTPA Study (NJS), a recent experimental evaluation of a large scale U.S. training programme, to learn what the earnings of participants would have been had they not participated.[1] The Job Training Partnership Act (JTPA) programme is typical of many government job training programmes around the world in terms of both its target population and the types of services it provides (see Heckman *et al.*, 1999). Control group members were

---

[1] See Bloom *et al.* (1993) and Bloom *et al.* (1997) for descriptions of the National JTPA Study.

eligible for, applied to and were initially accepted into the JTPA programme prior to being randomised out. Under certain conditions, their earnings represent the desired counterfactual.[2] For adult males, the control group data reveal that the dip in mean earnings is primarily transitory. For the other demographic groups considered, control group earnings grow above pre-programme levels in the period following random assignment.

We show that this post-random-assignment earnings growth among the controls imparts a strong upward bias to before-after estimators of programme impact. Early evaluators who used these estimators falsely attributed to the programmes being evaluated improvements in earnings that would have oc-curred even in the absence of training.

A similar bias plagues conventional difference-in-differences estimators. We apply these estimators to two comparison groups composed of persons eligible for JTPA. The first consists of eligible non-participants (ENPs) at four training centres in the JTPA experiment. In many ways, this comparison group is ideal. The ENPs reside in the same local labour markets as the experimental treatments and controls, complete the same surveys, and are all eligible for JTPA.[3] The second comparison group of eligibles is drawn from the 1986 Full Panel of the Survey of Income and Programme Participation (SIPP). This sample resembles those used in earlier evaluations with the exception that programme eligibility can be precisely determined in the SIPP data because there is much more information on monthly income dynamics.[4]

Compared to the experimental impact estimates, the conventional differ-ence-in-differences estimators applied to either comparison group produce substantially biased estimates of programme impacts because the upward trend in post-programme earnings for controls is not found for comparison group members. That the earnings behaviour of the comparison groups does not correspond to that of the controls indicates that these groups do not provide the desired counterfactual. Furthermore, the earnings growth among controls after random assignment, along with the pre-programme dip, makes the difference-in-differences estimator quite sensitive to the specific periods over which 'before' and 'after' are defined.

The failure of simple comparison group estimators suggests that the design

[2] Heckman (1992), Heckman and Smith (1993, 1995) and Heckman et al. (1999) discuss in detail the conditions under which experimental control group data provide the desired counterfactual. In short, these conditions are: (1) that random assignment be correctly conducted, so that control group members do not receive the experimental treatment; (2) that there is no 'randomisation bias' such that the programme operates differently or serves different persons due to random assignment; and (3) that the control group members do not receive substitute treatments from other sources that are similar to the experimental treatment. Bloom (1991) and Bloom et al. (1993) provide evidence in support of (1) for the NJS. Heckman, Khoo, Roselius and Smith (1996) report that there is little evidence of randomisation bias in the JTPA experiment. Heckman, Hohmann et al. (1998) present evidence of violations of (3) for those control group members (about a third of the total) recommended to receive classroom training. Substitution is fairly low among the remaining controls.

[3] Heckman and Roselius (1994a) show that most comparison groups used in practice lack at least one, and often all, of these features. Heckman, Ichimura, Smith and Todd (1998) present evidence on the importance of using the same survey instruments and drawing participants and comparison group members from the same local labour market.

[4] See the Appendix for a more detailed data description.

of successful estimators may benefit from a deeper understanding of the programme participation process. Partly due to data limitations, early analysts focused on earnings as the outcome measure of interest and on declines in the opportunity cost of taking training as the key determinant of programme participation (see Heckman, 1978, Heckman and Robb, 1985, 1986, Ashenfelter and Card, 1985, and the survey in Heckman *et al.*, 1999). Even if this model is a valid description of the programme participation process, conditioning on eligibility does not suffice to make comparison group members comparable to controls. While eligible adults sometimes experience a dip in earnings prior to the decision to participate in the programme, their dip differs from that experienced by the controls in both its timing and intensity. The two dips differ because the dip among the controls results primarily from unemployment dynamics while the dip among the eligibles results primarily from reductions in earnings conditional on employment (Heckman *et al.*, 1998). This mismatch helps account for the bias and instability in the conventional difference-in-differences estimator applied to earnings gains.

Unemployment dynamics and not earnings or employment dynamics, drive participation in training programmes. Unemployment dynamics are only weakly related to earnings dynamics. For example, persons who re-enter the labour force and become unemployed have no change in their earnings but increase their likelihood of participation in training programmes. Job training programmes such as JTPA appear to operate as a form of job search. This is not surprising given that many of the services they offer – such as job search assistance and on-the-job training at private firms – are designed to lead to immediate employment.

We also show that a number of additional factors such as age, schooling, marital status and family income are important determinants of programme participation. Our evidence explains the failure of econometric methods based on the assumption that earnings histories drive programme participation and suggests the value of investigating alternative econometric strategies that exploit information on unemployment dynamics along with the additional factors determining programme participation to control for self-selection bias in programme participation.

We use our model of programme participation to develop cross-sectional matching estimators and a conditional (on the probability of participation) nonparametric version of the difference-in-differences estimator that improve on the performance of conventional before-after and difference-in-differences methods. These methods reduce the estimated selection bias compared to what is obtained from conventional methods. Conditioning on labour force status histories plays a crucial role in reducing selection bias for adult men. However, substantial bias still remains.

The plan of the paper is as follows. Section 1 presents new evidence on the earnings of the experimental control group from the National JTPA Study. Section 2 compares the earnings dynamics of the comparison group samples to those of the controls and indicates the implications of their differing earnings patterns for the design and performance of difference-in-differences estimators of programme impact. Section 3 analyses the determinants of programme participation. Section 4 demonstrates that the richer models of programme participation are effective in reducing selection bias in non-experimental estimates of programme impact. The final section summarises the implications of our analysis for future evaluations of labour market programmes.

1. The Pre-programme Dip and the Before-After Estimator

In this section, we examine the mean earnings of randomised-out JTPA participants, and consider their implications for before-after estimators of programme impact. Figs 1a to 1d display the mean earnings of eligible applicants accepted into the programme but randomly denied access to services. This group is labelled 'Controls' in Figs. 1a to 1d.[5] Month 't' in this case represents the month of random assignment, which coincides with the month of eligibility determination for most controls.[6] The data show a large dip in the mean earnings of control group members for all four demographic groups: adult males and females (age 22 and above) and male and female out-of-school youth (ages 16–21). In each case, the dip reaches its lowest point in the month of random assignment. Ashenfelter (1978) first noted this pre-programme dip in the earnings of participants in job training programmes, and it has subsequently been found to be a feature of virtually all training and adult education programmes (Heckman et al., 1999).

The pattern of recovery from the pre-programme dip has important practical consequences for the performance of before-after estimators, which compare post-programme earnings to pre-programme earnings to measure the effect of the programme. Define the impact of the programme as the effect of the programme on participants, compared to what they would have earned without participating in the programme. If the decline in earnings prior to month 't' is transient, before-after comparisons will *overstate* the impact of the programme on earnings if the earnings decline occurs in the period used to measure pre-training earnings. On the other hand, if the decline in mean earnings is persistent, before-after comparisons will *understate* the impact of the programme if the decline occurs during the period used to measure pre-training earnings. Fig. 1a reveals that the mean earnings decline for adult males is largely transient, while Figs 1b to 1d reveal that post-programme earnings grow well above pre-programme levels for the other three demographic groups. The timing of the earnings dip indicates that valid before-after comparisons will require more than a year of pre-programme data for adults. Even with sufficient pre-programme data, post-programme earnings growth among controls implies a large upward bias in before-after estimators of programme impact for all groups but adult males.

---

[5] Patterns are similar for the full set of 16 training centres in the National JTPA Study. We focus on the four centres at which the ENP sample was drawn.

[6] In some cases, lags in the intake process may cause the month of random assignment to lie one or two months after the month of eligibility determination.

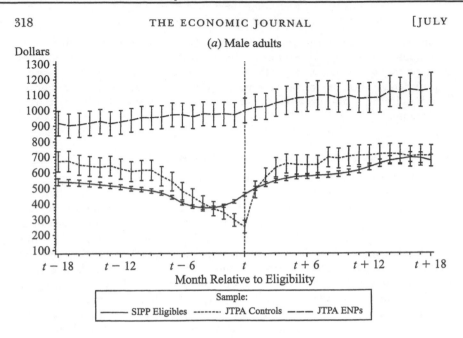

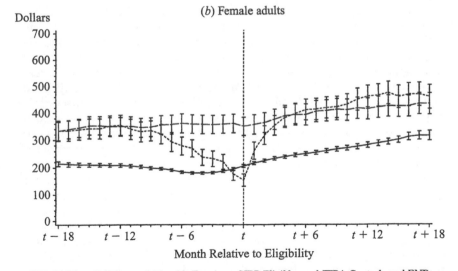

Fig. 1. *Mean Self-Reported Monthly Earnings: SIPP Eligibles and JTPA Controls and ENPs*
Notes: SIPP uses all JTPA–eligible person–month observations of respondents present in both the first and last months of the panel. Controls are randomised–out participants from the National JTPA Study. Observations based on quasi-rectangular sample. ENPS are JTPA–eligible non-participants at the same sites as the controls from the National JTPA Study. Observations based on quasi-rectangular sample. Standard error bars +/− 2 standard errors of the means.

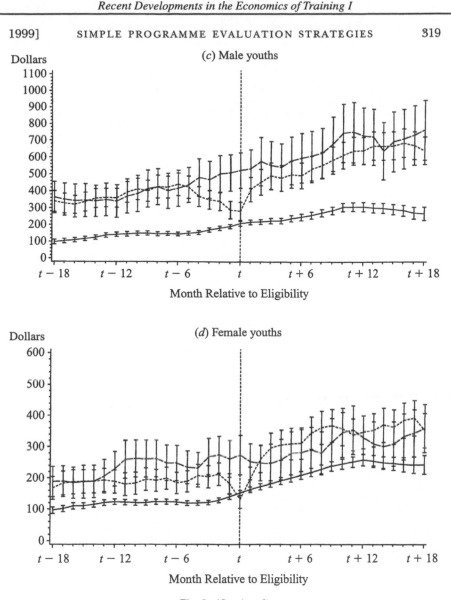

Fig. 1. *(Continued)*

More precisely, let Y_{0a} denote earnings without training in the period after month 't' ($a > t$) and Y_{1a} denote earnings with training in the period after month 't'. Let $D = 1$ for persons who apply and are accepted into JTPA and $D = 0$ otherwise, and let $R = 1$ for persons who are randomised into the experimental treatment group (conditional on $D = 1$) and $R = 0$ for persons randomised into the experimental control group. Then the experimental impact is defined as:

Table 1

Before-After and Difference-in-differences Impact Estimates

NJS control and treatment group and ENP samples and SIPP eligible sample. Estimates in dollars of earnings per 18 months. Estimated standard errors in parentheses

Before period	After period	Experimental estimate*	Before-after estimate†	Diff-in-diffs estimate (ENP)‡	Diff-in-diffs estimate (SIPP)‡
		Adult Males			
$t - 18$ to $t - 1$	$t + 1$ to $t + 18$	656.93 (562.78)	3108.98 (511.25)	922.89 (1143.08)	N.A.
$t - 15$ to $t - 1$	$t + 1$ to $t + 15$	601.51 (578.83)	3413.89 (512.78)	1501.74 (1144.06)	851.26 (559.09)
$t - 12$ to $t - 1$	$t + 1$ to $t + 12$	529.75 (586.53)	3592.49 (512.52)	1994.42 (1141.67)	1163.95 (544.36)
$t - 15$ to $t - 13$	$t + 13$ to $t + 15$	953.74 (703.98)	2626.14 (693.13)	−807.58 (1351.88)	−347.21 (784.59)
$t - 18$ to $t - 16$	$t + 16$ to $t + 18$	937.18 (687.96)	1854.91 (697.06)	−1960.56 (1342.43)	N.A.
		Adult Females			
$t - 18$ to $t - 1$	$t + 1$ to $t + 18$	845.17 (370.54)	3171.83 (317.11)	2188.61 (536.84)	N.A.
$t - 15$ to $t - 1$	$t + 1$ to $t + 15$	877.88 (368.53)	3078.08 (315.99)	2236.26 (537.80)	2059.30 (329.08)
$t - 12$ to $t - 1$	$t + 1$ to $t + 12$	928.02 (366.41)	2986.58 (313.45)	2269.11 (537.48)	2106.32 (322.75)
$t - 15$ to $t - 13$	$t + 13$ to $t + 15$	753.15 (481.93)	3413.24 (425.47)	1989.68 (632.21)	1870.15 (440.78)
$t - 18$ to $t - 16$	$t + 16$ to $t + 18$	811.95 (476.98)	3600.43 (424.58)	1878.65 (631.71)	N.A.

* Experimental estimates include only treatments and controls at the four training centres at which detailed information on controls and eligibles non-participants was collected. The experimental estimates presented are cross-section estimates obtained by differencing treatment and control mean earnings in the 'after' period. Note that with experimental data the expected values of the cross section and difference-in-differences estimators are the same.

† The before-after estimates are obtained by subtracting control group mean earnings in the 'before' period from treatment group mean earnings in the 'after' period.

‡ The difference-in-differences estimates consist of the difference between the change in mean earnings for the treatment group between the 'before' and 'after' periods and the change in mean earnings for the comparison group (either SIPP or ENP) between the 'before' and 'after' periods. Treatment group mean earnings in the 'before' period are estimated using control group mean earnings in the 'before' period.

$$E(Y_{1a}|R = 1, D = 1) - E(Y_{0a}|R = 0, D = 1). \qquad (1)$$

This is just the difference in mean earnings between the experimental treatment and control groups in period a after random assignment. Under the assumptions that justify random assignment, this parameter estimates the effect of treatment on the treated.[7,8]

The non-experimental before-after estimator converges to:

Experimental estimate*	Before-after estimate†	Diff-in-diffs estimate (ENP)‡	Diff-in-diffs estimate (SIPP)‡
		Male Youth	
−1060.02	2498.51	−1214.98	N.A.
(658.69)	(527.17)	(1404.83)	
−1134.38	2014.13	−1156.27	349.10
(690.22)	(540.16)	(1430.55)	(581.61)
−1035.84	1486.05	−978.22	−154.12
(694.07)	(559.63)	(1472.85)	(592.99)
−1500.32	4665.60	−2065.06	1855.96
(884.89)	(647.23)	(1675.42)	(701.56)
−1387.61	4836.80	−1957.95	N.A.
(843.04)	(667.81)	(1756.79)	
		Female Youth	
−112.83	2641.68	1180.19	N.A.
(432.68)	(322.33)	(742.50)	
−96.70	2452.41	1313.47	1031.85
(440.35)	(328.15)	(754.56)	(359.06)
−148.89	2223.29	1327.33	904.51
(445.28)	(333.17)	(773.33)	(355.72)
292.14	3492.87	1302.14	1163.15
(583.40)	(435.97)	(885.76)	(478.07)
−105.99	3683.81	490.73	N.A.
(603.27)	(427.29)	(918.57)	

Notes: Some values for the SIPP are omitted due to the limited length of the panel.
The top 1% of monthly earnings are trimmed for each demographic group in each of the SIPP, ENP, Control and Treatment group samples.
The Control group and ENP samples include only persons with a valid earnings observation in month $t − 18$ and in month $t + 18$. The Treatment group sample includes only persons with a valid earnings observation for month $t + 18$ (no earnings information is available for the Treatment group prior to month t). The SIPP eligible sample includes only persons with valid earnings information in the first and last months of the panel.
The SIPP eligible sample consists of person-months rather than persons.

Samples sizes	Adult males	Adult females	Male youth	Female youth
treatments	1,271	1,464	736	804
controls	453	599	230	289
ENPs	401	885	85	154
SIPP eligibles	10,864	19,606	2,167	3,311

$$E(Y_{1a}|R = 1, D = 1) - E(Y_{0b}|R = 0, D = 1), \qquad (2)$$

where the subscript b denotes the period before month 't' $(b < t)$, and where

---

[7] See Heckman (1992), Heckman and Smith (1993, 1995) and Heckman *et al.* (1999) for discussions of these assumptions.

[8] Heckman (1997), Heckman and Smith (1998) and Heckman *et al.* (1999) consider the limitations of this parameter and discuss other parameters of interest to evaluators.

the pre-random-assignment earnings of the control group are used to proxy the pre-random-assignment earnings of the treatment group. The mean bias that results from using (2) in place of (1) to estimate the impact of treatment on the treated is

$$E(Y_{0a}|R = 0, D = 1) - E(Y_{0b}|R = 0, D = 1), \tag{3}$$

the difference between the pre-programme earnings of participants and what their post-programme earnings would have been, had they not participated.

Table 1 presents before-after estimates based on the JTPA data. The first two columns define the 'before' and 'after' periods used in each estimator. The experimental impact for the 'after' period is given in column three for adults and column seven for youth, and the before-after estimates appear in column four for adults and column eight for youth. (The numbers in the remaining columns are defined later in this paper). For all demographic groups and for all base periods, the before-after estimate substantially exceeds the experimental estimate. For example, the eighteen-month before-after estimate for adult males is $3,109 compared to an experimental estimate of $657. Note that, for adult males, the group with the largest pre-programme dip and the smallest (relative) post-programme earnings growth for the controls, the before-after impact estimate is substantially larger for before periods that include the pre-programme dip than for those that do not.

Can we do better by using a difference-in-differences estimator? We now address this question using two comparison groups selected according to the intuitively appealing criterion that included persons be eligible for the programme but not participate in it.

2. Comparison Groups and the Conventional Difference-in-Differences Estimator

In this section, we first describe the eligibility rules for JTPA that define our two non-experimental comparison groups of eligibles. We show that the earnings patterns of the two comparison groups differ in important ways from the pattern found for controls. Conditioning on eligibility alone does not eliminate bias. As a result, conventional difference-in-differences estimators based on comparison groups of eligibles are both biased and unstable.

2.1. *The JTPA Eligibility Rules*

Economic disadvantage is the primary eligibility condition for JTPA training. It consists of an individual having either low family income in the six months prior to application or current participation in a means-tested social programme.[9,10]

___

[9] As defined in the Job Training Partnership Act, economic disadvantage arises if at least one of the following criteria are met: (1) low *family* income in the six months prior to application; (2) current receipt of cash public assistance such as Aid to Families with Dependent Children (AFDC) or general assistance; and (3) current receipt of food stamps. According to the U.S. Department of Labor (1993a), in Program Year 1991 (July 1991 to June 1992), around 93% of JTPA participants qualified because

The key features of the eligibility rules are the dependence on family (rather than individual) income and the short six-month window over which income is summed to determine eligibility. The six-month window allows highly-skilled workers to become eligible for the programme after only a few months out of work.[11],[12]

Barnow (1993) shows that there are slight differences between the eligibility criteria for JTPA and those of its predecessor programmes.[13] All major training programmes in the United States have focused on displaced workers, persons with low incomes and transfer recipients. Furthermore, our evidence on the determinants of participation suggests that many differences in eligibility rules across programmes will have little impact on the types of persons participating. In particular, because recently unemployed persons and persons re-entering the labour force are much more likely to select into the JTPA programme than other eligibles, differences in eligibility rules across programmes that do not affect the eligibility status of the unemployed will have only a limited effect on the composition of programme participants.

2.2. *Comparing the Earnings Patterns of Eligibles and Participants*

We now compare the mean earnings patterns of the two comparison groups of programme eligibles and the experimental controls from the National JTPA Study. The eligible non-participant, or 'ENP', comparison group is drawn from the same local labour markets as the controls and has earnings data collected using the same survey instrument. In contrast, the 'SIPP' comparison group is a national sample drawn from a major U.S. panel data set. Both comparison groups are composed exclusively of persons eligible for JTPA. Differences in the time series of mean earnings between a comparison group and the controls generally produce bias in the difference-in-differences estimator.

Figs 1 *a* to 1 *d* display the mean individual earnings of the controls and the two comparison groups of eligibles. For the comparison groups, month '*t*' is

they were economically disadvantaged. Similar measures of economic disadvantage have formed the basis of eligibility for most U.S. job training programmes.

[10] A second, and much less important, avenue to JTPA eligibility is an 'audit window' that allows up to 10% of participants at each training centre to be non-economically-disadvantaged persons with other barriers to employment such as limited ability in English. Due to the subjective nature of these barriers, the eligibles examined here consist only of persons eligible via economic disadvantage.

[11] Devine and Heckman (1996) present an extensive discussion of the JTPA eligibility rules, their variation over time and across states, and the implications of this variation for the composition of the eligible population.

[12] The implementation of the general rules described here varies somewhat across localities, as states and training centres have some discretion over exactly what constitutes family income and what constitutes a family. Devine and Heckman (1996) show that such differences are too small to affect the patterns discussed here. The eligibility rules described here are those in place at the time our data were collected. Since that time some marginal changes have been made. See Devine and Heckman (1996) or U.S. Department of Labor (1993*b*).

[13] The JTPA programme replaced the CETA (Comprehensive Employment and Training Act) programme which had earlier replaced the MDTA (Manpower Development and Training Act) programme.

the month of measured eligibility. Adult male and adult female SIPP eligibles display a dip in mean earnings centred in the middle of the six-month window over which components of family income are summed to determine JTPA eligibility, although the dip for women is much less pronounced. Devine and Heckman (1996) prove that the JTPA eligibility rules generate such a dip for stationary family income processes; since adult earnings are typically a large component of family income in low-income families, this pattern also shows up in graphs of individual earnings for adult eligibles. In contrast, youth in the SIPP eligible sample experience no dip in mean individual earnings. These demographic differences in earnings dynamics indicate that, except for adult males, eligibility depends crucially on the earnings behaviour of other family members. For adult SIPP eligibles, mean earnings recover from their decline because the eligibility rules for JTPA (and many other programmes) operate to include persons temporarily suffering adverse economic circumstances.

Comparing the mean earnings of the SIPP eligibles to those of the JTPA controls from the National JTPA Study, we find substantial differences between the two groups. Among adults, the magnitude of the dip is larger for the controls, whose dip is centred at month 't' rather than three or four months earlier. Among youths, only the controls show any dip at all. This evidence strongly suggests that while the JTPA eligibility rules clearly affect the mean earnings patterns observed for all eligibles, additional behavioural factors are required to account for the dip observed for programme participants.

Adult male and female ENPs show no dip in mean earnings during the period prior to month 't'. Smith (1997a) demonstrates that the absence of a dip for this group results from the structure of the survey instrument used to gather earnings information on the ENPs. This survey instrument smooths away all within-job variation in earnings. Such variation is an important component of the dip observed among the SIPP eligibles. It plays a relatively small role in the earnings dip for the controls, most of which results from the effects of job loss, which are captured by the survey. A better survey would have revealed a greater decline in earnings for both the ENPs and the controls.[14] Furthermore, with the exception of male youth, the ENPs do not experience earnings growth after month 't' to match that found for the controls or, to a lesser extent, for the SIPP eligibles.

The differences between the earnings patterns of the controls and the two comparison groups prior to month 't', and the post-'t' divergence in mean

---

[14] See Smith (1997a, b) and the extended data appendix (available on request) for a more detailed discussion of these issues and of the difference in mean earnings levels between the SIPP eligibles and the ENPs. In brief, differences in observed characteristics do not explain the difference in mean earnings levels between the ENP and SIPP samples of eligibles. Instead, non-response bias among the ENPs (low income persons are more likely to attrit from the sample), local labour market factors, differences in the distribution of calendar months of eligibility and differences in the way the underlying survey instruments measure hours worked and income from overtime, tips, bonuses and commissions account for the differences in mean earnings levels, with the relative importance of these factors varying by demographic group.

earnings due to earnings growth among controls, produce the failure of conventional difference-in-differences estimators. Using the notation already defined, the population version of the conventional difference-in-differences estimator is defined as:

$$[E(Y_{1a}|D = 1, \ R = 1) - E(Y_{0b}|D = 1, \ R = 0)]$$
$$-[E(Y_{0a}|D = 0) - E(Y_{0b}|D = 0)]. \quad (4)$$

The estimator is implemented by replacing population expected values with their sample analogs.[15]

Table 1 presents conventional difference-in-differences estimates of the impact of training on earnings constructed using the ENP (columns 5 and 9) and SIPP eligible (columns 6 and 10) comparison samples. These estimates reveal a general pattern of upward bias relative to the experimental impact estimates. Furthermore, the differences in the earnings patterns across groups – in particular the pre-programme dip and post-random-assignment earnings growth experienced by the controls – lead to a high degree of sensitivity to the choice of 'before' and 'after' time periods used to generate estimates. For example, for adult males, the estimates using the twelve months before and after month 't' are dominated by the pre-programme dip and so are positive. In contrast, the estimates using months 16 to 18 before and after month 't' are dominated by the post-random-assignment earnings growth of the controls, and so are negative.

Heckman, Ichimura, Smith and Todd (1998), Heckman and Todd (1996) and Heckman and Roselius (1994a,b) show that the failure of the conventional difference-in-differences estimator for these comparison groups persists when the estimates are adjusted for differences in observable characteristics.

3. The Determinants of Participation in JTPA

Heckman (1978) developed a model of programme participation that is applied by Ashenfelter and Card (1985). The model is summarised in Heckman *et al.* (1999). It focuses on earnings changes as determinants of participation. This emphasis was a natural consequence of Ashenfelter's discovery and reflects the limited data available to early analysts. This line of thought produced a set of longitudinal estimators that use earnings histories to eliminate differences between participants and non-participants. These estimators were extensively developed in Heckman (1978) and Heckman and Robb (1985). We have just shown that simple versions of these estimators are not effective. The evidence presented in Heckman *et al.* (1999) indicates that more sophisticated versions do not perform any better.

---

[15] This estimator is widely used and a number of economists in the past decade have claimed credit for inventing it. Heckman and Robb (1985, 1986) discuss it among the many estimators they examine. Ashenfelter (1978) uses it and Campbell and Stanley (1966) discuss and apply it. See their Section 14 on multiple time series.

A central principle of the evaluation literature introduced in Heckman and Robb (1985) is that knowledge of the determinants of programme participation should guide the appropriate choice of a non-experimental estimator. The early literature assumed that earnings dynamics drove the participation process and used longitudinal estimators tailored to that assumption. A major finding reported in this paper is that it is unemployment dynamics that drive programme participation and not earnings dynamics. Once this is recognised, progress can be made toward solving the problem of devising a good non-experimental estimator for evaluating job training and adult education programmes.

3.1. *The Important Role of Labour Force Status Dynamics*

We now show that unemployment histories do a better job of predicting participation among eligibles than alternative measures based on earnings or employment, particularly for groups other than adult men. This evidence helps to account for the disappointing performance of econometric evaluation models that assume that programme participation depend solely on earnings or employment histories.

The top panel of Table 2 presents participation rates calculated using the ENP and control data. Labour force status – whether a person is employed, unemployed or out of the labour force – plays a key role in determining the probability of participation in the JTPA programme for all four demographic groups. In every case, those unemployed in the month of measured eligibility have by far the highest probability of application to, and acceptance into, the JTPA programme.[16] This over-representation of the unemployed among participants implicitly suggests that participants place a fairly low value on the services provided by JTPA, as they are willing to participate, in general, only when the opportunity costs are low, because they are not working, and the benefits are high, because they are looking for work.

Going back over spells, we find that both the labour force status in the month of measured eligibility or random assignment and the labour force status in the preceding spell affect the probability of participation in JTPA. The two most recent labour force statuses during the period including month '*t*' and the six preceding months define a set of nine labour force status patterns. For example, the pattern labelled 'Emp→Unm' refers to persons who were unemployed in month '*t*' but whose most recent labour force status during the preceding six months was employment. Repeated patterns such as 'OLF→OLF' indicate persons with the same labour force status in month '*t*' and in all six preceding months.

The bottom panel of Table 2 displays participation rates conditional on

---

[16] Sandell and Rupp (1988) find that the unemployed have a higher probability of JTPA participation than the employed or those out of the labour force in their comparison of national samples of JTPA participants (drawn from administrative data) and programme eligibles (constructed using the CPS).

Table 2

Rates of Participation in JTPA Conditional on Eligibility by Labour Force Status and Labour Force Status Transition

NJS ENP and Control Group samples

	Adult males	Adult females	Male youth	Female youth
	Labour force status at 't'			
Employed	0.0137	0.0197	0.0221	0.0204
	(0.0007)	(0.0010)	(0.0019)	(0.0021)
Unemployed	0.1171	0.1017	0.0484	0.0868
	(0.0106)	(0.0056)	(0.0068)	(0.0109)
OLF	0.0392	0.0197	0.0300	0.0201
	(0.0041)	(0.0010)	(0.0053)	(0.0017)
	Labour Force Status Transitions			
Emp→Emp	0.0084	0.0140	0.0166	0.0115
	(0.0007)	(0.0011)	(0.0019)	(0.0017)
Unm→Emp	0.0496	0.0483	0.0615	0.0444
	(0.0080)	(0.0074)	(0.0163)	(0.0131)
OLF→Emp	0.0551	0.0269	0.0228	0.0316
	(0.0122)	(0.0048)	(0.0053)	(0.0082)
Emp→Unm	0.1433	0.1330	0.0631	0.1446
	(0.0165)	(0.0120)	(0.0128)	(0.0447)
Unm→Unm	0.0967	0.0948	0.0333	0.0631
	(0.0142)	(0.0100)	(0.0097)	(0.0159)
OLF→Unm	0.1182	0.0693	0.0400	0.0725
	(0.0377)	(0.0089)	(0.0161)	(0.0206)
Emp→OLF	0.1032	0.0355	0.0713	0.0332
	(0.0268)	(0.0049)	(0.0385)	(0.0071)
Unm→OLF	0.1363	0.0500	0.0289	0.0240
	(0.0171)	(0.0107)	(0.0181)	(0.0106)
OLF→OLF	0.0275	0.0166	0.0146	0.0155
	(0.0040)	(0.0011)	(0.0051)	(0.0020)

Notes: The entries in the table are the conditional proportions participating calculated using the controls and ENPs under the assumption that the population participation rate is 0.03.

Labour force status transitions are defined by looking backward in time starting in month 't' and ending in month '$t - 6$'. The second status in each pattern is the status in month t. The first status is the most recent prior status within the indicated time period. Thus, 'Emp→Unm' indicates persons unemployed at 't' but whose most recent preceding labour force status within the prior six months was employed. Repeated patterns such as 'Emp→Emp' indicate persons with the same labour force status from '$t - 6$' to 't'.

these labour force status transitions. Several interesting patterns emerge. First, substantial variation in participation rates exists among persons who do not work in any of the seven months up to and including month 't'. For all four demographic groups, the participation rate of persons persistently out of the labour force during this period lies well below that for persons unemployed for all seven months, and for persons who transit into or out of the labour force.

Second, for groups other than male youth, job leavers have a higher probability of programme participation if they remain in the labour force after leaving their jobs than if they do not. Third, for adult females and male youth, programme participation rates are higher among job gainers who found a job while unemployed than among those who found a job while out of the labour force. Finally, for adult males the participation rate of persons persistently out of the labour force substantially exceeds that of continuously employed persons. For the other three demographic groups, these two participation rates are roughly equal.

The importance of unemployment, and transitions into unemployment, as predictors of participation in JTPA is shown graphically in Figs 2a to 2d, which show the fraction of the ENPs and controls in each of the three labour force statuses – employed, unemployed and out of the labour force – in the months surrounding random assignment (or RA, for the controls) and measured eligibility (or EL, for the ENPs). For each of the four demographic groups, the fraction unemployed in the control group increases during the period leading up to month 't', as individuals transit into this status, with the result that the unemployed are over-represented among participants in each case.

3.2. *Alternative Labour Market Variables*

The National JTPA Study data contain a far richer set of variables than those available to previous analysts. Table 3 contrasts the data available from the NJS with that available in Ashenfelter (1978), Ashenfelter and Card (1985), LaLonde (1986), Bryant and Rupp (1987) and Dickinson *et al.* (1987). In this section we examine a variety of labour market variables to see which ones perform well using a common measure of predictive performance. We seek to determine the key behavioural determinants of participation, to form the cornerstone of an econometric model that successfully corrects for selection bias.

Table 5 summarises our evidence on the performance of various predictors of programme participation. Definitions of the variables used in the estimation appear in Table 4. We consider fifteen specifications broken down into four groups. The first group contains two specifications limited to background variables; these specifications serve as a benchmark. The remaining groups are for specifications based on employment, earnings and labour force status variables, respectively.

Each row of Table 5 presents the fraction of the control and ENP observations predicted correctly using a given set of regressors. Estimated standard errors for the prediction rate appear in parentheses. For each specification, separate equations are estimated and reported for each of the four demographic groups.[17] The reported fraction of correct predictions consists of the

[17] In an appendix available on request, we show that (1) the relative performance of the alternative specifications is robust to removal of the background variables; (2) the 0.03 cutoff value typically lies close to that which maximises the equal-weights prediction rate; and (3) changing the cutoff value from 0.03 to either 0.01 or 0.05 does not affect the relative performance of the various labour market variables at predicting programme participation.

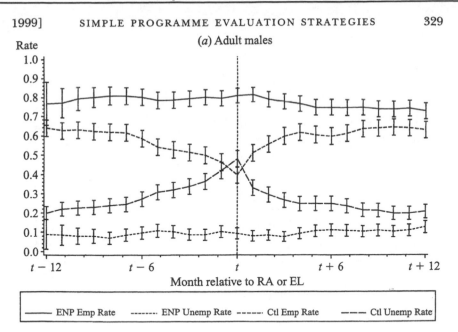

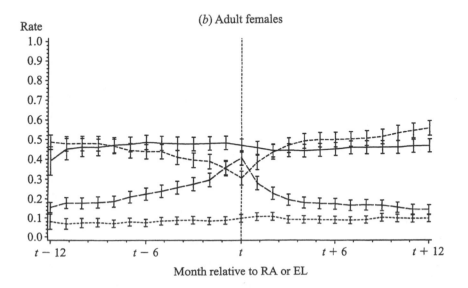

Fig. 2. *Monthly Employment and Unemployment Rates JTPA Controls and ENPs*

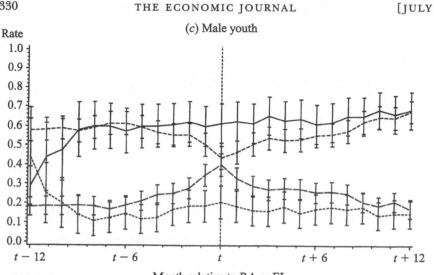

(c) Male youth

Rate

Month relative to RA or EL

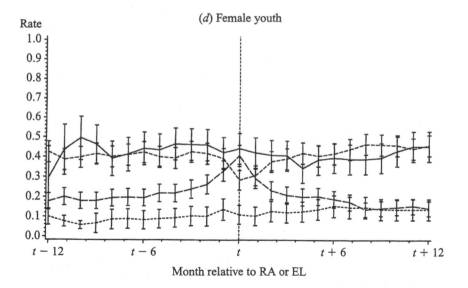

(d) Female youth

Rate

Month relative to RA or EL

Fig. 2. *(Continued)*

Notes:
Controls are randomised-out participants from the National JPTA Study. Observations based on quasi-rectangular sample.
ENPs are JPTA-eligible non-participants at the same sites as the controls from the National JPTA Study. Observations based on quasi-rectangular sample.
Standard error bars +/− 2 standard errors of the means.

Table 3

Data Available in Studies of Employment and Training Programmes

	Ashenfelter (1978)	Ashenfelter and Card (1985)	LaLonde (1986)	Bryant and Rupp (1987)	Dickinson *et al.* (1987)	NJS
Demographic variables						
Age	Yes	Yes	Yes	Yes	Yes	Yes
Sex	Yes	Yes	Yes	Yes	Yes	Yes
Race or ethnicity	Yes	Yes	Yes	Yes	Yes	Yes
Years of schooling	No	Yes	Yes	Yes	Yes	Yes
Marital status	No	Yes	Yes	Yes	Yes	Yes
Transfer programme participation variables						
AFDC receipt	No	No	No	No	No	Yes
Food stamp receipt	No	No	No	No	No	Yes
Labour market variables						
Pre-training hours	No	No	2 Years (Annual)	No	No	5 Years (Monthly)
Post-training hours	No	No	2 Years (Annual)	No	No	2 Years (Monthly)
Pre-training earnings and employment	5 Years (Annual)	5 Years (Annual)	2 Years (Annual)	2 Years (Annual)	2 Years (Annual)	5 Years (Monthly)
Post-training earnings and employment	5 Years (Annual)	2 Years (Annual)	2 Years (Annual)	2 Years (Annual)	2 Years (Annual)	2 Years (Monthly)
Pre-training labour force status	No	No	No	No	No	1 Year (Monthly)
Post-training labour force status	No	No	No	No	No	2 Years (Monthly)
Local labour market	No	No	No	No	No	Yes
Other variables						
Family income	No	No	No	No	No	Yes

Notes: NJS refers to studies based on the National JTPA Study data. In addition to this paper, these include Heckman, Ichimura, Smith and Todd (1998), Heckman and Smith (1997), Heckman and Todd (1996) and Heckman and Roselius (1994 *a,b*), among others.

Ashenfelter (1978), Ashenfelter and Card (1985), Bryant and Rupp (1987) and Dickinson *et al.* (1987) had Social Security earnings data matched to samples of programme participants and to comparison groups constructed from the Current Population Survey. Lalonde had self-reported data on Supported Work experimental treatment and control group members, along with self-reported data on PSID sample members and Social Security earnings data on CPS comparison group members. The NJS studies have available constructed monthly earnings measures based on self-reported information about job spells for experimental control group members and for a comparison group of eligible non-participants at four of the 16 training centres in the study.

simple average of the control and ENP correct prediction rates. This weighting is consistent with a symmetric loss function for misclassifications in the two groups.[18] A person is predicted to be a control if his or her estimated

---

[18] Note that if the population-weighted prediction rate is used, then a correct prediction rate of 0.97 can be achieved by predicting everyone to be an ENP.

Table 4
Definitions of Labour Market Measures

Background Specifications

1. The background (BKGD) specification includes race and ethnicity indicators, age category indicators, years of completed schooling category indicators, marital status indicators, and an indicator for the presence of a child less than six years of age. These variables are included in most of the other specifications as well.

2. The family income specification adds a categorical measure of family income based on the earnings in the 12 months prior to the baseline interview of all family members living in the same household as the sample member at the time of the interview.

Employment Measures

1. 'Employment at 't'' is an indicator for whether or not the person was employed in the month of random assignment or eligibility determination.

2. 'Employment transitions' are the four patterns formed by the employment status at 't' and the most recent previous employment status in months '$t-1$' to '$t-6$'. The patterns are continuously employed, job loser, job gainer and continuously not employed.

3. 'ETC' indicates categories of the number of transitions from employment to non-employment or vice versa in the 24 months prior to the baseline interview.

4. '18 month job spells' indicates categories of the total number of job spells in the 18 months prior to random assignment or eligibility determination.

5. '48 month job spells' indicates categories of the total number of job spells in the 48 months prior to random assignment or eligibility determination.

Earnings Measures

1. 'Earnings in '$t-1$' to '$t-6$'' are own total earnings in each of the six months prior to random assignment or eligibility determination.

2. 'Earnings in '$Q-1$' to '$Q-4$'' are own total earnings in each of the four quarters prior to random assignment or eligibility determination.

Labour Force Status Measures

1. 'LFS at 't'' is the labour force status (employed, unemployed, or out of the labour force) in the month of random assignment or eligibility determination.

2. 'Time in labour force status' is the number of months in the labour force status at random assignment or eligibility determination. There are separate variables for each status: employed, unemployed, and out of the labour force. For each status, there is a continuous variable for 0–6 months and an indicator variable for greater than six months in the status.

3. '2 Quarter LFS' consists of patterns formed by constructing quarterly labour force measures for the two quarters prior to random assignment or eligibility determination. That is, the statuses are first aggregated within quarters, with employment having precedence over unemployment and unemployment over OLF, and then combined into one of nine possible sequences.

4. '6 Month LFS2' is the two most recent labour force statuses in the seven months up to and including the month of random assignment or eligibility determination as defined in the text.

probability of participation exceeds 0.03, the assumed fraction of participants in the population.[19]

The first group presented in Table 5 includes specifications based solely on demographic background variables as defined in Table 4. The two specifications differ only in that the second includes a categorical family income

---

[19] Hunt *et al.* (1984) estimate that 1.85% of persons eligible at some time during calendar year 1983 participated in JTPA. Sandell and Rupp (1988), using administrative data on JTPA participants from the Job Training Quarterly Survey for Programme Years 1984 and 1985, along with data on persons eligible for JTPA constructed using the March 1986 CPS, estimate an annual participation rate of 2.3% among persons eligible at some time during a given year. This estimate may be broken down into separate estimates of 1.6% for adults age 22 to 64 amd 5.1% for youth age 16 to 21.

1999]   SIMPLE PROGRAMME EVALUATION STRATEGIES   333

Table 5
JTPA Participation Probability Equations: Prediction Cutoff Value = 0.03

Mean proportion correctly predicted. Estimated standard errors in parentheses. NJS ENP and control samples.

Specification	Adult males	Adult females	Male youth	Female youth
Background				
Background (BKGD)	0.7010	0.6363	0.5968	0.6172
	(0.0116)	(0.0100)	(0.0226)	(0.0185)
BKGD + Family income	0.7453	0.6317	0.6372	0.6240
	(0.0111)	(0.0101)	(0.0219)	(0.0185)
Employment specifications				
Employment at 't' (No BKGD)	0.7457	0.5842	0.5868	0.5638
	(0.0110)	(0.0099)	(0.0226)	(0.0179)
BKGD + Employment at 't'	0.7664	0.6543	0.6295	0.6361
	(0.0108)	(0.0100)	(0.0223)	(0.0184)
BKDG + Employment transition	0.8043	0.6650	0.6387	0.6756
	(0.0101)	(0.0100)	(0.0220)	(0.0179)
BKGD + ETC	0.7700	0.6761	0.6779	0.6599
	(0.0107)	(0.0098)	(0.0216)	(0.0181)
BKGD + 18 month job spells	0.7129	0.6390	0.6384	0.6331
	(0.0115)	(0.0100)	(0.0217)	(0.0184)
BKGD + 48 month job spells	0.7086	0.6632	0.6110	0.6427
	(0.0116)	(0.0100)	(0.0224)	(0.0183)
Earnings specifications				
BKGD + Earnings in '$t-1$' to '$t-6$'	0.7901	0.6589	0.6308	0.6124
	(0.0103)	(0.0099)	(0.0222)	(0.0186)
BKGD + Earnings in '$Q-1$' to '$Q-4$'	0.7933	0.6464	0.6152	0.5986
	(0.0102)	(0.0100)	(0.0224)	(0.0187)
Labour force status specifications				
LFS at 't' (No BKGD)	0.7542	0.6831	0.6008	0.6632
	(0.0109)	(0.0093)	(0.0225)	(0.0159)
BKGD + LFS at 't'	0.7714	0.6960	0.6393	0.6365
	(0.0107)	(0.0098)	(0.0221)	(0.0178)
BKGD + Time in labour force status	0.8016	0.7049	0.6417	0.6954
	(0.0101)	(0.0097)	(0.0220)	(0.0174)
BKGD + 2 quarter LFS	0.7517	0.6611	0.6241	0.6536
	(0.0110)	(0.0100)	(0.0223)	(0.0182)
BKGD + 6 month LFS2	0.8104	0.7003	0.6724	0.6878
	(0.0100)	(0.0098)	(0.0213)	(0.0176)

BKGD includes race, age, years of schooling, marital status, and presence of a child less than six years of age.

variable. The first specification predicts remarkably well, especially for adult males. Adding family income improves the prediction rate for males but not for females.

The specifications in the second group include employment-related variables. The first specification in this group includes only an indicator variable for whether or not the person is employed in month 't'; this specification has a surprisingly high prediction rate. The second specification adds the background variables, which increases the prediction rate for all four groups relative to either the background variables alone or the employment indicator alone. The greater predictive power of the employment variables for adult males compared to the other three groups is a major finding, and motivates our search for other determinants of participation.

The third specification includes an employment transition variable that is similar to the labour force status transitions but combines persons who are unemployed and out of the labour force. For adult males, but not the other three groups, employment transitions do almost as well as labour force status transitions at predicting programme participation. The fourth specification in this group, denoted 'ETC' in Table 5, includes a categorical variable based on the number of transitions from employment to non-employment (or vice-versa) in the twenty-four months prior to month 't'. This specification has the highest prediction rate overall for male youth. The last two specifications include categorical variables based on the number of job spells during the 18 or 48 months prior to month 't'; these specifications perform relatively poorly.

The third group includes specifications based on earnings-related variables. The two specifications include monthly earnings in each of the six months prior to month 't' and quarterly earnings in each of the four quarters prior to month 't'. The earnings history variables predict programme participation moderately well for adult males, but much less well for the other three groups. We examine a number of other earnings-based variables, including more complicated variables based on earnings patterns in the months prior to month 't', and none perform particularly well. For this reason, we do not discuss them here. Earnings patterns alone are relatively poor predictors of programme participation, especially for groups other than adult males. This is not surprising for youth or re-entrant women who have no earnings. It is an important finding which helps account for the disappointing results reported in Ashenfelter and Card (1985), who implement a longitudinal non-experimental evaluation strategy using earnings histories.

Specifications including detailed labour force status variables comprise the final group in Table 5. The first two specifications include indicators for labour force status in month 't', with and without the background variables. Both predict far better than the corresponding specifications involving employment at 't'. Distinguishing between non-employed persons who are and are not looking for work (*i.e.*, between the unemployed and those out of the labour force) is crucial in successfully predicting programme participation. The other three specifications incorporate variables measuring the dynamics of labour force status. For adult males, the specification based on the two most recent labour force statuses has the highest overall prediction rate. For women, it is a close second to the specification based on the amount of time in the most recent labour force status. For male youth, it is a close second to the specification based on the employment transition variable.

In comparing across specifications in Table 5, the prediction rates of certain pairs of specifications often cannot be statistically distinguished. However, the broad pattern of the table is clear. With the exception of the employment transition variable for male youth, specifications based on recent labour force dynamics that explicitly separate the unemployed from those out of the labour force do better at predicting programme participation than those based on employment or earnings.

3.3. *Multivariate Analysis*

This section presents a multivariate analysis of the determinants of participation in the JTPA programme conditional on eligibility using the data on experimental controls and ENPs from the National JTPA Study.[20] Our multivariate analysis reveals the central role of recent labour force status dynamics in determining programme participation, as well as the contributing role of other factors such as age, schooling, marital status and family income. We focus on the labour force status transition variables that we find do a better job of predicting participation in JTPA than other measures based on earnings or employment histories.

Table 6 reports estimates of logit models of participation in JTPA. The table includes coefficient estimates, estimated standard errors and mean numerical derivatives (or finite differences in the case of indicator variables). Coefficient estimates and estimated standard errors account for the choice-based nature of the sample.[21]

The results for adult males and adult females show that the coefficients for all eight of the labour force status pattern indicators are statistically significantly different from zero. For both groups, the smallest coefficient is on the indicator variable for those persistently out of the labour force; their participation probabilities differ the least from those of the persistently employed, who constitute the omitted group. The relative effects of the labour force status patterns parallel the ordering of univariate participation rates in Table 2.

Older adults have a lower conditional probability of participation which is consistent with the view that returns to training decline with age. The effect of completed schooling on the probability of participation shows a hill-shaped pattern, with adults with fewer than 10 or more than 15 years of schooling having differentially low estimated participation probabilities. Heckman and Smith (1997) show that this pattern results from low rates of programme awareness among those with little schooling, and low rates of participation conditional on awareness among the highly educated.

Currently married adults of both sexes are relatively less likely to participate than those who have never married, while those whose marriage ended more than two years ago are relatively more likely to participate. The effect is especially strong for adult women for whom training programmes often provide a bridge back into the labour force following divorce. Receipt of food stamps has a positive effect on the participation probability for both groups, while participation in welfare (AFDC receipt) has a negative effect. Because nearly all AFDC recipients also receive food stamps, the coefficients on the

---

[20] Heckman and Smith (1997) present a more detailed analysis of the JTPA participation process in which the participation process is decomposed into a series of stages such as eligibility, awareness, application and acceptance into the programme.

[21] We use standard methods as exposited in Amemiya (1985).

Table 6
JTPA Participation Probability Estimates

Weighted logit equation – dependent variable: control status. NJS ENP and control samples

Variable	Coefficient	Standard error	Numerical derivative	Coefficient	Standard error	Numerical derivative
	Adult males			Adult females		
Black	0.149	0.273	0.004	0.234	0.174	0.006
Hispanic	-0.256	0.308	-0.006	0.345	0.192	0.009
Other race-ethnic	0.394	0.409	0.011	0.262	0.337	0.007
Age 30–39	-0.458	0.228	-0.012	-0.294	0.139	-0.008
Age 40–49	-0.982	0.297	-0.022	-0.229	0.180	-0.006
Age 50–54	-0.400	0.394	-0.011	-0.349	0.281	-0.009
Highest grade < 10	-0.541	0.272	-0.012	-0.498	0.154	-0.012
Highest grade 10–11	0.354	0.266	0.010	-0.063	0.162	-0.002
Highest grade 13–15	0.711	0.311	0.023	0.168	0.201	0.005
Highest grade > 15	-1.373	0.416	-0.022	-0.414	0.389	-0.011
Currently married	-0.522	0.263	-0.012	-0.904	0.184	-0.019
Married 1–24 months ago	-0.029	0.637	-0.001	0.564	0.225	0.021
Married > 24 months ago	1.240	0.487	0.052	1.263	0.199	0.064
Child age < 6 years	-0.217	0.311	-0.005	-0.245	0.133	-0.006
Received AFDC at ' *t* '	-1.196	0.511	-0.020	-0.758	0.205	-0.019
Received food stamps at ' *t* '	0.560	0.244	0.015	0.452	0.174	0.013
Unemployed→Employed	1.927	0.322	0.043	1.556	0.276	0.034
OLF→Employed	2.083	0.418	0.051	0.988	0.320	0.016
Employed→Unemployed	3.239	0.330	0.136	2.825	0.244	0.121
Unemployed→Unemployed	2.766	0.412	0.094	2.621	0.263	0.101
OLF→Unemployed	3.787	0.490	0.199	2.146	0.297	0.065
Employed→OLF	2.684	0.626	0.087	1.214	0.271	0.022
Unemployed→OLF	3.633	0.774	0.179	1.991	0.339	0.055
OLF→OLF	1.186	0.411	0.016	0.770	0.222	0.011
Family Income $3K–9K	-0.347	0.364	-0.011	0.543	0.207	0.016
Family Income $9K–15K	-0.025	0.400	-0.001	0.162	0.284	0.004
Family Income >$15K	-1.599	0.474	-0.034	0.029	0.269	0.001
	Male youth			Female youth		
Black	0.410	0.384	0.014	0.742	0.303	0.021
Hispanic	-0.494	0.492	-0.011	0.457	0.351	0.011
Other race-ethnic	-1.846	0.899	-0.028	-1.058	0.650	-0.014
Age 19–21	0.153	0.347	0.004	-0.535	0.265	-0.016
Highest grade < 10	0.589	0.441	0.015	-0.394	0.324	-0.011
Highest grade 10–11	0.673	0.385	0.018	-0.235	0.351	-0.007
Highest grade > 12	-0.164	0.598	-0.003	0.084	0.365	0.003
Currently married	0.298	0.461	0.009	-0.563	0.346	-0.013
Div-Wid-Sep	-0.439	0.817	-0.010	0.241	0.403	0.008
Child age < 6 years	-1.059	0.498	-0.021	-0.241	0.260	-0.007
Received AFDC at ' *t* '	-0.721	0.730	-0.015	-0.988	0.363	-0.025
Received food stamps at ' *t* '	-0.046	0.441	-0.001	1.363	0.337	0.052
Unemployed→Employed	2.125	0.482	0.089	1.599	0.466	0.030
OFC→Employed	-0.166	0.511	-0.002	1.394	0.449	0.023
Employed→Unemployed	1.593	0.442	0.051	3.218	0.472	0.149
Unemployed→Unemployed	1.162	0.579	0.030	2.379	0.473	0.070
OLF→Unemployed	1.000	0.597	0.024	3.018	0.509	0.126
Employed→OLF	2.016	0.633	0.080	1.554	0.421	0.028
Unemployed→OLF	0.993	0.774	0.023	1.106	0.725	0.016
OLF→OLF	0.191	0.567	0.003	0.709	0.414	0.008
Family Income $3K–9K	1.450	0.574	0.058	-0.466	0.452	-0.010
Family Income $9K–15K	0.110	0.602	0.002	0.031	0.528	0.001
Family Income >$15K	0.048	0.642	0.001	1.423	0.441	0.068

Notes: Number of observations: 1,552 adult males, 2,438 adult females, 530 male youth and 701 female youth.

For adults, the logit model also includes training centre indicators and a constant.

For adults, the omitted race group is whites, the omitted age group is age 22–29, the omitted highest grade completed category is exactly 12 years, the omitted marital status category is never married, the omitted labour force status transition pattern is 'Employed→Employed' and the omitted family income category is less than $3,000.

For youth, the omitted age group is 16–18. Other omitted categories the same as for adults.

Labour force status transition patterns are defined by looking backward in time starting in month 't' and ending in month '$t - 6$'. The second status in each pattern is the status in month 't'. The first status is the most recent prior status within the indicated time period. Thus 'Employed→ Unemployed' indicates a person unemployed at 't' but whose most recent labour force status within the prior six months was employed.

AFDC receipt indicators should be interpreted as the effect of receiving both types of assistance rather than just food stamps. Finally, adult male eligibles with family incomes over $15,000 in the past year are relatively less likely to participate while adult females with family incomes between $3,000 and $9,000 have the highest probability of participation.

The same basic patterns are found for male and female youth. In particular, the labour force status pattern variables play a key role in determining participation for both groups.[22]

The fundamental importance of labour force status dynamics in determining participation is clearly evident even in a more general statistical model. For adult women, changes in the life cycle dynamics of the family, especially divorce, childbearing, and the entry of children into school are also important. A number of other factors including age, schooling, marital status and family income also help to determine participation for all demographic groups.

4. Selection Bias and the Determinants of Participation in JTPA

In this section we show how the knowledge gained from our analysis of the determinants of participation in JTPA can be used to improve the performance of non-experimental evaluation methods in estimating the impact of JTPA on earnings. We focus here on two strategies that compare participants and non-participants based on their observed characteristics. The counterfactual for a given participant is estimated by the outcomes experienced by non-participants with the same or 'similar' observable characteristics.

Both methods are based on 'selection on observables' (see, *e.g.*, Heckman and Robb, 1985) and rest on assumptions regarding the relationship between

---

[22] Absent from the specifications reported here are measures of the state of the local economy at each of the four training centres. We estimated models including both county-level monthly unemployment rates averaged over the counties served by each centre, and interactions between these unemployment rates and the centre indicators. These variables never attained statistical significance and never had a noticeable impact on the proportion of correct predictions. One reason for this is that the number of ENPs whose month of measured eligibility occurs in a given calendar month depends not only on the size of the eligible population in that month, but also on the administrative schedule of the firm conducting the surveys. A second reason is that the flow into the programme, as measured by the number of persons randomly assigned in each calendar month, depends on other factors beyond the local economy, including the academic schedule of the community colleges that provide much of the JTPA training at these centres.

earnings and programme participation conditional on observed character-istics. They allow us to exploit in a structured way what we have learned about the determinants of participation in the preceding sections. The cross-section matching estimator assumes that conditional on a vector of observed charac-teristics $\mathbf{X}$, D is independent of the non-participation outcome Y_{0a}. In formal terms, it is assumed that

$$(Y_{0a} \perp\!\!\!\perp D)|\mathbf{X},$$

where $\perp\!\!\!\perp$ denotes independence. As noted by Heckman and Robb (1986), and Heckman, Ichimura, Smith and Todd (1998), in order to use matching to estimate the parameter 'treatment on the treated' it is only necessary to assume conditional mean independence so that conditional on $\mathbf{X}$,

$$\mathrm{E}(Y_{0a}|\mathbf{X}, D = 1) = \mathrm{E}(Y_{0a}|\mathbf{X}, D = 0).$$

Selective differences in non-participation outcomes are assumed to be elimi-nated by conditioning on $\mathbf{X}$. The nonparametric conditional difference-in-differences estimator introduced in Heckman, Ichimura and Todd (1997, 1998) and Heckman, Ichimura, Smith and Todd (1998) assumes that, condi-tional on $\mathbf{X}$, selection bias in Y_0 is the same in particular periods before and after the participation decision, so that, conditional on $\mathbf{X}$, it can be differenced out. In formal terms, the method assumes that in the population,

$$\mathrm{E}(Y_{0a}|\mathbf{X}, D = 1) - \mathrm{E}(Y_{0a}|\mathbf{X}, D = 0)] -$$
$$[\mathrm{E}(Y_{0b}|\mathbf{X}, D = 1) - \mathrm{E}(Y_{0b}|\mathbf{X}, D = 0)] = 0,$$

so that (4), augmented by conditioning on $\mathbf{X}$ identifies $\mathrm{E}(Y_{1a} - Y_{0a}|\mathbf{X}, D = 1)$, the effect of treatment on the treated, where the b and a subscripts again denote periods before and after month 't'. As noted in Heckman and Robb (1985, 1986), this estimator assumes that common time (or age) effects operate on treatment and comparison group members so they can be differenced out.

Whereas matching is assumed to eliminate the bias in the post-programme period, the conditional difference-in-differences estimator assumes the same cross-section bias in periods a and b so that differencing the outcomes between a and b eliminates the common bias component. Note that the conventional difference-in-differences estimator considered earlier is a crude version of this estimator in which the only conditioning variable is eligibility for JTPA.

Rosenbaum and Rubin (1983) demonstrate that under general conditions, conditioning on $\mathbf{X}$ is equivalent to conditioning on the probability of participa-tion $\Pr(D = 1|\mathbf{X}) = P(\mathbf{X})$. In this case, $P(\mathbf{X})$ replaces $\mathbf{X}$ in the assumptions justifying the matching estimator. Heckman, Ichimura and Todd (1997, 1998) develop a nonparametric difference-in-differences estimator that also condi-tions on $P(\mathbf{X})$. They develop the statistical properties of the matching and nonparametric difference-in-differences estimator when $P(\mathbf{X})$ is estimated.[23] We use their asymptotic theory to produce the estimates and standard errors reported below.

---

[23] Rosebaum and Rubin (1983) assume that $P(\mathbf{X})$ is known rather than estimated.

A general definition of the matching estimator for the impact of treatment on the treated presented in Heckman *et al.* (1999) is:

$$\widehat{M_a}(S) = \sum_{i \in I_1} [Y_{1ai} - \sum_{j \in I_0} W_{N_0, N_1}(i, j) Y_{0aj}], \text{ for } P(\mathbf{X}) \in S,$$

where Y_{1ai} denotes earnings with training in the post-programme period for participant i, Y_{0aj} denotes earnings without training in the post-programme period for non-participant j, N_1 is the number of programme participants, N_0 is the number of persons in the comparison group, and I_1 and I_0 are sets of indices for participants and comparison group members, respectively. $W_{N_0, N_1}(i, j)$ is the weight attached to comparison group member j in constructing the counterfactual outcome for participant i. These weights sum to one for each participant so that $\sum_{j \in I_0} W_{N_0, N_1}(i, j) = 1$ for all i. The set S is the 'common support' of $P(\mathbf{X})$ – that is, the subset of $(0, 1)$ for which values of $P(\mathbf{X})$ are present in both the participant and comparison group samples.[24] Matches for each participant are constructed by taking weighted averages over comparison group members.

Matching estimators differ in the weights they attach to members of the comparison group (Heckman, Ichimura and Todd, 1997). For example, 'nearest-neighbour' matching sets all the weights equal to zero except for that on the comparison group observation with the estimated probability of participation closest to that of the participant being matched, whose weight is set to one.

In contrast, the commonly-used kernel matching approach uses the weights:

$$W_{N_0, N_1}(i, j) = \frac{G_{ij}}{\sum_{k \in I_0} G_{ik}},$$

where $G_{ik} = G[(X_i - X_k)/a_{N_0}]$ is a kernel function and a_{N_0} is a bandwidth parameter.[25] Kernel matching is a local averaging method that reuses and reweights all of the comparison group observations in constructing the estimated counterfactual outcome for each treatment sample member. Relative to nearest-neighbour matching, kernel matching reduces the variance of the matching estimate by making use of information from additional non-participant observations. At the same time, it increases the bias in small samples because the additional observations are more distant, in terms of their probabilities of participation, from the observation being matched.

The matching estimates we report in Table 7 are based on the local linear matching method developed in Heckman, Ichimura and Todd (1997, 1998) and Heckman, Ichimura, Smith and Todd (1998). Local linear matching

[24] The region of common support consists of those values of $P(\mathbf{X})$ such that the smoothed densities of $P(\mathbf{X})$ in both the $(D = 1)$ and $(D = 0)$ samples are above a trimming level $\hat{q}$. Formally, $S = \{P(\mathbf{X}): \hat{f}[P(\mathbf{X})|D = 1] > \hat{q}$ and $\hat{f}[P(\mathbf{X})|D = 0] > \hat{q}\}$, where $\hat{f}$ is a smoothed density of $P(\mathbf{X})$ obtained using a standard kernel density estimator. Appendix C of Heckman, Ichimura and Todd (1997) discusses the choice of $\hat{q}$ and reports that the bias estimates are sensitive to the value of $\hat{q}$ only for small samples, such as that for male youth.

[25] a_{N_0} satisfies $\lim_{N_0 \to \infty} a_{N_0} \to 0$. Precise conditions on the rate of convergence needed for consistency and asymptotic normality of the matching estimators used here are presented in Heckman, Ichimura and Todd (1997).

Table 7

Estimated Selection Bias in Nonexperimental Estimates of the Impact of JTPA Training on Earnings in the 18 Months after Random Assignment Using Alternative Estimators

Estimated standard errors in parentheses. NJS ENP and control samples.

	Unadjusted mean difference	Coarse I probabilities	Coarse II probabilities	Coarse III probabilities	'Best predictor' probabilities
	Adult males				
Local linear matching	−6,066	−5,238	−2,988	−450	684
	(846)	(972)	(1,008)	(1,494)	(1,152)
Conditional difference-in-differences	−6,066	576	2,592	774	936
	(846)	(1,404)	(1,098)	(1,710)	(1,332)
	Adult females				
Local linear matching	594	198	396	576	720
	(468)	(558)	(522)	(630)	(684)
Conditional difference-in-differences	594	306	36	414	486
	(468)	(558)	(540)	(702)	(702)
	Male youth				
Local linear matching	360	36	144	306	126
	(1,026)	(936)	(936)	(1,260)	(954)
Conditional difference-in-differences	360	666	486	612	396
	(1,026)	(1,008)	(972)	(1,062)	(864)
	Female youth				
Local linear matching	864	648	738	1,116	144
	(648)	(648)	(630)	(756)	(756)
Conditional difference-in-differences	864	936	828	504	306
	(648)	(630)	(630)	(702)	(702)

Source: Heckman, Ichimura and Todd (1997), Tables 6(*a*) and 6(*b*).
The best predictor probabilities for all four demographic groups contain indicator variables for training centre, age, race and ethnicity, years of schooling, marital status, children less than six and labour force status transitions. The model for adult males also includes an indicator for past vocational training, the number of household members, earnings in the month of random assignment or measured eligibility (RA or EL) and indicators for the number of jobs held in the 18 months prior to RA and EL. The model for adult females includes an indicator for recent schooling, earnings in the month of RA or EL, and indicators for the number of employment transitions in the 24 months prior to RA or EL. The model for male youth includes average earnings in the six months prior to RA or EL and in the 12 months prior to RA or EL and average positive earnings in the 6 months prior to RA or EL. The model for female youth includes average earnings in the 12 months prior to RA or EL.

differs from kernel matching in the addition of a linear term in the probability of participation when constructing matches. To understand the method, note that one can construct the kernel estimate of the counterfactual outcome for participant i by running a weighted regression using all of the comparison group observations with non-zero weights with Y_{0aj} as the dependent variable. The regression contains only an intercept term and the estimated intercept is the kernel estimate of the counterfactual outcome for participant i. Local linear matching works the same way except that the weighted regression for each participant i includes both an intercept term and a linear term in the probability of participation. This smooths out the estimate of the intercept and has desirable statistical properties if the underlying model is smooth.[26]

We use local linear weights instead of more conventional kernel weights because local linear estimators converge at a faster rate at boundary points and adapt better to different data densities. The boundary behaviour is potentially important in our context because many observations in both groups have values of $P(\mathbf{X})$ close to the boundary value of zero.[27]

The conditional on $P(\mathbf{X})$ difference-in-differences estimator is defined as:

$$\widehat{D_{a,b}}(S) = \sum_{i \in I_1} \left[(Y_{1ai} - Y_{0bi}) - \sum_{j \in I_0} W_{N_0, N_1}(i, j)(Y_{0aj} - Y_{0bj}) \right]$$

$$= \widehat{M_a}(S) - \widehat{M_b}(S),$$

where $\widehat{M_b}(S)$ is constructed using the same weights as $\widehat{M_a}(S)$ but is calculated using pre-programme earnings data as the outcome measure.[28]

There are two ways in which what we learned in Section 3 about the determinants of programme participation can help improve the performance of non-experimental evaluation methods. The first insight is that, for probabilities of participation based on the specification in Table 6, which incorporate the important labour force status transition variables, there are many participant $(D = 1)$ observations for which the ENP comparison group contains no non-participant $(D = 0)$ observations with the same or similar probabilities of participation. Put more simply, P-comparable non-participants are unavailable for many participants.

Heckman, Ichimura and Todd (1997) and Heckman, Ichimura, Smith and Todd (1996, 1998) refer to this as the 'common support' problem, as the empirical supports of the distributions of participation probabilities differ between participants and non-participants. They show that the failure of the common support condition accounts for a substantial fraction of the selection bias in simple cross-section comparisons of the earnings of participants and non-participants. Moreover, they show that imposing the common support condition substantially reduces selection bias in a variety of cross-sectional non-experimental evaluation procedures, including several variants of matching, conditional (on $P(\mathbf{X})$) difference-in-differences and the Heckman (1979) 'two step' procedure.

The second way in which a better understanding of the determinants of participation helps to improve the performance of non-experimental evaluation

---

[26] The exact form of the weight for local linear matching is:

$$W_{N_0, N_1}(i, j) = \frac{G_{ij} \sum_{k \in I_0} G_{ik}[P(X_k) - P(X_i)]^2 - \{G_{ij}[P(X_j) - P(X_i)]\} \left\{ \sum_{k \in I_0} G_{ik}[P(X_k) - P(X_i)] \right\}}{\sum_{j \in I_0} G_{ik} \sum_{k \in I_0} G_{ij}[P(X_k) - P(X_i)]^2 - \left\{ \sum_{k \in I_0} G_{ik}[P(X_k) - P(X_i)] \right\}^2}.$$

[27] However, Heckman, Ichimura and Todd (1997) show that other matching methods yield similar results.

[28] See Heckman, Ichimura and Todd (1997, 1998) or Heckman, Ichimura, Smith and Todd (1998) for more detailed descriptions of both estimators and formal analyses of their statistical properties.

methods is by providing probabilities of participation that are more likely to satisfy the assumptions underlying the matching and conditional difference-in-differences evaluation methods. The importance of understanding the determinants of participation is demonstrated by the results presented in Table 7.

4.1. *Estimates*

Table 7 presents estimates of the extent of selection bias (the difference between the experimental estimate and the estimate that would be yielded by a non-experimental estimation procedure) for the parameter treatment on the treated, $E(Y_{1a} - Y_{0a}|\mathbf{X}, D = 1)$, when matching and conditional difference-in-differences methods are applied to the experimental controls and ENPs from the JTPA data to estimate the impact of JTPA participation on earnings in the 18 months after random assignment.[29],[30] Table 7 contains four panels, one for each demographic group. For each demographic group, there are five columns and two rows. The first column presents the unadjusted mean difference in outcomes between the experimental controls $(D = 1)$ and the ENPs $(D = 0)$. This difference represents the selection bias present in the simple estimator that compares the unadjusted mean earnings of participants and eligible non-participants in the post-programme period.

The remaining four columns present the selection bias present in non-experimental estimates based on probabilities of participation constructed using successively richer sets of conditioning variables, $\mathbf{X}$. The probabilities in the 'Coarse I' column are based only on a small set of demographic variables.[31] The 'Coarse II' column augments the demographic variables with earnings in the year prior to month 't', while the 'Coarse III' column augments the demographic variables with the labour force status transition variables that we find to be crucial in determining participation in JTPA for all four groups. The final column presents estimates based on the 'best predictor' probabilities constructed by Heckman, Ichimura, Smith and Todd (1998).[32]

---

[29] We report the estimated selection bias here, rather than the impact estimates as in Table 1, because we lack the data on Xs required to construct the probabilities of participation for the experimental treatment group. This in turn means that we are unable to impose the common support condition on the treatment group data. The bias is calculated by replacing the earnings values of the experimental treatment group in the post-programme period with the earnings values of the experimental control group in the same period in the formulas for the local linear matching and conditional difference-in-differences estimators.

[30] A similar analysis could be conducted using the SIPP as the source of the comparison group. See Heckman, Ichimura, Smith and Todd (1998) for estimates using this framework for three SIPP comparison groups constructed using different sample inclusion criteria. Heckman and Roselius (1994*a,b*) construct SIPP comparison samples based on matching the local labour market characteristics of the controls.

[31] The exact **X** for each set of participation probabilities are defined in the notes to Table 7.

[32] The **X** used for these best predictor probabilities are rough supersets of those used in Table 6, with some variables (e.g., marital status for adult males) measured slightly differently, a small number of variables omitted (e.g., family income for adult males), and a few others added. These **X** were iteratively selected for each demographic group based on two criteria: improvements in the prediction rate and the statistical significance of the individual variables in the participation logit. See the discussion in Appendix C of Heckman, Ichimura, Smith and Todd (1998) for more details. The slight differences between these estimates and those reported in Table 6 do not affect any of the conclusions of this paper.

The first row in Table 7 for each demographic group presents estimates from local linear matching, which assumes that Y_0 is mean independent of D conditional on $P(\mathbf{X})$, so there is no selection bias in any period. The second row presents estimates from a nonparametric conditional difference-in-differences estimator, which assumes that the selection bias in Y_0, conditional on $P(\mathbf{X})$, is the same in symmetric quarters around month 't', so that it can be differenced out.

Several important patterns emerge from the estimates in Table 7. First, for adult males, either estimation method, even if applied using the 'Coarse I' probabilities based on only a few demographic variables, substantially reduces selection bias relative to the unadjusted difference in means. This indicates that conditioning on eligibility alone is easily improved on by conditioning on basic demographic variables.

Second, the strongest effect of using the probabilities of participation based on labour force histories is for adult men. For them, adding the labour force status transition pattern variables to the set of $\mathbf{X}$s used to construct the participation probabilities, which corresponds to moving from the 'Coarse I' probabilities to the 'Coarse III' probabilities, reduces the selection bias from $-\$5,238$, a figure even larger than the biases found in Table 1, to only $-\$450$. In contrast, for the other three demographic groups the bias from the 'Coarse I' probabilities is not statistically different from that from the 'Coarse III' or the 'best predictor' probabilities.

Our analysis does not provide a definitive answer as to why the pattern of bias in Table 7 for the local linear matching estimator is so different for adult males compared to the other demographic groups. Three factors may be at work: (1) The unadjusted mean bias for adult males is substantially larger than it is for the other three groups, for which it is not statistically distinguishable from zero. Thus, it may be that the effects of the matching for the other groups are dwarfed by the sampling variation. (2) Looking back to Table 5, the improvement in the prediction rate that results from adding the labour force status transition variables to the background variables – that is, in going from the 'Coarse I' specification to the 'Coarse III' specification – is around 0.11 for adult males but only about 0.07 for the other three groups. Thus, these variables may be more important in explaining participation, and controlling selection bias, for adult males. (3) The overall prediction rate for adult males in Table 5 is always about 0.10 higher than for the other three demographic groups. We conjecture that this is because family factors, which are not measured well in our data, affect participation more strongly for the other three groups than for adult males. It may be that conditioning on these other factors as well as on the labour force status transition variables is required in order to observe substantial bias reduction for groups other than adult males.

Third, for all four demographic groups, the biases resulting from all four models for the probability of participation are roughly the same for the conditional (on $P(\mathbf{X})$) variant of the difference-in-differences estimator, and are never statistically distinguishable from zero at conventional significance levels. For adult males, this method produces a substantial improvement over the unadjusted mean difference, and suggests that, given conditioning on at least the demographic variables in the 'Coarse I' probabilities, much of the bias is constant over time in the sense of being roughly equal in symmetric intervals around the month of random assignment or measured eligibility. In contrast, for the other three demographic groups, the lack of any statistical difference between the unadjusted mean differences and the conditional on $P(\mathbf{X})$ difference-in-differences estimates of the bias suggests that little if any of the conditional bias is constant over time, or is equal in symmetric intervals around month 't'.

Fourth, with the exception of the adult males, for whom the conditional difference-in-differences estimator yields smaller estimated bias, there is no systematic difference in the extent of bias reduction in the two estimators considered here.

5. Summary and Conclusions

Using rich data on randomised-out control group members from a recent experimental evaluation of the JTPA programme, we examine the earnings patterns of persons who would have participated except they were randomised out. Combining the control group data with two comparison groups of persons eligible for JTPA, we consider the implications of the control (and comparison) group earnings patterns for commonly used before-after and conventional difference-in-differences estimators. In addition, we use these rich data sources to gain a deeper understanding of the determinants of participation in training programmes. Six main findings emerge from our analysis.

First, a pre-programme dip in the mean earnings of participants is found for all demographic groups in the JTPA data. It is a feature of the pre-programme earnings of participants in many social programmes (Heckman *et al.*, 1999). Second, earnings data on the experimental control group reveal that the dip in mean earnings for participants is not mean-reverting except for adult males. In the other three groups, programme participants would experience earnings growth in the post-programme period even if they did not participate. This growth leads to substantial upward bias in before-after estimators of programme impact.

Third, comparison groups of programme eligibles exhibit different pre-programme and post-programme earnings patterns than experimental control group members. That is, conditioning on eligibility status for the programme results in a comparison group that does not represent the desired counterfactual outcome that participants would experience if they did not participate. Using two separate comparison groups of eligibles, we show that these differences in earnings patterns lead to substantial bias in conventional difference-in-differences estimators of programme impacts. Furthermore, these estimators exhibit striking instability with respect to changes in the 'before' and 'after' time periods used to construct them. The nonparametric conditional difference-in-differences estimators introduced in Heckman, Ichimura and Todd (1997, 1998) perform much better than the conventional difference-in-differences estimator.

Fourth, labour force status transitions, particularly transitions into unemployment from employment or from outside the labour force, drive participation in JTPA among programme eligibles. Earnings changes are only weak predictors of programme participation. The emphasis on earnings declines as predictors of programme participation in the previous literature reflects the lack of available data in earlier studies and helps to account for the disappointing performance of some of the earlier longitudinal evaluation strategies that use lagged earnings to control for selective differences between participants and non-participants.

Our evidence suggests that the model of programme participation developed by Heckman (1978) and Heckman and Robb (1985) and applied by Ashenfelter and Card (1985) and others should be amended. That model emphasises changes in the opportunity costs of earnings foregone as the major determinant of participation in training programmes. The evidence suggests that it is changes in labour force (and for adult women marital and family) status that predict participation in programmes. Heckman *et al.* (1999) develop a model of labour force dynamics and training that extends the original Heckman model to account for the lessons of this paper.

Fifth, based on our findings of the importance of labour force status dynamics in determining participation in JTPA training, we investigate the performance of two estimators – the method of matching and a nonparametric conditional difference-in-differences estimator introduced in Heckman, Ichimura and Todd (1997, 1998). Especially for adult males, we find that both local linear matching and the conditional (on the probability of participation) nonparametric version of the method of difference-in-differences substantially reduce the extent of selection bias in nonexperimental estimates of the impact of training on earnings. Furthermore, we find that for adult males, but not for the other three demographic groups, conditioning on labour force status transitions plays an important role in reducing the level of selection bias.

Sixth, the methods used in this paper are based on selection on observables in the sense of Heckman and Robb (1985, 1986). They reduce, but do not eliminate selection bias. The nonparametric selection bias estimator proposed and implemented in Heckman, Ichimura, Smith and Todd (1998) does not assume selection on observables. It is a promising candidate for investigation in future non-experimental evaluations of social programmes.

University of Chicago and American Bar Foundation

University of Western Ontario

Date of receipt of first submission: October 1997
Date of receipt of final typescript: January 1999

Appendix: Data Description

A.1. *SIPP Sample of JTPA Eligibles*

We draw our national sample of persons eligible for JTPA from the 1986 Panel of the Survey of Income and Program Participation (SIPP). The SIPP is a continuing longitudinal self-weighting survey of the non-institutional population of the United States with a focus on current income and participation in social programmes. The 1986 panel covers the period from October 1985 to March 1988.

We use eligibility Definition B in Devine and Heckman (1996), which captures only eligibility via economic disadvantage. We establish the eligibility status of each person in each month after the seventh month of the panel for which data are available. Eligibility cannot be established with certainty during the first six months of the panel because the requisite six months of prior data on family income are not available. To match the ENP sample, we exclude persons outside the 16 to 54 age range and those enrolled in junior high or high school. The graphs in Figs. 1*a* to 1*d* and the estimates in Table 1 use a rectangular sample consisting of all eligible person-months of persons present in both the first and last months of the panel. We exclude observations with earnings imputed by the Census Bureau, as these imputations appear to be unreliable.

A.2. *Eligible Non-Participant (ENP) Sample*

The ENP sample is based on a sample of dwelling units drawn from the areas served by four of the sixteen training centres in the JTPA experiment: Corpus Christi, TX, Fort Wayne, IN, Jersey City, NJ and Providence, RI. At each centre, the sampling frame excluded low poverty areas containing up to, but not more than, 5% of those with incomes at or below 125% of the poverty level in 1980. In the remaining areas served by each centre, dwelling units were selected at random.

Attempts were made to collect data on all JTPA-eligible persons in the sampled dwelling units who were (1) eligible for JTPA via economic disadvantage, (2) 16 to 54 years of age, (3) not in junior high or high school and (4) not permanently disabled. Persons in the resulting sample had months of measured eligibility between January 1988 and December 1989. Only ENPs with valid earnings values for the 18th month before and the 18th month after measured eligibility were used in Figs. 1*a* to 1*d* and for the difference-in-differences estimates in Table 1. The slightly different rectangular sample defined in Heckman, Ichimura, Smith and Todd (1998) is used for Fig. 2. All ENPs with valid values for the relevant variables were used for the participation rates in Table 2 and the logit estimates in Tables 5 and 6.

A.3. *Experimental Treatment and Control Group Samples*

The experimental treatment and control group samples consist of persons randomly assigned at the four training centres in the JTPA experiment at which the ENP sample was drawn. Control group members were excluded from JTPA services for 18 months after random assignment. At the Corpus Christi and Fort Wayne centres, random assignment began in December 1987 and concluded in January 1989, while in Jersey City and Providence it ran from November 1987 to September 1989.

Controls with valid values of monthly earnings for the 18th month before and the 18th month after random assignment, and treatment group members with valid values for the 18th month after random assignment (no pre-random assignment data were collected for them), were used for Figs. 1*a* to 1*d* and for the estimates in Table 1. The slightly different rectangular sample defined in Heckman, Ichimura, Smith and Todd

(1998) is used for Fig. 2. All controls with valid values for the relevant variables were used for the participation rates in Table 2 and the logit estimates in Tables 5 and 6.

A.4. *Imputations*

Missing values due to item non-response were imputed for the variables included in the estimation of the JTPA participation equations in Tables 5 and 6. Missing values of dichotomous variables were replaced with the *predicted probabilities* estimated in a logit equation. Missing values of indicator variables corresponding to categorical variables with more than two categories were replaced by the *predicted probabilities* obtained from a multinomial logit model. The models used to produce the imputations included indicators for race/ethnicity, age categories, receipt of a high school of diploma or GED and training centre, as well as interactions between control status and these variables. These variables were chosen because they had no (or very few) missing values in the sample. Imputed values were constructed separately for the four demographic groups.

References

Amemiya, Takeshi. (1985). *Advanced Econometrics*. Cambridge, MA: Harvard University Press.
Ashenfelter, Orley. (1978). 'Estimating the effect of training programs on earnings.' *Review of Economics and Statistics*, vol. 60, pp. 47–57.
Ashenfelter, Orley and Card, David. (1985). 'Using the longitudinal structure of earnings to estimate the effect of training programs.' *The Review of Economics and Statistics*, vol. 67, pp. 648–60.
Barnow, Burt. (1993). 'Getting it right: thirty years of changing federal, state, and local relationships in employment and training programs.' *Publius: The Journal of Federalism*, vol. 23, pp. 75–91.
Bassi, Laurie. (1983). 'The effect of CETA on the post-program earnings of participants.' *Journal of Human Resources*, vol. 18, pp. 539–56.
Bassi, Laurie. (1984). 'Estimating the effect of training programs with non-random selection.' *The Review of Economics and Statistics*, vol. 66, pp. 36–43.
Bloom, Howard. (1991). *The National JTPA Study: Baseline Characteristics of the Experimental Sample*. Bethesda, MD: Abt Associates.
Bloom, Howard, Orr, Larry, Cave, George, Bell, Stephen and Doolittle, Fred. (1993). *The National JTPA Study: Title IIA Impacts on Earnings and Employment at 18 Months*. Bethesda, MD: Abt Associates.
Bloom, Howard, Orr, Larry, Bell, Stephen, Cave, George, Doolittle, Fred, Lin, Winston and Bos, Johannes. (1997). 'The Benefits and Costs of JTPA Title II-A Programs.' *Journal of Human Resources*, vol. 32, pp. 549–76.
Bryant, E. and Rupp, Kalman. (1987). 'Evaluating the impact of CETA on participant earnings.' *Evaluation Review*, vol. 11, pp. 473–92.
Campbell, Donald and Stanley, Julian. (1966). *Experimental and Quasi-Experimental Designs for Research*. Chicago, IL: Rand McNally.
Devine, Theresa and Heckman, James. (1996). 'The structure and consequences of eligibility rules for a social program.' In (Solomon Polachek, ed.), *Research in Labor Economics*, Volume 15, pp. 111–70. Greenwich, CT: JAI Press.
Dickinson, Katharine, Johnson, Terry and West, Rebecca. (1987). 'An analysis of the sensitivity of quasi-experimental net impact estimates of CETA programs.' *Evaluation Review*, vol. 11, pp. 452–72.
Heckman, James. (1978). 'Dummy endogenous variables in a simultaneous equations system.' *Econometrica*, vol. 46, pp. 931–59.
Heckman, James. (1979). 'Sample selection bias as a specification error.' *Econometrica*, vol. 47, pp. 153–61.
Heckman, James. (1992). 'Randomization and social program evaluation.' In (Charles Manski and Irwin Garfinkels, eds.), *Evaluating Welfare and Training Programs*, pp. 201–30. Cambridge, MA: Harvard University Press.
Heckman, James. (1997). 'Instrumental variables: a study of implicit behavioral assumptions used in making program evaluations.' *Journal of Human Resources*, vol. 32, pp. 441–62.
Heckman, James, Hohmann, Neil and Smith, Jeffrey, with Khoo, Michael. (1998). 'Substitution and dropout bias in social experiments: a study of an influential social experiment.' *Quarterly Journal of Economics*, forthcoming.
Heckman, James, Ichimura, Hidehiko, Smith, Jeffrey and Todd, Petra. (1996). 'Sources of selection bias

in evaluating social programs: an interpretation of conventional measures and evidence of the effectiveness of matching as a program evaluation method.' *Proceedings of the National Academy of Sciences*, vol. 93, pp. 13416–20.

Heckman, James, Ichimura, Hidehiko, Smith, Jeffrey and Todd, Petra. (1998). 'Characterizing selection bias using experimental data.' *Econometrica*, vol. 66, pp. 1017–98.

Heckman, James, Ichimura, Hidehiko and Todd, Petra. (1997). 'Matching as an econometric evaluation estimator: evidence from evaluating a job training program.' *Review of Economic Studies*, vol. 64, pp. 605–54.

Heckman, James, Ichimura, Hidehiko and Todd, Petra. (1998). 'Matching as an econometric evaluation estimator.' *Review of Economic Studies*, vol. 65, pp. 261–94.

Heckman, James, Khoo, Michael, Roselius, Rebecca and Smith, Jeffrey. (1996). 'The empirical importance of randomization bias in social experiments: evidence from the national JTPA study.' University of Chicago, unpublished manuscript.

Heckman, James, LaLonde, Robert and Smith, Jeffrey. (1999). 'The economics and econometrics of active labor market programs.' In (Orley Ashenfelter and David Card, eds.), Handbook of Labor Economics, Volume III, forthcoming. Amsterdam: North-Holland.

Heckman, James and Robb, Richard. (1985). 'Alternative methods for evaluating the impact of interventions.' In (James Heckman and Burton Singer, eds.), *Longitudinal Analysis of Labor Market Data*, pp. 156–245. Cambridge: Cambridge University Press.

Heckman, James and Robb, Richard. (1986). 'Alternative methods for solving the problem of selection bias in evaluating the impact of treatments on outcomes.' In (Howard Wainer, ed.), *Drawing Inference From Self-Selected Samples*, pp. 63–107. Berlin: Springer-Verlag.

Heckman, James and Roselius, Rebecca. (1994a). 'Evaluating the impact of training on the earnings and labor force status of young women: better data help a lot.' University of Chicago, unpublished manuscript.

Heckman, James and Roselius, Rebecca. (1994b). 'Nonexperimental evaluation of job training programs for young men.' University of Chicago, unpublished manuscript.

Heckman, James and Smith, Jeffrey. (1993). 'Assessing the case for randomized evaluation of social programs.' In (Karsten Jensen and Per Kongshoj Madsen, eds.), *Measuring Labour Market Measures: Evaluating the Effects of Active Labour Market Policies*, pp. 35–96. Copenhagen: Danish Ministry of Labour.

Heckman, James and Smith, Jeffrey. (1995). 'Assessing the case for social experiments.' *Journal of Economic Perspectives*, vol. 9, pp. 85–110.

Heckman, James and Smith, Jeffrey. (1997). 'The determinants of participation in a social program: evidence from JTPA.' University of Chicago, unpublished manuscript.

Heckman, James and Smith, Jeffrey. (1998). 'Evaluating the welfare state.' In (Steiner Strom, ed.), *Econometrics and Economic Theory in the 20th Century: The Ragnar Frisch Centennial*. Cambridge: Cambridge University Press for the Econometric Society Monograph Series, pp. 241–318.

Heckman, James and Todd, Petra. (1996). 'Assessing the performance of alternative estimators of program impacts: a study of adult men and women in JTPA.' University of Chicago, unpublished manuscript.

Hunt, Allen, Rupp, Kalman and Associates. (1984). 'The implementation of title II-A of JTPA in the states and service delivery areas: the new partnership and program directions.' *Proceedings of the Thirty-Seventh Annual Meeting of the Industrial Relations Research Association*, pp. 85–92.

LaLonde, Robert. (1986). 'Evaluating the econometric evaluations of training programs with experimental data.' *American Economic Review*, vol. 76, pp. 604–20.

Rosenbaum, Paul and Rubin, Donald. (1983). 'The central role of the propensity score in observational studies for causal effects.' *Biometrika*, vol. 70, pp. 41–55.

Sandell, Steven and Rupp, Kalman. (1988). 'Who is served in JTPA programs: patterns of participation and intergroup equity.' Research Report RR-88-03, National Commission for Employment Policy.

Smith, Jeffrey. (1997a). 'Measuring earnings dynamics among the poor: a comparison of two samples of JTPA eligibles.' University of Western Ontario, unpublished manuscript.

Smith, Jeffrey. (1997b). 'Measuring earning levels among the poor: evidence from two samples of JTPA eligibles.' University of Western Ontario, unpublished manuscript.

U.S. Department of Labor. (1993a). *Job Training Quarterly Survey: JTPA Title IIA and III Enrollments and Terminations During Program Year 1991 (July 1991–June 1992)*. Employment and Training Administration, Office of Strategic Planning and Policy Development, Division of Performance Management and Evaluation.

U.S. Department of Labor. (1993b). *Title II Eligibility Documentation*. Employment and Training Administration.

[21]

ELSEVIER

Labour Economics 9 (2002) 187–206

LABOUR
ECONOMICS

www.elsevier.com/locate/econbase

A nonexperimental evaluation of training programs for the unemployed in Sweden

Håkan Regnér*

Swedish Institute for Social Research, Stockholm University, S-106 91 Stockholm, Sweden

Abstract

This study uses a unique administrative database to evaluate employment training program effects on three samples of Swedish adult males. Alternative nonexperimental models suggest both positive and negative relationships between training and annual earnings. Model specification tests decisively reject the fixed-effect model, but not the random-growth model, which shows that specification tests can reject misspecified models. The chosen model predicts no effects or significantly negative earnings effects of the training program. One explanation for this result is that some participants may have enrolled in the program not for the purpose of making a human capital investment, but for the purpose of collecting unemployment insurance benefits. © 2002 Elsevier Science B.V. All rights reserved.

JEL classification: J31; J38
Keywords: Nonexperimental evaluation; Specification tests; Labor market policies; Employment training programs; Unemployment insurance benefits

1. Introduction

For many years, participation in employment training programs has been an important part of the unemployment experience of Sweden. Training is a central component of Swedish labor market policy, which focuses on active policies instead of passive income-support measures. Participation in training averaged 0.8% of the labor force between 1980 and 1985 and then grew steadily to 2.0% by 1992. This growth reflects policymakers' increased emphasis on employment training and their decreased emphasis on public relief

* Tel.: +46-8-162154; fax: +46-8-154670.
E-mail address: hakan.regner@sofi.su.se (H. Regnér).

0927-5371/02/$ - see front matter © 2002 Elsevier Science B.V. All rights reserved.
PII: S0927-5371(02)00013-1

188					*H. Regnér / Labour Economics 9 (2002) 187–206*

work as a strategy for addressing adult unemployment.[1] This strategy has gained attention outside Sweden and has even been recommended as a tool to reduce the persistent unemployment observed in many European countries (see, e.g. Layard et al., 1991).

Despite the extensive use of training, little is known about program effectiveness. There are four nonexperimental econometric studies of the impact of employment training in Sweden, all conducted on the program as it was run before 1985 (Björklund and Moffitt, 1987; Edin, 1988; Axelsson, 1989; Ackum, 1991). The sample sizes are generally small, the precision of the impact estimates is low, and alternative models produce different program earnings effects. These findings coincide with those reported in many US studies (e.g. Lalonde, 1995).

The problems with these nonexperimental studies have made it difficult to draw conclusions about the impact of Swedish training programs. A similar finding from nonexperimental evaluations of US programs has lead researchers to recommend social experiments to evaluate training programs (e.g. Ashenfelter and Card, 1985; Lalonde, 1986; Barnow, 1987).[2] Heckman and Hotz (1989) reach a different conclusion about the reliability of such evaluations. They argue that the reported sensitivity of the nonexperimental estimates merely results from applying inappropriate models to the data. To address the problem of sensitivity of nonexperimental estimates, Heckman and Hotz develop a strategy for testing among alternative models and then choosing the appropriate estimated training effects. Their results are encouraging because if their approach works, it can serve as a tool in situations where a randomized experiment cannot be conducted.[3] Strangely, no further studies of employment training programs have used the test strategy suggested by Heckman and Hotz.

This paper is concerned with two issues. First, what are the average earnings impacts of Swedish training programs for the unemployed? Second, is it possible to use the Heckman and Hotz testing strategy to choose among alternative nonexperimental estimators?

The paper has three main findings. First, model specification tests reject the fixed-effect model, but not the random-growth model, showing that specification tests can provide guidelines for a choice among estimated training effects. Second, the chosen model predicts that employment and training programs had negative effects on earnings for adult males who participated in the early 1990s. Third, institutional factors related to the unemployment insurance system might explain the estimated earnings effects of the training program.

Sections 2 and 3 present the empirical models and the model specification tests. Section 4 describes the institutional framework, and Section 5 presents the data. Section 6 reports

---

[1] Public relief work was the main policy for the unemployed during the 1980–1985 period, with up to 1.5% of the labor force participating in the policy. The incidence of relief works has trended downward in the 1980s, and in the 1990–1995 period, participation averaged 0.4%. In 1998, training was still the most important program for unemployed adults.

[2] See Heckman and Smith (1995) for discussions of problems with the experimental approach and Björklund and Regnér (1996) for solutions to some of the problems.

[3] In general, policymakers are reluctant to accept the idea of randomly excluding persons from training. Doolittle and Traeger (1990) report that training sites involved in the National Job Training Partnership Act (JTPA) Study conducted in the US were concerned with the ethical implications of the experiment.

impact estimates of training, and Section 7 the results of specification tests. Section 8 concludes the paper.

2. The empirical models[4]

Conventional nonexperimental evaluations of training programs generally start with the following equations for earnings and program participation decision:

$$Y_{it} = X_{it}\beta + D_i\alpha_t + \theta_{1i} + t\theta_{2i} + v_{it}; \tag{1}$$

$$D_i^* = Z_i\eta + \varepsilon_i, D_i = 1 \quad \text{iff } D_i^* > 0; \quad D_i = 0 \text{ otherwise.} \tag{2}$$

In Eq. (1), yearly earnings of individual i in period t, Y_{it}, is a function of a vector of individual characteristics, X_{it}, such as age and schooling; a dummy variable that indicates if the individual has participated D_i; and an error that includes a person-specific fixed effect, θ_{1i}, a person-specific time trend, $t\theta_{2i}$, and a transitory disturbance, v_{it}. The coefficient on D_i, denoted α_t, represents the impact of participation in training in period t. This is the parameter of interest.

Eq. (2) specifies the participation decision, wherein individuals participate in training if the latent variable D_i^* exceeds zero. The latent variable is a function of observed Z_i (which may include X_i variables) and unobserved ε_i variables. It is well known that we have a selection bias problem in the estimation of α_t when a stochastic relationship exists between D_i and the person-specific fixed effect or time trend, or between D_i and the transitory component of the error term.

This paper uses three nonexperimental models. The first model assumes that the selection bias is due merely to observed differences between trainees and the comparison group. It is assumed that the inclusion of observed selection variables, Z_i, into the earnings equation is sufficient to adjust for selection bias (Barnow et al., 1980). This suggests the following control function model:[5]

$$Y_{it} = X_{it}\beta + Z_i\delta + D_i\alpha_t + v_{it}. \tag{3}$$

The second model is the standard fixed-effect model.[6] It assumes that the selection bias is due to the unobserved individual-specific component, θ_{1i}, which is fixed over time. It also assumes that there is no person-specific time trend θ_{2i}, or that the trend is present, but

---

[4] Heckman and Hotz (1989) provide a detailed description of the models in this section.

[5] This is the linear-control function model, which belongs to a class of control function models. The frequently used two-step model developed by Heckman (1979) also belongs to this class of models (see Heckman and Robb, 1985).

[6] This model has been used in many empirical studies. For example, see Axelsson (1989) for a Swedish study, Raaum and Torp (1997) for a Norwegian study, Westergaard-Nielsen (1993) for a Danish study, and Barnow (1987) for an overview of American studies.

190   *H. Regnér / Labour Economics 9 (2002) 187–206*

unrelated to participation in the program conditional on $(X_{it}-X_{is})$. Taking first differences removes the fixed effect:

$$Y_{it} - Y_{is} = D_i\alpha_t + (X_{it} - X_{is})\beta + (v_{it} - v_{is}), \tag{4}$$

where s is a time period prior to training and t is a time period after training. The third model is the random-growth model. The model eliminates the selection bias that results from both the person-specific fixed effect and the person-specific time trend, θ_{2i}.[7] First differences eliminate the fixed effect and second differences eliminate the growth component. This gives the following empirical model:

$$(Y_{it} - Y_{is}) - (t-s)(Y_{is} - Y_{i,s-1}) = \alpha_t D_i + [(X_{it} - X_{is}) - (t-s)$$
$$\times (X_{is} - X_{i,s-1})]\beta + (v_{it} - v_{is})$$
$$- (t-s)(v_{is} - v_{i,s-1}) \tag{5}$$

An advantage with the models presented in this section is that they are robust to choice-based sampling, i.e. situations where trainees are overrepresented relative to their proportion in the population. This characterizes most nonexperimental data sets and, in particular, the data set used in this study.

3. The model specification tests[8]

The Heckman and Hotz (1989) testing strategy consists of two parts. The first component exploits the properties of the pretraining data, and the second component that places restrictions on the underlying econometric model.[9] The rationale for the first test is that, before training, training cannot affect earnings and, thus, the participation dummy should not affect preprogram earnings. That is, we test the null hypothesis that $\alpha=0$ in preprogram earnings equations. The model is rejected if α is statistically significantly different from zero. The test can be applied to all of the models in the previous section.

The second test exploits the restrictions implied by the models. While there are no testable restrictions implied by the linear-control function model, the fixed-effect and random-growth models do invoke testable assumptions. Both models presume that the correlation between the error term and the participation dummy is zero for all possible differences and that the error is not serially correlated. We test this restriction by including Y-values in the outcome equation from preprogram years other than those specified by the

---

[7] This model has not previously been used in any Swedish study. To my knowledge, Heckman et al. (1987, 1998) are the only published studies that have applied the model, and they used American data.

[8] The importance of testing nonexperimental models was recognized early by Ashenfelter (1978), Bassi (1983, 1984), and Ashenfelter and Card (1985). Heckman and Hotz (1989) were the first to suggest a general testing strategy that can be applied to a class of nonexperimental models.

[9] There is a third part of the testing strategy, but it requires access to data on an experimental control group. As a result, only the first two parts can be used in any nonexperimental study. See Lalonde (1986) for an early study using experimental data to evaluate the performance of nonexperimental models.

H. Regnér / Labour Economics 9 (2002) 187–206   191

original equations. Under the null hypothesis, the coefficients on these variables are equal to zero.

There are two general problems with the tests. First, the model restriction test can be applied only to models that impose restrictions beyond those required to estimate the training effects (i.e. to overidentified models). This means that the tests cannot detect whether or not a model that does not impose such restrictions (a just-identified model) is misspecified. Second, the validity of the preprogram test hinges on the assumption that models that successfully adjust for preprogram earnings differences between participants and comparison group members will also do so in the postprogram period. If the selection between the groups occurs on postprogram differences that are independent of preprogram differences, a model that is not rejected by the preprogram test might actually be misspecified. Also, for the same reason, models that are rejected by the test may actually be free from selection bias in the postprogram period.

4. Institutional framework

The National Labor Market Board is the central body for all labor market policies in Sweden, and the country is served by 24 County Labor Market Boards and a nationwide system of about 360 Public Employment Offices. The offices administer and implement all labor market policies. Individuals who want to participate in active labor market programs or to collect unemployment benefits must be registered at an office and must be actively seeking jobs.[10] The offices are obliged to inform all unemployed persons about eligibility rules, training benefits, and other program-related issues. The basic training eligibility condition is unemployment or running the risk of becoming unemployed. In addition, applicants for employment training must be over age 20. Based on these conditions, most unemployed persons are entitled to the program.

The training program is divided into vocational and nonvocational courses. Training can occur in the ordinary public education system or at special training agencies in the private or public sector. That is, it is possible to receive classroom training in occupational skills as well as courses identical to those in the ordinary educational system at the high school and university levels.

All training is free of charge, and participants receive a daily taxable training benefit that covers 5 days/week. The benefit levels depend on eligibility for unemployment compensation and age (see below). Additional benefits are available to cover literature, travel expenses, and costs for housing if participants cannot live at home while participating in training. In these respects, participation in employment training programs is far more advantageous than participation in the ordinary educational system.[11]

---

[10] Swedish labor force surveys report that about 87% (95%) of all unemployed persons used the services of employment offices in 1989 (1994).

[11] The average total costs for one trainee is about SEK 106,000 (US$16,012). About 60% of these costs are training benefits. The average yearly costs for students in compulsory and upper-secondary school are about SEK 53,000 (US$8006) and 63,000 (US$9,517), respectively. The US dollar (German mark)-to-Swedish crown exchange rates were 5.92 (3.67) in 1990, 5.99 (3.63) in 1991 and 6.62 (3.76) in 1992.

192   *H. Regnér / Labour Economics 9 (2002) 187–206*

Unemployment compensation is provided in two forms: unemployment insurance (UI) benefits or cash assistance (CA).[12] In the former system, there are several certified tax financed UI funds that are run by the trade unions at the industry and occupational levels.[13] Benefits are paid to unemployed persons who have been members of a UI fund for at least 12 months (the *membership requirement*). In addition, members of a UI fund must have worked for at least 4 months (16 weeks) during the 12-month period preceding the unemployment spell (the *work requirement* rule). Individuals who fulfill these two requirements receive a daily benefit that covers 5 days/week. Those under age 55 are entitled to compensation for a maximum of 300 days and those over 55 for a maximum of 450 days. This represents about 60 (90) calendar weeks, because only workdays count. The maximum daily compensation varied (in real prices) between SEK 610 and SEK 619 (today, this amounts to about US$68) during the period covered by this study.

The CA scheme provides benefits for unemployed persons who meet the work requirement, but not the membership requirement of a UI fund. Individuals under age 55 are entitled to CA for 150 days, while those over 55 receive CA for 300 days. The daily cash allowance is much lower than the UI benefits and varied between SEK 214 and SEK 217 (today this amounts to about US$24) during the period covered by this study.[14]

Persons who participate in employment training programs receive a daily taxable training benefit 5 days a week. Persons who are eligible for UI benefits receive the same amount during training as they would have received, had they been unemployed. Persons who are not eligible for UI benefits, but are over age 20 or below age 20, and have children, receive about 60% of the stipulated maximum amount of the former group. Persons not eligible for UI benefits, and not in the group with children just described, receive training benefits about the level of the CA scheme.

The work requirement rule in the UI system can be fulfilled by participation in employment training. This means that there are additional economic incentives to enroll in employment training programs in Sweden. These incentives were particularly strong during the period covered by this study, because almost no other programs were available for those who wanted to qualify for UI benefits.

There are at least four groups for whom the economic incentives to enroll in training were strong:

1. Members of UI funds whose expiration date is approaching can enter a 4-month course, and after completion collect UI benefits for another 60 weeks.

---

[12] This refers to the benefit system that was valid during the period covered by this study. During the 1987–1992 period, 66% of the unemployed collected UI benefits, 10% collected CA benefits, and 25% were without benefits.

[13] The government subsidizes about 95% of the expenditure. Membership fees cover the remaining 5%. Membership fees vary across UI funds, but are rarely above 0.5% of monthly earnings. Union membership is not a requirement.

[14] When compensation from UI or CA runs out, individuals can apply for means-tested social assistance benefits. The level of these benefits can be higher than the UI or CA benefits. But to collect the assistance benefits, applicants first must use up all of their savings, sell off valuable possessions, and even move to less expensive housing.

2. UI fund members who have not fulfilled the work requirement can do so by taking part in 4 months of training.
3. Persons who are aged 20 and eligible for CA, but not members of a UI fund, receive higher benefits in employment training programs than when unemployed.
4. Persons who are eligible neither for UI benefits nor for CA receive at least the minimum level of training benefits.

5. Data

The data used in this study come from a new panel database designed for evaluations of employment training (Regnér, 1997). The database covers the 1987–1992 period and contains data from administrative records kept by the National Labor Market Board (AMS) and Statistics Sweden (SCB). AMS keeps records of unemployed persons and participants in labor market programs, while SCB keeps various records of all persons living in Sweden.

Data on trainees and comparison groups were collected from the same administrative records. There are three random samples of trainees who left a course in December of 1989, 1990, and 1991, respectively. For the 1989 sample, there are 2 years of preprogram data (1987 and 1988) and 3 years of postprogram data (1990, 1991 and 1992). The 1990 and 1991 samples have more years of preprogram data available, but fewer years of postprogram data.

The data also include two comparison groups formed by a simple matching technique. The matching variables are age, gender, region in the country (county) and pretraining labor market status (unemployed or participation in labor market programs).[15] The county variable guarantees that nonparticipants come from the same local labor markets as the trainees.[16] Nonparticipants who match on all variables are included in the comparison group. One comparison group consists mainly of recently unemployed persons, and the other includes persons with unemployment spells of various durations. The latter comparison group is used in this study.[17]

The analyses focus on adult males who were living in Sweden in every year since 1987. Nonparticipants who received training benefits in the year participants took their courses are excluded. By invoking this restriction, I know for sure that the comparison group did not participate in training or in any other program (in which participants receive training benefits)[18] during the year when participants took their

---

[15] Persons were mainly unemployed, part-time employed or in temporary jobs before entering training or a comparison group.

[16] See Heckman and Smith (1999) for a discussion of the importance of selecting a comparison group with individuals from the same labor markets as participants.

[17] Regnér (1993) includes results based on the other comparison group. The impact estimates are lower, but no significant differences result from using one comparison group rather than the other. Also, the results of the specification tests are about the same. See also the discussion in Regnér (1997).

[18] During the year covered by this study, individuals could receive training benefits when they participated in vocational rehabilitation and job search activities.

194   *H. Regnér / Labour Economics 9 (2002) 187–206*

training.[19] The outcome measure is annual earnings in years following the end of the training. Earnings in this study include income from work, sick pay, and parental benefits.[20] Earnings do not include UI benefits or training benefits. There is no information on working hours.

Table 1 reports sample characteristics of training participants and comparison group members. It also describes the set of control variables used in the analyses. "Work experience" and "skilled worker" are based on individuals' own assessments of their experiences and skills in a particular field.[21] In the 1989 and 1990 samples, trainees are less experienced and skilled than members of the comparison group. There is a significantly larger share of disabled persons among training participants than among nonparticipants.[22] Again, this concerns mainly the 1989 and 1990 samples.

Preprogram earnings are higher for trainees who participated in the program in 1990 and 1991, compared to earnings for nonparticipants, and significantly so for the 1991 sample. Postprogram earnings for nonparticipants are higher for all samples and significantly larger for the 1990 and 1991 samples of nonparticipants. Training participants experience a dip in earnings mainly in the year of training. Explanations could be that many persons were employed part-time or had been unemployed for only a short time before the program. Many training participants in the US have experienced a preprogram dip in earnings, and earnings have, therefore, been seen as a potential determinant of program participation (e.g. Ashenfelter, 1978; Heckman and Smith, 1999; Heckman et al., 1999). Note that postprogram earnings are lower than preprogram earnings for participants as well as nonparticipants. This earnings pattern is similar to that of displaced workers in the US, and it may suggest a loss of specific human capital or rents from a former good job match that are not recovered (e.g. Jacobson et al., 1993).

Table 2 reports mean unemployment insurance benefits during the 1987–1992 period and percentages receiving benefits in each year. The UI benefit level is somewhat higher for nonparticipants than participants in all preprogram years (except for the immediate preprogram years—1988 for the 1989 sample, 1989 for the 1990 sample, and 1990 for the 1991 sample). The UI benefit level is significantly higher for comparison group members than for participants in the year when participants receive training for the 1989 and 1990 samples, and higher, but not significantly so for the 1991 sample. This suggests that nonparticipants were mainly looking for jobs when trainees took their courses. Mean UI benefits are significantly larger for participants than comparison group members in

---

[19] Sixteen percent of nonparticipants in 1989 received training benefits in the year before they enter the comparison group. The percentages for nonparticipants in 1990 and 1991 are 10.4 and 4.8, respectively. About 30% of trainees received benefits before the year they are observed in the program. I have reestimated all models excluding persons who received benefits in preprogram years, but the conclusions reached in this study are not affected.

[20] Parental benefits are earnings-related benefits to parents who are on leave to care for children. See Albrecht et al. (1999) for a detailed discussion of the Swedish parental leave system.

[21] Individuals state whether they have no, some, or good work experience, and whether they are skilled workers or not when they register with an employment office.

[22] The data include an indicator of being disabled or not. This variable has been constructed from data collected by personnel at the employment office. Disability refers to cardiovascular and respiratory diseases, hearing and vision problems, physical and psychical handicaps, among others.

H. Regnér / Labour Economics 9 (2002) 187–206   195

Table 1
Sample means of variables used in the analyses

Variables	1989		1990		1991	
	Trainees	Comparison group	Trainees	Comparison group	Trainees	Comparison group
(1) Earnings						
1987	114.6 (74.3)	114.3 (75.1)	121.9 (73.1)	115.9 (80.3)	140.7 (71.7)*	127.1 (84.8)*
1988	113.7 (74.8)*	123.2 (76.6)*	129.3 (75.1)	121.9 (82.5)	145.9 (75.6)*	137.0 (84.8)*
1989	107.4 (76.5)	115.3 (76.2)	130.8 (74.8)	127.7 (83.9)	151.9 (77.2)*	142.0 (86.2)*
1990	**108.5 (79.2)***	**119.5 (78.1)***	111.4 (75.4)	117.8 (81.1)	138.6 (78.7)	133.4 (87.9)
1991	**99.9 (80.5)**	**108.4 (87.9)**	**84.3 (75.3)***	**97.4 (84.0)***	79.2 (78.5)*	101.3 (80.9)*
1992	**90.4 (84.1)**	**98.0 (88.6)**	**83.9 (77.7)***	**94.3 (86.5)***	**71.0 (74.6)***	**84.0 (79.9)***
(2) Age	35.6 (7.1)	35.2 (7.4)	35.5 (8.0)	35.5 (8.1)	36.1 (7.8)	36.3 (7.7)
(3) Percent married	0.36	0.35	0.36	0.34	0.37	0.39
(4) Percent foreign citizens	0.14*	0.10*	0.13*	0.09*	0.07*	0.11*
(5) Percent disabled	0.34*	0.22*	0.26*	0.17*	0.17*	0.13*
(6) Percent high school education	0.41	0.40	0.45*	0.37*	0.48*	0.41*
(7) Percent university education	0.06*	0.11*	0.07*	0.15*	0.07*	0.11*
(8) Percent members of a UI fund	0.64	0.63	0.61	0.62	0.74	0.70
(9) Percent some work experience	0.25	0.26	0.25	0.27	0.27	0.24
(10) Percent good work experience	0.21*	0.38*	0.30*	0.41*	0.46*	0.54*
(11) Percent skilled workers	0.35*	0.45*	0.40	0.44	0.52	0.52
(12) Percent living in the northern part of Sweden	0.32	0.33	0.31	0.29	0.29	0.27
(13) Percent living in a big city	0.28	0.29	0.30	0.31	0.29	0.29
Number of persons	627	544	748	786	951	875

Standard deviations are in parentheses. Earnings are in thousands of 1995 SEK. Means are calculated for respective sampling year if a variable is observed in more than 1 year. The average course length was 16 weeks for trainees in 1989, 35 weeks for trainees in 1990, and 32 weeks for trainees in 1991. Personnel at an employment office measure variables 4–11 when individuals register at an office. The other variables come from administrative records at Statistics Sweden. Bold values indicate postprogram years. An asterisk (*) indicates that mean values and frequencies differ significantly between the groups.

postprogram years. That is, the pattern in postprogram years is opposite to that in preprogram years.[23]

If training were a way to become eligible for UI benefits, one would expect an increase in the percentages collecting benefits in the year following training. The frequencies in

---

[23] The average unemployment rate was 2% in 1987 and 4.8% in 1992. At the county level, the unemployment rate varied between 1.1% and 4.8% in 1987 and between 4.0% and 8.3% in 1992. The variable set R3, described in detail in the notes to Table 3, includes regional unemployment rates.

Table 2
Unemployment insurance (UI) benefits in thousands of 1995 SEK and percent receiving benefits, 1987–1992

Year	1989		1990		1991	
	Trainees	Comparison group	Trainees	Comparison group	Trainees	Comparison group
1987	13.4 (26.2)	15.0 (29.0)	9.5 (22.7)*	11.5 (24.4)	8.7 (21.5)*	11.1 (24.1)*
1988	15.7 (28.4)	14.1 (26.1)	10.0 (22.6)	11.3 (23.4)	8.1 (20.9)*	9.0 (21.2)*
1989	18.8 (29.2)*	24.2 (33.8)*	12.5 (25.7)	11.6 (24.4)	6.8 (17.9)	8.5 (21.5)
1990	**21.4 (32.1)***	**17.1 (27.8)***	16.2 (27.4)*	20.6 (31.0)*	12.5 (26.3)	11.4 (25.3)
1991	**19.8 (32.9)***	**17.4 (31.6)***	**33.5 (42.7)***	**23.6 (36.2)***	26.6 (34.4)	30.7 (38.0)
1992	**26.5 (42.5)**	**25.5 (39.9)**	**33.9 (42.8)***	**25.7 (40.0)***	**54.7 (51.3)***	**38.1 (44.3)***
Percent receiving UI benefits						
1987	30.1	29.0	22.6	28.2	21.0	24.6
1988	34.6	32.7	24.1	27.9	19.8	24.0
1989	44.8	49.4	31.6	28.9	19.4	21.8
1990	**48.9**	**42.1**	42.5	45.7	28.1	28.6
1991	**38.1**	**31.9**	**54.9**	**43.9**	53.4	55.9
1992	**39.4**	**39.7**	**51.3**	**39.3**	**68.9**	**54.7**

Standard deviations are in parentheses. Bold values indicate postprogram years. An asterisk (*) indicates that mean UI benefits differ significantly between the groups.

Table 2 show that the percentage is larger in the first postprogram year than in other years. The percentage of benefit receivers increases faster among trainees than among non-trainees from the year before the program to the first postprogram year. These changes are statistically significant for the 1990 and 1991 samples. One interpretation of these differences is that some trainees may have enrolled in employment training not for the purpose of making a human capital investment, but for the purpose of collecting post-training UI benefits.

6. Estimates of the impact of training

Table 3 reports impact estimates of training for adult males who left the program in December 1989, 1990, and 1991. All earnings effects are obtained holding the slope coefficients the same for participants and nonparticipants. Looking at the results for the 1989 sample, we see that the impact estimates exhibit the same degree of instability as those reported in most previous studies. The fixed-effect specification based on data from 1987 and two specifications of the linear-control function model predict significantly negative training effects in both the first (1990) and the second (1991) year after the program. In contrast, the random-growth model predicts significantly positive program effects.[24] The fixed-effect model is sensitive to the choice of base year, and alternative specifications of the linear-control function model (described in the notes to Table 3) produce different results. Obviously, these results exemplify a typical nonexperimental situation where specification tests are needed.

---

[24] All of the models indicate a significantly negative relationship between regional unemployment rates and individual earnings for all samples.

H. Regnér / Labour Economics 9 (2002) 187–206   197

The results for the 1990 sample do not vary as much as the results for the 1989 sample. In addition, the random-growth specification no longer produces large positive effects. The fixed-effect and linear-control function models predict significantly negative relationships between participation in employment training programs and earnings in both outcome years. These models are not particularly sensitive to alternative specifications,[25] and the precision of the estimates is rather high. For example, the variation of the fixed-effect estimates (calculated as the width of a 95% confidence interval) is about 10% of annual earnings in the first postprogram year. The precision of the random-growth estimates is lower, and the random-growth model is sensitive to the choice of base year. The specification that uses preprogram data from 1987 and 1988 suggests effects similar to the fixed-effect model, while the other specification predicts insignificant program effects. Moreover, the impact estimates of training are model dependent, ranging from -0.2 to -24.3. Even so, all models predict that training had no, or even negative, effects on earnings both 1 and 2 years after the program.

Similarly, the results for the 1991 sample do not vary as much as the results for the 1989 sample.[26] All models predict negative effects of employment training on earnings for the 1991 sample of adult males.[27] The fixed-effect model is not sensitive to the choice of base year, but the random-growth model is. The linear-control function model is not particularly sensitive to alternative specifications. The precision of the linear-control function and of the fixed-effect estimates is high, while the precision of some random-growth estimates is low. In all, the results suggest that training had a negative effect on earnings for participants in the early 1990s. We can get an idea of the magnitude of the negative effects by relating the average of the estimated earnings effects to the highest level of preprogram earnings. This suggests a loss in earnings of about 10%.

7. Results of the model specification tests

Table 4 reports probability values (p-values) for model specification tests applied to the alternative models for the three samples. The p-value is the probability of obtaining the actual outcome, given that the null hypothesis is correct. Hence, a low p-value implies a rejection of the null hypothesis and the related model. Looking first at the results for the 1989 sample of adult males, we see that the preprogram test rejects the fixed-effect model and all, but one, specification of the control function model. The specification that is not rejected is the one that includes the full set of controls other than lagged earnings. The model restriction test also rejects the fixed-effect model. The data do not allow the tests to be applied to the random-growth model for this sample.

---

[25] The exception is the control function model that includes the full set of control variables other than earnings. That model yields an insignificant earnings effect.

[26] I have estimated various specifications of the traditional selection model developed by Heckman (1979). The results are extremely sensitive to alternative specifications of the model and the estimated standard errors are very large. The model is not appropriate for the data used in this study.

[27] These results are in stark contrast to those reported for participants in the early 1980s by Axelsson (1989), but are in line with those reported for participants in the 1970s and the early 1980s by Edin (1988) and Ackum (1991).

Table 3
Estimates of training effects for adult males who completed a course in December 1989, 1990, and 1991

Variable sets	1989			1990					1991			
	Fixed-effect estimates		Random-growth estimates	Fixed-effect estimates			Random-growth estimates		Fixed-effect estimates		Random-growth estimates	
	$s=1988$	$s=1987$	$s=1988,$ $s-1=1987$	$s=1989$	$s=1988$	$s=1987$	$s=1989,$ $s-1=1988$	$s=1988,$ $s-1=1987$	$s=1989$	$s=1988$	$s=1990,$ $s-1=1989$	$s=1989,$ $s-1=1988$
1990 Earnings												
R1	−1.1 (4.8)	−11.7 (5.0)	18.1 (9.4)									
R1–R2	−0.9 (4.8)	−11.5 (5.0)	17.7 (9.4)									
1991 Earnings												
R1	1.5 (5.2)	−8.8 (5.2)	30.2 (12.8)	−16.2 (4.4)	−20.5 (4.6)	−19.3 (4.5)	−7.0 (8.2)	−24.3 (10.4)				
R1–R2	1.8 (5.2)	−8.5 (5.2)	30.1 (12.8)	−16.2 (4.4)	−20.7 (4.6)	−19.6 (4.5)	−7.3 (8.2)	−24.3 (10.4)				
1992 Earnings												
R1	2.7 (5.4)	−7.5 (5.5)	40.6 (15.9)	−13.4 (4.7)	−17.8 (4.9)	−16.5 (4.8)	−0.5 (10.9)	−23.1 (13.1)	−23.1 (4.4)	−22.1 (4.3)	−8.5 (8.2)	−26.0 (10.3)
R1–R2	2.6 (5.4)	−7.9 (5.5)	40.0 (15.8)	−13.5 (4.7)	−18.1 (4.9)	−16.9 (4.8)	−0.2 (10.9)	−23.2 (13.1)	−23.3 (4.4)	−22.0 (4.4)	−9.1 (8.2)	−26.8 (10.4)

H. Regnér / Labour Economics 9 (2002) 187–206   199

	Linear control function estimates			Linear control function estimates		Linear control function estimates
	1990 Earnings	*1991 Earnings*	*1992 Earnings*	*1991 Earnings*	*1992 Earnings*	*1992 Earnings*
R1	−11.7 (4.5)	−9.2 (4.8)	−7.8 (5.0)	−13.9 (4.0)	−11.1 (4.1)	−12.4 (3.6)
R1–R2	−11.8 (4.3)	−9.0 (4.7)	−7.9 (4.9)	−14.2 (4.0)	−11.4 (4.1)	−12.3 (3.6)
R1–R3	−2.9 (4.2)	−0.5 (4.6)	1.3 (4.8)	−12.5 (3.7)	−8.7 (3.9)	−13.0 (3.4)
R1–R4	−1.9 (4.2)	0.6 (4.5)	2.9 (4.7)	−10.9 (3.7)	−7.4 (3.2)	−12.3 (3.4)
R1–R4, except lagged earnings	−3.9 (4.5)	−1.1 (4.7)	1.0 (4.9)	−8.1 (4.0)	−5.0 (4.1)	−9.9 (3.5)

R1 includes age (linear and higher order terms) and marital status. R2 includes area of residence (county dummies) and regional rate of unemployment. R3 includes lagged earnings, foreign citizenship, disability, member of a UI fund, and work experience. R4 includes education (high school and university) and self-reported worker skill level. Estimated standard errors are in parentheses. Earnings are in thousands of 1995 SEK. R^2 is in the range of 0.004–0.08 for the fixed-effect model, 0.008–0.01 for the random-growth model, and 0.04–0.23 for the linear-control function model. Different specifications of the fixed-effect model give similar results. The random-growth model using data from 1988 and 1987 yields similar impact estimates as the model using data from 1990 and 1989 for the 1991 sample, but the precision is somewhat lower.

Table 4
P-values from specification tests of nonexperimental models

1989 — Fixed-effect model

Preprogram test using preprogram earnings

	s=1988, s−1=1987
R1	0.004
R1−R2	0.004

Model restriction tests

	1990 Earnings s=1988	1991 Earnings s=1988	1992 Earnings s=1988
R1	0.000	0.000	0.000
R1−R2	0.000	0.000	0.000

1990 — Fixed-effect model

Preprogram test using preprogram earnings

	s=1989, s−1=1988	s=1988, s−1=1987
R1	0.137	0.594
R1−R2	0.122	0.638

Model restriction tests

	1991 Earnings s=1989	1992 Earnings s=1989
R1	0.000	0.000
R1−R2	0.000	0.000

1990 — Random-growth model

Preprogram test using preprogram earnings

	s=1989, s−1=1988, s−2=1987
R1	0.197
R1−R2	0.201

Model restriction tests

	1991 Earnings s=1989, s−1=1988	1992 Earnings s=1989, s−1=1988
R1	0.688	0.275
R1−R2	0.726	0.287

1991 — Fixed-effect model

Preprogram test using preprogram earnings

	s=1989, s−1=1988	s=1988, s−1=1987
R1	0.709	0.110
R1−R2	0.705	0.108

Model restriction tests

	1992 Earnings s=1989
R1	0.000
R1−R2	0.000

1991 — Random-growth model

Preprogram test using preprogram earnings

	s=1990, s−1=1989, s−2=1988	s=1989, s−1=1988, s−2=1987
R1	0.191	0.214
R1−R2	0.181	0.230

Model restriction tests

	1992 Earnings s=1990, s−1=1989	s=1989, s−1=1988
R1	0.749	0.963
R1−R2	0.748	0.956

H. Regnér / Labour Economics 9 (2002) 187–206   201

Model restriction test

	Model restriction test on preprogram earnings $s=1989$, $s-1=1988$	Model restriction test on preprogram earnings $s=1990$, $s-1=1989$, $s-1=1988$		Model restriction test on preprogram earnings $s=1990$, $s-1=1989$, $s-2=1988$
		1989 Earnings	1988 Earnings	1988 Earnings
R1	0.000	0.000	0.000	0.881
R1–R2	0.000	0.000	0.000	0.854

Linear-control function model

Preprogram test using preprogram earnings

	1988 Earnings	1989 Earnings	1989 Earnings	1988 Earnings	1988 Earnings
R1	0.015	0.562	0.006	0.078	0.010
R1–R2	0.022	0.601	0.007	0.092	0.008
R1–R3	0.020	0.871	0.084	0.085	0.692
R1–R4	0.021	0.873	0.119	0.100	0.558
R1–R4, except lagged earnings	0.297	0.067	0.006	0.647	0.014

The results of the model restriction test are identical for other combinations of preprogram earnings and other specifications of the fixed-effect models.

Turning to the 1990 sample, we see that the preprogram test rejects neither the fixed-effect model nor the random-growth model. The test does reject all specifications of the linear-control function model other than the one using R1–R4 as control variables. The model restriction test rejects the fixed-effect model, but not the random-growth model. Taken together, the tests suggest that the random-growth model and one control function model might adjust properly for selection bias. Table 3 reveals that both specifications of the random-growth model indicate that training has negative effects for participants in 1990, and that the magnitude of the effects differs depending on the preprogram years employed to construct the estimates. The random-growth model estimated using the earlier years of preprogram data is not subject to testing, as it is just identified given the available data. Thus, this is a situation where we need some additional information in order to identify which of the specifications provides the best estimate of the earnings effect. It seems as if only data from a properly conducted experiment can provide such information.[28] Note, however, that the linear-control function model that passes the preprogram test suggests large negative earnings effects of the program. Qualitatively, this result coincides with the one from the just-identified version of the random-growth model.

The results of the specification tests applied to models estimated for adult males in 1991 are also encouraging. The preprogram test does not reject either the fixed-effect model or the random-growth model. The model restriction test rejects the fixed-effect model, but not the random-growth model. There are more years of pretraining data for the 1991 sample and, therefore, the model restriction test can also be applied to preprogram earnings. This test also does not reject the random-growth model. Taken together, the tests again reject the fixed-effect model, but not the random-growth model.[29] From Table 3, we see that the selected model predicts negative earnings effects of the training program. The impact estimates vary among alternative specifications of the model, although the selected models lead to identical policy conclusions, namely that employment and training programs may not be the most effective way to improve the skills of workers who have lost their jobs.

There are various explanations for the estimated negative effects of training for the 1990 and 1991 samples. One explanation is that training is less effective than active job search. Another is that training signals low productivity and is used as a screening device by employers. It is also possible that participants enrolled in the program to become eligible for UI benefits after the program.[30] It is difficult to analyze these explanations. However, by using information on UI benefits, I can conduct at least two analyses of the potential explanation that some participants may have enrolled in training in order to collect UI benefits after the program. First, if some persons enrolled in training for the UI benefits, there should be a positive relationship between the training dummy and the UI

---

[28] Heckman and Hotz (1989) used data on a control group to construct such an additional test. They also compared the nonexperimental impact estimates with experimental impact estimates, which, given random assignment, amounts to the same thing. It is also evident from recent studies of the JTPA program that experimental data are crucial when analyzing the performance of various nonexperimental models (see, e.g. Heckman et al., 1998).

[29] Axelsson (1989) reports large positive effects of training based on a fixed-effect model.

[30] Naturally, it is also possible that the data lack information about important factors that affect program participation.

H. Regnér / Labour Economics 9 (2002) 187–206

Table 5
The relationship between training participation and UI benefits, and estimated training effects for members of a UI fund and nonmembers

Outcome measure and samples	Adult males 1989			Adult males 1990			Adult males 1991		
	Fixed-effect estimates	Random-growth estimates	Linear-control function estimates	Fixed-effect estimates	Random-growth estimates	Linear-control function estimates	Fixed-effect estimates	Random-growth estimates	Linear-control function estimates
1990	s=1987	s=1988, s−1=1987	*1990*						
(A) UI benefits	6.1 (2.1)	−3.9 (4.4)	5.5 (1.8)						
(B1) Members of a UI fund	−18.1 (6.1)	22.4 (12.1)	−8.8 (5.2)						
(B2) Nonmembers	−0.1 (8.6)	10.8 (14.8)	9.4 (7.0)						
1991			*1991*	s=1987	s=1989, s−1=1988	*1991*			
(A) UI benefits	4.2 (2.2)	−8.7 (6.0)	3.6 (1.9)	12.1 (2.1)	4.5 (3.8)	10.8 (2.0)			
(B1) Members of a UI fund	−13.0 (6.6)	40.1 (16.4)	−7.8 (6.0)	−29.5 (5.5)	−12.9 (10.4)	−15.5 (4.8)			
(B2) Nonmembers	−1.2 (8.9)	14.5 (20.2)	8.7 (7.6)	−4.5 (7.5)	−3.3 (13.1)	−4.4 (6.0)			
1992			*1992*	*1992*		*1992*	s=1988	s=1989, s−1=1988	*1992*
(A) UI benefits	2.7 (2.7)	−13.1 (7.6)	2.8 (2.5)	10.4 (2.3)	7.5 (4.9)	9.1 (2.1)	19.1 (2.3)	20.7 (4.1)	16.5 (2.2)
(B1) Members of a UI fund	−17.1 (6.9)	45.2 (24.2)	−7.8 (6.0)	−23.3 (5.9)	−3.7 (13.9)	−9.5 (5.0)	−25.0 (5.0)	−37.9 (12.2)	−13.3 (4.0)
(B2) Nonmembers	7.9 (9.3)	25.2 (25.6)	20.8 (7.6)	−6.9 (8.1)	2.7 (17.5)	−5.3 (6.4)	−22.4 (7.9)	10.4 (18.8)	−10.2 (6.4)

Estimated standard errors are in parentheses. Row A reports impact estimates of training on UI benefits. Rows B1 and B2 report impact estimates on earnings for members of a UI fund and nonmembers, respectively. Control function models include R1–R4. Fixed-effect and random-growth models include R1–R2.

benefits in the first postprogram year. The results reported in Table 5 (row A) show that there is a significant positive relationship between training participation and UI benefits for all samples except for the 1989 sample.

Second, if some persons enrolled in training to become eligible for a new period of UI benefits, impacts on earnings should be lower (less positive or more negative) for members of a UI fund than for nonmembers. The reason is that only persons who are members of a UI fund before entering the program can become eligible for another period of UI benefits by participating in the program. Table 5 (rows B1 and B2) shows that the estimated impacts of training are lower for UI fund members than for nonmembers, but because of large standard errors, few estimates are statistically significant and the results of the specification tests are ambiguous. Even so, the large differences in point estimates between the groups indicate that training effects might be lower for those with strong economic incentives to enroll in training than for other participants. In all, the results suggest that the institutional setting of Swedish labor market policy might explain the observed negative effects of the training program.

8. Concluding remarks

The results in this study show that the Heckman and Hotz (1989) testing strategy can help solve the problem of choosing among alternative nonexperimental models. The tests decisively reject the frequently applied fixed-effect model for three samples of adult males, but do not reject the random-growth model for two samples. Unfortunately, the estimated effect varies among different specifications of the random-growth model. This result suggests that either the sample sizes are too small, that better nonexperimental data might be required to solve the problem, or that we need experimental data to choose among nonexperimental estimators. However, a majority of the estimated training effects reported in this study are qualitatively consistent with one another. This suggests that it might be worthwhile addressing issues related to the quality of nonexperimental data before trying to persuade policy makers to agree on experimental evaluations.

Even though the results vary among alternative nonexperimental models, it is possible to argue that training had no, or even negative, effects 1 year after the program for adult males who participated in the early 1990s. The reason is that the models selected by the specification tests all suggest that training had no, or significantly negative, effects on earnings. One explanation for this result is that some training participants may have enrolled in the employment training program not for the purpose of making a human capital investment, but for the purpose of collecting unemployment insurance benefits after the program. This suggests that the well-known Swedish active labor market policy has in fact been rather passive.

Acknowledgements

I thank Anders Björklund, Robert Lalonde, Oddbjørn Raaum, Jeffrey Smith, and anonymous referees for helpful comments.

References

Ackum, S., 1991. Youth unemployment, labor market programs and subsequent earnings. Scandinavian Journal of Economics 93 (4), 531–543.

Albrecht, J., Edin, P.-A., Sundström, M., Vroman, S., 1999. Career interruptions and subsequent earnings. A reexamination using Swedish data. Journal of Human Resources 34 (2), 294–311.

Ashenfelter, O., 1978. Estimating the effect of training programs on earnings. Review of Economics and Statistics 60 (1), 47–57.

Ashenfelter, O., Card, D., 1985. Using the longitudinal structure of earnings to estimate the effects of training programs. Review of Economics and Statistics 67 (4), 648–660.

Axelsson, R., 1989. Svensk arbetsmarknadsutbildning en kvantitativ analys av dess effekter. Umeå Economic Studies, vol. 197. University of Umeå, Sweden.

Bassi, L., 1983. The effect of CETA on the post-program earnings of participants. Journal of Human Resources 18 (4), 539–556.

Bassi, L., 1984. Estimating the effect of training programs with non-random selection. Review of Economics and Statistics 66 (1), 36–43.

Barnow, B., 1987. The impact of CETA programs on earnings. Journal of Human Resources 22 (2), 157–193.

Barnow, B., Cain, G., Goldberger, A., 1980. Issues in the analysis of selectivity bias. Discussion paper #600-60, Institute for Research on Poverty, University of Wisconsin-Madison.

Björklund, A., Moffitt, R., 1987. The estimation of wage gains and welfare gains in self selection models. Review of Economics and Statistics 69 (1), 42–49.

Björklund, A., Regnér, H., 1996. Experimental evaluation of European labor market policy. In: Schmid, G., O'Reilly, J., Schömann, K. (Eds.), International Handbook of Labor Market Policy and Evaluation. Edward Elgar, Aldershot, UK.

Doolittle, F., Traeger, L., 1990. Implementing the National JTPA Study. Manpower Demonstration Research, New York, United States.

Edin, P.A., 1988. Individual consequences of plant closure. PhD dissertation, Department of Economics, Uppsala University.

Heckman, J., 1979. Sample selection bias as a specification error. Econometrica 47 (1), 153–161.

Heckman, J., Hotz, J., 1989. Choosing among alternative nonexperimental methods for estimating the impact of social programs: the case of manpower training. Journal of American Statistical Association 84 (408), 862–874.

Heckman, J., Robb, R., 1985. Alternative models for evaluating the impact of interventions. In: Heckman, J., Singer, B. (Eds.), Longitudinal Analysis of Labor Market Data. Cambridge Univ. Press, Cambridge.

Heckman, J., Smith, J., 1995. Assessing the case for social experiments. Journal of Economic Perspectives 9 (2), 85–110.

Heckman, J., Smith, J., 1999. The pre-programme dip and the determinants of participation in a social program: implications for simple program evaluation strategies. Economic Journal 109 (457), 313–348.

Heckman, J., Hotz, J., Dabos, M., 1987. Do we need experimental data to evaluate the impact of manpower training on earnings? Evaluation Review 11 (4), 395–427.

Heckman, J., Ichmura, H., Smith, J., Todd, P., 1998. Characterizing selection bias using experimental data. Econometrica 66 (5), 1017–1098.

Heckman, J., Lalonde, R., Smith, J., 1999. The economics and econometrics of active labor market programs. In: Ashenfelter, O., Card, D. (Eds.), Handbook of Labor Economics, vol. 3A. Elsevier, Amsterdam.

Jacobson, L., Lalonde, R., Sullivan, D., 1993. Earnings losses of displaced workers. American Economic Review 83 (4), 685–709.

Lalonde, R., 1986. Evaluating the econometric evaluations of training programs with experimental data. American Economic Review 76 (4), 604–620.

Lalonde, R., 1995. The promise of public sector-sponsored training programs. Journal of Economic Perspectives 9 (2), 149–168.

Layard, R., Nickell, S., Jackman, R., 1991. Unemployment: Macroeconomic Performance and the Labour Market. Oxford Univ. Press, Oxford.

206   *H. Regnér / Labour Economics 9 (2002) 187–206*

Raaum, O., Torp, H., 1997. Labour market training in Norway — effect on earnings. Report no. 46/97, Stiftelsen for samfunns-og næringslivsforskning, Oslo.

Regnér, H., 1993. Choosing among alternative nonexperimental models for estimating the impact of training; New Swedish evidence. Working Paper 8/1993, Swedish Institute for Social Research, Stockholm University.

Regnér, H., 1997. Training at the job and training for a new job: two Swedish studies. Dissertation series no. 29, Swedish Institute for Social Research, Stockholm University.

Westergaard-Nielsen, N., 1993. The effects of training — a fixed effect model. In: Jensen, K., Madsen, P.K. (Eds.), Measuring Labour Market Measures. Ministry of Labour, Copenhagen, Denmark.

[22]

ELSEVIER

Labour Economics 9 (2002) 433–450

www.elsevier.com/locate/econbase

The effect of training on search durations: a random effects approach

Anders Holm

Department of Sociology, University of Copenhagen, Linnégade 22, 1361 Copenhagen K, Denmark

Received 1 July 2000; received in revised form 1 August 2001; accepted 1 October 2001

Abstract

After 7 months of search for apprentice vacancies, Danish vocational students are offered training. The training program has two purposes. One is to assist students in their search for apprentice vacancies and the other is to give the students the possibility of completing their education through the training program rather than through an ordinary apprenticeship. Thus, the training program may attract both students with low as well as high transition rates into apprentice vacancies. Controlling for observed as well as unobserved heterogeneity is therefore important when estimating the effect of the program. Empirically, it turns out that when applying a traditional hazard model, the training program is seen to decrease the hazard rate to apprenticeship vacancies. However, when correcting for selection bias by jointly modelling the allocation process to training as well as hazard rates to apprentice vacancies by a random effect model, the training program is seen to increase hazard rates significantly. © 2002 Elsevier Science B.V. All rights reserved.

JEL classification: C41; I21; J64
Keywords: Hazard rates; Training; Unobserved heterogeneity

1. Introduction

We study the effect of a training program. The purpose of the training program is to assist vocational students in finding an apprentice vacancy and to offer the students an opportunity to complete the entire vocational education through the training program in case the student never finds an apprentice vacancy. The motivation for the analysis is an

---

E-mail address: anders.holm@sociology.ku.dk (A. Holm).

434   *A. Holm / Labour Economics 9 (2002) 433–450*

apparent paradox. The students who choose training seem to have, on average, lower transition rates to apprentice vacancies than those who reject training.

Assume that completing the vocational education through the training program is only a second-best solution in terms of future earnings compared to completing the vocational education through an ordinary apprenticeship. In this case, the decision to enter the program is a trade-off between a higher probability of completing the vocational education by entering the program and higher future earnings by completing the vocational education as an apprentice outside the program. We should then expect the students who enter the training program to possess relatively low transition rates into apprenticeships.

If the training program attracts students with lower abilities in terms of finding an apprentice vacancy, then an indicator variable for program participation in a simple hazard rate model to apprentice vacancies will capture both any true effects from the program, as well as the fact that students on the program have lower average abilities than students off the program. The combined empirical effect of the indicator variable in this case might thus be either positive or negative. However, if it is possible, conditional on observed regressors and unobserved explanatory variables to separately model the choice of training and the transition process to apprentice vacancies, then it is possible to estimate only the true program effect through the program indicator variable in the hazard rate model to apprentice vacancies. This is a standard result in the economic literature on training.

A substantial part of this literature is concerned with wage or employment per period effects of training (see e.g. Ashenfelter and Card, 1985; Lynch, 1992) but a number of papers study the effects of training on hazard rates, e.g. the seminal paper by Gritz (1993), but also papers by Mealli et al. (1996), Eberwein et al. (1997) and Bonnal et al. (1997).

However, irrespective of the type of response variable, the training literature is extensive (see the recent overview by Heckman et al., 1999). In this literature, the importance of the nature of the training program is stressed in terms of correcting for selection bias. Identification of the econometric model often happens through identifying assumptions on the expected difference on the response variable from participation in training versus nonparticipation. For instance, applying the popular difference-in-difference estimator requires an assumption of identical changes in means of the response variable from participation for both participants as well as nonparticipants.[1]

The duality of identifying restrictions is assumed on the effects of training on the response. The standard Heckman estimator, introduced in Heckman (1979), is only valid in the case of identical hypothetical effects of training on all individuals, both those actually entering the training program, as well as those who do not, had they entered. In case of individual effects of training, both, in terms of interaction effects between training and observed explanatory variables as well as interaction effects between training and

---

[1] This estimator requires at least repeated cross-section data. Unfortunately, this is not available for this study. Furthermore, we also have right-censoring, as our response variable is a duration. Even though there is a test of genuine training effects for duration data similar to the difference-in-difference estimator (see van den Berg, in press), this test requires variation in duration to training, which is also not available to this study. Hence, in this study, we must rely on cross-sectional estimators. However, as all students have identical search histories until entering the data, some simplification of the selection problems is achieved. Furthermore, this study illustrates what can be achieved with data that are typically available.

unobservables, this estimator will not correct for all selection bias. In this paper, we do test for whether there are such differences, and although it is stated in Heckman et al. (1999) that this test almost always concludes that there are individual effects, we find in this study that the null of no individual differences is accepted. This greatly simplifies both interpretation of the estimated effect of training and also how this effect should be estimated, as the standard Heckman estimator is now useful, however, translated into duration models.

In this paper, this is accomplished by including random effects in the hazard model as well as into the model for the choice of training. The random effects are allowed to be correlated. In formulating such a model, identification of the training effects relies on the functional forms and instrumental variables, i.e. variables that affect the probability of entering training, but not the hazard rate to apprentice vacancies. In this study, two such instrumental variables are available. The first instrumental variable is a binary indicator variable separating those regions where an admission test was enforced and where some students were subsequently denied access to the training program, and regions where the test was not enforced. Furthermore, another variable, whether the student has a voluntary 10th grade from lower secondary school, might be used as an instrumental variable. The reason for believing that the educational indicator variable is a credible instrumental variable is as follows: there is little reason to believe that the 10th grade (baseline) is of immediate relevance to employers in their choice of apprentices because all students searching for apprentice vacancies have graduated from their first year of vocational schooling on top of a potential 10th grade. However, according to the note on the 10th grade in Section 3, there is reason to believe that students with the 10th grade have a higher preference for training than other students.

Using the random effects model, we find a positive and significant effect of the training program. Therefore, it seems that the apparent negative effect of the training program, which has been found using a conventional hazard model, is due to selection bias and that once this has been accounted for, a positive effect of the training program appears.

The rest of the paper is organized as follows: Section 2 explains the training program and the context of the program in more details. In Section 3, we show and discuss the data set available for this study. In Section 4, we discuss why we should expect negative selection bias using conventional models and Section 5 presents a random effects model that takes into account selection bias, with results being discussed in Section 6. Finally, there are some concluding remarks in Section 7.

2. Vocational education and training

In order to understand the purposes of the training program, this section will briefly introduce the Danish vocational educational system as of the early 1990s.

More than half of a youth cohort choose vocational education as opposed to upper secondary school or no further education at all. Vocational education in Denmark consists of two parts. First, a publicly provided basic year of formal schooling and secondly, an apprenticeship period of 2 years. The students must find an apprentice vacancy them-selves. The apprentice period involves on-the-job training with a wage of approximately

436   *A. Holm / Labour Economics 9 (2002) 433–450*

half the minimum wage, which is also roughly equivalent to the youth social welfare benefit. Wages are the same in all apprenticeships. The apprentice period terminates with a final examination, and conditionally on passing this, the student has obtained his "degree".

As all students leave school on the same date, there tends to be a cluster of students searching for vacancies each year, when a new cohort starts searching. Adding to this number of 'new' students are, of course, students from previous cohorts who have not yet obtained an apprentice vacancy since the completion of their vocational education.

In 1990, the Danish Ministry of Education established a training program to assist students in finding apprentice vacancies. The program was offered to students who graduated from vocational school in June 1990 (22,254 students) and who had not found an apprentice vacancy by January 1991 (7917 students). Students still searching at this point in time were offered complementary training. This is the training program analyzed in this paper.

The program was established as a swift political agreement in the parliament and was not expected by the students searching for apprentice vacancies.[2] This is important in the context of this paper since there is then no need to consider strategic behavior of the students prior to entering the training program, such as deliberately delaying their search for apprentice vacancies to be able to enter the program.

The students can only be admitted to the program when it starts. Thus, students who reject training cannot change their minds regarding the program and enter later in the search process. Furthermore, the training centers were only to allow admission to the program after students had passed an eligibility test. Criteria for passing this test were identical for all schools. However, in most schools, this test was not enforced and in these schools, no students were denied admission. But in few regions, some schools did enforce the test and rejected a number of students. These students could not get admission to other training centers either. Therefore, there is a regional variation in the average type of students entering the training program. This variation in admission practices corresponds to an experimental design, which might improve the identification of the true effect of training (see e.g. Ham and Lalonde, 1991).

In order for the students to complete their vocational education through the training program, they must spend 2 years in the program. The students entering an apprenticeship from the training program have time spent on the program subtracted from the time they should otherwise have spent as an apprentice. Therefore, it takes 2 years for all students entering the training program to complete their vocational education.

If students on the program find an apprenticeship or are offered one through the employer network of the vocational schools, they must accept this vacancy and leave the program. This reflects the intention of the program to reduce time spent searching for ordinary apprenticeships. However, this restriction was not severely enforced and was also hard to administer for the schools. While on the program, the students have to follow a full-time training schedule and as compensation, they receive a grant equal to the wage paid in an ordinary apprenticeship.

---

[2] The time from when the program was announced and until students were introduced was less than 2 months.

A. Holm / Labour Economics 9 (2002) 433–450 437

The training program consists of workplace-like situations in the various fields in which vocational training takes place, e.g. carpentry, office work, salesmanship and various specializations in these fields. It also covers classes in both technically related material as well as more general material such as Danish literature, math, etc. The technical part is also an integrated part of an ordinary apprenticeship where for some short periods, the apprentice leaves the employer to follow classes. However, ordinary apprenticeships cover far less general material.

3. Data on students on and off training

In this section, we will look at the data available for this study. Data are generated by a survey conducted by The Institute of Local Government Studies-Denmark, in late 1991. The data are random samples of searching students who left the initial year of schooling in June 1990 and who were offered training in January 1991.

Out of 7917 students searching at that time, 1225 students were interviewed. After removing observations with missing values, 1205 observations were included in the data set. Of these, 701 entered training and 504 did not.

In Table 1, we show means and standard deviations in the data.

From the table, some differences between trainees and nontrainees show up. We see that, on average, students on the training program are younger and conduct their search for apprentice vacancies in areas with lower unemployment compared to those who reject training. But these differences in means are small.

There is a larger fraction of students on the program who have a voluntary 10th grade from secondary school,[3] denoted as 10th GRADE, compared to the nontrainees, but fewer with education beyond secondary school, FURTHER EDUCATION. Students on training have, on average, slightly lower grades, GRADE, from secondary school.

Admission to the training program is administered differently in different regions. This is measured by a binary indicator variable, REGION, taking the value of 1 in the regions where some students were denied admission, and 0 otherwise. For students on the program, 10% attended the initial vocational schooling and search in regions where schools have denied students admission to the program against 8% for students not in the training program. This difference in percentages seems at odds with what should be expected. However, schools that enforced the eligibility test were typically situated in regions with higher numbers of applicants.

About 24% of the students drop out of the program before finding an apprentice vacancy. This is indicated by a binary indicator variable, DROP, which takes the value of 1 for those who drop out of the program and 0 otherwise. In the data, there is information about how long it takes for drop outs to find an apprentice vacancy, but no information

---

[3] The voluntary 10th grade is a special feature of the Danish educational system and therefore deserves a comment. The 10th grade does not in itself lead to further qualifications, but is meant as an extra year in which students have more time to make choices on further education without leaving the educational system all together. We know that students with the 10th grade have weaker scholastic abilities than other students (Jensen et al., 1997) but perhaps, also a higher preference for schooling than other students.

Table 1
Summary statistics of the data

Variable	Mean	Standard deviation	Minimum	Maximum
Students off the training program				
DURATION (days)	407.8	77.45	228	806
Fraction censored	0.63	–	0	1
AGE (years)	19.8	3.65	17	54
UNEMPLOYMENT (%)	11	2.65	4.6	18
GRADE (0–13 scale)	7.9	0.84	5.8	10
REGION	0.08	–	0	1
9th GRADE or less	0.27	–	0	1
10th GRADE	0.59	–	0	1
FURTHER EDUCATION	0.14	–	0	1
NO GRADE	0.37	–	0	1
EMPLOYMENT	0.1	–	0	1
MALE	0.45	–	0	1
INDUSTRY	0.56	–	0	1
Students on the training program				
DURATION (days)	416.6	72.77	228	806
Fraction censored	0.70	–	0	1
AGE (years)	19.4	2.35	14	32
UNEMPLOYMENT (%)	10.9	2.35	4.5	17
GRADE (0–13 scale)	7.8	1.05	0.6	10.5
REGION	0.1	–	0	1
9th GRADE or less	0.24	–	0	1
10th GRADE	0.68	–	0	1
FURTHER EDUCATION	0.08	–	0	1
NO GRADE	0.38	–	0	1
EMPLOYMENT	0.01	–	0	1
MALE	0.44	–	0	1
DROP	0.24	–	0	1
INDUSTRY	0.56	–	0	1

about the time they leave the program. Therefore, in the following estimations, drop outs either have to be categorized as trainees or controls or have to be completely excluded from the analysis. In this analysis, we choose to include them in the group of students in the program. This is further discussed in footnote 15.

Training in manufacturing, building, and construction is separated from training in administration and business by a binary indicator variable, INDUSTRY, taking the value of 1 for business and administration and 0 otherwise. From the table, it is seen that there is no measurable difference between trainees and nontrainees by INDUSTRY.

Students holding an unskilled job when offered training is indicated with the binary indicator EMPLOYMENT.

From the table, we also see that a large fraction of students (70% of the trainees and 63% of the nontrainees) have right-censored spells. Among these spells, there will only be modest variation in spell lengths as the origin of all spells is identical, and all spells are sampled within a few months. Hence, the large fraction of right-censored spells is likely to inflate standard errors in a duration model estimated on this sample.

A. Holm / Labour Economics 9 (2002) 433–450   439

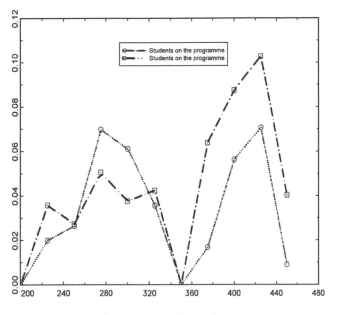

Fig. 1. Kaplan–Meier hazard rates.

In order to inspect hazard rates to apprentice vacancies for trainees and nontrainees, we show Kaplan–Meier estimates in Fig. 1 below.[4] One reference to Kaplan–Meier hazard rates is Lancaster (1990).

From the figure, we see that hazard rates on and off the program differ.[5] A likelihood ratio test for identical hazard rates has a p-value of 0.0002 (test statistic of 33.6 with 10 degrees of freedom). A likelihood ratio test for identical hazard rates until 340 days and different hazard rates thereafter, has a p-value of 0.192 (test statistic of 741 with 5 degrees of freedom). This implies that for the first 340 days of search, there is no significant difference between hazard rates on and off the program, but for more than 340 days, the hazard rate is lowest for students on the program. The sharp drop in the hazard rate for both trainees and nontrainees at 350 days reflects the fact that during the summer vacation, no matches are made between employers and students on apprenticeship contracts. The drop in the hazard rate towards the end of the sample period is probably the result of increasing competition for vacancies from a new cohort of searching students graduating the following year. This increases competition

---

[4] Although durations are measured in days, Kaplan–Meier hazard rates in Fig. 1 are based on grouped data in order to avoid insignificant scatter.

[5] Note also the large maximum value of search for both students on and off training in Table 1. This is because, although the survey was conducted during October and November 1991, some students returned questionnaires very late, and reported very long durations of search. However, because these few and very large values of duration are considered unreliable, all observations of more than 500 days (end of November 1991) are right-censored at this date in the following analysis. None of these observations reported a transition into an apprentice vacancy.

440   *A. Holm / Labour Economics 9 (2002) 433–450*

for apprentice vacancies among old and new entrants and thus decreases the probability of obtaining an apprentice vacancy for the cohort of the study. There are no data on the following cohort.

4. A search model approach

In this section, a search model is developed to explain why we should expect that students on the program have lower transition rate into apprentice vacancies compared to students outside the program.

For students accepting the training offer, there are two ways of completing their vocational education; either by finding an apprentice vacancy thus interrupting the training program, or simply by completing their vocational education through the training program, entirely replacing the apprenticeship period by training. Therefore, it takes 2 years, in the following denoted as $\tilde{t}$, for all students entering the training program to complete their vocational education. Thus, there is, by construction of the training program, no uncertainty of the duration until the completion of their vocational education for students accepting the training program. But there is uncertainty on whether it will involve time as an ordinary apprentice.

For students declining the training offer, duration until the completion of their vocational education now consists of time searching for an apprentice vacancy, t, and 2 years as an apprentice, $\tilde{t}$, amounting to a total time of $t + \tilde{t}$ until their vocational education is completed. Therefore, for students rejecting training, there is inherent uncertainty of the duration until the completion of the vocational education.

Let R_y, $y = 0,1$ denote the (expected) value of entering the labor market with a completed vocational education, i.e. both the first year of schooling and a completed apprenticeship period. Subscript 0 denotes entering the labor market without entering the training program and 1 denotes entering through the training program, and perhaps, also an ordinary apprenticeship.

Assume that agents have an infinite planning horizon so that search time for apprenticeship vacancies has no influence on the value of R_y, $y = 0,1$. Finally, let ρ denote an individual discount rate.

If for simplicity we denote the income (or utility) during search, training, or as an apprentice by a common factor[6] C, we can write the total income or utility of accepting training as

$$I_1 = \int_0^{\tilde{t}} C e^{-\rho t} dt + e^{-\rho \tilde{t}} R_1 = \frac{(1 - e^{-\rho \tilde{t}})}{\rho} C + e^{-\rho \tilde{t}} R_1, \tag{4.1}$$

where the first term of the last expression is the discounted value of income, while training and the last term is the discounted value of entering the labor market with a completed vocational education, completed through or partly through training.

---

[6] This is of course a simplifying assumption. But in many cases, it might be close to real labor market conditions as youth social benefit, student grants, and often, also wages for unskilled youth are not very different. Furthermore, relaxing this assumption will not affect the conclusion of this section.

A. Holm / Labour Economics 9 (2002) 433–450 441

Assuming that offers of apprentice vacancies are received according to an exponential distribution with rate λ, the expected income or utility from declining training when offered is then

$$I_0 = E\left(\int_0^{t+\tilde{t}} Ce^{-\rho s}\,ds + e^{-\rho(t+\tilde{t})}R_0 \right)$$

$$= \int_0^{\infty} \left[\frac{(1 - e^{-\rho(s+\tilde{t})})}{\rho} C + e^{-\rho(s+\tilde{t})}R_0 \right] \lambda \exp(-\lambda s)\,ds$$

$$= \frac{(\rho + \lambda) - \lambda e^{-\rho\tilde{t}}}{\rho(\rho + \lambda)} C + \frac{\lambda}{\rho + \lambda} e^{-\rho\tilde{t}} R_0, \qquad (4.2)$$

where the first term inside the bracket on the last line is the expected income while searching for (until t) and being an apprentice (from t to $\tilde{t}$), and the last term is the discounted value of entering the labor market with a completed vocational education, completed without training.[7]

If the student search outside training for an infinite period, he will receive a total discounted income of $\frac{C}{\rho}$. Eq. (4.2) implicitly assumes that the student will accept any apprentice vacancy if he receives an offer, and offers are identical by assumption.[8] Acceptance happens if the discounted total income from completing a vocational education is larger than discounted income from searching for an infinite period, i.e. $\frac{1 - e^{-\rho\tilde{t}}}{\rho}C + e^{-\rho\tilde{t}}R_0 > \frac{C}{\rho} \Rightarrow R_0 > \frac{C}{\rho}$.

From Eqs. (4.1) and (4.2), we also see that a necessary condition for any student to reject training is $R_0 > R_1$, i.e. lifetime income with a completed vocational education outside the training program must exceed lifetime income with a vocational education through, or partly through, the training program. This is because it takes more time to complete vocational education without training than with training. Hence, if $R_0 \leq R_1$, all students should enter the program. The reason why we should expect $R_0 > R_1$ is that some employers might use training as a negative screening device and thereby be more reluctant

---

[7] Note that if $\lambda \to \infty$, that is, if the students have extremely high arrival rates of vacancies or, putting it differently, almost certain of finding one immediately, $I_0 \to I_1$ except for potential differences between R_0 and R_1.

[8] If apprenticeship offers are heterogeneous, the observed hazard rate will be the product of an offer rate combined with an acceptance probability, as discussed in Mortensen (1986) for ordinary job-search models. We should definitely expect that jobholders outside the training program have lower acceptance probabilities than other students. Also, we could expect that students entering the program have higher acceptance probability than nonparticipants, as students entering the program have, in principle, to be prepared to accept any offered apprentice vacancy, once offered. As mentioned in Section 2, this was not enforced. However, students entering the program were informed that they had to accept any vacancy offered and are therefore more likely to have a higher acceptance probability.

As we have no data that allow us to empirically distinguish between acceptance probabilities and offer rates, we shall not pursue this discussion further here. But we should note that if observed hazards are lower for students on the program compared to students off the program, and the students on the program have higher acceptance probabilities, this leads us to believe that the differences in hazard rates reflect even larger differences in offer rates.

442   *A. Holm / Labour Economics 9 (2002) 433–450*

to hire students who have completed their vocational education through the training program. Anyhow, we know from the data that some students reject training, even students without any current employment.

In order to study the implications of Eqs. (4.1) and (4.2) for the allocation process to training, we will look at how students with different characteristics value training differently. Defining $\Delta I = I_1 - I_0$ and differentiating ΔI with respect to the arrival rate of apprentice vacancies, λ, we get

$$\frac{\partial \Delta I}{\partial \lambda} = -\frac{\partial I_0}{\partial \lambda} = e^{-\rho \tilde{t}} \frac{C - R_0 \rho}{(\rho + \lambda)^2}.$$

Applying the condition needed for apprenticeships to be attractive for students at all $\frac{C}{\rho} < R_0$, we get $\frac{\partial \Delta I}{\partial \lambda} < 0$. In words: the higher the arrival rate of apprentice vacancies, the relatively less attractive the training program will appear to the student. Students with high arrival rates of apprentice vacancies tend to reject training, whereas students with low arrival rates tend to accept training. Hence, this model predicts that the average duration of search for apprentice vacancies is shorter for students off training compared with students on the training program, because students with high arrival rates are, on average, off training. Conversely, students with low arrival rates are, on average, on the program.[9] Therefore, we expect students with characteristics associated with low arrival rates of apprentice vacancies to choose training. This makes it vital to control for all the important characteristics determining the arrival rates. If all these characteristics are not included in the data as explanatory variables, we will get a negatively biased estimate of the effect of training. Therefore, we will introduce a random effects model that will take into account possibly excluded covariates determining the hazard rate to an apprenticeship vacancy.

5. A hazard model with training

In this section, we shall outline an econometric hazard rate model that will allow for selection effects into the training program. Before training is offered, hazard rates are assumed to be captured by one model. After training is offered, hazard rates for those

---

[9] This theory does not explain how search behavior might be affected by participation. Assume there are set-up costs, e.g. habits, switching from the training program to an apprentice vacancy. We may then find that students are prepared to enter an apprentice vacancy if they have been in the training program for only a short duration because the time spent as an apprentice will be long enough to balance set-up cost, e.g. in terms of more specific training, but not if they have been in the program for longer durations where the training program is near its completion, and where time as an apprentice will be short. In this case, we expect search intensity for apprentice vacancies for trainees to decrease over time. This would lead to a corresponding decrease in the hazard rate for trainees compared to nontrainees. This was also what was seen in the Kaplan–Meier hazards in Fig. 1 in Section 3. However, as it will be seen in Section 6, hazard rates for nontrainees are higher for all durations, once observed heterogeneity is accounted for. Therefore, this discussion will not be pursued further.

students who reject the offer of training are still assumed to be captured by this model, whereas hazard rates for those who accept the offer of training are now assumed to be captured by an alternative hazard rate model. In the following, let y denote a binary indicator equal to 1 if the student accepts training and 0 otherwise. We define T as a variable measuring duration of search from leaving the initial year of vocational schooling.[10] The duration after leaving vocational school and until training is introduced as t^*. Note that t^* is fixed and has the same value for all students. We can now write the following hazard rates: $\theta_0(t|x,v;\beta) = \theta_0^0(t)\theta(x\beta)v$ for all t where $y = 0$ and $\theta_1(t|x,v;\beta) = \theta_1^0(t)\theta(x\beta)v$ for $T > t^*$ where $y = 1$ and where x is a row vector of time invariant explanatory variables and β is a vector of corresponding coefficients. Finally, v is a random effect capturing the effect of unobserved heterogeneity in the hazard rate model.[11]

From the hazard functions, we get survivor functions conditional on $T > t^*$:

$$P(T \geq t \mid T > t^*, Y = y, v) = \exp\left(-\left(\Lambda_y(t;v) - \Lambda_y(t^*;v)\right)\right)$$
$$= S_y(t \mid t^*; v),$$

for $y = 0,1$[12], with $\Lambda_y(t;v) = \int_0^t \theta_y(s;v)ds, y = 0,1$, being the integrated hazard function[13], also conditional on the random effect v and with the notation $\theta_y(t;v)$ meaning $\theta_y(t|x,v;\beta)$, $y = 0,1$.

To complete the selection model set up, we extend the allocation model to training by a random effect, u, to get

$$P(Y = y) = F(z\pi + u)^y(1 - F(z\pi + u))^{1-y} = G(y;z\pi + u),$$

for $y = 0,1$ with $F(\cdot)$ being the logistic distribution function, z is a vector of explanatory variables, and π is the corresponding vector of coefficients, and finally u is a random effect. The two random effects in the model, u,v, are correlated with joint density function $h(u,v)$.

---

[10] As opposed to the previous section where t denoted time from when the program was offered.

[11] However, according to the literature mentioned in Section 1 (e.g. Heckman et al., 1999), this set-up might not take into account all selection bias, not even in the presence of experimental data and plausible instrumental variables. If there are individual effects of training, and the students based their choice of training on the knowledge of this, including a multiplicative random effect in the model will not account for all selection bias. Therefore, we have, in preliminary modelling, allowed for interaction effects between random effects, explanatory variables, and the hazard baseline for both groups of students. However, as all these interactions turned out to be insignificant, we proceed by only allowing training to affect hazard rates through separate base lines.

[12] To see this, write:

$$P(T \geq t \mid T > t^*, Y = y) = \frac{P(T \geq t \mid Y = y)}{P(T \geq t^*)} = \frac{\exp\left(-\left(\int_0^{t^*} \theta_0(s;v)ds + \int_{t^*}^t \theta_y(s;v)ds\right)\right)}{\exp\left(-\int_0^{t^*} \theta_0(s;v)ds\right)}$$
$$= \exp\left(-\left(\Lambda_y(t;v) - \Lambda_y(t^*;v)\right)\right).$$

[13] The integrated hazard rate function captures the accumulated information of the hazard rate process, up to time t.

444   *A. Holm / Labour Economics 9 (2002) 433–450*

Identification of the effect of training in this model depends on functional forms of the model, as well as instrumental variables. This is discussed in Section 1.

Modelling unobserved heterogeneity is somewhat complicated by the fact that we do not observe students at the outset of their search spell, but only durations for students who have durations exceeding at least t^*. Thus, we are interested in finding $h(v,u \mid t > t^*)$. In Appendix A, we show that on the assumption of a proportional piecewise exponential hazard rate model, this is

$$h(u,v \mid t > t^*) = \frac{\exp(-\theta(\beta x)v)h(u,v)}{\displaystyle\int e^{-\theta(\beta x)v}h(v)\,\partial v},$$

where $h(\cdot)$ is the marginal density of v.

5.1. Parameterization

To allow for a very flexible baseline hazard, we adopt the piecewise exponential hazard framework for θ_y^0, $y=0,1$ that is θ_y^0 are constant within say $1,\ldots,H$ intervals, but may vary between intervals. We can write the integrated baseline hazard as

$$\Lambda_y^0(t) = \sum_{h=1}^{h=\kappa} \theta_{yh}^0 \Delta t_h + \theta_{y\kappa+1}^0 (t - t_\kappa),$$

where Δt_h is the length of the hth interval, θ_{yh}^0 is the baseline hazard in the hth interval, and κ is the number of the last interval for which the observation is observed completely and t_κ is the endpoint of the κth interval. This yields

$$\Lambda_y^0(t) - \Lambda_y^0(t^*) = \sum_{h=l}^{h=\kappa} \theta_{yh}^0 \Delta t_h + \theta_{y\kappa+1}^0 (t - t_\kappa) = \sum_{\tilde{h}=1}^{\tilde{h}=\tilde{\kappa}} \theta_{y\tilde{h}}^0 \Delta t_{\tilde{h}} + \theta_{y\tilde{\kappa}+1}^0 (t - t_{\tilde{\kappa}})$$

assuming that t^* is at the endpoint of Δt_l, and by rearranging according to $\tilde{h}=h-l-1$ and $\tilde{\kappa}=k-l-1$. Hence, we get

$$S_y(t \mid t^*;v) = \exp\left(-\theta(x\beta + v)\left(\sum_{\tilde{h}=1}^{\tilde{h}=\tilde{\kappa}} \theta_{y\tilde{h}}^0 \Delta t_{\tilde{h}} + \theta_{y\tilde{\kappa}+1}^0 (t - t_{\tilde{\kappa}})\right)\right).$$

As we have no information on the functional form of $h(\cdot,\cdot)$, a nonparametric discrete distribution is assumed following the work of Lindsay (1983), with past applications in econometric hazard models (see, e.g. Meyer, 1990; Gritz, 1993).[14] That is, we represent the

---

[14] Consistency of a nonparametric representation of an unknown distribution of heterogeneity in the case of a Weibull hazard rate model is shown by Heckman and Singer (1984).

A. Holm / Labour Economics 9 (2002) 433–450   445

unknown distribution of u,v by a nonparametric distribution with a finite number of points of support. Here, e_1 and e_2 represent a pair of discrete points of support with probability $p(e_1,e_2)$. To get the unconditional log-likelihood based on observed variables, t,y, given $T>t^*$, we must sum over all possible values of e_1,e_2, take logs, and sum over n observations (ignoring censoring for simplicity):

$$l^J = \sum_{i=1}^{n} \ln\left(\sum_{j=1}^{J} f_y\left(t_i \mid t^*,e_{1_j}\right) G\left(y_i; z_i\pi + e_{2_j}\right) p\left(e_{1_j}, e_{2_j} \mid T > t^*\right) \right) \qquad (5.1)$$

with $f_y(t \mid t^*,v) = \theta_y(t,v)S_y(t \mid t^*,v)$, $y = 0,1$. This is the log-likelihood from which parameter estimates will be obtained. It is conditional on the number of points of support, J. This number can be determined in the following way: let l_i^J be individual contributions to the log-likelihood using J mass points and define the following function $D = \sum_{i=1}^{n} [l_i^1/l_i^J - 1]$, where the upper part of the fraction is individual contributions to the log-likelihood using only one mass point in the model and the lower part is individual contributions to l_i^J using J mass points for the nonparametric representation of the unknown bivariate mixing distribution.

By a theorem of Lindsay (1983), the value of J yielding $D = 0$ provides an optimal mixing distribution in the sense that a mixing distribution including a higher number of mass points will not yield a higher value of the semi-parametric likelihood.

6. Results

In this section, we will present results from estimating the joint allocation and hazard rate model based on Eq. (5.1) in the previous section. We shall present two types of results. First, we shall present estimates using a conventional model ignoring the random effects. Secondly, we shall present results from estimation of the hazard rate model with random effects as described in the previous section. For this model, obtaining $D = 0$, two mass points were required. This indicates the presence of significant unobserved heterogeneity, and hence, potential selection bias. All results are reported in Table 2.

First, we offer a few comments on the logit models. It is striking that the two grade variables (GRADE and NO GRADE) change signs between the two estimated logit models. The reason for this reversed effect of grades on the allocation process to training could be explained as follows: assume that the negative effect in the model without random effects 2 is driven by a tail effect from students with very low grades on the program, as indicated by the descriptive statistics in Table 1. If these students also have low hazard rates to apprenticeships, it is possible that this correlation is captured by the random effect in the model allowing for these effects. In fact, as we shall see below, it turns out that there are some students with very high probability of entering the training program and very low hazard rates due to unobserved heterogeneity.

Table 2
Estimation results of the training model

Variable	No random effects		Random effects	
	Coefficient	Standard error	Coefficient	Standard error
Logit choice model[a]				
Constant	2.4597 **	0.8467	− 0.1132	0.4177
AGE	− 0.4342 **	0.2198	− 0.4880	0.2975
REGION	0.2693	0.2061	0.6255 *	0.3374
INDUSTRY	− 0.0106	0.0382	0.2398 *	0.1311
9th GRADE	− 0.3411	0.2311	− 0.7693 **	0.3548
FURTHER EDUCATION	− 0.5533 **	0.2117	− 0.4572 **	0.2315
GRADE	− 0.1548 **	0.0774	0.0411	0.0384
NO GRADE	− 1.0740	0.6496	0.1420	0.3274
Piecewise exponential duration model				
AGE	− 0.5657 **	0.2381	− 0.4960 **	0.2440
UNEMPLOYMENT	− 0.0350 *	0.0194	− 0.0405 **	0.0198
GRADE	0.2392 **	0.0739	0.2221 **	0.0760
NO GRADE	1.8198 **	0.5952	1.7182 **	0.6128
DROP	0.9506 **	0.1430	0.9110 **	0.1470
EMPLOYMENT	− 1.3279 **	0.4143	− 1.3222 **	0.4159
θ_{11}^0 (200–300 days)	− 2.9613 **	0.8181	− 2.9724 **	0.8249
θ_{12}^0 (301–400 days)	− 2.7733 **	0.8173	− 2.7586 **	0.8224
θ_{13}^0 (401– days)	− 2.0730 **	0.8157	− 2.0363 **	0.8212
θ_{01}^0 (200–300 days)	− 2.5838 **	0.8233	− 3.9262 **	0.9355
θ_{02}^0 (301–400 days)	− 2.2132 **	0.8232	− 3.5548 **	0.9346
θ_{03}^0 (401– days)	− 1.2298	0.8190	− 2.5716 **	0.9301
Bivariate mixture distribution				
e_{11}	–	–	0	
e_{12}	–	–	− 2.8971 **	1.0501
e_{21}	–	–	0	–
e_{22}	–	–	1.3983 **	0.4632
p_1	–	–	0.5741	–
p_2	–	–	0.4259 **	0.1035
Likelihood ratio tests	χ^2 (df)	*p*-value	χ^2 (df)	*p*-value
No regressors	97.7 (13)	0.000	104.4 (16)	0.000[b]
Identical baseline hazard rates	32.0 (3)	0.000	14.2 (3)	0.003
Identical regressors on and off training	8.76 (6)	0.188	15.2 (9)	0.086[c]
Proportionality of hazard rates	10.9 (12)	0.538	11.2 (12)	0.512

The * and ** denote significance at the 10% and 5% levels, respectively.

[a] The parameters reported in Table 2 for the logit model with random effects had been divided by the implicit estimate of the variance of the random effect in the logit model (see Pickles and Davies, 1989). This makes them comparable with the estimates reported for the logit model without random effects. Inference is unaffected by the scaling of the parameters.

[b] In this case, the test covers both exclusion of the observed regressors as well as the random effects.

[c] This includes testing for identical distribution of the random effects on as well as off training.

In terms of identification of the effects of training, the low significance of the variable REGION, capturing differences in program admission, is problematic as it was supposed to serve as an instrumental variable. However, the variables 9th GRADE and FURTHER EDUCATION are both significant at a 5% level in the logit model with random effects, but insignificant in the hazard rate model (and hence excluded from this part of the model). These variables also serve as instruments.[15]

We now turn to comment the results for the hazard rate model. The baseline hazard rates in the estimated models are constant in the following intervals, measured in days: (200–300), (301–400) and (401–).[16] Recall that the impact of the training program happens through the difference between the baseline hazards rates, $\theta_{1h}^0 - \theta_{0h}^0$, $h = 1,2,3$. As we have arrived at a final model where the explanatory variables have the same coefficients on as well as off training, we can write the relation between hazard rates on and off training as: $\theta_1(t_h \mid x,v) / \theta_0(t_h \mid x,v) = \exp(\theta_{1h}^0 - \theta_{0h}^0)$, where t_h belongs to the hth interval on the time scale.

By far, the most notable difference between the conventional model and the random effects model is that the negative program effect changes into a positive effect of the training program using the random effects model. The hazard rate on training is only between 43% and 68% of the level of the hazard rate off training, when estimated using the estimates from the conventional model,[17] whereas the baseline hazard rates off the program is only between 31% and 68% of the hazard rates on the program, using the estimates from the random effects model. This is seen from the third panel of Table 2: the baseline parameters for students off the program are larger than the corresponding parameters for students on the program, when looking at the conventional model, and vice versa, when looking at the model with random effects.

The difference between the baseline hazards on and off training is significant for both models. This is seen from likelihood ratio tests of uniform baselines. The test statistic for the conventional model has a p-value less than 0.000 and the similar p-value for the random effects model is 0.003. Note that it is mostly the baseline hazard rates for students off the program that has changed from the conventional model to the model with random effects. The interpretation of this could be that the bias in the estimates of the effect of the training program in the conventional model is more or less due to a fraction of students off the training program with very high hazard rates to vacancies, due to unobserved characteristics. Once the presence of these students has been accounted for through the random effects, we obtain comparable groups of students off and on training given observable characteristics. If this is the case, we should expect to find the largest changes in the hazard rates for students off training.

This interpretation is also supported by the discussion of the estimates of the random effects below where we find that the students with unobserved characteristics yielding a high probability of rejecting training also have unobserved characteristics associated with high hazard rates to apprentice vacancies.

---

[15] It is hard to test the exogenity assumption of educational indicators as there are not a lot of other potential instruments in the data. However, gender is a significant variable in explaining the choice of education, but is insignificant in both the allocation and hazard model, and hence, excluded in the models reported here. We have obtained predicted values of the educational indicators from a multinomial logit regression using gender as the only explanatory variable. We then performed a Wald test of exogeneity, using predicted values of the educational indicators against observed values in the logit model for allocation to training. This yielded a p-value of 0.147 (test statistic of 2.1 with 1 degree of freedom). Hence, exogeneity of the educational indicators is not rejected.

[16] Alternative intervals and adding more intervals did not improve the model fit significantly.

[17] A similar pattern was also found from the Kaplan–Meier estimates of Section 2, however, only for durations longer than 340 days.

Besides the changing effect of training, there are only minor changes in the estimates of the regression parameters reported in Table 2 between the model with and without random effects. However, note that the variable DROP, indicating students who have entered training but subsequently dropped out, has decreased in absolute value in the random effects model compared with the conventional model. This could indicate that DROP partly represents unobserved effects when used in the conventional model.[18]

The fourth panel of Table 2 reported the estimated discrete points of support and associated weights for the nonparametric distribution of unobserved heterogeneity.[19] From the table, we see that two mass points were sufficient to capture the significant features of the distribution of unobserved heterogeneity. As there are two mass points, we can speak of two main types of students observed with probabilities 0.426 and 0.574. We might denote them as types 1 and 2. Compared to type 1 students, type 2 students are more likely to accept training. This is indicated by $e_{22} > e_{21}$, which by the logistic function implies a higher probability of choosing training for type 2 students than for type 1 students. Moreover, it is also more difficult for type 2 students to find an apprenticeship, as $e_{12} < e_{11}$. This means that the hazard rate for type 2 students is lower than for type 1 students.

Finally, from the estimated mass points representing the random effects, we see that there is a negative correlation between the random effects terms in the model, because the largest value of the mass point in the hazard model corresponds to the smallest value in the allocation model and vice versa.

Summarizing, it seems that the apparent counterproductive effect of the program according to the conventional model reported in Table 2 is due to a nonrandom allocation of students to training. Students with the lowest unobserved qualifications in terms of finding an apprentice vacancy also have a higher probability of choosing the training program. Correcting for this feature, we find a significant positive effect of the program.

7. Conclusion

In this paper, we have analyzed hazard rates for students searching for an apprentice vacancy for the completion of their vocational education. As finding an apprentice vacancy is difficult for the students, a training program is offered to students searching for vacancies. The purpose of the training program is twofold. First, it is to assist

---

[18] Both the variables EMPLOYMENT and DROP could be considered endogenous, as they are the results of decisions related to the search process. They are included in the model because they have a significant impact on hazard rates and might prove valuable in disentangling unobserved heterogeneity. However, excluding them from the model does not change the qualitative conclusions of the model regarding the effects of training. Also, excluding the drop outs entirely from the analysis did not alter the qualitative conclusions of the analysis, i.e. a significant negative effect of the program when unobserved heterogeneity was not allowed for and a positive effect when this is allowed in the model.

[19] In order to obtain these, it must be taken into account that the log-likelihood is not necessarily concave. Therefore, different starting values for the parameters in the model have been tried until convergence to a global maximum of the log-likelihood function was achieved.

students in searching for an apprenticeship vacancy, and secondly, it gives them the opportunity of completing their vocational education altogether through the training program. The last purpose somewhat distorts the aggregated effect of the training program on hazard rates to apprentice vacancies. Just looking at Kaplan–Meier hazard rates, or the effect of training on hazard rates estimated through a conventional piecewise constant proportional hazard model, yields a picture where students on the training program in general have a lower hazard rate for obtaining an apprentice vacancy compared to students off the program. By invoking a random effects model to remove possible selection bias from allocation to training, we obtain a quite different picture. Now, we estimate a positive and significant effect of the training program on the hazard rate of finding an apprenticeship vacancy.

Acknowledgements

I wish to thank two anonymous referees and the editor Dan A. Black for many valuable comments and suggestions which have improved the paper. Finally, I would like to thank Gerard van den Berg for helpful comments on an earlier version of the paper.

Appendix A

In this appendix, we shall derive the joint density of random effects, u,v, under the assumption of a proportional piecewise exponential duration model, conditional on survival at least until t^*. First, we obtain the joint probability of survival until t^* and the two random effects

$$P(T > t^*, u, v) = P(T > t^* \mid v)h(u,v) = e^{-\Lambda_0(t^*)}h(u,v),$$

where $e^{-\Lambda_0(t^*)}$ is a shorthand notation for $e^{-\Lambda_0(t;v)}$. Using the last expression, we get the conditional density of u,v by dividing the above expression by the marginal probability of $T > t^*$. This is obtained by integrating out u,v from the joint probability above

$$h(u,v \mid T > t^*) = \frac{P(T > t^*, u, v)}{P(T > t^*)} = \frac{e^{-\Lambda_0(t^*)}h(u,v)}{\int\int e^{-\Lambda_0(t^*)}h(u,v)\partial v \partial u}$$

$$= \frac{e^{-\Lambda_0(t^*)}h(u,v)}{\int e^{-\Lambda_0(t^*)}h(v)\partial v} = \frac{\exp(-\theta(\beta x)\delta v)h(u,v)}{\int \exp(-\theta(\beta x)\delta v)h(v)\partial v},$$

where $\delta = \Lambda_1^0(t^*) = \sum_{h=1}^{h=l} \theta_{1h}^0 \Delta t_h$ (as t^* is at the end of Δt_l). Now

$$\frac{\partial h(u,v \mid T > t^*)}{\partial \delta} = 1; \forall \delta.$$

450   *A. Holm / Labour Economics 9 (2002) 433–450*

Hence, no parameters defining δ can be identified when only observing values of $T>t^*$. Hence, we normalize $\delta = 1$ and an expression of the density of the random effects conditional on survival until t^* is

$$\frac{\exp(-\theta(\beta x)v)h(u,v)}{\int \exp(-\theta(\beta x)v)h(v)\partial v}.$$

References

Ashenfelter, O., Card, D., 1985. Using the longitudinal structure of earnings to estimate the effect of training programs. Review of Economics and Statistics 67, 648–660.

Bonnal, L., Fougere, D., Serandon, A., 1997. Evaluating the impact of French employment policies on individual labour market histories. Review of Economic Studies 64, 683–713.

Eberwein, C., Ham, J.C., LaLonde, R.J., 1997. The impact of being offered and receiving classroom training on the employment histories of disadvantaged women: evidence from experimental data. Review of Economic Studies 64, 655–682.

Gritz, R.M., 1993. The impact of training on the frequency and duration of employment. Journal of Econometrics 57, 21–51.

Ham, J.C., Lalonde, R.J., 1991. Estimating the effect of training on employment and unemployment durations: evidence from experimental data. National Bureau of Economic Research Working Paper, 3912, 1–36. November.

Heckman, J., 1979. Self-selection as a specification error. Econometrica 47, 153–162.

Heckman, J., Singer, B., 1984. A method for minimizing the distributional assumptions in econometric models for duration data. Econometrica 52, 271–320.

Heckman, J.J., Lalonde, R.J., Smith, J.A., 1999. The economics and econometrics of active labor market programs. In: Ashenfelter, O., Card, D. (Eds.), Handbook of Labor Economics vol. 5A. Elsevier, Amsterdam, NL.

Jensen, T., Mogensen, K., Holm, A., 1997. Valg og veje i ungdomsuddannelserne. AKF Forlaget. AKF publishers, Copenhagen, (in Danish, with a summary in English).

Lancaster, T., 1990. The Econometric Analysis of Transitions Data. Cambridge Univ. Press, Cambridge, UK.

Lindsay, B.G., 1983. The geometry of mixture likelihoods: a general theory. The Annals of Statistics 11, 86–94.

Lynch, M.L., 1992. Private-sector training and the earnings of young workers. The American Economic Review 82, 299–312.

Mealli, F., Pudney, S., Thomas, J., 1996. Training duration and post-training outcomes: a duration-limited competing risk model. The Economic Journal 106, 422–433.

Meyer, B.D., 1990. Unemployment insurance and unemployment spells. Econometrica 58, 757–782.

Mortensen, D., 1986. Job search and labor market analysis. In: Ashenfelter, O., Layard, R. (Eds.), Handbook of Labor Economics, vol. 2. North-Holland, Amsterdam, NL, pp. 849–920.

Pickles, A.R., Davies, R.B., 1989. Inference from cross-sectional and longitudinal data for dynamic behavioural processes. In: Hauer, J. (Ed.), Urban Dynamics and Spatial Behaviour. Kluwer Academic Publishing, Amsterdam, NL, pp. 136–151.

van den Berg, G., et al., 2001. Duration models, specification, identification and multiple durations. In: Heckman, J.J., Leamer, E.E. (Eds.), Handbook of Econometrics, vol. 5A. Elsevier, Amsterdam, NL.

[23]

Jahrbücher f. Nationalökonomie u. Statistik (Lucius & Lucius, Stuttgart 1999) Bd. (Vol.) 219/1+2

Employment Effects of Publicly Financed Training Programs – The East German Experience

Beschäftigungseffekte von Fortbildungs- und Umschulungsmaßnahmen in Ostdeutschland

By Florian Kraus, Patrick Puhani* and Viktor Steiner, Mannheim

JEL J64, J68

Publicly financed training, evaluation studies, employment effects, sample selection, east Germany.

Fortbildungs- und Umschulungsprogramme, Evaluation, Beschäftigungseffekte, Stichprobenselektion, Ostdeutschland.

Summary

We analyze the effectiveness of publicly financed training and retraining programs in east Germany as measured by their effects on individual re-employment probabilities after training. These are estimated by discrete hazard rate models on the basis of individual-level panel data. We account for unobserved individual heterogeneity in both the training participation and outcome equation. The latter differentiates between transitions into "stable" and "unstable" employment after the completion of a training program. Our findings are that in the first phase of the east German transition process, when the institutions delivering the training programs were being set up, there are no positive effects of training on the probability to find stable employment. For the period of September 1992 to November 1994, when the institutional structure for the programs was in place, we find positive effects of both on-the-job and off-the-job training for women, and positive effects of off-the-job training for men.

Zusammenfassung

Die individuellen Beschäftigungseffekte öffentlich finanzierter Fortbildungs- und Umschulungsmaßnahmen (FuU) in Ostdeutschland werden mit Hilfe individueller Panel-Daten anhand diskreter Abgangsratenmodelle geschätzt. Für unbeobachtete individuelle Heterogenität wird sowohl in der Selektions- als auch in den Ergebnisgleichungen kontrolliert. Letztere unterscheiden zwischen Übergängen in „stabile" und „instabile" Beschäftigung nach Abschluß der FuU-Maß-

---

* Patrick Puhani is also a Research Affiliate at the Centre for Economic Policy Research (CEPR), London, UK, the Institute for the Study of Labor (IZA), Bonn, Germany, and a Research Fellow at The William Davidson Institute at the University of Michigan Business School, Ann Arbor, MI, U.S.A.

nahme. Es zeigt sich, daß während der Aufbauphase der FuU-Maßnahmen keine positiven Effekte auf die Wahrscheinlichkeit, eine stabile Beschäftigung zu finden, zu verzeichnen sind. Nach der Aufbauphase, d. h. für den Zeitraum September 1992 bis November 1994, werden positive Effekte sowohl inner- als auch außerbetrieblicher FuU-Maßnahmen für Frauen und positive Effekte außerbetrieblicher FuU-Maßnahmen für Männer geschätzt.

1. Introduction

Publicly financed training programs (PFTP) form an important part of "active" labor market policies in east Germany. Compared to west Germany and most other OECD countries, the number of participants in and expenditures on such programs have been very high. They peaked in 1992 when a yearly average stock of about 500,000 people participated in such programs. Subsequently, this number declined substantially and stabilized at a level of about 200,000 participants. Compared to west Germany, where about the same number of people participated in publicly financed training programs in the year 1996, this is still an astonishingly large number given the much smaller east German labor force. In 1996, average expenditures per participant were about DM 34,000 and total gross cost in that year amounted to almost DM 4,7 billions, which was only a little less than for west Germany. Net costs per trainee as calculated by the Federal Labor Office (*Bundesanstalt für Arbeit*) by deducting expenditures saved on unemployment benefits and contributions to the social security system were about DM 11,000; total net costs of PFTP in east Germany amounted to almost DM 2,3 billion in that year.

While PFTP are widely viewed as a prerequisite for preventing unemployment in east Germany to increase from its already high level, the effectiveness of these programs in improving individual re-employment prospects is surprisingly little discussed in the public policy debate. Evaluation of PFTP and other labor market programs is only in the beginning in Germany. Since experimental data which would allow identification of the average training effect with less arbitrary assumptions are generally not available in Germany, the few empirical studies have to rely on non-experimental data of modest size and informational content. These evaluation studies are based on two techniques. First, microeconometric models which try to take into account potential selectivity in program participation along the lines of Heckman and Robb (1985), Heckman and Hotz (1989). Second, the statistical matching approach associated with Rubin (1979) and Rosenbaum and Rubin (1983, 1985). For east Germany, these studies yield conflicting results concerning the employment effects of PFTP. It is not clear whether these differences derive from the particular methodology employed, the evaluation criteria used, or the different data sets and time periods analyzed.

By applying the microeconometric approach to evaluate the employment effects of PFTP in east Germany, we follow the traditional econometric literature. However, in contrast to previous research, we distinguish between "stable" and "unstable" employment after participation in PFTP, which we contrast with the employment prospects of an unemployed person not participating in training. In addition, by estimating the outcome models for PFTP participants and non-participants separately, and by testing for selection on unobservables without making a parametric distributional assumption on the joint distribution of the error terms in the PFTP participation and outcome equations, our econometric modelling approach is less restrictive than traditional econometric approaches. In the next section, we briefly describe the structure and development of PFTP in east Germany. Previous studies of the employment effects of PFTP in east Germany are surveyed in section 3. Our evaluation methodology is set out in section 4, and the data are described in section 5. In section 6 we present the estimation results, and section 7 concludes.

2. The Development and Structure of Publicly Financed Training Programs in East Germany

Publicly financed training is considered an important part of "active" labor market policy by the German government and the Federal Labor Office. After unification, PFTP have been extended tremendously to ease the east German transition process. In view of the dramatic employment decline in east Germany PFTP have not only been used as means of investing in partially obsolete human capital inherited from the socialist past, but also to keep people off the dole and to avoid social hardship associated with long-term unemployment (see Buttler and Emmerich 1994).

The scope of PFTP in east Germany is unique in both the national and international context (see, e.g. OECD 1993, 1997, Puhani and Steiner 1996). Figure 1 shows the development of participants in and expenditures on publicly financed training in east Germany after reunification.[1] In the first period of the transition process, PFTP were massively built up both in terms of expenditures and participants. At that time, the great majority of all participants were trained on a full-time basis. Thereafter, the government scaled the programs down until 1994, when quarterly expenditures on training as well as the number of participants stabilized. The recent reduction of public expenditures resulted in a marked reduction in the number of participants to about 150,000 by the end of 1997.

The legal basis for PFTP is the Work Support Act (*Arbeitsförderungsgesetz*, AFG). For east Germany, this law came into effect together with German Economic, Monetary, and Social Union on July 1st, 1990. However, there were, and there still are, some important special regulations that only refer to east Germany. Aside from the AFG, there are special regulations by the Federal Ministry of Labor and Social Affairs or the Board of Governors (*Verwaltungsrat*) of the Federal Labor Office (*Bundesanstalt für Arbeit*), especially the so-called "*Anordnung Fortbildung und Umschulung*" which was amended in 1993. The Federal Labor Office is hierarchically structured into regional and local labor offices. Within the rules set out in the AFG and the special accompanying regulations as well as the budget allocated to them, the local labor offices decide to whom a PFTP is offered.

In principle, this decision depends on whether training is considered "necessary" to reintegrate an unemployed person into work. However, in order to ease the transition process and to avoid the hardship associated with long-term unemployment, the rules were interpreted in a very flexible way in east Germany, so that virtually everybody hit or threatened by unemployment had a chance of receiving public support for training, at least during the first phase of the transition process. In practice, there are certain equity-driven criteria in the selection of participants in publicly financed training. In

---

[1] If not stated otherwise, the mentioned facts are taken from the official bulletin of the Federal Labor Office (Amtliche Nachrichten der Bundesanstalt für Arbeit), various issues.

Employment Effects of Publicly Financed Training Programs · 219

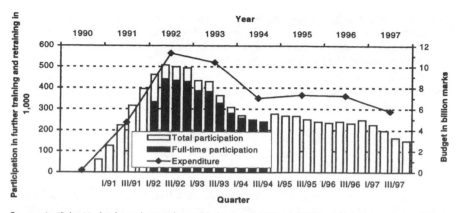

Source: Amtliche Nachrichten der Bundesanstalt für Arbeit (Official Bulletin of the Federal Labor Office); various issues.

Figure 1: Expenditures on and participants in PFTP (1990–1997)

particular, women, older and disabled workers are named as target groups for training to facilitate their transition into employment (Blaschke, Plath, and Nagel 1992).

There are clear incentives to join a training program once an offer is received from the labor office. First, the labor office has the right to suspend the payments of unemployment benefits if such an offer is rejected by the unemployed person. Second, the labor office offers a special allowance during training called *Unterhaltsgeld*. This allowance was 73 % (65 %) of previous net earnings for those with (without) children before December 1993 and equal to the respective income replacement ratio for the unemployed of 67 % (60 %) afterwards. In addition, the period this allowance is paid does not count into the eligibility period for unemployment benefits. Provided an individual fulfilled the criteria mentioned before, he or she was entitled to PFTP until December 1993, whereas the decision to offer training has become more discretionary on the side of the labor office since then.

In general, three types of PFTP can be distinguished: short training courses, continuous training in an old occupation, and retraining. Short training courses lasted up to six weeks and were dominated by courses which provided job search skills and information about work opportunities, or improve basic skills of the unemployed. For this type of PFTP, a completed vocational qualification or work experience was generally not required. These courses, which were disproportionately taken by women in the first phase of the transition process, were abolished in 1993, but several similar short-term courses which are taken by a relatively small number of people remain in effect. On the other hand, retraining and, especially, continuous training have become quantitatively more important during the transition process. While the shares of courses devoted to retraining in east Germany was almost 60 % in 1993, it declined to less than 40 % in 1996. Correspondingly, the share of courses offering continuous training increased to almost 60 % by 1996.

For retraining, the maximum duration of the course is normally two years and is completed with a publicly approved examination. About two thirds of all retraining courses effectively last between one and two years, while the great majority of all courses offering continuous training fall between 7 and 12 months (more than 60 % in 1996). These courses are limited to a maximum duration of one year unless they provide a publicly approved examination. Overall, the distribution of the duration of training courses changed considerably over time. While more than 40 % of all publicly financed training courses in 1991 lastet less than 4 months, and only about 18 % more than 12 months, these shares changed to, respectively, 16 % and 30 % in 1994 (Müller and Plicht 1997, Table 85).

The compostion of participants in PFTP also changed considerably during the transition process. The share of participants entering a PFTP from unemployment increased from 75.3 % in 1992 to 95.9 % 1994, while the share of formely long-term unemployed participants increased from 13.2 % to 34 % (Eichler and Lechner 1996, Table 3.8). Participation rates also differ by gender, age and education. As for gender, the higher participation rates of females correspond to their higher unemployment share of about 60 %. Normalizing participation rates by relative group size shows that a disproportionately large share of people without vocational qualification and younger people are participating in PFTP. As these differences already indicate, participation in PFTP is probably a highly selective process and this poses a difficult problem for the evaluation of the effectiveness of PFTP. There have been several attempts to overcome this problem in the evaluation studies for east Germany, to which we now turn.

3. Previous Empirical Studies for East Germany

There are several recent studies evaluating the employment effects of PFTP in east Germany, the main results of which we summarize in this section. These studies use non-experimental data and are based on either microeconometric models or the so-called statistical matching approach, or both. In the former approach the effect of participation in a PFTP on some outcome variable, like an individual's future unemployment probability, is modelled. Potential selectivity in PFTP participation is usually corrected using standard econometric methods along the lines of Heckman and Robb (1985) and Heckman and Hotz (1989). Studies based on the statistical matching approach associated with Rubin (1979) and Rosenbaum and Rubin (1983, 1985) try to overcome the fundamental selectivity problem by constructing a comparison group of non-participants with the same observable characteristics as the group of participants and then compare the average outcome variable. The data used in these studies either come from the Socio-Economic Panel for east Germany (GSOEP-east) or the Labor Market Monitor (LMM). The GSOEP is a widely used panel data set[2], the LMM which is also used in this study will be briefly described below.

The various studies also differ with respect to the observation period, the evaluation criteria used and the specification of the outcome variable. On the basis of a discrete-time hazard rate model estimated on the GSOEP-east, Pannenberg (1995) finds that participation in PFTP had no significant effect on the transition rate from unemployment in the first phase of the east German transition process (1990–1992), whereas in a subsequent study (Pannenberg, 1996) he finds a significantly positive effect for the

---

[2] Details on the GSOEP can be obtained from the webserver of the German Institute of Economic Research (DIW) in Berlin (http://www.diw-berlin.de/soep/).

period 1990 to 1994. In this latter study, the author also tests for selectivity bias in the outcome equation. On the basis of the pre-program test proposed by Heckman and Hotz (1989), the hypothesis that training participants and non-participants differ significantly in their employment chances before the training course cannot be rejected. Hence, it is not clear whether the positive correlation between this variable and the unemployment transition rate found in this study can be interpreted in a causal sense.

Potential selectivity bias is controlled for in the microeconometric studies by Fitzenberger and Prey (1996, 1997, 1998) on the basis of the LMM covering the period 1990 to 1994. Estimating differences in employment probabilities between participants and non-participants before and after participation in PFTP, these authors interpret their results as indicative for positive employment effects of PFTP provided outside the firm, whereas there seem to be no positive effects of publicly financed training if provided within the firm. That is, the positive employment effects of PFTP reported by these authors refer to a difference-in-difference interpretation in the sense that participants' employment probabilities relative to those for non-participants before PFTP were worse than after the program (for a similar approach see Heckman, Ichimura and Todd 1997, pp. 612 ff). On the basis of the LMM, Fitzenberger and Prey (1998) compare the employment effects of PFTP derived from a microeconometric model with those obtained from the statistical matching approach and conclude that they do differ, but due to the large confidence bands associated with the matching technique in relatively small samples, these differences are not statistically significant.

In contrast, applying statistical matching techniques, Lechner (1996) concludes on the basis of the GSOEP-east that there have been no significant positive average effects from PFTP on the employment probability of participants in the period 1990 to 1994. The difference to the results obtained by Fitzenberger and Prey may derive from Lechner's use of the GSOEP-east, which is considerably smaller than the LMM used by the former authors. Alternatively, it may also be related to the different application of the matching procedure by these authors. Lechner constructs the control group in such a way that its average employment probability before entrance into a PFTP is not statistically different from that of group of participants. In contrast, Fitzenberger and Prey allow for remaining differences in this probability between the two groups after matching and interpret them in the difference-in-difference sense referred to above.

Staat (1997) also uses the GSOEP-east but estimates effects of PFTP on the duration on unemployment on the basis of a hazard rate model. Instrumenting the training participation dummy in the hazard rate model to account for potential selectivity-bias, the author finds no statistically significant effects of PFTP on the duration of unemployment. The author also investigates whether training has an effect on the stability of employment found after the program and finds rather negative results. Overall, his results suggest that participants in PFTP are worse off than those who did not participate in such programs.

Finally, applying several popular estimation procedures, Hübler (1997a) shows on the basis of the LMM for the period 1993 to 1994 that the estimated effects of PFTP seem to be rather sensitive to the particular methodology employed. As in Fitzenberger and Prey (1996, 1997, 1998), the author also finds that participants' employment probabilities before PFTP were significantly lower than those of non-participants. Furthermore, effects of PFTP within one respectively two years differ, and these effects also differ by gender. Whereas employment prospects of men participating in PFTP improve within two periods, there seems to be a negative employment effect for females associated with an increased transition rate out-of-the-labor-force. Hence, it seems important to account for gender differences when evaluating the employment effects of PFTP.

The diversity of the existing studies makes it difficult to trace back the different results on special features of any study. Nevertheless, the analyzes using the LMM, all find some positive effects of the east German training measures (Hübler 1997a, Fitzenberger and Prey 1996, 1997, 1998). The fact that Lechner (1996) finds no significant employment effects of PFTP could be related to his use of the GSOEP-east, because the relatively small number of observations available in this data set makes the identification of any significant effects based on the statistical matching approach difficult. In contrast, using the same data set but a microeconometric model, which yields more efficient, if possibly inconsistent estimates, could explain the positive employment effect of PFTP reported by Pannenberg (1996). However, this conflicts with the results obtained by Staat (1997) on the basis of the same data set and a similar econometric approach.

In the following, we present our own study of the employment effects of PFTP which is based on a microeconometric model estimated on data from the LMM. As described in the next section, the model differs in various aspects from those used in the studies reviewed above.

4. Evaluation Methodology

In order to evaluate the employment effects of PFTP one needs to define an appropriate observable outcome variable, specify how PFTP might affect this variable and account for other observable and unobservable factors which may affect the outcome variable aside from training. Our methodological approach differs from previous studies with respect to the definition of the outcome variable, in that we explicitly distinguish between different forms of employment after the completion of a training course. As the most important criterion for the public evaluation of PFTP in east Germany is its potential to increase the future re-employment probability of formerly unemployed people, we compare the re-employment chances of trainees with the counterfactual outcome had they remained unemployed instead of entering a training course. This focus differs from other studies reviewed in section 3, which do not restrict the comparison group to the unemployed. A particularly difficult problem arises from the potential selectivity of participation in PFTP, i.e., its dependence on similar factors which also determine the outcome variable. In the following, we propose a new approach to overcome this problem.

4.1. Treatment of Selection Bias

The essence of the sample selection problem is that participants in PFTP may differ from the non-participants, who act as the comparison group, in both observed and unobserved characteristics. If this potential selectivity-bias is not taken into account, one is likely to obtain biased estimates of the employment effects of training programmes. The standard econometric solution to this problem is to correct for potential selectivity-bias in the outcome equation on the basis of a training participation equation estimated for the combined sample of participants and non-participants in training. More formally, we can write the outcome and participation equations as

$$Y^*_{ijt} = X'_{it}\beta_j + \delta_j D_{it} + u_{it}$$

$$D^*_{it} = Z'_{it}\gamma + v_{it}$$

Y^*_{ijt} is the latent index which defines the outcome variable of interest for individual i. In our context, this outcome is the hazard rate from either unemployment or training into labor force state j, i.e., the conditional probability to leave unemployment (training) for that state in time period t, given the individual has been unemployed (in a PFTP) until time t. The second equation refers to the selection into training, where D^*_{it} is the latent index which determines the transition from unemployment into training at time t for individual i. Selection bias can arise through a correlation between u and Z (selection on observables), or through a correlation between u and v (selection on unobservables).

As for the *selection on observables*, it can be treated by the linear control function estimator (see, for example, Heckman and Hotz 1989). The idea here is to assume that the conditional expection of u given X and Z is linear in Z. In this case, including the Z variables in the outcome equation controls for selection on observables.[3] To account for *selection on unobserables*, we assume the following error-components specification for the outcome and selection (training participation) equations

$$u_{it} = \varepsilon_i + \eta_{it}$$

and

$$v_{it} = \mu_i + \xi_{it}$$

ε_i and μ_i are time-invariant individual effects with expectations $E(\varepsilon_i) = E(\mu_i) = 0$, and variances $E[(\varepsilon_i)^2] = \sigma^2_\varepsilon$ and $E[(\mu_i)^2] = \sigma^2_\mu$. η_{it} and ξ_{it} are identically and independently distributed error terms which vary both with time and across individuals, with $E(\eta_{it}) = E(\xi_{it}) = 0$, and variances $E[(\eta_{it})^2] = \sigma^2_\eta$ and $E[(\xi_{it})^2] = \sigma^2_\xi$. Furthermore, we assume that error components in each equation are uncorrelated with each other and that the time-varying component is serially uncorrelated.

If we impose the restriction that the covariance between u_{it} and v_{is} is constant for all t and s, it can be shown that the correlation between the error terms in the PFTP participation and the respective outcome equation has a rather small upper-bound (see the appendix). In particular, in the case where we have no unobserved individual heterogeneity in both the participation and outcome equations, this bound is given by $1/T$ where T is the total number of intervals (months) observed. In our application $T = 50$ months, which implies an upper bound for the correlation coefficient of 0.02. In the appendix we also show numerically that the correlation between u and v becomes negligible if there is no unobserved heterogeneity in either of the two equations.

---

[3] To condition on observable factors (or some function of them) is also the basis for the statistical matching approach. In principle, this approach can be extended to account for certain types of unobservables as well (see *Heckman, Ichimura* and *Todd* 1997).

As we show below on the basis of the estimated heterogeneity components in the outcome and the PFTP participation equations, the effects of unobserved heterogeneity are in fact negligible in our application. Hence, it seems safe to ignore unobserved heterogeneity in the estimation of the employment effects of PFTP and control for selectivity by including the same observed variables as in the participation equation in the outcome equation.

4.2. Specification of the Outcome and Participation Equations

We specify our outcome and participation equations as duration models.[4] Compared to most of the studies summarized in section 3 this has the great advantage that both the time spent in a PFTP and the time between its completion and the beginning of a subsequent employment spell are considered in the estimation. Thus, both calendar-time effects and process-time effects ("duration dependence") can be taken into account in the comparison of future employment outcomes of PFTP participants and previously unemployed non-participants. As Ham and LaLonde (1996) stress, this may be important in order to effectively control for selectivity bias if the outcome variable relates to the duration of (un-)employment. Because the duration data are only observed in monthly intervals in the LMM we specify discrete hazard rate model to account for the large number of ties.

The hazard rate for transitions from unemployment or training into labor force state j in discrete time t is the probability (Pr) of exit into state j at time t conditional on the event that the person has remained in unemployment (training) up to time $t - 1$. In our application, the j exit states are training, employment, and other labor force states in the PFTP *participation model* and "stable" employment, "unstable" employment, and non-employment in the *outcome models*. The definition of the exit state space differs between the participation and outcome models. In the participation model, we specify the transition rate from unemployment into PFTP with employment and other labor force states as the remaining exit states. Other labor force states include short-time work, retirement, unemployment, and out-of-the-labor-force.

The distinction between the exit states in the outcome models is intended to capture the effect of training on the stability of the subsequent employment spell to some extent, given the relatively short observation period. These states are defined as

- *stable employment*: the person finds *regular* employment and is still employed in the twelfth month after the PFTP or training spell ended. Regular employment does not include short-time work, public works or vocational training.
- *unstable employment*: the person finds a regular job during the twelve months after the end of the spell but leaves it before the end of the twelve-months' period.
- *non-employment*: the person is not regularly employed for even one month during the twelve-months' period after the spell ended, where employment in PFTP and public works programs are also included in this category.

If the person is still in training or unemployment at the end of the observation period, or if the employment status is missing at least for one out of the twelve months for any reason, spells in the outcome models are treated as *right-censored* in the estimation.

---

[4] For similar applications see *Ridder* (1986), *Gritz* (1993), *Ham* and *LaLonde* (1996), *Hujer, Maurer* and *Wellner* (1997a, 1997b), and *Staat* (1997).

Note that there is a given "risk period" of 12 months for each observation starting immediately after the end of the training (unemployment) spell. This is a very important condition for comparability of the outcome variable, which is often not observed in evaluation studies based on comparisons of outcomes at particular points in time, as is the case for pure panel studies. Our definition of stable employment takes into account that, due to the well-known length-bias in stock-sampling, someone who is employed at a particular point in time is likely to be observed in the middle of a relatively long employment spell (see also Winter-Ebmer and Zweimüller 1996). Hence, an interrupted employment spell of, say, six months at the end of the risk period of twelve months is to be interpreted differently with respect to an individual's employment stability compared to a completed six-month employment spell, i.e. non-employment at the end of the risk period.

Of course, we cannot tell whether an employment spell is really stable because we do not observe the employment history of the people in our sample after November 1994. However, our classification procedure at least assures that those who find employment within the first twelve months after their training or unemployment spell, but lose their job before the twelfth month, are correctly identified as not having gained stable employment within the risk period. Indeed, using the likelihood ratio test for equality of two states in the multinomial logit model proposed by Cramer and Ridder (1991), we found that stable and unstable employment according to our classification are in fact two distinct categories.

For the PFTP participation and outcome models, the hazard rate is formally defined as

$$\lambda_{jk}(t \mid x_{it}, \varepsilon_{im}) = \Pr[T_{ik} = t, J = j \mid T_{ik} > t - 1, x_{it}, \varepsilon_{im}]$$

where k denotes the kth spell in unemployment or training, j denotes the jth exit state, ε captures unobserved individual heterogeneity, which has a distribution with m mass-points, and x_{it} is a time varying vector of observed covariates. Note that there can be more than one unemployment or training spell per person, and these spells are correlated due to the heterogeneity term. The distribution of ε is specified non-parametrically with the restrictions

$$E[\varepsilon_i] = \sum\nolimits_{m=1}^{M} \Pr(\varepsilon_{im})\varepsilon_{im} = 0, \text{ and } \sum\nolimits_{m=1}^{M} \Pr(\varepsilon_{im}) = 1,$$

where M is the number of discrete mass-points necessary to account for unobserved heterogeneity in the sample (see, e.g., Heckman and Singer 1984). It is assumed that ε is orthogonal to the time-varying covariates x_{it}.

The hazard rate in the kth spell in unemployment or PFTP into state j at time t is specified as

$$\lambda_{jk}(t \mid x_{it}, \varepsilon_{im}) = \frac{\exp(a_{jt} + \beta_j' x_{it} + \varepsilon_{im})}{1 + \sum_{l=1}^{J} \exp(a_{lt} + \beta_l' x_{it} + \varepsilon_{im})},$$

where a_{jt} are process time dummy variables specifying a non-parametric baseline hazard. Assuming the spells of different persons are independent, the likelihood function for the sample is given by

$$L = \prod_{i=1}^{n} \sum_{m=1}^{M} \Pr(\varepsilon_{im}) \prod_{k=1}^{K_i} \prod_{j=1}^{J} [\lambda_{jk}(t_i \mid x_{it}, \varepsilon_{im})]^{\delta_{ikj}} \prod_{\tau=1}^{t_i-1} (1 - \lambda_k(\tau \mid x_{i\tau}, \varepsilon_{im}))$$

where δ_{ijk} equals one if the kth spell of individual i ends in state j at time t, and zero otherwise.

We estimate a participation model for the transition from unemployment into training and two outcome models. The first outcome model refers to the transition of trainees into stable employment and other labor force states, respectively. The second outcome model refers to the transition of unemployed non-trainees into stable employment and other labor force states. By estimating the outcome models for the group of participants and the group of non-participants separately, we allow the coefficients of all explanatory variables to differ between the two groups.[5]

4.3. Cumulated Transition Probabilities

We define the employment effect of PFTP as the difference of the cumulated transition probability *(ctp)* into employment within the first 12 months after the end of training and unemployment, respectively. Formally, the cumulated transition probability after t months is defined as

$$ctp_j(t) = \sum_{\tau=1}^{t} S(\tau \mid x_{i\tau})\lambda_j(\tau \mid x_{i\tau}),$$

with

$$S(t \mid x_{i1} \ldots x_{it_i-1}) = \sum_{m=1}^{M} \Pr(\varepsilon_{im}) \prod_{\tau=1}^{t-1} (1 - \lambda(\tau \mid x_{i\tau}, \varepsilon_{im}))$$

and

$$\lambda_j(t \mid x_{it_i}) = \frac{\sum_{m=1}^{M} \Pr(\varepsilon_{im}) \times \lambda_j(t_i \mid x_{it_i}, \varepsilon_{im}) \times \prod_{\tau=1}^{t-1} (1 - \lambda(\tau \mid x_{i\tau}, \varepsilon_{im}))}{S_i(t \mid x_{i1} \ldots x_{it-1})},$$

where S denotes the survivor function and λ_j is the transition rate into state j in discrete time τ. The survivor function gives the probability of still remaining in unemployed (training) after t months. The 12-months' *ctp* into stable employment of person i thus is the probability that person i has found stable employment within the first 12 months after the beginning of the training or unemployment. The 12-months' *ctp* for the transition into unstable employment and non-employment have an analogous interpretation.

The definition of the *ctp* explicitly takes into account the time someone has spent in training and thus allows one to directly compare the outcome of a PFTP and an unemployment spell. Given the distribution of the duration of PFTP and the length of the observation period available to define a common risk-period (see section 4.2), it seems sensible to define the *ctp* for a period of 12 months. Since the great majority of all training spells end within this 12-months' period, we also take into account that a

---

[5] This is equivalent to estimating the model jointly for trainees and non-trainees with all explanatory variables interacted with the training dummy.

PFTP is typically not terminated prematurely even if a job offer would become available during the course.

For each person, S and λ can be derived given parameter estimates from the discrete hazard rate models described above. The simulated *ctp* for both groups can then be obtained by plugging the x_t-variables of the trainees into the outcome model for the unemployed non-trainees. This gives the 12-months' *ctp* for the trainees had they not received training. Given that our controls for observed and unobserved characteristics effectively remove all differences other than training between the two groups, the difference in the distribution of the *ctp* between trainees and the simulated distribution had the trainees stayed unemployed can be interpreted as the causal employment effect of training.

5. Data and Variables

The Labor Market Monitor (*Arbeitsmarktmonitor*, LMM) of the Institute of Labor Market Research (*IAB*) of the German Federal Labor Office is a representative panel survey of the east German working-age population. The panel contains eight waves. They refer to the months of November 1990, March 1991, July 1991, November 1991, May 1992, November 1992, November 1993, and November 1994. In the first wave about 0.1 percent of the working-age population or 10,751 persons had been interviewed. Extra samples were added to the original sample in waves 5 and 6. All of these persons were interviewed in each wave following their admission into the sample, except they died, moved to west Germany or refused finally to answer.[6] Nevertheless, the sample size shrunk down to 5,377 in wave 8 (November 1994).

The LMM contains information on socio-economic characteristics like age and education, participation in all ALMP measures, and the employment status. From the first wave onwards the interviewees were asked when they participated in training measures and whether they received a training allowance (*Unterhaltsgeld*) from the labor office. From this information we constructed spells on the labor force state with monthly information. The spells were constructed for the period of January 1989 to November 1994. The following table shows the distribution of exits from unemployment and training. The exit state in the training participation model refers to the employment state in the first month after the transition from the unemployment state. For the outcome models, the exit state are defined as described in section 4.2.

The same set of control variables is included in both the participation and the outcome models. Aside from personal characteristics they include firm size, industry and regional dummies, indicators of an individual's previous employment history, and income variables. Definitions and means of these variables are given in Tables A1 and A2 of the appendix. In case of the unemployment benefit variables, the unemployed usually give the amount of benefit they receive at the date of interview. The replacement ratio is estimated by dividing the amount of unemployment benefit by the estimated wage. This estimated wage is obtained from an empirical wage equation which is not reported here, but available from the authors upon request. All amounts are in 1990 real Deutsche Marks.

---

[6] A general introduction to the LMM is provided by *Hübler* (1997b).

Table 1: Target labor force states in the participation and outcome (unemployment and training) models

exit into	participation model spells	participation model percent	unemployment model spells	unemployment model percent	training model spells	training model percent
stable employment	–	–	518	16.73	604	34.63
employment (full- or part-time)	818	23.35	–	–	–	–
training	553	15.79	–	–	–	–
other labor force states	703	20.06	–	–	–	–
unstable employment	–	–	151	4.88	79	4.53
non-employment	–	–	724	23.39	241	13.82
right censored	1,429	40.79	1,702	54.99	820	47.02
total	3,503	100.00	3,095	100.00	1,744	100.00

Source: LMM; own calculations.

We split the observation period into two subperiods, viz. January 1989 to August 1992, and September 1992 to November 1994, respectively. The reason for this split is the fact that in the first period training measures were just being set up in east Germany, and there were many complaints about the bad quality of the training programs at that time. In particular, the courses were quite general and did not really focus on the specific needs of the trainees (see section 2). This changed in the second period, when the institutional structure of the training programs became settled. This development obviously suggests that a structural break may have occurred between the two periods.

We control for differences in on-the-job and off-the-job training by including a dummy variable for off-the-job training. As can be seen from Table A1, about two-thirds of training participants in our sample were trained off the job. Since we already distinguish between two subperiods as well as between men and women, it does not seem feasible to estimate the equations separately for on-the-job and off-the-job trainees.

6. Estimation Results

6.1. Sample Selectivity

We test for potential selectivity-bias due to the presence of unobserved heterogeneity by comparing the maximum likelihood value between models with a different number of mass-points for the heterogeneity component in both the participation and outcome equations. In addition, we use the Akaike Information Criterium (AIC). The values of (minus two-times) the natural logarithms of the log likelihood (LnLik) and the AIC from our estimated hazard rate models (see Tables A3 and A4 in the appendix) are given in the following table.[7]

---

[7] This transformation of the maximum log-likelihood forms the basis of the standard likelihood-ratio test. For the null hypothesis of no unobserved heterogeneity, the likelihood ratio statistic violates standard regularity conditions and its distribution is therefore not known (see, e.g., Gritz 1993). AIC is defined as $AIC = LnLik - k$, where k is the number of parameters in the model. The decision rule is to take the model with the highest AIC (see, e.g., Greene 1997, p. 401).

Table 2: Tests for unobserved heterogeneity in the PFTP participation and outcome models

unobserved heterogeneity	training model		unemployment model		participation model	
	− 2LnLik	AIC	− 2LnLik	AIC	−2LnLik	AIC
0 mass-points	7398.23	−3806.12	11733.90	−6015.95	15206.95	−7953.57
2 mass-points	7391.82	−3804.91	11727.02	−6014.51	15203.31	−7955.03
3 mass-points	7391.82	−3806.91	11727.02	−6016.51	−	−

Source: Estimated hazard rate models (see Tables A3 and A4 in the appendix).

According to the AIC, we have two heterogeneity mass points in both the training and unemployment model. However, as Table 3 shows, the estimated heterogeneity components are not significantly different from zero in both models. Indeed, $\Pr(\varepsilon_1)$ is not significantly different from zero, and $\Pr(\varepsilon_2)$ is not significantly different from one.

These constellations for the ε-values and the $\Pr(\varepsilon)$ estimates indicate that the unobserved heterogeneity component is superfluous, and the comparison of the likelihoods indeed showed only negligible differences in the parameter estimates between the models with and without unobserved heterogeneity. Based on these results, we decided to choose the models without unobserved heterogeneity. Furthermore, no unobserved heterogeneity could be detected in the participation model. Hence, in accordance with the discussion above, we assume that, after conditioning on the set of observable explanatory variables in the participation model, we do not face a severe selectivity selection problem in our estimations.

6.2. Participation in Training

For the sake of brevity, detailed estimation results from the participation equation are not reported in this paper but are available from the authors upon request. Here, we just summarize some of the most important estimation results. It is a general result that only few variables are significant in the participation estimation. This confirms the view that, given a few qualifications, the training programs did not have a very strong target group orientation in east Germany. People over 50 years of age have very low chances of receiving training, which makes sense for efficiency if not equity reasons. There are, however, slight differences between the first and the second period. In the first period, both men and women under 35, but especially those under 25, had higher chances of receiving training than people between 36 and 50. In the second period, there is no difference between these age groups. As to the impact of occupational qualification on training participation, there are differences between men and women. Whereas men with a university degree have better chances of getting into a public training program than men with lower, occupational degrees, the occupational qualification plays hardly any role for women. An exception is that women without any qualification have low chances to get into training in the first period, but the coefficient becomes insignificant in the second period. A further interesting observation is that people with previous training spells have high chances to receive further training if they become unemployed again. This is a common finding for countries where ALMPs are also used as a social policy instrument (OECD 1997). This observation casts doubt on the efficient use of these programs.

230 · F. Kraus, P. Puhani and V. Steiner

Table 3: Estimates of the heterogeneity components for the outcome models with two mass-points

| | training model | | unemployment model | |
	estimate	t-value	estimate	t-value
ε_1	− 0.0005	− 0.0901	− 0.0008	0.0060
ε_2	0.0004	0.0016	0.0007	0.0000
$Pr(\varepsilon_1)$	0.4433	1.3683	0.4539	0.0109
$Pr(\varepsilon_2) = 1 - Pr(\varepsilon_1)$	0.5567	1.7186	0.5461	0.0131

Source: Estimated hazard rate models (see Tables A3 and A4 in the appendix).

As can be seen from Figure 2, most formerly unemployed participants of PFTP in east Germany are selected into the program between their sixth and twelfth month in unemployment. This suggests that training programs do have some targeting focus in east Germany, namely on the long-term unemployed. Alternatively, the increase in the transition rates after six, and to a lesser extent also after nine months, in the second period could be related to the exhaustion of unemployment benefits. Although the transition rates differ only slightly for men and women in the first period, women clearly are more likely to get into training in the second period. This is unsurprising, as the female share in unemployment increased and it was considered politically opportune to expand their share in PFTP accordingly.

6.3. Employment Effects

Estimation results for our hazard rate models are given in Tables A3 and A4 in the appendix. In order to improve on the efficiency of the estimation, we reduced the number of parameters by excluding all variables with associated t-values of less than 1.64 in a first-round estimation. The reported results are the second-round estimates. All explanatory variables are included as interactions with a dummy for gender and a time-

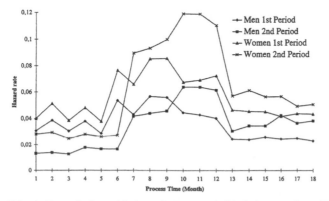

Source: Estimated hazard rate models; hazard rates are calculated at mean values of the explanatory variables for the respectives sub-groups; see text.

Figure 2: Hazard rates from unemployment into PFTP

period dummy, and there is no global constant in the model. In essence, this specification almost amounts to estimating the models separately for all four groups. We have, however, specified a common baseline hazard in the outcome models in order to keep the number of estimated coefficients at a reasonable level, given the number of available observations. In the following, we discuss the effects of training on the probabilities to find stable employment or to become non-employed subsequently to the training course. Because of the small number of observations on exits into unstable employment (*cf.* Table 1), we prefer not to interpret the results referring to this state.

As for the effects of training on the chances to regain stable employment, Figure 3 plots the distributions of the cumulated 12-months' transition probability (*ctp*) into stable employment for both men and women in both the first and the second period. All these cumulated transition probabilities were calculated on the basis of the group of formerly unemployed trainees, and are thus directly comparable (see our discussion in section 4.3).

For the first period, the figure shows that both men and women were better off staying on the dole than participating in PFTP. This is especially true for men and holds irre-

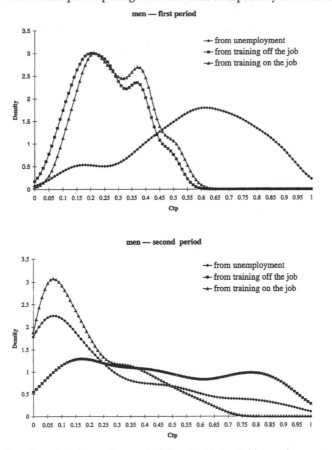

Figure 3a: Cumulated transition probability (*ctp*) into stable employment (Kernel density estimates)

232 · F. Kraus, P. Puhani and V. Steiner

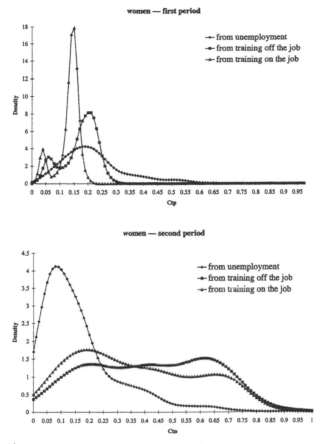

Figure 3b

spective of whether training occurred on-the-job or off-the-job. Hence, our estimation results confirm the widespread belief that PFTP were not very effective in their introduction period. Things changed in the second period, where in terms of re-employment opportunities both men and women were better off in training than in unemployment. However, men are only better off in training off-the-job, whereas both off-the-job and on-the-job training show positive employment effects for women.

Overall, the evidence on the effectiveness of PFTP to bring participants back into the first labor market is mixed for men, with clear signs of improvements in the second period for women. This conclusion is somewhat modified if the effect of training on the hazard rate into non-employment is also taken into account. Even if PFTP were ineffective in getting people directly back to work, they still may have positive effects if they keep participants searching for work and prevent them from dropping out-of-the-labor-force. As Figure 4 shows, this is clearly the case for both men and women in both periods as far as transitions into non-employment relate to transitions out-of-the-labor-force and not, say, into public works programs. One explanation for this finding

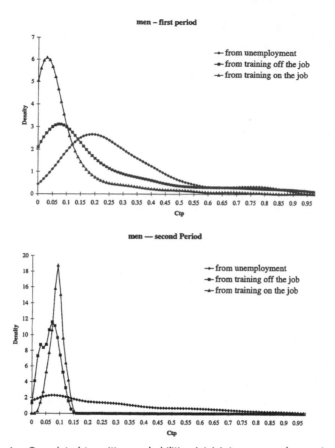

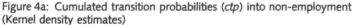

Figure 4a: Cumulated transition probabilities (*ctp*) into non-employment (Kernel density estimates)

is that a PFTP could renew the entitlement to unemployment benefits and thus create strong incentives to stay on the register longer than non-participants. Hence, it seems difficult to evaluate the efficiency of PFTP on the basis of the participants' lower hazard rate out-of-the-labor-force.

So far, we have compared the marginal distributions of the *ctps* of trainees with their counterfactual distribution had they stayed unemployed without training. The three-dimensional graphs of Figure 5 show the distribution of winners and losers from participating in PFTP, where the plots have to be interpreted in the following way. Take a point on the unemployment axis, say 0.2. If you slice the mountain at that point parallel to the training axis, you get the conditional distribution of the *ctps* into stable employment after training for the unemployed who would have had a *ctp* of 0.2 without training. Obviously, if the mountain were just a diagonal slice from the north-west to the south-east of the cube, then training would have no effect whatsoever.

For women in the first period, we see that irrespective of the *ctp* in unemployment, the great mass of *ctps* from training is concentrated around 0.2 to 0.3. Hence, in the first period

234 · F. Kraus, P. Puhani and V. Steiner

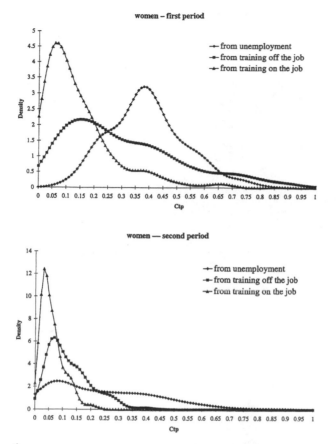

Figure 4b

training seems to have made female trainees more equal in terms of their employment prospects than they were before. As a we have seen above, the overall employment effect was negative, though. In the case of men in the first period, the picture looks qualitatively similar, although the distribution of the *ctps* is more dispersed here. In the second period, the situation is more complicated. Overall, around 80 percent of all women lie right of the diagonal in the area where training has led to an improvement in employment prospects. For men, about 50 percent of all cases seem to be better off through training.

7. Summary and Conclusions

Previous research on the employment effects of publicly financed training and retraining programs (PFTP) in east Germany has yielded mixed results. To some extent, this can be related to the use of different data sources and methodological approaches. Following the microeconometric approach to the evaluation of the employment effects of these programs, we have estimated hazard rate models taking into account the exact

men – first period

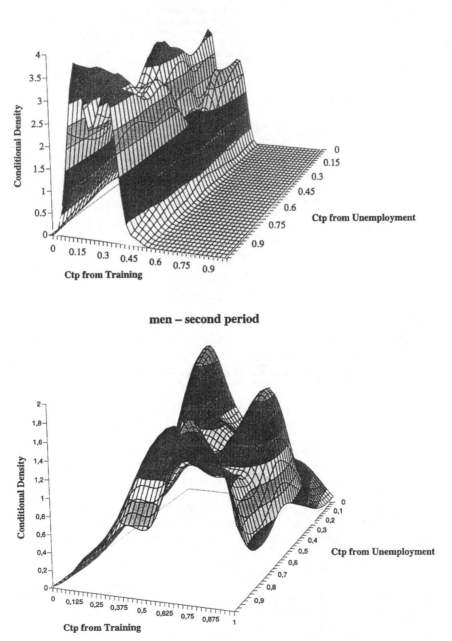

men – second period

Figure 5a: Distributions of cumulated transition probability (*ctp*) into stable employment from training conditional on ctp from unemployment (Kernel density estimates)

women – first period

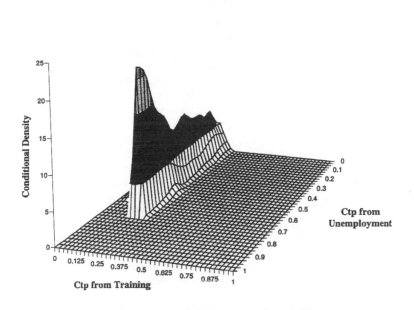

women – second period

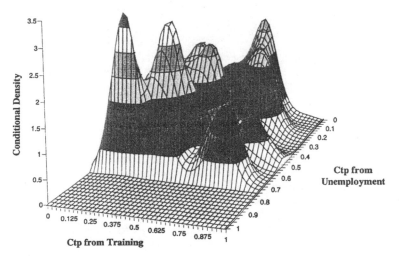

Figure 5b

timing of events and distinguished between stable and unstable employment subsequently to participation in a PFTP. The employment effects of PFTP are estimated separately for men and women and for two subperiods on the basis of the Labor Market Monitor covering the period 1990 to 1994. We have accounted for selection bias by controlling for a fairly large number of observable characteristics and also allowing for unobserved heterogeneity in both the outcome and participation equations. In all estimated equations, unobserved heterogeneity seems to be of little quantitative importance. Given this result, we show that the correlation between the error terms in the participation and outcome equations is rather small. This implies that, after controlling for a large number of observable characteristics in the outcome equations, selectivity-bias is likely to be negligible in our application.

In accordance with most previous research, we do find positive employment effects of PFTP in east Germany. However, these effects differ both by gender and between the first and second time period. For the first period, we find that staying unemployed increased the chances of finding stable employment relative to participating in PFTP. At that time, an infrastructure for effective training programs was not yet in place, and a large share of PFTP consisted of courses of very short duration offering only basic job counselling information. In the second period, when the institutional structure of the training programs was in place, both on-the-job and off-the-job training increased the probability of finding stable employment. For both men and women, there is also some evidence that PFTP have kept participants searching for work and prevented them dropping out-of-the-labor-force in both periods.

Although our results show at least for some groups positive employment effects, they do not imply that the unemployed population as a whole would have been worse off without this system of large-scale PFTP. It may well be that trainees have displaced other workers not offered training by the labor office. Furthermore, there are substantial net fiscal costs per trainee, which are financed through social security contributions, thus increasing labor costs and potentially reducing the demand for labor. Although potentially important for the overall evaluation of PFTP, such macro effects could not be taken into account in our evaluation of the microeconomic effects of these programs.

Acknowledgement

Financial support from the German Science Foundation (DFG) under the project "Arbeitsmarktdynamik im ostdeutschen Transformationsprozess" is gratefully acknowledged. We thank Herbert S. Buscher, Hermann Buslei, François Laisney, Friedhelm Pfeiffer, Elke Wolf and the participants of the University of Munich Economic Faculty Seminar for helpful comments.

In addition, we are grateful to the session participants at the Econometric Society European Meeting in Berlin 1998, the European Economic Association Annual Meeting in Berlin 1998, the European Association of Labour Economists Annual meeting in Blankenberge 1998, the *Verein für Socialpolitik* (German Economic Association) Annual Meeting in Rostock 1998, and our discussant Charles Brown, University of Michigan, for helpful comments at the Econometric Society Winter Meeting in New York City 1999. Moreover, we thank an anonymous referee for helpful suggestions.

We also thank Avo Schönbohm, Anja Triebe and Kathrin Gresser for excellent research assistance. Any remaining errors are our own responsibility.

Appendix

Derivation of an Upper Bound for the Correlation of the Errors in the Participation and Outcome Equations

In section 4.2, we have specified the error terms in the outcome and participation equation as

$$u_{it} = \varepsilon_i + \eta_{it}$$

and

$$v_{it} = \mu_i + \xi_{it}$$

where the error terms are distributed as specified in the text. From this specification it follows that

$$\mathrm{cov}[u_{it}, u_{is}] = \mathrm{cov}[\varepsilon_i + \eta_{it}, \varepsilon_i + \eta_{is}] = E[(\varepsilon_i + \eta_{it})(\varepsilon_i + \eta_{is})] - E[\varepsilon_i + \eta_{it}]E[\varepsilon_i + \eta_{is}]$$

$$= E[\varepsilon_i\varepsilon_i + \varepsilon_i\eta_{it} + \varepsilon_i\eta_{is} + \eta_{it}\eta_{is}] - 0 = E[\varepsilon_i\varepsilon_i] = \sigma_\varepsilon^2 = \text{constant} \quad \forall t \neq s,$$

and, analogously,

$$\mathrm{cov}[v_{it}, v_{is}] = \sigma_\mu^2 = \text{constant} \quad \forall t \neq s.$$

Imposing the restriction

$$\mathrm{cov}[u_{it}, v_{is}] = \mathrm{cov}_{u,v} = \text{constant} \quad \forall t,s,$$

we get the following correlation matrix of the residuals

$$\mathrm{Corr}_{u,v} = \begin{bmatrix}
1 & \rho_\varepsilon & \cdots & \rho_\varepsilon & & & & \\
\rho_\varepsilon & 1 & & \rho_\varepsilon & & \rho_{u,v} & & \\
\vdots & & \ddots & \vdots & & & & \\
\rho_\varepsilon & \rho_\varepsilon & \cdots & 1 & & & & \\
& & & & 1 & \rho_\mu & \cdots & \rho_\mu \\
& & & & \rho_\mu & 1 & & \rho_\mu \\
& \rho_{\mu,v} & & & \vdots & & \ddots & \vdots \\
& & & & \rho_\mu & \rho_\mu & \cdots & 1
\end{bmatrix}$$

with $\rho_\varepsilon = \sigma_\varepsilon^2/\sigma_u^2$, $\rho_\mu = \sigma_\mu^2/\sigma_v^2$, and $\rho_{u,v} = \mathrm{cov}_{u,v}/(\sigma_u \times \sigma_v)$.

For $\rho_\varepsilon = \rho_\mu = 0$, the eigenvalues of this matrix are $2(T-1)$ times 1, $1 + T\rho_{uv}$, and $1 - T\rho_{uv}$. Because this matrix has to be positive definite, all eigenvalues have to be positive. From $1 + T\rho_{uv} > 0$ and $1 - T\rho_{uv} > 0$, it follows that $(1 + T\rho_{uv})(1 - T\rho_{uv}) = 1 - T^2 \rho_{uv}^2 > 0$ implying $1/T > | \rho_{uv} |$. Thus, in the case of no unobserved heterogeneity in both the participation and the outcome equation, $1/T$ is the upper bound for ρ_{uv}. If there is unobserved heterogeneity in either equation, that upper bound for ρ_{uv} can

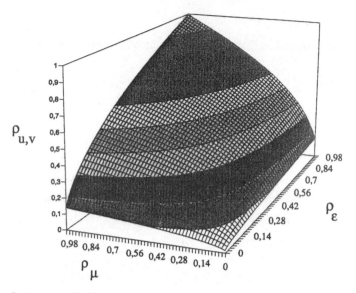

Source: own calculations.

Figure A: Upper bound for the correlation between u and v for $T = 50$

be found numerically by increasing ρ_ε and ρ_μ in the correlation matrix until it is no longer positive definite.

Figure A shows the result of this calculation for the upper bound of ρ_{uv}. As the plot shows, for either ρ_ε or ρ_μ equal to zero the upper bound for the correlation between u and v becomes very small.

Table A1: Descriptive statistics for the training model

Variable	Men 1st period	Men 2nd period	Women 1st period	Women 2nd period
age $<=25$	0.21	0.11	0.14	0.11
$25 <$ age $<= 35$	0.27	0.26	0.32	0.34
age > 50	0.10	0.15	0.12	0.13
married	0.67	0.70	0.72	0.72
with children	0.55	0.78	0.70	0.88
no vocational training	0.03	0.03	0.03	0.04
semi-skilled worker	0.03	0.02	0.02	0.01
master craftsman/technician	0.09	0.10	0.04	0.04
vocational college	0.20	0.17	0.19	0.28
university degree	0.20	0.28	0.10	0.14
20–200 employees	0.05	0.11	0.04	0.12
200–2000 employees	0.13	0.09	0.05	0.07
more than 2000 employees	0.04	0.03	0.06	0.02
primary sector	0.03	0.03	0.01	0.02

continued ./.

240 · F. Kraus, P. Puhani and V. Steiner

Table A1: Descriptive statistics for the training model (ctd.)

Variable	Men 1st period	Men 2nd period	Women 1st period	Women 2nd period
construction industry	0.04	0.03	0.01	0.01
tertiary sector	0.09	0.17	0.04	0.22
public employee	0.06	0.10	0.05	0.16
training off the job	0.72	0.72	0.83	0.74
Mecklenburg-Vorpommern	0.16	0.14	0.13	0.12
Brandenburg	0.13	0.14	0.11	0.16
Sachsen-Anhalt	0.14	0.18	0.19	0.15
Thüringen	0.17	0.14	0.22	0.15
Berlin (East)	0.09	0.07	0.07	0.09
previously in short-time work	0.32	0.08	0.26	0.06
previously in unemployment	0.25	0.17	0.48	0.34
previously out of the labor force	0.05	0.08	0.05	0.09
previous duration in short-time work	2.68	0.72	2.02	0.62
previous duration in employment	5.25	16.70	2.49	12.57
previous duration in unemployment	1.05	1.23	2.55	2.88
previous duration out of labor force	0.34	0.48	0.20	0.75
entry in the first quarter of a year	0.39	0.20	0.33	0.20
entry in the second quarter of a year	0.27	0.26	0.29	0.25
entry in the third quarter of a year	0.24	0.26	0.21	0.32
current quarter is the first of the year	0.20	0.18	0.18	0.18
current quarter is the second of the year	0.34	0.23	0.42	0.17
current quarter is the third of the year	0.26	0.14	0.22	0.18
current year is 1992	0.41	0.12	0.48	0.12
public income maintenance/ expected earnings	0.66	0.71	0.66	0.77
public income maintenance (in DEM)	911.53	1197.28	635.69	913.27
unemployment rate	7.38	9.10	14.65	19.26
month in process time, first period				
month 3–6	0.39	0	0.39	0
month 7–9	0.19	0	0.16	0
month > = 10	0.17	0	0.19	0
month in process time, second period				
month 2	0	0.10	0	0.07
month 3	0	0.07	0	0.05
month 4	0	0.05	0	0.05
month 5–6	0	0.06	0	0.07
month 7	0	0.08	0	0.11
month 8–9	0	0.05	0	0.07
month 10–12	0	0.06	0	0.07
month 13–15	0	0.07	0	0.12
month > = 16	0	0.23	0	0.28
mean duration	5.82	9.27	5.87	11.53
(subsample size/sample size) × 100	24.23	12.84	35.55	27.39

Note: Variables indicating durations are given in months, unemployment rates are given in percent.
Source: LMM, waves 1–8; own calculations.

Table A2: Descriptive statistics for the unemployment model

Variable	Men 1st period	Men 2nd period	Women 1st period	Women 2nd period
age < = 25	0.15	0.11	0.13	0.08
25 < age < = 35	0.26	0.20	0.32	0.25
age > 50	0.27	0.29	0.21	0.28
married	0.62	0.61	0.74	0.75
with children	0.52	0.46	0.69	0.61
no vocational training	0.05	0.07	0.09	0.10
semi-skilled worker	0.09	0.06	0.05	0.06
master craftsman/technician	0.11	0.12	0.03	0.04
vocational college	0.16	0.14	0.16	0.14
university degree	0.12	0.18	0.05	0.07
20–200 employees	0.20	0.29	0.20	0.24
200–2000 employees	0.17	0.16	0.15	0.16
more than 2000 employees	0.06	0.04	0.05	0.04
primary sector	0.10	0.10	0.07	0.07
construction industry	0.07	0.10	0.02	0.02
tertiary sector	0.17	0.23	0.28	0.34
public employee	0.17	0.14	0.16	0.19
previously not in employment	0.47	0.34	0.49	0.39
Mecklenburg-Vorpommern	0.14	0.13	0.14	0.12
Brandenburg	0.18	0.16	0.14	0.16
Sachsen-Anhalt	0.18	0.16	0.16	0.17
Thüringen	0.17	0.17	0.18	0.16
Berlin (East)	0.06	0.11	0.08	0.05
previously in short-time work	0.18	0.10	0.18	0.15
previously in job creation measure	0.02	0.12	0.01	0.08
previously in retraining or further training	0.05	0.11	0.09	0.23
previously out of the labor force	0.06	0.09	0.15	0.10
previous duration in short-time work	1.84	1.17	1.80	1.96
previous duration in employment	8.36	10.08	7.31	8.30
previous duration in job creation measurement	0.10	1.40	0.07	1.10
previous duration in retraining or further training	0.25	1.40	0.42	2.75
previous duration out of the labor force	0.47	1.03	1.31	1.10
entry in the first quarter of a year	0.25	0.14	0.26	0.15
entry in the second quarter of a year	0.18	0.25	0.22	0.31
entry in the third quarter of a year	0.33	0.33	0.30	0.29
current quarter is the first of the year	0.24	0.10	0.25	0.07
current quarter is the second of the year	0.17	0.19	0.20	0.18
current quarter is the third of the year	0.29	0.10	0.29	0.08
current year is 1992	0.22	0.28	0.33	0.22
unemployment benefits/ expected earnings	0.39	0.60	0.44	0.64
unemployment benefits (in DEM)	466.68	718.00	411.87	599.06
unemployment rate	6.73	9.18	13.25	19.33

continued ./.

242 · F. Kraus, P. Puhani and V. Steiner

Table A2: Descriptive statistics for the unemployment model (ctd.)

Variable	Men 1st period	Men 2nd period	Women 1st period	Women 2nd period
month in process time, first period				
month 2	0.13	0	0.12	0
month 3	0.16	0	0.11	0
month 4	0.09	0	0.09	0
month 5	0.10	0	0.10	0
month 6	0.08	0	0.08	0
month 7	0.04	0	0.07	0
month 8–9	0.07	0	0.09	0
month 10–12	0.07	0	0.08	0
month > = 13	0.05	0	0.08	0
month in process time, second period				
month 7–9	0	0.18	0	0.19
month 10–12	0	0.14	0	0.12
month 13–18	0	0.13	0	0.15
month > = 19	0	0.10	0	0.21
mean duration	4.55	8.67	5.54	11.70
(subsample size/sample size) × 100	24.23	12.84	35.55	27.39

Note: Variables indicating durations are given in months, unemployment rates are given in percent.
Source: LMM, waves 1–8; own calculations.

Table A3: Training model: exit into stable employment and into non-employment

	Exit into stable employment		Exit into non-employment	
	coeff.	t-value	coeff.	t-value
men, first period				
constant	−3.8910	−10.04	−5.5161	−4.24
age < = 25			−2.2000	−2.60
age > 50			1.2181	2.35
married	0.8506	2.67	−1.1640	−2.57
with children	−0.3673*	−1.82		
master craftsman/technician			1.4404	2.45
training off the job			1.2048	2.27
Mecklenburg-Vorpommern	−0.7429*	−1.81		
Thüringen	−0.6533*	−1.78		
previously in short-time work			2.2029	4.38
current year is 1992			−0.5008	−1.16
public income maintenance	0.3057	0.84	−0.0006	−0.92
unemployment rate			0.0911	0.91

continued ./.

Table A3: Training model: exit into stable employment and into non-employment (ctd.)

	Exit into stable employment		Exit into non-employment	
	coeff.	t-value	coeff.	t-value
men, second period				
constant	−0.8279*	−1.78	−5.3706	−8.47
married			−0.2764	−0.67
training off the job	1.2488	6.18		
Mecklenburg-Vorpommern	0.6937	2.69		
previously out of the labor force	−1.2196	−2.84		
previous duration in employment	0.0223	5.11		
previous duration in unemployment	−0.1518	−4.26		
current quarter is the first of the year	−0.6858	−3.68		
current quarter is the third of the year	−0.6348	−3.33	−0.9195	−1.55
current year is 1992	−0.7211	−3.22		
public income maintenance			−0.0005*	−1.93
income maintenance/ expected earnings in employment	0.0479	0.19		
unemployment rate	−0.1592	−3.63		
women, first period				
constant	−4.4800	−8.61	−3.0135	−5.21
age < = 25	−0.4545	−3.12	−1.4669	−3.92
25 < age < = 35			−0.7866	−3.40
age > 50			0.5853	2.15
master craftsman/technician			0.9247*	1.77
training out of the job	0.4798	1.46	1.0861	3.13
Berlin (East)			−0.6559	−1.62
previously in short-time working			1.0748	3.56
previously in unemployment	0.1356	0.49	0.3552	1.33
entry in the third quarter of a year			−1.0930	−4.10
public income maintenance	0.2871	0.58	−0.0017	−3.49
women, second period				
constant	−0.6721	−2.30	−4.3373	−6.43
age < = 25	−0.6309	−2.08*	−1.7244	−3.52
25 < age < = 35			−0.9154	−3.32
no vocational training			0.6315	1.45
tertiary sector	−0.6043	−2.33		
public employee	−0.7657	−2.63		
training out of the job			0.8771	2.10
previously in short-time working	1.5529	3.57		
previously out of the labor force	−1.2632	−3.23		
previous duration in unemployment				
previous duration in short-time working	−0.1498	−3.16		
previous duration in employment	0.0249	5.30		
previous duration in unemployment	−0.1703	−4.63	−0.0142	−0.76
entry in the first quarter of a year	−0.4199*	−1.89		
current quarter is the first of the year	−0.8725	−3.97	−1.2792	−3.07
current quarter is the second of the year	−0.6051	−2.88		
current quarter is the third of the year	−0.3822	−2.03	−0.4339	−1.50

continued ./.

244 · F. Kraus, P. Puhani and V. Steiner

Table A3: Training model: exit into stable employment and into non-employment (ctd.)

	Exit into stable employment		Exit into non-employment	
	coeff.	t-value	coeff.	t-value
women, second period				
current year is 1992	−0.9749	−4.21		
public income maintenance/	−0.5989	−2.23	−0.0019	−5.51
expected earnings in employment				
month in process time, first period				
month 7−9	0.3550*	1.70		
month in process time, second period				
month 2	−0.5978	−3.58*	1.7333	3.10
month 3	−1.0558	−4.98		
month 4	−1.1284	−4.74		
month 5−6	−1.4519	−6.97	1.2840	2.27
month 7	−0.7978	−3.35	2.0330	3.61
month 8−9	−1.3646	−5.80*	1.8114	3.42
month 10−12	−1.4767	−6.61	1.4851	2.70
month 13−15	−1.3528	−6.00	2.0004	3.84
month > = 16	−1.8560	−10.00	1.5606	3.08

Note: Shaded values indicate statistical significance at the 5 %, a star at the 10 % level.
Source: LMM, waves 1−8; own calculations.

Table A4: Unemployment model: exit into stable and into non-employment

	Exit into stable employment		Exit into non-employment	
	coeff.	t-value	coeff.	t-value
men, first period				
constant	−3.0293	−7.02	−4.2624	−13.15
age > 50	−1.4998	−5.71	0.4823	2.66
married	0.6346	3.42	0.5473	2.79
with children			−0.4396	−3.04
no vocational training	−0.6838	−1.53		
semi-skilled worker	−0.4942	−1.45		
master craftsman/technician	0.3263	1.34	0.4100	2.02
university degree			0.2711	1.26
20−200 employees			0.7861	3.55
200−2000 employees			0.8748	3.89
more than 2000 employees			0.9836	2.84
previously not in employment	−0.5919	−2.91		
Mecklenburg-Vorpommern	−0.5571	−2.33		
Sachsen-Anhalt			0.3819*	1.92
previously in retraining or further training	1.0858	4.27		
previously out of the labor force	−1.0263*	−1.84	0.3182	1.05
previous duration out of the labor force	0.1189	3.91		
entry in the first quarter of a year	−0.4488	−2.05	−0.7952	−3.44

continued ./.

Table A4: Unemployment model: exit into stable and into non-employment (ctd.)

	Exit into stable employment		Exit into non-employment	
	coeff.	t-value	coeff.	t-value
men, first period				
entry in the second quarter of a year	-0.8324	-3.00	-0.6837	-2.90
entry in the third quarter of a year	-0.4696	-2.16	-0.4734	-2.41
current quarter is the second of the year			-0.5936	-2.73
unemployment benefits/expected earnings	0.1635	0.49		
unemployment benefits			0.0000	-0.20
unemployment rate	0.0942	2.23	0.0914	2.38
men, second period				
constant	-2.1978	-2.16	-5.8529	-10.55
25 < age < = 35	0.4264	1.24		
age > 50	-2.1026	-3.94	0.6543	-2.22
married	0.6974	2.05		
with children			-0.3315*	-1.75
no vocational training			0.3745	0.63
master craftsman/technician	1.4678	4.32		
vocational college			0.6081*	1.93
primary sector	-1.7042	-2.41		
tertiary sector	0.5936*	1.77		
previously not in employment	-1.6262	-3.99		
Mecklenburg-Vorpommern	1.3857	2.31		
Thüringen	0.8529	2.06		
previously in job creation measure			1.5434	2.17
previously out of the labor force			0.3198	0.70
previous duration in employment	-0.0369	-2.63		
previous duration in job creation measure	-0.0823	-2.15	-0.1807	-2.15
entry in the first quarter of a year	-1.5453	-3.06	-0.9413	-2.00
entry in the second quarter of a year	-1.6224	-3.30	-0.6065	-1.63
entry in the third quarter of a year	-1.1090	-2.68		
current quarter is the first of the year	1.8376	2.83		
current quarter is the second of the year	1.6099	2.45	1.5910	3.65
current quarter is the third of the year	1.0392	2.45		
current year is 1992	1.9371	3.82	2.6793	6.93
unemployment benefits/ expected earnings in employment	0.6133	0.83		
unemployment benefits			0.0003	0.75
unemployment rate	-0.3138	-3.56		
women, first period				
constant	-3.5176	-16.22	-4.5875	-19.96
age > 50	-1.2512	-4.54	0.3172	2.61
with children	-0.3209	-2.58		
no vocational training			-0.5208	-2.69
semi-skilled worker	-0.7464*	-1.94	-1.1948	-3.66
vocational college	0.4169	2.10		
university degree	1.0012	4.32		
more than 2000 employees			0.4028	1.62

continued ./.

246 · F. Kraus, P. Puhani and V. Steiner

Table A4: Unemployment model: exit into stable and into non-employment (ctd.)

	Exit into stable employment		Exit into non-employment	
	coeff.	t-value	coeff.	t-value
women, first period				
tertiary sector	0.6773	3.88		
public employee	−0.2596	−1.19	−0.2514	−1.54
Mecklenburg-Vorpommern			−0.2511	−1.36
Thüringen			−0.3174*	−1.92
previously in retraining or further training			0.5962	3.33
entry in the second quarter of a year			−0.3960	−2.76
current quarter is the first of the year			0.6540	4.67
current quarter is the third of the year			0.6346	4.78
current year is 1992			−0.5502	−3.56
unemployment benefits/ expected earnings in employment	0.0180	0.06		
unemployment benefits			0.0001	0.37
unemployment rate			0.0826	4.63
women, second period				
constant	−4.1261	−10.29	−7.6350	−15.17
age < = 25			0.7704	2.10
age > 50	−1.2415	−3.33	0.4556*	1.77
with children			0.3301	3.08
no vocational training	0.7016*	1.88		
construction industry	1.3168	2.44		
previously not in employment	−0.5881	−1.97		
Thüringen			0.2495	0.97
previously in short-time working	1.6278	2.93	0.6274	2.27
previously in retraining or further training	1.7504	3.55*	1.6612	4.17
previously out of the labor force			1.2457	4.02
previous duration in short-time work	−0.0691*	−1.91		
previous duration in retraining or further retraining	−0.1066	−2.04	−0.1384	−2.85
entry in the first quarter of a year	−1.8874	−4.37		
entry in the second quarter of a year	−1.3153	−3.69		
entry in the third quarter of a year	−0.6736	−2.27	0.5874	2.80
current quarter is the second of the year			1.1572	4.10
current year is 1992	1.3128	4.92	2.1354	7.67
unemployment benefits/expected earnings	−0.4868	−1.40		
unemployment benefits			0.0015	3.83
month in process time, first period				
month 3			0.4310	2.85
month 4−6			0.5931	4.74
month >n = 7			0.6562	5.19
month in process time, second period				
month > = 7	0.3599*	1.76	0.5640	3.25

Note: Shaded values indicate statistical significance at the 5 %, a star at the 10 % level.
Source: LMM, waves 1−8; own calculations.

References

Blaschke, D. and *E. Nagel* (1995), Beschäftigungssituation von Teilnehmern an AFG-finanzierter beruflicher Weiterbildung, Mitteilungen aus der Arbeitsmarkt- und Berufsforschung (MittAB), 2/95, 195–213.

Blaschke, D., H.-E. Plath, and *E. Nagel* (1992), Konzepte und Probleme der Evaluation aktiver Arbeitsmarktpolitik am Beispiel Fortbildung und Umschulung, Mitteilungen aus der Arbeitsmarkt- und Berufsforschung (MittAB), 3/92, 381–405.

Buttler, F. and *K. Emmerich* (1994), Kosten und Nutzen aktiver Arbeitsmarktpolitik im ostdeutschen Transformationsprozeß; Schriften des Vereins für Socialpolitik, 239/4, 61–94.

Cramer, J. S. and *G. Ridder* (1991), Pooling States in the Multinomial Logit Model, Journal of Econometrics, 47, 267–272.

Eichler, M. and *M. Lechner* (1996), Public Sector Sponsored Continuous Vocational Training in East Germany: Institutional Arrangements, Participants, and Results of Empirical Evaluations, Discussion Paper No. 549–96, Fakultät für VWL und Statistik, University of Mannheim.

Fitzenberger, B. and *H. Prey* (1996), Training in East Germany, An Evaluation of the Effects on Employment and Wages, CILE Discussion Paper 36–1996, University of Konstanz.

Fitzenberger, B. and *H. Prey* (1997), Assessing the Impact of Training on Employment, The Case of East Germany, ifo-Studien – Zeitschrift für empirische Wirtschaftsforschung, 43(1), 69–114.

Fitzenberger, B. and *H. Prey* (1998), Beschäftigungs- und Verdienstwirkungen von Weiterbildungsmaßnahmen im ostdeutschen Transformationsprozeß: Eine Methodenkritik, in: F. Pfeiffer and W. Pohlmeier (eds.): Qualifikation, Weiterbildung und Arbeitsmarkterfolg, Nomos Verlag, Baden-Baden.

Greene, W. (1997), Econometric Analysis, 3rd ed., Prentice Hall, New Jersey.

Gritz, R. M. (1993), The Impact of Training on the Frequency and Duration of Employment, Journal of Econometrics, 57, 21–51.

Ham, J. C. and *R. LaLonde* (1996), The Effect of Sample Selection and Initial Conditions in Duration Models: Evidence from Experimental Data on Training, Econometrica, 64, 175–205.

Heckman, J. J., H. Ichimura, and *P. Todd* (1997), Matching as an Econometric Evaluation Estimator: Evidence from Evaluating a Job Training Programme, Review of Economic Studies, 64, 605–654.

Heckman, J. J. and *J. Hotz* (1989), Choosing Among Alternative Nonexperimental Methods of Estimating the Impact of Social Programs: The Case of Manpower Training, Journal of the American Statistical Association, 84, 862–874.

Heckman, J. J. and *R. Robb* (1985), Alternative Methods for Evaluating the Impact of Interventions, in: J. Heckman and B. Singer (eds.): Longitudinal Analysis of Labor Market Data, Cambridge University Press, New York, 156–245.

Heckman, J. J. and *B. Singer* (1984), A Method for Minimizing the Impact of Distributional Assumptions in Econometric Models for Duration Data, Econometrica, 52, 271–320.

Hübler, O. (1997a), Evaluation beschäftigungspolitischer Maßnahmen in Ostdeutschland, Jahrbücher für Nationalökonomie und Statistik, Bd. 216/1, 22–44.

Hübler, O. (1997b), Der Arbeitsmarkt-Monitor des IAB, in: R. Hujer, U. Rendtel, and G. Wagner (eds.): Wirtschafts- und sozialwissenschaftliche Panel-Studien. Datenstrukturen und Analyseverfahren, Sonderhefte zum Allgemeinen Statistischen Archiv, 30, 149–168.

Hujer, R., K.-O. Maurer, and *M. Wellner* (1997a), The Impact of Training on Unemployment Duration in West Germany – Combining a Discrete Hazard Rate Model with Matching Techniques, Frankfurter Volkswirtschaftliche Diskussionsbeiträge, Arbeitspapier Nr. 74, Johann Wolfgang Goethe-Universität Frankfurt/Main.

Hujer, R., K.-O. Maurer, and *M. Wellner* (1997b), Estimating the Effect of Training on Unemployment Duration in West Germany – A Discrete Hazard-Rate Model with Instrumental Variables. Frankfurter Volkswirtschaftliche Diskussionsbeiträge, Arbeitspapier Nr. 73, Johann Wolfgang Goethe-Universität Frankfurt/Main.

Lechner, M. (1996), An Evaluation of Public Sector Sponsored Continuous Vocational Training Programmes in East Germany, Discussion Paper No. 539–96, Fakultät für VWL und Statistik, University of Mannheim.

Müller, K. and *H. Plicht* (1997), Entwicklung und Struktur der AFG-finanzierten beruflichen Weiterbildung, in: H. Bielenski et al. (eds.): Der Arbeitsmarkt Ostdeutschlands im Umbruch, Datensätze, Methoden und ausgewählte Ergebnisse des Arbeitsmarkt-Monitors 1989–1994, Beiträge aus der Arbeitsmarkt- und Berufsforschung, 210, Nürnberg.

OECD (1993), Employment Outlook, Paris.

OECD (1997), Lessons from Labour Market Policies in the Transition Countries, Paris.

Pannenberg, M. (1995), Weiterbildungsaktivitäten und Erwerbsbiographie, Eine empirische Analyse für Deutschland, Studien zur Arbeitsmarktforschung, Campus, Frankfurt/New York.

Pannenberg, M. (1996), Zur Evaluation staatlicher Qualifizierungsmaßnahmen in Ostdeutschland: Das Instrument Fortbildung und Umschulung (FuU), Discussion Paper Nr. 38, Institute for Economic Research Halle, IWH.

Puhani, P. A. and *V. Steiner* (1996), Public Works for Poland? Active Labour Market Policies During Transition, ZEW Discussion Paper No. 96–101.

Rosenbaum, P. R. and *D. B. Rubin* (1983), The Central Role of the Propensity Score in Observational Studies for Causal Effects, Biometrica, 70(1), 41–50.

Rosenbaum, P. R. and *D. B. Rubin* (1985), Constructing a Control Group Using Multivariate Matched Sampling Methods that Incorporate the Propensity Score, The American Statistician, 39, 33–38.

Ridder, G. (1986), An Event History Approach to the Evaluation of Training, Recruitment and Employment Programmes, Journal of Applied Econometrics, 1, 109–126.

Rubin, D. B. (1979), Using Multivariate Matched Sampling and Regression Adjustment to Control Bias in Observational Studies, Journal of the American Statistical Association, 74, 318–328.

Staat, M. (1997), Empirische Evaluation von Fortbildung und Umschulung, Schriftenreihe des ZEW, Nomos Verlagsgesellschaft, Baden-Baden.

Winter-Ebmer, R. and *J. Zweimüller (1996),* Manpower Training Programmes and Employment Stability, Economica, 63, 113–130.

Dr. Viktor Steiner, ZEW, P.O. Box 10 34 43, D-68034 Mannheim, Germany.
e-mail: steiner@ zew.de

[24]

Econometrica, Vol. 64, No. 1 (January, 1996), 175–205

THE EFFECT OF SAMPLE SELECTION AND INITIAL CONDITIONS IN DURATION MODELS: EVIDENCE FROM EXPERIMENTAL DATA ON TRAINING

By John C. Ham and Robert J. LaLonde[1]

We investigate the separate effects of a training program on the duration of participants' subsequent employment and unemployment spells. This program randomly assigned volunteers to treatment and control groups. However, the treatments and controls experiencing subsequent employment and unemployment spells are not generally random (or comparable) subsets of the initial groups because the sorting process into subsequent spells is very different for the two groups. Standard practice in duration models ignores this sorting process, leading to a sample selection problem and misleading estimates of the training effects. We propose an estimator that addresses this problem and find that the program studied, the National Supported Work Demonstration, raised trainees' employment rates solely by lengthening their employment durations.

Keywords: Duration models, job training, sample selection.

1. INTRODUCTION

GOVERNMENT SPONSORED EMPLOYMENT and training programs frequently improve the labor market prospects of economically disadvantaged women.[2] Often, this improvement results largely from increases in post-program employment rates rather than from increases in wages or in weekly hours for those who work (Gueron and Pauly (1991)). Less is known, however, about how these programs generate these employment gains. Training may raise employment rates because it helps unemployed former participants find jobs faster by improving their job search skills. Alternatively, training may be effective because it helps employed participants retain regular jobs by improving their work habits. Because the

[1] We are grateful to John Abowd, David Card, Christopher Flinn, Joseph Hotz, Lawrence Katz, George Jakubson, Kris Jacobs, Tony Lancaster, Angelo Melino, Bruce Meyer, Robert Moffitt, Kevin M. Murphy, Thomas Mroz, Robert Porter, Joseph Tracy, Robert Topel, James Walker, and two anonymous referees for helpful discussions and comments. We owe an especially large debt to James Heckman, Bo Honore, and Geert Ridder. Seminar participants at British Columbia, Chicago, Georgetown, Michigan, Northwestern, Pittsburgh, Stony Brook, Toronto, Virginia, and Yale made many useful suggestions. William Anderson, Lee Bailey, Susan Skeath, and especially Kris Jacobs and Tan Wang provided excellent research assistance. The Social Science and Humanities Research Council of Canada, the Industrial Relations Section at Princeton University, and the Graduate School of Business at the University of Chicago, and NSF (SES-9213310) generously supported this work. Part of this research was carried out while Ham was a visitor in the Economics Department at Northwestern and he would like to thank the department for its support and hospitality. We emphasize that we alone are responsible for any errors.

[2] Both experimental and nonexperimental evaluations of government sponsored training administered during the past three decades consistently find that these programs raise the earnings and employment rates of adult women. By contrast, these evaluations usually find that these programs do not benefit adult men and youths. For surveys of these studies see Barnow (1987), Gueron and Pauly (1991), and LaLonde (1995).

176 J. C. HAM AND R. J. LALONDE

services provided by government-sponsored training programs vary widely, we would not be surprised to find that these programs have varying impacts on employment and unemployment durations. To better understand how training raises employment rates, we develop an econometric framework for estimating the separate effects of training on the durations of participants' subsequent employment and unemployment spells.

There are several reasons why such estimates should interest policy makers and analysts. First, by distinguishing between training's impacts on employment and unemployment durations, our estimates enable us to look into the "black box" and learn how training works. This distinction is helpful to analysts interested in understanding training's effects within the context of theoretical models of job search behavior, firm hiring decisions, and employee turnover.

A second and more immediate benefit of our estimates is that they may aid in the design of new training programs. Policy makers generally would prefer to combine a service that helps participants find jobs with one that helps them hold on to their jobs, as opposed to combining two services that each help trainees leave unemployment. Alternatively, policy makers may prefer to fund a program that lengthens employment durations as opposed to one that shortens unemployment durations, because the former program is likely to lead to more stable job histories and greater human capital accumulation. Unfortunately, it is not possible to make such policy decisions if we only know the effect of training programs on employment rates.

A final benefit of our approach is that we can use our estimates to predict the effect of a program beyond the sampling frame. We can do this by simulating our econometric model or by calculating the steady state employment rate (the ratio of the expected duration of an employment spell to the sum of the expected durations of an employment spell and an unemployment spell). This application should be useful to program evaluators because trainees usually are followed for only one or two years after leaving the program and there is reason to believe that the long-run effects of many programs differ from their short-run effects.

In this paper we apply our econometric framework to data on disadvantaged women from a social experiment. The advantage of data from a randomized experiment is that among the population of eligible program volunteers, a woman's training status is uncorrelated with her unobserved heterogeneity. Therefore, simple comparisons between trainees' and controls' employment rates yield unbiased estimates of training's effect on the probability of employment. However, a similar comparison between the durations of trainees' and controls' employment and unemployment spells, or their hazard rates out of those spells, yields potentially biased and economically misleading estimates of the effect of training. Although program administrators used random assignment to create the treatment and the control groups, there is no reason to believe that the treatments and controls experiencing subsequent employment and unemployment spells are random subsets of the experimental sample. In fact, we present strong evidence below that the samples of individuals in new spells are *not* random subsets of the experimental sample. Consequently, even when using experimental data, evaluations of training's effect on employment and unemployment durations require a formal statistical model.

Our empirical findings may be summarized as follows. First, we find that using only new employment and unemployment spells creates a sample selection problem that contaminates the experimental design and thereby yields misleading estimates of the training effects. Second, our econometric framework successfully addresses this sample selection problem. This finding is important because there is no practical modification to the experimental design that would eliminate this problem in our data. Third, although this problem requires a formal statistical model, random assignment provides crucial identifying information in a relatively complex econometric model. Finally, the social experiment studied in the paper—the National Supported Work (NSW) Demonstration—raised trainees' employment rates because it helped those who found jobs to keep them. This program had no effect on the rate at which individuals left unemployment.

The remainder of the paper proceeds as follows. Section 2 discusses the problems that occur when experimental data are used to make inferences about the effect of training on employment and unemployment durations. Section 3 focuses explicitly on the NSW program to illustrate the issues discussed in Section 2. Section 4 constructs an econometric model that formally addresses the problems raised in the previous sections. Section 5 reports our empirical findings. Section 6 concludes the paper.

2. DURATION ANALYSIS WITH EXPERIMENTAL DATA

An appealing feature of social experiments is that they yield easily derived estimates of a program's impact on a variety of policy-related outcomes. In these experiments, program administrators randomly assign eligible applicants either into a treatment group—whose members are offered program services—or into a control group—whose members are denied access to these services. A woman's experimental status is, by construction, independent of her other characteristics, and thus the difference between the treatment and control groups' mean employment rates or earnings provide an unbiased estimate of the program's impact. Additional controls for differences among women's characteristics do not affect (asymptotically) the estimated impact although they can affect its standard error.

Alternatively, when a program does not incorporate an experimental design, the evaluation of its impact becomes much more complex. In such a setting, researchers first must construct a comparison group of persons who did not participate in the program, and then specify a statistical model that simultaneously accounts for the selection process into training and for the process that generates the outcomes of interest (Ashenfelter and Card (1985), Heckman and Robb (1985), Card and Sullivan (1988)). In practice, the estimated outcomes of such programs have been sensitive to how researchers constructed their comparison groups and how they specified their econometric models. Indeed, the sensitivity of nonexperimental estimates has generated a debate about their

178　　　　　J. C. HAM AND R. J. LALONDE

reliability for policy-making purposes (Burtless and Orr (1986), LaLonde (1986), Fracker and Maynard (1987), Heckman and Hotz (1989), Manski and Garfinkel (1992)).

However, when we turn from the question of whether training is effective to the question of how or why it works, even with experimental data we often must rely on nonexperimental methods like those described above. Consider, for example, a typical employment and training program for disadvantaged individuals in which volunteers are unemployed when they are randomly assigned to training at the baseline. At that time, the treatments leave unemployment and enter training for a period of t^* weeks. Afterwards, program evaluators follow their progress in the labor market for an additional $T - t^*$ weeks. By contrast, the controls remain unemployed at the baseline and then are followed for a total of T weeks. Suppose that the subsequent experimental evaluation demonstrates that training significantly raised participants' earnings in week T. Assume for expositional purposes that training did not affect weekly hours of work (conditional on employment status) in a given period. Instead, it achieved these earnings gains (i) by raising employment rates and/or (ii) by raising hourly wage rates, and we wish to estimate these two effects.

Measuring the effect of training on employment rates is straightforward. Program evaluators obtain an unbiased estimate of the average effect during week T simply from the difference between the treatment and control groups' employment rates. Likewise, a seemingly intuitive way to measure the effect of training on wages is to compare the two experimental groups' mean wages during week T. However, if training affected the treatments' employment rates, this simple estimator of the wage effect is biased. This bias arises because we observe wages only for the employed, and because an individual's employment status depends on his or her experimental status as well as other observed and unobserved characteristics.

To see how this bias arises, suppose further that individuals differ in only two respects: their training status and whether or not they are high school dropouts. In addition, assume that an individual's dropout status is not observed by the econometrician and that dropouts have lower employment rates and lower wages than high school graduates. Suppose that when training raises employment rates, a larger fraction of trainees who are dropouts find jobs than is the case for controls who are dropouts. Because the employed trainees are (on average) less educated, the difference between their mean wages and those of the employed controls underestimates the effect of training on wages. This bias arises because the outcome of interest, hourly wages, is missing for some individuals and whether it is missing depends on an individual's experimental status and unobservables (dropout status). As a result, training status is (negatively) correlated with the unobservables in the sample of employed persons, and this correlation prevents us from obtaining an unbiased estimate of the average treatment effect by simply comparing the mean hourly wages of the employed treatments and controls.

It is worth observing in our hourly wage example that (i) there is no correction to the experiment that will solve this missing data problem and (ii) this problem does not imply that random assignment is of no use in examining the effect of training on hourly wages. To estimate this effect with experimental data, we must model the selection process into employment using a nonexperimental approach such as that suggested in Heckman (1979). By contrast, to estimate the wage effect with nonexperimental data, we must model not only (i) the selection process into employment but also (ii) the (more difficult) selection process into training. Consequently, the availability of experimental data significantly simplifies the task of estimating the effect of training on hourly wages.[3]

A similar but more complicated problem arises in our example when we examine how training increased employment rates. In this case, we wish to observe the effect of training on the length of new employment and unemployment spells. Consider first the effect of training on employment spells. A natural way to proceed is to compare the treatments' and controls' experiences in these spells. However, there is no reason to believe that during the sampling frame we will observe comparable fractions of treatments and controls who are dropouts in employment spells. On the one hand, training may make it relatively easier for treatments to leave unemployment in a given period, especially for treatments who are high school dropouts. This would tend to increase the fraction of treatments in new employment spells who are dropouts relative to members of the control group that experience these spells. On the other hand, the trainees have only $T - t^*$ periods to find a job after they leave training, whereas the controls have all T^* periods to find employment, and this difference may lead to a higher fraction of controls being dropouts in employment spells. Unless these effects cancel out, the fraction of employed treatments and controls who are dropouts will differ, and training status will be correlated with unobservables (dropout status). As a result, random assignment will be contaminated in the sample of women experiencing employment spells, just as it was contaminated in the comparison of hourly wage rates.

---

[3] It is interesting to ask whether we can say training "causes" wages in the sense of Holland (1986), Rubin (1986), and the papers cited therein. It is clear that interpreting training as causing employment status appears consistent with this literature, because offering individuals training can be (i) manipulated (Rubin, p. 962) and (ii) offered as a treatment in an experiment (Holland, p. 954). Our example of the effect of training on wages differs from Holland's discussion in that he assumes that the outcome of interest is observed for each individual, while in our example, wages are missing nonrandomly. Therefore, even though offering training is a manipulable treatment in an experiment, it is not in general possible to construct an experiment to simply measure the effect of training on wages, and it is not clear whether one should describe training as causing wages in Holland's sense. We leave this as an open issue and continue to use the terminology of the "effect of training on wages" and "the effect of training on unemployment duration" in what follows. We note that Holland's and Rubin's use of the word "cause" is narrower than that used in much of economics. For example, it probably would not be consistent with Holland's paper to speak of the effect of time spent studying on grades or test scores. The problem is that time spent studying can not be directly manipulated, even though it may be indirectly affected by randomly assigning individuals to a treatment group that (i) received computers or (ii) was assigned to additional mandatory study periods. (See Holland's discussion on pp. 954–955.) We are grateful to an anonymous referee for drawing our attention to the Holland paper.

180   J. C. HAM AND R. J. LALONDE

Direct comparisons between the treatments' and controls' unemployment spells may involve even more serious biases. The treatments' unemployment spells are truncated at the baseline when they enter training, and they begin fresh or new unemployment spells when they finish training at t^*. By contrast, after random assignment the controls remain in their unemployment spells and continue to look for a regular job. For a control to experience a fresh unemployment spell, she must leave the unemployment spell in progress at the baseline to begin a new job, and then subsequently leave employment for unemployment within the sampling frame. However, in a sample of disadvantaged persons, many controls will not leave the unemployment spell in progress at the baseline during the sampling frame. (In what follows we will refer to these spells as interrupted.) Further, among those controls who leave this unemployment spell, some will not leave their subsequent fresh employment spell. As a result, the number of controls with fresh unemployment spells will be much smaller than the number of treatments with such spells. More importantly, if dropout status does not have a large effect on employment duration, it is likely that the controls who experience fresh unemployment spells will be predominantly those with high school degrees, since these controls are more likely to exit their interrupted unemployment spell.

If we could treat remaining time (after the baseline) in an interrupted unemployment spell as equivalent to time in a new unemployment spell (that began after the baseline), we could use the interrupted spells to avoid the missing data problem for the controls' spells. However, as we discuss in some detail below, time remaining in interrupted spells is not comparable to time spent in new spells if there is (i) duration dependence and (ii) unobserved heterogeneity. We find that both of these conditions hold in our data and believe that they are likely to hold when evaluating other employment and training programs targeted to economically disadvantaged persons. To address the contamination of random assignment in the samples of those experiencing fresh employment and unemployment spells, we must model the treatments' and controls' entry into such spells.

In the discussion above, we have ignored an additional problem that arises even if the fractions of high school dropouts and graduates were identical among the treatments and controls experiencing fresh unemployment (employment) spells. In practice, training takes time, sometimes as much as one year. As a result, some of the controls' fresh spells take place when the treatments are in training. Therefore, the treatments' and controls' spells will correspond to different local demand conditions, violating the premise underlying experimental evaluations that a women's training status is independent of her other characteristics. We could avoid this problem by comparing the probability that treatments and controls leave a fresh unemployment (or employment) spell during the same calendar week. However, we then would face the difficulty that because the treatments and controls started these spells at different calendar times, duration dependence and unobserved heterogeneity ensures that these exit probabilities will differ in general even in the absence of a treatment effect. We do not focus on this complication because (at least in principle) it may be addressed using standard econometric models for transition data (Lancaster (1990)), whereas these models cannot deal with unobserved differences between the samples of treatments and controls who enter fresh employment and unemployment spells. Below we show that the standard approach can be very sensitive to the latter problem.

We should emphasize that even though we must use nonexperimental methods to address these questions, our task is made much easier when program administrators randomly assign eligible applicants into either a treatment or a control group. In any nonexperimental analysis of the effect of training on the duration of employment and unemployment spells, we would have to simultaneously model (i) the nonrandom selection process into training and (ii) the nonrandom selection into fresh employment and unemployment spells. Because we have experimental data we need only address the second of these problems. Given that we believe that it is very difficult to model the selection into training, we view the availability of experimental data as extremely beneficial.

3. THE EFFECT OF TRAINING ON EMPLOYMENT HISTORIES

To illustrate the potential importance of the points raised in the previous section, we examine training's impact on participants in the National Supported Work (NSW) demonstration. This program provided work experience to a random sample of eligible AFDC women who volunteered for training.[4] The remaining volunteers did not receive training and thus formed the control group. Women in the treatment group usually were guaranteed 12 months of subsidized employment in jobs in which productivity standards were raised gradually over time. Most jobs were in clerical or services occupations and paid slightly below the prevailing wage in the participants' labor markets. When their subsidized jobs ended, the trainees were expected to enter the labor market and find regular jobs.

Despite similar preprogram employment rates, the trainees' postprogram employment rates substantially exceeded those of the control group members. As shown by Figure 1, the trainees' and controls' preprogram employment rates were essentially identical and were declining during the two years prior to the baseline.[5] After the baseline, the employment rates of the two groups diverged as the trainees entered NSW jobs and the controls sought regular unsubsidized employment. The employment rates of the two groups approached each other as the trainees' terms in supported work ended or they voluntarily dropped out of the program. Nevertheless, in the 26th month, or more than a year after the typical trainee had left the program, the employment rates of the trainees exceeded those of the control group by 9 percentage points. Therefore, the

---

[4] See the Appendix for more details about the NSW sample used in this study, and Table A, which provides the means of the trainees' and controls' demographic and pre-baseline employment characteristics. For an in-depth discussion of the program and its costs, see Hollister et al. (1984).

[5] Those unfamiliar with training program data may be surprised by the growth in the controls employment rates after the baseline. However, this pattern is a consistent feature of the data used in training evaluations and reflects the program's eligibility criteria (Ashenfelter (1978)).

182   J. C. HAM AND R. J. LALONDE

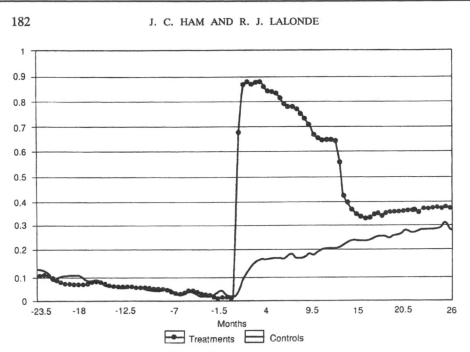

FIGURE 1.—Employment rates of AFDC women in the NSW Demonstration.

experimental evaluation shows that at least in the short run, NSW substantially improved the employment prospects of AFDC participants.

The NSW demonstration achieved these employment gains by helping trainees to hold on to their jobs longer and/or to find jobs faster, thereby increasing the length of their employment spells and/or reducing the length of their unemployment spells. To begin our analysis of these effects of training, we examine the Kaplan-Meier survivor functions for the treatments' and controls' employment and unemployment spells in Table I.[6] The first two columns of the table indicate that 65 percent of the trainees' employment spells lasted six or more months compared with only 57.3 percent of the controls' spells. When we follow standard practice and compare the experience of treatments and controls in fresh unemployment spells in columns three and five of Table I, we see that 73 percent of the treatments are still in an unemployment spell after a duration of 6 months compared to only 61.3 percent of the controls. Thus training appears to be a mixed blessing since it increases the length of both employment and unemployment spells.

Unfortunately, as previously noted, such a simple analysis of the treatments' and controls' employment histories may be misleading First, the possibility that the treatments and controls faced different demand conditions is particularly

[6] In practice many of the employment and unemployment spells are not completed during the sample period (i.e., they are right censored). Therefore, we cannot simply compare their mean durations, especially because the treatments spend on average half the sampling frame in training.

SAMPLE SELECTION AND INITIAL CONDITIONS

TABLE I

EMPIRICAL SURVIVOR FUNCTIONS
(Proportion Remaining Employed or Unemployed)

	Employment		Unemployment		
Months	Treatments (1)	Controls (2)	Treatments (3)	Controls: All Spells (4)	Controls: Fresh Spells (5)
1/2	0.968	0.929	0.955	0.949	0.929
	(.013)	(.018)	(.013)	(.011)	(.023)
1	0.929	0.848	0.910	0.914	0.895
	(.019)	(.026)	(.018)	(.015)	(.028)
2	0.839	0.761	0.864	0.843	0.791
	(.027)	(.030)	(.021)	(.019)	(.039)
3	0.787	0.687	0.817	0.807	0.756
	(.031)	(.033)	(.024)	(.021)	(.039)
4	0.733	0.648	0.778	0.781	0.728
	(.033)	(.034)	(.025)	(.022)	(.039)
5	0.670	0.603	0.746	0.756	0.672
	(.034)	(.034)	(.026)	(.022)	(.041)
6	0.650	0.573	0.730	0.725	0.613
	(.035)	(.035)	(.027)	(.023)	(.043)

Notes: The calculations in Column 4 include spells in progress at the baseline. (In the spells in progress, duration is measured from the baseline.) Those in Column 5 use only unemployment spells that begin after the baseline. The standard error calculations account for "right censoring" of the data.

pertinent in the present case because participants entered NSW as the economy was recovering from the 1974–75 recession. As a result, the controls encountered significantly worse labor market conditions during the portions of their spells that occurred while the treatment group received training.[7]

More importantly, as also observed in Section 2, an experimental design ensures only that the entire sample of treatments and controls are random draws from the same population. It does not ensure, for example, that the subsamples of treatments and controls experiencing employment spells are drawn randomly from the same population. To explore this possibility, we present in Table II the mean characteristics of treatments and controls experiencing different types of spells. As shown by columns one and two, these figures suggest that treatments experiencing employment spells are younger, less skilled, less likely to have ever been married, and have fewer weeks of work in the previous two years. Because these characteristics usually are associated with shorter employment durations, the NSW demonstration may have had an even larger impact on these durations than that suggested by the Kaplan-Meier estimates in Table I.

A similar problem arises in the fresh unemployment spells. As shown by columns three and five of Table II, the treatments and controls experiencing

---

[7] As noted in Section 2, we could avoid this problem (but encounter others) by using only the post-training data for treatments and controls. We do not focus on this problem here since standard parametric models should be able to deal with it.

　　　　　J. C. HAM AND R. J. LALONDE

TABLE II

INDIVIDUAL AND SPELL CHARACTERISTICS

Variable	Employment		Unemployment		
	Treatments (1)	Controls (2)	Treatments (3)	Controls: All Spells (4)	Controls: Fresh Spells (5)
Age	33.77	34.73	33.21	34.98	34.36
	(.60)	(.63)	(.51)	(.45)	(.72)
Schooling	10.42	10.55	10.18	10.11	10.50
	(.14)	(.17)	(.13)	(.13)	(.20)
H.S. Dropout	.62	.60	.71	.71	.63
	(.04)	(.04)	(.03)	(.03)	(.05)
Kids under 18	2.29	2.41	2.26	2.30	2.40
	(.10)	(.12)	(.09)	(.08)	(.15)
Never Married	.38	.30	.39	.33	.34
	(.04)	(.04)	(.03)	(.03)	(.05)
Proportion Black	.83	.78	.86	.82	.82
	(.03)	(.04)	(.02)	(.02)	(.04)
Prior Experience	2.46	4.09	2.82	2.91	5.04
	(.63)	(.65)	(.40)	(.42)	(.87)
Proportion	.17	.13	.15	.18	.12
Never Employed	(.03)	(.03)	(.02)	(.02)	(.03)
Number of Women	149	138	222	266	92
Number of Spells	185	198	269	374	126

Notes: All employment spells and trainees' unemployment spells begin after the baseline. The controls' spells in column 4 include both unemployment spells that are in progress at the baseline and that begin after the baseline. The statistics in column 5 include only spells that begin after the baseline. Prior experience is measured as the number of weeks worked during the two years prior to the baseline. See Appendix Table A for the means and standard errors of the full samples of treatments and controls. The numbers in parentheses are the standard errors.

fresh unemployment spells have quite different characteristics. The controls are significantly better educated than the treatments. Further, the controls had substantially more work experience during the previous two years. The latter difference in prior experience is quite important because it results from both observed and unobserved differences between treatments' and controls' characteristics.

The differing employment dynamics of the treatments' and controls' employment histories leads to this sample selection problem in fresh unemployment spells. Approximately 70 percent of the trainees leave NSW for a fresh unemployment spell. By contrast, for a control to have a fresh unemployment spell, she must first complete the unemployment spell in progress at the baseline, and then complete an employment spell before the end of the sample period. Not surprisingly, only one-third of the controls reach a fresh unemployment spell during the sampling period. Hence, the standard approach in event history studies of using only fresh spells leads to a sample of above-average controls.

We potentially could eliminate this sample selection problem for the controls by treating time spent after the baseline in an interrupted unemployment spell as equivalent to time spent in a fresh unemployment spell. Indeed, we see from comparing columns three and four of Table I that when we make this assumption, 73 percent of both the trainees' and the controls' unemployment spells lasted at least 6 months. Moreover, a comparison of columns three and four of Table II indicates no substantial differences between the treatments and this expanded sample of controls. However, data on remaining time in interrupted unemployment spells are comparable to data from fresh unemployment spells only in the absence of duration dependence and our empirical work below reveals substantial evidence of duration dependence.

We could allow for duration dependence in our treatment of an interrupted spell by conditioning on the prebaseline duration in the spell. Unfortunately, this approach is inappropriate in the presence of unobserved heterogeneity. In general, it will contaminate the experimental design, because the controls' heterogeneity distribution is implicitly conditioned on the prebaseline duration (Heckman and Singer (1984a, p. 108, footnote 20)). By contrast, the trainees' interrupted spells end when they are assigned into the treatment group at the baseline, and as a result their heterogeneity distribution is not conditioned on the prebaseline duration. This problem is particularly important because it causes the treatments and controls to have different heterogeneity distributions in a case in which the benefit of random assignment is that it insured that these distributions were the same. As a practical matter, conditioning on the start date for the interrupted spells leads to a survivor function for the controls that is very similar to that based only on the fresh spells. The reason for this result is that we usually only observe controls early in their unemployment spells when they are in the midst of a fresh spell. By contrast, when we observe the controls at the baseline, they usually have already spent a substantial amount of time in their interrupted unemployment spell.

The problems associated with using only the controls' fresh spells may be compounded by the selection process for trainees.[8] As noted above, most trainees become unemployed when they leave NSW, but some move directly into a regular job. Further, some of these trainees do not experience a subsequent spell of unemployment during the sample period. As shown in columns one and three of Table II, trainees with employment spells are more skilled than those with unemployment spells. Consequently, the sample of trainees with unemployment spells excludes women with "above average" characteristics.[9] Therefore, using only fresh spells to estimate the effect of training on unemployment durations causes us to compare above-average controls to below-average treatments.

As noted in the previous section, standard models of transition data can mitigate some of the foregoing problems by conditioning on demand variables and on observed characteristics, and by allowing for unobserved heterogeneity

---

[8] For the sake of simplicity, we abstracted from this complication in our example in Section 2. However, the addition of sorting on the part of the treatments does not eliminate the selection problems discussed there.

[9] The difference in prior experience between the treatments and controls in columns one and two indicates that there also may be selection bias in employment spells. In our empirical work, we do not find any evidence that this bias is large.

186   J. C. HAM AND R. J. LALONDE

that is uncorrelated with these observed characteristics. However, because these models explicitly assume that the unobserved heterogeneity is uncorrelated with the observed variables, they cannot account for the effects of unobserved variables that are correlated with a person's training status. In order to follow standard empirical practice, we would have to adopt one of the following two implausible assumptions: (i) there is no duration dependence in unemployment spells; or (ii) in the sample experiencing fresh unemployment spells, unobserved heterogeneity is uncorrelated with a woman's training status. We now turn to a statistical model that avoids both of these assumptions.[10]

4. ECONOMETRIC MODEL

There are several different ways to use the NSW data to construct a likelihood function for the treatments' and controls' employment histories. One approach utilizes both the postbaseline data and the two years of available prebaseline data. Unfortunately, this strategy leads to an extremely intricate likelihood function, even for simple specifications of the hazard functions, because of the NSW's complex eligibility criteria. The program administrators required participants to be unemployed when they volunteered for training and to have been unemployed for at least three of the six months prior to the baseline.

A second approach is to use the exact likelihood for the post.baseline data without conditioning on the starting date of the interrupted spells. Unfortunately, this likelihood function also is extremely complicated.[11] A third approach also utilizes only the postbaseline data, while conditioning on the starting date of the interrupted spells for the controls. As noted in the previous section, this approach will produce inconsistent estimates in the presence of unobserved heterogeneity. In light of these drawbacks, we follow Heckman's and Singer's (1984a) suggestion and define a separate hazard and heterogeneity term for the interrupted spells.

4.1 Contribution of the Controls' Employment Histories

To facilitate our development of the likelihood function, we begin by describing the employment history for a hypothetical member of the control group. As shown by Figure 2, when a woman volunteers for training at the baseline (or experimental time 0), she has been unemployed for T periods. After the

---

[10] Standard models also cannot deal with the contamination to random assignment that arises from conditioning (on the prebaseline duration) in the controls' (i) hazard for the interrupted spells and (ii) heterogeneity distribution. A referee has suggested that it may be possible to deal with this problem by conditioning both the treatments' and controls' heterogeneity distributions on prebaseline duration. This suggestion is beyond the scope of our paper and we have not explored it.

[11] See Ham and LaLonde (1991) for derivations of both of these likelihood functions. One might expect that using the prebaseline data would alleviate our initial conditions problem. But it simply moves this problem back two years and yet still requires us to model the eligibility rules that volunteers had to satisfy in order to be admitted into the experimental sample.

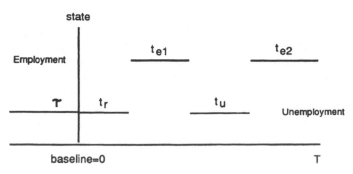

FIGURE 2.—Employment history for a hypothetical control.

program administrators randomly assign her to the control group, she remains in that spell for an additional t_r periods. She next experiences an employment spell lasting t_{e1} periods followed by a fresh unemployment spell lasting t_u periods. Finally, she begins another employment spell which is in progress at the end of the sampling frame and thus is censored after t_{e2} periods.

To form the likelihood function for this control's employment history, we must define the transition rates out of each of the types of spells depicted in Figure 2. In what follows we work in discrete time and define these transitions rates for person i as follows:[12]

$$(1a) \qquad \lambda_{ji}(t|\theta_{ji}) = \left(1 + \exp(-y_{ji}(t))\right)^{-1},$$

where

$$(1b) \qquad y_{ji}(t) = \beta_j X_i(t + t^*) + y_j D_j + \delta_{1j}\log(t) + \delta_{2j}\log(t)^2 + \theta_{ji}.$$

In (1) the subscript j denotes the type of spell. Accordingly, $j = r$ denotes an interrupted unemployment spell; $j = u$ denotes a fresh unemployment spell; and $j = e$ denotes a fresh employment spell. The spell begins at calendar time t^* and t is its current duration. The vector X_i includes both personal characteristics and demand variables. Among the personal characteristics are age, years of schooling, whether or not the woman dropped out of high school, the number of children less than 18, race, and marital status.[13] The demand variables are monthly nonagricultural employment and the number of persons receiving unemployment benefits. We measure both demand variables as log deviations from SMSA means. The dummy variable D_i equals 1 when a woman belongs to the treatment group and 0 otherwise. To capture the effects of duration

---

[12] The hazard in (1a) is conditioned on the $X_i(\ )$ variables, which could in principle contain the entire history up to this period. For notational ease we make this conditioning implicit and condition explicitly only on θ.

[13] We also experimented with adding age-squared, and dummy variables for whether a woman was of Hispanic origin or currently married. None of these variables had a coefficient that was significantly different from zero, nor did the addition of the variables affect the results.

188   J. C. HAM AND R. J. LALONDE

dependence, we used log duration and its square.[14] Finally, we represent the unobserved characteristics by a scaler random variable θ_{ji}. Because we leave the mean of θ_{ji} unrestricted, the parameter vector β_j does not include an intercept. In Section 4.3, we discuss our different specifications for the joint distribution of these heterogeneity terms across different types of spells.[15]

Using the foregoing transition rates, we can now define the contribution to the likelihood for the hypothetical control depicted in Figure 2. (In what follows we drop the i subscript.) The contribution of the fresh employment and unemployment spells is straightforward (Flinn and Heckman (1983)). The contribution of the first employment spell and the fresh unemployment spell in Figure 2 conditional on θ_j is given by

$$(2a) \qquad f(t_{e1}|\theta_e) = \lambda_e(t_{e1}|\theta_e) \prod_{k=1}^{t_{e1}-1} (1 - \lambda_e(k|\theta_e))$$

and

$$(2b) \qquad f(t_u|\theta_u) = \lambda_u(t_u|\theta_u) \prod_{k=1}^{t_u-1} (1 - \lambda_u(k|\theta_u)).$$

(Unless otherwise noted, all contributions to the likelihood are conditional on the realization of the unobserved heterogeneity.) The contribution of the right-censored employment spell in Figure 2 is given by

$$(3) \qquad S(t_{e2}|\theta_e) = \prod_{k=1}^{t_{e2}} (1 - \lambda(k|\theta_e)).$$

As indicated above, modeling the exact contribution of the unemployment spell in progress at the baseline is very complicated and we follow Heckman's and Singer's suggestion and let this spell have its own hazard and heterogeneity term. Therefore, the contribution for the interrupted spell in Figure 2 is given by

$$(4) \qquad f_r(t_r|\theta_r) = \lambda_r(t_r|\theta_r) \prod_{k=1}^{t_r-1} (1 - \lambda_r(k|\theta_r)).$$

Combining the information on the hypothetical control's interrupted and fresh spells, we arrive at the overall *unconditional* contribution to the likelihood

[14] We also controlled for higher order polynomials of log duration, but these terms were never significant. The quadratic term was significant only for the transition rates from fresh employment spells. Because the quadratic term was not significant for the transition rates from interrupted or fresh unemployment spells, we dropped it for these transition rates. We also used time dummy variables instead of log duration and log duration squared to capture the effects of duration dependence (Ham and Rea (1987), Meyer (1990)). This alternative specification had no effect on any of the estimated coefficients, including that for training status. Finally, a referee has noted that it may be advantageous to make an adjustment when using a polynomial in log duration in a *continuous* time model (see Lancaster, Imbens, and Dolton (1987)).

[15] We always assume that θ_{ij} is constant across spells of the same type.

function given by

$$(5) \qquad \mathscr{L}(t_r, t_{e1}, t_u, t_{e2}) = \int f_r(t_r|\theta_r) f_e(t_{e1}|\theta_e) f_u(t_u|\theta_u)$$

$$\times S_e(t_{e2}|\theta_e) \, dG_1(\theta_r, \theta_e, \theta_u)$$

where $G_1(\cdot)$ is the distribution function for θ_r, θ_e, and θ_u.

Of course there are other labor market histories than that depicted in Figure 2, but their contribution to the likelihood is analogous to (5). However, because such a large percentage of controls never left their interrupted spell during the sample period, it is worth describing their contribution to the likelihood function. The *unconditional* contribution of such an employment history is given by

$$(6) \qquad \mathscr{L}(T) = \int S_r(T|\theta_r) \, dG_r(\theta_r)$$

where T is the length of the postbaseline sample period,

$$(7) \qquad S_r(T|\theta_r) = \prod_{k=1}^{T} (1 - \lambda_r(k|\theta_r)),$$

and $G_r(\theta_r)$ is the marginal distribution function of θ_r.

4.2 *Contribution of the Treatments' Employment Histories*

We now turn to the treatment group's contribution to the likelihood function. In contrast to a control's interrupted spell, a treatment's unemployment spell ends when she is randomly assigned into training. As shown for a hypothetical treatment in Figure 3, we find that after the program administrators randomly assign her to the treatment group, she remains in the program until training ends after S^* periods. She then experiences a fresh unemployment spell lasting t_u periods. At the end of this spell she begins an employment spell that is still in progress at the end of the sampling frame and thus is censored at t_e periods.

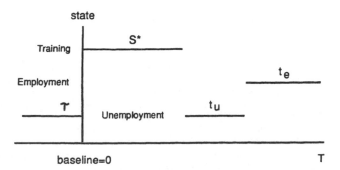

FIGURE 3.—Employment history for a hypothetical treatment who completes training.

190   J. C. HAM AND R. J. LALONDE

The treatments usually were eligible for up to 12 months of training, but approximately one half dropped out of the program early to go to a regular job or to unemployment. Therefore, the treatments' contribution to the likelihood function must account for their time in training and whether or not they left training early for employment or unemployment. In order to model these possibilities, we use a multiple exit framework to describe the transition into employment or unemployment after s periods of training. Accordingly, we write the conditional probability of dropping out of training into employment in week t_{se} as

(8) $\qquad \lambda_{se}(t_{se}|\theta_{se}) = (1 + \exp(-y_{se}(t_{se})))^{-1},$

where

(9) $\qquad y_{se}(t_{se}) = \beta_{se}X(t_{se} + t^*) + h_{se}(t_{se}) + \theta_{se},$

and where the baseline for this individual occurs at calendar time t^* and $h_{se}(t_{se})$ is a polynomial in log duration. Likewise we assume that the conditional probability of dropping out of training to unemployment in week t_{su} is given by

(10) $\qquad \lambda_{su}(t_{su}|\theta_{su}) = (1 + \exp(-y_{su}(t_{su})))^{-1},$

where

(11) $\qquad y_{su}(t_{su}) = \beta_{su}X(t_{su} + t^*) + h_{su}(t_{su}) + \theta_{su},$

and where $h_{su}(t_{su})$ also is a polynomial in log duration.[16]

The individual in Figure 3 completes training and does not drop out early. Thus the training period contributes

(12) $\qquad S_s(S^*|\theta_{su}, \theta_{se}) = \prod_{k=1}^{S^*} (1 - \lambda_{su}(k|\theta_{su}))(1 - \lambda_{se}(k|\theta_{se})).$

The contributions of the treatments' subsequent fresh employment and unemployment spells are straightforward and analogous to those of the controls' spells. Thus the *unconditional* contribution is given by

(13) $\qquad \mathscr{L}(S^*, t_u, t_e) = \int S_s(S^*|\theta_{su}, \theta_{se})f_u(t_u|\theta_u)S_e(t_e|\theta_e)\, dG_2(\theta_{su}, \theta_{se}, \theta_u, \theta_e)$

where $G_2(\theta_{su}, \theta_{se}, \theta_u, \theta_e)$ is the joint distribution function for $\theta_{su}, \theta_{se}, \theta_u, \theta_e$.

To calculate the contribution for a trainee who drops out of the program early, consider the employment history shown in Figure 4. This woman drops out of training after t_{se} periods to begin a regular job. This employment spell lasts t_e periods, and is followed by an unemployment spell that is censored at the end of the sampling frame after t_u weeks. The contribution of this woman's training

---

[16] The data indicated the need for $h_{se}(t_{se})$ to be a second order polynomial in log duration and $h_{su}(t_{su})$ to be a sixth order polynomial in log duration.

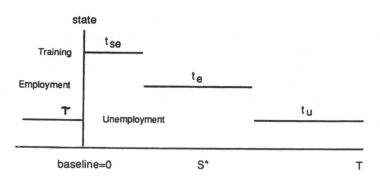

FIGURE 4.—Employment history for a hypothetical treatment who drops out of training.

spell is given by

$$(14) \qquad f_{se}(t_{se}|\theta_{se}, \theta_{su}) = \lambda_{se}(t_{se}|\theta_{se}) \prod_{k=1}^{t_{se}-1} (1 - \lambda_{se}(k|\theta_{se}))(1 - \lambda_{su}(k|\theta_{su})).$$

Therefore, the *unconditional* contribution of the employment history is given by

$$(15) \qquad \mathscr{L}(t_{se}, t_e, t_u) = \int f_{se}(t_{se}|\theta_{se}, \theta_{su}) f_e(t_e|\theta_e) S(t_u|\theta_u) \, dG_2(\theta_{se}, \theta_{su}, \theta_e, \theta_u).$$

4.3 *Specification of the Heterogeneity Distributions*

To estimate the effect of training on employment and unemployment dura-tion, we maximize the likelihood formed by combining the contributions of the treatments' and controls' spells (Ridder and Verbakel (1984)). The resulting likelihood function is relatively complex and computationally demanding as it depends on five different parameter vectors ($\beta_r, \beta_u, \beta_e, \beta_{su}, \beta_{se}$) and five differ-ent heterogeneity terms ($\theta_r, \theta_u, \theta_e, \theta_{su}, \theta_{se}$).

We estimate this model under the following assumptions about the unob-served heterogeneity:

(A1) *There is no unobserved heterogeneity, and thus*

$$(16) \qquad \theta_j = \alpha_j, \quad j = se, su, r, u, e,$$

where α_j is a fixed intercept.

(A2) *Unobserved heterogeneity is independent across spells and is drawn from a two-point distribution*[17]

$$(17) \qquad \begin{aligned} \theta_j &= \theta_{j1} \quad \text{with probability } P_j, \\ &= \theta_{j2} \quad \text{with probability } 1 - P_j, \end{aligned}$$

where $j = r, u, e$.

---

[17] In all but (A5) below, we assume that θ_{se} and θ_{su} follow a one factor structure with one intercept normalized to zero and one loading factor normalized to one.

(A3) *The unobserved heterogeneity components* $(\theta_{su}, \theta_{se})$, θ_e *are independent of each other and of* θ_u *and* θ_r. *Further* θ_u *and* θ_r *follow the one-factor structure*

$$(18) \qquad \theta_j = \alpha_j + c_j \theta^*,$$

where $j = u$, *r and* θ^* *is drawn from a two-point distribution. (In this specification and in* (A4) *and* (A5) *below, we normalize* $\alpha_u = 0$ *and* $c_u = 1$.)

(A4) *The unobserved heterogeneity terms* $(\theta_{su}, \theta_{se})$ *are independent of* θ_u, θ_e, *and* θ_r. *Further* θ_u, θ_e, *and* θ_r *follow the one-factor structure given by* (18).

(A5) *All heterogeneity terms follow the one-factor structure given by* (18).[18]

Assumptions (A1) and (A2) imply that there will be no selection bias from using only fresh employment and unemployment spells in estimation. Our discussion of the survivor functions in Table I and of the means of the treatments' and controls' characteristics in Table II suggests that these assumptions are inappropriate within the current parametric framework.

The Assumptions (A3) through (A5) allow us to address the sample selection problem. Assumption (A3) focuses on the idea that the crucial correlation is between the controls' interrupted spells and fresh unemployment spells. Assumption (A4) allows for the possibility that there is additional sample selection bias arising from treating the unobservables in the employment spells as independent from unobservables in the interrupted and fresh unemployment spells. For example, controls who leave an interrupted spell and enter an employment spell may have above average unobserved characteristics. Finally, Assumption (A5) addresses the possibility that there is sample selection among the treatments depending on how they leave training. For example, we would expect treatments who drop out of training for employment to have above-average unobserved characteristics.

In our empirical work, we obtain estimates for two different specifications of the interrupted spell hazard, λ_r. In the first case, we do not condition on the time spent in the interrupted spell before the baseline. In the second case, we do condition on the time spent in the spell prior to the baseline. Specifically, in this later case, we measured duration in the interrupted spells from the beginning of those spells and not from the baseline. We noted above that if we use the same hazard and heterogeneity distribution for the fresh and interrupted unemployment spells (with duration in the latter spells measured from the beginning of the spell), we will contaminate the experimental design. However, when we allow the interrupted spells to have their own hazard,

[18] The project was quite computationally demanding and thus we generally stayed with the assumption that θ^* was drawn from a two-point distribution. However, we did try to add a third point of support for one of our more complex models. Even though we tried several starting values, we could only achieve a trivial increase in the likelihood. Given that we could not find a role for a third point of support in one of our most complicated models, we maintained the assumption that θ^* was drawn from a two-point distribution in our other specifications.

accounting for time in this spell prior to the baseline simply helps us obtain a better approximation to the interrupted spell hazard and a greater degree of (empirical) identification by exploiting the variation in this variable among the control group members. Therefore, our alterative specifications for λ_r should provide a check on the robustness of our results.

In an earlier version of the paper (Ham and LaLonde (1991)), we estimated the model under Assumptions (A3) through (A5) for the case in which we do not condition on prebaseline duration and α_j is restricted to zero in (18) for all j. This restriction places a proportionality restriction on the intercept terms for a woman of a given type. For example, this restriction constrains the constant in the interrupted hazard to be c_r times the intercept in the fresh unemployment spell and to be c_e/c_r times the intercept in the fresh employment spell. Our estimates under Assumptions (A3), (A4), and (A5) generally produced quite similar estimates for the cases in which (i) we condition on prebaseline duration in the interrupted spells; (ii) we do not condition on prebaseline duration and do not restrict $\alpha_j = 0$ in (18); and (iii) we do not condition on prebaseline duration and restrict $\alpha_j = 0$ in (18). Accordingly, we present results for the case in which we condition on prebaseline duration in the interrupted spell. The only real difference among the estimates occurred when we estimated the full one-factor model (A5) and did not condition on prebaseline duration in the interrupted spells nor imposed the restriction that $\alpha_j = 0$ in (18). In this case we essentially lost identification.[19] Although it is hard to generalize from one data set, these results suggest that the prebaseline duration data provide important identifying information. Further, in the absence of such information, it may be necessary to impose additional restrictions such as placing a proportionality restriction on the intercepts.

5. ESTIMATES OF THE TRAINING EFFECT

We first present estimates of the training effects assuming no heterogeneity (A1) or independent heterogeneity (A2) among spells. These assumptions imply that we can obtain consistent estimates of the training effect using only the fresh spells. Next, we show how incorporating information on the controls' interrupted spells affects our estimates of the fresh unemployment hazard using Assumption (A3). Then we examine the effect of including information from the interrupted spells on our estimates of both the fresh employment and unemployment hazards using Assumption (A4). Finally, we include the treatments' training

---

[19] We found three distinct optima. One looked very similar to the estimates presented below in columns three and five of Table IV. For the other two optima, the estimates implied that one of the hazards was zero (for one of the mass points of distribution) in the sense of being smaller than e^{-66}; moreover, in each case the maximization algorithm appeared to be exploiting the fact that as it changed the heterogeneity distribution, the computer was treating a hazard for one heterogeneity term as equal to zero. One of these optima yielded training effects quite similar to those in Table IV. However, the other optima yielded a large positive training effect in the employment hazard and a large negative training coefficient in the unemployment hazard.

194   J. C. HAM AND R. J. LALONDE

TABLE III

ESTIMATED TRAINING EFFECTS USING FRESH SPELLS

| | Employment | | Unemployment | | | |
| | | | Fresh Spells Only | | Fresh and Interrupted Spells Combined | |
Variable	(1)	(2)	(3)	(4)	(5)	(6)
Training Status	−.394	−.425	−.382	−.374	−.191	−.105
	(.155)	(.180)	(.166)	(.208)	(.129)	(.156)
Log Duration	.212	.155	−.453	−.299	−.503	−.353
	(.246)	(.258)	(.075)	(.119)	(.055)	(.082)
Log Duration Squared	−.168	−.113	—	—	—	—
	(.069)	(.085)				
Controls for Unobserved Heterogeneity	No	Yes	No	Yes	No	Yes
Log Likelihood	−852.7	−851.6	−768.1	−765.5	−1416.4	−1411.9

Notes: All models also include controls for age, years of schooling, a woman's high school dropout status, number of children under 18, marital status, race, and a woman's SMSA's establishment employment and unemployment insurance recipients. Local employment and unemployment are defined as the log deviations from site means. Appendix Table B presents the estimated coefficients for these variables. The standard errors are in parentheses.

spells and estimate the complete likelihood function based on the heterogeneity distribution defined by Assumption (A5).

5.1 *Results from Standard Models*

As was suggested by the empirical survivor functions in Table I, the estimated training effects based on the fresh spells imply that training lowered both the probabilities of leaving employment and unemployment. Column one of Table III presents the coefficient (and standard error) of the training dummy variable and the duration terms from the employment hazard when θ_e is constant, while column two presents the same estimates when this heterogeneity term is assumed to come from a discrete distribution with two points of support. (The full set of parameter estimates is contained in Appendix Table B.) The estimate of −.394 implies that training increased expected employment duration by approximately 11 months. In columns three and four of Table IV, we present the corresponding estimates for the unemployment hazard. The estimate of −.382 implies that training increased expected unemployment duration by approximately 40 months.[20]

Although the estimated effect of training on unemployment durations is not credible, the other estimated coefficients are economically plausible. As shown

[20] We calculated the estimated differences in trainees' and controls' expected durations using the parameters from the estimated hazard functions which ignore unobserved heterogeneity.

SAMPLE SELECTION AND INITIAL CONDITIONS   195

TABLE IV

ESTIMATES OF THE TRAINING EFFECT BASED ON ALTERNATIVE
HETEROGENEITY ASSUMPTIONS

	Fresh Unemployment Hazard			Employment Hazard	
	(1)[a]	(2)[b]	(3)[c]	(4)[b]	(5)[c]
Training	−.073	−.062	.024	−.365	−.403
Status	(.209)	(.207)	(.217)	(.159)	(.156)
Log Duration	−.357	−.370	−.357	.207	.212
	(.070)	(.095)	(.091)	(.246)	(.246)
Log Duration	—	—	—	−.163	−.168
Squared				(.069)	(.069)
Log Likelihood	−1401.2	−2251.9	−2994.4	−2251.9	−2994.4
Log Likelihood					
No Heterogeneity	−1410.2	−2262.8	−3007.9	−2262.8	−3007.9

Notes: See notes to Table III; estimates in the table correspond to the assumptions described below and in the text. In column (1) the log likelihood refers to the contribution of the fresh and interrupted unemployment spells. In columns (2) and (4) it refers to the contribution from employment spells as well as that from the interrupted and fresh unemployment spells. In columns (3) and (5) the log likelihood refers to the contribution of all spells (i.e., including the training data).
[a] (A3), where the heterogeneity terms for r and u follow the one-factor structure given by (18). Under (A3) the corresponding estimates for the employment hazard are from the model with independent heterogeneity, reported in column 2 of Table III.
[b] (A4), where the heterogeneity terms for r, u, and e follow the one-factor structure given by (18).
[c] (A5), where all heterogeneity terms follow the one-factor structure given by (18).

by Appendix Table B, individuals have longer unemployment spells if they are older, less educated, or African-American. In addition, adverse local labor market conditions also seem to increase the duration of unemployment. By contrast, the only personal characteristic besides training status that significantly affects the employment hazards is high school dropout status. Women who are high school dropouts experienced significantly shorter employment spells. Finally, we find substantial duration dependence both in the unemployment and employment hazards. The quadratic term in the employment hazard reflects the tendency in the data for the hazard to rise during the first few weeks in a new job before declining in subsequent weeks.

In light of training's positive impact on employment rates, the finding that training impaired a woman's ability to find a job is surprising. However, a more plausible conclusion to draw from the analysis of fresh spells is that the training coefficient merely reflects the selection problem discussed above. Moreover, we would not expect the problem to be resolved by accounting for observed characteristics and unobserved heterogeneity (in column four), because the standard approach to unobserved heterogeneity assumes that the heterogeneity terms are independent of the explanatory variables, including training status. We have argued above that our sample selection problem contaminates the experimental design and thereby causes a woman's training status to be correlated with the heterogeneity term in the fresh unemployment hazard.

An informal way of avoiding this selection problem is to include the controls' interrupted spells in the analysis and to assume that the fresh and interrupted spells have the same hazard function.[21] Of course, this procedure is valid only under the strong assumption of no duration dependence in the unemployment hazard. If this assumption is inappropriate, including interrupted spells involves trading off the bias from misspecification—that is, treating time remaining in an interrupted spell the same as time remaining in a fresh spell—against the sample selection bias that results from excluding these interrupted spells.

As shown by column five, when we use the same hazard for both the interrupted and fresh unemployment spells, the estimated training effect in the unemployment hazard falls by one half in absolute value and is no longer statistically significant at standard confidence levels. However, we also find strong evidence of duration dependence, and this result is not simply caused by unobserved heterogeneity. As shown in column six, when we account for unobserved heterogeneity, the magnitude of the duration dependence coefficient declines but nonetheless remains substantial and statistically significant. The existence of duration dependence indicates that it is inappropriate to use the same hazard function for the interrupted and fresh unemployment spells.

5.2 Results from Models Allowing for Sample Selection

The findings in Table III underscore the potential importance of sample selection and motivate consideration of the more complicated statistical framework developed in this paper.[22] We first obtain estimates based on Assumption (A3) where the heterogeneity terms θ_u and θ_r follow the one-factor structure given by (18) and are independent of θ_e, θ_{se}, and θ_{su}. As shown in column one of Table IV, now training has almost no effect on the transition rate out of a fresh unemployment spell.[23] This result contrasts with the corresponding estimate in column four of Table III, which indicated that training substantially increased unemployment durations. Further, this result is essentially identical to the one obtained when we forced the interrupted and fresh spells to have the same hazard function (in column six of Table III). This finding suggests that the bias that results when we follow standard practice and discard the interrupted spells

---

[21] For the estimates presented in Table III, we measure the duration in the spells as time spent unemployed since the baseline. Alternatively, if we use the total duration of these spells, which includes time spent unemployed prior to the baseline, the estimated training effect is similar to that reported for fresh spells in column three. If there were no unobserved heterogeneity, this alternative approach would be appropriate. But, as discussed in Section 3, in the presence of such heterogeneity, conditioning on prebaseline duration contaminates the experimental design.

[22] In what follows, we allow the interrupted and fresh unemployment spells to have different hazard functions.

[23] Given Heckman and Singer's (1984b) results suggesting that our approach is likely to do a poor job of recovering the heterogeneity distribution, we do not discuss the parameter estimates for this distribution.

is more serious than the bias that results when we treat the two types of spells as having the same hazard function.

We next impose Assumption (A4) where the heterogeneity terms θ_e, θ_u, and θ_r follow the one factor structure (18) and are independent of the terms associated with the training spells (θ_{su}, θ_{se}). As shown by column two of Table IV, when we correct for selection bias in this fashion, training again has no effect on unemployment durations. However, as shown by column four, training continues to significantly lengthen employment durations.

Finally, we account for the potential selection bias arising from the treatments' exit from training by adopting Assumption (A5) and using the one-factor structure (18) for all the heterogeneity terms. Column three of Table IV contains the coefficient for the training dummy for the fresh spell unemployment hazard, while column five contains the estimate of the training coefficient for the employment hazard. Comparing columns two and three, we see that the training dummy in the unemployment hazard is still essentially zero. Comparing columns four and five, we see that the training coefficient in the employment hazard also is unchanged and is still quite significant. (As shown by Appendix Table B, we also find that the estimated coefficients for the other independent variables are unaffected by changing the assumed heterogeneity structure.)

Our estimates that account for sample selection indicate that training significantly increased the duration of employment spells, while it had no effect on the duration of unemployment spells. These findings make considerably more economic sense than the results based only on fresh spells, which suggest that training substantially raised unemployment duration. Our results also indicate that initial conditions problems are of more than theoretical interest in event history studies, and that policy conclusions based on these studies may be quite sensitive to how researchers deal with such problems.

5.3 Tests of Model Specification

We also considered goodness-of-fit tests for our estimates under the assumption of independent heterogeneity (A2), which ignores selection bias and the full factor model (A5), which accounts for selection bias. We initially had hoped to test these models by comparing the predicted employment rates generated by them to the actual employment rates from a resurvey of NSW women. This survey was conducted during the Fall of 1979, which for most women was nearly one year after the end of the original sampling period. Although the resurvey sought to interview a random sample of the NSW treatments and controls, we found substantial evidence of attrition bias in the resurvey data. Not only were the nonrespondents younger than the respondents, but their employment rates during the original sampling period also were significantly different. For the controls, by the 26th month after the baseline, the nonrespondents' employment rates were only one half as large as those of the respondents. For the treat-

198   J. C. HAM AND R. J. LALONDE

TABLE V

ACTUAL AND PREDICTED EMPLOYMENT RATES

			Months Since the Baseline				Chi-Square Statistic
	(1) 21	(2) 22	(3) 23	(4) 24	(5) 25	(6) 26	(7)
Controls:							
Actual	.282	.289	.297	.301	.320	.289	—
Predicted: Model (A5)	.269	.273	.278	.284	.290	.295	9.22
							(.16)
Predicted: Model (A2)	.267	.271	.277	.283	.290	.295	9.47
							(.15)
Treatments:							
Actual	.367	.364	.382	.385	.385	.382	—
Predicted: Model (A5)	.341	.346	.353	.359	.365	.371	3.02
							(.81)
Predicted: Model (A2)	.360	.364	.369	.373	.378	.382	2.24
							(.90)

Notes: We calculated the predicted employment rates generated by our model under the Assumptions (A5) and (A2) as defined in the text. The figures in the table are the means of each woman's predicted employment probabilities in each period. The chi-square statistic is for the joint hypothesis that the difference between the actual and predicted employment rates equal zero during months 21 through 26. The numbers in parentheses are the "*p*-values."

ments, the nonrespondents employment rates grew during the last nine months of the original sampling period, while the respondents employment rates remained constant during that period. Thus the resurvey data appears to contain above-average controls and below-average treatments, and thus are inappropriate for goodness-of-fit tests.

We then carried out goodness-of-fit tests for the employment rates in the last six months of the period used for estimation. Specifically, we tested the joint hypothesis that the difference between the predicted and actual employment rates for the treatments were zero in each of the six months preceding the end of the sample. We also carried out this test for the controls. We followed the approach of Heckman and Walker (1990) and used Monte Carlo simulation to calculate the employment probability for an individual over the period.[24] As shown by Table V, we find that the full specification (A5) and the independent heterogeneity (A2) yield predicted employment rates for both treatments and controls that are nearly identical to the actual rates during the last six months of the sampling frame. Thus, we cannot distinguish between the models using goodness-of-fit statistics in the sample used for estimation. In retrospect, this result is perhaps unsurprising because both models have a relatively large

---

[24] As in the Heckman and Walker (1990) study, our test statistics do not reflect the error in estimation of the parameters of the likelihood function because of the computational resources this would require.

number of parameters with which to fit the sample period data. In the absence of a random sample in the resurvey data, goodness-of-fit statistics do not help us distinguish between the models.

6. CONCLUSIONS

In this paper we found that NSW raised employment rates because it helped women who found jobs remain employed longer than they would have otherwise. Our finding is in keeping with the program's objectives and is encouraging because longer employment spells may lead to greater human capital accumulation. Such a possibility suggests that the short-term program effects should persist and might even increase over time. A recent study by Couch (1992) supports this conjecture. Using quarterly Social Security earnings data, he reports that the NSW treatments had significantly greater earnings than the controls more than seven years after the NSW program ended. Thus, our study suggests that short sampling frames contain information that program evaluators might use to draw inferences about the long-term effects of training. Such a contention needs, of course, to be explored further in future research.

We conclude with a final point concerning the value of an experimental design when evaluating training's effect on employment and unemployment durations. The complexity of the estimator developed in this paper does not reflect a shortcoming of the experimental design. Indeed, in a nonexperimental setting this problem is much more complex. For example, Gritz (1993) uses the National Longitudinal Survey to evaluate the impact of public sector training on employment and unemployment durations. His study differs from ours in two fundamental ways because he does not have an experimental design.[25] First, because he does not condition the heterogeneity distribution on being eligible for training, his study addresses a more ambitious question than ours, namely, what effect training would have on a randomly chosen member of the labor force. Second, because he must allow for individuals entering training both before and during his sampling frame, he faces a much more complex task in accounting for selection bias. Not surprisingly, Gritz finds that government-sponsored training substantially increases unemployment duration and decreases employment duration. He acknowledges that these findings may reflect the failure of his econometric model to account fully for selection bias.[26]

In contrast to Gritz, we analyze the effect of training only among those who were eligible volunteers for the NSW program. Given the characteristics of individuals likely to participate in government-sponsored training programs, we

---

[25] He must also aggregate across different training programs.

[26] See Ridder (1986) for an evaluation of Dutch training programs with nonexperimental data. As Ridder explicitly notes, he is forced to make strong identifying assumptions because he lacks a control group and must instead rely on pre/post comparisons between unemployment durations.

do not see this as a limitation of our study. Moreover, for this group of eligible volunteers, random assignment assures that an individual's heterogeneity is independent of her training status. Because the experimental design eliminates the need to account for selection into training, we must simply model how the controls leave their interrupted unemployment spells and how the treatments leave their training spells. As our results indicate, this task is clearly much more manageable than Gritz's. Therefore, although the experimental design does not eliminate the need for a formal econometric model, it does give us sufficient leverage to obtain economically meaningful results.

Dept. of Economics, University of Pittsburgh, Pittsburgh, PA 15260, U.S.A.
and
Dept. of Economics, Michigan State University, East Lansing, MI 48824, U.S.A.,
and National Bureau of Economic Research, Cambridge, MA 02138, U.S.A.

Manuscript received November, 1991; final revision received February, 1995.

APPENDIX
DESCRIPTION OF NATIONAL SUPPORTED WORK DATA

I. *Source of Data and Documentation*

The data used in this study were obtained from the Employment and Earnings File of the Supported Work Evaluation Study Public Use File. This file was prepared under Contract Number 33-36-75-01 to the Manpower Demonstration Research Corporation. The record layout and definitions of the variables in the public use file can be found in Technical Document No. 8 "Constructed Variables Derivation for the Supported Work Evaluation Study Public Use File: Employment and Earnings File," Mathematical Policy Research, Inc. and Social and Scientific Systems, Inc., December, 1980. This paper uses data for the AFDC women who participated in the Demonstration.

II. *Eligibility Requirements and Data Collection*

To qualify applicants had to be currently unemployed, to have been unemployed for a total of at least three of the previous six months, to have received AFDC payments for thirty of the previous thirty-six months, and to have no preschool children. Eligible applicants who volunteered for Supported Work were randomly assigned into a treatment or a control group during 1976 and 1977. The experiment was run in seven sites: Atlanta, Georgia; Chicago, Illinois; Hartford, Connecticut; Newark, New Jersey; New York City, New York; Oakland, California; and in several locations in Wisconsin.

All participants, including the control group members, were interviewed when admitted into the program. Among the information collected in these interviews were the woman's age, years of schooling, whether she was a high school dropout, number of children under 18, marital status including whether she had ever been married, and race. In addition, retrospective data on a woman's employment status were obtained in semimonthly intervals for the two years prior to the baseline. This information was used to calculate the respondent's number of semimonthly periods of employment experience in the two years prior to the baseline. Another question determined the number of weeks since a woman's last regular job, which was used to construct a variable for whether a woman had held a regular job since she was 16 years old.

SAMPLE SELECTION AND INITIAL CONDITIONS   **201**

Both treatments and controls were interviewed at nine-month intervals following the baseline. These interviews collected information on each woman's employment status in semimonthly intervals during the previous nine months. These data were used to construct the length of spells of employment and unemployment during the twenty-six months following the baseline. Some women with a twenty-seven month interval had employment data for only twenty-six months because their interview took place before the end of the month. The post-baseline employment histories in our study extend for fifty-two semimonthly periods. The sample used in the study consists of only those women with a baseline and three nine-month interviews and who satisfied the two employment related eligibility criteria for the program. Unfortunately, less than 40 percent of the sample was interviewed after twenty-seven months due to program costs. In addition, not every woman who participated in the program as either a treatment or a control appears to have satisfied the employment-related eligibility criteria. However, these factors do not affect the integrity of the experimental design since treatments and controls were affected equally. Nevertheless, the sample available for this study was greatly reduced. There were 275 women in our treatment group and 266 women in our control group. All of these women volunteered for the program during 1976. The means and standard errors of the women's demographic characteristics are presented in Table A.

The labor demand variables used in the paper were collected from various issues of *Employment and Earnings* published monthly by the U.S. Department of Labor. We used the deviation around the site mean of total payroll employment and number of persons receiving unemployment insurance to proxy for labor market conditions in each woman's city at a point in time.

III. *Miscellaneous Issues*

A. *Deleting Ineligibles*: There were thirty-four women—nineteen trainees and fifteen controls— whose employment histories prior to the baseline were inconsistent with two intended eligibility requirements of the program. Nearly all of these women were unemployed in less than three of the

TABLE A

CHARACTERISTICS OF TREATMENTS AND CONTROLS

	Treatments (1)	Controls (2)
Age	33.67	34.98
	(.47)	(.45)
Schooling	10.17	10.11
	(.11)	(.13)
H.S. Dropout	.70	.71
	(.03)	(.03)
Number of Kids	2.25	2.31
	(.08)	(.08)
Never Married	.38	.33
	(.03)	(.03)
Black	.85	.82
	(.02)	(.02)
Prior Experience[a]	2.59	2.91
	(.34)	(.42)
Never Employed[b]	.16	.18
	(.02)	(.02)
Number of Women	275	266

[a] Prior experience is the number of weeks of employment in the two years prior to the baseline.
[b] Never employed is a dummy variable indicating that the woman has not had a regular job since she was 16 years old.

J. C. HAM AND R. J. LALONDE

six months prior to the program; some also were employed at the baseline. When these women are put back into the sample there are 294 trainees and 283 controls. Ham and LaLonde (1990) present the average durations and empirical survivor functions for this slightly larger sample. The program's effect on employment rates is unaffected by which sample we choose to use.

Excluding these women should not affect the integrity of the experimental design as long as "ineligible" women were no more likely to be assigned to the treatment group than to the control group. We focus on the program effects for this "eligible" sample in this paper partly because there are relatively few cases of ineligibles, and because we would have too few data points to estimate a separate hazard for interrupted employment spells.

B. No-Shows: There were fourteen treatment group members in our sample who volunteered and were randomly assigned into training but never showed up for supported work. We treat these no-shows as trainees throughout the analysis. To exclude these women from the analysis would contaminate the experimental design. Therefore, the training effect measures the impact on the

TABLE B
ESTIMATES OF EMPLOYMENT AND UNEMPLOYMENT HAZARD FUNCTIONS

A: Full Set of Estimates for Table III

Variables	Employment Spells		Fresh Unemployment Spells		All Unemployment Spells	
	(1)	(2)	(3)	(4)	(5)	(6)
Training status	−.394	−.425	−.382	−.374	−.191	−.105
	(.155)	(.180)	(.166)	(.208)	(.129)	(.156)
Age	−.013	−.016	−.009	.009	−.016	−.018
	(.011)	(.013)	(.012)	(.015)	(.009)	(.011)
Schooling	.049	.056	.125	.149	.150	.169
	(.051)	(.062)	(.063)	(.078)	(.068)	(.054)
H.S. Dropout	.398	.472	.306	−.427	−.335	−.437
	(.199)	(.238)	(.219)	(.277)	(.163)	(.200)
Kids under 18	.010	.009	−.037	−.024	.030	.052
	(.055)	(.066)	(.060)	(.073)	(.045)	(.053)
Never Married	.075	.028	−.148	−.182	−.243	−.284
	(.167)	(.205)	(.182)	(.238)	(.134)	(.167)
Black	.060	.065	−.391	−.458	−.386	−.469
	(.191)	(.225)	(.210)	(.275)	(.153)	(.191)
Area Employment	1.78	1.10	4.60	3.36	.531	1.15
	(3.78)	(4.18)	(4.24)	(4.83)	(3.10)	(3.38)
Area Unemployment	.651	.669	−.117	−.135	−1.26	−1.19
	(.431)	(.447)	(.511)	(.531)	(.368)	(.385)
Log Duration	.212	.155	−.453	−.299	−.503	−.353
	(.246)	(.258)	(.075)	(.119)	(.055)	(.082)
Log Duration^2	−.168	−.113	—	—		
	(.069)	(.845)				
θ_1	−3.15	−2.78	−2.91	−2.21	−3.16	−2.34
	(.817)	(1.03)	(.946)	(1.36)	(.694)	(.885)
θ_2	—	−4.12	—	−3.81	—	−3.94
		(1.19)		(1.36)		(.862)
μ	—	.181	—	−1.24	—	−1.68
		(1.20)		(1.50)		(.836)
−Log L	852.7	851.6	768.1	765.5	1416.4	1411.9

SAMPLE SELECTION AND INITIAL CONDITIONS

TABLE B Cont.

ESTIMATES OF EMPLOYMENT AND UNEMPLOYMENT HAZARD FUNCTIONS

B: Full Set of Estimates for Table IV

Variable	Excluding Training and Employment Spells — Unemployment		Excluding Training Spells — Unemployment			Including Training Spells — Unemployment		
	Interrupted (1)	Fresh (2)	Interrupted (3)	Fresh (4)	Employment (5)	Interrupted (6)	Fresh (7)	Employment (8)
Training status	—	−.073	—	−.062	−.365	—	.025	−.403
		(.201)		(.207)	(−.159)		(.217)	(.156)
Age	−.021	−.009	.021	−.010	−.012	.020	−.0097	−.012
	(.018)	(.013)	(.019)	(.013)	(.011)	(.017)	(.013)	(.011)
Years of schooling	.200	.150	.207	.145	.057	.205	.150	.055
	(.088)	(.072)	(.089)	(.072)	(.053)	(.086)	(.072)	(.052)
Kids under 18	.223	−.035	.220	−.033	.018	.221	−.041	.018
	(.077)	(.067)	(.078)	(.066)	(.056)	(.076)	(.067)	(.056)
Black	−.596	−.422	−.618	−.420	.051	−.603	−.442	.038
	(.263)	(.246)	(.265)	(.241)	(.194)	(.257)	(.025)	(.193)
Never married	−.224	−.140	−.284	−.155	.088	−.222	−.101	.095
	(.267)	(.211)	(.309)	(.215)	(.171)	(.265)	(.212)	(.169)
H.S. dropout	−.595	−.516	−.606	−.503	.366	−.590	−.559	.373
	(.304)	(.264)	(.308)	(.264)	(.202)	(.298)	(.259)	(.201)
Local employment	−5.76	4.71	−4.61	4.50	2.17	−5.20	5.27	2.46
	(5.54)	(4.50)	(5.67)	(4.47)	(3.81)	(5.48)	(4.50)	(.382)
Local unemployment	−2.50	−.189	−2.44	−.198	.599	−2.42	−.206	.617
	(.619)	(.521)	(.617)	(.520)	(.435)	(.614)	(.517)	(.433)
Log duration	−.803	−.357	−.816	−.370	.207	−.807	−.357	.212
	(.198)	(.097)	(.197)	(.095)	(.246)	(.194)	(.091)	(.246)
Log duration squared	—	—	—	—	−163	—	—	−168
					(.069)			(.069)
Constant: α_j	5.71	0	6.27	0	−2.22	5.27	0	−2.59
	(3.07)		(3.34)		(1.07)	(2.81)		(.976)
θ_1	−3.76		−2.27			−2.14		
	(1.11)		(1.05)			(1.05)		
θ_2	−2.23		−3.67			−3.78		
	(1.06)		(1.11)			(1.10)		
μ	2.03		−1.99			−2.11		
	(.329)		(.368)			(.313)		
Loading	2.08	1.0	2.28	1.0	.329	1.97	1.0	.191
	(.652)		(.732)		(.221)	(.517)		(.173)
Log L	−1401.2		−2251.9			−2994.4		
Log L, No heterogeneity	−1410.2		−2262.8			−3007.9		

Notes: See notes to Table III. The term μ is defined as $P_1 = e^u/(1 + e^u)$. In Panel B, the "loading" factors are the c_j terms in equation (18), where c_u is normalized to equal 1.

204   J. C. HAM AND R. J. LALONDE

employment opportunities of the treatment group members of the opportunity to participate in supported work.

C. *Supported Work Participation*: Trainees were guaranteed a subsidized supported work job for nine to eighteen months. Initially productivity and attendance standards for the participants were less than would be expected on a regular job, but these standards were raised by the program administrators over time. Some participants either left the program voluntarily or were asked to leave because of poor performance before their term expired. For the sample used in this paper, 75 percent of the participants had left by the 13th month and 95 percent were out of the program by the 17th month.

REFERENCES

ASHENFELTER, ORLEY (1978): "Estimating the Effect of Training Programs on Earnings," *Review of Economics and Statistics*, 60, 47–57.

ASHENFELTER, ORLEY, AND DAVID CARD (1985): "Using the Longitudinal Structure of Earnings to Estimate the Effect of Training Programs," *Review of Economics and Statistics*, 67, 648–660.

BARNOW, BURT (1987): "The Impact of CETA Programs on Earnings: A Review of the Literature," *Journal of Human Resources*, 22, 157–193.

BURTLESS, GARY, AND LARRY ORR (1986): "Are Classical Experiments Needed for Manpower Policy?" *Journal of Human Resources*, 21, 606–639.

CARD, DAVID, AND DANIEL SULLIVAN (1988): "Measuring the Effect of CETA Participation on Movements in and out of Employment," *Econometrica*, 56, 497–530.

COUCH, KENNETH (1992): "New Evidence on the Long-Term Effects of Employment and Training," *Journal of Labor Economics*, 10, 380–388.

FLINN, CHRISTOPHER J., AND JAMES J. HECKMAN (1983): "The Likelihood Function for the Multi-state-Multiepisode Model in 'Models for the Analysis of Labor Force Dynamics'," in *Advances in Econometrics*, Vol. 2, ed. by R. L. Basmann and G. F. Rhodes. Greenwich, CT: JAI Press.

FRACKER, THOMAS, AND REBECCA MAYNARD (1987): "Evaluating Comparison Group Designs with Employment-Related Programs," *Journal of Human Resources*, 22, 194–227.

GRITZ, MARK (1993): "The Impact of Training on the Frequency and Duration of Employment," *Journal of Econometrics*, 57, 21–51.

GUERON, JUDITH, AND EDWARD PAULY (1991): *From Welfare to Work*. New York: Russell Sage Foundation.

HAM, JOHN, AND ROBERT J. LALONDE (1990): "Using Social Experiments to Estimate the Effect of Training on Transition Rates," in *Panel Data and Labor Market Studies*, ed. by J. Hartog, G. Ridder, and J. Theeuwes. North-Holland: Elsevier Science Publications, 157–172.

———— (1991): "Estimating the Effect of Training on Employment and Unemployment Durations: Evidence from Experimental Data," NBER Working Paper No. 3912.

HAM, JOHN C., AND SAMUEL A. REA, JR. (1987): "Unemployment Insurance and Male Unemployment Duration in Canada," *Journal of Labor Economics*, 5, 325–353.

HECKMAN, JAMES (1979): "Sample Selection Bias as a Specification Error," *Econometrica*, 47, 153–161.

HECKMAN, JAMES J., AND V. JOSEPH HOTZ (1989): "Choosing Among Alternative Nonexperimental Methods for Estimating the Impact of Social Programs: The Case of Manpower Training," *Journal of the American Statistical Association*, 84, 862–874.

HECKMAN, JAMES, AND RICHARD ROBB (1985): "Alternative Methods for Evaluating the Impact of Interventions," in *Longitudinal Analysis of the Labor Market Data*, ed. by J. J. Heckman and B. Singer. Cambridge: Cambridge University Press.

HECKMAN, JAMES J., AND BURTON SINGER (1984a): "Econometric Duration Analysis," *Journal of Econometrics*, 24, 63–132.

—— (1984b): "A Method for Minimizing the Impact of Distributional Assumptions in Econometric Models for Duration Data," *Econometrica*, 47, 247–283.

HECKMAN, JAMES, AND JAMES WALKER (1990): "The Relationship between Wages and Income and the Timing and Spacing of Births: Evidence from Swedish Longitudinal Data," *Econometrica*, 58, 1411–1441.

HOLLAND, PAUL W. (1986): "Statistics and Causal Inference," *Journal of the American Statistical Association*, 81, 945–960.

HOLLISTER, R., P. KEMPER, AND R. MAYNARD, EDS. (1984): *The National Supported Work Demonstration*. Madison: University of Wisconsin Press.

LALONDE, ROBERT J. (1995): "The Promise of Public Sector-Sponsored Training Programs," *Journal of Economic Perspectives*, 9, 149–168.

—— (1986): "Evaluating the Econometric Evaluations of Training Programs with Experimental Data," *American Economic Review*, 76, 604–620.

LANCASTER, TONY (1990): *The Econometric Analysis of Transition Data*. Cambridge: Cambridge University Press.

LANCASTER, TONY, GUIDO IMBENS, AND PETER DOLTON (1987): "Job Separations and Job Matching," in *The Practice of Econometrics-Studies on Demand, Forecasting, Money and Income*, ed. by Risto Heijmans and Heintz Neudecker. Boston: Kluwer Academic.

MANSKI, CHARLES, AND IRWIN GARFINKEL (1992): "Introduction," in *Evaluating Welfare and Training Programs*, ed. by Charles Manski and Irwin Garfinkel. Cambridge: Harvard University Press.

MEYER, BRUCE (1990): "Unemployment Insurance and Unemployment Spells," *Econometrica*, 58, 757–782.

RIDDER, GEERT (1986): "An Event History Approach to the Evaluation of Training, Recruitment, and Employment Programs," *Journal of Applied Econometrics*, 1, 109–126.

RIDDER, GEERT, AND WIM VERBAKEL (1984): "On the Estimation of the Proportional Hazards Model in the Presence of Unobserved Heterogeneity," Report 17/84, Faculty of Actuarial Science and Econometrics, University of Amsterdam.

RUBIN, DONALD (1986): "Comment: Which Ifs Have Causal Answers," *Journal of the American Statistical Association*, 81, 961–962.

[25]

Economica (1996) **63**, 113–30

Manpower Training Programmes and Employment Stability

By Josef Zweimüller*† and Rudolf Winter-Ebmer†‡

* *Institute for Advanced Studies, Vienna, † University of Linz, Austria, and ‡ Centre for Economic Policy Research, London*

Final version received 30 March 1994.

We evaluate Austrian labour market policy focusing on its possible effects upon recurrent unemployment. Without properly considering the selection processes for public training programmes, misleading results emerge. Taking the participation decision into account in a bivariate probit setting, Austrian manpower training programmes turn out to be a sort of 'catching up': (i) disadvantaged and less motivated job-seekers are given priority in enrolment into training programmes, and (ii) participation in such courses improves employment stability significantly.

Introduction

Most industrialized countries spend non-negligible amounts on 'active labour market policies', such as direct job creation, employment subsidies and labour market training programmes. Among these policy measures, manpower training programmes (MTPs) are of high importance. In most countries the budgetary funding of MTPs has been increasing, in both absolute and relative terms.[1]

In the United States, MTPs are designed mainly to increase the earnings capacity of the 'working poor'. Consequently, the main focus of evaluation studies is on the wage effects of MTPs. This is different from Europe, where unemployment has been persistently high, and MTPs are seen by many as a key to improving work opportunities of the unemployed and other groups facing high unemployment risks. As a result, MTPs are implemented to affect the subsequent employment opportunities of participants.

This is also true for Austria. Austria's position as a low-unemployment country has eroded, and the share of problem groups among the unemployed increased during the 1980s. Although MTPs are not used as extensively as in, for instance, Scandinavia, they are quantitatively important and are the most heavily used 'active' measures. It is the aim of this paper to study the employment effects of Austrian MTPs.

Despite the widespread use of MTPs in European countries, econometric evidence on the employment effects of measures is scarce, although this has been changing of late.[2] Available studies differ in the sample design (experimental/non-experimental data) and in the group analysed (unemployed/youth) as well as in the indicators that measure the success of the programmes.[3]

It is often claimed in the evaluation of programmes that non-experimental data are misleading. Objections to this method stem from the fact that training participants are a non-random (self-selected) sample. Comparing a sample of MTP-enrolled individuals ('treatments') with a control group ('controls') with similar observable characteristics will lead to biased estimates: it is likely that unobservable characteristics will differ systematically between the two groups.[4]

Whereas traditional non-experimental studies ignore these differences, more recent approaches address the issue of sample selectivity directly. This is done by applying appropriate methods for the correction of sample selection bias.[5] The studies by Main and Shelly (1990) as well as Ackum (1991) apply these methods to study MTP effects on wages in the United Kingdom and Sweden, respectively. Both estimate a MTP participation function and include a selectivity correction term in the wage regressions for trainees and controls. This guarantees unbiased estimates of coefficients in wage equations,[6] which are used to assess the effectiveness of training programmes.

Our approach is similar in spirit, but differs from these studies in one important respect. Rather than looking at *wages* after MTP participation, our aim is to evaluate training effects on subsequent employment experience. This makes things more complicated because of the choice of a suitable indicator of success.

Basically, there are two variables that seem to be obvious candidates for modelling potential training effects: (i) re-employment probability (i.e. unemployment duration after MTP enrolment), which should reveal the short-term effects of training; and (ii) stability of employment following MTP participation, which should reveal the longer-term effects of training.

Torp (1994) analyses the effects of MTPs in Norway on employment duration in the 12 months following a fixed base-line date. In this study, the expected value of the dependent variable is obviously the product of the two interesting indicators mentioned above: the expected employment duration during the respective period, given that the individual holds a job, and the re-employment probability.

Unfortunately, the comparison of re-employment probabilities between treatments and controls, as discussed in Ham and LaLonde (1990), turns out to be very problematic. This is so even if there are no systematic differences in unobservable variables between the two groups, so that sample selectivity problems can be ignored. Consider two identical groups, which differ only in their MTP enrolment status, and assume that there is negative duration dependence in unemployment spells. A comparison of hazard rates of treatments (calculated from 'fresh' spells after the end of training participation) with the hazard rates of controls (calculated from spells in progress) will then bias the estimates in favour of positive MTP effects. We will observe shorter unemployment spells for treatments even if there is no training effect—simply as a consequence of state dependence.[7]

Concentrating on the second possible effect of training seems to be more fruitful. Instead of using duration models and analysing the duration of subsequent employment spells, we adopt a different method. We define subsequent employment experience as a dichotomous variable. A work history is assumed to be 'unstable' if the individual rejoins the unemployment register within a given 'risk period', and is considered to be 'stable' otherwise. The main advantage of this procedure is that it enables us to deal with the sample selection issue in a convenient way. Our problem is reduced to the joint determination of two (0, 1) events: training participation and employment stability.

The paper is organized as follows. In Section I we discuss the importance of MTPs in Austria relative to other countries and then describe the institutional features characterizing Austria's MTPs. Section II describes the data, with particular reference to the construction of the relevant employment indicator, and shows preliminary evidence without proper consideration of sample selection issues. After a discussion of technical issues, including the econometric methodology and problems of identification, Section III presents our main empirical results. We conclude that, taking selective training enrolment into account, MTPs have strong positive effects on participants' employment careers in Austria.

I. INSTITUTIONAL BACKGROUND

Table 1 displays national expenditures on labour market policies, with special reference to training measures. In Austria, the total amount spent on labour market policies (including 'passive' measures such as unemployment insurance and early retirement provisions) is comparatively low. In 1986, the period to which our study refers, Austria spent 1·48% of GDP on labour market policies, compared with considerably more than 2% of GDP in other European countries, e.g. Germany, France, the Netherlands, Sweden or the United Kingdom. This is due in part to persistently lower unemployment rates in Austria than in most of OECD-Europe. If one considers the corresponding figure per percentage unemployed, then Austria's expenditure (0·48% of GDP per 1% unemployment) is the highest among all countries listed in Table 1, apart from Sweden.

TABLE 1

EXPENDITURES ON LABOUR MARKET POLICIES, SELECTED COUNTRIES, 1986

Country	Unemployment rate (%)	Expenditure (% of GDP)		
		Training*	Total active	Active and passive
Austria	3·1	0·29	0·41	1·48
Germany	8·0	0·79	0·99	2·34
France	10·5	0·68	0·74	3·07
Netherlands	13·2	1·02	1·08	3·99
Sweden	2·2	1·60	1·86	2·66
UK	11·8	0·58	0·89	2·57
US	7·0	0·23	0·24	0·83

* Includes special programmes for young and disabled.
Source: OECD (1988).

Much of this expenditure, however, is devoted to passive measures, in particular for early retirement provisions, from which Austria has made heavy use.[8] As in the other countries listed in Table 1, about one-third of total expenditure goes to active measures. (Again, Sweden is the exception.)

The main part of active labour market policies consists of training measures. It should be noted that the figures in Table 1 also include special programmes for young and disabled persons, which may not necessarily be training programmes. As far as the Austrian figure is concerned, however, the proportion of such expenditure is negligible (Bundesministerium für Arbeit und Soziales 1986).

According to the Ministry of Social Affairs, the goals of training programmes are broad; they range from inhibiting future unemployment to providing the skills necessary for structural change and to support problem groups, such as the disabled, young and long-term unemployed. Consequently, MTPs supplied by the public labour market administration are rather heterogeneous. They include general programmes intended to inhibit the depreciation of skills, to teach the skills required for a new occupation, to restore and maintain work morale and labour market attachment of participants and simply to provide skills for job search, as well as more specific measures such as training for specific jobs, and training for specific tasks within firms.[9]

To be eligible for participation a person must be unemployed, or face the risk of becoming unemployed. Since the Austrian Ministry of Social Affairs does not specify the eligibility criteria more narrowly, this leaves a great deal of discretion to the programme administrators (Bundesministerium für Arbeit und Soziales, n.d.). The guidelines instruct the public servants actively to offer training to the unemployed who lack specific skills, and in particular to individuals with placement disadvantages (school dropouts, the long-term unemployed, the disabled, women with long work interruptions).

During training participation, individuals receive compensation which amounts to the level of unemployment benefits. If necessary, the administration supports additional costs accruing from participation (e.g. travel costs or increased cost of living). Courses are financed from the budget for labour market administration.

II. Data and Preliminary Results

The data we use concern a representative 2% sample of Austrian unemployed males[10] who left the unemployment register in 1986 either directly after a training episode or after an unemployment spell. As we are interested in employment stability, we restrict the population to Austrian citizens below the age of 52 to exclude disturbing influences from early retirement schemes and foreign workers' legislation. The data are administrative data from the files of Austrian labour offices. The sample was drawn in spring 1988 and covers the unemployment history as well as the occurrence of training episodes for all individuals in the sample back to the introduction of electronic unemployment service in the early 1980s.

To evaluate training effects, we look at the occurrence of repeat unemployment spells within a period of 12 months, beginning with the day after the 1986 spell, in order to take an equal 'risk period' into consideration. Strategies and opportunities of workers may be different: some may find a new job during course participation, others may remain unemployed after completion of the programme. However, a possible unemployment episode immediately after a training spell should not be counted as a repeat spell, but as a logical continuation of the previous spell, interrupted by a training programme. Individuals 1 to 4 of Figure 1 are included in the final sample because they left the register in 1986, allowing room for an observation period of 12 months. Note that training attainment in 1986 is not a precondition for entering the sample (person 4). Those who did not manage to find work in 1986—even if they completed a course in this year (person 5)—had to be excluded from the sample. The

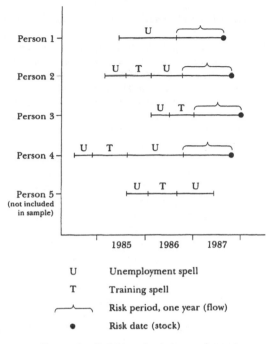

U	Unemployment spell
T	Training spell
⌒	Risk period, one year (flow)
●	Risk date (stock)

FIGURE 1. Definition of repeat unemployment.

study is therefore representative for unemployment-leavers in 1986. In the case of a stationary state,[11] the structure of unemployment-leavers is constant over time; this refers to enrolment as well as to the number of short- and long-term unemployed (compare persons 4 and 5).

Owing to the importance of tourism in Austria, seasonal unemployment contributes a substantial portion to total unemployment rates. This phenomenon is particularly relevant when issues of recurrent unemployment are studied. For this reason, we excluded persons who were engaged in occupations prone to seasonal unemployment—agriculture, construction and tourism—from the analysis.[12] Our remaining sample consists of 1945 unemployment leavers, 5·8% of whom received manpower training in the course of this episode. Of these trainees, 45·5% suffered a repeat spell within 12 months compared with 46·4% of controls. The difference in the unemployment probability is statistically insignificant (χ^2-value of 0·02).

To model recurrent unemployment econometrically, let y_i be an index for the risk of unemployment repetition, which is assumed to be positive if the individual joined the unemployment register again within a period of one year (flow measure) and 0 or negative if not. Assume that y_i is determined by

(1) $y_i^* = \alpha d_i + \beta x_i + \varepsilon_i,$

where d_i is a dummy variable, taking the value 1 if the individual was enrolled in training and, 0 otherwise, and x_i is a vector of individual characteristics and labour market variables. If ε_i, the error term, follows the standard normal distribution, the coefficients of interest, α and β, can be estimated by the standard probit model.

This is only one way of modelling recurrent unemployment. The chosen procedure leaves out the length of a repeat unemployment spell: any repeat spell is weighed equally regardless of whether it lasts five days or one year. To control for spell length, we define a second success indicator of the programmes: we count a repeat spell if the individual is unemployed on the day exactly one year after the 1986 spell (stock measure; see Figure 1). The stock measure produces an over-representation of the long-term unemployed; the probability that a person is counted as unemployed at a point of time is higher, the longer the spell is ('length bias': Salant 1977); therefore, the duration component gets more weight. Using this definition, 28·9% of trainees experienced a repeat spell compared with 23·3% of controls, which results in a significant *negative* impact of training programmes in the aggregate (χ^2-value of 6·56). A further possibility would be to ask how often an individual has become unemployed during a year. This concept was not followed because it is empirically untractable in a bivariate setting, where training selection is taken into account.

To control for population heterogeneity, several personal characteristics like age, marital status and education are included in the regressions. In addition, local and occupational labour market conditions are accounted for by unemployment–vacancy (U–V) relations; the past employment career of the job-seeker is modelled by the tenure of his last job before the 1986 spell and by his last unemployment spell as well as the unemployment record in the preceding three years, i.e. excluding the 1986 spell.[13]

From the point of view of job search theory, the expected earnings replacement ratio (expected unemployment benefits in relation to expected labour income) should be a major determinant of unemployment entry. For administrative reasons, information about benefits exists only for those who suffer a repeat spell. To overcome this problem, we estimated a selectivity-corrected OLS regression for the replacement ratio on the sub-sample of the recurrent unemployed. Expected replacement ratios were then calculated using these consistently estimated regression coefficients for the whole sample.[14]

A look at Table 2 draws a pessimistic picture of the efficiency of these policies.[15] The coefficient of the training dummy is insignificant in the flow case and even significantly *positive* at the 10% level for the stock measure of repeat unemployment. However, to conclude that training programmes were ineffective, one would have to assume that the training selection process had no relation to the probability of recurrent unemployment—an assumption we should test for.

III. CORRECTING FOR SELECTIVE ENROLMENT INTO TRAINING

Econometric issues

The selection problem arises because trainees are not chosen randomly from the population. If unobservable variables that determine selection for a training programme are correlated with those affecting the future unemployment outcome, there is a simultaneity problem. Consider the following simultaneous-

TABLE 2
RECURRENT UNEMPLOYMENT*

	Flow	Stock	Mean
Training (0, 1)	−0·073	0·226*	0·058
	(0·128)	(0·133)	
Age: −25 (0, 1)	−0·189*	−0·127	0·373
	(0·099)	(0·108)	
Age: 26–30 (0, 1)	−0·201**	−0·147	0·205
	(0·092)	(0·100)	
Age: 46–52 (0, 1)	0·338***	0·366***	0·089
	(0·119)	(0·123)	
Hard-to-place (0, 1)	−0·029	0·150*	0·197
	(0·075)	(0·081)	
Married with children (0, 1)	−0·179*	−0·068	0·307
	(0·101)	(0·109)	
Schooling: primary (0, 1)	0·006	0·075	0·399
	(0·063)	(0·069)	
Schooling: higher or university (0, 1)	−0·278***	−0·067	0·077
	(0·129)	(0·145)	
Tenure last job (days) × 10^{-3}	−0·106***	−0·078***	0·759
	(0·023)	(0·026)	(1·414)
Duration of last unemployment spell (days) × 10^{-2}	0·056	0·139***	1·191
	(0·043)	(0·046)	(1·506)
(Duration of last unemployment spell)^2 × 10^{-4}	−0·004	−0·009**	3·686
	(0·004)	(0·004)	(14·471)
Cumulated unemployment duration 3 years before 1986 (days) × 10^{-2}	0·101***	0·075***	1·045
	(0·018)	(0·019)	(1·672)
Expected replacement ratio (%)	0·021**	0·019**	54·0
	(0·008)	(0·009)	(6·27)
City size >100,000 and <1,000,000 (0, 1)	−0·283***	−0·215**	0·174
	(0·088)	(0·100)	
City size >999,999 (0, 1)	−0·186**	−0·033	0·202
	(0·079)	(0·087)	
Occupational U–V relation × 10^{-2} (%)	0·008	0·008	8·484
	(0·006)	(0·007)	(4·855)
Regional U–V relation × 10^{-2} (%)	0·007	0·013	7·558
	(0·008)	(0·008)	(4·268)
Constant	−1·196	−2·033	
Log L	−1283·2	−1022·1	
LR test	119·0***	95·4***	
N	1945	1945	

* Dependent variable: flow: repeat unemployment within one year (0, 1); stock: repeat unemployment at the reference date (0, 1); standard errors in brackets. *(**, ***): significant at 10 (5, 1)% level.

equations model:

(2a) $y_i^* = a d_i^* + b x_i + e_i$ $y_i = 1$ if $y_i^* > 0$

                                            $y_i = 0$ otherwise,

(2b) $d_i^* = c z_i + u_i$ $d_i = 1$ if $d_i^* > 0$

        $E(e_i u_i) \neq 0$ $d_i = 0$ otherwise.

Equation (2a) is identical to (1) except that the training indicator, d_i^*, is a continuous rather than a dichotomous variable. Equation (2b) models training selection: c is a parameter vector, measuring the influence of training determinants summarized in the vector z_i; u_i is an error term. Note that (2a, b) is a recursive system. Since we look at the unemployment experience of an individual *after* participation in a training programme, the likelihood of his being selected for a training programme, d_i^*, influences the risk of his suffering repeat unemployment, y_i^*, but not vice versa.

The estimation of (2a, b) can be carried out by a two-stage procedure, analogous to two-stage least squares. In the first stage we run a univariate probit over (2b). This yields coefficients $\hat{c}$, from which an estimator for the training index, $\hat{d}_i^* = \hat{c}z_i$, can be calculated. In the second stage, we use $\hat{d}_i^*$ as a regressor in another univariate probit for equation (2a), to obtain an asymptotically consistent estimate of a, the parameter of our primary interest. The estimate $\hat{a}$, though consistent, is not asymptotically efficient. To estimate the standard error of $\hat{a}$ correctly, we have to use the asymptotic variance–covariance matrix. This is reported in Maddala (1983, pp. 246–7).

The second method of dealing with the selectivity issue is to run a bivariate probit model of the following form:

(3a) $y_i^* = ad_i + \beta x_i + \varepsilon_i,$

(3b) $d_i^* = \gamma z_i + \mu_i,$

where y_i^* and d_i^* are defined as before.

The major difference between models (2a, b) and (3a, b) is that in the former the training variable enters the repeat unemployment equation as the continuous index, d_i^*, whereas in the latter it is the dummy variable, d_i, that influences the risk of recurrent unemployment. Model (2a, b) assumes that it is the *intention* (or the likelihood) to participate in a training programme that influences the future unemployment outcome; this may reflect the motivation of the trainee, the availability of programmes, and/or the interests of the programme administrator. In model (3a, b), on the other hand, it is the *occurrence* of a training episode, that is the actual participation (or non-participation) in a programme, which is the relevant variable.[16] Furthermore, in model (3a, b) the correlation of error terms in the two equations can be directly estimated.

Below, we will report the result of both models. From the above discussion, however, it should be clear that measuring the effectiveness of training programmes requires an analysis of the impact of actual participation in training. Consequently, it is model (3a, b) that is the appropriate one for the present problem.

Identification

In order to get reliable estimates of the interesting parameters of the simultaneous-equations system (2a, b) and (3a, b), respectively, we have to take a closer look at the determinants of training enrolment, and to specify the identifying restrictions of the model.

In general, the actual enrolment procedure consists of three different stages: the availability of training programmes at a certain point in time, the eligibility of the individual, and the decision of the unemployed to participate. The estimation of the enrolment equation can only be based on a reduced-form of these three influences.

The trainee-control differences, which are most difficult to handle, are mainly motivation and immediate pre-training labour market position and earnings. American studies often assume that the motivation of trainees is superior to those of controls. This can be deduced from the behaviour of 'no-shows'—persons who were eligible for a programme and did not show up, or dropped out within the first few days—a group often preferred as a control group (Cooley *et al.* 1979). On the other hand, if programme administrators are paid or evaluated according to the post-programme earnings and employment records of their clients, they have an incentive to 'cream' (Bassi 1984, p. 37), i.e. to choose the best among those eligible.

Trainees have typically experienced a decline in their earnings, both absolutely and relative to any comparison group selected, in the period immediately preceding treatment (Ashenfelter and Card 1985, p. 648); the same applies to employment ratios (Card and Sullivan 1988, p. 501). Problems may arise especially if these 'dips' are the consequence of negative transitory components, whereas permanent components[17] may be larger than those of the controls (Cooley *et al.* 1979, p. 124). Modelling enrolment should take these considerations into account.

Identification of the unemployment equation in the two-stage model is accomplished if at least one regressor in (2b) can be excluded from (2a). The bivariate model is identified if at least one regressor in any of the two equations does not appear in the other one. In our empirical results, the training equation includes all variables, which also appear in the unemployment equation. The only exception is the earnings–replacement ratio: we assume that the ratio between unemployment benefits and expected wages influences only the unemployment outcome. This can be justified by the fact that payments to the unemployed do not vary with their trainings status.[18]

Moreover, we concentrate on the forecasts concerning the long-run state of the labour market within districts. This variable should have no systematic effect on the current unemployment experience of individuals, but it is likely to determine current supply of training measures, as well as the choice of the unemployed to join a programme. Availability of courses should be the result of planning in advance, taking into account the long-term state of the labour market. It is also rational, from the point of view of the unemployed, to join a training programme if labour market problems are expected to be permanent rather than transitory. This is why we used 'projected employment change in district in 1991' as the relevant labour market variable in the training equation. Furthermore, elapsed unemployment duration is treated differently in the two equations. In the training equation, only unemployment days up to the entry into a training programme are considered, whereas for the unemployment equation, jobless days immediately after a training spell are counted as well. Of course, the two measures coincide in the case of no training.

Concerning the remaining variables in the training equation, care has been taken to include control variables in both equations in the same way. To overcome 'dips' in pre-training experience mentioned above, past employment and unemployment records in the three years preceding the 1986 spell are taken into account. In addition, matching of programme demand and supply should be facilitated in a 'thick market' (city size). As motivation and certain special qualifications of participants are partly observed by the programme administrator but are unobservable for the analyst, they should be picked up by the error structure, i.e. the coefficient of correlation.

Results

Training attainment   Table 3 presents our results. The coefficients of the training equation were obtained from the bivariate probit model using the flow measure in the unemployment equation. The results are almost identical to the stock specification and the univariate probit used for the two-stage procedure, respectively. To save space they are not reported here. It has to be remembered that training attainment arises from a reduced-form equation incorporating the supply of training slots and the demand thereof. Past unemployment—the length of the 1986 spell as well as cumulated joblessness in the preceding three years—raises training entry considerably. The former effect should not be surprising because it implicitly refers to a 'cumulative probability of training', whereas the latter can be interpreted as an enrolment procedure.[19]

The variables schooling and age are not significant; the point estimates correspond to prior expectations and recent UK studies: less training with higher age, but more retraining for already well educated individuals (Booth 1991, Greenhalgh and Stewart 1987). Men with dependent children attain fewer training measures.[20] City size does not play the expected role: the unemployed residing in Vienna receive significantly fewer training opportunities than those in small or medium-size cities. Several reasons may be responsible for this. Job-matching for individuals holding rare occupations will be easier in a big city, and thus retraining will be less necessary. On the other hand, fewer training slots may be available in Vienna because it has better labour market conditions than the rest of the country.

The focusing of manpower training plans shows up clearly in the variable 'projected employment change in district for 1991'. Bad forecasts for a district lead to an increase in training opportunities.

Effect of MTPs on recurrent unemployment   Columns (2) and (3) of Table 3 report the results of the unemployment equation by using the bivariate probit specification when the dependent variable is constructed as the flow measure (column (2)) and as the stock measure (column (3)).

From an econometric point of view, the results should be compared with two independent probit equations, the coefficient of correlation ρ being the important parameter. Both Wald and likelihood ratio (LR) test imply that the hypothesis $\rho = 0$ can be rejected at the 5% level. After correcting for observable characteristics, the positive coefficient of correlation suggests that people with unfavourable expected employment careers will be more frequently selected for training. There is no evidence of a strategy of choosing the best among potential participants, but, rather on the contrary, evidence of a support of disadvantaged or less motivated persons by programme administrators. This corresponds to the guiding principles of Austrian labour market policy (Bundesministerium, n.d.) stressing the promotion of problem groups.[21]

TABLE 3

RECURRENT UNEMPLOYMENT WITH SELECTIVE TRAINING ENROLMENT[2]

	Bivariate probit			2-stage probit	
	Training (1)	Flow (2)	Stock (3)	Flow (4)	Stock (5)
Training	—	−1·261** (0·599)	−1·338*** (0·329)	−0·006 (0·092)	0·263*** (0·095)
Age: –25 (0, 1)	0·083 (0·135)	−0·158 (0·098)	−0·077 (0·101)	−0·189* (0·099)	−0·134 (0·108)
Age: 26–30 (0, 1)	0·101 (0·146)	−0·170* (0·091)	−0·091 (0·099)	−0·201** (0·092)	−0·172* (0·101)
Age: 46–52 (0, 1)	−0·268 (0·218)	0·291** (0·122)	0·283** (0·125)	0·337** (0·122)	0·446*** (0·127)
Hard-to-place (0, 1)	−0·088 (0·126)	−0·040 (0·074)	0·114 (0·081)	−0·030 (0·077)	0·196** (0·083)
Married with children (0, 1)	−0·332** (0·146)	−0·195** (0·099)	−0·115 (0·104)	−0·178* (0·106)	0·004 (0·113)
Schooling: primary (0, 1)	0·009 (0·109)	0·004 (0·063)	0·064 (0·068)	0·006 (0·063)	0·075 (0·069)
Schooling: higher or university (0, 1)	0·259 (0·193)	−0·240* (0·133)	−0·007 (0·146)	−0·278** (0·130)	−0·112 (0·146)
Tenure last job (days) × 10⁻³	0·004 (0·046)	−0·100*** (0·023)	−0·068*** (0·026)	−0·100*** (0·023)	−0·079*** (0·026)
Duration of last unemployment spell (days) × 10⁻²	—	0·076* (0·042)	0·166*** (0·045)	0·053 (0·058)	0·042 (0·061)
(Duration of last unemployment spell)² × 10⁻⁴	—	−0·004 (0·004)	−0·009* (0·005)	−0·004 (0·004)	−0·005 (0·004)
Unemployment duration 1986 until training (days) × 10⁻²	0·185*** (0·075)	—	—	—	—
(Unemployment duration 1986 until training entry)² × 10⁻⁴	−0·007 (0·007)	—	—	—	—
Cumulated unemployment duration 3 years before 1986 (days) × 10⁻²	0·053* (0·029)	0·104*** (0·017)	0·081*** (0·018)	0·100*** (0·019)	0·059*** (0·020)
Expected replacement ratio (%)	—	0·019** (0·008)	0·015* (0·008)	0·021** (0·008)	0·018** (0·009)
City size >100,000 and <1,000,000 (0, 1)	0·083 (0·158)	−0·250*** (0·089)	−0·155 (0·099)	−0·284*** (0·088)	−0·217** (0·100)
City size >999,999 (0, 1)	−0·384*** (0·142)	−0·218*** (0·080)	−0·103 (0·090)	−0·186** (0·086)	0·056 (0·094)
Occupational U–V relation (%) × 10⁻²	−0·007 (0·011)	0·006 (0·006)	0·005 (0·007)	0·008 (0·006)	0·009 (0·007)
Regional U–V relation (%) × 10⁻²	0·001 (0·015)	0·010 (0·007)	0·016** (0·008)	0·007 (0·007)	0·009 (0·008)
Projected employment change in district for 1991 (%)	−0·026** (0·011)	—	—	—	—
Constant	−1·760	−1·048	−1·756	−1·204	−1·429
ρ		0·580** (0·294)	0·796*** (0·190)	—	—
Log L		−1685·3	−1422·3	−1283·4	−1019·6
LR test		171·8***	145·6***	118·7***	100·4***
LR test for bivariate specification		4·9**	7·1***	—	—
N		1945	1945	1945	1945

[2] See notes to Table 2. The regression results for the training equation refer to the bivariate probit (flow). Means and standard deviations of variables are reported in Table 2, except for projected employment change (−1·74, 5·45).

Taking enrolment in courses into consideration does not change the parameters of the repeat unemployment equations (*cf.* Tables 1 and 2) except for one: the training dummy. Here the coefficients change dramatically, indicating a high and significant improvement in employment stability for both definitions of repeat unemployment.[22]

These results can be contrasted with those obtained from a two-stage probit, where the training indicator enters as a continuous variable constructed from the stage 1 probit on training (columns (4) and (5)).[23] The estimated MTP effects contrast strongly with those obtained in the bivariate probit, but they almost exactly reproduce the estimates obtained in Table 1, where selectivity was not taken into account: training is found to have no or even negative effects on subsequent unemployment experience. From the above discussion, however, it should be clear that the results of a two-stage probit are misleading. To evaluate MTP effects, the focus has to be on actual training participation, rather than on the likelihood of being selected This is why the subsequent discussion focuses on the bivariate probit results. It might be interesting to calculate the quantitative effect of training on unemployment probabilities for a given reference case. This is done in Table 4. The reference case refers to an individual with characteristics equal to the sample means for continuous variables, and equal to zero for dummies.

TABLE 4

REPEAT UNEMPLOYMENT PROBABILITIES OF DIFFERENT TYPES OF
SAMPLE MEMBERS (FLOW)

Training	Treatments		All		Controls
	No[a]	Yes[b]	No[c]	Yes[d]	No[e]
Reference[f]	93·7	54·0	58·0	15·6	55·5
Age 26–30	90·0	44·1	51·6	12·0	48·2
Age 46–52	97·8	72·1	68·6	23·2	67·4
Married with children	93·4	52·7	50·5	11·4	49·0
Higher education	86·7	37·6	48·9	10·7	44·4
Tenure last job +1 year	93·2	52·3	56·7	14·7	54·1
Unemployment duration +100 days	93·4	53·2	60·4	17·0	57·1
Cumulated unemployment +100 days	94·7	57·5	62·0	18·1	59·4
Replacement ratio +10%	95·9	62·4	65·0	20·3	62·8
City size >100,000 and <1,000,000	88·5	40·9	48·5	10·5	45·1
City size >999,999	93·4	52·9	49·7	11·1	48·3

[a] $\Phi(\beta x_i, \delta z_i; r)/F(\delta z_i)$. $F(\ )$ denotes the univariate cumulative density of the standard normal distribution.
[b] $\Phi[(\alpha + \beta x_i), \delta z_i; r]/F(\delta z_i)$.
[c] $F(\beta x_i)$.
[d] $F(\alpha + \beta x_i)$.
[e] $\Phi(\beta x_i, -\delta z_i; -r)/(1 - F(\delta z_i))$.
[f] For the reference case, continuous variables were taken at means; dummies are set at zero, using col. (2) of Table 3.

As Heckman and Robb (1985, p. 161) point out, the coefficient of the training dummy may give answers to two distinct questions. The evaluator of manpower programmes wants to know above all whether participants have experienced perceptible improvements in their labour market position. Training enrolment lowers repeat unemployment risk of a typical trainee from 93·7% to 54·0% (columns (1) and (2) in Table 3; computations refer to the flow definition of repeat unemployment only). This remarkable reduction emphasizes the effectiveness of such policies.

The second question extends the problem to the whole population: what would be the impact of training on a randomly chosen job-seeker, irrespective of his enrolment status?[24] For the reference case, our results predict a reduction in recurrent unemployment probability from 58% to 15·6% (columns (3) and (4)). These calculations may serve as a benchmark for the implementation of any qualification measures not addressed to special problem groups.

In addition to these two hypothetical questions discussed by Heckman and Robb (1985), a third emerges quite naturally, i.e. the actual outcome of treatments versus controls (columns (2) and (5)): 55·5% of average non-participants can expect a repeat spell of unemployment in contrast to 54·0% of trainees. This leads us back to the beginning, where, neither in aggregate figures nor in the preliminary regression results of Table 1, could any appreciable differences between treatments and controls be detected; in particular, no positive training impact was found.

Now we are able to explain this observation. Job-seekers with high base risks of repeat unemployment are given priority for training (see columns (1) and (5)); participating in these courses can be seen as a 'catching-up' process, narrowing the risk gap between the respective groups considerably.

Other determinants of repeat unemployment   Age has a crucial impact on unemployment probability. Coefficients in Table 3 measure the effect relative to the age-group 31–45. Younger individuals face a lower unemployment risk (which is not significant for ages 25 and lower), but older individuals are significantly more at risk of becoming unemployed. Table 4 shows that trainees in the age group 26–30 are 9·9 percentage points (=54·0−44·1) less likely to rejoin the unemployment register than 31–45-year-old people. The corresponding value for members of the control group is 7·3 percentage points (=55·5−48·2); for individuals aged 46 and older, the unemployment probability for treatments (controls) is 18·1 (11·9) points lower than the base case. Trainees who are married and have children face a slightly lower risk of suffering a repeat spell (1·3 percentage points), whereas for married controls the probability is considerably lower (6·5 points). This difference arises because family status is an important determinant of selection into training. A higher level of education significantly reduces the chance of becoming recurrently unemployed. This is especially the case for treatments whose unemployment risk is 16·4 points lower than the reference. The corresponding figure for non-trainees is 11·1 points.

Potential effects of past employment history are captured by duration of the 1986 unemployment spell, tenure in the last job, and the cumulated duration of unemployment in the three years preceding the 1986 spell. A more stable job in the past has a tendency to reduce the current unemployment risk, but the effect is quantitatively not very large. One additional year of tenure in the last job reduces the unemployment probability for both groups by somewhat more than 1 percentage point. The duration of unemployment in 1986 is an important determinant both of training attainment and of recurrent unemployment. This is why a higher duration of unemployment has different effects on treatments and controls. For treatments, the net effect of an increase of 100 days in unemployment is a negligible decrease in the unemployment probability, whereas for controls it increases by about 2 points. A more unfavourable employment history, however, unambiguously results in a higher chance of repeat unemployment both for treatments and for controls: 100 days more of unemployment before 1986 increase repeat unemployment probability by about 4 percentage points.

The results also include the earnings–replacement ratio, defined as the relation between unemployment benefits and expected wages. Increasing the replacement ratio by 10 percentage points raises the probability of unemployment from 54·0% to 62·4% for treatments and from 55·5% to 62·8% for controls. This is consistent with search theory.

Furthermore, a broader supply of jobs in larger communities decreases the unemployment risk for treatments and controls. The unemployment risk is lowest in cities with more than 100,000 and less than 1 million inhabitants; here, the risk for treatments is 13·1 percentage points lower than in smaller communities, whereas for controls the reduction is only slightly above 10 percentage points. Apart from the variables discussed above, we included a dummy variable for individuals who are disadvantaged because of health or mobility problems ('hard-to-place'). This variable turns out to be insignificant in all regressions. One reason might be legislation for handicapped, which taxes employers who do not obey employment quota for these groups. Another reason might be the efforts of the labour exchange officers, who offer special services to these groups. Similarly, the regional as well as the occupational relationship between unemployment and vacancies were insignificant in most cases. The coefficients show the expected sign in all regressions, but are insignificant.

TABLE 5

TEST OF IDENTIFYING RESTRICTIONS IN BIVARIATE PROBIT MODEL

	Flow		Stock	
	1	2	3	4
Training equation				
Expected replacement ratio	0·014	—	0·008	—
	(0·009)		(0·009)	
Projected employment	−0·026**	−0·022*	−0·021**	−0·021**
change in district for 1991	(0·011)	(0·012)	(0·011)	(0·012)
Unemployment equation				
Expected replacement ratio	0·021*	0·020**	0·018**	0·016*
	(0·008)	(0·008)	(0·008)	(0·008)
Projected employment	—	0·009	—	0·003
change in district for 1991		(0·007)		(0·008)
Training	−1·408***	−1·075	−1·361***	−1·312**
	(0·500)	(0·747)	(0·306)	(0·366)
LRT with model in Table 3	1·0	2·0	0·6	0·2

Finally, in Table 5 we test the identification restrictions used for the bivariate probit model. In Table 3 we excluded the replacement ratio from the training equation and the variable 'projected employment change' from the unemployment equation. We proceed to test the robustness of our results by always relaxing one of the two zero restrictions.[25] The expected earnings–replacement ratio has a significant impact on the subsequent unemployment probability, but does not affect training enrolment. These results hold irrespective of whether the stock or the flow measure of repeat unemployment is chosen, and are independent of the appearance of projected regional employment change in the unemployment probit.

Similarly, the latter variable significantly influences training but fails to have an impact on the unemployment risk. In all cases, the effect of training on unemployment is comparable in magnitude, and in three out of four cases also in significance, to those reported in Table 3. These results underline the appropriateness of the identifying restrictions of our model.

IV. CONCLUSIONS

We have shown that clear-cut evaluation results of manpower training programmes can be obtained using rather standard econometric methods. Appropriate modelling of the training selection rule is of crucial importance. Austrian labour market policy turns out to be a sort of 'catching-up' strategy: (i) disadvantaged and less motivated unemployed are given priority in programme enrolment, and (ii) participation in such courses improves employment stability considerably.

ACKNOWLEDGMENTS

Valuable comments by R. Buchegger, B. Dickens, J. Ham, G. Ridder, M. Riese, G. Ronning, P. Ruud, T. Rothenberg, I. Walker, K. F. Zimmermann and seminar participants at Munich, Oslo, ESPE Pisa, EEA Cambridge and EUI Florence are gratefully acknowledged. This research was supported by the Austrian 'Fonds zur Förderung der wissenschaftlichen Forschung' under the projects S44 and J0548-SOZ.

NOTES

1. See OECD (1988), where labour market policies of 22 OECD countries are surveyed. For policies adopted in the UK, see Carruth and Disney (1989); for the FRG, Disney (1989); and for Sweden, Johannesson (1989).
2. Studies dealing with this issue include Main (1991), Main and Shelly (1990) and Greenhalgh and Stewart (1987) for Britain, Westergard-Nielsen (1993) for Denmark, Ridder (1986) for the Netherlands and Torp (1993) for Norway. Card and Sullivan (1988), Ham and LaLonde (1990), Gritz (1993) and Kaitz (1979) analyse the US experience. For time-series studies, see Haskel and Jackman (1988) and Lehmann (1993) for the UK, as well as Bellmann and Lehmann (1990) for the FRG.
3. Compare the comprehensive survey by Dolton (1993).
4. See e.g. LaLonde (1986), who shows that empirical results obtained from experimental data differ strongly from those obtained from traditional non-experimental methods.
5. For a discussion of these methods and their application to programme evaluation, see Heckman and Robb (1985) and Heckman *et al.* (1987).
6. This is the familiar two-step procedure, initially proposed by Heckman (1979).
7. Ham and LaLonde (1990) point out that the exclusion of spells in progress does not solve the problem; instead, it raises the issue of selection bias. They also present evidence from the National Supported Work experiment: mean unemployment duration for treatments is lower than post-baseline durations of all controls but higher if spells in progress are eliminated for the control group.
8. As a result, labour force participation rates of elderly males are among the lowest in the OECD countries. For an analysis of retirement behaviour of this group, see Zweimüller (1991).
9. There are also job placement programmes, which pay wage subsidies to employers, or pay the whole wage bill for the participants. The impact of these measures is not analysed in the

present paper. See Lassnig *et al.* (1990) for wage subsidies and Schuh (1992) for wage effects of Austrian MTPs.
10. Similar results for females may be obtained in Winter-Ebmer and Zweimüller (1992b).
11. In 1986 the labour market for males was almost stationary: the rate of unemployment rose by 0·2 percentage points, and mean spell duration increased by 10 days compared to 1985.
12. Regression results, including persons with seasonal occupations, may be obtained from the authors upon request.
13. Those who did not participate in the labour force for the whole observation period—school-leavers—were eliminated.
14. The calculations are more fully described in Winter-Ebmer and Zweimüller (1992a). Expected labour income was computed on the basis of standard human capital wage functions, controlling for occupational and regional wage differentials. The Austrian Micro Census June 1983 is the database.
15. The effect of all other variables on repeat unemployment are discussed below (see Table 3).
16. This problem of intention versus occurrence was the subject of previous discussion. Landes (1968) tried to assess the effect of anti-discrimination legislation on the wages of blacks. Using a 'fair-employment' dummy (indicating whether or not a state had an equal opportunity law) in a wage regression, he found that blacks earn higher wages in states with anti-discrimination laws. This approach was criticized by Stigler (quoted in Maddala 1983, p. 130), who mentioned that it is not the presence (i.e. the 'occurrence') of such legislation but the sentiments of the population (i.e. the 'intention') that lead to higher wages. Maddala (1983, p. 125), on the other hand, offers fertilizers as a counter-example, where the 'occurrence' rather than the 'intention' is a determinant of some other outcome (in his case, the production of hybrid seed).
17. This applies in particular to earnings, but may also be relevant to volatile labour demand.
18. In some countries, e.g. Sweden, unemployment benefits are contingent upon participation in active labour market policy measures. This is not the case in Austria.
19. Allen *et al.* (1991), using hazard rate methods, calculate falling instantaneous probabilities for seeking training over elapsed unemployment duration in the UK. This leads to a rising cumulative probability of unemployed persons having sought training during a given period of unemployment, a pattern (stemming from demand considerations alone) that would be compatible with our reduced-form estimates.
20. Again, compare similar results for company or job-related training for the UK by Green (1993), Booth (1991) or Greenhalgh and Stewart (1987).
21. Different results concerning motivation of trainees can be found in Allen *et al.* (1991), where—contrary to this approach—only the demand for training is studied.
22. The bivariate probit results, including persons engaged in seasonal occupations, yield somewhat lower but still significant negative training coefficients. The coefficient of correlation is also lower.
23. The coefficients of the stage 1 probit on training are not reported. They are almost identical to those obtained from the bivariate procedure (col. (1)).
24. If selection for training is independent from the unemployment risk the two questions coincide.
25. This procedure is not possible in the two-stage model, because here identification of the recurrent unemployment equation rests on the inclusion of instruments in the first-stage training equation. We report therefore the coefficient of 'projected employment change' in the first-stage equation: 0·012 (0·016) for the flow measure and 0·009 (0·013) for the stock (standard errors in parentheses).

REFERENCES

ACKUM, S. (1991). Youth unemployment, labour market programs and subsequent earnings. *Scandinavian Journal of Economics*, **93**, 531–43.

ALLEN, H. L., McCORMICK, B. and O'BRIEN, R. J. (1991). Unemployment and the demand for training. *Economic Journal*, **101**, 190–201.

ASHENFELTER, O. (1978). Estimating the effect of training programs on earnings. *Review of Economics and Statistics*, **60**, 47–57.

—— and CARD, D. (1985). Using the longitudinal structure of earnings to estimate the effect of training programs. *Review of Economics and Statistics*, **67**, 648–60.

BASSI, L. (1984). Estimating the effect of training programs with non-random selection. *Review of Economics and Statistics*, **66**, 36–43.

BELLMANN, L. and LEHMANN, H. (1990). Active labour market policies in Britain and Germany and long-term unemployment: an evaluation. Paper presented at the EALE conference, Lund, Nuremberg.

BOOTH, A. L. (1991). Job-related formal training: who receives it and what is it worth? *Oxford Bulletin of Economics and Statistics*, **53**, 281–94.

Bundesministerium für Arbeit und Soziales (1986). *Programmbudget der Arbeitsmarktverwaltung*, Vienna.

—— (n.d.). *Betreuungsplan*. Vienna.

CARD, D. and SULLIVAN, D. (1988). Measuring the effect of subsidized training programs on movements in and out of employment. *Econometrica*, **56**, 497–530.

CARRUTH, A. and DISNEY, R. (1989). The evaluation of 'active' labour market policies. University of Kent at Canterbury, Working Paper no. 89/14.

COOLEY, T. F., McGUIRE, T. W. and PRESCOTT, E. C. (1979). Earnings and employment dynamics of manpower trainees: an exploratory econometric analysis. In F. E. Bloch (ed.), *Research in Labor Economics*. Greenwich, Conn.: JAI Press, Supplement 1, pp. 119–48.

DISNEY, R. (1989). Labour market policies towards the adult unemployed in Germany: an overview. University of Kent at Canterbury, Working Paper no. 89/15.

DOLTON, P. J. (1993). The econometric assessment of training: a review. Mimeo, University of Newcastle.

GREEN, F. (1993). The determinants of training of male and female employees in Britain. *Oxford Bulletin of Economics and Statistics*, **55**, 103–22.

GREENHALGH, C. and STEWART, M. (1987). The effects and determinants of training. *Oxford Bulletin of Economics and Statistics*, **49**, 171–90.

GRITZ, M. R. (1993). The impact of training on the frequency and duration of employment. *Journal of Econometrics*, **57**, 21–52.

HAM, J. C. and LALONDE, R. J. (1989). Estimating the effect of training on the incidence and duration of unemployment: evidence on disadvantaged women from experimental data. Mimeo, University of Toronto, June.

—— and —— (1990). Using social experiments to estimate the effect of training on transition rates. In J. Hartog *et al.* (eds.), *Panel Data and Labor Market Studies*. Amsterdam: North-Holland, pp. 157–72.

HASKEL, J. and JACKMAN, R. (1988). Long-term unemployment and the effects of the community programme. *Oxford Bulletin of Economics and Statistics*, **50**, 379–404.

HECKMAN, J. J. (1979). Sample selection bias as a specification error. *Econometrica*, **47**, 153–61.

—— and ROBB, R. (1985). Alternative methods for evaluating the impact of interventions. In J. Heckman and B. Singer (eds.), *Longitudinal Analysis of Labor Market Data*. Cambridge University Press.

——, HOTZ, J. V. and DABOS, M. (1987). Do we need experimental data to evaluate the impact of manpower training on earnings? *Evaluation Review*, **11**, 395–427.

JOHANNESSON, J. (1989). On the composition and outcome of Swedish labour market policy. EFA/Delegation for Labour Market Policy Research, Swedish Ministry of Labour, Stockholm.

KAITZ, H. B. (1979). Potential use of Markov process models to determine program impact. In F. E. Bloch (ed.), *Research in Labor Economics*. Greenwich, Conn.: JAI Press.

LALONDE, R. (1986). Evaluating the econometric evaluations of training programs with experimental data. *American Economic Review*, **76**, 604–20.

LANDES, W. (1968). The economics of fair employment laws. *Journal of Political Economy*, **98**, 507–52.

LASSNIG, L. *et al.* (1990). *Wirkungen von vermittlungsfördernden Maßnahmen*. Vienna (Forschungsberichte aus Sozial- und Arbeitsmarktpolitik 42): Bundesministerium für Arbeit und Soziales.

LEHMANN, H. (1983). The effectiveness of the Restart Programme and the Enterprise Allowance Scheme. Discussion Paper no. 139, Centre for Economic Performance, London School of Economics.

MADDALA, G. S. (1983). *Limited Dependent and Qualitative Variables in Econometrics*. Cambridge University Press.

MAIN, B. G. M. and SHELLY, M. A. (1990). The effectiveness of the Youth Training Scheme as a manpower policy. *Economica* **57**, 495–514.

MALLAR, C. D. (1977). The estimation of simultaneous probability models. *Econometrica*, **45**, 1717–22.

OECD (1988). *Employment Outlook*. Paris.

RIDDER, G. (1986). An event history approach to the evaluation of training, recruitment and employment programmes. *Journal of Applied Econometrics*, **11**, 109–26.

SALANT, S. W. (1977). Search theory and duration data: a theory of sorts. *Quarterly Journal of Economics*, **91**, 39–57.

SCHUH, A.-U. (1992). Evaluation der Wirkung der Teilnahme an der Aktion 8000 auf das Lohnein-kommen. Mimeo, Institute for Advanced Studies, Vienna.

TORP, H. (1994). The Impact of Training on Employment: Assessing a Norwegian Labour Market Programme. *Scandinavian Journal of Economics*, **96**, 531–50.

WESTERGARD-NIELSEN, N. (1993). Effects of training: a fixed-effect model. In *Measuring Labour Market Measures*. Copenhagen: Ministry of Labour.

WINTER-EBMER, R. and ZWEIMÜLLER, J. (1992a). Do they come back again? Job search, labour market segmentation and state dependence as explanations of repeat unemployment. *Empirical Economics*, **17**, 273–92.

—— and —— (1992b). Sind Schulungsmaßnahmen ein wirkungsvolles Mittel zur Bekämpfung individueller Arbeitslosigkeit? *Wirtschaftspolitische Blätter*, Vienna, 695–700.

ZWEIMÜLLER, J. (1991). Earnings, social security legislation and retirement decisions: the Austrian experience. *Applied Economics*, **23**, 851–60.

[26]

Review of Economic Studies (1997) **64**, 683–713
© 1997 The Review of Economic Studies Limited

0034-6527/97/00300683$02.00

Evaluating the Impact of French Employment Policies on Individual Labour Market Histories

LILIANE BONNAL
CRESEP, Université d'Orléans and GREMAQ, Université des Sciences Sociales, Toulouse

DENIS FOUGÈRE
CNRS and CREST, Paris

and

ANNE SÉRANDON
LIRHE, Université des Sciences Sociales, Toulouse

First version received March 1994; final version accepted February 1997 (Eds.)

This paper deals with the evaluation of some public employment policies set up in France during the 1980's to improve the labour market prospects of unskilled young workers. The evaluation implemented in this paper is restricted to the impact of such public measures on durations and outcomes of subsequent spells of unemployment and employment. The econometric study is conducted with non-experimental longitudinal microdata recording individual labour market histories. A particular attention is paid to the differential effects of various types of measures, according to the educational level of recipients. Programmes involving a higher level of on-the-job training, such as alternating work/training programmes in private firms, are principally beneficial to the less educated young workers. In contrast, for more educated young workers, "work fare" programmes in the public sector decrease the intensity of transition from the subsequent unemployment spell to regular jobs; for that subgroup, "work fare" programmes may act as a signal of low employment performance.

I. INTRODUCTION

This paper deals with the evaluation of public employment policies set up in France during the 1980's to improve the labour market prospects of the most disadvantaged and unskilled young workers. This evaluation, however, is restricted to the impact of youth employment schemes on subsequent unemployment and employment durations of recipients. For that purpose, we estimate a reduced-form multi-state multi-spell transition model that includes participation in these programmes as an additional state. In this framework, participation in a programme (or "training") is allowed to affect the transition rates out of the state that follows the programme, and distinct types of programmes (namely, programmes in the public sector vs. programmes in the private sector) are allowed to have differential effects. Moreover, our model allows for possibly related unobserved heterogeneity in the specifications of all transition rates, thus capturing the potentially selective nature of training enrolment. The empirical analysis makes use of non-experimental longitudinal micro data collected by INSEE (Institut National de la Statistique et des Etudes Economiques, Paris) from 1986 to 1988. These data are based on administrative records supplemented by a series of four interviews over one and a half years; they provide information on the dates of entry into training programmes and on durations of subsequent spells of employment and unemployment.

Our paper is directly connected with previous studies estimating effects of programme participation by using individual transition data (see, for example, Ridder (1986), Card and Sullivan (1988), Ham and Lalonde (1990, 1996), Gritz (1993)). Three types of motivation justify this approach:

• firstly, for disadvantaged or unskilled groups of workers, it seems more natural to focus on re-employment rates rather than on earnings gains for which empirical evidence is less clear (see Bassi (1983) or Ashenfelter and Card (1985), for example); moreover, because public employment programmes are directed at individuals, they have to be evaluated at the individual level, with the use of longitudinal micro data;

• secondly, there is an obvious interest in estimating separately the effects of programmes on subsequent durations of unemployment and employment; Ham and Lalonde (1996, p. 176) point out that separating these effects allows the comparison of different programmes: for example, "policy makers may prefer to fund a programme that lengthens employment durations as opposed to one that shortens unemployment durations, because the former is likely to lead to more stable job histories and greater human capital accumulation"; moreover, estimating the two kinds of effects is necessary to evaluate the long-run impact of these programmes. These considerations are particularly well adapted to the situation of the French labour market, which was characterized during the last fifteen years by the coexistence of different public employment programmes, long-term employment contracts (roughly speaking, "regular jobs") and short-term employment contracts (roughly speaking, "temporary jobs");

• finally, the main advantage of individual labour market transition data is that they include multiple spells per respondent; it is well known that, in the mixed proportional hazard (MPH) model for single-spell duration data, the identification of unobserved heterogeneity and duration dependence relies crucially on the multiplicative nature of the transition rate (see Elbers and Ridder (1982) and Ridder (1990)); more recently, Honoré (1993) has shown that this identification result is still valid in MPH multi-spell models without lagged duration dependence, under rather general assumptions on the joint distribution of the unobserved heterogeneity terms; this identifiability argument shows that it is very well possible to deal with the endogeneity of programme participation and to obtain reliable training effect evaluations with non-experimental continuous-time transition data.[1]

Papers by Ridder (1986) and Gritz (1993) are the most important previous studies examining the effects of programme participation on labour market histories with the use of non-experimental transition data. Our paper differs from them in several aspects. For example, Ridder (1986) does not control for unobserved heterogeneity; moreover, he considers that the selection of programme participants is an exogenous process, only affected by the labour force state reached just before entering the programme. Obviously,

---

1. It has been argued that, in order to be able to evaluate the effects of training programmes, it is necessary to have data from a social or natural experiment. However, contributions by Heckman and Hotz (1989), Heckman (1990), Dubin and Rivers (1993) and Ham and Lalonde (1996) emphasize the potential biases inherent in experimental studies: generally, random assignment does not eliminate all biases due to endogenous selection, especially in multi-stage training programmes. This limitation reduces the prior advantage of experimental data.

this last assumption is inappropriate: the selection is generally made by programme administrators, but also by employers participating in the programme (or offering jobs subsidized through this programme), and finally by workers themselves, who either accept or refuse offers to participate. Our empirical analysis is much more comparable with the study made by Gritz (1993). Like Gritz, we treat participation in a programme as a separate (possibly recurrent) state of a continuous labour market transition process, and we allow entry rates into programmes to depend on an unobserved individual random covariate which is possibly correlated with unobserved heterogeneity terms affecting rates of transition to other states. Moreover, when estimating the effects of programme participation on the transition rates out of the state which follows the programme, we distinguish between the effects of different types of programmes (essentially, programmes in the public sector vs. programmes in the private sector). However, contrary to Gritz, we stratify the sample with respect to the educational level and so we can produce empirical evidence on the beneficial effects of "on-the-job" training programmes for the less educated young workers. A time-varying covariate indicating qualification to receive unemployment insurance benefits through the unemployment spell is also introduced, and we study the sensitivity of parameter estimates to assumptions concerning the distribution of the unobserved heterogeneity components. Finally, our statistical modelling attempts to reduce the endogenous stock sampling bias due to the fact that the respondents are drawn from the stock of individuals who were unemployed at a particular date. It also takes into account the attrition bias due to endogenous exits from the panel. To correct such biases, we apply the methodology recently introduced by Van den Berg, Lindeboom and Ridder (1994).

Table 1.1 presents the main features of youth training programmes which were in effect in France during the late 1980's. Most of these programmes were launched before, but the numbers of participants increased greatly after the 1986 Emergency Plan for Youth Employment ("Plan d'Urgence pour l'Emploi des Jeunes"). This Plan introduced strong incentives for private firms offering training places (see Table 1.1) and facilitated the development of programmes with alternating spells of work and training ("formations en alternance", for which we propose the term "alternating work/training programmes"). For instance, the lower age limit for entry into such programmes has been lowered from 18 to 16 years, while the upper age limit for entry into the apprenticeship system has been raised from 20 to 25 years. To simplify, we can distinguish between two types of programmes: the alternating work/training programme provided by private firms (including apprenticeship, qualification and adaptation contracts, and "courses for preparation to the working life"; see Table 1.1), and the "workfare" programme provided by the State and the public sector (including community jobs and "courses for the 16-to-25 years old"; see Table 1.1). In this second type of programme, the amount of vocational and specific training is generally lower than in the first type. Then the main question we address in this paper is the following: can we also differentiate these two types of programme when we consider their impacts on durations and outcomes of subsequent unemployment and employment spells? Results show that these impacts depend crucially on the initial educational level of trainees. Programmes involving a higher level of on-the-job training, such as alternating work/training programmes in private firms, are principally beneficial to the less educated young workers, who may increase their human capital and work experience through these programmes. In contrast, for more educated young workers, "workfare" programmes in the public sector decrease the intensity of transition from the subsequent unemployment spell to regular jobs; for that subgroup, "workfare" programmes may act as a signal of low employment performance.

Section II gives some descriptive statistics on the sample. Section III presents the transition model and the likelihood function we estimate. Results are commented upon in Section IV. Our conclusions are summarized in the last section.

TABLE 1.1

Summary table of main programmes for youth employment in France during the period 1986–1988

Programmes	Durations	Objectives	Eligible workers	Potential employers	Amount of training	Wage levels	Employer incentives
Apprenticeship contracts	Temporary employment contracts (between 1 and 3 years)	To provide a specific training giving a formal qualification or allowing to take examination for national diploma after completion	Young people without any diploma or without any formal qualification	All private firms in craft, trade and industrial sectors	At least 400 hours of training for non-college graduates; at least 1500 hours of training for college graduates	The apprentice is paid by the firm, the wage depends on age and seniority in the contract (between 17 and 75% of the legal minimum wage)	Firms are exempted from paying social security contributions
Qualification contracts	Temporary employment contracts (between 6 and 24 months)	Idem	Idem	All private firms	At least one quarter of the contract duration	Idem	Firms are exempted from paying social security contributions and the employer training tax
Adaptation contracts	Either temporary employment contracts (from 6 to 12 months) or permanent employment contracts	To provide a specific training (adapted to the job occupied)	Young people with a formal qualification but who have difficulties to find a job	Idem	At least 200 hours in the case of a temporary contract; for permanent employment contracts, it depends both on the job and on the young worker's qualification	The wage is paid by the firm; it is at least equal to the legal minimum wage	Firms are exempted from paying the employer training tax but have to pay social security contributions (since July 1987)
Courses for preparation to the working life (SIVP)	Non-renewable temporary contracts	To give a formal qualification (adapted to existing jobs)	Young people with no work experience or unemployed for more than one year	Idem	Training provided either by the firm or by a government training centre	Trainees receive a lump-sum from the state and a complementary allowance from the firm	Firms are exempted from paying social security contributions
Community jobs (TUC)	Non-renewable temporary employment contracts (from 3 to 12 months or 24 months since 1987)	To help young people to find a regular job	Young workers between 16 and 21 years old or long term unemployed between 22 and 25 years old	State or local administration, public institutions, non-profit making associations, ….	No formal or specific training	Trainees are paid by the state and receive a fixed payment (about 1250FF) and sometimes an allowance from the firm	
Training courses for 16 to 25 years-old	Courses with a duration between 6 and 9 months	To facilitate social and professional integration	Young people leaving the educational system without any qualification	Courses take place in state training centres	Between 550 and 700 hours of training	Trainees receive a lump-sum from the state	

BONNAL *ET AL.*   INDIVIDUAL LABOUR MARKET HISTORIES   687

II. THE DATA

The data used for this study are provided by the "Suivi des Chômeurs" survey collected by INSEE (Paris). The sample was drawn randomly in August 1986 from the files of the public employment service ("Agence Nationale Pour l'Emploi" or ANPE).[2] About 8000 unemployed people were sampled but only 7450 could be reached at the first interview. Individuals were interviewed four times, in November 1986, May 1987, November 1987, and finally May 1988. At the first interview, respondents were asked to give information on their labour market status between August and November 1986, and in particular on the time already spent in the unemployment spell sampled in August 1986 and on their status before entry into that spell. The data record retrospectively month after month, between November 1986 and May 1988, the events corresponding to individual transitions in the labour market. For that study, we consider only young men who were less than 26 years old in August 1986 and for whom it is possible to observe an accurate and relevant date of registration in the ANPE files. Table 2.1 gives descriptive statistics for this sub-sample which contains 1337 individuals.

TABLE 2.1

Descriptive statistics

Variables	Min	Max	Mean	Standard deviation
French nationality	0	1	0·9289	
Age in November 1986	15	26	21·17	2·66
Skill level				
Unskilled blue-collar worker	0	1	0·5086	
Skilled blue-collar worker	0	1	0·2094	
White-collar worker	0	1	0·1810	
Other levels	0	1	0·1010	
Educational level				
No diploma	0	1	0·5033	
Technical school certificate	0	1	0·3029	
High school diploma and above	0	1	0·092	
Non-response	0	1	0·1017	
Reason of entry into the sampled unemployment spell				
End of a temporary employment contract	0	1	0·3119	
Lay-off	0	1	0·1511	
Quit	0	1	0·2034	
First entry	0	1	0·3336	
(including after military service)				
Individual characteristics in August 1986				
Qualification for UI	0	1	0·25	
Previous participation to a programme	0	1	0·16	
Duration of the sampled unemployment spell	1	79	13·36	11·67
(without right-censored spells)				

Figure 2.2 presents Kaplan–Meier estimates for survival functions of durations in successive spells (without correction of the stock-sampling bias). These curves show that, during the first year of occupation, the exit rate from training programmes is lower than the exit rate from temporary jobs: for instance, in the first spell observed after the sampled unemployment spell, the mean duration of a programme is about four months while the mean duration of a temporary job is approximately three months. The exit rates from

2. These files include all unemployed people registered at the ANPE who were looking either for a full-time or part-time permanent job, or a full-time or part-time temporary job in August 1986. These requirements do not correspond to the definition of unemployment given by the International Labour Office.

688   REVIEW OF ECONOMIC STUDIES

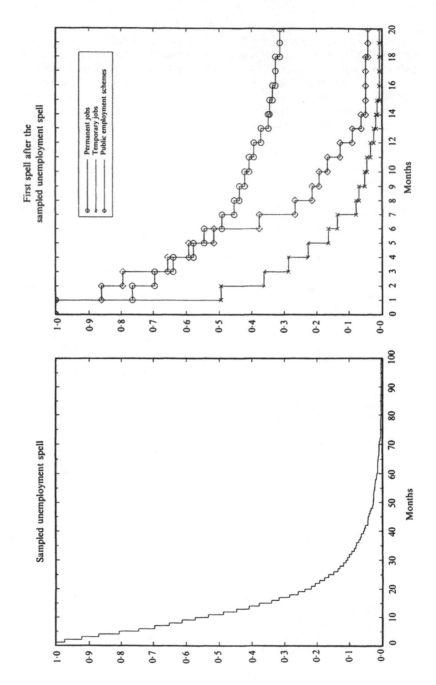

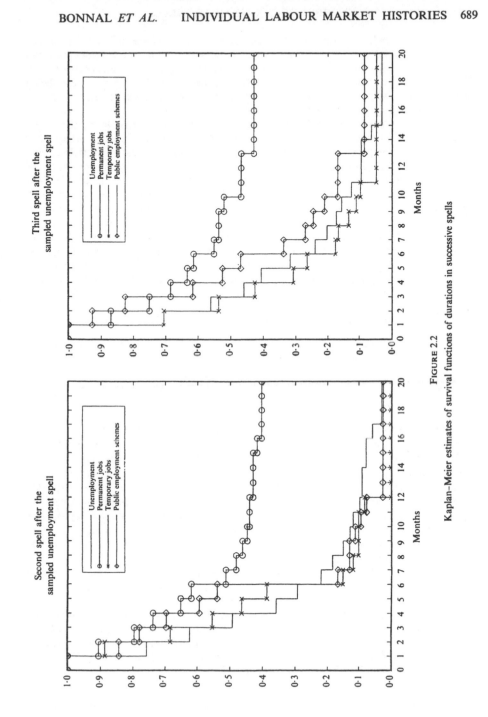

FIGURE 2.2

Kaplan–Meier estimates of survival functions of durations in successive spells

unemployment spells occurring after the second observed spell are higher than the exit rate from the initial unemployment spell: this could be due either to a heterogeneity bias (long-term vs. recurrent unemployment) or to the small length of the observation period. This last problem could also affect the results, because some of the programmes being evaluated have durations that are potentially longer than the sampling frame (e.g. the apprenticeship programme includes contracts of up to three years).

Figure 2.3 gives a general description of the transitions experienced by the young male subsample between August 1986 and May 1988. In this figure, we consider three employment states: permanent employment (UDC), temporary employment (LDC), and employment resulting from a public employment policy (PEP). Because of the small numbers of corresponding transitions, we do not make any distinction between the different kinds of public employment policies, such as TUC, SIVP, "qualification" or "adaptation" contracts, . . . described in the introduction. Moreover, besides the usual states of unemployment (U) and out-of-labour-force (OLF), we treat the phenomenon of attrition as a particular state of the transition process. Individuals who leave the panel through attrition do not re-enter the sample at following interviews. Consequently, attrition (A) is an absorbing state.

Because public employment policies are mainly oriented towards low-educated or low-experienced young people, we have stratified the young male subsample according to the educational level. Four groups may be distinguished (see Table 2.1):

- the first one has no diploma (less than 9 years of schooling): it represents 50·33% of the sample,
- the second one gets a technical school certificate (called a C.A.P. or a B.E.P. in France, and obtained after 11 years of schooling): 30·3% of the sample get such a diploma,
- the third group corresponds to young men holding at least a high-school diploma (more than 12 years of schooling): it represents 9·2% of the subsample,
- finally, 136 individuals (10·17%) gave no information on their education level.

Figure 2.4 shows the proportions of these four subgroups who were unemployed, employed either in a permanent job, a temporary job or a public employment programme each month from August 1986 to May 1988 (these proportions are calculated without incorporating the individuals having moved to attrition). It is obvious that, for the highly educated people, the unemployment rate is lower at the end of this period, while their rate of employment in permanent jobs is higher (65% vs. 30% for the young men with no diploma). Now let us consider the proportions in jobs resulting from public employment policies: they are higher for young men without a diploma or non-respondents. For young men with at least a high-school diploma, the proportion in PEP jobs is around 10% at the end of the observation period.

One objective of our study is to compare programme effects for different educational levels. Consequently, we concentrate the statistical analysis on the most represented strata: males without a diploma and males with a technical school certificate satisfying the age condition for programme participation.[3] Descriptive statistics giving numbers of individual transitions over the observation period show that these two groups move more intensively between labour force states than the highly educated people. For instance, the maximum number of transitions recorded over this period is equal to 11, indicating that young males with a low educational level are highly mobile.

---

3. To simplify, we keep males who are more than 16 years old in August 1986 and less than 26 in May 1988.

BONNAL *ET AL.* · INDIVIDUAL LABOUR MARKET HISTORIES 691

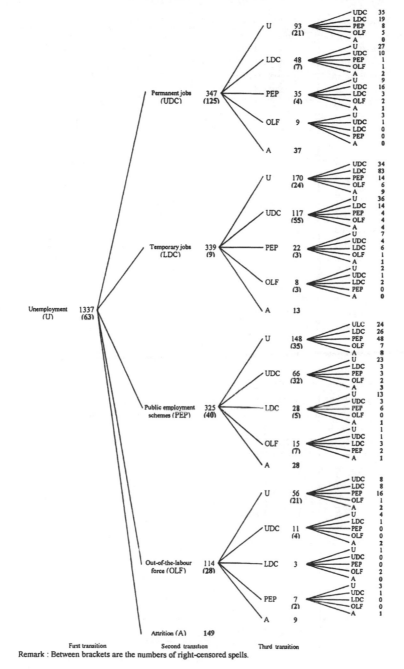

First transition   Second transition   Third transition

Remark : Between brackets are the numbers of right-censored spells.

FIGURE 2.3

Frequencies of the first three transitions

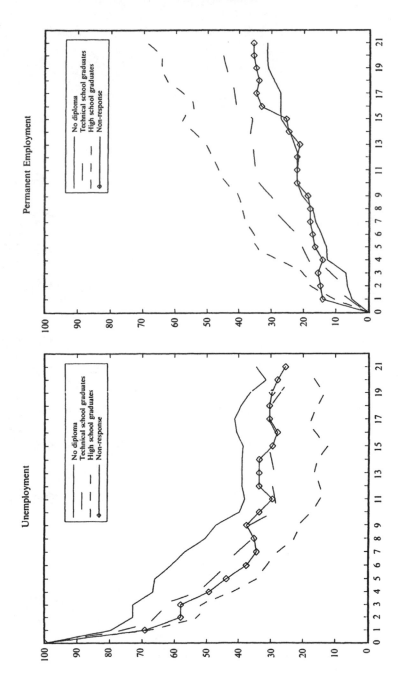

BONNAL *ET AL.* INDIVIDUAL LABOUR MARKET HISTORIES 693

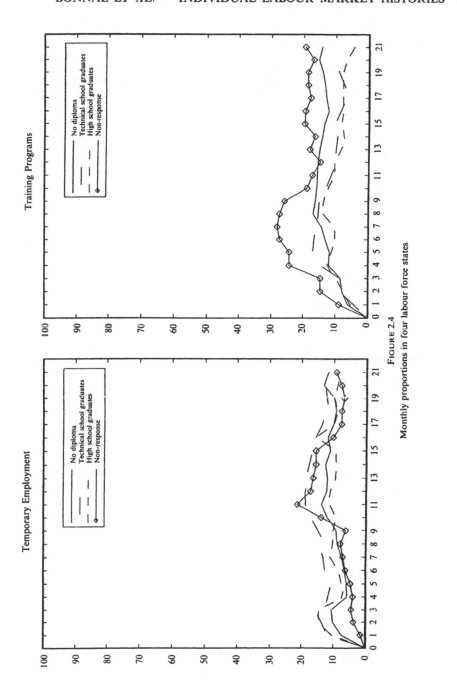

FIGURE 2.4

Monthly proportions in four labour force states

III. MODELLING INDIVIDUAL LABOUR MARKET TRANSITIONS

III.1. *General framework and notations*

We suppose that each worker in the population is subject to a participation process[4] Y_t describing his current state in the labour market at time t ($t \geq 0$). Considering the problem to be analysed and the specificities of our data set, we assume that the process Y_t takes its values at any instant t in the discrete state space $E = \{j \in \mathbb{N}, 1 \leq j \leq 6\}$, where the index j labels the following states:

1. unemployment,
2. employment in a job with an unlimited duration contract (permanent employment),
3. employment in a job with a limited duration contract (temporary employment),
4. employment in a job resulting from a public employment policy (PEP job),
5. out-of-labour force state,
6. attrition state.

In fact, the survey permits us to distinguish between five kinds of PEP jobs: apprenticeship contracts, adaptation and qualification contracts, community jobs (T.U.C.), initiation courses (S.I.V.P.), and courses for 16-to-25 year-olds. But considering the small numbers of observed transitions, we aggregate the different kinds of PEP jobs into one state. The attrition state is an absorbing state which can be reached only after the sampling date T_0 (August 1986). The index l is used for indicating the rank order of a spell in any individual event history. This index can take a positive or negative integer value: $l = 0$ refers necessarily to the unemployment spell sampled at T_0, $l = 1$ corresponds to the first spell (if any) observed after this sampled unemployment spell, $l = -1$ corresponds to the spell just preceding this unemployment spell, and so on. Consequently, the maximal value taken by l for an individual observation indicates the number of transitions experienced by the worker after the sampling date T_0. Individual participation histories are retrospectively observed at times T_1 (November 1986), T_2 (May 1987), T_3 (November 1987) and T_4 (May 1988). Any "complete" (without attrition) history is right-censored at T_4. A transition to attrition may occur at any time between T_{m-1} and T_m ($m = 1, \ldots, 4$), and not at times $T_0, \ldots, T_4$ exactly. For a worker,[5] τ_l denotes the random date of entrance into the lth spell of his observed participation history: consequently, Y_{τ_l} is the state occupied by an individual during the lth spell of his history, and $U_l = \tau_{l+1} - \tau_l$ is a (positive) random variable representing the time spent by the worker in this lth spell.

In our data set, individuals are sampled in the unemployed population at date T_0 (August 1986): consequently, the worker has already spent a time $\bar{U}_0 = T_0 - \tau_0$ in unemployment at this date. This sojourn time $\bar{U}_0$ is obviously an incomplete (right-censored) duration: then $R_0 = U_0 - \bar{U}_0 = \tau_1 - T_0$ denotes the residual duration of the sampled unemployment spell ending with a transition to state Y_{τ_1} at time τ_1.

For simplifying the model, we assume that individual transitions in the labour market do not directly depend on calendar time through seasonal or business cycle effects.[6] Moreover they are supposed to be independent of the worker's age. This is mainly for practical

---

4. For a general presentation of the econometric treatment of transition data, see for example the textbook by Lancaster (1990) or surveys by Florens and Fougère (1992) or Fougère and Kamionka (1992*b*).

5. We delete the person-specific index to simplify formulas.

6. Obviously, this is a strong (and probably unrealistic) assumption: however, Fougère and Kamionka (1992*a*) found empirical evidence of the relative time-homogeneity of individual transition intensities over the period 1986–1988 in France. For the incorporation of seasonal and business-cycle effects in duration or transition models, see De Toldi, Gouriéroux and Monfort (1995) or Imbens and Lynch (1992).

reasons: including age as a covariate in the twenty-five possible transitions would unreasonably expand the already long list of coefficients to be estimated. To some extent, the effects of age at entry into the sample will be captured by the unobserved heterogeneity term; however, we must recognize that a random term is an imperfect substitute to age.[7]

Consequently, the individual time axis may be scaled so that its origin ($t=0$) is set equal to the date at which a worker enters the labour market for the first time: then τ_l measures the time difference between this entry date (which is observed in the data set) and the date at which the individual experiences his lth transition in the labour market. As an illustration of the sampling scheme, Figure 3.1 represents a realization of the labour market transition process described above. This figure shows that the worker is firstly unemployed for a duration $U_{-2}=\tau_{-1}$, then is employed in a temporary job with a duration equal to $U_{-1}=\tau_0-\tau_{-1}$, then enters once again unemployment (where he is sampled at date T_0 and surveyed at date T_1) for a duration equal to $U_0=\tau_1-\tau_0$, then finds a job under an "adaptation-type" contract whose duration is $U_1=\tau_2-\tau_1$, and then moves to a permanent job in which he stays for a duration greater than $\bar{U}_2$: this last duration is right-censored at date T_4 by the end of the observation schedule.

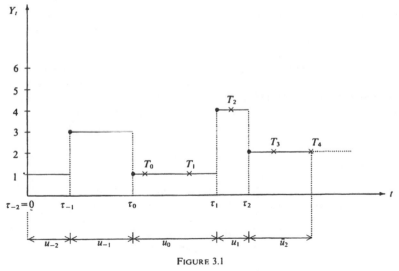

FIGURE 3.1

A realization of the labour market transition process Y_t

III.2. *Distribution of the individual transition processes*

Now we assume that individual labour market transitions are governed by intensity functions of the mixed proportional hazard (MPH) type (see Elbers and Ridder (1982) and Ridder (1990) for the presentation and the identifiability of MPH models applied to single-spell duration data, and Flinn and Heckman (1982, 1983), Aalen (1987) and Honoré

---

7. In less-parameterized versions of the econometric model, we introduced among covariates affecting rates of exit from unemployment a dummy variable indicating if the worker's age was greater than 21 years old at the beginning of the unemployment spell. Generally, this variable was found to have no statistically significant effect.

(1993) for extensions of such models to multi-state multi-spell duration data). More specifically, we assume that the intensity of transition to state k after a sojourn duration equal to u_l in state j ($j \neq k$), during the lth spell of his labour market transition process, is defined by

$$h_{jk}(u_l | \beta_{jk}, X_{jk}(\tau_l + u_l), v_{jk}) = h_{jk}^{(0)}(u_l) \exp[\beta'_{jk} X_{jk}(\tau_l + u_l)] v_{jk} \quad \text{for } k \neq j, \qquad (1)$$

where:

- $h_{jk}^{(0)}(\cdot)$ is a positive baseline intensity function, whose form may depend on the origin (j) and destination (k) states, but not on the rank order (l) of the current spell in the transition history,
- $X_{jk}(\cdot)$ is a vector of time-varying individual covariates whose value at the transition time ($\tau_l + u_l$) is supposed to affect a move from state j to state k ($k \neq j$) through a vector of unknown parameters β_{jk} (to be estimated),
- and v_{jk} is a positive random variate with c.d.f. F_{jk}, whose specification may depend on states j and k but not on the rank order of the spell, and which is intended to capture the effect of individual unobserved heterogeneity on transition from state j to state k.

Given the number of possible transitions, we restrict the size of the multivariate random vector (v_{jk}) by assuming that $v_{jk} = v_k$, for any $j \in E$, which means that the heterogeneity term affecting the intensity of transition from state j to state k ($k \neq j$) is specific to the destination state k. This last assumption implies, for example, that an individual with a relatively high value for the unobserved component v_5 has a loose attachment to the labour market and is more likely to move to the non-participation state, whatever the state (employment or unemployment) he currently occupies. Alternatively, an unskilled or disadvantaged worker should have much more willingness to accept subsidized course-type jobs or training programmes and so have a higher value for the unobserved component v_4.

The vector of time-varying covariates $X_{jk}(\cdot)$ can be decomposed into two sub-vectors $X_{jk}^0(\tau_l)$ and $X_{jk}^1(\tau_l + u_l)$:

- the value of the first one $X_{jk}^0(\tau_l)$ is fixed at the date of entrance into the lth spell and then remains constant through the spell: typically, this vector includes time-independent covariates and also covariates describing the past individual history in the labour market (number of previous spells of unemployment, total sojourn duration in these spells, last state occupied, ...);
- the second sub-vector of covariates $X_{jk}^1(\tau_l + u_l)$ incorporates covariates varying through the lth spell; in our application, we consider exclusively one such covariate: an indicator process $Z(\tau_l + u_l)$ taking the value one if the state occupied by the individual during the lth spell of his transition process is unemployment and if he is still receiving unemployment insurance benefits after a time u_l spent in this spell, the value zero otherwise. However, the survey does not give any information on the amount of these benefits and on the duration of the period of qualification to receive unemployment insurance.

Using assumptions made on X_{jk}, the transition intensity (1) may be written

$$h_{jk}(u_l | \beta_{jk}, X_{jk}(\tau_l + u_l), v_k) = h_{jk}^{(0)}(u_l) \exp[\beta_{jk}^{0\prime} X_{jk}^0(\tau_l) + \gamma_{jk} Z(\tau_l + u_l)] v_k, \qquad (2)$$

where

$$\beta_{jk} = (\beta_{jk}^{0\prime}, \gamma_{jk})', \ X_{jk}(\tau_l + u_l) = [X_{jk}^0(\tau_l), Z(\tau_l + u_l)]',$$

and

$$Z(\tau_l + u_l) = \begin{cases} 1 & \text{if } u_l \leqq D_l, \\ 0 & \text{elsewhere.} \end{cases}$$

D_l is the potential duration of qualification for unemployment insurance benefits during the lth spell if this spell is an unemployment spell, i.e. $j = 1$ (if $j \neq 1$, D_l is necessarily equal to zero and $Z(\tau_l + u_l)$ is constantly zero through the lth spell). Consequently, the conditional density function (3) of the duration in state j during the lth spell, given that this spell starts at time τ_l and ends at time $\tau_l + u_l$ with a transition to state k, is (see Fougère and Kamionka (1992b, pp. 474–475) for a proof)

$$g_{jk}(u_l | \beta_j, X_j(\tau_l + u_l), v) = h_{jk}(u_l | \beta_{jk}, X_{jk}(\tau_l + u_l), v_k)$$

$$\times \exp\left(-\int_0^{u_l} \Sigma_{k'=1,\, k' \neq j}^{K} h_{jk'}(t | \beta_{jk'}, X_{jk'}(\tau_l + t), v_{k'}) dt\right)$$

$$= h_{jk}^{(0)}(u_l) \exp\left[\gamma_{jk} Z(\tau_l + u_l) + \beta_{jk}^{0t} X_{jk}^{0}(\tau_l)\right] v_k$$

$$\times \exp\left(-\Sigma_{k'=1,\, k' \neq j}^{K} \exp\left[\beta_{jk}^{0t} X_{jk}^{0}(\tau_l)\right] v_k\right.$$

$$\times \left\{ Z(\tau_l + u_l) \exp(\gamma_{jk'}) \int_0^{u_l} h_{jk'}^{(0)}(t) dt + (1 - Z(\tau_l + u_l)) \right.$$

$$\times \left. \left(\exp(\gamma_{jk'}) \int_0^{D_l} h_{jk'}^{(0)}(t) dt + \int_{D_l}^{u_l} h_{jk'}^{(0)}(t) dt \right) \right\}\right), \qquad (3)$$

where the vectors $\beta_j, X_j(\cdot)$ and v are defined by $\beta = [\beta_{jk}]_{k \neq j}, X_j(\cdot) = [X_{jk}(\cdot)]_{k \neq j}, v = [v_k]_{k \in E}$, and where $K = 6$ if transitions to attrition state are allowed, $K = 5$ otherwise. The conditional density function defined in (3) is the likelihood contribution of the lth spell when it is not right-censored (i.e. when $\tau_{l+1} = \tau_l + u_l \leq T_4$). When the lth spell ends after T_4, the contribution of this right-censored spell to the likelihood function is

$$S_j(T_4 - \tau_l | \tau_l, \beta_j, X_j(T_4), v)$$

$$= \text{prob}(u_l > T_4 - \tau_l | \tau_l, \beta_j, X_j(T_4), v)$$

$$= \exp\left(-\int_0^{T_4 - \tau_l} \Sigma_{k'=1,\, k' \neq j}^{K} h_{jk'}(t | \tau_l, \beta_{jk'}, X_{jk'}(\tau_l + t), v_{k'}) dt\right), \qquad (4)$$

where $S_j(\cdot | \cdot)$ is the conditional survival function of the duration in state j. If an individual moves to the attrition state during the lth spell between two successive interview dates T_{m-1} and T_m ($m = 1, \ldots, 4$), then the contribution of this spell to the likelihood function is

$$\text{prob}(u_l \in \,] T_{m-1} - \tau_l, T_m - \tau_l [\,| \tau_l, Y_{\tau_l} = j, \beta_j, X_j(T_{m-1}), v)$$

$$= S_j(T_m - \tau_l | \tau_l, \beta_j, X_j(T_{m-1}), v) - S_j(T_{m-1} - \tau_l | \tau_l, \beta_j, X_j(T_{m-1}), v). \qquad (5)$$

However some difficulty may appear in the treatment of transitions towards the attrition state. In fact, suppose an individual is observed to leave the panel between two consecutive interviews. The model states that there is a positive probability that the individual makes one or more labour market transitions between the last interview at which he participated and the moment at which the duration of panel survey participation is completed. Past states should affect the exit rate out of the panel, so every time a transition is made, the exit rate out of the panel should change. The easiest way to avoid this difficulty is to make the exit rates out of the panel independent of past labour market states.[8]

III.3. *Correction of the stock sampling bias*

It is well known that sampling from the stock of unemployed people at a given date T_0 may induce biased estimates for parameters of the distribution of durations in that state or in subsequent states (employment, out-of-labour force, etc.). The bias has two components: firstly, a length-bias due to the fact that the sampling probability of a given spell is generally proportional to its elapsed duration (or length), and secondly, an inflow-rate bias, resulting from the dependence of this probability on the rate of transition into unemployment at the starting date τ_0 of that spell.[9]

Like other data sets used in similar studies (see, for example, Ridder (1986), Van den Berg, Lindeboom and Ridder (1994)), the INSEE survey does not register the individual transition history $\Omega(\tau_0)$ preceding the entry into the unemployment spell sampled at T_0, with the exception of the information on the state occupied just before entering this unemployment spell. For circumventing this problem, one way is to assume that the entry rate into unemployment does not depend directly on the calendar time, but factorizes in terms of v_1 (the unobserved heterogeneity term affecting the intensities of transition towards unemployment) and $X(\tau_0)$, which denotes the vector of individual covariates at the time of entry into unemployment (see Van den Berg, Lindeboom and Ridder (1994, p. 424)). In other terms, if $q(\cdot \mid \cdot)$ denotes the inflow rate, then we assume that

$$q(\tau_0 \mid v_1, X(\tau_0)) = q_1(v_1) \times q_2(X(\tau_0)) \propto v_1 \times q_2(X(\tau_0)), \qquad (6)$$

with $q_1(\cdot) > 0$ and $q_2(\cdot) > 0$. Recalling that $\bar{U}_0 = T_0 - \tau_0$ denotes the time already spent in unemployment by an individual at the sampling date, then the probability that an individual with a given unobserved heterogeneity term v and a given covariate vector $X(\tau_0)$ is in the stock of unemployed people at T_0 equals

$$P_s(v, X(\tau_0)) = \int_0^\infty q(\tau_0 \mid v, X(\tau_0)) \, \text{prob} \, (U_0 > \bar{U}_0 \mid v, X(\tau_0)) d\bar{U}_0$$

$$\propto v_1 \times q_2(X(\tau_0)) \times \int_0^\infty \exp\left\{-\sum_{k=2}^5 \int_0^{\bar{U}_0} h_{1k}(t \mid \beta_{1k}, X_{1k}(\tau_0), v_k) dt\right\} d\bar{U}_0.$$

Consequently, the probability to be sampled in the stock given the observable heterogeneity only is

$$P_s(X(\tau_0)) = \int_{v \in \Lambda} P_s(v, X(\tau_0)) f(v \mid \alpha) dv, \qquad (8)$$

---

8. We thank a referee for this suggestion.
9. Papers by Ridder (1984), Van den Berg, Lindeboom and Ridder (1994) and Gouriéroux and Monfort (1992) develop statistical analysis of such biases in the context of unemployment duration models.

where $f(\cdot \mid a)$ is the joint density function of the vector v and Λ is the support of the distribution of v. Finally, the likelihood contribution of an individual with covariates $X(\tau_0)$ at entry and with observed transition history $(\tau_l, Y_{\tau_l})_{l=0,1,...,\bar{L}}$ is the conditional density of this sequence given that the individual was in the unemployment stock at date T_0, $\bar{L}=0, 1, 2, \ldots$ being the number of transitions observed for this individual before T_4. So this likelihood function has the general form

$$\mathscr{L}((\tau_l, Y_{\tau_l})_{l=0,1,...,\bar{L}} \mid X(\tau_0), \beta, \alpha)$$

$$= \left[\int_{v \in \Lambda} q(\tau_0 \mid v_1, X(\tau_0)) S_{Y_{\bar{L}}}(T_4 - \tau_{\bar{L}} \mid \beta_{Y_{\bar{L}}}, X_j(T_4), v) \right.$$

$$\times \left\{ \prod_{l=0}^{L} g_{Y_{l-1}, Y_l}(u_{l-1} \mid \beta_{Y_{l-1}}, X_{Y_{l-1}}(\tau_{l-1} + u_{l-1}), v) \right\} f(v \mid a) dv \right] \times [P_s(X(\tau_0)]^{-1}$$

$$\propto \left[\int_{v \in \Lambda} v_1 \times S_{Y_{\bar{L}}}(T_4 - \tau_{\bar{L}} \mid \beta_{Y_{\bar{L}}}, X_j(T_4), v) \right.$$

$$\times \left\{ \prod_{l=0}^{L} g_{Y_{l-1}, Y_l}(u_{l-1} \mid \beta_{Y_{l-1}}, X_{Y_{l-1}}(\tau_{l-1} + u_{l-1}), v) \right\} f(v \mid a) dv \right]$$

$$\times \left[\int_{v \in \Lambda} v_1 \left(\int_0^\infty \exp \left\{ -\sum_{k=2}^{5} \int_0^{\bar{U}_0} h_{1k}(t \mid \beta_{1k}, X_{1k}(\tau_0), v_k) dt \right\} d\bar{U}_0 \right) f(v \mid a) dv \right]^{-1}, \quad (9)$$

where Y_l is the state occupied during the lth spell of the observed transition history. Given formulas (2), (3) and (4), a standard maximum likelihood procedure allows to obtain consistent estimates of $\beta = (\beta_{jk})_{k \neq j}$, of parameters of baseline hazard functions $h_{jk}^{(0)}$ and of parameters α of the joint density $f(\cdot)$ of the vector v.

III.4. *Specification issues*

Besides the introduction of a time-varying unemployment benefits entitlement variable, we allow the baseline rates of transition from unemployment to permanent or temporary employment and to PEP jobs to be piecewise constant. More precisely, we assume that

$$h_{1k}^{(0)}(u) = \exp(\delta_{0k}) \qquad \text{if } u \leq 6 \text{ months,}$$

$$= \exp(\delta_{0k} + \delta_{2k}) \quad \text{if } 6 < u \leq 12 \text{ months,} \qquad \text{for } k = 2, 3, 4. \quad (10)$$

$$= \exp(\delta_{0k} + \delta_{3k}) \quad \text{if } u > 12 \text{ months,}$$

This specification allows for possible non-monotone evolutions of the exit rates from unemployment, without increasing dramatically the number of parameters. All other transition intensities are supposed to be constant through time. For the distribution of the unobserved heterogeneity vector $v = (v_k)_{k=1,...,K}$, we consider two alternative assumptions. Firstly, following Flinn and Heckman (1982), we assume that components $(v_k)_{k=1,...,K}$ are generated by a common normally distributed random variate w such as

$$v_k = \exp(a_k w), \quad (11)$$

where $w \sim I\mathcal{N}(0, 1)$.

Obviously, this specification allows unobserved explanatory variables v_k to be mutually dependent. However, this dependence is too restrictive, because correlation between log v_k and log $v_{k'}$ ($k' \neq k$) can only equal 0, 1 or -1, according to the fact that $\alpha_k \alpha_{k'} = 0$, $\alpha_k \alpha_{k'} > 0$ or $\alpha_k \alpha_{k'} < 0$. A way of producing more flexible dependence is to assume that components v_k have discrete multivariate distributions with a finite number of points of support. For instance, Van den Berg (1995) examines the range of values that correlation of the duration variables can attain in bivariate mixed proportional hazard models. It turns out that when the bivariate vector of unobserved heterogeneity terms has a bivariate discrete distribution with two or more points of support for each component, and the locations of these points are not fixed in advance, then all possible values can be reached. On the other hand, when this vector has a log-normal distribution, then the range of values that can be attained is smaller.

In our model, a six-dimensional discrete distribution would be burdensome, but it is still possible to estimate without too much computational difficulty a two-factor loading model in which

$$v_k = \exp(\alpha_{k1} w_1 + \alpha_{k2} w_2), \tag{12}$$

and

$$\text{prob } \{(w_1, w_2) = (w_{11}, w_{21})\} = p_1,$$
$$= (w_{12}, w_{21})\} = p_2,$$
$$= (w_{11}, w_{22})\} = p_3,$$
$$= (w_{12}, w_{22})\} = 1 - p_1 - p_2 - p_3,$$
$$w_{ij} \in \mathbb{R}, \qquad i, j = 1, 2.$$

For this second model, we have to estimate K couples $(\alpha_{k1}, \alpha_{k2})$ of parameters, four points of support w_{ij} and three probabilities of the form

$$p_i = \frac{\exp(\mu_i)}{1 + \sum_{j=1}^{3} \exp(\mu_j)}, \qquad i = 1, 2, 3. \tag{13}$$

The test for model selection developed by Vuong (1989) may be used here as a criterion of choice between the two alternative models (11) and (12). These two models are overlapping and their intersection is the model without unobserved heterogeneity. Consequently, the selection test is the two stage sequential test proposed by Vuong (1989, p. 321).

IV. RESULTS

As explained in Section III, the different public measures are aggregated into one state, called "public employment programmes" (PEP). So the statistical model allows for transitions among six states, which are unemployment (U), regular employment with an unlimited duration labour contract (UDC), temporary employment with a limited duration labour contract (LDC), employment in a public employment programme (PEP), out-of-labour force (OLF), and attrition (A).[10] Here we consider strata composed of men who were less than 26 years old in November 1986 and who get either a technical school certificate or no diploma at all. Table 4.1 contains parameters estimates of models (11)

---

10. In the subsample of young men holding a technical school certificate, attrition state is omitted because of the small number of concerned transitions; transitions towards the attrition state are treated as right-censored spells.

BONNAL *ET AL.*　　INDIVIDUAL LABOUR MARKET HISTORIES　701

and (12) (denoted models A and B, respectively) with individual heterogeneity and correction of the stock sampling bias. Covariate vectors include a time-varying variable indicating if the individual is qualified for the unemployment insurance (UI) system during each month of the unemployment spell, and also dichotomous variables indicating the state occupied just before entering the current state. Among previous states, we make the distinction between four types of employment programmes:

- qualification, adaptation or apprenticeship contracts,
- public interest jobs (TUC).
- courses for preparation to the working life,
- other courses.

IV.1. *Transition intensities*

The results show that the previous occurrence of a public employment programme affects only some transition intensities. The sign and the magnitude of the statistically significant effects depend on the type of programme which has been previously followed. Introducing unobserved heterogeneity terms improves the adequacy of the models.[11] The result of the Vuong test for model selection is inconclusive: models (11) and (12) cannot be discriminated given the data. Generally, parameter estimates do not vary much from one model to the other. However, they differ significantly for some variables of interest.[12] Let us first comment upon the results which are stable. The impact of programmes on subsequent unemployment durations depends crucially on the educational level. For young men without a diploma (the least educated group), the previous occurrence of an apprenticeship, qualification or adaptation contract induces a higher intensity of transition from unemployment to regular (UDC) jobs, while it has no effect on the same transition for young men with a professional education level. At the same time, the experience of a community job in the public sector (TUC) has no effect on the intensity of transition from unemployment to regular or temporary employment for the sample without a diploma, while it decreases significantly this transition intensity for young men with a professional or technical diploma. In a sense, these results provide a first criterion for ranking different public employment programmes. Obviously, whatever the educational level is, training programmes in the private sector (respectively, in the public sector) have the most favourable (respectively, the poorest) impact on unemployment outcomes. Programmes involving a higher level of on-the-job training, such as apprenticeship or qualification contracts, are essentially beneficial to the less educated young people, who may increase their human capital and work experience through these programmes. In contrast, for more educated young men, programmes in the public sector (TUC jobs) decrease the intensity of transition from the subsequent unemployment spell to regular employment: one possible explanation of this result is that participation in such programmes may act as a signal of low employment performance, especially for young people who have initially received some professional education.[13] Another noticeable result is the high degree of state recurrence, in spite

---

11. Parameter estimates for the model without unobserved heterogeneity are not presented here. For each model with unobserved heterogeneity, a likelihood ratio test leads to the strong rejection of the nested model without unobserved heterogeneity.

12. This fact confirms the results of Heckman and Singer (1984) who gave evidence on the sensitivity of parameter estimates obtained from econometric models for single duration data to assumed functional forms for the distribution of unobserved variables.

13. This result was also found by Gritz (1993), but with a relatively small number of government trainees and without distinguishing between different levels of education.

TABLE 4.1 (beginning)

Transition intensities from unemployment

Variables	Young men without any diploma ($N=672$)		Young men with a technical school certificate ($N=405$)	
	Model A	Model B	Model A	Model B
$U \to UDC$				
Intercept	−4·269 (0·489)	−4·299 (0·098)	−4·115 (0·674)	−3·888 (0·124)
Intercept 6–12 months	−0·506 (0·140)	−0·490 (0·100)	−0·126 (0·120)	−0·080 (0·120)
Intercept >12 months	−0·363 (0·171)	−0·319 (0·093)	−0·044 (0·067)	0·250 (0·119)
Qualification for UI	0·047 (0·438)	−0·255 (0·098)	0·300 (0·754)	0·138 (0·124)
Previous occurrence of:				
QC, AC, App	*0·979 (0·606)*	1·606 (0·120)	−0·264 (1·221)	−0·059 (0·156)
TUC	−0·120 (0·390)	0·000 (0·116)	−0·753 (0·360)	−0·746 (0·152)
SIVP	0·485 (0·239)	0·840 (0·117)	0·493 (0·343)	0·416 (0·147)
Other courses	0·300 (0·339)	0·538 (0·113)	0·045 (0·494)	−0·190 (0·150)
UDC	0·902 (0·151)	0·922 (0·093)	0·386 (0·201)	_0·389 (0·118)
LDC	0·403 (0·186)	0·405 (0·094)	*0·334 (0·200)*	0·341 (0·114)
$U \to LDC$				
Intercept	−3·343 (0·813)	−3·107 (0·101)	−3·445 (0·333)	−3·658 (0·131)
Intercept 6–12 months	−0·151 (0·209)	−0·197 (0·094)	−0·011 (0·203)	−0·113 (0·113)
Intercept >12 months	−0·411 (0·178)	−0·446 (0·095)	0·069 (0·175)	−0·077 (0·125)
Qualification for UI	−0·912 (0·461)	−1·275 (0·101)	−0·134 (0·276)	−0·178 (0·127)
Previous occurrence of:				
QC, AC, App	0·167 (1·065)	0·383 (0·121)	−0·752 (0·914)	0·032 (0·157)
TUC	0·131 (0·219)	0·086 (0·114)	−0·772 (0·343)	−0·828 (0·152)
SIVP	1·010 (0·315)	0·718 (0·116)	0·227 (0·559)	0·371 (0·148)
Other courses	−0·255 (0·397)	−0·186 (0·116)	0·855 (0·587)	1·360 (0·149)
UDC	−0·363 (0·131)	−0·386 (0·101)	0·165 (0·148)	0·152 (0·124)
LDC	0·537 (0·160)	0·523 (0·089)	0·660 (0·156)	0·750 (0·108)
$U \to PEP$				
Intercept	−4·619 (0·792)	−4·844 (0·100)	−3·257 (0·727)	−3·074 (0·123)
Intercept 6–12 months	−0·006 (0·161)	0·066 (0·096)	−0·303 (0·230)	−0·328 (0·132)
Intercept >12 months	0·088 (0·191)	0·223 (0·092)	0·153 (0·145)	*0·221 (0·126)*
Qualification for UI	0·688 (0·704)	0·766 (0·099)	−0·521 (0·696)	−0·664 (0·123)
Previous occurrence of:				
QC, AC, App	1·229 (0·362)	0·795 (0·118)	0·359 (0·749)	0·663 (0·155)
TUC	0·912 (0·078)	0·877 (0·108)	1·334 (0·380)	1·280 (0·139)
SIVP	0·805 (0·330)	0·610 (0·115)	1·123 (0·181)	1·130 (0·144)
Other courses	0·294 (0·317)	0·160 (0·111)	0·853 (0·229)	0·633 (0·148)
UDC	−0·420 (0·134)	−0·458 (0·101)	−0·417 (0·344)	−0·440 (0·133)
LDC	*−0·205 (0·126)*	−0·186 (0·094)	−0·528 (0·234)	−0·489 (0·126)
$U \to OLF$				
Intercept			−4·003 (0·888)	−3·777 (0·117)
Qualification for UI			1·477 (1·001)	1·369 (0·117)
$U \to A$				
Intercept	−4·421 (1·182)	−4·921 (0·104)		
Qualification for UI	−0·544 (1·210)	−0·403 (0·104)		

of the introduction of time-constant unobserved heterogeneity into the model. For example, the previous experience of a regular job just before the entry into the current unemployment spell increases the probability of transition to another regular job at the end of the current unemployment spell. The same recurrence effects appear for temporary jobs and youth employment programmes. With these data and with this reduced-form model, it is difficult to know if these recurrence effects are mainly due to workers' preferences or to the selection carried out by employers during the hiring process: nevertheless, they could be compatible with a segmented labour market in which past employment histories provide information on applicants to future employers, and which may result,

BONNAL *ET AL.*   INDIVIDUAL LABOUR MARKET HISTORIES   703

TABLE 4.1 (intermediate)

Transition intensities from regular and temporary jobs

Variables	Young men without any diploma (N=672)		Young men with a technical school certificate (N=405)	
	Model A	Model B	Model A	Model B
UDC→U				
Intercept	−3·003 (0·117)	−2·227 (0·086)	−3·266 (0·061)	−3·259 (0·105)
Previous occurrence of:				
SIVP	−0·363 (0·591)	−0·777 (0·119)	−0·836 (1·079)	−0·672 (0·155)
Other PEP jobs	0·320 (0·317)	−0·050 (0·114)	0·828 (0·210)	0·877 (0·142)
LDC	0·119 (0·446)	*0·176 (0·108)*	−0·437 (0·355)	−0·588 (0·140)
UDC→LDC				
Intercept	−3·966 (0·117)	−4·277 (0·103)	−4·078 (0·138)	−4·057 (0·135)
Previous occurrence of:				
PEP jobs	*−1·240 (0·653)*	−1·513 (0·120)		
LDC	−2·210 (0·365)	−1·738 (0·119)	−0·438 (0·136)	−1·041 (0·145)
UDC→PEP				
Intercept	−4·556 (0·162)	−4·179 (0·108)	−4·510 (0·363)	−4·750 (0·136)
Previous occurrence of:				
PEP jobs	0·583 (0·671)	0·097 (0·118)		
LDC			−1·131 (1·087)	−0·894 (0·154)
UDC→OLF: Intercept	−5·992 (0·482)	−6·280 (0·118)	−5·321 (0·249)	−5·422 (0·143)
UDC→A: Intercept	−4·406 (0·219)	−4·500 (0·109)		
LDC→U				
Intercept	−1·625 (0·265)	−1·636 (0·080)	−1·891 (0·120)	−2·146 (0·095)
Previous occurrence of:				
PEP	−0·936 (0·485)	−1·084 (0·117)	−1·462 (0·278)	−1·319 (0·153)
UDC	−0·663 (0·211)	−0·430 (0·110)	*−0·363 (0·219)*	−0·226 (0·141)
LDC→UDC				
Intercept	−2·625 (0·288)	−3·017 (0·093)	−2·447 (0·155)	−2·288 (0·106)
Previous occurrence of:				
PEP	−1·115 (0·703)	−1·056 (0·120)	0·038 (0·391)	−0·367 (0·151)
UDC	−0·643 (0·329)	−0·810 (0·115)	0·169 (0·358)	−0·087 (0·143)
LDC→PEP				
Intercept	−4·663 (0·367)	−4·753 (0·114)	−4·213 (0·300)	−3·962 (0·133)
Previous occurrence of:				
PEP	1·854 (0·497)	1·702 (0·119)	0·995 (0·515)	0·881 (0·152)
LDC→OLF: Intercept	−4·813 (0·579)	−4·614 (0·117)	−4·789 (0·263)	−4·695 (0·143)
LDC→A: Intercept	−4·139 (0·286)	−4·096 (0·114)		

through this signalling process, in the confining of workers with different productive abilities in different types of jobs.

The results concerning transitions from regular (UDC) jobs reveal that, for young people with a technical school certificate, the previous occurrence of a programme in the public sector with neither formal nor specific training is related to a higher intensity of transition from regular employment to unemployment than other types of programmes (namely, SIVP and apprenticeship, qualification or adaptation contracts): this result may be explained by the fact that regular jobs offered by employers to young people after a training period in the firm have better attributes than the ones offered to young people having just experienced a programme in the public sector, and so that they generate better matches and longer subsequent employment durations. Moreover, a young worker with no experience who was previously in a programme (whatever its type) or in a temporary job and who is currently employed in a regular job moves less frequently to a temporary job than if he was previously unemployed.

TABLE 4.1 (end)

Transition intensities from PEP and OLF states

Variables	Young men without any diploma ($N=672$)		Young men with a technical school certificate ($N=405$)	
	Model A	Model B	Model A	Model B
$PEP \rightarrow U$: Intercept	**−2·424 (0·044)**	**−2·668 (0·080)**	**−2·532 (0·139)**	**−2·594 (0·108)**
$PEP \rightarrow UDC$: Intercept	**−3·394 (0·210)**	**−3·368 (0·098)**	**−3·094 (0·068)**	**−3·232 (0·121)**
$PEP \rightarrow LDC$: Intercept	**−4·501 (0·652)**	**−4·766 (0·111)**	**−4·290 (0·455)**	**−4·328 (0·141)**
$PEP \rightarrow OLF$: Intercept	**−5·010 (0·537)**	**−5·976 (0·116)**	**−4·287 (0·286)**	**−4·295 (0·141)**
$PEP \rightarrow A$: Intercept	**−4·494 (0·371)**	**−4·612 (0·109)**		
$OLF \rightarrow U$: Intercept	**−2·944 (0·094)**	**−2·958 (0·100)**	**−2·943 (0·086)**	**−3·033 (0·133)**
$OLF \rightarrow UDC$: Intercept	**−5·018 (0·262)**	**−5·278 (0·118)**	**−4·535 (0·353)**	**−4·756 (0·150)**
$OLD \rightarrow LDC$: Intercept	**−5·567 (0·702)**	**−5·789 (0·119)**	**−5·223 (0·577)**	**−5·572 (0·152)**
$OLF \rightarrow PEP$: Intercept	**−4·557 (0·454)**	**−4·671 (0·116)**	**−4·810 (0·399)**	**−4·971 (0·152)**
$OLF \rightarrow A$: Intercept	**−4·985 (0·283)**	**−5·348 (0·117)**		
α_1	−0·067 (0·263)		−0·021 (0·126)	
α_2	−0·203 (0·311)		0·234 (0·170)	
α_3	**−0·889 (0·078)**		**−1·016 (0·079)**	
α_4	0·316 (0·499)		−0·253 (0·261)	
α_5	0·215 (0·641)		**−0·244 (0·107)**	
α_6	**0·682 (0·350)**			
α_{11}		**−0·592 (0·084)**		**0·259 (0·075)**
α_{21}		**0·258 (0·079)**		−0·114 (0·084)
α_{31}		**−0·357 (0·090)**		**−1·794 (0·139)**
α_{41}		**−0·875 (0·107)**		**−0·302 (0·098)**
α_{51}		**−2·199 (0·119)**		**−0·561 (0·076)**
α_{61}		**0·453 (0·094)**		
α_{12}		0·041 (0·062)		**−0·694 (0·104)**
α_{22}		**−0·682 (0·087)**		**0·645 (0·106)**
α_{32}		**−1·276 (0·104)**		**0·730 (0·121)**
α_{42}		**0·404 (0·083)**		**0·656 (0·118)**
α_{52}		0·155 (0·114)		**0·808 (0·099)**
α_{62}		**0·944 (0·104)**		
μ_1		**−0·319 (0·109)**		**−0·467 (0·137)**
μ_2		**−0·680 (0·112)**		**−0·499 (0·149)**
μ_3		**0·346 (0·112)**		**−4·244 (0·150)**
ω_{11}		**−0·491 (0·070)**		**−0·799 (0·099)**
ω_{12}		**1·592 (0·117)**		**1·550 (0·142)**
ω_{21}		**−0·883 (0·080)**		**−0·741 (0·105)**
ω_{22}		**0·962 (0·101)**		**1·077 (0·120)**
Log-likelihood	−10,536·76	−10,519·93	−5807·58	−5790·77

Notes. Meaning of abbreviations for Table 4.1: QC, AC, App: Qualification Contract, Adaptation Contract, or Apprenticeship Contract.
Remark. In Table 4.1, figures between brackets are standard deviations. Bold type style indicates a 5% significance level while italic type style means a 10% one.

Baseline piecewise-constant intensities of transition from unemployment are not much modified when the distributional assumption on the unobserved heterogeneity terms changes. Intensities of transition from unemployment to regular employment or to temporary employment are decreasing for young men with a very low educational level, while they are constant for young men having a professional diploma. For this last group and at that time (1986–1988), long-term unemployment did not reduce the chances of getting a regular (or a temporary) job: from this viewpoint, long-term unemployment was only

BONNAL *ET AL.*   INDIVIDUAL LABOUR MARKET HISTORIES   705

unfavourable to the least-educated young workers. Under assumption (11), i.e. when the individual random effects are supposed to be log-normally distributed, the intensity of transition from unemployment to training programmes is constant through the unemployment spell. However, when these random effects are assumed to have a bivariate discrete distribution with two points of support (model B), this transition intensity increases slightly after twelve months: this could be due to a decline of the reservation wage which makes training programmes more acceptable over a longer period of unemployment, or to the fact that subsidized jobs in the public sector (community jobs, for example) are more frequently offered to long-term unemployed people.

Finally, the estimated effects of the time-varying covariate indicating qualification for the UI system through the unemployment spell is sensitive to the distributional assumption concerning unobserved heterogeneity, except in the case of the intensity of transition from unemployment to temporary employment which is lower for low-educated young workers before time of benefit exhaustion.[14] In general, qualification for UI has no effect or a negative effect on the rates of exit from unemployment. However, when young unemployed men with no educational diploma are still qualified for the UI system, they are transiting more intensively to programmes (the corresponding estimating parameter is significant with model B). This last result could be due to an incentive effect resulting from the legislation concerning eligibility rights to the UI system. More precisely, when an unemployed young worker qualified for UI accept to enter into a programme, the UI payment is interrupted during the programme, but the worker keeps his remaining rights to UI if he re-enters unemployment at the end of the programme.

In model A, most of the estimates of parameters α_k associated with the unobserved Gaussian heterogeneity term are not significantly different from zero: according to this model, selection into programmes does not depend on unobservable covariates. On the contrary, estimates of parameters α_{kj} in model B imply that unobservables have significant effects on programme entry. More precisely, estimates of correlations between random heterogeneity terms show that selection into programmes is "negative" for young men without any diploma: this means that, in this subgroup, individuals who are unexpectedly likely to enter programmes are also unexpectedly likely to enter unemployment. At the opposite, selection is "positive" for young men holding a technical school certificate: here, individuals who are unexpectedly likely to enter programmes are also unexpectedly likely to be hired in permanent jobs.

IV.2. *Some useful indicators*

Estimated transition intensities may be used to calculate some summary indicators of the magnitude of programme effects. We concentrate here on the conditional probability that some state k directly follows state j ($k \neq j$) and on the conditional probability of becoming long-term unemployed, given that a programme has been previously experienced. Given the importance of the self-selection issue in assessing the effects of training programmes, we report estimates of these conditional probabilities after elimination of the effects of unobserved heterogeneity on transitions towards the programmes. For that purpose, we calculate these indicators as expectations of conditional probabilities over the unconditional distribution of the unobserved heterogeneity. Under the assumptions of the model,

---

14. This result could be explained by a change in the search behaviour of low-educated young workers through their unemployment spell: once they are no more qualified for the UI system, they could be more disposed to accept temporary jobs, which are more frequent but often associated with lower wages.

these expectations may be viewed as the conceptual equivalent of random assignment to the different programmes.

When covariates do not vary during the lth spell in state j, the conditional probability that state k follows state j $(k \neq j)$, given the value $X(\tau_l)$ of individual covariates at time τ_l of entry into the current spell in state j, is equal to

$$\Pi_{k|j}(X(\tau_l)) = \int_{w \in W} \Pi_{k|j}(X(\tau_l), w) f(w) dw, \tag{14}$$

where

$$\Pi_{k|j}(X(\tau_l), w) = \int_0^{+\infty} h_{jk}(u \mid X(\tau_l), w) S_j(u \mid X(\tau_l), w) du. \tag{15}$$

In equation (14), W (respectively, f) denotes the support of the distribution (respectively, the density function) of the random heterogeneity term w. When w has a discrete distribution, the integral in equation (14) is substituted for a simple sum over the points of support of w. If the origin state j is different from unemployment $(j \neq 1)$, the assumption of time-constant baseline transition intensities implies that

$$\Pi_{k|j}(X(\tau_l), w) = \frac{h_{jk}(X(\tau_l), w)}{\sum_{k' \neq j} h_{jk'}(X(\tau_l), w)}, \qquad j \neq 1. \tag{16}$$

If the origin state is unemployment $(j = 1)$, assumption (10) implies that

$$\Pi_{k|1}(X(\tau_l), w) = \frac{h_{1k}^{(1)}}{\sum_{k' \neq 1} h_{1k'}^{(1)}} [1 - \exp\{-6 \sum_{k' \neq 1} h_{1k'}^{(1)}\}]$$

$$+ \frac{h_{1k}^{(2)}}{\sum_{k' \neq 1} h_{1k'}^{(2)}} \exp\{-6 \sum_{k' \neq 1} h_{1k'}^{(1)}\}[1 - \exp\{-6 \sum_{k' \neq 1} h_{1k'}^{(2)}\}]$$

$$+ \frac{h_{1k}^{(3)}}{\sum_{k' \neq 1} h_{1k'}^{(3)}} \exp\{-6 \sum_{k' \neq 1} (h_{1k'}^{(1)} + h_{1k'}^{(2)})\}, \tag{17}$$

where

$$h_{1k}^{(l)} = \exp(\delta_{0k} + \delta_{lk} + \beta_{1k}' X(\tau_l)) v_k, \qquad l = 1, 2, 3, \tag{18}$$

with $\delta_{1k} = 0$ for identification, v_k being alternatively defined by equations (11) and (12). These probabilities are calculated by using ML parameter estimates of the models (11) and (12) for unemployed workers not qualified for the UI system and for workers currently occupied in a regular job. In the case of an unemployed worker who is eligible to the UI system, we have to consider the potential duration T of his eligibility period. For instance, in 1986 in France, if an unemployed worker was employed between 3 and 6 months, 6 and 12 months or more than 12 months during the year preceding his entry into unemployment, the length of his UI elegibility period was 3, 8 and 14 months, respectively. People who were previously employed in a community (TUC) job were generally not qualified

BONNAL *ET AL.* INDIVIDUAL LABOUR MARKET HISTORIES 707

for UI once they re-entered unemployment. For example, when the eligibility period is greater than 12 months (for instance, $T=14$ months), the conditional probability that a spell in state k follows directly the current spell of unemployment is equal to

$$\Pi_{k|1}(X(\tau_I), T, w) = \frac{h_{1k}^{(1)*}}{\sum_{k' \neq 1} [h_{1k'}^{(1)*}]} [1 - \exp\{-6\sum_{k' \neq 1} h_{1k'}^{(1)*}\}]$$

$$+ \frac{h_{1k}^{(2)*}}{\sum_{k' \neq 1} [h_{1k'}^{(2)*}]} \exp\{-6\sum_{k' \neq 1} h_{1k'}^{(1)*}\}[1 - \exp\{-6\sum_{k' \neq 1} h_{1k'}^{(2)*}\}]$$

$$+ \frac{h_{1k}^{(3)*}}{\sum_{k' \neq 1} [h_{1k'}^{(3)*}]} \exp\{-6\sum_{k' \neq 1} (h_{1k'}^{(1)*} + h_{1k'}^{(2)*})\}$$

$$\times [1 - \exp\{-(T-12)\sum_{k' \neq 1} h_{1k'}^{(3)*}\}]$$

$$+ \frac{h_{1k}^{(3)}}{\sum_{k' \neq 1} [h_{1k'}^{(3)}]} \exp\{-6\sum_{k' \neq 1} (h_{1k'}^{(1)*} + h_{1k'}^{(2)*}) - (T-12)\sum_{k' \neq 1} h_{1k'}^{(3)*}\},$$

where

$$h_{1k}^{(l)*} = \exp(\delta_{0k} + \delta_{lk} + \beta_{1k}' X(\tau_I) + \gamma_{1k})v_k, \qquad l = 1, 2, 3, \tag{19}$$

$h_{1k}^{(l)}$ being defined in (18). Calculations of these probabilities for $0 < T \leq 6$ and $6 < T \leq 12$ are not reproduced here.

Moreover, the probability of becoming long-term unemployed (i.e. to be unemployed for a period greater than 12 months) given the length T of the UI eligibility period is equal to

$$S_1(12|X(\tau_I), T) = \int_{w \in W} S_1(12|X(\tau_I), T, w) f(x) dw, \tag{20}$$

where

$$S_1(12|X(\tau_I), T, w) = \exp\{-6\sum_{k' \neq 1} (h_{1k'}^{(1)*} + h_{1k'}^{(2)*})\}, \qquad \text{if } T > 12,$$

$$= \exp\{-\sum_{k' \neq 1} [6h_{1k'}^{(1)*} + (T-6)h_{1k'}^{(2)*} + (12-T)h_{1k'}^{(2)}]\}, \quad \text{if } 6 < T \leq 12,$$

$$= \exp\{-\sum_{k' \neq 1} [Th_{1k'}^{(1)*} + (6-T)h_{1k'}^{(1)} + 6h_{1k'}^{(2)}]\}, \qquad \text{if } 0 < T \leq 6,$$

$h_{1k}^{(l)}$ and $h_{1k}^{(l)*}$ being defined in (18) and (19), respectively.

Tables 4.2.a and 4.2.b show that these indicators are very sensitive to the distributional assumption on the unobserved heterogeneity terms. For the subsample of young men with a low level of education, the choice of a bivariate discrete distribution (model B) results in a much higher (respectively, lower) estimate of the expected probability of moving to a permanent job (respectively, to another training programme) at the end of the unemployment spell which follows participation to a training programme. However, the estimate of the expected probability of becoming long-term unemployed is not as sensitive to this specification assumption. For the young male subsample with a technical school certificate, the results are strictly different: the estimate of the expected probability of becoming long-term unemployed is more sensitive to the assumption concerning unobserved components than the estimates of the expected probabilities of transition from unemployment to other

TABLE 4.2.a

Probability of unemployment outcomes according to the state previously occupied
(percentages)

Young men without a diploma

Previous state	First entry	TUC	Other PEP		SIVP		LDC		QC, AC, App		UDC	
Potential duration of UI eligibility (in months)	0	0	3	8	3	8	3	8	8	14	8	14
Probability of transition to												
UDC												
Model without heterogeneity	16·5	12·4	25·0	25·2	17·0	17·8	18·1	20·4	25·6	24·7	43·1	43·9
Model A	17·5	10·4	21·1	22·2	13·8	15·1	18·6	20·6	24·9	25·1	40·3	41·7
Model B	19·0	17·1	31·8	33·8	27·3	29·9	22·4	25·0	50·1	51·3	46·2	48·2
LDC												
Model without heterogeneity	59·7	48·4	35·7	29·7	50·0	40·3	64·7	57·4	17·2	14·0	31·4	27·4
Model A	46·1	43·0	37·8	29·4	51·1	43·8	50·9	45·9	21·9	18·5	25·6	22·4
Model B	47·0	45·8	33·6	28·9	43·1	36·8	48·2	43·0	20·3	17·3	22·8	19·6
PEP												
Model without heterogeneity	11·5	28·5	24·7	30·6	25·2	33·9	8·8	12·7	49·8	55·4	12·7	15·2
Model A	16·7	29·4	24·7	29·8	24·1	31·1	12·8	15·5	44·5	49·1	14·8	17·1
Model B	8·7	15·0	11·8	14·9	12·6	16·5	7·8	20·2	16·9	19·2	8·9	10·6
prob (Unemp > one year)												
Model without heterogeneity	35·9	32·6	44·2	45·7	23·2	26·4	24·4	32·0	23·4	21·4	42·3	44·8
Model A	45·2	30·8	40·7	43·0	17·8	20·7	31·4	36·7	20·7	20·6	43·5	46·1
Model B	34·3	29·8	35·5	41·9	20·8	26·2	28·3	36·1	19·5	22·8	41·2	46·6

TABLE 4.2.b

Probability of unemployment outcomes according to the state previously occupied
(percentages)

Young men with a technical school certificate

Previous state	First entry	TUC	Other PEP		SIVP		LDC		QC, AC, App		UDC	
Potential duration of UI eligibility (in months)	0	0	3	8	3	8	3	8	8	14	8	14
Probability of transition to												
UDC												
Model without heterogeneity	12·2	3·8	10·9	12·7	14·0	16·4	14·2	16·2	12·2	12·7	22·4	23·0
Model A	16·5	4·5	10·5	11·1	15·7	16·6	19·5	18·9	12·6	12·6	21·8	21·5
Model B	19·1	5·0	9·7	9·8	15·3	16·1	23·1	21·4	13·2	13·2	23·9	22·9
LDC												
Model without heterogeneity	42·2	11·6	33·5	27·7	23·5	19·5	52·5	42·7	14·3	12·4	26·1	22·8
Model A	33·1	10·0	35·4	33·1	20·7	19·4	41·8	36·3	13·2	12·2	27·0	25·1
Model B	27·3	8·8	37·9	36·8	19·4	18·7	32·2	29·6	17·3	16·8	21·0	20·0
PEP												
Model without heterogeneity	30·1	74·3	33·3	27·8	41·9	34·9	23·2	8·3	32·6	27·9	12·6	10·8
Model A	33·8	75·4	32·5	26·2	41·8	33·8	12·6	9·5	31·4	26·6	12·5	10·5
Model B	35·9	75·3	27·9	22·1	39·3	32·2	17·8	10·1	28·8	25·4	11·7	9·6
prob (Unemp > one year)												
Model without heterogeneity	21·7	11·4	10·1	10·7	7·4	8·1	11·6	11·6	21·6	19·3	18·7	16·2
Model A	28·7	13·9	11·2	9·9	10·3	9·2	19·6	15·3	22·4	18·8	18·2	14·7
Model B	18·8	7·3	7·3	6·7	5·0	5·1	13·6	10·6	10·1	9·0	12·5	10·1

states. In spite of the high sensitivity of estimates, it appears that the estimates of these expected probabilities vary significantly with the types of programmes previously experienced. For example, for young men without any diploma, the expected probability of becoming long-term unemployed for the ones who were previously participating to a "workplace" training programme (like a qualification, adaptation or apprenticeship contract) is half of the same probability calculated for the ones who were previously participating "courses for the 16-to-25 years old" (called "other PEP" in Tables 4.2) or who enter the labour market for the first time. The efficiency of workplace programmes in the private sector is strengthened by the fact that, for the low-educated people, the expected probability of getting a permanent (UDC) job at the end of the current unemployment spell is much higher if they were previously participating to workplace programmes: on the contrary, this probability is low when they enter the labour market for the first time or when they were previously employed in community jobs (TUC). In terms of these indicators, the benefits of alternating work/training programmes are less pronounced for young men with a higher educational level (see Table 4.2.b). Moreover community jobs reduce significantly their chance of getting a regular job at the end of the current unemployment spell. Indeed this chance is higher for a young man entering the labour market for the first time. However community jobs and programmes characterized by low training levels, such as "courses for preparation to the working life" (SIVP) and "courses for the 16-to-25 years old" (other PEP), are associated with lower expected probabilities of becoming long-term unemployed and with shorter unemployment spells which in turn end up frequently with a re-entry into a training programme: for instance, 75% of unemployment spells occurring after employment in community jobs are directly followed by re-entries into programmes.

Moreover let us notice that, when entering the labour market, young men holding a technical school certificate are more likely to have access to a training programme than less educated young males. So it is clear that participation in training programmes is highly selective. Finally, let us notice that the expected probability of becoming long-term unemployed does not increase significantly with the duration of the period of qualification for UI.

Table 4.3 contains estimates of the expected probabilities of transition from regular jobs according to the state previously occupied. First of all, let us remark that the expected probability of a transition to unemployment is higher for young men previously participating to programmes in the public sector (TUC and other courses) than for those previously participating to alternating work/training programmes in the private sector (SIVP and contracts). On the whole, the expected average duration of a regular employment spell (or equivalently the expected probability that it exceeds one year) is higher when it has been preceded by an alternating work/training programme in the private sector.[15]

V. SUMMARY AND CONCLUSIONS

This analysis has focused on the short-term impact of youth employment programmes set up in France during the 1980's on the labour market trajectories of recipients, especially on durations of their subsequent spells of unemployment and employment. Our study, using non-experimental transition data, has paid particular attention to the possible effects

---

15. As a referee pointed out, omitting the age covariate may lead in particular to an overestimate of the permanence of employment spells for the sample as a whole.

REVIEW OF ECONOMIC STUDIES

TABLE 4.3

Probability of transitions from regular (UDC) jobs
(percentages)

Destination state	Previous state			
	U+OLF	LDC	SIVP+ Contracts	Other courses+ TUC
Unemployment (U)				
N.d.				
Model A	47·8	64·6	39·1	51·9
Model B	41·9	57·4	25·5	50·8
T.c.				
Model A	52·0	54·0	33·4	69·8
Model B	43·3	41·8	30·4	59·3
Temporary jobs (LDC)				
N.d.				
Model A	23·5	3·6	27·4	19·0
Model B	22·7	5·1	29·8	7·1
T.c.				
Model A	26·9	27·9	36·2	17·5
Model B	33·7	25·5	39·0	26·2
Training programmes (PEP)				
N.d.				
Model A	10·8	12·3	12·7	15·2
Model B	8·4	9·1	11·4	11·1
T.c.				
Model A	14·4	7·5	20·9	8·6
Model B	15·5	27·1	20·8	9·5
prob (UDC> one year)				
N.d.				
Model A	28·7	34·9	34·3	20·6
Model B	32·7	36·8	41·4	40·0
T.c.				
Model A	39·9	55·6	51·6	22·2
Model B	36·1	55·5	43·8	21·3

Notes. Abbreviations for education levels: N.d. (no diploma), T.c. (technical school certificate).

of unobserved individual heterogeneity on rates of transition towards programmes, thus capturing the potentially selective nature of training enrolment. A special emphasis has been put on the differential effects of various types of programmes (roughly speaking, workplace programmes in the private sector vs. "workfare" programmes in the public sector), according to the educational level of individuals. Estimates show that:

(a) According to their nature and the amount of training they involve, youth employment programmes have different effects on the recipients' trajectories; for instance, participation in alternating work/training programmes in the private sector increases the intensity of transition from the following unemployment spell to regular employment for young males with a low educational level, while it has no effect on the same transition for young men holding a technical school certificate; at the same time, the experience of a "workfare" programme in the public sector (e.g. a community job) has no effect on the intensity of transition from unemployment to regular jobs for the least educated young people, while it decreases significantly this transition intensity for young men with a vocational diploma; so participation in these programmes may act as a negative signal at

BONNAL *ET AL.*   INDIVIDUAL LABOUR MARKET HISTORIES   711

higher educational levels; however, for this subgroup of people, community jobs are associated with a lower average duration of unemployment and with a highly probable re-entry into programmes; simultaneously, a regular job preceded by an alternating work/training programme in the private sector has a higher expected duration than a regular job following a community job or a course in a public training centre; moreover, it ends less frequently with a transition to unemployment;

(b) Participation in programmes is highly selective; it depends firstly on the state currently occupied (for instance, for young men holding a technical school cert-ificate, transitions from unemployment to programmes are more frequent than transitions from temporary employment to programmes); it depends also on the educational level of young workers (the least educated ones move less intensively from unemployment to programmes); finally, it depends on past occurrences of programmes, but also on individual unobserved heterogeneity (at least, when we assume that this random heterogeneity follows a bivariate discrete distribution with two points of support); let us notice that we can only detect first-order effects of past programme occurrences[16]; consequently, programme participation has a very short-term impact on individual labour market histories;

(c) The duration of the period of entitlement to unemployment insurance (UI) does not increase the expected duration of unemployment spells; when they are still qualified for UI, the least educated young workers enter programmes more intensively; this could be due to an incentive effect resulting from the legislation on UI. Once again, this result is only verified under the assumption of a bivariate discrete distribution for the unobserved heterogeneity terms.

Obviously many other questions could be addressed. In particular, one could try to examine the effects of exemptions from social contributions as incentives for firms to hire young workers in alternating work/training programmes. One could also try to know if firms substitute these subsidized jobs to regular or temporary ones. These questions are beyond the scope of this study, primarily because they require informations on firms which are not available in the data set we use. Finally, one could be interested in measuring the effects of introducing these programmes on the employment prospects of young workers as a group, and then in discussing the equilibrium effects of such policies. This could be done by estimating displacement effects which result from the fact that a transition into a workplace programme by any one worker affects the job-finding prospects of any other worker by filling a vacancy. The impossibility of ascertaining the importance of such an issue is clearly a limitation of the current research approach.

Acknowledgements. This is a revised version of CREST Working Paper 9417. We wish to thank for their helpful comments participants at the RES-CEMFI Conference "On the Evaluation of Training Programs" (Madrid, September 1993), especially James Heckman, Joe Hotz, and Gerard van den Berg, and also participants at the 1993 Asset Meeting (Barcelona, October 1993), at the CORE (Louvain-la-Neuve) and CREST (Paris)

16. In additional estimates which are not reported here, we have introduced among covariates affecting transitions from unemployment a dummy variable indicating if the individual has participated to a training programme before the spell preceding entry into the current unemployment spell; this variate appears to have no significant effect on rates of exit from unemployment, while its introduction leaves relatively unchanged the effects of a training period occurring just before the current unemployment spell. However, our test is subject to some criticism: because data contain no information on the participation history preceding the spell which occurred just before the sampled unemployment spell, we restricted the estimation of models with "second-order" effects to subsequent unemployment spells, which are more likely observed for more mobile individuals.

712   REVIEW OF ECONOMIC STUDIES

Econometric Seminars, and at the 1994 ESEM (Maastricht, August 1994). We have benefitted from the suggestions of the Managing Editor, Manuel Arellano, and from the comments of two anonymous referees, which
improved substantially the paper. We are indebted to Carmen Olmos for her excellent computing assistance.
This research has benefitted from a grant from the French Ministry of Labour (Ministère du Travail, de l'Emploi,
et de la Formation Professionnelle). The usual disclaimer applies.

REFERENCES

AALEN, O. O. (1987), "Mixing Distribution on a Markov Chain", *Scandinavian Journal of Statistics*, 14, 281–289.
ASHENFELTER, O. and CARD, D. (1985), "Using the Longitudinal Structure of Earnings to Estimate the Effect of Training Programs", *Review of Economics and Statistics*, 67, 648–660.
BASSI, L. (1983), "The Effect of CETA on the Post-Program Earnings of Participants", *The Journal of Human Resources*, 18, 539–556.
CARD, D. and SULLIVAN, D. (1988), "Measuring the Effect of Subsidized Training Programs on Movements In and Out of Employment", *Econometrica*, 56, 497–530.
DE TOLDI, M., GOURIÉROUX, C. and MONFORT, A. (1995), "Prepayment Analysis for Securitization", *Journal of Empirical Finance*, 2, 45–70.
DUBIN, J. A. and RIVERS, D. (1993), "Experimental Estimates of the Impact of Wage Subsidies", *Journal of Econometrics*, 56, 219–242.
ELBERS, C. and RIDDER, G. (1982), "True and Spurious Duration Dependence: The Identifiability of the Proportional Hazard Model", *Review of Economic Studies*, 49, 403–409.
FLINN, C. J. and HECKMAN, J. J. (1982), "Models for the Analysis of Labor Force Dynamics", in Basmann, R. and Rhodes, G. (eds.) *Advances in Econometrics*, Vol. 1 (Greenwich: JAI Press), 35–95.
FLINN, C. J. and HECKMAN, J. J. (1983), "The Likelihood Function of the Multivariate-Multiepisode Model", in Basmann, R. and Rhodes, G. (eds.) *Advances in Econometrics*, Vol. 2 (Greenwich: JAI Press), 225–231.
FLORENS, J. P. and FOUGÈRE, D. (1992), "Point Processes", in Mátyás, L. and Sevestre, P. (eds.) *The Econometrics of Panel Data, Handbook of Theory and Applications* (Dordrecht: Kluwer Academic Press), 316–352.
FOUGÈRE, D. and KAMIONKA, T. (1992a), "A Markovian Model of the French Labour Market", *Annales d'Economie et de Statistique*, 27, 149–188.
FOUGÈRE, D. and KAMIONKA, T. (1992b), "Individual Labour Market Transitions", in Mátyás, L. and Sevestre, P. (eds.) *The Econometrics of Panel Data, Handbook of Theory and Applications* (Dordrecht: Kluwer Academic Press), 470–508.
GOURIÉROUX, C. and MONFORT, A. (1992), "Duration Models and Generation Effects" (Working Paper CREST no. 9125, INSEE).
GRITZ, R. M. (1993), "The Impact of Training on the Frequency and Duration of Employment", *Journal of Econometrics*, 57, 21–51.
HAM, T. and LALONDE, R. (1990), "Using Social Experiments to Estimate the Effect of Training on Transition Rates", in Hartog, J., Ridder, G. and Theeuves, J. (eds.) *Panel Data and Labor Market Studies* (Amsterdam: North-Holland), 157–172.
HAM, T. and LALONDE, R. (1996), "The Effect of Sample Selection and Initial Conditions in Duration Models: Evidence from Experimental Data on Training", *Econometrica*, 64, 175–205.
HECKMAN, J. J. (1990), "Alternative Approaches to the Evaluation of Social Programs: Econometric and Experimental Methods", Invited Lecture, 6th World Congress of the Econometric Society, Barcelona, Spain.
HECKMAN, J. J. and HOTZ, J. (1989), "Choosing Among Alternative Non-Experimental Methods for Estimating the Impact of Social Programs; The Case of Manpower Training", *Journal of the American Statistical Association*, 84, 862–874.
HECKMAN, J. J. and SINGER, B. (1984), "A Method for Minimizing the Impact of Distributional Assumptions in Econometric Models for Duration Data", *Econometrica*, 52, 271–320.
HONORÉ, B. E. (1993), "Identification Results for Duration Models with Multiple Spells", *Review of Economic Studies*, 60, 241–246.
IMBENS, G. W. and LYNCH, L. (1992), "Labour Market Transitions over the Business Cycle" (Working Paper, Harvard University).
LANCASTER, T. (1990), "The Econometric Analysis of Transition Data" (Cambridge: Cambridge University Press).
RIDDER, G. (1984), "The Distribution of Single-Spell Duration Data", in Neumann, G. R. and Westergard-Nielsen, N. (eds.) *Studies in Labor Market Analysis* (Berlin: Springer Verlag).
RIDDER, G. (1986), "An Event History Approach to the Evaluation of Training, Recruitment and Employment Programs", *Journal of Applied Econometrics*, 1, 109–126.
RIDDER, G. (1990), "The Non-Parametric Identification of Generalized Accelerated Failure Time Models", *Review of Economic Studies*, 57, 167–182.

VAN DEN BERG, G. J., LINDEBOOM, M. and RIDDER, G. (1994), "Attrition in Longitudinal Panel Data and the Empirical Analysis of Dynamic Labour Market Behavior", *Journal of Applied Econometrics*, **9**, 421–435.
VAN DEN BERG, G. J. (1995), "Association Measures for Durations in Bivariate Hazard Rate Models", *Journal of Econometrics* (forthcoming).
VUONG, Q. (1989), "Likelihood ratio tests for model selection and non-nested hypotheses", *Econometrica*, **57**, 307–333.

Name Index

The International Library of Critical Writings in Economics